The EUROPEANS IN AUSTRALIA

Alan Atkinson was born in Sydney and grew up in southern Queensland. He was an undergraduate at Sydney University and has a PhD from the Australian National University in Canberra. This is his tenth book. Others include *Camden: Farm and Village Life in Early New South Wales* (1988), which helped to introduce new forms of social history to Australia, and *The Commonwealth of Speech* (2002), an argument about history writing in the twenty-first century and about the links between the national past and present.

He also has a master's degree in education from the University of Dublin. From 1981 to 2008 he was employed at the University of New England, New South Wales, a university with distinctive teaching traditions, and more recently as senior tutor at St Paul's College, Sydney University. He has been a Fulbright scholar and a visiting fellow at the universities of Cambridge, London and Melbourne, and at the Australian National University. He is married to Catherine Pound, with three adult children.

For CP

The EUROPEANS IN AUSTRALIA

VOLUME THREE: NATION

ALAN ATKINSON

UNSW PRESS

A UNSW Press book

Published by
NewSouth Publishing
University of New South Wales Press Ltd
University of New South Wales
Sydney NSW 2052
AUSTRALIA
newsouthpublishing.com

First published 2014

10 9 8 7 6 5 4 3 2 1

National Library of Australia Cataloguing-in-Publication entry
Author: Atkinson, Alan.
Title: The Europeans in Australia. Volume 3: Nation/Alan Atkinson.
ISBN: 9780868409979 (paperback)
ISBN: 9781742241500 (ePub/Kindle)
ISBN: 9781742246833 (ePDF)
Notes: Includes bibliographical references and index.
Subjects: Australia – History – 20th century.
Dewey Number: 994

Design Josephine Pajor-Markus
Cover design Di Quick
Cover image WC Piguenit (Australia, b. 1836, d. 1914), *The flood in the Darling 1890* (1895), oil on canvas, 122.5 x 199.3 cm, courtesy of the Art Gallery of New South Wales.
Printed and bound by CPI Group (UK) Ltd, Croydon, CR0 4YY

This book is printed on paper using fibre supplied from plantation or sustainably managed forests.

UNSW Press wishes to acknowledge the generous support of the Macquarie Group Foundation.

Contents

Foreword

I

This is the third and last volume of *The Europeans in Australia*. It covers the period from the 1870s to the end of World War One or, as I call it, the Great War, the name used by those who endured it. It is usual for historians to break Australia's story in 1901, the year of Federation, which is understood to be the end of the beginning and the foundation period of a new kind of existence. By finishing instead with the War, I have attempted to tell a different story. So the War appears as the tragic culmination of several extraordinary decades, including the Federation years, and as an event which made a much deeper mark on the Australian people than did anything else, including Federation. At the same time, Federation and the War were two parts of a single experience. The choice to go no further than the War, which was part of the scheme of writing from the start, comes partly from the need to show that however unmistakable the signs of continuity might be the subject of these volumes was another world.

The whole book, the three volumes, therefore covers one and a quarter centuries, from the beginning of British settlement, when the invaders really were Europeans in Australia, to the point when they became, in their hundreds of thousands, Australians in Europe, themselves beating back invasion. This has been the work of about twenty years, from 1993 to 2013. Even during the 1990s, when the writing was well underway (volume 1 was published in 1997 and volume 2 in 2004), it was not perfectly clear to me where it was all headed. There was a set of themes and there was a plan, in the sense of a structure with some symmetry to it, and the writing has never wandered far from that overall patterning. All the same, the deeper logic of *The Europeans in Australia* has only slowly, and towards the end, pushed to the surface.

The book belongs to those two decades between 1993 and 2013, which like the period of Federation and the War has been a great turning-point time in the Australian experience. The 1990s was the decade of the High Court judgments in Mabo (1992) and Wik (1996), both redefining Indigenous land rights. It is hard to overstate the luminous engagement with Australia which those two judgments seemed at the time to represent, and yet they are barely household words today, so completely have we moved to another angle of the turning point. With those two judgments the High Court offered a trenchant comment on the whole process of European settlement. It also crystallised for Australia the possibility of 'moral community', as Tim Rowse (now a senior research fellow at the Australian National University) explained at the time, or in other words a national consensus based on a common, complex understanding of entitlement to land. Moral community is a term which, as Rowse said, reiterates 'commonwealth', the ideal of 1901, but post-Mabo it expresses even larger hopes.[1]

The High Court judgments were also founded on the Common Law. By weaving Indigenous understanding of land use ('native title') into the law as administered by the courts, law which from a settler perspective went back to Henry II and Alfred, the court posed fundamental questions about land and people, ownership and use, but also about communication, since all these things are shaped by the way the various inhabitants dealt with each other.

The question of moral community at one level or another crops up over and over throughout the three volumes, at least as a possibility – often a failed one. Sometimes it is a matter of Black and White, but more often it is a matter of wondering about the idea itself, within an Australian landscape. At the heart of each volume there are three chapters headed 'Men and Women', 'Black and

White' and 'God and Humanity'. In each of them moral community is the main point.

Moral community is, again, about the way people communicate. The years from 1993 to 2013 saw the arrival of mass electronic communication, an event more vast and sudden than any other in human history. The World Wide Web had been invented in Australia's bicentennial year. At that point, email was already in use among a few, and with the coming of the reader program Eudora, also in 1988, email started to be a real alternative to postage. In 1994 the web became fully accessible, with the first of a series of user-friendly browsers, in 1998 Google was launched, and in 2004 Facebook. When human beings start dealing with each other by fundamentally different means (not just message but also medium) the human condition itself changes. It has certainly done so this time and, whatever the change has done for moral community, it has coloured the kind of questions we ask about humanity in the past.

In some ways this great transformation looks like the culmination of something which has been going on for some time (though it will look more like a transition to our grandchildren). Early European settlement in Australia, in the last years of the eighteenth century, coincided with a revolution in common literacy centred on Europe and North America, and with remarkable developments in the technology and logistics of long-distance communication. In the first two volumes there was therefore a preoccupation with all the paraphernalia of print, postage and mass publication. In this final volume there is detail on self-awareness in speech (accent and articulation), on the ways of the telephone and on educational reform, including the usefulness of maps and the way we read them, and on 'scientific management' and 'efficiency'. (Inverted commas are called for because meanings have shifted.) When a certain critical number of the Europeans in Australia could grasp in their minds the map of Australia, then, and only then, Federation could go ahead by popular consent. Then, too, scientific management could be applied to the whole continent. When new ideas about management and governance came into play, then so did top-down centralisation. The War similarly depended on a mass understanding of maps and on putting efficiency first.

All the time, real human beings were embracing, resisting, creating and digesting these changes. Moral community (and commonwealth) is also about the way people agree to share things, to prosper together. This is particularly obvious in the light of Mabo and Wik. In these three volumes the question reaches to the agreements made by ocean castaways to ensure survival, to the commons scattered across Australia during the second half of the nineteenth century, to the 'village settlements' of the 1890s, and to life in the trenches during the War. Most obviously, it is an idea which speaks to marriage and family life, and to the ecology of the ordinary household.

The post-Indigenous settlement of Australia was a process woven through with wonderful ingenuity, from the First Fleet itself, which was a triumph over distance, to the dazzling inventiveness of the late nineteenth century and of Federation, which was about space more than distance. It was not all triumph. Fighting with distance and space takes its toll. Every gain was also a loss. In working forwards, in trying to create bigger and bigger communities and networks, there was a powerful temptation to devalue the sense and sensuality of the face to face and the small scale. On top of that, different expectations were placed on men and on women. Manhood was supposed to be shaped by large horizons and womanhood by small ones. So the making of big nations was often a vexed issue for women.

These three volumes have done little more than point to these questions, and in a fairly idiosyncratic fashion. It is a task which had to be tried, as a contribution to redeeming the promise of Mabo and Wik. The historian Nicholas Brown, writing in *The Cambridge*

History of Australia (a book which seems to make much the same attempt at redemption), suggests that '[i]t is unlikely that future historians will find in Australia at the beginning of the twenty-first century the vibrant civic culture rediscovered at the beginning of the twentieth'.[2] Certainly, during the decade after Mabo the republican debate and then (worse) the 'History Wars', each in different ways, blocked and corrupted the rich conversation implicit in both High Court judgments. It is not so much a matter of politics and policy. It is a matter of the bigger questions those judgments pointed to, and of deep undercurrents easily overlooked in chasing things that matter much less.

II

'I am sick to death of cleverness', says Jack Worthing, in *The Importance of Being Earnest*. 'Everybody is clever nowadays. You can't go anywhere without meeting clever people. The thing has become an absolute public nuisance.' At the time Oscar Wilde wrote this play (it was first staged in 1895), the Europeans in Australia, like everyone else, put enormous faith in cleverness. The men and women responsible for the Federation of the Australian colonies worshipped it. They wanted it everywhere. For the first time ever, an extensive, many-faceted, hands-on literacy had become a virtue everyone could aspire to, more or less. This volume makes a lot of that point.

It was much the same throughout the twentieth century. Tests of IQ (*Intelligenzquotient*, or Intelligence Quotient) began in France and the United States in the century's very first years, to test cleverness, and they were to be one of its typical and lasting inventions. The twentieth century was a century in love with numerical measurement, and more than any other numerical measurement IQ tests seemed to touch the core of individual potential and individual destiny.

After several generations of testing, in 1981 one of those working in the area, James Flynn, afterwards professor of political studies at the University of Otago, asked the world an important question. Mean IQ had always been set at 100. So how was it that psychologists testing IQ had been forced to change the position of that mean continuously from the beginning to the present? And why were the changes always in the same direction? In every country where testing was done an IQ of 100 at any one time was markedly below the IQ of 100 later on. Intelligence (as tested) was understood to be congenital and free of cultural input, and yet everywhere people seemed to be becoming steadily more intelligent. As Flynn put it, after looking at all possible explanations, it was only possible to conclude that, for some reason, there were 'massive IQ gains from one generation to another'. They were always at the same rate. To all appearances we were much cleverer than our immediate forebears had been. We were steadily drawing away from the generation which had started the tests, Oscar Wilde's generation, and presumably even further away from those who had lived before that.[3]

This is the Flynn Effect. Pointing it out made Jim Flynn famous. The process of change was already well underway during the period covered by this, the third and last volume of *The Europeans in Australia*. Beyond these paragraphs I have nothing to say about the Flynn Effect specifically, but it is clearly relevant to all that follows. It is one of the most complicated things to have happened to humanity, and fundamental to the way the Europeans in Australia started to understand themselves from the 1870s. It was central to the way they made themselves into a single people.

The change in IQ results was not due to a change in intelligence overall. It was a sign of greater efficiency in dealing with abstractions, logic and hypotheses, and it is symptomatic of the larger field of brain activity made possible by technologies associated with paper and ink (and more recently, no doubt, by reading online). Flynn speaks of 'a scientific perspective', but the increased capacity goes beyond science. It also stretches our minds, bit by bit, to embrace much bigger spaces and much longer periods of time. Through reading we can hold imagination still within particular periods and places, and among personalities, utterly different from our own. Reading also makes detailed introspection possible. As the great commentator on language Walter Ong said, the written word gives us a place from which to see into the chasm which divides the external objective world from the world of interior self.[4] We do not just look out from within ourselves. We also see ourselves looking out. In the period covered by this volume, educated men and women, taken with their own enlarged ability, made a hobby of introspection. They were also deliberately taught to be more sharply conscious of the sound of their own voices – and, in an age of racism, the colour of their own skins. Self-awareness was a fad, a symptom of well-read sophistication.

Of course, such skills have always been with us, at least a little. But mass literacy and the inventions linked with it, overlaying and complicating all the old attitudes built into oral conversation, meant that they became more completely part of our way of life. Beyond a certain point that makes a profound difference. Speech remains deeply important, and vastly more common than writing in dealings day to day. But our relationship with abstraction, with thought as a thing, has mutated as it has gained hold and as it has dug in more deeply. In a recent book, *The Better Angels of Our Nature* (2011), the American cognitive psychologist Steven Pinker gives a good account of the way wide reading, including novels, takes the individual into the lives and minds of others so as to extend the 'circle of empathy'.[5] This can mean an intellectualised sense of our group (or what we are told is our group), as with racism, or it can go further into something like 'the brotherhood of man'. It is the basis of humanitarianism. It deeply affects the relationship between the sexes, sometimes seeming to both reinforce and weaken sexism at the same time. There was a deep energy in all such issues during the period covered by this volume.

In 1983, in *Imagined Communities*, Benedict Anderson used much the same argument in explaining the nineteenth-century rise of the idea of the nation.[6] As much as any other single text, *Imagined Communities* sets the agenda for this whole book.

In the foreword to volume 1, I said that *The Europeans in Australia* as a whole – all three volumes – would be a description of 'the day-to-day intellectual notions associated with life as an Australian among Australians'. Also, I said, '[t]his history is about voices and language'. The first volume concentrated on what I called 'different forms of conversation'. I meant two things, but it is hard to disentangle them – namely, conversations of pen and paper and, on the other hand, 'the narrow and ephemeral conversations, the living, burning, sharp-edged exchanges of individuals face to face'.[7]

I did that in volume 1. Volume 2 carried the story into the middle decades of the nineteenth century. In that volume, I wrote on what I called 'a revolution in communications', due to a large but still limited expansion of literacy. The glorious result of this revolution was the beginning of the self-awareness already mentioned, a type of 'self-overhearing', which gave educated men and women a far sharper sense of themselves in the world. The well read – but the effect pushed out wider and wider – began to see how the written word could turn the world upside down, or rather inside out. This was an age of system. How wonderful to invent and even just to comprehend system! Nearly everyone, in greatly varying degrees, engaged with the interconnectedness of their universe. They saw larger, more numerous and more intricate patterns and abstractions.

In volume 3 all this is continued, as much as I have been able to manage, into the early twentieth century. Pen and paper, print and postage, and many, many more books created that interconnectedness. Such things remade imagination, because they made it easier to envisage with the mind's eye as well as to hear with the mind's ear. Thinking in abstract terms, using words like 'system', became a mark of status, especially for men. Women were usually more hesitant. Instead, women were quicker, from the period around 1850, to see reading and writing as a way of freeing themselves from the places to which their gender bound them. (This is clear from statistics on literacy.) They were more given to network than to hierarchical abstraction. As a result, they patterned their circumstances in distinctive ways and gave an altered slant to established mediums.

Of course, we see the Flynn Effect as improvement. So did most, but not all, nineteenth-century men and women. It was one of the great aims of school and university reform in the fifty years before the Great War. It looks like mental emancipation – the embracing of perfect objectivity. Really, as Michael Polanyi said long ago about the Copernican revolution (which put the sun at the centre of the universe rather than the earth), for all its prodigious brilliance the immediate aim of this shift was 'to satisfy a different human affection' – namely, 'man's delight in abstract theory'. Flynn, too, takes a cooler approach. He speaks only of 'new habits of mind' – new and not always better. Given that these new habits led, for instance, directly to the Great War, he is right to be cautious.[8]

III

Another set of ideas which has been an inspiration for the following pages is found in Peter Brown's book *The Rise of Western Christendom*. Brown is Rollins professor of history at Princeton. *The Rise of Western Christendom* appeared first in 1995 and came out again in a revised edition in 2003. The new version involved a good deal of rewriting. According to Brown, a 'dam burst' of research had been done in his area after 1995, and at the same time larger questions had emerged. In a sense he had had to start again.[9]

Though less ambitious and less learned than Brown's book, *The Europeans in Australia* has been shaped by the same current priorities, especially this final volume, and it has been pushed about by its circumstances in the same way. For Brown the big challenge was to get rid of the idea that Europe, or at least Western Europe, has always had a single mighty destiny. The older understanding, pre-Brown, made unity unquestionably good. It was providential. Under that rubric, disunity meant bigotry, petty-mindedness and war. In tracing the early story of Christianity in Europe, Brown talks instead of 'localization', and he suggests that being and thinking local was not necessarily a failure of humanity. On the contrary, the local was rich with a particular kind of humanity, with its own way of mingling emotion and intelligence. The great achievement of Christianity, says Brown, was to build a bridge between the local and the universal, so as to combine familiar ties (the essence of the gospel message, as in 'love thy neighbour') with 'loyalty to the idea of a wider Christendom'.[10]

Brown talks of this creation of Christendom as an extraordinary achievement. Ideals that can do what early Christianity did, thanks to the limitlessly subtle writing of St Paul, reconciling the small with the vast, are amazing evidence of human potential. In the first volume I spoke of settlement in Australia as an extension of Christendom. By the time covered by volume 3 that possibility was very deliberately challenged. Australian Federation shows how there were now other ways to proceed.

This is the angle I take in the following pages. Australian Federation was a great achievement too. In the last part of the nineteenth century, the Europeans in Australia, struck by their sudden ability to bridge distance and space, busied themselves with ideas about size. Changed ways of communicating meant changed possibilities and obligations in that respect. They were not alone. Everywhere there were efforts to make groups of humanity bigger and bigger, stretching over larger spaces. The *Barrier Miner*, a leading newspaper at Broken Hill, the mining city in far western New South Wales, put it well in June 1898:

> Here there is combination and there federation; an industrial union, one of the grandest in the world, is beaten by a wider-spreading federation of employers; the churches, suffering from wasted efforts, come together in organic union; members of Parliament, representing similar interests, agree to a pledge of solidarity; companies displace firms, and trusts displace companies – federation, union, combination everywhere; and everywhere only vanquished by still larger federations. The race is not to the swift nor the battle to the strong. They only win in these latter days who are united.[11]

The great question, as with early Christianity, was how to preserve the interests of the small, including the love of neighbours, within the interests of the vast – how to combine without killing off the combining parties.

Federation, and not just federation for colonies, was the most ingenious answer, because it made various sovereignties and collective freedoms possible all at the same time. The United States had done the same thing much less self-consciously a century earlier, and for many (the eminent Tasmanian Andrew Inglis Clark, for instance) the United States was the model for Australia. As James Bryce, British scholar, politician and mountain climber, put it, America was 'a Commonwealth of commonwealths, a Republic of republics, a State which, while one, is nevertheless composed of other States even more essential to its existence than it is to theirs'.[12] Bryce's formulation meant a lot to the Australians.

As a means of squaring the circle, in late-nineteenth-century Australia, Federation was very like Mabo and Wik, and for its time just as sophisticated. Both formulations also draw on the rich idea of nation, as something sovereign – something self-justifying – and also as a hypothesis throwing open many large questions. How big can a nation be and still make sense? Is a nation possible without a single unrivalled government to define it? Can a nation have a conscience? Can a nation have a soul, or at least a spiritual essence? Can it have a single, genuinely representative voice? An enlarged nation (enlarged in its geographical dimensions, its total population or its diversity) forces minds to expand, and, as I say, this volume, like the previous two, is a story of mental expansion.

One central figure is the Sydney feminist Rose Scott, who loved the land, in its beauty and variety, and also the people who lived in and by it, but hated the idea of continental government. Hers is still an important possibility. In his talk of moral community, Tim Rowse quoted Hobbles Danayarri, a Mudburra man of Wave Hill, in the Northern Territory: 'Because I'm saying, we the one with the land. Sitting on the land, Aboriginal people. You got nothing. All you government'.[13]

But there was a lot Rose Scott did not see. This volume, especially towards the end, concentrates on the various ways in which inhabitants of the continent saw, or did not see, or did not see through (in both senses) the different possibilities of a nation, using what everyone was starting to call brainwork.

IV

In writing this book I have had three main benefactors. At the start, the Australian Research Council gave me funding for five years of uninterrupted research, which was an enormous and essential boon, and the University of New England topped that up. UNE also gave me a place to work in for most of that time. This volume in particular makes much of the bush, and being at a bush university, and such a good one, has been a great help – on top of a bush upbringing. More recently I have benefited enormously from the kind attention and forbearance of the warden and fellows of St Paul's College, at the University of Sydney, especially the inimitable and unlimitable warden Ivan Head. From the college, the vigour and generosity of its internal life, and its powerful intellectual traditions, I have also gained a great deal, as will be obvious to those who know where to look.

To live several years among students is to understand better John Keats's plan at the age of twenty-two: 'I will clamber through the Clouds and exist'.[14] And to understand that is to understand better the Federation of the Australian colonies, which was partly driven by the young. It goes without saying that the volume also owes a great deal to my own children, Tom, Catherine and Elizabeth, for the same reason and much more profoundly. Thanks to them too for the way they have lived through this work.

The volume divides itself roughly into three large topics, and there are debts attached to the way I have dealt with each. Running through the whole there is the slow-moving, generational turnover of habit, thought and attachment to the continent, including, towards the end, its wildlife. Historians interested in the way the settler people adjusted to their surroundings nearly always focus on landscape and human artefacts. They say little about wildlife, and yet human beings can identify with other living creatures at least as readily as with inanimate surroundings. Animals figure largely in this volume – livestock to start with and wildlife later on. Noises made by animals were part of the common soundscape, which means that, like many apparently trivial things, they are essential to our broad historical understanding of the past. It is likely that the noise of the bush made a sharper impact than its appearance did on its European invaders. Children's stories written around the turn of the century were the first thoroughgoing attempt to come to grips with bush sounds, a project which women writers especially took to heart, some of them finding help in Indigenous understanding.

In the area of sensibility in general, I have been guided by the writings of Meg Vivers, especially her ideas about 'inscape' (taken from Gerard Manley Hopkins) and her richly perceptive exploration of the difference between men's and women's ideas of space, in the setting of the colonial frontier.[15] Bain Attwood's work has underpinned concerns with the rights and wrongs of exclusive attachment to the land, from the settler perspective, informed by a sense of ongoing negotiation and contradiction. Australian history writing now looks to parallels and comparisons beyond Australia much more usefully than it used to do, as part of the boundless networking of ideas mentioned earlier. Attwood's writing shows how well that approach can work on the page, and also the importance of precise moral judgment. Deborah Bird Rose's brilliant book *Dingo Makes Us Human* does the same with the Indigenous viewpoint.[16]

However, Rose's work is just one example of the remarkable flowering of Indigenous history in Australia since the 1970s. No other body of historical scholarship seems quite so rich, and it has enlightened other areas as well. The inspiration can be traced to Mabo and beyond.

My understanding of the geopolitics of the continent in the pre-Federation period has been greatly helped by Anne Coote's writing on the way the colonies thought of themselves as nations. (Anne Coote has also written a short piece on common attitudes to wildlife in the nineteenth century.)[17] Ray Evans's work on Queensland – not only his book on race, *Fighting Words*, but also his volume in the Cambridge collection of state histories – has made an essential difference too.[18] And as usual, so has the remarkable writing of Henry Reynolds. Geopolitics runs right through Reynolds's work, including his early classic, *The Other Side of the Frontier*. In this volume I have made use especially of his master's thesis on the history of colonial Tasmania, and his *North of Capricorn*, written forty years later, about the other side of the continent. *North of Capricorn* shows what questions become possible when you start, like Peter Brown with Europe, by imagining Australia in parts rather than as a preordained unity.[19]

Links between city and bush are central. Two learned articles on that subject, by Graeme Davison and by John Hirst, published in the same issue of *Historical Studies* (now *Australian Historical*

Studies) in 1978, are leading examples of the deep infrastructure a book like this has to have.[20]

In every case, the few authors named stand out from a much larger number.

In my arguing about the way the Europeans in Australia were drawn together at the time of Federation, Stuart Macintyre's book *A Colonial Liberalism: The Lost World of Three Victorian Visionaries* was especially useful. It reinforces a belief in the variability of methods and traditions from one colony to the next and it casts essential light on the tradition most fundamental to the making of the Commonwealth – namely, the protectionism associated in different ways with David Syme, George Higinbotham and Charles Henry Pearson. Macintyre's book also has a particularly fresh and easy method of tracing ideas through word and deed together. The same is true of Frank Bongiorno's *The People's Party*, on Victorian radicalism before and after Federation. I hope that some years of knowing and reading Frank, in all his multiple interests, have made an impact on this volume.[21]

Sylvia Lawson's work on the *Bulletin* in *The Archibald Paradox* shows that words are deeds. The *Bulletin* has a central place in the engine, or animal, I have called 'organised intelligence' (a label taken from the great English writer HG Wells). Like many other things, the *Bulletin* figures less than it should in these pages, but I have carried Lawson's way of dealing with it into other, related lines of inquiry. The evidence of Australian ingenuity in other areas, as presented in particular by Ann Moyal, has been inspirational in the same way.[22]

Drawing the Global Colour Line, by Marilyn Lake and Henry Reynolds, has provided pointers for the wider geographical setting attempted in this book. Even more obviously, Lake's earlier work *Getting Equal: The History of Australian Feminism* has shaped a crucial part of the argument towards the end, together with what she says about men 'giving birth' to the nation.[23] Bob Birrell's

Federation: The Secret Story, pointed out to me some years ago by Frank Bongiorno, offers just the right sort of detailed big picture for coming to grips with the architects of Federation and their businesslike idealism. But then, in another way, so does John Hirst's *Sentimental Nation*, which has also been a foundation text.[24]

As for the Great War, in getting a sense of its dimensions and meaning, I have used a variety of Australian sources. The big picture, however, comes from authorities overseas. William Philpott's *Three Armies on the Somme* I found especially useful, together with a collection published in 2000 called *Great War, Total War: Combat and Mobilization on the Western Front, 1914–1918*.[25] However, Bill Gammage's *Broken Years*, first published in 1974, continues to inform and inspire, as the original Australian classic in its field, and so does Ken Inglis's *Sacred Places*. The issue of post-War memory of mourning has been an area of strength in Australian history (the writing of Stephen Garton and of Joy Damousi, for instance), but it has been largely beyond the reach of my argument.[26] Nevertheless, I have used John Moses's understanding of the origins of Anzac Day, with its implication that religious faith and ceremony have a central place in understanding the War. Joan Beaumont's *Broken Nation: Australians and the Great War* appeared too late for me to use.[27]

In the overall shaping of the argument for this volume, besides Anderson's *Imagined Communities*, I owe a great deal to two books in particular: Richard Sennett's *The Fall of Public Man*, which I first read a long time ago, and Stephen Kern's *The Culture of Time and Space, 1880–1918*. Both have rounded out ideas of subjectivity and 'the view from within' which are central to the whole book. *Is History Fiction?*, a great book by Ann Curthoys and John Docker, has also done a lot to strengthen the general approach.[28]

At the very end of writing, the new *Cambridge History of Australia*, already mentioned, helped very considerably in fine-tuning and testing the overall picture. Ultimately, I, and surely most Australian historians, have been profoundly influenced by Manning

Clark, who showed that it was possible for a scholar not just to reimagine the national story but also to do it in ways that ask questions about humanity itself.[29] Half a century before him, Charles Bean, historian of the Great War, did the same.

Among various archives repositories in which I have found material for this volume, I am especially indebted to the Mitchell Library (State Library of New South Wales) and the National Library of Australia. The availability of online sources has made the writing of this volume very different from that of volumes 1 and 2. A glance at the notes will show how much I have relied on Trove, the digital copying project orchestrated by the National Library.

I have not sought much help from research assistants. However, Eve Vincent found some useful material for me in Melbourne, for which I am very grateful, and in Sydney, Yvonne Perkins has made a very significant difference, tying her own perceptive research on the Federation period, its moral and religious dimensions, to my own inquiries.[30]

Large debts indeed are owed to those who have read the typescript all the way through before publication, remarkably quickly and carefully – namely, Nicolas Rothwell, Stuart Macintyre, Marian Quartly, Mark McKenna, Frank Bongiorno and Stephen Foster. Marian's guidance, especially, goes a long way back. Thanks also, very much, to Phillipa McGuinness at NewSouth Publishing. The book would not have been possible at all without her encouragement, and more essentially her remarkable patience. The many peculiarities of style which have survived an extraordinarily patient, precise and painstaking copyediting by NewSouth Publishing come from my belief that every book exists, more or less, within the 'commonwealth of speech'.[31]

And first and last, my wife, and the commonwealth of two. How deep, rich and complicated that contribution is. Catherine Pound has energised and sustained these volumes, at great cost, and made them worth finishing.

EXPLORING

The relativity revolution ... dates from 1905 and 1915 ... While struggling with puzzles involving electricity, magnetism and light's motion, Einstein realized that Newton's conception of space and time, the cornerstone of classical physics, was flawed. Over the course of a few intense weeks in the spring of 1905, he determined that space and time are not independent and absolute, as Newton had thought, but are enmeshed and relative in a manner that flies in the face of common experience. Some ten years later, Einstein hammered a final nail in the Newtonian coffin by rewriting the laws of gravitational physics. This time, not only did Einstein show that space and time are part of a unified whole, he also showed that by warping and curving they participate in cosmic evolution. Far from being the rigid, unchanging structures envisioned by Newton, space and time in Einstein's reworking are flexible and dynamic.

The two theories of relativity [specific in 1905 and general in 1915] are among humankind's most precious achievements, and with them Einstein toppled Newton's conception of reality. Even though Newtonian physics seemed to capture mathematically much of what we experience physically, the reality it describes turns out to be not the reality of our world. Ours is a relativistic reality.[1]

Brian Greene, *The Fabric of the Cosmos*

1

The Elements

I

Charles Edwin Woodrow Bean was the first to write the story of the Australians in the Great War, 1914–18. The way he told that story was coloured by what he had learnt about Australia in the years before fighting broke out. Bean did more than anyone else to cut and polish the hero image of the Anzac, but long before he did that he already had clear ideas about the land and people. He was a lawyer who had become a journalist, and five years before the War he had been sent to western New South Wales by the *Sydney Morning Herald* to report on the wool industry at ground level. It was his second trip to this part of the country and he made himself at home among all the glassy heat. Travelling by train and coach to Bourke and then by steamship, the *Dreadnought*, along the tree-shaded, sweet-breezy, snag-ridden waters of the River Darling, he gathered a mass of thoughts about wool and sheep, and he added to what he already knew about language, labour, housing, jokes, animal peculiarities, the usefulness and beauty of the inland trees, the possibilities of irrigation, and the ease with which, in those bright, hard places, men died of thirst.

'*Dreadnought*', the name, was a joke. The dreadnoughts were warships built as part of Britain's preparation for conflict with Germany, and the river people were putting their small vessel on a par with the greatest fighting ships the world had ever seen. Bean liked this kind of chaffing. He was also, he said, 'passionately fond of children'. A boy he called 'the Imp' (real name Ern Bentley) was the *Dreadnought*'s steward. The Imp's face was half-hidden by a shabby hat. He displayed, said Bean, 'the white sailor jumper and monkey jacket, the bare knees, sturdy brown shins, and crumpled socks of an Australian youngster'. One night, when the ship was tied up, two crewmen stepped ashore to settle a quarrel. Everyone else went to watch. The Imp came late, loudly announcing his arrival.

> With the strange simplicity of outback Australians [Bean wrote], the men listened to him exactly as to one of themselves.
>
> 'You're just in time, son,' said the big deck-hand, with a sly glance at Bill [one of the combatants], who ... had been getting the worst of it. 'Bill here's about your size. He'll put 'em on with you.'
>
> 'What 'm I going to say to his mother if I damage him?' retorted the Imp.

The Imp was a musician. That night in the saloon he played his mouth organ. It was an 'awful instrument', Bean said, but this enigmatic child touched it gently, lingering lightly from note to note. The sound hung like a harvest of stars against the stillness of the night. It cast a charm on its listeners, cutting a gash in the tangible world, according to Bean, and revealing another world, infinitely lovely. '[O]ne felt as if a curtain had been raised ever so little,' he said, 'and one realised just for a second that one was looking through at something beyond'.[1]

Bean hungered for glimpses like this of the sublime and exquisite, and also of the brave and terrible – for 'something beyond'. He longed for the 'strangely simple' aspects of humanity that played about the edges, or maybe at the half-hidden heart, of Australian life. Picking over small places, he looked for a vastness of feeling in each man and woman. Bean was more than just a historian of wartime. Like many who figure in the following pages, he saw the continent as a single large stage for playing out a drama central to the history of the world. Australia for Bean was a problem, and one with an infinite number of halfway solutions. He went no further west than Broken Hill, but he sensed beyond that point, beyond the Darling's feeble line of water, which was both highway and boundary, a kind of vacancy, a place empty of civilisation and of moral light – though oppressed with sun. He had travelled inland to gather knowledge about a region very little known to the men and women who lived along the coast. He saw it as a place of destiny. The territory threaded by the Darling was, as another Australian writer said in the same year, 'the borderland of savagery', a place '[f]ar removed from the law-bewitched nerve-centres of population'. For Bean too it was a border, though still part of 'civilized Australia'. It was the land even further out (or in) that puzzled and intrigued him. He called it 'Central Australia' or 'the Centre'. But, he said, it was hardly Australia at all.[2] It was the middle. But it was also beyond the edge.

Afterwards, during the War, he transferred his inquiries to the hearts of people, especially men. His eagerness to know, and the contradictions he discovered, were much the same.

In the Centre, Bean alleged, even the mails came no more than twice a year. (In fact, four times was common.) 'The King's writ may run', he said, 'but it does not run very often ... The only justice can be such as a strong manager metes out among strong men'. A station manager, for instance, the boss of many parched acres, 'never woke or slept', so Bean fantasised, 'without a revolver, and he generally kept it by his shoulder to save unnecessary waste of time'. Think of the authority that went with such isolation. Think of the power multiplied by years of existence in 'the black's country' – and multiplied too by the hundreds of miles that lay between such a manager and any useful town. The White men under that manager's authority were few. Bean recounted a story told, so he said, by a typical boss. 'Once in his life ... he had to settle which of two men was in the wrong ... He settled – and the man whom he judged to be wrong he never saw again.'[3] It sounds almost as if there was another place, even further away than the Centre, into which desperate men dropped and vanished.

The idea of a centre within the Centre, or beyond it – as John Milton says, 'in the lowest deep a lower deep', a point without order, an age before the beginning of history, in nineteenth-century terms a fourth dimension (see later) – was a ruling theme of European life, including European life in Australia, during the years covered by this volume.[4] The century ahead was to throw up forms of traffic and communication more dazzlingly rapid than anything men and women had ever known, types of human power remarkably vast and disorder beyond imagining – evil worse than evil. This volume deals with Australia up to the time of the Great War. It therefore tells of peculiar beginnings.

Bean was not the first to think in longing and visionary ways about the Centre. An earlier generation had imagined an inland sea, a green and shining spot, which would welcome all that was best about European civilisation. Since then, during the later decades of the nineteenth century, as ideas about the single landmass further unfolded, that image had turned itself inside out. In the years of Bean's youth, Australian thoughts were vexed with bleaker possibilities. The key to this understanding can be found in the most popular type of contemporary novel – crystallised, that is, in fiction. In London in 1885 a former British colonial official, Henry Rider Haggard, published a story called *King Solomon's Mines*. Haggard's heroes pushed for many days across a scorching desert (where their lips cracked when they smiled) and over a freezing mountain (14 or 15 degrees below zero) into the heart of Africa, looking for legendary diamond mines that had been worked by King Solomon. They found physical and moral desolation – the remains of an ancient empire, and a people who could tell them only that the great ruins roundabout were made by 'the wise men of old time'.

King Solomon's Mines was called 'the most amazing book ever written'. Within a year it had sold over 30,000 copies in England and had passed through thirteen editions in the United States. It made the same impression in Australia. It galvanised the imagination of the European world and for a generation hundreds of stories were produced, both fact and fiction, modelled on it.[5] The formula was simple. There was a journey deep into some vast landmass. A body of men drove hard into the unknown – Africa, Australia, South America – and somewhere there, beyond the reach of our familiar civilisation and in a different kind of time, another world revealed itself, alien, corrupt and terrifying. Life itself was in a state of suspension. Joseph Conrad's famous story, *The Heart of Darkness* (1902), about Africa, was the finest example. Remember too Bram Stoker's *Dracula* (1897) – not at first a bestseller – which started and ended with journeys, increasingly frightening, into a barely known corner of Europe, to the fortress of 'the Un-Dead'.

In Australia, tales of 'extraordinary tribes of blacks', highly sophisticated but cut off from the world and far beyond the White man's frontier, had circulated by word of mouth since the 1850s.[6] The example of *King Solomon's Mines* showed how such tales could be written up, varnished with gothic detail and sold to advantage. Readers had to imagine such people suddenly discovered by men (even women) such as themselves. The result was a stream of new novels: *The Secret of the Australian Desert* (1894) by Ernest Favenc (an explorer himself), *An Australian Bush Track* (1896) by David Hennessey, *The Last Lemurian* (1898) by George Firth Scott, *The Lost Explorers: A Story of the Trackless Desert* (1907) by Alexander Macdonald, and many more.

Why now? Where, at that time, did the thrill of such stories come from? Joseph Conrad has been called 'the first modern novelist in England' because of the way he showed human character on its own, with all convention cut away. In Conrad's words, imagination in this new age was drawn to the 'purely psychological' – to 'the expectation of some essential disclosure as to the strength, the power, the horror, of human emotions'. Readers were forced from bright and comfortable habitats into their own 'heart of darkness'.[7] They slid into the void of their inner selves, or into the possibility of so far unsuspected selves. They danced with their own mortality. In earlier centuries, sailors who went far enough from Europe were supposed to fall off the edge of the earth. Here, now, was another kind of vertigo, a moral void. It was not long before many of the Europeans in Australia, boys and girls in the 1880s and '90s, went on to be soldiers and nurses in the Middle East and in France. After their long journey, they found the same sort of thing there.

Honoré de Balzac had lived one or two generations earlier, but he was another favourite author of the moment. (A forty-volume English translation of his work appeared in 1896.) Balzac's story of Colonel Chabert captured exactly the sense of suspended animation felt in reading these books. Chabert, the hero, was buried alive in a mass grave on the field of the Battle of Stuttgart in 1814. Waking up, he found himself among a knotted mass of limbs: 'I heard – or I thought I heard, I will assert nothing – groans from the world of the dead among whom I was lying. Some nights I still think I hear stifled moans'.[8] Escaping from the grave, he found himself still dead in the minds of former friends. They thought he was a ghost or impostor. From life among the dead, he stepped into death among the living.

Thinking could be very morbid. Obsession with childhood and youth (see later on) was mirrored by obsession with menacing age and death. The two ends of human experience shaped each other. (In *Dracula* they interpenetrate.) Whole cities could seem alive and dead at the same time. In Nathaniel Hawthorne's *The Marble Faun*, nineteenth-century Rome was encrusted with smells, the smell of mould and the smell of sour-bread, for instance, freshly baked.

Young people fill the story, and yet the city was 'a long decaying corpse' thick with 'dust and fungus growth'.[9] In Thomas Mann's *Death in Venice* (1912), also full of the beauty of youth, old buildings, all elegance, oozed sweet stench.

This was the age of Australian Federation, and Australian fancy fixed on the Centre as the pivot of a new national domain. (In the early twenty-first century for the same sort of reasons the Centre is called 'the zero-point of national identity'. That word 'identity' is too mean.) It was a place out of time, dead and alive. Ralph Tate, professor of natural science at the University of Adelaide, relying on 'book knowledge', imagined the MacDonnell Ranges near Alice Springs as an 'insular mass' with plants and animals predating Australia's current wildlife – species which should have been extinct. He imagined life, or pseudo-life, untouched by the changes happening everywhere else.[10] Charles Bean said much the same about the places he saw beyond the immediate reach of the Darling, with its happier smells of mud and moistness. '[O]ut here,' he said, 'in the real Australia, there survive some of the old trees that have been run off the face of the world by the fierce competition elsewhere, trees with thin feathery jointed fingers of leaves such as you can only see in fossils elsewhere'. There was elsewhere and there was us. These 'cenotaphs of species dead elsewhere', said the poet Bernard O'Dowd, defined the continent. Similarly, Arthur Conan Doyle wrote a novel, *The Lost World* (1912), set in the Amazon Basin, featuring prehistoric animals and semi-humans with 'cold inexorable light blue eyes'.[11]

As for the Aboriginal people, they were understood as the primitive possessors of a place as rich as King Solomon's mines. They lacked self-awareness and sense of purpose, or what the German philosopher Georg Hegel called *Geist*, the consciousness possessed by higher humanity. They danced, but in repetition, like a machine. The view of William Austin Horn, mining magnate and philanthropist, was typical: 'The Central Australian aborigine is the living representative of a stone age ... He has no traditions, and yet continues to practise with scrupulous exactness a number of hideous customs and ceremonies which have been handed from his fathers, and the origin or reason of which he knows nothing'. Ages ago the Black man had reasons for the things he did. Now he was a re-enactor. Dancing, dancing, dancing, as a puppet of time. Like Colonel Chabert, he had no hope of proving he was really alive. This was a common idea about Aboriginal people, and about Chinese too. It was an idea which shadowed the process of Australian nationality. Australia as a whole, said another writer, was 'a museum of living antiquities', 'a little modified fragment of ... [the] Middle Age of the earth'.[12] And yet it was the newest nation.

This nation was all future, but the Aboriginal people could have no future. Their system of existence, it was said, fell to pieces on exposure to the living air and to newness. According to an American anthropologist, 'The Australian tribes are melting away before the touch of civilisation'.[13] (It was a common image. Bram Stoker's 'Un-Dead' dissolved at the moment of defeat.) The main excitement in the latest novels, in *King Solomon's Mines*, *The Heart of Darkness*, *The Lost Explorers*, came from that moment, that mutual touch of youth and age, newness and death, the happy idiom and up-to-date weapons of today and the primeval responses of a people out of time. The Australian nation stood, in contrast, for life at its fullest.

A mounted constable remembering fights among the golden gorges of Central Australia put it well. '[T]he Martini-Henry carbines [invented in 1877, used also in the Zulu War] ... were talking English', he said, 'in the silent majesty of those great eternal rocks'.[14]

Tales like these were good fun. They were 'ripping yarns'. But they also took you into 'something beyond'. They summed up the European sense of Australia as a single mass – one continent, one battlefield, one theatre – with one eternally parched, eternally dazzling Centre-stage. They could be fiction. But they seemed true. As late as 1909 someone as straightforward as Charles Bean, who must have read them as a boy, could scatter their echoes, like the rattle of carbines, through his writing. These stories show, or help to show, how the continent as a whole – past, present and future – was imagined by the Europeans who lived in it. On such thoughts something very large was built.

II

It is said that Australia (unlike, say, the United States) was not a nation born in revolution. That is not completely true. During the last part of the nineteenth century a sense of extraordinary novelty was in the air. The creation of the Commonwealth in 1901 tapped that feeling. The interest in death and in 'something beyond' matched a heightened idea of life's possibilities. Emerging from shadows, defeating menace, taking control, using brains – those were the best things about being Australian.

The cultivation of human intelligence is part of the long interweaving of speech and literacy, a central point in these three volumes. Generation by generation, as men and women became more thoroughly literate, as trained intelligence of this sort became a common tool, habits of talk and habits of reading and writing became more and more subtly and powerfully interconnected. Until the 1870s knowledge about the Centre had been gathered spasmodically, from explorers and long-distance drovers, most of them no more than venturing to its edge. The Overland Telegraph, completed between Port Augusta and Port Darwin in 1872, was by far the most substantial European invasion of the Centre so far. Here was writing coded for instant transmission across vast distances.

The line had to be regularly checked and maintained, and repeater stations were built at intervals along it, each with a small resident team of men, servants of the new technology. These stations served a range of purposes. By the end of the 1870s the station at Alice Springs, for instance, housed a barometer and a weather gauge, and the officer in charge was expected to check readings at three-hourly intervals each day, from nine in the morning to nine at night. His observations, transmitted by telegraph, became part of the South Australia–wide monthly meteorological record.[15]

Among the speech-driven Aboriginal people of the Centre, the telegraph sparked a rearrangement, or at least an extension and intensification, of customary movements. Europeans doubted that Aborigines could change, but the people at the Centre proved to the contrary. Here, unlike in many other parts of Australia, the movement of the invaders was slow enough for them to take advantage of it. The stations became meeting places, where a certain amount of water and food was available. In the words of Edward Stirling, an amateur anthropologist,

> As frequently happens in the dry regions of Australia it is the advantages offered by the presence of permanent water that has [*sic*] been the prime inducement to select a particular locality for a settlement both by whites and blacks, and in the case of the latter, the presence of the white man offers additional inducements in the way of gifts or unconditional trifles of food.[16]

Grazing properties, now spreading further out because communications were better, had the same effect. Aborigines joined in the seasonal mustering and droving of livestock, in shepherding and shearing, and as cameleers. Among their older occupations, the needs of ritual and livelihood had always overlapped. The timing of both ritual and livelihood shifted accordingly.[17]

During the previous two or three generations there had already been some major disturbances in the rhythm of Aboriginal life. Epidemics of smallpox had spread several times from the north, started among Makasan sailors camping on the beach, most recently in 1858. For some reason, this disease affected women more than men, and where more women than men died, old patterns of relationship and belief had to be rearranged, a transformation hurried forward by the impact of the telegraph.[18] New ceremonies emerged. The people gathered in larger numbers and from longer distances. They began to expect immensely new things. A dance of great complexity called the Mudlunga was invented among Aborigines in Queensland north-west of Mt Isa, possibly in the 1890s, and it was carried from people to people as far as Lake Eyre and so to the Great Australian Bight. One dancer, whom the Europeans called Mick McLean, remembered long afterwards the first performance of the Mudlunga near the Diamantina River in about 1901 (this is a translation from his own language):

> There was a place ... Narani we call it, [white people] call it 'Seven Mile'. That's where they danced the Mudlunga ceremony in the creek so that a vast number of people should see this Mudlunga. That is how they all got to see something special, sensational, a new corroboree which they had never seen before.

Onlookers were very deliberately gathered together: '[O]ld men from my mob were on their way to Kanowana to fetch people from there for the Mudlunga. They went to Kanowana, to Yarawarawarga country to collect them for the Mudlunga – it was just like mustering'. The dancers were painted in red ochre and black manganese, they wore horns like bullocks, and they sang in a tongue from another part of the country, a tongue foreign to themselves and to their listeners. Even the way listeners turned up was new – the way they were persuaded, more forcibly than in earlier days. '[T]hey drove us like cattle.'[19]

'[I]t was just like mustering.' '[T]hey drove us like cattle.' The noise of droving – pushing forwards, shouted orders, the odd bark of a dog plus the sharp moan of the cattle, the spasmodic tumult which goes with the moving of livestock – was a noise which echoed through that age. Droving was long-distance work, and few things did more than droving to unify the Europeans in Australia. The Mudlunga united people, even when they spoke different languages. Mick McLean was a stockman, so he knew about droving.[20] He knew about the inclinations of cattle, about their instinctive movements, large and small, about pushing and guiding, gathering and drafting, using a willing few to move the mass. It was a continent-wide skill. It was like managing democracy.

As a drover, Mick McLean had been initiated in a business with ancient origins in Europe. Long ago, Dafydd Jones, for instance, an eighteenth-century Welshman, was employed in the cattle trade to London. A convert to Methodism, he wrote hymns, but his thoughts were a drover's thoughts. He sang in Welsh about gathering souls for judgment. 'They all came', he said, 'from the East, West, North and South to unlimited Sion', like streams of cattle drawn to one point – to the everlasting waters. So with Mudlunga. The Aboriginal people did not think of a Christian paradise, but their dance seemed to forecast devastating revenge by Aboriginal people on the invaders.[21] The taste of startling freshness – of being herded and hurried towards something new – was certainly much the same.

Among the Aborigines, trading patterns were already large. Now they were larger. Valuable objects made their way over vast distances – from the Kimberley, say, in the far north-west, even to central Queensland. Also, more trouble was taken with the objects themselves, and richer pieces were exchanged. There were pearl-shell pendants from the north coast, obtained from Makasans. Stone knives, sometimes of white chalcedony, were especially prized. They were made longer and more elaborate, and it may be that additional quarries were opened up. Sacred *tjuringa* (flat ornamented pieces of wood or stone) seem to have been produced in larger numbers, with new ornamentation and new uses. There was an expanding market among the people in the goods of the Europeans themselves, such as tobacco, glass and metal, including lengths of wire and billycans. Broken in pieces, the white porcelain insulators on the telegraph line were used for trimming spearheads.[22]

For the White people, the building of the Overland Telegraph was something like the building of an observation station on the moon. It had enormous intellectual implications. The line, linked with a submarine cable in the north, brought the rest of the world within reach. But it was also possible now, with an awareness of the telegraph, to think of yourself standing in the middle of the country, at that Centre '[d]ark with excessive bright', as Milton says, and looking outwards.[23] You could let your intellectual eye sweep across the continent as a whole. For this and other reasons (see later), Europeans could now imagine Australia more clearly as one landmass, as a united network of communications, as one tangle of problems and one sheet of answers. The people as a whole could be imagined as a single enterprise, belonging to one great crystalline vacancy. A world made dangerous and difficult in 'ripping yarns' was rendered almost smooth and simple by the telegraph.

The line was used like a clue within a maze by men overlanding sheep and cattle. In 1872 the Englishman Ernest Giles took advantage of it to explore the country to the west of Alice Springs. 'My object', he said, '... was to force my way across the thousand miles that lay untrodden and unknown, between the ... telegraph line and the settlements upon the Swan River'. Giles was not infected by the morbid pessimism of the 'ripping yarns'. (Those were to come a little later.) In 'that unknown space', he said, as he summed up his thoughts before starting,

> [t]here was room for snowy mountains, an inland sea, ancient river, and palmy plain, for races of new kinds of men inhabiting a new and odorous land, for fields of gold and

> golcondas of gems, for a new flora and a new fauna, and, above all the rest combined, there was room for me![24]

Golconda was the name of a granite fortress in India which was a famous place for trading diamonds, diamonds being the White man's chalcedony. Giles made five expeditions between 1872 and 1876, and he twice managed to reach the west coast. There was no snow or diamonds, but plenty of saltbush and mulga.

The power of the telegraph hovered over these apparently empty spaces. Close enough, you heard the singing of the wire. Telegraph lines, first built in Australia in 1853, had begun as a technological miracle. Within thirty years, they made up a complicated network extending through all the settled parts of the continent, and useful for directing all kinds of activity. Agents and employees were managed like puppets through the wires. 'I've been hunting wild geese', said a character in the novel *An Outback Marriage*, by Andrew Barton 'Banjo' Paterson.

> That's what I do most of my time now. The old man – Grant, you know – my boss – he's always hearing of mobs of cattle for sale, and if I'm down in the south-west [of New South Wales] the mob is sure to be up in the far north-east, but it's all one to him. He wires to me to go and inspect them quick and lively before someone else gets them, and I ride and drive and coach hundreds of miles to get at some flat-sided pike-horned mob of brutes without enough fat on them to oil a man's hair with.[25]

Such traffic created overland stock-routes, connecting the various colonies across what was otherwise a blank wilderness. The country north of Adelaide, for instance, was linked to south-west Queensland mainly by the Birdsville Track, which became a regular thoroughfare when the South Australian government sank artesian bores along the way. Its hub was Maree, a railhead town populated by Muslim cameleers from Afghanistan and adjacent places, and with a mosque of timber and thatch for the telling of stories from elsewhere.[26]

III

During the last part of the nineteenth century, Britain had seven antipodean colonies. Five made up the Australian mainland and two, New Zealand and Tasmania, were archipelagos. In wealth and population New South Wales and Victoria were by far the biggest. Their capital cities, Sydney and Melbourne, were unique within the empire, smaller than London and two or three more cities in Britain itself, but beyond anything else in the queen's dominions. Sydney was three generations old, but Melbourne had grown to its prodigious size – 473,000, according to the 1891 census (Sydney had 383,000) – within living memory.[27] For a generation, Melbourne was virtually the British capital of Australasia, but the 1890s depression hit Melbourne hard and as a result Sydney drew ahead. City life on the scale of Sydney and Melbourne was a true phenomenon, exhilarating for some and frightening for others. Such vast numbers, tightly packed, posed large questions for the future of humankind.

For some men and women these questions had gloomy answers. It was an article of faith, at least among romantics, that man – true man – was a solitary and occasionally dangerous being, best left alone, away from crowds. '[D]o you notice how,' asks Joseph Conrad in *Lord Jim*, 'three hundred miles beyond the end of telegraph cables and mail-boat lines, the haggard utilitarian lies of our civilisation wither and die, to be replaced by pure exercises of imagination, that have the futility, often the charm, and sometimes the deep truthfulness of works of art?'[28] Many readers, especially men, might have murmured, 'Yes indeed'. Cities were contingent. The elemental was to be found at the end of long, barely travelled tracks.

And yet the 'deeply true' came in many forms, rural and urban, ancient and new, male and female. Sydney, for instance, the original site of British settlement, was a starting point for telegraph cables and mail-boat lines such as Conrad spoke of. It was named after a former British cabinet minister, and as we travel back, away from Australia's Centre, through the city of Sydney to that city's namesake, we find that Lord Sydney was descended from the Sidneys of Penshurst, in Kent, the most famous of whom was Sir Philip Sidney, Elizabethan courtier, soldier and poet, mortally wounded fighting in the Netherlands in 1586. European civilisation offered few things more noble than the story of Sidney's death. Fainting on the field, he refused a drink of water, giving it to another wounded like himself, saying (so the tale goes), 'Thy necessity is yet greater than mine'.[29]

Philip Sidney's Penshurst, with its golden-stoned castle encircled by two rivers, was utterly different from Australia's bone-dry Centre. Ernest Giles's report of his travels west of Alice Springs in 1872 underlines the difference. One day in October it was 33 degrees Celsius in the shade and death from thirst was likely:

> We found some large rocky places, where water might remain for weeks, after being filled; but when such an occurrence ever had taken place, or ever would take place again, it was impossible to tell. We had wandered into and over such frightful rocky and ungodly places, that it appeared useless to search farther in such a region, and it seemed utterly impossible for water to exist in it at all.

Giles hoped to meet with the inhabitants of the country. He thought they might help, repeating a fraction of Philip Sidney's nobility. On previous days the party had seen smoke, from campfires and from the systematic firing of spinifex. And on that day too, 'the natives were about, burning, burning, ever burning; one would think they were of the fabled salamander race, and lived on fire instead of water'. But he knew the Blacks drank 'from the hollow spouts of some trees and from the roots of others'.[30] They possessed, to his mind, almost miraculous resources.

Among the Europeans in all the colonies, as settlement stretched further inland, or outback, the unpredictability or simple absence of water became a fundamental problem. Dryness and drought were the themes of gossip and quarrelling, of widespread cooperation and of ambitious government policy. During the first months of 1875 in Victoria and New South Wales the lack of moisture was dramatically difficult. Men and women wondered at the power of the country to change its face in a matter of weeks, or even days. The land confounded and destroyed itself in tides of fire.

In late January, Bendigo, one of Victoria's main cities, was surrounded by seven bushfires, 'almost enclosing the district in a terrible circle of flame'. Nearer Melbourne, a line of flame 32 kilometres long lit up the Grampians, and Mt Macedon, as the train passed by at midnight, was seen to be alight from top to bottom; to men and women looking from the windows, '[t]he appearance of the mountain on fire … was grand in the extreme'. In Melbourne itself, the temperature was officially (but inaccurately) reported at 146 degrees Fahrenheit (63 degrees Celsius). Along the Murray, in 'the Land of Flame', as a local paper called it, the air was so 'freighted with smoke' that it was hard to see at all, 'and all vestige of vegetation has long since disappeared'. A fortnight later fiercely hot winds combined with extraordinary dust storms. St Arnaud, north-west of Melbourne, was dark all morning with dust, which was then enfolded in storm clouds, in a mingling of elements 'awfully grand'. The after-effect of such disasters was a country in mourning, as the people put it: clothed in black.[31]

In Victoria several people were burnt to death. Mary Ellis and David, her husband, were farmers at Bulabul Creek, near

Inglewood, north-west of Bendigo. They had been married several years but had no children. They were part of an extended family in the neighbourhood that had come from Nova Scotia, a far cooler country, nine years before. They were Presbyterian and were probably typical of the stern-minded, hard-working Scottish and Northern Irish settler communities that dotted rural Victoria. On the afternoon of 20 January, as fire tore towards their farm, Mary and some friends saw a haystack in danger and ran to beat it out. There was no 'heart of darkness' for them, but a heart of light, which dazzled as they struggled. '[T]he fire caught her clothes,' according to a newspaper reporter, 'and she was immediately enveloped in flames … Everything was burnt off her and she received such severe injuries that she died in a few hours afterwards'.[32]

Sights on the horizon – fire, smoke, dust – were more urgent than they were for later generations. The Ellises, assuming they were churchgoing Presbyterians, must have known the story from Exodus in which God guided his people towards the Promised Land with a pillar of smoke by day and a pillar of fire by night. Many ancient peoples signalled with smoke, including Aborigines. But success in reading smoke signals depended on a good knowledge of the land and of the sky on which the messages were written. By the 1870s, Europeans had some of that skill. It intrigued Mary Cameron, a little girl in south-west New South Wales (afterwards the writer Mary Gilmore). Faraway dust-clouds carried messages of long-distance movement, and she called the dust 'our news sheet'. '[E]very kind of hoof made a differently shaped rise, and every speed a different roll; every variation in hoof-mass raised a greater or less volume, and a greater or less height, hang, and fall again to earth.'[33]

The movement of bushfires, in fevered brightness against the sky, was much more challenging. Here, in particular, Europeans had much to learn. Aborigines used fire often, clearing old grass and undergrowth, and they could usually stop it getting out of control.

They prevented massive bushfires by managing the incipient flame with small branches, back-burning and, where fragments trickled forwards, squatting to beat out each small flare. Mary watched them as they measured each movement:

> Having the confidence of habit they allowed the fire freedom where it seemed less dangerous. In one such fire [as she recalled] they concentrated on the sides, letting the centre flame run forward. But far in advance of this ran lubras [women] hunkering down over their half-yard-wide flares. Behind the first row a second line was at work, and behind this a third, each fire opposite the gaps between the forward ones.

According to Rosa Praed, a Queenslander, '[A]ll the flimsinesses of life are torn into shreds by the wild forces of nature which reign in the bush'.[34] But the wild forces were differently understood by Black and White.

The summer and autumn of 1874–75 made up an extraordinary period of disasters. A better understanding of the country seemed more urgent by the day. In November in New South Wales, some parts of the landscape were devastated not just by serious and sometimes fatal fires, but also by grasshopper plagues. Hordes appeared first to the far north-west, between the River Darling and Cooper's Creek. They swept in vast numbers over the Darling, Lachlan and Murrumbidgee plains and exhausted themselves around Deniliquin. In that town all the gardens were destroyed. On fruit trees only stones remained, 'skinned … as completely and as cleanly as though they were boiled'.[35]

One tragedy after another suggested to the Europeans in Australia the helplessness of humanity in this new world. All the horrors attendant on fire were summed up during the same summer in the story of the burning of the immigrant ship *Cospatrick*, off the Cape of Good Hope, a disaster which featured in all Australian newspapers late in 1874 and was felt with pain in a land of immigrants. The loss of life, including more than 100 families, was beyond any previous accident of its kind, 'a record', it was said, 'of woe, suffering, and disaster such as it has seldom been the fate of humanity to encounter'. The fire, starting in a cabin to forward, had swept in an instant through the ship, killing many straightaway, pushing others into the sea and destroying most of the lifeboats. As a later popular song put it,

> With frantic cries they rent the air
> They rushed on deck, no help was there.
> All through the ship the flames did sweep
> And many plunged into the deep.

Only one boatload was rescued, after weeks at sea, and of the five people still left in it two were mad. In the end they had been living off the bodies of the dead.[36]

Ironically, 1875 was also a year of torrential rain. In March, in New South Wales and Queensland, there was disastrous flooding, and storms at sea caused havoc among ships. Blinded in a downpour, the steamer *Gothenburg* struck and sank on the Great Barrier Reef, with the loss of all eighty-five passengers and most of the crew. Its rigging was found above water, bedecked with a comforter, a mattress and a lady's shawl. In the Hunter Valley, north of Sydney, parts of the river rose 50 feet (15 metres), and, among other tragedies, the speaker of the New South Wales Legislative Assembly William Munnings Arnold was drowned when his little boat overturned. At Maitland, said a reporter, '[n]o language can adequately describe the misery and destitution ... For miles around nothing is to be seen but water'. In Melbourne, in spite of the early heat and drought, this was one of the wettest years on record.[37]

Was this a country where human beings would always suffer

vast, unpredictable disasters? Or might settlers here hope to see, more than anywhere else in the world, the triumph of intelligent cooperation over the vagaries of nature – intricate, self-assured work, extended through the continent? In spite of floods, water was usually the one thing needful – continuously necessary in sustaining life and often urgent in putting out fires – and altogether the control of water, whether scarce or superfluous, was the main challenge of the day. Major drought afflicted large parts of the continent for most of the period between 1880 and 1903, climaxing with the most severe and comprehensive lack of moisture since first settlement.[38]

Searching for a straightforward solution, and certain that water ought to be an ever-present fact of life, the Europeans in Australia turned their minds first to the possibility that a permanent reservoir lay in easy reach – most obviously under their feet. Here was a great intellectual effort. Shortly after these disasters, for instance, Thomas Kingsmill Abbott, police magistrate at Gunnedah, north-west of Sydney, carried out a survey of underground water sources on the Liverpool Plains roundabout where he lived. He asked squatters a variety of questions about the wells and springs on their land, with the hope of gathering 'reliable facts as to the flow of water beneath the surface of the earth'. This inquiry had been instigated by Henry Chamberlain Russell, government astronomer and meteorologist in Sydney, and its main point was to work out how rainfall patterns affected the flow of subterranean water. Russell was not alone in his belief that the Australian soil, for many hundreds of metres down, must be laced through with channels. Rain fell over the catchment of the upper Darling in quantities far beyond what the surface rivers could account for, even allowing for soakage and evaporation. Where did it go?

Abbott's findings added to the confusion. There were certainly aquifers of apparently unlimited resource, but understanding how they operated was another matter. A spring on Bando Station, he said (and his finding seems dubious today), was certainly affected by the weather, but in baffling fashion. 'On bright sunny days the flow is only about 120 gallons [540 litres] per hour, and on dull cloudy days (although no rain may be falling) the outflow sometimes reached 400 gallons per hour.' Otherwise, as far as he could see, the weather seemed to make very little difference. Another spring on the same station had only gushed in great quantities since the clearing of a nearby forest of eucalypt. At Garrawilla, there was a remarkable natural fountain throwing up 9600 gallons an hour. Even before it reached the surface you could hear it rushing underfoot, rain or shine.[39]

The notion of rivers and wells that went down, down, down, echoing to an infinite depth, had an appeal a long way beyond men like Russell. Remember Samuel Taylor Coleridge's sacred river Alph, which 'ran / through caverns measureless to man / down to a sunless sea'. Among the current generation, the great American psychologist William James had written of our internal selves in the same way. This was our own Centre,

> this dumb region of the heart in which we dwell alone with our willingnesses and unwillingnesses, our faiths and fears. As through the cracks and crannies of caverns those waters exude from the earth's bosom which then form the fountain-heads of springs, so in these crepuscular depths of personality the sources of all our outer deeds and decisions take their rise.[40]

That idea of internal fertility, enclosed in 'dumbness', triggered imagination in powerful ways. In Australia, weather experts, and men and women on the land, liked it for their own reasons, but so did many others. Maybe not all was dead in the unknown parts of the continent. In *The Last Lemurian*, George Firth Scott spoke of 'a pool of mystery' at the Centre, edged with rich grass and broad-leaved trees, and fed by a waterfall. It had no outlet or overflow, and it seemed to Scott's adventurers to be linked underground to a continent-wide network of rivers and pools.

The Great Artesian Basin, an enormously valuable resource of underground water lying under most of the eastern half of the continent, was discovered in 1878, and its dimensions were clear by the end of the century. But scientifically established fact made the thirsty imagination of settlers even more eager for stories. In David Hennessey's tale *An Australian Bush Track*, a similar oasis, 'the most weird, uncanny-looking bit of scenery I have ever put eyes on in Australia', was watered from below. And in Rosa Praed's *Fugitive Anne*, there was a sweet fragment of water called Maianbar or 'the Deep Tank', just as remote from settled places. Small in circumference, and memorably blue, Maianbar was fed by a buried stream and to the Aboriginal mind, at least, was 'bottomless'.[41]

If there is one thing that makes its mark on the imagination of a people bred in dryness it is the idea of endless water – reliable streams above ground or below, or else perfectly predictable rain. The image of the overshadowed creek bed shining black and as deep as fancy allows, proof against all outside accident, is hard to forget once it makes its mark. We had a pool like that where I grew up, in southern Queensland. It was too deep for safe paddling, too deep for anything except efforts of imagination.

IV

Joseph Furphy, one of Australia's greatest writers, spoke at this moment of a national wealth waiting to be tapped, of an 'unconfined, ungauged potentiality of resource'. He could see the land yielding something of its secrets, material and spiritual, to anyone who could read the 'ideographic prophecy' written on its surface.[42] There were already, by 1880, various ways of using natural wells. TK Abbott reported that water from the well at Garrawilla was dammed and then pumped to 'one of the most extensive sheep-washing establishments in the Colony'. At three or four places windmills drew the water from beneath the surface, but primitive 'whips' were more common. That is to say, a forked stick was set in the ground and a long pole balanced on it, with a weight at one end and a rope and bucket on the other. Elsewhere, there were horse-powered 'whims', originally meant for draining mines. Abbott was sure that much more might be done with proper drilling and encased bores. He was hopeful, he told HC Russell, that '[t]here are rivers in the earth'. It ought to be possible to trace them, measure their depth and make them useful.[43]

Russell must have received Abbott's report with mixed feelings, because it did not demonstrate exactly how ingenuity could be applied to the problem of water shortage. Russell himself was one of the most ingenious Australians of his time. Born in the Hunter Valley in 1836, he had spent his working life in Sydney and at fifty had been elected a fellow of the Royal Society of London, the most distinguished association in the scientific world. As New South Wales government astronomer from 1870 to 1904 he was a leader on the charting of the southern skies. He made his earliest mark in international circles with his photographs of the transit of Venus in 1874, taken from his observatory at Dawes Point, in Sydney. He was especially interested in double stars, and 500 new ones were spotted from Dawes Point while he was in charge. But it was his work with the weather that made him most important for generations to come.

The best educated Europeans were just starting to wonder about the deep interconnectedness of the natural world.[44] Russell was one of the first anywhere to think carefully about meteorology as something global, partly because he wanted to make his knowledge of the southern hemisphere fit with European understandings. He was also a pioneer in asking questions with a vertical perspective. That is, he was convinced of what he called 'the intimate relations which subsist between the earth's atmosphere and the sun's surroundings', and, at a lower level, between events in the atmosphere and events below the surface of the earth.

He worked with teams of both amateurs and professionals. As an astronomer, he needed expensive equipment, which was available mainly in Sydney. But as a meteorologist, he spread his net far afield, and his sources of information included a host of untrained and semi-trained people throughout New South Wales. '[K]nowing what important questions could only be answered by statistics about rain, rivers and evaporation', he said, 'I began at once to collect them and educate the people to keep rain records'. The process depended on two vital items of technology, the rain gauge and the telegraph. Gauges made of copper or glass and with inch markings down the side could now be bought by anyone over the counter, though at first their dimensions varied by as much as 10 per cent. By 1881 Russell was using 290 amateur observers throughout New South Wales, each equipped with a gauge and sending in regular reports. By 1898 he had 1600 – and by this time all their gauges measured a standard 8 inches (20 centimetres) around.[45]

Every colony except Tasmania had a government astronomer whose duties involved keeping weather records. From a meteorological point of view, Russell in Sydney and Robert Ellery in Melbourne were the leading figures. With Charles Todd in Adelaide, they started a three-point system of weather telegrams that allowed them to assemble large maps of weather movement – not only patterns of dryness and moisture, which were critical to life itself, but also temperature and wind movement. Their approach depended on gathering information, but also on distributing it – accurately, systematically and as widely as possible. They imprinted larger patterns of thought about the weather among all kinds of men and women.

This was knowledge democratised, a defining project of the age. It was based on a rich combination of writing and speech, on high literacy and a massive increase in all sorts of publications, but also copious human traffic, steam driven, which meant wider travel and interaction. It was a project going back to the seventeenth century and to Sir Francis Bacon, but never so close to reality as now. As the Melbourne poet Bernard O'Dowd put it, it was a project 'gradually but surely transferring political power, art, literature, knowledge, amusement, and all the things that go to make up life in the larger sense, from the possession of the privileged classes to that of the mass of people'. As later chapters show, on this foundation and in various parts of the world including Australia, there was built something utterly new, which HG Wells called 'organised intelligence', an engine of thought going beyond the education of the individual.[46] Interconnected and self-nourishing, almost organic, driven by unfamiliar efficiencies in communication, this collective effort created and recreated nations. It had a mighty impact on Australia and it explains the Federation of the six colonies in 1901.

Meteorological work such as these men were engaged in had some practical application, especially for shipowners, farmers and graziers, although for the time being information was usually too generalised and too late to be very useful. In fact, the effort was so far driven mainly by curiosity and imagination. More specifically, it was driven by that generation's hunger for vastness, a second theme running through this volume. This was vastness grasped only by minds stretched through a long effort of literacy.

One of HG Wells's short stories written in the 1890s – short, but brilliantly original – shows how minds were now engaged with the power they could see in the skies, and with the immensity of time and space. 'The Star' is a story with hardly a human being in it. It is reminiscent of the paintings of the Englishman JMW Turner (who died in 1851), which were canvases filled with living light. Wells told of the movements through space of a great lump of rock, almost self-willed in its approach page by page closer to earth. 'So the star, with the wan moon in its wake, marched across the Pacific, trailed the thunderstorms like the hem of a robe, and the growing tidal wave that toiled behind it, frothing and eager, poured over island and island and swept them clear of men.'[47] It was a long time since anyone had written about the forces of nature as if they were titans or gods, as careless about humanity as cattle were about insects underfoot. This was an age of deified nature. The dazzling power described by Wells, beyond any human notion of right and wrong, was the kind that excited HC Russell. The possibility of measuring it and even harnessing it – binding Titan – excited him even more.

How was it to be measured? In October 1875 Russell came back from a visit to Britain and the United States, where he had looked at new ways of drawing and publishing weather maps. Fourteen months later he had worked out his own method of publishing, the first such venture in any British colony, and probably the first anywhere in the world to be done daily. He used the *Sydney Morning Herald*, depending to start with on information sent in from stations throughout his own colony and from several places beyond, including Melbourne, Adelaide and Brisbane. First of all, it was necessary to think of the continent and its surrounding seas and oceans as one great arena of daily activity. It had to be imagined as a single stage for drama of the kind described by Wells. New South Wales, Victoria and South Australia were the obvious places to start, but something much bigger was called for.

In other countries, maps of this kind were redrawn for each periodic survey. Russell invented a single printing block with small holes into which symbols could be inserted, and it took only an hour each day to update his block for the press. Each map (of the south-east mainland only) showed the state of the weather at nine o'clock on the morning before. Eventually, Russell added daily synopses for all the colonies, from New Zealand to Western Australia. With Ellery and Todd, he also published forecasts.[48]

All this was wonderfully intriguing, and it drew in ever more people drunk with ideas about size and predictability. Among increasing numbers it was normal now to think in broad and yet exact terms about the weather. Russell also sent to the *Herald* monthly summaries, in which he tried to match large weather patterns with the worries natural to anyone who owned livestock, crops and gardens. For instance, in early February 1877:

> January has been extremely hot and dry throughout most parts of the colony. The heat has ranged from 100° to 125° [38–52 degrees Celsius] in the shade, the latter temperature having occurred at Bourke during the middle of the month ... The stations on the Macquarie River are reported to be dry, and with scarcely any grass, and at Dubbo the country is very bare. In fact, unless it frequently rains during the summer months, the intense heat of the sun very soon parches the ground, and causes the grass to disappear.[49]

No longer was the weather just the obvious place-bound unpredictable work of Providence, managed by running eyes along the horizon. Now this elemental experience was to be bound by literacy and by general rules.

After measurement came control. In the United States, James Pollard Espy, 'the Storm King', had written a book called *The Philosophy of Storms*, in which he said that rain could be induced by the updrafts of hot air from large-scale burning. As Russell, deeply knowledgeable about American meteorology, explained, '[F]armers began the practice of making large heaps of brushwood on each farm, and when they wanted rain lighting them altogether'. It was not an experiment he recommended for his own country. He had seen too many bushfires whose only sequel was scorching, vacant sky.[50]

In spring 1879, Russell organised a three-day conference in Sydney, where he and his two Australian colleagues consulted with their opposite number in New Zealand, James Hector, on ways of making their work more useful and precise. Russell was interested in two great spaces – two enormous playing fields for the sport he loved best – the Tasman Sea (which is why New Zealand was important) and the Australian inland. He wanted to know how the weather was linked from one arena to the other, and, thanks to the submarine cable lately laid across the Tasman, that question could now be tackled. It was already obvious that most atmospheric disturbances came sweeping across Australia from the west. By way of illustration, Todd reminded the Sydney meeting of a recent hurricane. It had made its first Australian impact on the north-west coast at Christmastime 1878. By New Year's Eve, its presence was felt by the barometer at Eucla, at the western end of the Great Australian Bight, with an aftermath registering at Hobart on 2 January.

Imagine this extraordinary march of power, so much more vast than any hitherto known to humanity – 'a slow progressive motion over the Australian continent', as Todd put it (like Wells's star), 'emerging from the coast at about the Great Bight, and occupying twenty-four hours in passing from the Great Bight to Hobart Town'.[51] 'Slow' he might call it. As he knew himself, there was nothing quicker on the earth's surface, except for the telegraph.

Measurements made along the Overland Telegraph, running through the Centre of the continent, made it possible to predict weather along the east coast, and east-coast weather shaped in turn weather in and across the Tasman. This was obvious, but the talk in Sydney broadened the picture. Russell wanted more stations in western New South Wales. Todd, in turn, thought that if he had good information from points to his westward, he 'should be able to give the easterly colonies timely warning of approaching gales'. This meant bringing in Western Australia. Hector, the New Zealander, spoke of Queensland: '[I]t would be from that quarter they would receive early notice of the origin and progress of the dangerous and suddenly-occurring cyclones that crossed the north part of New Zealand'. For Ellery, from Melbourne, Tasmania held the key. The pattern would be complete 'if Hobart Town observations were discussed in connection with … movement on the western coast of Australia, and the subsequent weather on the east coast'.[52]

Such a business meant regular gathering of detail across enormous spaces. In the United States (an area of comparable size), national meteorology was the job of the Army Signal Corps. It was done by the corps because the members of that body knew about communications, including telegrams. Also, in America only the military could cast a reliable net of correspondence over the distances involved, leaping easily from state to state.[53] In the British empire, however, especially Australia, initiatives like these came from the civilian employees of the Crown, including men like Russell. The public service, from colony to colony (later chapters repeat the point), was an engine of intricate, multiplying power.

The antipodean meteorologists stressed the importance of 'weather telegrams'. Two kinds of message were currently sent by telegraph, with government messages taking priority over private ones. Weather telegrams were classified as private, because they were only about science. And yet, they could contain urgent public news. As Ellery said, delay might make weather information useless: 'Weather telegrams were of no value to shipping and the commercial interest unless they were transmitted punctually'. They therefore ought to go before all other private messages. Coloured paper was part of the answer, because it made the messages stand out among the uncoloured mass in the telegraph office.[54]

Weather telegrams were humble things. But they represented a kind of intellectual revolution. Science and technology were promoted as a part of government, underlining the authority of men like Russell. Many less well known individuals were involved in the same transformation, as they went each morning to see what dew or rain had trickled into their glass or green-brown copper gauges. This, plus pink or blue paper, was a democracy of knowledge.

Russell's view was not just global. He also thought historically. He was intrigued with theories about weather cycles and he longed to be able to show beyond a shadow of a doubt that rain and drought appeared in preordained patterns, 'like the vibrations in musical notes'. In a paper given before the Royal Society of New South Wales in 1876 he canvassed all possibilities, from cycles of two years in Tasmania to fifty-six in England. He gradually convinced himself that nineteen years was the right answer for his own colony, and he set himself up as a fortune teller for graziers wanting advice. Meteorology was not a thoroughly exact science, he warned. But he boasted that everyone who used his predictions with common sense did well. One, he said, had profited to the extent of £250,000.[55]

Russell's historical inquiries went back to the first years of settlement at Sydney Cove. He also used the stories of Aboriginal people, plus patterns of vegetation, as evidence of the unfolding of good times and bad. He could see an enormous complexity, cycles of varying length from place to place, within Australasia and beyond. But then, taking the broadest possible view, as he said in 1876, 'we must ever bear in mind that the solar system is not stationary – it is rolling on into the unknown regions of space'.[56] Surely this meant that in spite of Russell's hunger for a fixed answer, everything was fluid, or, as near contemporary Albert Einstein might have said (see the quotation which opens this part of the book), a 'relativistic reality'?

Surely the vibrations were not music at all, as Russell suggested, but titanic chaos? Surely the meteorological future of the world was hidden in perfect darkness – as weird and uncanny as David Hennessey's oasis in *An Australian Bush Track*, as bottomless as Rosa Praed's pool in *Fugitive Anne*? Russell's mind, trained in old-fashioned habits of certitude, shrank from that idea. The older he got, the more sure he was about his eternal cycles. Unlike Charles Bean, he did not luxuriate in unlimited mystery. He could not imagine 'something beyond'.

2

Australia's Rural Code

I

On occasion in the bush the usual bustle, the whispering concatenation common from immemorial time, was shattered with the rushing of cattle. Less vast than the sound of bushfires, this was also a commotion sharper, harder, more down to earth – the beating of feet, the trampling of small trees, the snapping of branches, the breathing, bellowing articulation of fear. These were surely single-minded beasts, wild eyes under heavy lashes intent on escape. But cattle can be less focussed than such fuss suggests. A horseman standing in the way, or even a clever dog in the right place, and they would prop and turn, scattering in other directions.

Horses rushed too, jostling hard bodies horse to horse in tight places, and bursting out like water in an unstopped spring. By the last quarter of the nineteenth century parts of the bush were infested with wild horses, and on the south-west slopes of New South Wales they were brutally culled. They were yarded and then released through a narrow gate, on each side of which a man stood with a blade from a pair of hand-shears attached to the end of a pole. Stomachs were slashed as the horses passed through, pushing against each other mad to escape, and each, pausing and stumbling, died slowly where it dropped.[1]

Mary Cameron (Mary Gilmore) spoke about the 1870s, when she was little, as years dense with livestock. With all the intellectual longing of her generation, she struggled with resentment to grasp things beyond the experience of girls and women, keen herself to escape. Her childhood image of grown men – her father, uncles and others, all the men that came and went about her home – was anchored in the fact that they had power over cattle, horses and sheep. They walked around with knowledge wonderfully unfenced in:

> In men [as Mary recalled] was life's continuity, for with them were the roads that went out back, [and] the mustering of cattle, each mustering an event telling alike of last year and of years to come. Theirs was the yarding and breaking of horses, which meant riders and work and saddles; and saddles meant endless talk, and talk of a kind that was full of the colour of life; talk that went like a broad river, sweeping in times and places and people as it flowed; talk that reached from Sydney to California, and that covered travel, endurance, seas, and oceans.

City streets too, in those days, she said, were redolent with men and livestock, 'and the rich smell of the hay-and-corn stores'. In Sydney there were horse bazaars 'within neighing distance', as Mary put it, of the GPO, and pigs squealed as men, never women, carried them from Circular Quay.[2]

White men pushed to the frontiers in company with livestock. It was livestock that justified their invasion. It was livestock that shaped the way they behaved among themselves, and whose aims and fears they lived for. Cattle, horses and sheep meant limitless movement, but they also made Australia a land of boundaries, because they had to be yarded and, later on, fenced about for classification and control. The animals themselves got accustomed to these limits in their own way. When cattle were being taken through a gate or across a bridge, said one old stockman, they 'should not be forced, but should be allowed to have a look & if just held quietly will usually go thro[ugh]'. They would then run well altogether. Livestock gave stockmen their habits of thought. When they counted stock through a gate the minds of men leapt in twos or threes to keep up, as the beasts squeezed through that boundary, and this method – grouping so as to help with computation – was transferred to, or maybe adapted from, other tasks.[3] The walls of woolsheds and the smooth timber in stockyards, where branding was done, were marked with strokes in charcoal or chalk, sometimes in rows of four crossed through with a fifth. Every two parcels made up ten.

The framework of settler society was underpinned by a pattern of obligations connected with stock. In droving, customs were interwoven with law. Joseph Furphy's story *Such Is Life* is full of this sense of obligation in the movement of stock, although different parties thought about things in different ways. Graziers contradicted themselves. They depended on the drovers and teamsters for their concerns, but still they resented the way they used up local pasture.

> 'Squatters hed orter fine grass f'r wool teams, an' glad of the chance,' observed Price, with unprintable emphasis.
>
> 'Lot of sense in that remark,' commented Mosey, with a similar potency of adjective.

The balladeer 'Banjo' Paterson told a similar story: 'From camp to camp and from run to run they battle it hand to hand / For a blade of grass and the right to pass on the track of the Overland'.[4]

Colonial governments laid down public stock-routes, like channels in an intricate irrigation system, set about with rules and customary obligations, and used not just for livestock traffic but also as a source of extra feed in drought. The pattern of tracks in New South Wales, managed by its Pastures Protection Boards, was unrivalled for intricacy anywhere else in the world. Armidale, in the north, for instance, was a meeting place for seven stock-routes, as well as being a railhead. The most important of them connected the western slopes and plains with coastal ports, but Armidale, 193 kilometres from the border with Queensland, the country of cattle, was also a staging post for livestock moving northwards.[5]

In several continents, including this one, there was still plenty of land unoccupied by such settlers, but livestock multiplied fast as more people and more capital, especially in Europe and North America, drove up demand for meat, hides and wool. The management of resources and the settling of property rights among graziers were fundamental issues, to be met by mixing principles and knowledge old and new. For the time being, it was not possible to distribute all the land to individuals in neat parcels secured by survey and title. On the Great Plains of the United States – Kansas, Wyoming, Montana and so on – cattlemen did without government coordination. Parties combined as 'cattlemen's associations', taking up parts of the open range for their shared use (though in law it belonged to no-one), organising joint musters ('roundups'), keeping out non-members, and only later getting the law to back them up.[6] In Argentina and Uruguay, in South America, the national economies depended largely on cattle hides and dried beef ('jerky'). Even the poor there begged on horseback. There too, no doubt, as in these colonies, individuals were identified and remembered by the horses they rode: 'It was a man on a big black horse', or 'It was a youth on a broken-down nag, lame in the near off foot'.

Comparisons with South America help our effort to understand the great changes imposed on rural life in late colonial Australia. In both South America and Australia rules came down from government more easily than they did in the United States. In Argentina, officials and a few large ranchers, *hacendados*, together worked out a 'Rural Code', promulgated in 1865. Argentina had just emerged from a bloody civil war, and the winning party had sealed its triumph by cutting, one by one, the throats of an entire enemy regiment. It was an unpromising start for the new regime (like culling redundant horses in New South Wales), but from this point the republic enjoyed several decades of extraordinary prosperity.[7] Reform meant not just new certainty in land use and cattle ownership, but forms of citizenship and contractual relations suitable for an egalitarian and liberal age. It fitted neatly with the international market. Fences were few, but the government cast a tight legal net over the country, so that every proprietor knew, or should have known, where his rights began and ended.

The minister responsible for Argentina's rural reform, Valentin Alsina, boasted that his invention was unequalled for enlightenment and scope anywhere on earth. It stretched from water rights and the branding of cattle to labour relations and the preservation of wildlife, from ostriches to armadillos.[8] The antipodean colonies each made an effort much the same – more piecemeal, more cautious, but in practical terms even more far-reaching. Here there was a similar revolution in thought and practice, an effort of intelligence, made up of a series of ingenious steps all geared to the better management and understanding of the land. Most of all they coped with vastness. They were parallel with the work done by HC Russell in his scanning of the skies.

The magic image of the bushman dances through those days. He seems free from any need to think beyond the task at hand. The poet Adam Lindsay Gordon, among many others, spelt it out:

> 'Twas merry in the glowing morn, among the gleaming grass,
> To wander as we've wander'd many a mile,
> And blow the cool tobacco cloud, and watch the white wreaths
> pass,
> Sitting loosely in the saddle all the while.
> 'Twas merry 'mid the backwoods when we spied the station roofs,
> To wheel the wild scrub cattle at the yard,
> With a running fire of stockwhips and a fiery run of hoofs;
> Oh! the hardest day was never then too hard![9]

But there was something calculated underneath this richly coloured way of life.

In 1840 Governor Sir George Gipps had compared the owners of livestock in New South Wales with 'the Arabs of the Desert'. It would be just as easy to rule their wanderings, he said, as it would be to keep the Arabs 'within a circle, traced upon their sands'.[10] He would have liked it better if the people kept still, or moved only so as to put down roots somewhere else, as they did in Europe. The idea that life on horseback might be a kind of citizenship – that men on the move mattered as much as families with settled homes and with all the paraphernalia of freehold title – was extremely hard to work through. It was tackled with cunning during the second half of the nineteenth century. The program to 'unlock the lands' – the 'free selection movement' that settled small farmers on soil hitherto monopolised by squatters – is famous. (See volume 2.) But something larger and more clever was happening at the same time.

Never before or since have the immigrant people thought so energetically, so whimsically, but so well about the vast, impersonal, almost abstract spaces at their command. Joseph Furphy once told of a visit to Sydney when he sat talking with a number of city journalists about life in the bush – pointing out to them the technical errors made by George Lambert in his magnificent 1899 painting of a wagon laden with wool bales, called *Across the Black Soil Plains*. (It still hangs in the Art Gallery of New South Wales.) 'I'll never forget', Furphy wrote home to a friend, 'the eager, hungry interest of those town fellows in anything connected with the grand silent expanses which you and I know so well'.[11] His listeners were apparently intrigued not just with great expanses, hard as they were to imprint with any human dimension, but also with the mechanical intricacies of rural life, and especially with proof of manly and practical intelligence. Such individuals, writers and readers of all kinds, wanted to know just how intricacies like these made their mark on vastness.

More than this, an entire generation was hungry to know and comprehend the country, as if it were the only way of comprehending – abstracting, identifying – themselves. Charles Bean's reports to the *Sydney Morning Herald*, a little later on, helped to feed the hunger. In fact, these chapters (volume 3 of *The Europeans in Australia*) are filled with such cases, of individuals putting ideas end to end, like a series of ladders, in a calculated effort to escape their own circumstances – bursting through gateways. Australia was both a bundle of power and a crystalline idea.

All this was part of a global drive in ideas, which ran through the books and newspapers circulating around the literate world. For nine centuries, said the great German historian Oswald Spengler, the Western soul had been yearning towards distance and infinity, and he made that pronouncement as a would-be prophet, speaking for his generation in what he saw as an age of apotheosis. The music of Europe proved it – the organ, for instance, which was unique in musical history, said Spengler, as a '*space-commanding* giant' (and largely, he added, a German invention). Geographers took the same approach. Mere space, abstractly understood, had become the end point for human destiny. In Paris, the Russian Jacques Novicow condemned the 'idolatry of square kilometres', and Camille Vallaux mocked the uselessness of his country's enormous claim on the Sahara Desert. But Americans agreed: 'big spatial ideas' were everything – and that was the consensus.[12] It was the Europeans in Australia, however, who best put their minds to the concentrated management of vastness.

So we find democracy itself reshaped. Democracy as it had evolved everywhere in the middle part of the nineteenth century was a type of government defined by cities and big towns. It was civic. One of its textbooks was George Grote's *History of Greece* (published in twelve volumes, 1846–56), which showed how the democracy of ancient Athens, a city-state, might be reimagined for the present.[13] This was the mid-century democracy of the

Australasian colonies (the mainland, Tasmania and New Zealand) shaped by the leading towns and townspeople. At its heart it was a democracy of voices within reach of each other. The end-of-century democracy, which brought about the Australian Commonwealth, was a democracy of space rather than place. It was a democracy of being. You could be born or reborn into it, and in the end you might die for it. You belonged to it all. It did not evolve through doing and talking, through labour, commerce and worship, as the earlier, town-centred type of democracy had done. It was another animal altogether.

In many parts of the country, the main value in land use was found not in the soil but in the imported creatures that seeped and flooded across its surface. Legal innovation dated from Governor Gipps's time, when members of the Legislative Council in Sydney, challenged by serious economic depression (and in spite of the governor), changed the way the law defined livestock as property. In 1843, legislation pushed through by William Charles Wentworth made it possible for graziers to raise money when the only security was wool still on the sheep's back. It also made it easier to mortgage sheep and cattle as if they were real estate.[14] Allowing security (a lien) on wool was especially radical.

The Common Law of England was in principle the foundation for colonial law, and in England the original and classic form of property was in land: 'real' rather than 'personal' estate, fixed rather than mobile. Under the Common Law, animals were included in personal estate, but domestic animals were distinguished from wild animals – *domitae naturae* (attached to a house) from *ferae naturae* (part of savage nature). William Blackstone, the great eighteenth-century authority on the Common Law, defined the first as animals 'seldom, if ever, found wandering at large', whereas the second were animals 'usually found at liberty'. There had to be some complicated exceptions. Wild animals in a private park or forest belonged to the owner as long as they stayed there, and animals more or less wild might be branded in case they escaped.[15] But none of this worked well in the nineteenth-century Antipodes. Fences were few and nearly all of the most valuable beasts were 'at large'. As for branding, before the 1860s English practice prevailed and only neighbours knew each other's brands. And yet in the colonies stock were already being driven over vast distances.

As with work on the weather – as with HC Russell and his intercolonial colleagues – the challenge was met by civilian employees of the Crown. Patrick Robertson Gordon was a taker of snuff, a joker, a singer and a skilled performer on the violin and tympani. His favourite party piece was the music hall song 'The Lively Flea'. He was also chief inspector of stock for Queensland. An amiable man, Gordon more than anyone else manufactured in his wide imagination an antipodean rural code.

In Queensland, riches, present and future, depended on the movement of cattle, sheep and horses across the land – whether driven, grazing on their own or rushing in a heavy pack. Gordon wanted a revolution in the management of space and in the definition of property on and in the land. This meant stretching imagination beyond points on the map, such as ports, towns, homesteads and railway stations. It meant comprehending somehow the empty spaces, 'the grand silent expanses' Furphy spoke of. This was a cartographic question, a matter of maps. It was also a geometrical-philosophical question. In Europe arguments were abroad, Ernst Mach and Émile Durkheim being leading names, which posed big questions about space. Was it absolute and objective, as Euclidean geometry made out? Or was it relative? Did it spring from individual and community perceptions, varying over time? Was it cultural, in other words? Was it rooted in our spatial selves, even, Mach said, in thoughts about our own skin, which was, after all, 'two-dimensional, finite, [but] unbounded'?[16]

In Australia space certainly took form as mere individuals walked, rode and sent messages over it, and as they learnt to use it. Gordon recognised that in this part of the world, simply from a practical point of view, spaces often mattered more than points. And yet, spaces so big were hard for the mind to hold on to – much more so than our own skin. That effort, an educating effort, meant managing boundaries – the boundaries of colonies, but also the boundaries of runs and paddocks, lease and freehold, stock-routes and reserves, with various points of entry and exit, all overlaid with a pattern of watercourses, natural and man-made.[17] With shorter historical experience, it was much harder to do then than it is today.

Gordon was a Scot and he had once been inspector of sheep in New South Wales under his compatriot Alexander Bruce, chief inspector for that colony. Every Scot knew the importance of the Border (with England), at one time for warfare and now for trade. Sir Walter Scott's story 'The Two Drovers' (1827) tells of Highlanders crossing 'the Scots dyke' with cattle for the English market:

> They are required to know perfectly the drove-roads, which lie over the wildest tracks of the country, and to avoid as much as possible the highways, which distress the feet of the bullocks, and the turnpikes, which annoy the spirit of the drover; whereas on the broad green or gray track which leads across the pathless moor, the herd not only move at ease and without taxation, but, if they mind their business, may pick up a mouthful of food by the way.

The skills of the colonial drover were just the same, and for drovers here the most important border lay between Gordon and Bruce – between Queensland and New South Wales. It was a border, as later chapters show, more potent than any in the Antipodes except the sea itself.[18]

These two colonies dominated the livestock trade. During the 1870s New South Wales had more cattle than any other colony, but it was soon overtaken by Queensland, where by the end of the 1880s the numbers reached nearly five million – roughly two-thirds of the continental total. In most colonies, as profits from wool shot up, sheep numbers increased as well, but more steadily than was usual for cattle, and with occasional lapses, mainly a result of disease, such as scab and pleuropneumonia, which sometimes forced the destruction of thousands to stop further infection. In South Australia and Western Australia cattle numbers started to multiply fast in the late 1880s, as herds moved into more remote parts and with new chances for overseas trade, thanks to the invention of shipboard refrigeration.[19] Many came from New South Wales into South Australia, and from Queensland across the top into the Kimberley, in Western Australia's northern corner.

Although they were in step for most large purposes, Bruce and Gordon had different priorities. Their brains worked differently. Bruce liked owners to be calculating. The men in his office knew him as 'Tiger', not because of any fierce passion but because when he had his teeth in something he hung on hard. One of Bruce's interests was the science of judging stock. He argued for a points system, with each beast's attributes scored separately and then added up – better, he thought, than trusting to a kind of instinctive overall judgment, such as old bushmen boasted of (though back, legs and so on were important to everyone). He wanted to see the agricultural societies of New South Wales talking about such issues and promoting better technical knowledge within their regions.[20] Gordon was more curious about old expertise, knowledge based on talk, and keener to take advantage of it. Rather than using science to root it out, he tried to fit the two types of intelligence, mouth intelligence and paper intelligence, together. He focussed not just on town-bred scholarship but also on the minutiae of the landscape and the space-making thoughts of the drover.

Victoria was another world again. There, the government did not think very creatively about cross-border negotiation and long-distance movement. In 1877 it even imposed a duty on meat and livestock coming from outside – a stock tax. It was meant to raise revenue and protect local industry, but it was also part of a cross-border battle with New South Wales. It was a tax on mobility, a 'most barbaric tax', according to the premier in Sydney.[21] In Sydney and Brisbane, borders were part of a tapestry of traffic. In Melbourne, as we see again later, thoughts about space were very different.

These vast animal migrations, much bigger than the norm in Europe, meant that ownership had to be differently pinned down. As early as the 1840s, in the time of Governor Gipps and following WC Wentworth's legislation mentioned earlier, a Legislative Council committee in Sydney had declared that although land was the staple property in England livestock was the staple property here. '[S]heep, cattle and horses', it said, 'should possess all the incidents of fixed property in England ... it is sound policy not to curtail those incidents, directly or indirectly, but to give them their fullest scope'.[22] This radical break was precipitated by the limitless rattle and rush of clattering hooves.

Take branding too. Traditionally, livestock had been marked with the owner's initials, like any other personal possession. It was a method usually good enough to settle local quarrels. When they were mixed up in grazing, as happened often, the mark could be seen at a glance. Even children and servants might have a horse or two branded with their initials. But brands might not mean much in courts of law. They could complicate quarrels rather than settle them. So many were alike – in New South Wales at least 280 owners used 'JC'. In that colony an epidemic of cattle theft led in 1862 to the idea of a single, central register of brands. Combined with the telegraph, this meant that actionable information about thefts could be broadcast quickly from border to border. But as so often in New South Wales, the authorities worked in a haphazard fashion. No-one was forced to list their brand, there was no restriction on methods of marking, and claimants for the same brand had to sort the problem out themselves, with unsatisfactory results.[23]

Gordon did a lot better in Queensland. He had standard marks. Each brand included one letter (a roman capital) and two standard figures, such as numerals, stars or diamonds. There were two rules: one owner one brand, and first in first served. The effect was immediate. Within twelve months Gordon's register was used, for instance, to sort out the claims of a servant girl named Anne Marinan, at Ipswich. Anne's employer said that he had branded her bay mare 'AM over M' on the near shoulder, but a neighbour said that the brand proved he – the neighbour – had bought the horse himself from Angus Matheson, his brother-in-law. Matheson's brand was registered and Anne Marinan's was not, so she lost. There was no room any more for servant girls dreaming up their own brands. This system of certifying the ownership of animals seems to have been unrivalled anywhere in the world.[24] Mary Gilmore remembered men's talk, 'like a broad river', free of any narrow horizons. When men like Gordon talked about branding, this was just the way they did it. Queensland, after all, was vast.

The Queensland register was so handy that copies were held by every country post office, 'for the free use of the settlers'. Set out at first as a list of brands in alphabetical order, so as to identify stock, it later appeared also as a list of names followed by brands, which made it 'a reliable country directory'.[25] Each brand identified an owner, his or her piece of Queensland and many other possessions besides. 'I have seen drays, yokes, implements, and tools going about branded with the owner's registered brand, and harness stamped with it', said the magistrate at Taroom, 322 kilometres north-west of Brisbane. It was a remark that delighted Gordon. Even station mailbags, in which mail was delivered and gathered at intervals, 'are sealed', the gentleman said, 'with the owner's brand'.[26]

II

The soil itself was branded with ironbark posts. Fencing, making this a land of boundaries, was another great change. Patrick Gordon wrote five books, and the first, published in 1867, before he came to Queensland, was about the virtues of fencing. At that time, fencing was still used mainly around homesteads, for home paddocks, and to stop stock from pushing into gardens and crops. Since the convict period, men had learnt to live in the bush, to understand the lie of the land and the ways of horses, sheep and cattle – adapting their own ways accordingly – to recognise boundary markers (streams, ridges, outcrops, trees) and, along these notional borders, to keep up a kind of diplomacy with men from neighbouring places.

The livestock of different owners, especially cattle, inevitably ran together, and there were settled methods of sorting them out. Gordon, pioneering a new age, described these methods in disparaging terms. At regular intervals – say, just after calving – stockmen got together for a general muster. A great herd was gathered at some central point. Men shouted, dogs barked, and the stock complained as one, in a single, vast, penetrating moan – a noise like some wild Pentecostal chant and hard to forget for anyone who has heard it. Then, said Gordon, 'it almost invariably happens that in the confusion occasioned by the mixing together of so many cattle in the stockyards, numbers of calves are separated from their mothers, and, on account of the difficulty in identifying them in this confusion, many pass from the possession of their rightful owners'. Each man, from his own knowledge, claimed what he thought belonged to his own herd. But an unduly large number, said the future chief inspector, fell to 'the less scrupulous and most noisy'. At length, '[t]he new possessor soothes his conscience by believing – and in frequent instances openly boasting – that he obtained them through being sharper than his neighbours'.

Besides the disorder and injustice, this was bad for the stock. Cattle grew wild in the unfenced wilderness and then, with their calves, they were knocked about during mustering and yarding, so that they took time to return to their best. That affected prices. In principle and in practice, the system itself was bad. '[D]oes it not appear preposterous in the extreme', asked the great codifier, 'that a man's property should be scattered throughout the length and breadth of the land (as cattle and horse stock at present are on open runs), entirely beyond his own immediate control, and in the power of his neighbours or others ...?' What city businessman would be so careless with his capital?[27]

Some graziers, especially in Victoria and southern New South Wales, were already fencing themselves in. For a few, with enough confidence and capital to look ahead, this meant mapping their acreage and laying down a pattern of fences in keeping with new theories about the way animals ought to be organised from paddock to paddock. But progress with boundary fences depended on agreement among neighbours. The exercise was so important, Gordon thought, that colonial governments should step in and enforce a general system of fencing throughout their territories.[28] As with brands, owners ought to be forced to agree among themselves, and with government officials.

This sweeping intellectual effort was all about anchoring European civilisation in Australian space. It was not just drawing lines. It was also stretching minds, and a long way beyond the old limits. It was starting to be commonly understood that intellectual muscles, if constantly exercised, did amazing things. During the 1850s the goldrushes had drawn population into the interior. During the 1860s a basic infrastructure had been established – roads, railways, telegraph. Clergy, newspaper writers, schoolteachers and police had started to work out customary patterns of order a long way from the capital towns. But not until the 1870s did the Europeans start to think through the more fundamental problems of settlement. (So this volume starts in the 1870s.) We were in a geographical age. Men and women wrestled with puzzles of space and distance. So did children, who had the usefulness of maps drummed into them at school. In each of the colonies these matters were tackled in particular ways, depending on position and resources. It all added up to a great jigsaw of invention. Australian Federation was itself jigsaw work.

Patrick Gordon was a Queensland equivalent of HC Russell. He thought of the continent as a stage for acting out a great drama. Together, their stories throw a strong light on the intellectual flowering which took place in this part of the world towards the end of the nineteenth century. There were certain fashionable ways of thinking and discussing problems which beautifully matched antipodean circumstances. It was all about marrying advanced ideas to the brainwork of the people at large – again, the democratisation of knowledge (or, as we see later, 'organised intelligence'). It was about speech and writing. It was about teaching and training. It was about vastness. It was about power: the power of the few – of experts sitting, most of them, in the capital cities – but also the power of the people.

Skilled in measuring both the new needs and the old habits of the people, civil servants set themselves to respond to those needs and habits. They led and followed at the same time in a complex dance of accountability. Gordon was always suggesting acts of parliament, or drawing them up himself, with the idea of forcing a tighter order on owners and drovers, giving them access to skilled advice and support, and making sure that those who used the best methods were not held back by others. Livestock and human beings were two parts of a single problem. In 1880 he published a *Drover's Guide*, an encyclopedia of all the legal provisions governing the movement of stock, first in Queensland and then, in later editions, throughout the other mainland colonies, except for Western Australia. Distribution in print of information like this became a standard service in Queensland. In 1891 the printers of the Barcaldine paper the *Western Champion* issued their *Almanack and Year Book* for the people of central Queensland. They apologised for the scant information about drovers' routes and about distances from water, as if this was printed detail to which country people were entitled. In 1893 Gordon himself put out a *Map of New South Wales Shewing Stock Routes, Tanks and Trucking Stations, Railways and Telegraph Lines*.

Gordon also had a system for gathering ideas and centralising knowledge. Facts, or pretended facts, about pasture – what grass was good, what was bad, and what was toxic – circulated freely in talk among graziers and drovers. Drawing on such talk, in 1887 Gordon and the government botanist Frederick Manson Bailey published a small book called *Plants Reputed Poisonous and Injurious to Stock*. Bailey had already written a *Handbook to the Ferns of Queensland*, *An Illustrated Monograph of the Grasses of Queensland*, *The Fern World of Australia* and *A Synopsis of the Queensland Flora*. This new book included information from all the colonies, but again it was mainly about Queensland. Part of its purpose was to assess the truth of rumour and to impose science on superstition, and some samples of vegetation, sent in from all parts, had been tested in Bailey's laboratory. The *Lotus australis*, a native with purple-pink flowers, had been judged good fodder years ago in South Australia, but in Queensland stock were herded carefully around it. Specimens were tested and seemed safe. A drover on the Warrego had told of thirty of his rams dying within minutes of eating *Dysphania myriocephala*. And yet, said Gordon and Bailey, '[w]e have no other evidence to lead to the conclusion that the plant is poisonous'. The wallflower poison bush (*Gastrolobium grandiflorum*) was certainly toxic for part of the year, but rumour said that it was safe when its chocolate-coloured flowers came out. Gordon and Bailey put the question to their readers. What was the truth?[29]

Information moved both ways. Good mail runs, plus the telegraph, meant that a net of inquiry could be cast among amateurs. Sometimes it simply meant asking them to keep an eye out while they worked. Sometimes it involved supplying them with standardised equipment. On the one hand, certainly, there was more professionalism, more reliance on strict training and expensive laboratory work. On the other hand, experts might devote themselves to gathering information from amateurs, carefully broadcasting results and enlightening all concerned.

III

Democratising knowledge was a little like socialism. Everything was shared, even when it was won by individual hard work. In fact, collaboration seemed to be the answer to all big problems. The drive towards individual free enterprise, all-powerful during the middle third of the nineteenth century, had started to weaken, or rather, as we see later, to mutate into much more subtle hopes of 'individuality'. One of the great achievements of this earlier emphasis on individual self-reliance was the free selection movement, started in the 1860s, which had led to the much wider distribution of land. Large quantities of Crown land once occupied by squatters and grazed by sheep and cattle had been 'unlocked' for the benefit of farmers and graziers with smaller means, who took up pieces of freehold on easy terms. There were parallels overseas, such as the Homestead Acts in the United States. They looked to individual effort, especially the individual man feeding and supported by his family.

Free selection put a farming population on the soil. It also reinforced the claims of squatters to land they really needed. But even while this movement was at its height, men and women had often been keen to work together, sharing resources and sharing information. Just as important (and now almost totally forgotten) were the commons – vast allotments of shared land – created all over the continent. In England for many generations town and village commons had been basic to rural life, but by this time most English commons had been converted to private property. For most of the nineteenth century economic orthodoxy hated any hint of property in common.[30] And yet, in newly conquered parts of the world common property made good sense. Like the Australian commons, the rangelands of the United States and the latifundia of South America were crucial to livelihood on the land.

Throughout the mainland colonies, from the 1850s, and more and more from the 1860s, enormous areas, often tens of thousands of acres (many thousands of hectares) were measured up as a shared resource for men and women with cattle, horses and sheep needing extra space, from the 32,000 acres at Dongara, where the Irwin River meets the Indian Ocean, to the 50,000 acres across the continent at Dalby, at the extreme north-east of the Murray-Darling Basin. As in England, they were often meant for the livestock of townspeople – butchers' herds, for instance. But in Australia the needs of farmers mattered more. According to Dongara's leading men, their common was to 'aid the farmer in his farming'. It was for 'such stock as can fairly be used on a farm, say cattle for dairying and a small number of sheep to feed off stubble'. '[A]ll over the colony commonages are set apart', said the West Australian premier. They were not to be 'altogether permanent' and would be phased out as the land was better settled, as settlers started to match their acreage to their livestock numbers. But for the time being they were essential.[31] It was another way of getting on top of all the new problems which followed from suddenly filling up a continent with livestock.

In Victoria the first of the Land Acts, 1860, was the work of Charles Gavan Duffy. Duffy spoke to small settlers about sharing land at a distance from their farms. '[T]hey invariably replied that such would be of the greatest benefit, as though their working cattle could not be sent to grass, they could send out their store cattle to fatten'. They could see how it would work: 'proper regulations would be made, and an overseer appointed, so that the distance would be nothing'.[32]

First, find a community that can agree to put its wealth together. Second, draw around that community an ineluctable line. Every common belonged to a certain group of men and women. They were supposed to have their names listed and to pay commonage fees. On well-managed commons, 'overseers' (sometimes called 'herdsmen' or 'rangers') managed the amalgamated herd. Good overseers made all the difference when it came to settling ownership and to making sure that new calves were given the right brand. At Cooma, in New South Wales, the common measured 15,000 acres. Its trustees were extremely efficient, even publishing their accounts in the *Government Gazette*. In a single year, 1872, their income was nearly £130, mainly from rent and fees for agistment, and most of it was used to pay their secretary, herdsman and assistant herdsman.[33] At Benalla, in Victoria, with 7632 acres, there were about thirty commoners, mostly with 200 or 300 acres each of their own, and up to twenty cattle to run with the rest. Again, the herdsman was paid from commonage fees – £40 in 1879.[34]

By 1870, in Victoria alone, nearly 2 million acres were common land. Most towns of any size had a common of 100 acres or more. There were also fifty-five 'goldfields commons' and 205 'farmers' commons'. They all had managers appointed by municipal councils, mining boards or the government.[35]

The story of the Australian commons shows how people thought and what their basic habits were. There were some differences from one colony to the next. Things in Victoria were tightly run from the centre. In 1877 a member of parliament in Melbourne suggested that the commoners should choose their managers. The idea was knocked back: 'endless squabbles would arise'.[36] In New South Wales, always less doctrinaire, squabbles were part of the system. Armidale had a common of about 3000 acres. In 1873, when a new law feebly attempted tighter discipline, a local writer poked fun at the local response. 'As far as could be gathered,' he said, 'there were no trustees of the Armidale common in existence, and the Mayor finding a letter directed to those mythical personages opened it'.[37] He then called a public meeting, at which someone pointed out that they were powerless in law. The meeting had not been announced beforehand in the *Government Gazette*, as it should have been. And even if it had been they were paralysed because only the commoners could elect a chairman, and only the chairman, once elected, could say who was a commoner and who was not. The only solution was to ignore the rules.[38]

Throughout the colonies, by the end of the century, nothing was more fundamental than the idea of a place properly bordered, and if not with fencing of wire or wood then with salt surf. The continent itself was a kind of common, set aside for a favoured few: 'Australia for the Australians!' By the 1880s there were already plans among visionaries for making some or all of the colonies into something like a common on a gigantic scale – a vast space, shared, managed and protected by its own people, individually self-sufficient and yet interdependent, or their elected trustees.

As Charles Bean put it, 'Australia is a big blank map, and the whole people is constantly sitting over it like a committee, trying to work out the best way to fill it in'.[39] Its boundaries would be policed against intruders. Its discoveries and inventions would be shared by everyone who could call themselves Australian. It would be our common, our commonwealth. Within its boundaries, trusting each other, we would all get rich together. When politicians talked about cooperation like this they usually had in mind trade and customs. But the movement of livestock and the sharing of knowledge mattered just as much. The mobility of animals over whatever distance – within each common, across the continent – was a major question of public order. So was the movement of ideas. The conversation went on from shore to shore, from top to bottom. At least, that was the great hope – the hope of some but not all. It all depended on trust.

The chief inspectors of stock in each colony were like the rangers of commons, but on a large scale. In November 1874, Patrick Gordon and Alexander Bruce organised a meeting in Sydney with their colleagues from Victoria, South Australia and Tasmania, to compare ways of dealing with contagious diseases among stock and to see how they could all work together. New Zealand, Fiji and Western Australia were asked to join in, and the meeting became an annual event. The Queensland government already led the way in funding scientific inquiry into diseases in stock, and its methods were henceforth encouraged in other places. Through these meetings, a type for intercolonial cooperation (copied by the meteorologists and numerous other civil servants), a single code of rules and a single system of stock inspection came about. A boundary of quarantine was thrown around all those colonies which agreed to come under inspection. Within that boundary, all were classed as 'clean'.[40]

IV

Until the mid-1870s, continent-wide, sheep and cattle were easily the most important source of general prosperity. Afterwards, city-based manufacturing started to pull ahead. Even then, however, vast sums were invested in animals and land. During most of the 1870s wool accounted for half the value of all exports from the colonies, and even when demand fell away, graziers kept pushing into untried territory, keen to make a return on money already spent. Drought hit income hard even in the better settled country, never mind the newly settled. This was therefore risky business.[41]

The cost of labour was a critical part of the equation. The power of invention was stretched to its limit, and it underpinned the effort to federate Australia. In Argentina, Valentin Alsina's rural code had included a tighter discipline for gauchos, or stockmen, with rules about vagrancy, gaucho crime and order in the workplace. Older regulations had enforced passports for gauchos moving about the country, to be used on pain of years in gaol. Now they were held in a kind of paid bondage.[42] Good profits from livestock involved major investment. To make it safe, the control of labour had to be just as weighty.

There were close parallels in Australia. Work in the bush was done by Aborigines, Pacific Islanders and Europeans. Aboriginal men and women had been working with livestock since at least the 1830s. By the 1870s and '80s, especially in newly settled parts, their efforts were critical. There was often no-one else. Also, they did the work well. Cattle work was said to be 'second nature' to Aborigines. This was the opinion of Walter Blomfield, a stockman and grazier who spent most of his life between northern New South Wales and central Queensland. 'They are taught when young', he said, 'to round up a mob of kangaroos, a covey of quail, a shoal of fish', so they could anticipate even the smallest animal movement. '[H]andling a mob of cattle means keeping them in a straight line for where you want them to go & not letting them wobble all over the place.' These were things Aboriginal stockmen understood.[43]

'You can't fatten bullocks at a trot', as Blomfield put it. He had a story about a cattle owner who insisted, against all good advice, that his animals should be kept at a smart trot and packed tight while they were on the move.

> [W]hen we were within five miles or so of the yard he would jog along home & leave us to *drive* the mob. As soon as he was out of sight the 'Abos' would move out on both sides giving the cattle more room. We never saw a beast linger when let walk along this way.

They got home, in fact, before the boss. Blomfield's moral was '[n]ever drive cattle but let them walk along. Never drive your hands either'. 'Banjo' Paterson catches the spirit of it in his image of Clancy of the Overflow, the archetypal drover: 'As the stock are slowly stringing, Clancy rides behind them singing'.[44] Singing or, just as easily, in silent meditation.

In the northern part of the continent, from Queensland through the Northern Territory of South Australia (as it then was) and into the Kimberley, everything depended on Aboriginal stockmen. 'I do not know what they [the graziers] could have done without them', said Frank Gillen, telegraph officer at Alice Springs.[45] But Aboriginal stockmen themselves were often driven hard. In the early days, the first dealings between Black and White were completely brutal, until leading men and women among the Aborigines made peace for their own small groups. Some were fed in return for working with stock, and the system came to depend on their labour being in constant supply.[46]

An inspector of police stationed in the Northern Territory described the recruiting method. It was called 'running them down'. That meant 'forcibly taking them from tribes to stations some distance away', where they were surrounded by 'wild' and alien Blacks, and had no-one but their boss to protect them. It was a method brought by cattlemen from western Queensland and was widespread in the North. Women and girls were caught in the same way, for use as wives.[47] The system of running them down went on until at least the 1890s, even where governments had begun to make their presence felt. Police were loosely scattered, and they took orders from graziers and government at the same time.

Methods closer to the towns were gentler. In south-east South Australia ration depots were set up to stop Aborigines killing stock. So they were drawn into dependence on the White man and made useful.[48] Later on, especially in Queensland, a stricter and more all-encompassing code was forced onto Aboriginal people. (See chapter 8.) In the end they were bound at least as tightly as the gauchos.

In Queensland too, from the early 1860s there were Pacific Islanders, or Kanakas, mainly from the New Hebrides (now Vanuatu) and Loyalty Islands. They worked largely on the sugar plantations, around Mackay, Maryborough and elsewhere, but also as shepherds. In 1881 there were more than 6000. Like Aborigines, Kanakas were originally forced into service in violent, arbitrary ways. The recruiting voyage of the *Hopeful*, in and around the Bismarck Archipelago in 1884, was described in a government report as 'one long record of deceit, cruel treachery, deliberate kidnapping and cold-blooded murder'. This particular report led to seven White men being tried before the Supreme Court in Brisbane. Two were condemned to hang, but death sentences in such cases were not supported by Queensland public opinion, and petitions carrying more than 28,000 names, including those of sixty members of parliament, forced the government to commute them to life imprisonment. As the governor, Sir Anthony Musgrave, explained to London, the *Hopeful*'s excursion was normal. The labour traffic, His Excellency said, was 'no better than slave hunting'. But 'the crime of these men is the crime of the community and of the government which has permitted such things to be possible'.[49] His hands were tied.

Many Islanders were tricked into the boats. Ro-bah-he, from Sudest Island, in the Louisiade Archipelago, was asked afterwards why he had left his wife. 'I no savez', he said. 'If I had been ashore I would not be here now; she would have stopped me.' When there was violence it was often because Islanders already aboard suddenly realised what was going on.[50]

As with the Aborigines, these methods could not last. As early as 1868 recruitment was codified. A system of contracts was drawn up. The men were to work for three years at a time, for at least £6 a year with rations. The agreements were to be fully explained to them by interpreters, and they were legal only if the men had signed up with 'full knowledge and understanding' of what was to happen. But interpreters were not impartial. Nor were the government agents who looked on.

It was the Islander men themselves (the survivors) – when they got home at last, told their stories to their friends and showed their money (though much less than European workers got) – who eventually civilised the trade. The people liked what they heard and by the late 1870s they started to organise themselves to meet future demand. 'It is simply impossible to kidnap a man there', said a government agent, talking about the New Hebrides. 'The moment your boat touches shore, you are entirely in the power of the men on the beach.' It was now normal, he said, for crowds of men to volunteer. At one island, as the boat rocked in the surf,

> the mate would say, 'me give you two musket for two boys [young men] and powder and shot' … [T]he man supposed to be the head man, would point out to one or two boys, and then they would bring the muskets and [the Islanders would] fire them off before accepting them, knowing perfectly well the value of weapons; and if they were satisfied, the two boys would come into the boat.

The men all wanted firearms. There was also what one missionary called 'the burning desire of the youth to see the world'. Even so, the number who died in Queensland (as many as three in every five on the estate of the Colonial Sugar Refining Company at Goondi, near Innisfail), thanks partly to callous masters, kept the risk high.[51]

V

Much the same was happening among Europeans themselves, and not just in Australia. A new style of bargaining was starting to take place when they took up jobs. White men and women had started to talk about their labour as if it were a kind of property. It was 'merchandise', they said, it was 'capital', and it was their own. It could be sold where they liked and at their own price.[52] They would not be driven. The idea that their labour, skilled or unskilled, might be valued like this was new to the mass of working men and women. It raised extraordinary possibilities. They became a class in themselves, an interest group with a single sense of right. They could assess and assert that right by combining, and the more of them the better. This was the 'new unionism'. A dramatic early demonstration of it took place in London's East End in 1887, when the women in Bryant and May's match factory went on strike against intolerable conditions. They won partly because of their own courage, but they also had the support of some top journalists, including Annie Besant, of the *Link*, and William Stead, of the *Pall Mall Gazette*, who translated their grievances into print.

Legitimised in black and white, and in influential periodicals, this new thinking about labour quickly caught on. In the more civil, more efficient world which labouring men and women looked forward to, they would let themselves be mustered, listed and organised. But unlike cattle they would do it for their own good and at their own pace. They would not be forced. In 1889 dockers at the Port of London managed an even more ambitious strike, lasting nearly five weeks. Again, good publicity was crucial. The dockers' strike caused enormous interest in Australia, where £30,000 was raised and sent to London for strikers and their families.

The careful herding of humanity, like the democratic marshalling of knowledge, was the order of the day. It could be used against authority or in cooperation with authority. Sometimes authority was taken so much by surprise that it hardly knew how to respond. A few working men showed enormous ingenuity in this process, and many started measuring their power among men like themselves. So democracy in Australia took on a new edge.

The old unions had been limited to skilled trades in big cities with stable and concentrated populations. It was another thing, under the new unionism, to muster thousands of individuals into permanent associations, especially in the colonies, where they were often on the move, chasing jobs. In Australasia in the 1880s the greatest organising genius of this sort was William Guthrie Spence. Spence started his involvement in unionism when he was living on the goldfields at Clunes, to the north of Ballarat, in Victoria.

In 1874 the Amalgamated Miners' Association was founded not far away, in Bendigo, mainly in response to the way mining had been taken over by big companies, which were very effective in keeping down wages. The AMA started slowly, but a fresh push was made in 1878, after a concerted move by mine owners to cut pay.

Solidarity was then taken to another level of sophistication. At Creswick, with Spence in the lead, a Miners' Union was formed and integrated with the AMA. Then in 1882 Spence became general secretary. There was an explosion in numbers, as news got about. It was usual for miners to spend part of each year shearing, and in 1886 the Australian Shearers' Union was formed, also with Spence in charge. By 1890 its members numbered 20,000 and the AMA's 25,000, each member carrying his ticket, or tickets (many must have belonged to both unions), wherever he went as proof of what he was.[53] It was his ticket, collated with books at headquarters, that let a man say he 'was union'.

As I say earlier, in Australia there were new laws and conventions about the ownership of mobile livestock. It was the same with mobile labour. In both cases, colonial borders set a particular challenge. Like the meteorologists in their dealings with the movements of the weather, union leaders had to keep in mind a number of colonies all at once. Nearly as much as the weather, the men were heedless of intercolonial boundaries. 'Before we began', said Spence, talking about the Shearers' Union, 'I laid down the principle that the Union must be intercolonial – must ignore political boundaries – and every member must carry his rights and privileges as a member with him, no matter what colony he was in'.[54]

The Australian Shearers' Union spread in the 1880s, first into the Riverina, in southern New South Wales, and then northwards to Cobar, Bourke and Moree. There were branches in South Australia by 1889. For a while there was also a branch in New Zealand. Union organisers followed the men, and the men followed the shearing from place to place with the rhythm of the seasons.

Many crossed the Tasman each November. In central Queensland the inland country – Hughenden, Clermont, Blackall, Barcaldine, Augathella – was dense with sheep by the 1880s, and skilled shearing was a high attribute of manhood. Blackall was the home of Jackie Howe, 'the greatest shearer that ever lived'. In 1892 Howe shore 321 sheep in seven hours and forty minutes (still a record). He was a keen union man, and part of the original campaign at Blackall.[55]

A shearer wanting to work all year round could start in central Queensland in January, move on to St George, near the border, and so into western New South Wales by June–July, ending up in the Riverina by springtime. In fact, few men took this route in its entirety. The Queensland–New South Wales border, the line between North and South which so intrigued the two chief inspectors of stock, was a crucial divide. Even for shearers, and therefore for unionists, it was a barrier. So the usual circuit took in Victoria (especially the northern and western districts), the Riverina and western New South Wales, and the eastern parts of South Australia.[56]

These hinterlands, the backblocks of three colonies, were really one. For this reason (as we see later), the three became the heartland of Federation. The federating effort was built on such myriad movements. Among the middle class too, trade and family ties steadily drew together these same vast spaces. Rural bank managers, for instance, transferred from branch to branch in the course of their careers, circulated within the same area.[57] Queenslanders, on the other hand, of all classes, tended to keep to themselves. A Queensland Shearers' Union began in 1886, at Blackall, and a Queensland Labourers' Union at Barcaldine in 1888. The two joined forces as the Amalgamated Workers' Union of Queensland in 1891, Jackie Howe being one of the leaders in this enlarging effort. Only with a special effort, and even then a somewhat guarded one, could Queenslanders look southwards. The North–South divide was a great fact of antipodean life. It ran right through the Federation story.

Towards the end of 1890, in a crisis with origins in Argentina, some leading banks in London collapsed, triggering a disastrous failure of credit throughout the colonies, the failure of banks on the spot (both British and Australian owned), a tragic loss of life savings among numerous small investors, the suicide of several businessmen and, for some years, widespread unemployment. It was the worst depression the colonies had ever seen, and a period of massive suffering. To start with, unionised working men were sure they would be rescued by their leaders. The price of wool had been falling for some time, and sheep owners struggled to control the cost of shearing. But it was a life-and-death battle on both sides. A few Chinese and, in Queensland, Pacific Islanders were available for work at very low rates, and other strike breakers were always on call, which made it possible for employers to impose greatly inferior pay and conditions. On the other hand, the dockers' strike in London, and the efforts in Australia to raise money in support, proved what could be done if only organisation and publicity, aided by post and telegraph, were good enough. In Queensland, the Australian Labour Federation (in fact a body of Queenslanders) took a sudden leap in membership. In August 1890 it reached 15,000.

The strength of the unions was tested straightaway by the great Maritime Strike, towards the end of that year. Shipping companies met the combined force of unionised seamen, wharf labourers and others along the coast from Cooktown, in north Queensland, to Adelaide, but mainly in Melbourne and Sydney. The ship owners won, which gave heart to other employers, and when shearing was about to start in central Queensland in January 1891 graziers refused demands that they take on only unionised men. Over the next five months the shearers gathered in camps, mainly around Clermont and Barcaldine. There they built up dynamic little communities all their own. One journalist called these camps 'a national danger'. In fact, they were quiet and orderly.[58] Each camp elected a governing committee and chairman. In some, a special vigilance committee organised pickets, policing the movements of the rest of the men and keeping them sober.

This was another field of remarkable ingenuity. There was hidden tension between union leaders and the men on the ground. The leaders tried to get all the shearers together into one or two big camps. The men refused and the issue was dropped. Among the men, like gathered with like. Each camp had its own preferences and policies, and the leadership gave each what it wanted. Men with horses camped apart from 'footmen'. Near Clermont, the camp at Sandy Creek was set up by 'Western men' – wild men and 'regular nomads' who had no family ties and who were keen to stick it out to the end. Nearby, at Wolfgang and Capella, there were married men, mainly locals, worried about violence and needing work. The nomads cooked for themselves, but the married men wanted home comforts. To keep these more domesticated individuals happy, the leadership let them have cooks and certain 'luxuries' – vegetables and dried fruit – on top of the basic flour, tea, sugar and beef.[59]

Discipline felt self-imposed. On the whole it was. The camps looked like little republics packed with apparently high-minded individuals. When police came to arrest men at Capella, there was a shout, 'Turn out, boys, and ring the bells', and an immediate din of horse bells everywhere. When early risers at the camp near Barcaldine found the place surrounded by troops, they woke the rest by crowing like roosters.[60]

No-one had a good word to say for the South. From a Queensland point of view, southern strike breakers were not just 'scabs' and 'blacklegs'. They were 'foreigners'. On the other hand, from a southern perspective, the striking shearers, in the words of one Melbourne labour leader, were 'firebrands' – 'very nasty fellows to deal with'.[61]

The hopes of the leaders were summed up in that magic word of the 1880s and '90s: 'federation'. It was a word which meant a lot more than the union of the colonies. The leaders wanted solidarity, and across the largest possible area. The federation of unions was the answer. It was the only way of marrying the sort of efficiency size could bring with the diversity of the people, their separate interests and habits. Large numbers, after all, were a challenge as well as a blessing. They stretched the gap between the leadership and the mass, and they threatened true democracy. Federation was the answer. Federation married power and local voices, efficiency and wide discussion, theory and experience, sameness and difference. Within Queensland alone, variety was enormous. With the federation of unions, a strong executive, made up of the best brains, could run in harness with an infinity of opinion on the ground.

WG Spence had made maximum use of the postal services and the telegraph in linking the leadership with many widely scattered men. In Queensland too, a wide-awake and forceful executive was crucial – for instance, in dealing with unions in the South. A strike centred on Jondaryan Station, on the Darling Downs, in the early months of 1890, showed how important it was that southerners be kept on side in this way. Otherwise, it would be overwhelmed with strike breakers – with 'foreigners' from across the border.[62]

There were always matters that needed local knowledge and input from the bottom. Effective recruitment depended on the local touch. The wonders of modern communication notwithstanding, it was impossible to overlook the power of ordinary talk, the small habits and ceremonies, and the old ways that shaped life face to face. For such reasons, the Australian Labour Federation formed district councils with considerable power in their own areas.[63] The men had to feel that their leaders were close enough to put food into their mouths. While the strike moved slowly towards its climax, the Queensland shearers were managed with wonderful skill, and keeping men well fed was critical. Living on 'the fat of the land', as they put it, kept them loyal.

It was bread and circuses, and circuses meant colour and noise. In a parade through Barcaldine five chairmen rode in front, one with a plumed hat and attendant bugler, and all of them sporting 'immense blue sashes'. They were followed by more than 1000 men marching in close order on horse and foot, and carrying the tools of their trade, including 'shears and wands dressed in wool'. Embroidered banners were carried high. In the midst of it all, two men rode on a wagon shearing sheep, with rouseabouts standing by with brooms and tar pot.[64]

It was an extraordinary demonstration of power. Tied to the land, these were a self-sufficient people. Marching, shouting, making speeches and ringing bells, these 'very nasty fellows' had the world at their feet. And yet by May the strike was broken, and they all had to think again. That thinking was to be part of the great agenda of the years ahead. Again, it was to be Federation (for or against), but it was something else as well. Election to the colonial parliaments of men who could speak up for interests of labour and, very quickly, the formation of Labour (from 1912 spelt 'Labor') parties throughout the colonies. An intercolonial conference worked out the way forward in 1900, and a federal party was formed when the original federal parliament met in May 1901.[65] The first political body with a signed-up membership across colonial boundaries, and a large one at that, federal Labour sprang from the communication networks men such as WG Spence had started.

3

The Commonwealth of Speech

I

Federation was about unity and variety, both at once, the one and the many. A good balance was hard to strike. Mary Gilmore loved Australia as one people, but she also loved variety. Looking back from an elderly vantage point in the 1930s to the time of her childhood, sixty years before, she mourned the loss of truly Australian habits of speech, the tapestry of sound which had disappeared since the Federation years. 'That mixture of Scotch, Irish, county-and-shire-English, with its interlarding of aboriginal words, its sprinkling of Californian Spanish and its Red Indian hunting and gold-digging terms': all had disappeared as fragments of another age, together with the bugles and blue sashes of striking shearers.[1]

Mary Gilmore blamed imported novels. It followed that the new habits of speech were foreign. She was partly right. The need to mimic people in books from abroad might explain the coming of new words and the death of old ones. But there was much more to it than that. Among the Europeans in Australia, the sounds themselves had been transformed. Their articulation was smoothed out so as to be much the same from shore to shore.

Voices were mechanised too. In Hobart in 1888 William Westgarth, once an eminent Melburnian but now an elderly gentleman just arrived from London, was told that someone wanted to speak to him 'through the telephone'. It seems to have been Westgarth's first experience of this wonder.

> I hied at once to the telephone room, and duly, as directed, put two wire-connected caps to my ears, and was all attention. I did hear a still small voice come up, as from the vasty deep; but, whether from some little deafness of age, or from the awe-inspiring of such unaccustomed things, I failed to make it out.[2]

Magic met aged cynicism. The 'vasty deep' was Shakespeare's term. In *Henry IV*, part 1, the Welsh prince Glendower says, 'I can call spirits from the vasty deep', and Hotspur, the northern lord, scoffs, 'Why, so can I, or so can any man, / But will they come when you do call for them?'[3]

The 'still small voice', on the other hand, was the prophet Elijah's description of the voice of God. It was an impression typical of first-time telephone listeners. So was the sensation of something otherworldly trickling up, tickling the ear, from a bottomless void. The voice in the handset, said a man in Melbourne, 'seemed to be refined and as it were, thinned away until the sounds seemed to come from fairy-like creatures in the recesses of the telephone'.[4] In mourning the end of old languages, Mary Gilmore was also talking about a thinning away. That meant pinpointing peculiarities of accent and pruning them back.

News of the invention of the telephone, including detail on the technology, reached the colonies late in 1877. For some years thereafter, the telegraph lines already in existence were used for telephone transmission. The other necessary equipment, for speaking and listening, was easily put together. (Even easier was the popular version, which many also tried, with two tins linked by a piece of string.) Through the telephone men fought to throw their voices as far as they could. Alfred Biggs, a schoolteacher at Campbell Town, central Tasmania, made himself heard at Launceston, 80 kilometres away, with telephone sets positioned at the two railway stations and using the telegraph line that ran along the track.[5] The various colonial governments were interested in the long-distance possibilities of the telephone as a means of drawing their people together. In Queensland, William Cracknell, superintendent of telegraphs, secured two up-to-date telephones directly from Alexander Graham Bell, the inventor in the United States, and made experiments viva voce with outlying parts.[6]

However, people started using telephones mainly to communicate within their own cities and towns. Messages that had once been carried by hand about town or else saved up for meeting could now be sent straightaway, mouth to ear. As an official in Launceston said, 'This system will bring the entire community [the local community, that is] of business and professional men together. Subscribers can sit in their offices and transact business, buy and sell goods, give and receive orders etc. in every quarter of the city'. Hence, each city, so it was said of the United States, became a new type of organism, interlaced with 'millions upon millions of live filaments that unite all the privacies of the organism – and destroy them in order to make one immense publicity!'[7]

Some of the first telephone connections were set up between the various branches of the one firm, but by 1880 businessmen were getting together to build exchanges, with switchboards, for use by any local firms and individuals who wanted to subscribe. In Sydney this was the effort of a few leading men, using the stock exchange premises in Bridge Street. In Melbourne, one man made a start alone. Henry Byron Moore, who built the telephone exchange in Wills Street, was a greyhound racer who wanted to send results from the track at Werribee, outside Melbourne, to city punters as quickly as he could. He soon found others just as keen for lightning communication. After only three years his Melbourne Telephone Exchange Company was sold to the government for £40,000.[8]

By this time there was a government exchange in every capital except Perth. Colonists looked to the Americans not just for the original invention but also for the best ways to use it. In the United States the switchboard operators were usually women, and the staff was female in all Australian cities except for Sydney, where the superintendent of telegraphs insisted on men. The exchange in Melbourne, purpose built of bluestone and brick, was an extraordinary phenomenon – a 'Palace of Winged Words', someone called it. A great cavern of a room, the only action it contained was in the women's hands, which moved in 'magic confusion' backwards and forwards across the switchboard, itself 22 yards (20 metres) long, flicking switches and pushing plugs into jacks.[9]

The women's eyes never wandered. Their model was the thirty-year-old telegraph system, but unlike the telegraph operators they used mouths and ears as well as hands. They were therefore more completely absorbed into the machinery. They were trained to keep their voices absolutely under control: '[t]here is no shouting or even excitement – no apoplectic strain into the machine's mouth'. This was a marketplace of voices, and yet the voices were wonderfully discreet and subdued, a 'low coo-ing tone, almost a whisper' – womanhood at its best, busy, disciplined, discreet. 'Although during the busy hours of the day probably nearly all the operators were talking at the same time', said a visitor to an American exchange, 'yet so low is the tone of their voices, that but little sound fills the room and the click of the apparatus is distinctly audible'. At the Wills Street exchange, according to a visitor, nothing could be heard, day in and day out, but 'a soft sighing murmur'. The women seemed to have perfect control of the wilderness of voices pressing in on them from the hidden depths of the machine, whatever the problems – abuse for a bad line, for having to wait or for having to finish when time was up.[10]

Feeling when it bubbled over was suppressed by the uniform politeness of the operators, or else cut off. A woman caller, it was said, 'is quick to wrath when crossed in her inquiries, snaps bitterly, but has it all over in a moment, while a man in a passion switches off as if crazy'.[11] Throwing down the handset, callers must have caught the mental echoes of their own voices in the silence of disconnection.

It took a long time for the telephone to be much used for long-distance communication. The calls were too expensive. For the same reason it took a long time for the telephone to be used much for chatting, and by women at home. As late as 1906 medical men complained that women did not understand telephones. They would ring up at the drop of a hat for advice on minor ailments, avoiding the need to visit and so, they thought, the doctor's bill. These were rich women. A writer in Brisbane's *Worker* at about the same time could only dream of the day when 'working people may also know the tinkle of the telephone'. On that day, she thought, something like social networking (as we would call it) would arrive, and the spread of news from individual to individual would circumvent the capitalist press. 'Labour women will be able to communicate with each other, and tell the latest news of the women at the barricades in Russia, and of the women's fight for the franchise in England.'[12] Both women and men would be freed by the telephone from narrow minds and narrow places.

Could Australia itself be something like a 'Palace of Winged Words', a true commonwealth of speech – not just because of telephones but also through the concentration on sound and its possibilities that telephones represented? The American essayist Ralph Waldo Emerson, grappling with the spirit of his own land, spoke about a level of awareness 'where the air is music'. We need to hear better, he said, in order to understand our country at its most profound. We need to be 'so finely organized that we can penetrate into that region' – that region of our consciousness where our national home is truly known. When that happened, that home (America in his case) would be a spoken poem.[13]

Joseph Furphy made the effort. In *Such Is Life*, Furphy tried to give Australia, and especially the borderland of the Murray River, to readers' eardrums. He offered the country as a bundle of timbre and touch. Furphy knew about what is now called soundscape (the aural version of landscape). Set in the early 1880s, his story is thick with accents, which the reader stumbles to follow – hearing him recreate a patchwork of voices such as Mary Gilmore knew. In a bushmen's camp 'the easy profanity, unconscious obscenity, and august slang of the back country scented the air like myall'. Nature too, said Furphy, was 'alive with sounds'. Invisible vibrations, in a ubiquitous, crisscross web (here Furphy was in lecturing mode), 'ripple, spread, percolate, everywhere; they penetrate and saturate all solids and gases, yet are palpable corporeally only to the tympanum of the ear, and mechanically (as yet) only to the diaphragm of the phonograph'.[14]

Developments in philology led to the spread of technical knowledge about pronunciation. There was an interest in phonetics and in the study of voices and of sound generally as a science. There were also new ways of denoting sounds, apart from the well-known letters. Just as there were keys and codes to be learnt for reading maps, there were keys and codes in phonography. You could see sound. Voices had pungency, like bodily smells. They summed up the people who spoke, as men, as women, as good or bad citizens. 'Man is but a lyre' – this is Furphy again, and by 'lyre' he also meant 'liar' – 'whatever else a man may sing, he always sings himself'. People dressed themselves in sound. They put on airs, or 'side'. Genteel accents had long been taught to a few of the socially ambitious.[15] Now large numbers became self-conscious about their voices. This was one way, and a very important way, of changing from the inhabitant of a small place to the member of a nation. All that space, all that desert stillness, was to be expressed by each human inhabitant in a complex manipulation of breath.

This was new knowledge and new sensibility of a wonderful

kind, truly 'something beyond' the world as we know it. And yet it was part of ourselves. Henry Chamberlain Russell sounded the same when he talked about weather patterns convulsing the atmosphere, 'like the vibrations in musical notes'.[16]

II

On the Darling River in 1908, amid watery breezes, Charles Bean talked with an elderly ship's captain. He was struck with the way the man spoke, with 'that old-fashioned, deliberate, gentle punctuation that makes every syllable almost seem a separate word'. Bean meant both old-fashioned English and old-fashioned Australian, because language in both countries was changing. During his boyhood at Bathurst, in central western New South Wales, Bean himself had made a deliberate effort to sound Australian, or what his ears then told him was Australian. Even at ten years old he thought the voices of educated English people sounded affected.[17] He had a good ear for this sort of thing, for the commonwealth of speech.

Schoolteachers were drawing antipodean children away from their old habits towards something neither Australian nor English, though they hoped it would be both. Bean thought that vowel sounds, especially 'a', 'o' and 'ow', were badly taught in government schools. Old accents had made those sounds pleasant to the ear, he said, and it was a pity to 'distort' them as the new generation of teachers was doing. He also liked the old habit of 'lengthening of the final "y" into something nearer to "ee" (perhaps it can be best represented by "ie" – prettie, verrie, reeallie)'. It was sad to lose such things.[18]

With the best will in the world, the reform of speech was random and open-ended. Results were unpredictable. School inspectors, doing their rounds when Gilmore and Bean were young, kept an ear out for the changes and made notes as they heard children reading aloud and talking in the playground. Some innovations, springing up and spreading among the people, were the opposite of what they wanted. But how to agree as to which was right and which was wrong?

In the 1880s, the old Darling River captain's habit of separating syllables was already disappearing. 'Setting' was spelt with two 't's and that was the way it had always been pronounced. Old-fashioned teachers insisted on 'set-ting'. 'The practice of pronouncing double *t*, double *r*, and double *g* together,' said a South Australian inspector, 'as if they were a double letter like *w*, is most strongly to be condemned'. But it was hopeless. Whole syllables were disappearing. In 1900, according to another inspector, 'ness-ary for necessary, eag'ly for eagerly, [and] you for your' were distressingly frequent.[19] It was survival of the fittest. There never was an age which saw so many old articulations pass into extinction.

Alexander Clark, another South Australian school inspector, was fascinated with the mix of tongues, but only as an object of curiosity. He believed it must pass.

> Some of our schools are markedly Cornish, others Hibernian [Irish], some Caledonian [Scots], &c. In one school, in an examination in geography, I noticed, almost without exception, that *cape*, *bay*, *Germein* [as in Port Germein], *plain*, &c., were sounded in the true Cockney fashion as *kipe*, *bye*, *Germine*, *pline*, &c., and with the characteristic lazy drawl. In another locality a short sound of *a* as in n*a*p is used in a sentence like the following, 'Our c*a*lf ate h*a*lf the gr*a*ss', and this with a half nasal twang, which sounds very oddly.[20]

In rural Victoria too, as someone else said, 'British dialects [had] not yet mingled into a common language'. In Melbourne, as in most big cities, habits of speech were ahead of everywhere else. But even there, when the offspring of parents from southern Scotland and northern Ireland stood up in class, the old metallic sharpness rang in teachers' ears. As in South Australia, certain habits stuck to certain places. Between Branxholme and Goroke, in the Victorian western districts, the letter 'r' seemed so soft as to 'do credit to a Parisian'. Teachers wanted every 'r' to be a distinct sound. 'Part' should be 'p-a-r-t'.[21]

Remote regions such as Furphy knew well showed a slowness all their own, 'a peculiar monotonous drawl or sing-song'. 'Banjo' Paterson explained what it was like. The 'far-out bushman' sometimes seemed to forget that he had anyone listening. Used to talking to himself, he would fall into long pauses, 'out of which he would come with a start and break in on other people's conversation, talking them down with a serene indifference to their feelings'.[22]

If you found such a man on his own in the bush and listened for a few days there were strange revelations. You heard a hint of the music of which Emerson spoke, of that 'something beyond' which Bean heard when a mouth organ played on the night waters of the Darling. Immensely lonely, the bushman would lay himself open. He offered piece by piece 'the whole of his former life, his family affairs, his luck and his disasters, his faults and his virtues', threaded through with his own brand of philosophical speculation. Bushmen were often readers and sometimes writers. Knut Dahl, a Norwegian biologist who travelled in the North, spoke of their ballads. It was 'a regular poetry', he said, 'existing in manuscript on scraps of paper and passed from man to man', and sung when bushmen got together with a little to drink. They were a mix of book learning and old ways of speech, gilded with 'melancholy tunes' and the cadence of the bush.[23]

Some feared that local accents would be even more varied in future, as generation after generation dug into particular spots, ranging from the remote bush to the cities. Schoolteachers had to work hard against this possibility, stamping out all local peculiarities. Everywhere, uniformity of speech was basic policy. Shaping the speech of the people was like laying out roads, railways and stock-routes. Voices were part of the commonwealth. They were common property. When we all spoke the same, we would be one nation. What we said could be harnessed to one purpose, mustered to one end.[24]

Everything was referred back to the 'standard' English accent, which was supposed to be the way 'thoughtful' people spoke in London. In order to impose the standard in England itself, a London writer prescribed two tests. One was '[t]he perfect distinction of minutely differing vowels' and the other was 'the clear enunciation of unaccented syllables'. And yet speech was changing in England too. Novelists, especially the fashionable 'realist' writers, explored the manifold variations of living speech, including speech of the latest kind. In doing so, as Mary Gilmore said, they spread the variations even further abroad.[25]

In fact, as I say, it was impossible to agree on what was correct. It was certainly understood that every letter was there to be pronounced. Take 'yabber', a colloquial word for 'talk'. The professor of modern languages and literatures at Melbourne University Edward Ellis Morris noted as an interesting fact that the Aborigines pronounced it 'yabba', without the final 'r' used by the settler people. It followed that the vowel sounds in 'may' and 'spade' should be different. The first was a diphthong, or two sounds, 'a' and 'y'. Why, asked an inspector, did teachers not understand that? But then, for some reason, the same man also complained about 'day' being pronounced like 'hay'.[26]

Every colony had problems with 'h'. In Victoria,

> [w]e [Victorians, that is] are in a fair way of becoming a nation without an h in our vocabulary. From the average choir you will be pretty sure to hear ''eaven' and ''ell', and ''oly, 'oly, 'oly'. The average porter shouts out ''Awthorn' and ''Awksburn', and the average cabman 'Emerald 'ill'.

And what about 'what'? It had changed to 'wat', with the old 'hw' (not 'wh') sound forgotten.[27]

And then there was 'the growing tendency of the rising generation' in Victoria, but everywhere else too, 'to drawl their words, and unduly broaden the vowels in pronunciation'. Young teachers said 'orizontul' and 'purpundickeller'. We have to work hard on 'the general speech of the people', said the South Australian inspector-general. We must become, said one of his men in the field, 'a pure English-speaking colony'.[28]

III

Purity and uniformity were two sides of the same coin, in language as in skin colour. Uniformity of race was purity of race. We had to all look the same and we had to all sound the same. For many years, even into the 1880s, each colony thought of purity of speech as its own problem. '[T]he distinguishing characteristics of Victorian pronunciation', said one school inspector, were a 'slight tendency to a nasal accent' and a 'want of crispness and distinctness in enunciation'. Maybe such defects could be blamed on the Victorian landscape and air, since even Victorian Aborigines committed the same errors.[29]

Uncorrected, the 'Victorian rustic' would be an object of fun in neighbouring colonies.[30] Did each colony have its own brand of 'rustic', its own 'national' peasantry? Not many teachers and inspectors moved from one colony to another, and only a few thought that the way the people talked, and what they talked about, might be exactly the same beyond each border.

Alexander Clark, the South Australian school inspector, was one of the few, having worked also in Sydney. He was a Scot, like the inspectors of stock mentioned in chapter 2, Patrick Gordon and Alexander Bruce. Cheerful and large hearted, he shared their interest in dealing across borders. 'Australians on the average', said Clark, 'speak better English than the people of England themselves'. That is to say, their speech was 'devoid of the marked pronunciations of Yorkshire, Lancashire, or Somerset, and even of the less objectionable peculiarities of London or American speech'. The geographical variations, though regrettable, were relatively small. '[T]he school children of Brisbane, Sydney, Melbourne, and Adelaide are much more nearly allied in speech than those of London, Plymouth, Leeds, and Newcastle.'[31] They could speak up anywhere.

By the end of the 1880s the continental dimension started to be of wider interest. Now there was talk of 'the Australian twang', the 'evil' which made 'cow' into 'keow' and 'lady' into 'liedy'. Its faults were 'worse than Yankeeisms'. 'Is the coming Australian to be identified under all skies as the owner of a slovenly and nasal dialect, with truncated vowels and frost-bitten syllables?'[32] The Australian language, good or bad, became one of the markers of continental nationhood, like racial purity, as I say, like the shades of sky and eucalyptus landscape. Rosa Praed described the whole parcel as 'one of the signs of a growing type'. 'It used not to be so noticeable.' The only things Mrs Praed liked about it were the 'slight fall of cadence and tendency to drawl' she heard among the women. A visiting Italian, Edoardo Sacerdote, who worked with Madame Melba – Nellie Melba, Australia's own diva – disagreed. Again, it was the women. He doubted whether Australia would produce many good tenors, but '[y]our sopranos', he said, 'are the same in quality as the Italian sopranos … It is the natural voice of Australia'.[33]

In 1894 the Sydney *Bulletin* offered its own view of Australian women's voices, in a piece of rollicking verse called 'The Austrylian Songstress'. The heroine was an aspiring singer who dilated upon 'nightingyles'.

> But not alone the letter A
> In vocal twists she turns and frets,
> Her other vowels get astray

When in her hurry she forgets.
'How can I love and bid thee *gow*?'
She asks, and echo answers 'How?'

The Australian accent came from Cockney habits of speech, or so the *Bulletin* said. In that sense, '[w]e imported it, long before rabbits, sparrows, snails, and other British nuisances'. But maybe it was something to be proud of. (The *Bulletin* was ever happy to contradict itself.) Americans had their own 'correct' accent. Maybe, very soon, the Australian twang would be just as proper, 'and pass as "good form"'.[34]

Habits of speech spread by osmosis, and voices even rhymed across ranks – which meant, to the jaundiced English ear, that everyone sounded vulgar. 'The barrister will not say, "May your Honor please", but "May-ee yer Honor please". The scientist will refer to "Me researches".' And yet, even here, we were not unique. In spite of all the elevating efforts, in England itself the 'vulgar' shaped the intonations of the 'thoughtful' at least as much as the other way around.[35]

Children learnt from each other. Teachers turned that fact to advantage, and a good deal of class time was taken up with 'simultaneous recitation', which meant the chanting of lessons. Reciting all together made children less shy. It gave them 'distinct enunciation, proper pitch … firmness and confidence'.[36] By speaking and listening all at once, drawing on 'the sympathy of numbers', boys and girls learnt to shape their voices to an ideal.[37]

Schoolteachers also knew that an individual can have more than one voice. Every day they heard children changing the way they spoke, as they went up or down the steps between classroom and playground. As they passed in and out of different settings they shuffled accents like cards in a pack. Their singing, their reading, their talking together, all were different. Girls spoke in ladylike tones to their teachers and differently to their friends. This was not quite so clear with boys. '[I]f they attempt to talk better than their companions', said Alexander Clark, 'they will be accused of "putting on side", and so to avoid remark they speak as their fellows do'. But all shaped their voices to a variety of pressures. In the copper-mining districts of South Australia the sons of Cornish immigrants spoke like their parents until they started school. Then they were led, Clark said, 'by persistent training ... to drop the peculiarities of the Cornish pronunciation'. And yet, as soon as they went down the mines themselves with their fathers they switched back to 'the *patois* of the miner'.[38]

Male and female voices settled down, fitting bit by bit into some larger whole. Whatever the lapses of youth, so Clark thought, most children were being trained to know better. '[W]hen they are wiser [they] will copy purer models, not only of grammar and style, but also pronunciation.'[39] Whatever they did, children were learning to listen to themselves. Whatever their audience, they could feel the jab of disapproval if their voices failed to fit.

So 'peculiarities' wore away. Poetry with bounding rhythm was wonderful for this purpose. The schoolbooks had a good deal of English verse, but reformers wanted more of 'our own Australian poetry'. The inspector at St Arnaud, in Victoria, suggested pieces by Charles Harpur, Adam Lindsay Gordon and Henry Kendall. The schoolbooks should also have passages on 'Australian fauna and flora' mixed up with verse which, when read aloud, would fill the air with 'a true Australian spirit'.[40]

Best of all was singing. In the Mother Country there were singing lessons in primary schools from 1873. Other parts of the empire quickly followed. To start with teachers hated it. It was too much like a game. It got out of control and they resented showing off their own stumbling efforts, singing aloud in front of giggling children. They pleaded incompetence – so often that someone suggested that the local climate must breed bad voices.[41]

In singing, even more than in poetry, there were demands for lines instilling a love of country, refined but powerful, disciplined but free. Victorian children were already singing Samuel McBurney's intricate cantata *Victoria*:

> Yes, fair, O fair is our native land,
> The home of our childhood's days,
> Victoria on the golden strand,
> Our songs of joy we raise.[42]

In Adelaide, the creation of the Thousand Voice Choir, a gathering of schoolchildren from in and around the capital which performed year after year, sung in complex harmony under the 'genial … and inspiriting' direction of Alexander Clark.[43] It was an extraordinary unity of young voices unrivalled across the continent. It was South Australia with one voice, and Clark was a herdsman par excellence. The sounds of his mustering, the very movement of his hands in front of all those fresh, open-mouthed faces, enunciated a happy discipline for South Australians.

With the new movement, McBurney and other men and women turned their thoughts to the larger nation. The 'Song of Australia'– 'There is a land where summer skies / Are gleaming with a thousand dyes' – by Caroline Carleton (music by Carl Linger) had long been sung in South Australia (but parodied as 'There is a land that's very hot / And calls are made on pint and pot'). It had been a kind of colonial national anthem, but by the 1890s it was being taken up as a 'Federal Anthem'.[44] This was the sound of the future. When children's lips learnt that drill children's hearts would follow.

IV

Talk was always male and female. Different sounds came from boys' and girls' mouths, as from men's and women's. Thomas Hardy, the English novelist, popular in Australia as he was at Home, had a sharp ear for manliness and womanliness in talk, which made his love stories rich and sensual. Like Mary Gilmore in Australia, Hardy hated the deadening uniformity enveloping the voices he heard about him. The new education, he said, with 'its silent and inevitable effacement, [was] reducing the speech of this country [England] to uniformity, and obliterating every year many a fine old local word'.[45] But it was difference of sex that drove his stories, and it applied as much to readers in Australia as to readers in England.

In Hardy's stories desire usually happened at first sight – or first touch or first sound. In *Desperate Remedies* a man and woman, still strangers, felt their clothes touch, her skirt with his nether garments. To a man, said Hardy, 'clothes are something exterior ... to a woman her dress is part of her body'. And so the touch 'sent a thrill' through the female party. '[T]o escape the sensation she moved away, though by doing so it was necessary to advance a little into the rain.'[46]

Hardy's voices carried something physical through vacant air itself. In *The Return of the Native* Eustacia Vye heard Clym Yeobright before she saw him. She was hidden beside the path he walked in the dark with two other women. 'They went by her, and at the moment of passing [they] appeared to discern her dusky form. There came to her ears in a masculine voice, "Good night!"' For his part Yeobright first noticed his beloved dressed as a Christmas mummer, looking like a boy but sounding distinctly female.[47]

In Australia, Joseph Furphy revelled in such things, except that he treated sex much less seriously than Hardy did. For him it was a joke. The best part of *Such Is Life* concerns Nosey Alf, the boundary rider. Alf's singing, heard in a lonely bark hut, was 'rich, soft, transcendent', and the violin accompaniment was 'both mystery and revelation' – again like the mouth organ Bean heard on the Darling River.[48] Furphy's description is epiphany. But listeners and readers are all fooled because Nosey Alf was really a woman.

Archibald Gilchrist, school inspector at Ballarat, remarked on 'the natural timidity which some girls show when they hear their own voices, while all around are silent'. A persistent teacher, he said, could draw them out. Certainly, except for singing, getting noticed, heard and understood was a supremely male virtue. It proved manly character, a clear head and an independent mind. School inspectors sometimes found it a virtue distressingly hard to come by in the bush. William Gates, at Shepparton, in the Victorian north, found out the difference when he lost his way on a country road. Too many boys answered his simple question 'Where am I?' with 'a half intelligible grunt'. Clear speech was a keystone of good citizenship. Charles Henry Pearson, in a government report in 1878, told Victorians to follow the example of the United States. In American schools, he said, '[m]ere children are taught to speak out so that they may be heard by a large number in a large room'. It was 'an immense advantage for a young man to have early become accustomed to the sound of his own voice', said an inspector, especially in a country like this (Victoria), 'where one may be called upon at any time to speak before his fellow-men'.[49]

Male and female might often look as if they were under the same regime. But it was hard for girls to believe that their voices mattered much, except at home, and not many women made a practice of speaking before strangers and crowds. If a woman had ideas she wanted broadcast she found a man to do it for her. Or she used pen and ink, in which, 'though [still] at a disadvantage, she can for herself utter her thoughts'. This was the assessment of Catherine Helen Spence, who was active in various areas of public life in South Australia from the 1870s. Miss Spence was always interested in voices. She took in more by ear, she said, than by eye – more by talking, that is, than by reading. She thought that free voices were the key to women's emancipation. How many girls and women learnt that lesson as they fought against the louder voices of brothers, male cousins and the like?

Mary MacKillop, Mother Mary of the Cross, felt a disabling deference even at the height of her career as founder and head of the Order of the Sisters of St Joseph of the Sacred Heart, the first religious order unique to the Antipodes.

> [L]ong and painful experience [she said] has taught me that I cannot trust my own effort to *speak* as candidly as I would desire ... [W]hen writing I feel alone with God and, as He knows all things, am not kept back by any fear of what He may think, or how regard what I am doing, but it seems to be a fault in myself which I cannot overcome *not to speak as I can write*.

Deeply revered within her own order, Mother Mary's authority in her letters to sisters in various parts of Australia and New Zealand, and to her church superiors, was gentle and certain. But, she said, '[e]ven when I have written what I wish to say I am often tempted to destroy it, anything rather than deliver it to the person for whom it is intended'.[50]

More even than the vote, the capacity to be heard made women into citizens. Catherine Spence was concerned at first with citizenship in South Australia, but then with citizenship of the Commonwealth. She taught herself to speak in public. Struggling to stop her knees giving way, she said, she worked out rules. 'Not having had any lessons in elocution, I trusted to my natural voice, and felt that in this new role the less gesticulation I used the better.' Genuine feeling was everything, she said, plus a wish to be 'humanly helpful'. Women speakers needed earnestness, 'a conviction that what you say is worth saying, and worth saying to the audience before you'. Too much drama made a person look ridiculous. Everything depended on hands and voice. 'However little action I may use I never speak in public with gloves on. They interfere with the natural eloquence of the hand.' And all talk should 'suit ... the tastes and capacity of the person you address'.[51]

This was all very polite. Even at their most eloquent, women's voices did not carry a sound of danger and excitement as men's could do. White men's talk might be shaped by hopes as beautifully terrible as the dreams of the Black men who danced the Mudlunga. Hopes of apocalyptic change were particularly strong among men in Queensland, where vastness, variety and the rawness of frontier life threw up a dense mix of brutality and hope. Charters Towers, inland from Townsville, was one of the richest goldfields on the continent. Its gold was deeply buried quartz, which meant steady but highly lucrative digging. The population built up more gradually here than in places with surface pickings, but in twenty years there were 20,000 people, more than Townsville and second only to Brisbane, and its network of clubs and societies, its newspapers and its sense of its own importance made Charters Towers a potent centre of politics. It called itself 'The World'.[52]

It was a republic of men. The journalist Frederick Vosper set the tone. In 1890 Vosper started the *Australian Republican*, eager, as he told his father in England, 'to excite some degree of public attention'. He was a careful thinker and widely read. Later on in Perth he was a fine parliamentarian. But at this point, in this vivid and remote oasis, he thrilled to popular speech making, glorying in the sound of his own voice. He was a man possessed, as the *Bulletin* put it, with 'a fine gift-o'-gab for the multitude'. '[H]e could rouse the crowd to the heights of enthusiasm, or play upon its hatred of anything tinged with injustice so as to draw a scowl on every face.'[53] This was what manly rhetoric was all about.

It was the same with the great shearers' strike in early 1891. At first the government in Brisbane stood apart. But after two months' agitation it decided that the shearers posed a fundamental threat to public order. Their behaviour was remarkably civil, in the circumstances, but their talk spelt disaster. When William Guthrie Spence was called on to explain to a royal commission in Sydney he assured the commissioners that it was play-acting. The leaders had to speak in sweeping terms, he said, about 'the reconstruction of society' and so on, because it was the only way of holding the attention of the rest. They wanted 'to create discussion'. And yet the leaders, including Spence, used the same scorching talk among themselves. There would be a 'great final struggle', they said, between labour and capital. It would be an 'Australian revolution'.[54]

The shearers disguised themselves in language. 'There is only one way to obtain a satisfactory result with the squatters', said one, 'and that is to take up arms and fight them ... 10,000 resolute bushmen behind 10,000 shear blades'. No revolutionary 10,000 showed up. At Clermont, according to a newspaper reporter, they said 'they are resolved to fight, win or die. They say they can only die once'. But then the same reporter was informed that when they said 'fighting' they did not really mean *fighting*. They meant disobedience, or passive resistance. '[P]ull the buggers out and we'll fuck them', yelled a shearer, when a vehicle carrying members of the Pastoralists' Association braved the crowd at Clermont. None was touched. Some men let themselves be arrested in perfect peace, except that there were calls from their mates: 'Take it easy, boys; ye are martyrs to the cause'.[55]

When some non-unionists arrived to shear, a unionist shouted, 'I wish there was a plug of dynamite under that dray'. They wished for many things. 'Better to see the last squatter and the last member of this hateful Government butchered', wrote Frederick Vosper in the *Australian Republican*, 'than to see one jot or one tittle of the sacred rights of the people lost'. In the cold light of day, or rather in the immobile heat of a Queensland summer, there was not a hint of butchering. A man named Davies spelt out to a mass meeting at Barcaldine a dream he had had, of Parliament House stormed by a mob and all the members butchered indeed. The ministers turned up at heaven's gates, 'but the guardian doorkeeper directed them all below'. Davies's listeners raised a happy shout. Their revolution was a many-times-recounted dream.[56]

Shearers' grievances were real. They faced hunger for themselves, wives and children. The callousness of many bosses was real too. But everything was embroidered with talk from a separate universe. Government and union representatives agreed that most of the excitement sprang from 'big hot words', but they could not agree as to whose words were hotter. The government, determined to win this argument at least, ordered the trial of thirty-five shearers at a special Supreme Court sitting at Rockhampton, and of the four trials three turned on the question of criminal talk.[57] One of the accused was James Martin. A witness had heard Martin say, '[I]f the Amalgamated Miners are prepared to back us, we are prepared to take the colony'. Martin was also supposed to have spoken contemptuously about 'Old Mother Brown', meaning the queen. (Gossip said that Queen Victoria had married her servant John Brown.) This was crucial evidence because Martin was charged with seditious language. Other witnesses remembered shearers 'yelling out in a very excited manner' at non-unionists as they turned up to shear. They called them 'scabs – blacklegs – gaol birds'.[58] This was manhood in extremis.

V

You could delight in your own voice before a great crowd of excited men, as Vosper did. Or you could attend to the way you talked, say, in order to improve your accent. Both were methods of making yourself an acceptable member of the commonwealth of speech. You could also listen to yourself in the sense of imagining a voice from your own soul. You could listen inwards for the still, small articulation of self trickling upwards as through a telephone. This was at the other end of the spectrum from '[p]ull the buggers out and we'll fuck them'. But for many (how many?) it was a better way of being Australian.

Abroad (not yet in Australia), psychology was a flourishing

science. Like meteorology, it still depended on the findings of the amateur, and the amateur's most convenient field of study was the inner self. Men and women 'analysed', a favourite word, by looking or listening inwards. Or else, standing at the precipice of self, they fell all of a sudden, unawares – for who, as Victor Hugo asked in *Les Misérables*, 'has not, at least once in his life plummeted into that dark cave of the unknown?' 'Experimental psychology' – the careful observation of other people in clinical conditions, especially 'abnormal' behaviour – was still very new. It was largely an invention of the 1890s, Sigmund Freud being one of its pioneers. Even then, investigating inwards still made more sense. Messages from within, from yourself, must be more reliable than messages from other people. Good pre-Freud psychologists worked with a kind of nervous subjectivity, living in a mirror.[59]

It is a good metaphor. In Lewis Carroll's *Through the Looking Glass*, published in 1871, Alice not only passed through the mirror to another place altogether. On the other side she was told that she was a figment of someone else's imagination.

Looking inwards in these new ways was like searching new continents or universes. What you did and what you found were so extraordinary that some identified consciousness (or was it conscience?) with God. God was not just the still, small voice heard by the prophet Elijah. These days he was also 'the Light', your own inner power.

And yet, looking inwards, you also discovered yourself to be an automaton – a whispering engine, moving in ever-predictable ways. Psychologists, both expert and amateur, were intrigued by how much the body could manage to do without the intervention of thinking. They tried to distinguish between the habitual, instinctive and/or mechanical and the deliberate aspects of human behaviour. The eminent psychologist William Carpenter quoted 'a trustworthy source' (a clergyman) who remembered seeing a lady playing the piano perfectly well at a party when she was so drunk that she was more or less asleep. Staff in telegraph offices, said Carpenter, did much the same. 'I have often found myself', said one telegraphist, 'indulging in trains of thought, or even listening to a conversation that might be going on near me, and yet continue to "receive" and "send" just as if I was giving my whole attention to the work'.[60] Telephonists were like that too. With a good deal of the new machinery, once you learnt the basic motions it was possible to get by without thinking much at all. Talking and thinking, body and brain, seemed decoupled. So what was the brain? Was it the seat of the soul or was it just a machine?

This was the new game of introspection. The Germans, who set many intellectual fashions, called it *Bildung*, inwardness – self-searching and/or self-realisation. Or rather it was part of *Bildung*, which was many faceted. For the Germans, following the philosopher Friedrich Schelling, this apprehension of self was the supreme and final task of humankind. Full achievement came, said Schelling, with the recognition by each person that the world itself, as it showed itself to us, was a creation of the self, of our own inner being.[61] Everyone tried it. In *A Laodicean: A Story of Today* (1881), Thomas Hardy told the tale of a young couple addicted to 'juvenile introspection'. They were constantly turning inwards, in an onanistic parade of self.[62]

Novelists loved it. *Niels Lyhne*, by the Dane Jens Peter Jacobsen, was reviewed in the *Bendigo Advertiser* in May 1894, though not yet translated. Niels Lyhne was oppressed by 'cold ideas and brain dreams'. In fact, these internal explorations made it hard to decide who you really were. 'How innocuous it all was,' Niels told himself, 'and empty, empty, empty! This chasing after yourself, craftily observing your own tracks – in a circle of course … angling after yourself, fishing yourself up in one curious disguise or another'. In George Gissing's *Born in Exile* (selling in Australia for two shillings) the hero, lowly born, learnt all the habits of a gentleman – dress, bearing, accent, vocabulary – and performed with mechanical correctness. But still he was suspended in self-doubt, barred from 'easy, well-bred intimacy', and wrecked in the end by his own inner tinkering.[63]

Up-to-date youths, male and female, explored their own characters and habits, thought about their own thinking, gloried in self-consciousness and skated on the ice surface, or wallowed in the warm bath, of self. The word 'introspection' had been invented 200 years before, but it had never meant as much as it did in these days. In earlier times men and women had needed self-knowledge as a way of accounting to God. Now they bounced off themselves. 'What am I like?' or rather, 'What do I seem like?' (same thing?), 'How do I look?', 'How do I sound?'

A man alone at night in the Australian bush, driving his herd, could make a kind of happy theatre of his inner self, exploring inwards to the centre.

> It is these long night watches [wrote the Scottish-born poet Will Ogilvie] that turn a man in on himself as it were, on himself and the Bush, himself and the Bush, these two only, until the Bush seems to become wedded to his heart, and his heart to the Bush, till the Bush at night, with its weird cries and its still more weird hush, becomes an actual part of himself.[64]

The South Australian Catherine Martin, writing fiction, made the bush into a mirror of inner being. Dead scrub, strangely lit, became a state of mind. Looking at the scrub, we are looking at desert wilderness within. '[M]ile after mile, with each tree bleached and bare', we find branches 'silky-gray and pure white against a deep blue background', and underfoot 'a sad gray-green, with wide patches of yellow sand'.[65]

Some inner explorers pushed themselves hard. The young Alfred Deakin, afterwards Australia's second prime minister, struggled daily. '[G]ive me thy guidance', Deakin said to his God, 'that I may fearlessly pierce into the depths of my own Being and open sanctuaries within its unexplored recesses'. 'I seek to burrow, to creep', he cried, '& to fly & feel in myself the diverse natures of animal man and spirit'. Born in Melbourne in 1856, Deakin taught himself to examine the fleeting movements of his own mind by complicated intellectual inquiry – the kind of journey, he thought (following Schelling), every civilised human being ought to make. He prepared himself thoroughly beforehand, like a sedentary version of Ernest Giles in his search for desert diamonds, and sometimes, like Giles, he found only sand and saltbush. 'In continual touch with sceptics & the theories of scepticism', he said, 'I have pursued at every turn the method of one who doubted the testimony of his own senses'. He demanded for himself strict perseverance and self-discipline, the 'patience of intellect'.[66]

Sceptics pointed out the dangers. The voice of consciousness, said the great English philosopher John Stuart Mill, was not, in fact, 'the voice of Nature and of God'. Nothing, Mill said, in human thinking was innate. Truth was not to be found at the centre of being. It was born of circumstance and education.[67] But the tide was against such teaching. *Bildung* promised wonders. Deakin, fifty years younger than Mill, tried to be sceptical in all things. But he was typical of his day. He worshipped 'the Light' within. It was an authority, he thought, that revealed itself to every honest man. He had no doubt that it was God, 'the Soul of the Unknown', 'the soul of my soul'. At the same time he yearned outwards, towards the 'infinite Infinity' – 'Thine everlasting lovely & aweful sky'. In his introspection, he mingled the vast within and the vast without, and made himself drunk with thinking about size and depth, '[with] the endless spheres of physical nature from the infinitely small to infinitely great greater and greatest … [to the] myriads of myriads of interstellar spaces & modes of being before one of which our vision & imagination sink appalled'. It was these ideas which gave Deakin purpose in life, as a politician. As a leader in the movement for the Federation of the Australian colonies, he recoiled at the idea of anything less than one perfectly formed continental people. Everything had to be united from shore to shore – 'a noble state as a temple to Thee & Thy glory in humanity'. To be happy with fragmentary things, with casual variety, showed meanness of soul. It was not the way to hear the voice of God.[68]

Listening always to yourself, various voices might rise from the depths. Every mind could be a whispering 'Palace of Winged Words'. Deakin discovered selves, various manifestations of his own consciousness, set like geological layers – his 'highest self', his 'lower self', his 'subliminal self' and so on. In 1890, when he was in his thirties, he tried to draw on the innocence of his own childhood. Through concentrated introspection he could still track down such innocence, he said, 'hidden like dew in flowery recesses'. And again, in 1913, the 'AD' (as he called himself) of 1890 lingered somewhere in the vasty deep, beneath more recent ADs. It was 'dead and buried', he said; 'only its ghost at times haunts my dreams'.[69]

VI

Children, by Deakin's definition, lived in the first stratum of self-awareness. Through singing at school, children imbibed the rudiments of introspection by learning to identify notes they heard in their own mouths against the background of those they heard around them.

> Now, children [said the good teacher in England to a class of beginners], we are going to learn the art of singing in tune ... This is a note [he sings 'ah'] ... Could not some of you sing a note? Hold up hands – those who can sing a note ... I want you now to distinguish *the same* note from a *different* one. Sing

> the *same* note as this ... Sing the same note as this ... Hold up hands – those who will sing me a note, and I will sing the same.[70]

Voices had a quality, a colour, a texture. Every child could learn to see and feel them. Like soap, the purer the better.

Sound well styled was a commodity. It was a garment. You could put it on and take it off. It had to fit the moment. In Australia, these new ideas were hurried into the schools, and reading was geared to a self-conscious feel for sound. At one time, reading (a distinct subject in the syllabus) had meant learning letters. Children had memorised first the alphabet, then syllables, then words set out on slates and paper. They moved from stand-alone symbols to sequential groups. Now, the work was different. Too much talk about marks in black and white seemed old-fashioned. Those dead hieroglyphs 'A', 'B', 'C' had to be brought to life. They had to be born again from young lips, teeth, breaths and tongues. It was 'Hold up hands – those who can pronounce this word'. Or else everyone was told to read aloud together. It did not take long, as a school inspector in Victoria put it, for children to start to 'think in sound'.[71]

The late nineteenth century was 'a pedagogical age'.[72] There was enormous interest not just in the way human characteristics were distributed over space, as in geography, but also in the way they evolved over time. Physical characteristics (race and genetic make-up) and moral and intellectual qualities were all parts of unfolding history. It seemed vital, even a matter of national survival, to understand how such things were passed down the generations, within families and from teachers to children. There were abundant theories about good teaching, and by the 1870s, in some of the colonies, authorities were congratulating themselves on 'marvellous improvements'. In Adelaide, the minister spoke of his own country (South Australia) stepping out to a brighter future, with 'an old-established system' being pushed aside by one of 'quite another character'.[73] There was still much to be done, but everywhere the schools were being transformed.

Children had to be exposed to nature. They had to feel the sounds they produced. Noise had to live in the mind's eye, just as in Hardy's *The Return of the Native* Eustacia Vye actually saw Clym Yeobright because of his 'masculine voice'. And yet, by some strange contradiction, at the same time children had to grow in understanding, refinement and skill by cutting themselves off from the crude, colloquial world they had grown up in. Somehow, they had to live within nature – to hold it to themselves, to hear it ringing in their lungs and mouths – in order to free themselves from it. They had to be 'lyres', as Furphy said, because 'whatever else a man may sing, he always sings himself'.

The new ways of teaching reading were tried first in the United States, but they were quickly taken up in Australia and in Britain, at least in principle. Some parents were sceptical. Slightly educated themselves, a few of them wanted their offspring to start as they had, on 'what was known as the A, B, C'. Some teachers were doubtful too. In 1871 the school inspector at Bathurst, New South Wales, found most of the teachers in his district still using 'the alphabetic or spelling method'. And yet, it was 'not only contrary to common sense, but … also uninteresting, tiring, and uncertain'.[74]

As with accent, it was always hard to know what a good tone of voice was. Again, the authorities themselves disagreed, and the rule bandied about the schools, 'Read as you would speak', only made things worse. In the bush, said an inspector at Wollongong, south of Sydney, 'many of the children speak in a dull monotone characteristic of the class to which they belong'. With the best will in the world teachers could not smarten it up.[75] And yet further south, at Bega, a colleague said how much he liked the 'natural intonation and inflection of voice' he heard among the little ones when they started. What a shame to replace it with more stilted tones! There would always be a big gap, a Tasmanian inspector pointed out, between the children's ordinary speech and the 'long and too often very involved sentences' they struggled with at school. Scant reading was done in most homes, in his colony at least. '[T]he diction of books is … practically a foreign tongue'.[76] And yet everyone said, 'Read as you would speak'.

Over and over, the main task, in school and in the larger world, was to make a bridge between familiar things and big aspirations. You had to absorb the big world into your own small brain. The small day-to-day world, the world of chat and face to face, had to find room for the print-powered world, the natural had to embrace the perfect, and the solid and comfortable had to come to terms somehow with the shadowy and clever.

Children themselves, if they had any imagination at all, could be carried away by 'the diction of books', excited by the majesty of big words and big sentences, especially read out in a masterful way. Masterful themselves in fits and starts, children could feel their own voices swelling into greatness. When he was little, Joseph Furphy decided to be a preacher after hearing how a Presbyterian minister could throw out biblical phrases, as in: 'What prrrivily sall brrring in d[am]nable herrresies', 'O h[el]l! whaurr is thy veectorrry?' and 'O generrration o' vipperrrs! Hoo sall ye escape the d[amnatio]n o' h[el]l?' Furphy had a rare ear for vocal eccentricities. But most children knew drama when they heard it, especially in galloping rhythm. Infected by it, some threw their whole bodies into reciting in class. '[They] can never refer to the "heart"', said one inspector, 'without giving an expressive pat on the left breast, or mention weeping without tracing the course of an imaginary tear-drop down the cheek'.[77] But this too was frowned on. They had to be more 'natural' when they read aloud.

In Victoria, enormous trouble was taken in training voices. And yet ordinary talk in the classroom was reined very tightly. The Victorian school system was highly centralised and theorised, and the teachers were trained to a pitch of perfection. They also worked under a particularly thorough system of 'payment by results', in which salaries partly depended on how well the children did in written examinations. All this gave rigidity to Victorian teaching. By the late 1880s the authorities in Melbourne had started to see that better things were happening – more was done with voices – over the border in anarchic New South Wales. In that colony, there was more to-ing and fro-ing in class, and the overall result, as a Victorian inspector admitted, was 'better and freer'. It encouraged 'brightness of manner and quickness of thought'. Out in the bush, some stockmen forced their cattle, but the wiser ones let them move at their own pace. New South Wales children seemed more familiar with the sound of their own voices in class, and they spoke with more confidence. In Victoria daily 'speed and smartness' were lost in the fight to be passable when exams came round.[78]

How to harness inborn things without hobbling them, how to measure without maiming – it was a challenge suddenly bigger than it had ever been.

A JIGSAW FOR A CONTINENT

With his two theories of relativity, Einstein united space, time, and gravity. But this success only encouraged him to think bigger. He dreamed of finding a single, all-encompassing framework capable of embracing all of nature's laws; he called that framework a *unified theory*. Although now and then rumors spread that Einstein had found a unified theory, all such claims turned out to be baseless; Einstein's dreams went unfulfilled.[1]

Brian Greene, *The Fabric of the Cosmos*

4

Tyrannous Freedom

I

On a winter day in 1885, in Hobart, Grace Clark, in her early thirties, sat down to read a letter just received from Joseph Witton, a lawyer about her own age, who wrote from Melbourne to congratulate her on having lately added to her family. It was her fifth baby. Witton was Tasmanian too, and he had been two years on the far side of Bass Strait. He was not married, and he missed the delights of the Clark family circle, at Rosebank, Battery Point. Mrs Clark smiled at his childish banter, which took her back to their drawing-room chats. 'I am getting rusty', said Witton, 'on the subject of infants. I never hear their soothing cries; I never press my lips on their very damp mouths; I never show proud, and rather anxious, mothers what an adept an old bachelor can be in the ancient art of "nussing"'. Keen to be nursing something, Witton had bought a Borneo monkey called Calvin. But Calvin died and Witton had buried him in a pets' cemetery next to a deceased pet turkey. 'Two keys that rust in the selfsame lock.' He was then adopted by a black cat. 'She came to me strangely one night as I was mooning by the fire in the sitting-room. She came and sat by me on the hearth rug. No one had seen her before. Can it be Calvin transmogrified?'[1]

The cat had white paws. So Witton rattled on. And she had 'eyes not like the gazelle's, for they were green and fierce'. Grace Clark must have known all about 'the gazelle'. It figured in William Wetmore Story's fashionably famous poem 'Cleopatra', a favourite, apparently, for recital in the drawing room at Rosebank. Story, an

American, has Cleopatra mourning the loss of Antony. No longer, 'fierce in a tyrannous freedom', would he and she fill each day with 'tiger passions'. The great queen had only the servile friendship of her maid and the doe-like antics of her pet:

> There – leave me, and take from my chamber
> That stupid little gazelle,
> With its bright black eyes so meaningless,
> And its silly tinkling bell!
> Take him, – my nerves he vexes,
> The thing without blood or brain,
> Or, by the body of Isis,
> I'll snap his thin neck in twain![2]

Maybe Grace Clark knew the lines by heart. Conversation at Rosebank sparkled with a love of high, strong feeling undercut by jokes like Witton's. It was also full of Story's America, its poetry, its religion and its ideals, harder, higher ideals, blood and brain combined, than those locally available. The new baby, Wendell Clark, seems to have been named in honour of two American Wendells, Oliver Wendell Holmes junior, the writer and judge, and his cousin, Wendell Phillips, a great antagonist of Black slavery.

Witton wrote to Mrs Clark's husband, Andrew Inglis Clark, a distinguished barrister and a former and future member of the Tasmanian parliament. He was also an Australian patriot, but he had an ambiguous relationship with the world beyond Tasmania. 'Small, spare, nervous, [and] active.' So he seemed to Alfred Deakin, the urbane and wide-horizoned Melburnian, and, among intercolonial colleagues in the campaign for Federation, 'somewhat awkward in manner and ungraceful in speech'.[3] At Rosebank, within the smaller circle of family and friends, these flaws vanished and Clark was another man altogether.

Melbourne, that epitome of southern cities, was passionless, so

Witton told Clark – meaningless like the eyes of the gazelle. 'There is a lot of sordid materialism in this place, old man. For its size and pretensions and blow there is little intellectual leaven or exalted emotion in it.'[4]

In Hobart, Witton had been one of the Minerva Club, a group of men, mostly young, who gathered with the Clarks at Rosebank to talk over books and ideas, thrilling to the 'exalted emotion' of verse like Story's. During the 1870s, following the discovery of large quantities of gold, silver and tin in the west and north-west of the island, Tasmania had started to emerge from decades of economic depression and unemployment. Population was shooting up and the people were casting about for a fresh sense of direction. 'The feverish spirit of change and unrest finds its way into every line of business', said the conservative Hobart *Mercury*, '[and] into all the professions, and is slowly but surely undermining the steady foundation on which society is built'.[5] The Minerva men felt no attachment to that 'steady foundation'. They belonged to a generation radically new. They called themselves 'the boys'. Andrew Clark was their 'padre'. They found in the Clarks – well read and strong minded – a type of inspiration lacking within the generation hitherto, and still, in power. The Minerva Club was 'Young Tasmania'.

George Edwards, another Minerva man, found work in Sydney. He was left cold by that gargantuan metropolis. The buildings, he said (also reporting back to Rosebank), were big, even four stories high, and obviously expensive. But the architecture was abominable. Civilisation seemed shallow. The Minerva Club was inspired by 'free thought', a readiness to question all received doctrine, especially orthodox ideas about religion, and there was plenty of 'free thought' in Sydney, said Edwards. But 'the stuff spoken in the name of free thought is philosophy in cap and bells and ignorance with scientific long clothes'.[6] It was nothing compared with young Hobart's richness of spirit.

In Tasmania the smallness of things ensured a balance between feeling and intellectual adventure. Size, including largeness of ideas, seemed to kill genuine feeling, that sentiment which, as Andrew Inglis Clark said, 'is the basis of more than one-half of human life'. Talk in the Minerva Club bound the tenderness of home and family to the great ideas of the day. Each took life from the other. Clark again: '[T]he root of a man's love for the country of his birth or his adoption is found in the love of his family and his home and in the affections which grow out of his personal association with the community in which he lives'. He quoted Wendell Phillips: 'I love inexpressibly these streets in Boston over which my mother led my baby feet, and if God grants me time enough, I will make them too pure for the footsteps of a slave'.[7] Hobart was Clark's Boston. The baby feet of his own newborn, his little Wendell, had a kind of political gravity to them. A true sense of justice was riveted to a host of feelings, global and local, from the brotherhood of man to the stickiness of babies.

Minerva men, with the rest of the European world at that moment, put their faith in children. One of them was James Rule, who in England had been involved in Chartist agitation for radical democracy. In Tasmania, Rule's ideas for a bright new world made their mark on bush schools. As the colony's chief inspector of schools and later director of education, he made it his mission to build schoolhouses in every populated part of the island. Between 1870 and 1890 the number nearly doubled and enrolments went up by 80 per cent. In similar intimate and painstaking fashion 'the boys' hunted for methods of expressing their love of country. Another was John Beattie, nature conservationist and photographer. For Beattie, Tasmania was the jewel of the universe.[8]

The club had its absentees, such as Witton and Edwards, but most members walked all their lives over well-known ground. Theirs was a patient affection. Victoria, on the other hand, was a place of impatience. Melbourne was faster even than Sydney. There was 'a general sense of movement, of progress, of conscious power' in Melbourne, said the journalist Francis Adams. The Melbourne man of business seemed hungrier for profit than the Sydneysider, and therefore much hungrier than the Tasmanian. 'The one [in Melbourne] is always in a hurry, the other [in Sydney] takes life more easily.'[9]

Joseph Furphy was well acquainted with northern Victoria and southern New South Wales. His book *Such Is Life* was born of border country, the Murray River, a land of conflicting forces largely controlled by Melbourne investors who bought up squatting runs far into the south-western third of New South Wales. Furphy's New South Welshmen, even of the poorer sort, looked south across the river to 'the Cabbage Garden' and at 'Victorian energy and greed'. Furphy himself was a failure in money terms. Like the Minerva men, he could see plenty of course-grained materialism and a sad lack of high feeling south of the Murray, and not just in Melbourne. Francis Adams called Victoria a country of logicians and engineers.[10]

Individuals such as Furphy and Adams thought of the continent as a single stage and a single landscape, and yet boundaries were part of the drama played out on that stage. Some focussed on a few crucial boundaries – not just the Murray, but also the Queensland border, the Tasman Sea and Bass Strait. For many, the old boundaries, not to mention all the small, well-settled places within, seemed eternally important.

We are all, in our groups and collectivities, parts of nature, said the great German polymath Johann Wolfgang van Goethe (1749–1832). Our boundaries and borders therefore are 'the real joints of nature'. The energy that runs along our edges tells us who we are.[11] That understanding was part of the common attitude of these days too.

In William Wetmore Story's poem, Cleopatra exulted in the cunning majesty of power. A breed apart, she dreamt herself into a tiger, bright, terrible, abroad with her mate (Antony transmogrified).

Then down to the fountain we loitered,
Where the antelopes came to drink;
Like a bolt we sprang upon them,
Ere they had time to shrink.

Strange to think of such fierce lines – 'We drank their blood and crushed them, / And tore them limb from limb' – read aloud with pleasure by the Clarks, within a circle wanting justice for the weak and with babies upstairs.[12] The love of brilliance set no limits. Boundaries and frontiers, but breaking them, crossing them, fitted the great priorities of the day. In Henry Rider Haggard's *King Solomon's Mines* (1885), the heroes, like the tiger, mark their passage into a new type of country with massive slaughter (nine elephants), and they too feast on antelope. It was all part of what was called 'the struggle for existence'.

In the years of Witton's exile each of the Australasian capital cities was the centre of its own world. It had its own past, its own memories, its own customs, its own habits, its own hinterland, its own wealth, its own civic culture, its own ambitions – ambitions sometimes tiger-like and tyrannously free. Melburnians aimed to make Victoria into 'a great nation'. Besides their rich capital, they possessed a landscape dense with country towns, including Geelong, Ballarat and Bendigo, which were almost cities. '[W]e must seek to be a nation at all points', said *The Age*, Melbourne's leading paper, '[in] agriculture, mining, manufacturing, trading and shipping'.[13] In proportion to available space, Victoria had four times the population of New South Wales and thirty times the population of South Australia and Queensland. The men who ruled from Melbourne thought there was not much they could not achieve within their own boundaries and beyond.

Since the 1870s the British territories set around the Tasman Sea had become the home of several infant nations – 'the countries of the southern empire'.[14] In Europe at the same time several old principalities, growing with unusual speed, swallowed up their neighbours. Sardinia-Piedmont was the powerhouse of Italian nationalism and from 1861 its king was king of all Italy, although it was the republican and democratic Giuseppe Mazzini who best represented the new nationalism – the nationalism of a willing people – to the world at large, including the Australian colonies. In northern Europe the Prussian monarchy was absorbing princely states roundabout, and the resulting German empire, from 1871, combined military muscle with intellectual brilliance. Germany loomed large in British thinking, and among many in Australia it was an intriguing model, but in many respects one to avoid. It had been created from above, by force. It was one of those 'new Empires arm'd and crown'd', said Henry Parkes, the politician-poet in New South Wales. There, 'how little all which men call great / Has bless'd men's homes, or form'd a happy state!'[15]

Victorians were reaching far beyond their own boundaries. Was Victoria to be a predator among its neighbours, an antipodean Prussia, a tiger among antelopes? Melbourne was the financial engine room of the Antipodes, investing enormous sums in the Riverina, Queensland, Tasmania and New Zealand. The Burke and Wills expedition to the Gulf of Carpentaria, in 1860–61, though a tragic failure, had been designed to make Victoria a force on Australia's northern coast, and in 1886–87 Melbourne men even gave serious thought to the Antarctic and to the revival of whaling, if only that icy shoreline could be properly explored.[16]

Melbourne had the ball at its feet. Witton might scoff at its 'size and pretensions and blow'. Throughout the British empire, 'the great Colony of Victoria' had a singular prestige. It had its 'national debt', its 'national gallery', its 'national railway policy'. Melbourne was credibly described as the ninth city in the world. (London, Paris and New York were the first three.) Its intellectual life was remarkable. Victorians were readers, with an unusual number of good libraries, bookshops and newsagents, and their reading was up to date. In many respects, Victorian country towns kept up with the capital, an unusual thing for Australia. Victorian country schools, for instance, were at least as good as those in Melbourne.[17]

Hobart might have boasted the Minerva Club, but Melbourne's intellectual leadership had more institutional weight and a much wider reach. The vital figures were George Higinbotham, attorney-general and judge, Charles Henry Pearson, historian, member of parliament and minister for education, and David Syme, owner and editor of *The Age*. Higinbotham had once been a journalist and he became a pamphleteer. His tough arguments about the ethical basis of public life gave him extraordinary prestige. Pearson's intellectual authority was hard to beat in the Antipodes and his international reach put Australia at the centre of debates about the future of humanity. As for Syme's *Age*, no other paper throughout the continent could match its power over local opinion.[18] These men might not always agree, but together they drove a remarkable engine of ideas. Alfred Deakin, who knew them all well, inherited their energy, carrying it into the project for Federation.

Worldwide, the great debates of the day were partly a clash of generations. In 1888 *The Age* spoke of a 'new generation' deliberately organising itself. 'The assumption of power by the Younger Generation', said Francis Adams, 'means a political revolution'. Deakin belonged self-consciously to that generation. Turning thirty-four, he acknowledged what he called 'manhood unfolded'. But, he said, 'I would wish to retain the hope, the enthusiasm of youth with such ripeness as my nature permits of at its maturity'.[19] Everywhere, the publishing business pushed the changeover, getting out not only new ideas but also new forms of thought, including, once again, the democracy of knowledge. At the cheap end, publishers were conjuring up a market among late teens and early twenties, with 'penny dreadfuls' (in England) and 'dime novels' (in the United States). Comic strip magazines started in a small way in the 1880s and '90s, and primitive comic cartoons appeared in the Sydney *Bulletin*. At the higher end, the 'new learning' was fully understood mainly by the young. At the two universities, Sydney and Melbourne, there were professors who managed it well: Charles Badham in Sydney, and CH Pearson in Melbourne. Their students idolised them. But anyone who read newspapers could sense the change.

Novelists loved the drama to be found in arguments between youth and middle age. In Europe, there was Ivan Turgenev's *Fathers and Sons*, Samuel Butler's *The Way of All Flesh* and George Eliot's *Middlemarch*. Small, agonising conflicts, points of irritation within millions of families, needled the world forwards. Victoria's younger goldrush immigrants, middle-aged by the 1870s, found themselves a target for the coming generation, and the hottest cauldron of debate was the square mile of 'the metropolis of the Southern Hemisphere'. 'New men' were very obvious in the ministry of Pearson's close associate Graham Berry, a radical nationalist of effervescent zeal, which came to power in May 1877.[20]

Harnessing the energies of the young, Victoria, as Pearson said, was 'the most ambitious' of the colonies. It was a community possessed, he said, of 'a sort of preternatural sagacity which all our neighbours must be more or less on their guard against'. And yet there was an adolescent, presumptuous, doctrinaire quality in its conversation. There was the certainty of youth and, as with the schools, too much reading and not enough talk free of reading. There was too much success too soon, or what a later age called a 'cognitive surplus', an energy bound to carry all before it, bound to do too much and bound to run too far. Victoria stood for unity, not variety, and it drove the scheme for making the colonies into one nation. Its young, or youngish, men sprinted in front, sworn to unity and chasing their own 'unified theory' (see the opening passage for this part of the book), for instance as members of the Australian Natives' Association, a ginger group for Federation.[21]

In Hobart, the Minerva Club met at the Clarks' house, probably in Grace Clark's drawing room. There was not much of such conversational domesticity, with the possibility of men and women talking together, among the leading lights in Melbourne. There, the meeting places were factories of thought, especially the university and the offices of *The Age* in Collins Street. At the university Pearson, lecturer in history and political economy, debated with a few of his best students, and at *The Age* young writers such as Alfred Deakin made a start in the propagation of ideas. All were men. Higinbotham and Pearson both worked for the dignity and rights of women. Pearson was founding head of the Presbyterian Ladies' College in East Melbourne, and he wanted perfect equality in male and female schooling. And yet the wives of such men contributed little. These agenda-setting Melburnians wanted women to be drawn in to the world of men, not the other way around. Among women there were too many tangential, half-formed, unscholarly, unfathomable questions. The 'boys' of the Minerva Club knew it, or sensed it, and for them, issues of social justice were interwoven with home life. Not so with this Melburnian leadership.

Charles Pearson was the epitome of Melbourne brilliance and a bundle of contradictions. Weighed down with pessimism, he thought of human existence as an endless struggle. Toughness was all, and in the end defeat was more than likely. '[T]he disintegrating forces of time', he said, 'will always be stronger in the long run than any given organisation'. These were the disintegrating forces which Henry Rider Haggard and other popular novelists loved to dwell on. To survive at all, men who loved their country had to be men of intellect, ever sharpening their methods. Their duty was to face forces which they could hardly hope to control. They had to organise, even in despair, to build a powerful state, guard its boundaries, keep up their own dignity and if possible push outwards. Getting as big as possible was the only hope. This was the gist of Pearson's great work, *National Life and Character*, which was read and admired around the world. They had to 'try to preserve the body politic as it exists, and recover for it what it has lost, or acquire what seems naturally to belong to it'. With telling originality, Pearson spelt out the 'national' purpose of Englishmen living in and near the Australian continent. 'We are guarding the last part of the world', he said, 'in which the higher races can live and increase freely, for the higher civilisation'.[22]

In this agenda, Melbourne was the key. Victoria was geographically small, but, as Graham Berry put it, they could expect soon, 'within her territory ... a matured public opinion that would govern the whole of the Australian colonies'. Victoria, said Berry, 'might be to Australia what the New England states were to the United States of America ... she might be great in ideas'. Those ideas, enriched by Pearson, Syme, Deakin and the others, should be spread over the continent by Victoria's sons, young men everywhere eager, Berry said, 'to found houses of business or pursue other means of self-aggrandisement'.[23]

It was Victoria's right, even her duty, to make her mark on her neighbours. A former premier of Queensland (and current treasurer), Sir Thomas McIlwraith, was only echoing the Victorians themselves when he suggested that a pan-continental Federation would be the same as the government of Victoria writ large. '"Just let it expand," they say, "until it covers the whole of Australia".' A former premier of Tasmania, Adye Douglas, put it differently. Victoria wanted to 'cripple' the others, or at least the smaller ones. '[She] has put her foot down upon us,' he said, 'and a big foot it is'.[24]

Tasmania had its own 'national' institutions and 'national' habits, but many Tasmanians understood that they had no future on their own. They lacked the energy of Victorians. Their political apathy they themselves called a 'national curse'. Mining had helped, but Tasmania's 'national' wealth still depended on agriculture, and even there its prospects were limited. Free trade treaties were attempted one by one with Victoria, New South Wales, Queensland, South Australia and New Zealand, but Tasmania always had too little to offer.[25]

There was talk in the island's north of stepping freely into the tiger's mouth – amalgamating with Victoria. The editor of the Launceston *Daily Telegraph* used the idea to attack Hobart. '[A]s a self-governing community,' he said, 'we are a failure'. '[O]ur grand national sources of wealth' would be better managed from Melbourne. However, in due course a larger option, a greater idea, the Melburnian dream with some important qualifications – 'a newer and broader nationhood' – intervened.[26]

II

It was a long way from the 'very damp mouths' of Grace Clark's babies to the desert air that cracked the lips of explorers such as Ernest Giles. It was a long way from the happy recitation of 'Cleopatra', amid the nursery, suburban and seaside noises of Battery Point – the squeal of seagulls – to the primeval chanting, the 'hideous customs and ceremonies', the mere survival, the 'disintegrating forces of time' distinguishing human life in the vast expanses at the Centre of Australia. The contrast was frightening. Men and women of settler descent thought that the cities, even when they chose to live outside them, were the lynchpin of public order. Even those who spent their lives a long way inland believed that the future of the colonial peoples depended on the coastal centres.

Governing such spaces was a massive challenge. In the 1860s and '70s bushrangers, from Ben Hall to Ned Kelly, had sometimes controlled entire towns and highways in defiance of government. Public servants such as Patrick Robertson Gordon, Queensland's chief inspector of stock, weaving their network of information and shared trust, had part of the answer. At the same time rural unionists such as William Guthrie Spence, who wanted to ignore political boundaries, complicated the question.

Improved communications technology meant that distance was mattering less. Thanks to all the new schools, the ability to write and read letters, and to make sense of newspapers, was nearly universal. Postal services were wonderfully efficient, and most men and women thought of their smooth operation as a common fact of life. The telegraph put people in touch on the instant, even from one side of the world to the other. Detailed messages were expensive and communication points – telegraph offices – were not always close by, but the telegraph created an impatience with distance. So did steamships and railway trains.

How should such people settle the great knot of ideas, the bundle of problems, which summed up the impact of a far-reaching state, and even more a multistate Federation? That was the first question. The second was, once they had settled it, how should they keep it all together for the long term?

The young were most at ease with the new ways, making sense of enormous geographical spaces and of the vast numbers of people who might be scattered through them. It was one of the main points of school curricula, and new writing in books and newspapers offered the same challenge. Among male youth such mastery was a test of manhood. Joseph Witton was happy with Tasmania, but 'the man is not really a man', said a Queenslander in 1891, 'who does not feel some impulse to belong to a great community – to a great nation'.[27]

It was a question of power, and of sharing in power, but it was also about knowledge and imagination. It was about using your brain, testing the muscles of the intellect. A good brain could live beyond its traditional limits, beyond habit. It broke out of the kind of places inhabited by Mary Gilmore, with her love of accents patterned like fine tapestry. It could handle far-off places and events. As Mary Gilmore said, in men was the 'talk that went like a broad river, sweeping in times and places and people as it flowed', talk that reached across continents and oceans.[28] There was a kind of confidence, real or seeming, that a girl like her could only wonder at.

The most powerful intellectual discipline of the day was geography. In its mass shaping of minds geography offered just the right kind of information and power. Geography was democratic knowledge, a science for everyman, for manhood – a source of stories, a jigsaw of adventure, and also a quick way of understanding all humanity. Or rather, said the Queensland statesman Sir Samuel Walker Griffith, it was 'not itself a science but rather a department in which various sciences are coordinated in such a way as to present a vivid picture of the different regions of the world, and a clear statement of the causes that determine the resemblances and contrasts of those regions'.[29] Geography was a foundation for new forms of history, anthropology and theories of race. It revealed great patterns of people, especially by race and nation, with vivid simplicity. It offered a god's-eye view of the world, past, present and future. It offered command.

Improved methods of printing first used in the 1830s meant that maps were now much more common. They could be reproduced in any handy size thanks to photolithography.[30] Maps appeared in some school textbooks, but teachers still relied mainly on large sheet maps hung on walls or draped over chairs. Children were not expected to have maps of their own, and these images of the world, dense with exotic shapes and tiny writing, were still slightly mysterious. Cartographic literacy – linking space on a map to the kind of space you could move about in – was a skill in its own right and it was highly prized.

Think for a moment about the way maps are read, and about the way their logic seeps into the minds of children. Maps are counter-intuitive. They tell about ownership and control, using boundary lines and various hatchings and colours. They tell about people moving about, with lines representing roads and railway tracks. They show people stepping across thresholds, where lines of movement meet lines of separation. They tell about hierarchies of place and space, and on paper some areas are assemblages of smaller ones. The key to each puzzle lies in different types of writing, and reading the markings is like reading the stars. It needs initiation.

The novelist Rolf Boldrewood – real name Thomas Alexander Browne – gave a neat account of the uses of geography in a story he wrote in the late 1880s called *A Sydney-Side Saxon*. The hero tells his own tale, starting with his childhood in rural poverty in England. As a boy, he had read Walter Scott's *Ivanhoe* (1820), one of the most popular novels of the day. His mind had been fired by Scott's description of a Saxon serf who had the lord and place he belonged to scratched on a brass collar around his neck. As his own imaginary collar, the nineteenth-century hero wore poverty and helplessness. He got that collar off by learning, especially geography.

> Any man or woman [he said] that can read and write, keep simple accounts, and understand a map, has got hold of the levers that move the world … I was sharp about geography, so I looked out Australia, and found that there were divisions or colonies with large cities and houses, just like other places.

He travelled to New South Wales. He was taken up by a helpful squatter, who saw how sharp he was and showed him a map of nearby runs. Hidden among the interwoven lines was a sliver of uncharted territory, about 7 miles by 5 (11 kilometres by 8), waiting to be possessed, and on it he made his fortune.[31]

Being 'sharp about geography' was a handy thing for working men too. About the time Browne (or Boldrewood) was planning his story, William Guthrie Spence told a tale about striking members of the Australian Shearers' Union. Local organisers in the Riverina realised that they needed to know the limits of the land owned by squatters. 'Maps were obtained,' said Spence, 'and in more than one place, when the squatter ordered men off his run, he was astonished to find them set him at defiance by camping within a few yards of the woolshed. They had located a road – or it may be a reserve – which he had forgotten existed'. They had found patches of public land where they could pitch their tents for as long as they liked. They were sharp too, in a way the world particularly admired. So, said Spence, '[t]he organizers saved the Union from defeat'.[32]

Browne said, '[a]ny man or woman', but thinking about big maps as 'levers that move the world' was less urgent for a woman. As Mary Gilmore knew, not many women were in a position to travel far under their own initiative. Browne's wife, Margaret, also wrote a book, *The Flower Garden in Australia*. She had a good sense of space, but space of a different sort. She offered advice to 'ladies and amateurs' on choosing and arranging trees, shrubs and flowers. The gardener must learn what suited her own part of the country, said Mrs Boldrewood (her pen name), 'what soil the various plants require; [and] whether they flourish in sun or shade, in heat or cold'. It was a kind of geography, a ladies' geography. Garden beds, preferably long and broad, should be set among avenues and shrubberies, and the gardener should give each plant its patterned place. Good borders made all the difference in directing the observer's eye, and tulips, said Mrs Boldrewood, in yellow, red and white, were wonderful for borders. 'Rich light soil is the best ... and give them a sunny position.'[33]

Like her husband, Margaret Browne wanted to show that shaping your life, taking command, meant understanding places. She made her universe in annual planting and watching for weeds. Maps of squatting runs were no good to her. She was probably interested in weather maps, such as those produced from about this time by the meteorologist Henry Chamberlain Russell, but only because they showed how continental, or maybe hemispherical, weather patterns might affect her tulips.

Great issues lived within this overlap between the intimate and the vast – the 'too narrow' heart, to use Alfred Deakin's assessment, of someone like Margaret Browne, and the aspirations of men like Thomas Browne and Deakin himself.[34] Some saw themselves managing in the interstices of kitchens and gardens. Others put their hope in continents.

It may be that Margaret Browne's intelligent planning added to her husband's stories, just as his imagination probably added to her thoughts about gardening. The tension between household and local life on the one hand and large spaces on the other was a problem of vast concern to the new generation. It gave arguments about Federation their main point, which it is the aim of this volume to investigate. If I make this clear by the end of this volume, the job will be done.

The pull between these two habits of thought figured in the way geography was taught at school. There were two approaches. One, invented by William Channing Woodbridge, a Connecticut teacher, in the 1820s, started with daily environment, requiring children to think as Margaret Browne did about the places they were familiar with, and then move step by step outwards so as to embrace the whole world. You began small. According to Charles Hinton, an English educationalist, the worst problems in teaching children come from such early work 'not being broken up small enough, so that the power [of the brain] is overweighted from the beginning. Instead of working in the fields and turning over the soil, it tries to move the most ancient landmarks'.[35]

The other method started with 'ancient landmarks'. In other words, it confronted childish intuition and turned it upside down. It began with the world and worked downwards and inwards, just as the 'Sydney-Side Saxon' did, first pinpointing Australia and New South Wales and afterwards the piece of soil that made him rich.

The top-down method was used in Victorian schools and it fitted the Melburnian empire-building style. Geography lessons started there in second class, with '[t]he continents, oceans, and larger seas, with their relative positions', and only afterwards filled in this enormous picture.[36] It was a bird's-eye view, or rather a view fit for tigers.

South Australian government schools used the Woodbridge method. Teachers were told to start with 'local geography', with the concerns of Margaret Browne. That meant drawing diagrams of the classroom, the school buildings and the neighbourhood, gathering knowledge of the landscape within easy reach. Children learnt the code by which they could change the real world to paper and back again, and when they had done that they were shown pieces of cartography on a larger scale. They were told about mountains, rivers and oceans they could never hope to see, except in cartographic form. As a school inspector put it, each boy and girl was first told 'something about his own neighbourhood, the hills that surround it, the creeks which flow through it, the seas which wash its shores', but all the time the teacher was 'leading his mind forward from the known to the unknown'.[37]

The great challenge lay in leaping between dimensions, and from the concrete to the abstract. As another inspector said, '[T]he advance from the geography of the neighbourhood in the first class to that of all South Australia in the second is a very great stride'. The jump beyond, he added, from Australasia to the wide world, was even harder. So the mind moved from the concrete to the map and from the map to the imagination. As Charles Hinton put it, at the ultimate point 'it is possible to create a sort of mental paper, which shall serve in place of the real paper'.[38]

Here were two radically different ways of understanding the reality of large spaces. One way, favoured by Victorians, asked big questions first. The other way, favoured by South Australians, started with small questions, gathering strength for sudden aggregation.

III

Through most of the 1870s and '80s the main aim in most schools, from Western Australia to New Zealand, was that children should master the geography of the colony, the 'nation', that is, they lived in. 'Australian boys and girls of twelve or thirteen years of age', said a New South Wales inspector, 'should be as thoroughly acquainted with the geography of their own country as European girls and boys are with theirs'. That meant that New South Wales children should know as much about New South Wales as, say, French children knew about France. At Grafton, near the Queensland border, boys and girls had drummed into them a few details about 'their own country' – 'the names of the rivers and ranges on the coast and a few of the more important capes and inlets', but next to nothing about any other countries, including even Queensland.[39]

There were good reasons for keeping things focussed at this level. Everything depended on the old capitals, on Brisbane, Melbourne, Adelaide and so on. The minds of the people had to be directed to those capitals, the only centres of power short of London. In the 1870s and '80s making everyone loyal to 'their own country' or nation, not just their town or region, was urgent. 'I am anxious', Henry Parkes, premier of New South Wales, told a bush audience, 'that we should, more and more, cultivate a feeling of free citizenship, a feeling of nationality, and have more of New South Wales and less of any particular district in which we live'. Victoria was small and compact, but even Victorian children needed a wider view, beyond Bendigo, Gippsland and so on, and a keener kind of patriotism. Maybe, said one school inspector, teachers should read them 'stories of the hardships and heroic endurance of our early pioneers, told in their own words'. These were stories about their nation, Victoria.[40]

New Zealanders tackled the same problem. Indeed, New Zealanders set a challenging pace. Administratively chaotic to start with, for years New Zealand was itself a federation, with up to ten provinces, each of them run by an elected superintendent and a provincial council. A governor and two-house parliament managed the whole affair, but most governing was done at the lower level. The discovery of gold in the 1860s made both islands much richer, and from 1870 Julius Vogel, first as treasurer and then as premier, led a massive program of immigration and public works, especially railway building. Redirected energy and purpose at the centre meant that in 1876 the provinces could be abolished and New Zealand became a single state. But old loyalties never really died.[41]

In Tasmania, Hobart and Launceston had been separately founded and in its very first years Launceston had known independence. Also, the large pastoral estates of the Tasmanian Midlands, full of fine houses and hierarchical habits, were very different from the mining settlements on the West Coast, where the people were mainly from across the Strait and much more egalitarian. Throughout the island, no-one deferred to Hobart. Unlike New Zealand, Tasmania had no provinces, but it did have full-bodied local government, beyond anything on the mainland. Local councils, elected on a high property franchise, had their own police, which were used to reinforce independence. Government inspectors checking matters of public health were sent packing by the constables, and council members looked after their own public works and presided in their own courts, disciplining each other's servants and all but the worst criminals.[42]

In Tasmania wealth seemed to belong not to the island as a whole but to the places that produced it. 'Why should money from one district be spent in another', demanded a leading Midlands gentleman. 'It was a complete setting aside of the principles of self-government, and an attempt to substitute a system of centralisation.' But all the colonies were now committed to 'a system of centralisation', and in Tasmania local independence slowly dwindled from the 1870s. With it went the influence of 'the little knot of fogies' who had ruled, or tried to rule, Tasmania so far.[43]

Andrew Inglis Clark's 'boys', the clever men, young and middle-aged, of the Minerva Club, were centralisers. But they were centralisers of the 1870s, centralisers of a less absolute sort than were to be found on the mainland. Local interests always mattered to them too. The challenge lay in bringing local feeling, with its tender affections and its homely, instinctive sense of right and wrong, into line with modern civilisation. It was all about feeling – that 'feeling of free citizenship' that Henry Parkes wanted to see drawing everyone together in his own country, in New South Wales.

Clark wanted to preserve this tenderness. But he had two other great projects. He wanted to convert Tasmania from a set of more or less hierarchical communities into one egalitarian state. And he wanted Australian Federation. It was a complicated, even a convoluted program. Hobart, the old capital, was pivotal. It stood between his own universe of small places, including the drawing room at Battery Point, on the one hand, and the continental nation, on the other. Progress started in 1879, when William Robert Giblin became premier. Taxation reform, more revenue and massive growth in public works, including railways and roads, pulled the island together. Giblin was Tasmania's answer to Julius Vogel. From 1887 Clark himself was the great reformer, as attorney-general and leader in the lower house. In one year he brought in 150 bills. He gave Tasmanians laws which were enforceable from shore to shore, covering mental illness, child custody, cruelty to animals, industrial relations (legalising trade unions) and much more. In his mind, the working class, above all, had a 'national' (Tasmania-wide) importance. The rights of the poor depended on the use of power in Hobart.[44]

Queensland had roughly similar problems. Along its east coast – nearly 3000 kilometres, taking a week to traverse even by steamship – was a chain of settlements, and many had more or less independent beginnings. Brisbane lay in the far south-east. Rockhampton, a day or two to the north, commanded a network of rich coastal valleys, plus vast sheep country around Longreach and Blackall, and abundant goldmines, especially at Mt Morgan. There was enough in Rockhampton's hinterland to support a separate colony. Rockhampton depended on Sydney at least as much as it did on Brisbane (just as Launceston, though subject to Hobart, looked to Melbourne). Further north again, Townsville stood at the centre of another vast area taking up two-thirds of Queensland's eastern coastline. It included not just sugarcane plantations, from Mackay to Cairns, but goldmining settlements at Charters Towers, Cloncurry and the Gulf.[45]

It was hard not to be impressed by Queensland. '[H]er noble extent of territory', said Henry Parkes in 1879, writing in the *Melbourne Review*, 'affords more than ample scope for the growth of a mighty nation'.[46] Queenslanders thought so too. Preserving the unity of a nation as vast as Queensland – much bigger and potentially much richer than many European states – called for skilled give and take, and agitation for independence, with new capitals at Rockhampton and Townsville, forced the Brisbane government to think about compromising for the greater good. From the 1870s there were several plans for 'financial separation', giving each province, North, Central and South, more control of its own resources, and during 1890–92 there were detailed plans for a 'federal union', the 'United Provinces of Queensland', with three governors, three parliaments, and three metropolises for public opinion to work in.[47]

At the same time, a 'system of centralisation' was also underway, and all Queenslanders were pressed to think as a single nation, the nation of Queensland. There was a Queensland National Bank with branches everywhere building wealth for the whole country. The Queensland National Association (Patrick Robertson Gordon was one of its founders) supported the bank by nudging forward wide-horizoned, well-informed investment. The QNA was mainly an agricultural society, but it concerned itself with mining and manufacturing. Its governing committee was all-inclusive. That is to say, it was truly national, with members from various commercial interest groups and from all quarters, from Cape York to the New South Wales border. It was a major effort to meet a major challenge, a strategy to stop Queensland, this 'mighty nation' of the future, from breaking into three.[48]

IV

When the Europeans in Australia agreed at the end of the 1890s to come together in a single federal 'commonwealth' (a story told later on), each colony brought to the table its own peculiarities, methods which had grown out of its own particular nation building. After the deed was done, it was pleasant to think that it had all been preordained – 'a temple to Thee & to Thy glory', as Alfred Deakin called it – a plan prefigured in the mind of God.[49] But differences had been deep. Differences of understanding, not just about colonial nationality but also on a smaller scale, were powerfully persistent.

Europeans had attached themselves to the land in many ways. The old capital cities were to go on generating their own habits, customs and patterns of power for many years to come, and smaller communities did the same.

The main issue of the day was not, in fact, the famous conflict between empire and nation, between Britain and Australia – 'the old dead tree and the young tree green', as the writer Henry Lawson put it. It went much deeper. When the Great War came, in 1914, when men had to decide whether to go away and fight, it hit home. The tension between empire and nation was trivial compared with the balance struck in every household, in every mind, between the needs of small places, of wives, parents and children, of old habits and old duties, and, on the other hand, the needs of places big beyond imagination, of nations and empires.

Changes in communications technology were pivotal. More completely than at any previous time, it was possible for innumerable men and women to feel an attachment – but what sort of attachment? – to innumerable others they could never meet. Individuals, if literate, could share feelings with strangers spread across enormous spaces. Reading, including the reading of maps, made that possible. It was the main method of imagining the wide world. By the late nineteenth century more than four-fifths of grown-up colonists could read. On the other hand, the smaller networks of family, town and city life, and the timbre and tenderness of ordinary conversation, were as powerful as ever. These two kinds of attachment overlapped, as in the life and work of the Brownes, husband and wife. But they could just as easily be at odds.

Except for the Roman Catholic Church, the British empire was unrivalled in the allegiance it commanded around the world. Geography, meteorology and various other mind-stretching configurations of earth and heaven proved the importance of the empire. With maps all about them, from 1883 antipodean children might read about the aging Queen Victoria in a passage that taught patriotism and geography both at once. 'As her birth-day comes round', it went, 'on the 24th of May, the prayer "God Save the Queen", uttered by English-speaking lips, greets the sun-rise every hour of the twenty-four, until the circuit of the world has been made'. Beginning in England, moving with the sun – like the meteor in HG Wells's story – across the Atlantic to the West Indies and Canada, and so to New Zealand, Australia, Hong Kong and Singapore, Bombay and Mauritius, Natal and the Cape, the prayer echoed in a cosmic roundelay. 'Anon Malta is reached, and one hour later the new dawn [on the 25th] tells the sentinels at Windsor that the joyous benediction has travelled with the sun-light from meridian to meridian round the globe.'[50]

Lessons of the same kind were taught about Australia. The same children might sing lines by the Bendigo poet William Gay, thrilling themselves with thoughts of the continent they lived in:

> From all division let our land be free
> For God has made her one: complete she lies
> Within the unbroken circle of the skies,
> And round her indivisible the sea
> Breaks on her single shore.[51]

In that generation magic lay in being one – individual, indivisible. On an imperial scale, imagine the high symmetry of the sun as it moved in a single sweep around the globe, across an empire united and unanimous, calling up a wave of loyal prayers as it passed westwards. Imagine too, around Australia's 'single shore', the circle of sky somehow mirrored in the perpetual noise of the breaking sea. The visions were dazzlingly abstract. They made the mind topple.

And yet. There were innumerable small communities scattered across the continent and islands in this quarter of the globe. Each had its own affairs and its own 'local geography'. In 1890, speaking of the possibility of Australian Federation, a member of parliament in Brisbane said, '[A]s a Queenslander I do not desire to give any power away that would keep us out of touch with the people'.[52] The need to keep in touch was the need for real democracy, as he saw it. It told against large schemes. Keeping in touch meant constant talking together. Never mind Deakin's temple to God's glory, raised in communion between his diary and himself. How was it possible for men and women to keep in touch like that, something like face to face, across the 'circuit of the world' and around the 'single shore'? How was it possible for them to make their own voices heard among those brilliant images now mirrored in the minds of millions?

Old ways of keeping in touch were concentrated in the capital cities. But inventive minds were struggling with unfamiliar ways of reaching out from each metropolis and from border to border. Men and women of a scholarly or scientific bent met and talked together, and if they wanted to make a public impact they set up formal associations. The leading groups were the royal societies. Each was a 'national' body. There had long been royal societies in Tasmania (founded 1843), Victoria (1860) and New South Wales (1866). Adelaide's Philosophical Society became a royal society in 1880, Queensland's in 1884. They were small versions of England's Royal Society, and they busied themselves with discussions, lectures and the distribution of papers on scientific matters, 'science' being broadly interpreted, linking themselves also with similar bodies overseas.[53] Like the universities in Sydney (founded 1850), Melbourne (1853), Adelaide (1874) and Tasmania (1890), the royal societies were designed to give each colony a place among the nations of the world.

There were 'national' museums. Most capitals had buildings used for the collection and display of natural history. But there were problems. For instance, the Queensland Museum was useful only to inhabitants of Brisbane and nearby places. Anywhere much to the north it meant nothing at all.[54] The royal societies did better because they used the methods of communication now on offer to spread enlightenment. Their meetings involved men living in or near each metropolis, but members, scattered far afield, received their learned papers by post. In 1885 the Royal Society of New South Wales had 493 full members. Four-fifths had been elected in the last ten years or so, which shows how these institutions were pushing ahead. Many of them lived a very long way from Sydney, including a few bush clergymen, the odd medical man and government surveyor, and a good number of graziers.

Allan Yeomans, and his brother, of Gilgoin Station near Brewarrina, in the far north-west of New South Wales, found near their homestead the 'Gilgoin meteorites'. Yeomans, a fellow of the society in Sydney, submitted them to HC Russell's trained eye, and Russell wrote a description for the society's *Journal*. Weighing about 70 pounds (30 kilograms) each, they had lain a couple of miles (3 kilometres) apart. Russell guessed that they had fallen quite separately. They had been lying so long, he said, that their surfaces, originally molten and smooth, had started to break up.[55] Russell's paper must have led other bush members to keep an eye out for meteorites as they walked over their paddocks. It was intriguing to think of deep patterning in the pebbles underfoot.

By the 1880s scholars in the European world were changing their broad sense of purpose. The 'new learning' fitted the habits of minds of the young, but some of the new work was very expensive, needing complicated equipment and government funding. As Russell said, '[I]f we are to keep pace with world', we had to spend money on science. (By 'we' he meant New South Wales.) His model was the intellectualised state of imperial Germany.[56] Laboratory work was beginning to be expected at universities, and in 1886 the University of Sydney appointed a young Englishman, Richard Threlfall, to its chair in physics, with just that expectation. Threlfall brought the latest methods from Cambridge and from Strasbourg, where he had just spent a summer in the laboratory of August Kundt, probably the best physics lab anywhere.

Threlfall was massively built. His feats on the rugby field led to professors being banned from playing because the crowds got overexcited. He also made an impact on Sydney Harbour, testing explosives in seawater. A marriage of brain and muscle, Richard Threlfall stood for the modern power of manly intellect. He thought that science was fundamental to national strength. Some day, he said, the thrusting intelligence of the modern researcher (*Geist des Forschers*) will be 'the supreme weapon in the fight of mankind against the forces of nature'. The lesson was vital for national survival. '[W]oe to that nation', he said, 'that learns it last'.[57]

Threlfall loved power and precision. He also liked up-to-date equipment, and physics was a science moving beyond the reach of the untrained and unfunded. With meteorology too, though the amateur observer was still essential, discoveries had to be centrally collated in order to mean anything, and the work was becoming steadily more elaborate. Research had to be coordinated for maximum impact. Here again Germany was a world leader. Even before the creation of the German empire, in 1871, cooperation among German-speaking states had quickened the pace of research. In New Zealand scientific activities had been drawn together, more or less, within the New Zealand Institute. But throughout the Antipodes it was obvious that something even more ambitious was needed, spanning the Tasman Sea and including all the scientific bodies on both sides. The meetings of meteorologists mentioned in chapter 1 showed how much could be done when scientists got together.

As with the meteorological meeting in 1879, the initiative came mainly from Sydney, this time from Archibald Liversidge, professor of geology and mineralogy at Sydney University. Working through his own royal society, Liversidge created the Australasian Association for the Advancement of Science, which met first in Sydney in spring 1888. Isolated for most of each year, colonial scientists emerged from such get-togethers with their written arguments refreshed and interpenetrated by talk, and with a new sense of what they could do.[58]

Despite Melbourne's larger magnificence, intercolonial associations were often Sydney-centred. Sydney's leaders were better at collaborating across borders, and in the other colonies there was less resentment of Sydney's ambitions. In Melbourne the most eager minds wanted union and uniformity. 'The air at present is full of federation', said some Melbourne University students in 1887. Why not, they asked their Sydney equivalents, merge the student unions at the two universities into a 'greater Union which shall embrace students of all our Australian Universities'? As with several other Melbourne initiatives, Sydney's answer was silence.[59]

In Melbourne they wanted ideals to be singular. In Sydney they were more attuned to negotiating boundaries. Melbourne was a powerhouse of ideas. Sydney was more like a clearing house.

Something like 850 men and women, no doubt mainly local, went to the Australasian Association lectures in Sydney, but speakers were principally interested in consulting among themselves and in widening their worldwide network. Certainly, the democratisation of knowledge was also part of the agenda, but achievements in that respect were slight.

It was left to others to popularise. In 1883 a Frenchman living in Sydney but familiar with Victoria and Queensland, Edmond Marin la Meslée, set up the Geographical Society of Australasia. La Meslée had just published in France his *L'Australie Nouvelle* (The New Australia). He was a geographer himself, and he saw geography as the key to the civilising process. For La Meslée, geography was not just a discipline; it was a world of knowledge, interesting and useful to every educated citizen. It was not just 'the dry facts of physical geography' but also ethnography, philology, hydrography and orography (the study of mountains in connection with weather). It was about 'the commercial and political relations of races, &c'. Geography was knowledge of the world, an intellectual command of men and affairs, but at the same time a system of understanding shaped for the minds of the masses.[60] Geography was, par excellence, knowledge democratised.

It was an extraordinary project. In La Meslée's eyes Australia was a kind of antipodean English-speaking France. He took after his compatriot the great historian Jules Michelet, whose massive *Histoire de France*, published in nineteen volumes between 1833 and 1869, had spelt out a new kind of patriotism, of national solidarity and collective power, open to every thinking man and woman (but especially man). As a people's thinker, Michelet had been a pioneer. His great idea was the idea of the nation. He wooed his own country in page after page of scholarship. He described the physical features of each French province, as if his fingers were tracing the form of his beloved, and each part was a means to an end, a key to the beauty of the whole. He took his readers around the frontiers, pointing out how Frenchmen were different from place to place, and yet they were still French. Watching her eternal borders, the points of invasion and resistance, France was ever France. He unveiled France, Michelet said, 'in the living unity of natural and geographical events'. 'I was the first to see her as a soul and as a person.'[61]

More prosaically, La Meslée tried to do the same for Australia. Michelet's story of the French provinces proved the 'inevitable and fated regularity' that created one country in the end. So did

La Meslée's vision of Australia. Here, he said, the 'provinces' (he insisted on that word) were 'little republics recognizing in principle the suzerainty of the mother-country, but completely self-governing'. The people varied from one to the next. 'They are the same men but they do not hold the same ideas.' But in truth, every fragment belonged to the implicit nation. It was the purpose of the Geographical Society to give all these scattered peoples 'a sense of national existence'. Like Threlfall, La Meslée knew the power of science and 'in Australia', he said, 'geography is a science that cannot wait'.[62]

In Michelet's France each Frenchman, in order to be truly French, had to rise above small places, including home and neighbourhood. He had to understand and speak French – a fifth of the French population still used local dialects – because language was 'the principal sign of national existence'. Born of his own patch of soil, he had to shake himself free. '[H]e will quit it, reject it, spurn it.' Local attachment made a man, in Alfred Deakin's terms, narrow of heart. No longer a Lyonnaise or a Breton, the Frenchman embodied in himself, said Michelet, 'a great country, through which he may count himself for something in the destinies of the world'.[63] It was an agenda for the young, for minds newly freed by reading, by hunting for wide horizons, as the 'Sydney-Side Saxon' did, and by breaking away from family life. Young men and women, but again, especially men, loved teachers who gave them lessons such as these.

The Geographical Society of Australasia was pieced together for this end. It would be a 'national association', said La Meslée. It would be formed with the help of 'the Australian people'. It would spread knowledge of 'our great country' among ourselves and abroad. The coming generation was hungering for such things. Our 'young men', said a Melbourne writer, were 'inspired with the idea which influences all young people of building up a new nationality'.[64] This French recipe was just the thing.

The young made easy connections between Australia and

France. The Australians and the French, said journalist Francis Adams, were the two peoples alone in the world who knew what equality was. With 'God Save the Queen' the only other option, in these colonies activists found a national song in the 'The Marseillaise', and they used it in protest marches and public meetings. The Queenslander Archibald Meston composed his own 'Australian Marseillaise'. Remember the Imp, the archetypal Australian boy in Charles Bean's story of the River Darling in chapter 1. Smart, impertinent, droll, man and boy at the same time, he mirrored *le petit* Gavroche, Victor Hugo's Parisian of the same age, in *Les Misérables* (1862). To some minds, Young Australia reflected Young France.[65]

Professor Threlfall liked to think just as the Germans did. For Threlfall, nations were fasces, or bundles of power – intelligentsia, businessmen, armies, government. But for democratic youth-and-future-oriented men and women it was more appealing to think like the French. It was more pleasant to gather up our 'provinces' in a single sweep of imagination, as one great rainbow-like abstraction. A French sense of 'national identity', of a nation with boundaries given by the Almighty, and with a single soul, unique, sacred and eternal, was to fire antipodean understanding for generations to come. William Gay's vision of Australia – 'God has made her one: complete she lies / Within the unbroken circle of the skies' – matched exactly Michelet's picture of France, even to the hint of lovely womanhood. When we at last stood up to fight for that 'unbroken circle', that image of beauty, then we would know who we were.[66] We, were we male, would be men. Were we women, the picture was not quite so clear.

This French slant echoed the way English writers in Shakespeare's time had charged their imagination with Italy, translating from Petrarch, Machiavelli and Castiglione, locating drama in Verona, Venice, Padua, Naples.[67] It was about national birth or rebirth, Elizabethan England and pre-Federation Australia. It was as if a new collective sense of self could not happen without a model as different as possible from old ways. Both cases, English and Australian, involved the idealisation of romance, contest, violence – ineluctable things, the stuff of youth. Seduced by such magic, who could still think that the old colonies, those city-states pieced together by middle-aged men, deserved to be called nations?

La Meslée hoped to spread information. He hoped to imbue 'the general public' with the kind of knowledge needed for the right brand of patriotism.[68] In this respect the Geographical Society was not a success. None of the founders really grasped the complexities of the great problem involved in Australian sense of place, and the society was not organised for any kind of two-way conversation between small places and the centre, between amateurs and experts. It had branches in every capital city, but each branch went its own way. There were publications and 'illustrated lectures', and to start with a lot was done to sponsor exploration. An expedition to the Centre in 1891–92, organised by the South Australian branch, found many hitherto unknown plants and animals, including 150 new species of insects.[69]

However, there was no systematic muster of the thoughts of 'the Australian people'. The society became just another set of city-based associations and the members talked among themselves.

And yet the time was ripe for gathering. With literacy now normal, with vastly more reading matter and highly efficient postage, new ways of communication were being worked out. Men, women and children, including the poor, could make themselves heard on a large stage as never before.

La Meslée would have done better if he had been a journalist. Wonderful things were being done among the men of the press in the 1880s, and by a few women, especially in Sydney. Louisa Lawson's paper, *The Dawn: A Journal for Australian Women*, produced monthly from 1888, was aimed at women and produced by women, including female compositors. It flourished in the 1890s, only closing in 1905. Directed at wives and mothers, housekeepers as well as compositors, it became the centre of a network of political activity. It demanded women's right to vote, inspired a women's club and linked Australian feminism to movements overseas. Lawson urged readers to write in. The *Dawn*'s pages featured women questioning other women before a scattered host of their kind.

More clever still was the Sydney *Bulletin*, and it too was a phenomenon of the 1880s. JF Archibald, one of the two founders and a continental patriot, hammered out from week to week a new method of mass contact, largely and deliberately male. He took to a brilliant pitch conversation in print, and the paper lived on contributions from its readers: '[e]very man can write at least one good book; every man with brains has at least one good story to tell, with or without brains, moves in a different circle and knows things unknown to any other man'.[70] Send them in. Tell your story.

The *Bulletin* ended up with many voices. They often ran at cross purposes, riven with irony and anarchy. But all their variety was attached somehow, like the hoped-for nation, to a single space (the continent plus Tasmania and New Zealand), a single past and a single future. A much-travelled Frenchman after La Meslée's time called the *Bulletin* '[t]he most scathing, most daring, the wittiest, the most impudent and best edited paper I know'. The 3000 copies of the first issue sold out. Eventually circulation reached the immense total of 100,000.[71] It was a White man's paper, and there was a copy for every fifteen or sixteen White men from Christchurch to Perth.

Archibald was born in Warrnambool, Victoria, and his original Christian names were John Feltham, but he told everyone he was born in France and he renamed himself Jules François. He was fired by the unflinching realism of the newest French writing, especially the stories of Émile Zola. He was more or less an atheist, and he was eager for the power of the individual man, secular, absolute, idealistic. That man, if he was a real man, should be possessed of a 'tyrannous freedom', a kind of spiritual hunger that ran back to the French Revolution and beyond. Francis Adams called that man 'Voltairean' and there was certainly a Voltairean mix of fire and ice, drought and flood, in Archibald's ideal.[72] 'Every man', said the *Bulletin*, 'knows things unknown to any other man'. Was that a recipe for loneliness or hope?

Archibald's nation, like Michelet's, was an idea already alive among readers. It needed only to be drawn out, and enamelled over with the infinite diversity of masculine imagination.

The *Bulletin* was pure Sydney. Boundaries and distance did not worry its writers. They were simply part of masculine knowledge. In its pages Queensland was 'Bananaland'. New Zealand was 'Maoriland'. They were faraway places, but they somehow all belonged. You could give them colloquial names. The *Bulletin* took stories from all quarters, it was sent Australasia-wide, and it was driven by a need to grasp, but not to swamp, the local and provincial. Its arrival in the mail each week, said Adams, was 'an event in the coast towns from Port Darwin to Perth, and it is the same in New Zealand'.[73] Conceived and born in Sydney, among city backstreets and boltholes, it pictured a continental people, vastly scattered and variously organised, as a set of actors on a single stage.

5

The Significance of Brain

I

Laurence Gronlund was a lawyer, a Dane trained at the University of Copenhagen but a member of the American bar living in Chicago. In 1884 he published his manifesto, *The Cooperative Commonwealth*, in which he argued that the United States should set an example to the rest of the world by making 'the Community' responsible for everything essential to decent livelihood. He meant American society as a whole, from shore to shore. He left government out. Every enterprise should be owned and managed by the men and women who worked in it. When that happened the old methods, management by force and fear, would die away. Gronlund's book was soon being sold for three shillings and fivepence in Australia and he was being spoken of as 'the rising prophet of the worker'.[1]

Imagination took off. In 1888, also in America, Edward Bellamy published *Looking Backward*, set in the year 2000. Bellamy's time traveller found the whole world governed cooperatively, in 'a loose form of federal union', with the United States in the lead. His book, like Gronlund's, sold worldwide. It cost one shilling in Australia, but in Brisbane it was serialised in the *Worker* and there was soon a Bellamy Society. Its very vividness seemed to prove that such things were inevitable.[2]

Leo Tolstoy, the great writer, pointed out that *Looking Backward* did not explain how the leap was to be made from present mess to future perfection. But in 1898 Bellamy published another book, called *Equality*, which included his famous 'Parable of the Water Tank'. In this little fable the rich and the poor were two antagonistic parties, bound together by dealing in water. There was one great tank. It was called 'the Market'. The rich paid the poor a penny for every bucket they brought to the tank and they got them to pay twopence for every bucket they took out for themselves. In due course the tank overflowed and so the poor got no more pennies. This was Bellamy's explanation for the depression of the 1890s, when boom led straight to massive unemployment, suffering and starvation. Only when the poor organised and used their brains did they see what to do. On that happy day, in the land of the water tank, 'every man said unto his fellow, "My brother", and every woman said unto her companion, "My sister" … And the practice of equality ennobled the people of that land forever'.[3]

The story would have made particular sense in Australia, where water was a fragile source of life. So fragile, said Alfred Deakin, that water supply should not be left to chance, to the vagaries of nature and free enterprise (charging twopence a bucket). It ought to be a matter of 'parental consideration on the part of the State'.[4] Newspapers said the same, and frequent drought drove the point home. In New South Wales in 1875, among drought and bushfires, the government was called on to set up 'a system of works' for the interior.[5] People in the cities too should have water guaranteed. With inequality, some would die of thirst. With equality, all would drink and therefore live.

In fact, at Burra, the copper-mining town in South Australia, someone wrote a skit on *Looking Backward* which pre-empted the 'Parable of the Water Tank'. The mayor, Frederick Holder, was made to say:

> It is not good that the people should carry the great fluid about the city in carts when we could manage to get it run to their very doors by a little skill; I will arise, therefore, and get

> me unto the great Council of the people, and say unto them, let us put our heads together and manage this affair … that the rich and the poor may be alike amply provided for.[6]

It was a joke, but that was in fact the way the job was done in Burra. All worked together. With larger planning such local authorities might be effectively backed up by government, and by the resources and ingenuity of the people as a whole. Death from thirst gave human urgency to the problem on West Australian goldfields. But everywhere house fires and bushfires could obliterate life and property just because there was no water to put them out.

Careful thought and 'a little skill' was the answer, plus serious expenditure. '[T]hose who would worthily guide public opinion and direct the application of public resources must earnestly work out the problem of water supply and distribution for the metropolis, and for the country districts.'[7]

Getting people to work together, not just willingly (that could be easy) but also effectively, was a massive challenge. Cooperation could do wonders in fighting fires. Sometimes it seemed almost instinctive. During his travels near the River Darling, Charles Bean noticed men joining in a wonderful spirit of self-sacrifice, working together without hesitation, when it came to bushfires. He told of a group looking up from their work and seeing a fire on a nearby place, beyond the horizon. They headed off to put it out. Their boss, getting home a bit later, harnessed the fire cart (a water tank on wheels) and followed. They all fought without stopping until the following morning, when the fire was under control. Then another blaze blew up in a different direction.

> They made for their horses, scuttled down the paddock and straight across country; galloped all the way – another seven miles [11 kilometres]. They were first in the field this time … [T]he fire-cart was fourteen miles behind at the other fire; but

> the spring-cart came up with water bags, and they began to drive the fire from its flank towards a road which was five miles ahead. And then, as soon as they could spare them, they sent back two men for fresh horses and the fire-cart.

The cart was filled with water at the homestead and got to the second fire at dawn next morning. It was all over by the second midday.

> Neither of those fires [Bean pointed out] was on the property on which that manager or those men worked. And men are not paid for subduing bush-fires ... They fought and galloped for forty-eight hours continuously as a matter of fellowship; thrashing the flames till they were blacker than sweeps; rushing in upon the fire for a few moments and then retiring choked and breathless ... Their eyes and throats were swollen and sore. Their tongues were twice the normal size and at times lolled out of their mouths. Such food as they had was brought them at their work by the people whose paddock was burning. Their drink was a little cold tea.

There was nothing unusual about this effort. '[M]ost of these men would wonder why anyone should bother to tell about it.'[8]

Bean put this all down to 'fellowship', which was another name for Bellamy's 'practice of equality' (not just the theory). It has also been called a 'democracy of manners'.[9] Equipment mattered too. These men would have struggled much longer without the water cart. There was also the ability to use the equipment to good effect. Volunteer fire brigades sprang up in communities throughout the colonies, especially Victoria, from the 1870s. They all relied on financial support, first from fire insurance companies and afterwards from colonial and local governments, for the equipment they needed, and they all trained hard.[10] If this was fellowship, it was the kind of fellowship that extended far beyond feeling and far beyond the men themselves. It depended on intelligent organisation.

Volunteer firemen cultivated cool efficiency. Drill was fundamental. In May 1879 Abraham Abrahams, chairman of the Fire Insurers' Association in Adelaide, surprised the city brigade with a midnight drill, afterwards sending a 'highly satisfactory' report to the press. He timed the whole brigade with military precision. One man, he said, had travelled the 1198 yards (1100 metres) from his home to the place of the fictional fire in nine minutes. Another covered 2176 yards in nine minutes and thirty seconds.[11] Efficiency on the spot was just as crucial, and groups were made to compete against each other, with someone measuring to the second how long it took to reel out each hose and send an arc of water onto the imaginary fire. Established volunteer groups showed new ones how to do it. The volunteers at Norwood, an Adelaide suburb, set a splendid example, in training and with the real thing. 'None have been sooner on the scene than they, and none have worked harder, or with more intelligence to contain the enemy.'[12]

But then there was the need for water, always the need for water. The men of the Adelaide brigade pushed themselves to the limit when some haystacks belonging to Thomas Elder, one of South Australia's richest citizens, at Morphettville, just outside the city, caught fire. But they were all lost for lack of water. A fireman told the story: 'We bursted hose after hose at the Hon. Mr Elder's haystack fire; still we persisted in our endeavours to play on the fire, yet without avail – we could only throw a feeble and straggling drop of water on the stacks'.[13] Such crises, some on a much larger scale, proved that in Australia water was not just the key to growth and progress. It guaranteed existence.

Alfred Deakin led the argument for redefining water in the Antipodes. Redefining itself was a cooperative effort. Water here was important in ways quite different from water in Britain, and yet the laws here, like the laws of property in livestock (chapter 2), were originally based on English principles. The livestock laws were turned upside down by Queenslanders and New South Welshmen, and the laws of water by Victorians. In England, water was plentiful. There, the law was geared to water's ancient usefulness as a source of energy (especially for mills), and owners had to be stopped from diverting it to the injury of their neighbours. In Australia, it had to be managed from beginning to end as a shared resource, because its scarcity could leave life in the balance.[14] It was necessary to sink or swim together, or rather everyone, from place to place, drank from the same small cup. English law did provide one obvious precedent, however. That was the precedent of the dry-land commons. The thousands of acres of commons created throughout Australia since the 1860s were modelled on the old English commons. They too were meant as shared wealth, to be managed by cooperation. This was to be the way with water. It was another kind of socialism.

In June 1886 Deakin presented to parliament in Melbourne the first of several bills designed to give Victorians a new understanding of what water really was. Water, like common land, was to be 'reserved' to the Crown for communal use and managed by local bodies called 'trusts'. Working with this invention, he said, in time, 'we [Victorians] shall compare in population as in wealth – as I hope we shall always continue to do in energy and enterprise – with any colony of the [Australasian] group, or any country of the world'.[15]

Even the English, with their different laws, had known that water was hard to pin down. In the words of the great codifier of the English Common Law, William Blackstone, it was 'a moveable, wandering thing'. No single owner could ever have more than 'a temporary, transient, usufructuary property therein'.[16] Deakin's invention abolished even this temporary and transient right. Water, reimagined, was to be used not just to preserve life but also to change the land. It was to create other types of work and other ways of living. This initiative, as Deakin said, was part of a 'new movement'.[17]

Deakin, the great innovator, meant a movement based on new ways of thinking. It was not altogether unique to Australia. In some respects it was part of something worldwide. The worship of pure free enterprise was over. It was qualified now by a belief in the virtue of joining forces, in brain power, expressed through individuality but also through 'fellowship' and 'the practice of equality'. Even free-enterprise enthusiasts had shifted their focus. One of the most distinguished was the politician Bruce Smith, the son (like Deakin) of goldrush parents, founder of the Victorian Employers' Union and author of *Liberty and Liberalism: A Protest against the Growing Tendency toward Undue Interference by the State, with Individual Liberty, Private Enterprise and the Rights of Property* (1887). '[C]ombined action by all', Smith said, was always more efficient 'than the separate action of ... several individuals acting independently'.[18] If Bruce Smith could make this compromise so could almost anyone.

II

The 'little skill' used at Burra involved managing human beings, their abilities, knowledge and imagination. It meant dividing humanity into parcels of power. Recall how Louisa Lawson ran the *Dawn*, drawing on the sisterly spirit of other women in every aspect of the paper's production. It was a classic combination of brain and heart. In Brisbane the radical journalist William Lane was the founding editor of the *Worker*, a union newspaper also run on cooperative lines. It was 'yours', Lane told his readers, 'your very own; you own it, you control it, you with your pennies thrown in a heap together'. The paper had been born, he said, of 'your mutual trust in one another'.[19]

Popular new books set out the ideal, but like Bean they tended to play down the brainwork needed, dwelling instead on fellowship and feeling. (Historians have tended to do the same.) Following

Gronlund and Bellamy, William Morris, artist and designer, one of the founders of English socialism, wrote *News from Nowhere* (1890), a story set in southern England and another bestseller among English-speaking peoples worldwide. The hero was another time traveller, a man of the 1880s who lived several days in a twenty-first-century utopia where even complete strangers called each other 'neighbour'. In this wonderful era still to come society was gilded with togetherness.

For Morris, as for Thomas Hardy (chapter 3), it was the moment when people met – their touching, the impact of one another's voices – which underpinned everything. That was 'the practice of equality' in the flesh. In the new age there was no false modesty. Bodies were frankly admired. A man's 'splendid form [was] at its best amidst the rhymed strokes of the scythes', and a woman's 'grey eyes [showed] light amidst the tan of her face'. Innocent and yet glowing sensuality was the order of the day. Everywhere there was face to faceness, a tapestry of talk and touch, from unreasoning lovers' passion to the 'frank friendly' kiss used in most common conversation.

There was no 'dreary introspective nonsense' in Morris's story. Life was lived on its surface. State power was nil and 'we discourage centralisation all we can'. It was all good moments and small places, and all threaded through by the wet, winding abundance of the River Thames, a highway, a bright bond, on which people rowed as easily as walking.[20]

Another version of the same thing, almost a satire, was Jerome K Jerome's story *Three Men in a Boat* (1889), set on the same stretch of water, the River Thames, but peopled by fools. Joseph Furphy too ran a river through *Such Is Life*, taking watery bungling several steps beyond Jerome and an instinct for humanity several miles beyond Morris. Furphy's river, the Murray, with its spongy reed beds and black lagoons, was 'alive with the "plump, plump" of bullfrogs and the interminable "r-r-r-r-r" of yabbies'.[21] In *Such Is Life*, as in *News from Nowhere*, there is no government, or none that matters. The endless landscape fits together because of the river. Even among the dryness, all is 'riverine'. The story brings to mind also the network of underground rivers, the echoing wells and bright, scattered springs which contemporary imagination conjured up for the Australian landmass. In the Australian dream, we would have one interlaced reservoir, one noble Murray, rich and unfailing, for a widely scattered people.

No-one would work hard in dream places like these. Alfred Deakin worked hard to make the dream real, just as he worked hard in unravelling the mysteries of his own inner self. Some said that Deakin's model of 'State Socialism' was too authoritarian, because government would be able to force everyone into cooperation. Deakin himself was afraid it must breed corruption. And yet, if things went well, this was an incoming tide on which all boats would rise together.[22] The unintelligent, lazy and narrow hearted must be guided by the rest.

Quite apart from the commons, a multifaceted cooperative movement was well underway throughout the various colonies. There were shops selling basic foodstuffs for labouring families and run on cooperative ('Rochdale') principles. Members each owned a share paid for in instalments, they bought at their own counter, and they divided up any profit. A Rochdale cooperative started in Brisbane in 1859. Others flourished among copper miners in South Australia and coalminers in New South Wales, the shared hardship of the men matched by the shared budgeting of their wives. There were cooperative dairies in the coastal valleys north and south of Sydney, and cooperative sugarcane mills in central Queensland.[23] The dairymen and sugar growers agreed among themselves that only shared effort and shared capital could get the job done. Cooperative schemes were crucial for survival in some parts of the country, and governments did their best to prop them up, passing laws to underwrite the principles of property involved.

During the 1880s a quick crowding of ideas and experiments worldwide heralded a revolution in thinking about what property was and what society was, or could be. The communitarian anarchism of the Russian prince Grigory Potemkin showed how far the splendour of hope might reach. The communism of Karl Marx, newly popular, was a harder, more intellectual vision, with a program for action.

These ideas were compounded by the appalling experience of the 1890s depression, which hit the Australian colonies hard. By 1893, most Victorian banks had failed and nearly a third of skilled labourers were out of work. Enormous suffering among hard-working people in what was meant to be a land of opportunity had already suggested something fundamentally wrong with the arrangement of society even before Edward Bellamy's *Equality*, with its parable of the water tank, reached these shores. Trade unionism had failed too, and the Brisbane journalist William Lane crystallised plans for a settlement of Australians in Paraguay, in which all property would be held in common and all would be equal. The power of civilised intelligence would devise conditions which would make all tyrannies, large and small, impossible. Old Australia had manifestly collapsed. This would be 'New Australia'.

A party of 220 was gathered by Lane and his followers with no trouble at all, setting sail in July 1893, followed by about 300 more. The pioneers were mainly Queenslanders, including labouring men from the bush, but there were educated idealists too. Mary Cameron (quoted in these pages several times already) had made her name as a poet with the Sydney *Bulletin*, and she went to Paraguay as a schoolteacher. She was married there to William Gilmore, one of a second shipload from Adelaide, and her wedding ring was a mutilated shilling.[24]

Cooperative settlements (but with individual title to land) were tried many times. In 1882 in New Zealand, John Ballance proposed gathering groups of families on perpetual leases of Crown land, their initial expenses funded by government, and later, as a cabinet minister, he settled several thousand families.[25] These 'village settlements' were variations of utopia, but it was always a question as to how much cooperation was realistic. In South Australia from 1886, farmers were sold 'homestead blocks' on easy terms and were told to go forth and build. Then, in 1893, provoked by the depression, the premier, Charles Cameron Kingston, embarked on more radical possibilities, new Australias *within* the old one. Land for crops, pasture, gardens and orchards was to be held in common, under perpetual lease. Each 'association' was to be a little republic, managing its own affairs and putting all profit into a single fund. Eleven were formed, with about 1750 individuals altogether. Most of the people were married couples and children, who aimed to live together in settlements strung along the banks of the Murray near the Victorian border.[26] The Murray again – a perpetual source of life.

Lane's people in Paraguay included George and Helen Birks, and their eight children, and two of Birks's brothers went with their families to Murtho, on the Murray. John Birks had kept a chemist's shop in Port Adelaide. He was secretary to the group and at Murtho he managed the garden. According to his daughter Elsie, who taught the children (as Mary Gilmore did in Paraguay), he 'would notify us at the school, if peas, strawberries, beans, etc would need picking tomorrow'. Then, after picking, he 'divided all such fruit and vegetables among us all, according to the size of family. We ran on Communistic Lines,' Elsie explained, '"from each according to his ability; to each according to his need"'. But for Elsie Birks the more intimate and ephemeral things were more important. They were the small signs of true fellowship, 'the familiar whistle … the cheery good-morning … the ready joke', plus the dancing, the organised singing and the swimming in the slow brown river.[27]

William Pember Reeves, a New Zealand socialist, visited the various Murray settlements during their salad days. He found

4000 acres (1600 hectares) cleared, irrigation works established, and crops and orchards planted. He was impressed. 'Communal blacksmiths, wheelwrights, bootmakers, and bakers were at work in their shops. Sawmills were noisy; bricks were being made; lime-kilns and drying-kilns had been put up.' There were new schools and substantial cottages. A smaller effort was made at Pitt Town, on the Hawkesbury River near Sydney. And yet, in every case, in spite of all the eagerness to start with, the sharing effort was abandoned within a few years. Where crops failed, there was no way to carry on. Where they did well, the money generated quarrels.[28]

At Murtho, where Elsie Birks was, the main problem was drought. One good year was followed by three very dry ones. Everything then was down to the river. The wheatfield, garden, orchard and vineyard were sustained by water pumped up and fed through a system of channels. But the settlers lacked bush experience. The site they had chosen had bad soil and a high riverbank, which multiplied the necessary effort. When labour was already scarce the pumping was done by shifts of four men each, sweating day and night, and even then the water reached the top in a feeble trickle.

When she first took the boat upriver to Murtho, Elsie Birks had been determined to prove that there was 'inherent good in human nature'. William Lane in Paraguay appealed to the 'warm heart of humanity'. But as one of Lane's people said, 'however workable communism may be for angels, we were not suited for it'.[29] At Murtho, beside the purposeful, purposeless, infinite, unyielding Murray, there was more warmth and tighter fellowship than in Paraguay. But skill and judgment were in short supply. And water.

III

Although William Morris might not like it, as I said in chapter 3 this was an age of introspection. Introspection, done correctly, made the brain feel like an engine, marvellously powerful, and the feeling was addictive. '[I]t is in the brain that everything takes place', said Oscar Wilde. Each brain was a continent, a universe. 'It is in the brain that the poppy is red, that the apple is odorous, that the skylark sings.'[30] 'Every man', as JF Archibald put it, 'knows things unknown to any other man'. That was thanks to the infinity of every brain.

'Brain' was a word whose moment had come. The brain was the seat and engine of individuality. 'You speak of your brain power being less *just now*', wrote Elsie Birks to a friend, as if his psychic fuel were running low. In earlier days, the soul had been the main register of human experience. Now it was the brain, its complexity, its efficiency, its productivity. The brain was a multilevelled cosmos, a mystery within, ever ripe for new things. A few, it is true, could see nothing in it. 'Brains!' said the queen's cousin Field Marshal the Duke of Cambridge. 'I don't believe in brains. You haven't any, I know, sir.'[31]

A century later, about the time I write, psychologists were to develop the idea of the brain as something whose cognitive operations use two systems. Some call them system 1 and system 2. We understand in two ways. One is habitual and easy, and the other is deliberate. System 1 'detects simple relations ... and excels at integrating information about one thing, but it does not deal with multiple topics at once, nor is it adept at using purely statistical information'. System 2 'can follow rules, compare objects on several attributes, and make deliberate choices between options'. It can also 'program memory to obey an instruction that overrides habitual responses'.[32] The two systems feed each other. With a much feebler sense of the neurological underpinning, reformers in the period of Federation spent vast resources cultivating system 2. They adored its implications.

'The most important machine is man,' wrote the great English economist Alfred Marshall, 'and the most important thing produced is thought'.[33] One of the leading authorities on the subject was Francis Galton, also English, who focussed on what he called 'genius', especially the way it was transmitted in families. Intellectual ability was an asset or a commodity, like physical appearance. And yet brains were democratic things. They belonged to everyone, and ability could also come by chance. In common parlance, to be 'brainy' was to be clever in an everyday sense, gifted with regard to system 2, but not necessarily theoretical and academic. It was to think well, but in a down-to-earth way. It was to confront with delight the problems of the moment. In Australia the land itself was '[u]niquely favourable to steady, brainy work'. 'Not only the best brain, but the most educated brain, must find its place on the farm. The day has gone by when merely imitative and routine farming can be successful.'[34]

Words such as 'brainy' and 'brainwork', if the newspapers are any guide, were several times more commonly used in the 1890s than they had been twenty years earlier (dwindling again after the Great War).[35] Public houses invited the lazy man to waste time 'soaking his brains', but in other institutions, especially schools, brains were disciplined and nourished. It was a blessing to discover, when a young colonial did well in English university exams, that 'Australian brains, if cultivated, [might be] ... as good as Australian muscle in competition with men of their race who remain in the Old Home'. 'I do not admit that there is any other element of national growth', said Sir Henry Parkes, five times premier of New South Wales, 'except an intelligent population'. As for Parkes himself, Alfred Deakin called him 'a full-blooded, large-brained, self-educated Titan'.[36]

In colonial schools, children were pushed towards 'mental arithmetic', just as they were pushed towards reading maps, both classic applications of system 2 and both ways of exercising and training their 'reasoning powers'. Mental arithmetic was highly demanding.[37] It called for a kind of concentration and self-reliance new to the school curriculum, for 'coolness of judgment and presence of mind'. One had to think ahead, step by step. As a Victorian inspector explained,

> [W]e may expect a mental picture to stand before the pupil, thus:–
>
> $$\frac{27 \times 18}{9}$$
>
> which by cancelling leads almost immediately to the answer.[38]

(Maps were also in a sense 'mental pictures'.) In fact, there were two moves within this problem. Dwelling on it beforehand the child was supposed to imagine in an instant how one step led to the other.

It was too hard for many. Brain power flickered low and progress faltered. Faced with blank looks, teachers tried shortcuts, or 'trick rules', which cut back the effort.[39] In map reading the default process was simply to memorise names.

In 1871 a book of famous significance was published in England called *The Theory of Political Economy*, whose author, William Stanley Jevons, had once been assayer at Sydney's Royal Mint. During his five years in Australia, Jevons had exercised his own brain on a variety of human problems, economic, climatic and geographic. He had also thought about the link between brainwork and government policy, especially in New South Wales. He wanted to know how highly trained minds could shape the government of nations, an important question when it came to building up a civil service and linking government to universities. It was exactly what they were doing in Germany, and what HC Russell, CH Pearson, Richard Threlfall and many others wanted in Australia.

Jevons's brain never stopped. He was also introspective. Still a young man in his antipodean days, he had tried to map out his own career. He weighed his mental energy, self-assessed, against his chances of doing well, and he hunted for nicely calibrated links between present and future, for tiny clues such as good detectives might seize on. Jevons had been the first to think systematically about the Australian weather. (Russell acknowledged his effort.) In one elaborate paper, 'On Clouds', he based predictions on some of the most common, insubstantial things in human experience.[40] This was new wisdom. It offered new ways of reading the country.

It was the same in the United States, a place, like Australia, which still seemed ripe for exploration. Nature threw patterns at the intelligent observer, as if to tease with sheer abundance. Henry Thoreau, the American writer, remarked in wonder in his diary how, after a violent night storm, gravel on a railway crossing was stratified. 'I can tell within a small fraction of a degree from what quarter the rain came … Thus', he said, 'each wind is self-registering'.[41] Science could build on observations like this, such as a bushman took for granted.

Jevons was also a statistician. In later life he was certain that everything of any long-term importance for humanity could be quantified. Even the vagaries of religious faith could be stated in quantitative terms, by counting church congregations, for instance. What an immense intellectual advantage we had over our ancestors! Human decisions had always been shaped by apparent relationships between cause and effect, the chance of one event leading to another. Now we were learning to measure that connection. We could count how often dice fell in certain patterns, and the result could be applied in every avenue of life:

> Who [asked Jevons] could have conceived that the investigation of petty games of chance would have led to the creation of perhaps the most sublime branch of mathematical science – the theory of probabilities? …
>
> Now there can be no doubt that pleasure, pain, labour, utility, value, wealth, money, capital, &c. are all notions

> admitting of quantity: nay, the whole of our actions in industry and trade certainly depend upon comparing quantities of advantage or disadvantage.[42]

The householder knew each morning how many loaves they would need that day from the baker, and who, asked the government statistician in Sydney, could have imagined that men such as himself might know with equal certainty 'the number of crimes to be committed during the [coming] year, the number of unfortunates who will commit suicide, the number of fires that will occur, the number of persons who will be carried from the streets to the hospital, and from the hospital to their final rest?'[43] The idea that numbers could underpin all activity, uniting past, present and future, was indeed sublime. It is reminiscent of the intricate calculations behind the Pyramids, and many similar quantifications of the eternal.

Among the Europeans in Australia, statistics had always mattered. The goodness and badness of the convicts had been totted up year by year – numbers reformed, numbers reoffending, numbers married, numbers cohabiting. Potential immigrants looking for government assistance had been quantified before being added to the population mix, male and female, young and old, labourer and artisan, Protestant and Catholic. Churches had been subsidised by numerical proportions. When Jevons was here, complaints about Chinese goldmining were stated in terms of numbers, especially population ratios. In Victoria, for twenty-five years (1853–78), the process of gathering such data had been raised to a high pitch of excellence and ingenuity by William Henry Archer, for most of that period registrar-general.[44] All the colonies, more or less, were statistical compositions.

In Australia everything seemed to hang on the way population grew, moved about and settled. (In Britain the numbers dying in city slums seemed to matter more.)[45] When democratic voting became the rule governments had to recalculate often, shifting electoral boundaries to keep up. There were two ways for a people's voice to be heard. There was tumult and revolution, and there was counting votes. The colonies of Australasia were world leaders in democratic method, and democracy is founded on mathematics.

In Tasmania the counting of votes in parliamentary elections as a precise guide to the will of the people was a subject taken up by Andrew Inglis Clark, partly as an intellectual challenge. Clark's scheme for preferential voting, called the Hare-Clark system (still used for some Australian elections) and later refined by Catherine Helen Spence, was designed partly to register as many preferences as possible. It was another way of making sure that small places, with their particular opinions, would not be blotted out by big ones – the central conundrum of the Federation project. Like Thoreau's night storm, democratic opinion would be 'self-registering'.

Since the start of the Industrial Revolution human populations had grown faster than ever before. In Britain statistical science was advancing quickly. Wrestling with numbers was a major challenge for government and public order. It was also the basis of a new kind of knowledge, and a nation's numbers were all the more interesting as they got bigger. Divided and subdivided over and over, big numbers kept their statistical significance, and with numerous groupings it was easier to think about small statistical shifts as a guide to the future. Aggregates, percentages and subdivisions were the up-to-date equivalent of entrails and tea-leaves. Statistical averages, especially, were treated as part of the basic character of every nation, every town and every quantifiable part of humanity.[46]

IV

And there is more. In gambling, individual need or whim could be fed into complicated mathematical equations, which again were all the more intriguing as numbers grew. In these colonies gamblers loved horseracing. Traditionally, bets had been taken on the track by bookmakers who set up stalls and dealt face to face with everyone. The business then started to be monopolised by a few men who knew how odds worked when totals were enormous. 'Leviathan' Jones in Sydney and JJ ('Double J') Miller in Melbourne regularly put together 'fifty-thousand pound books', and their popularity meant they could offer odds of 200 to 1.[47] In 1879 the totalisator machine, a mathematical calculator, appeared on racetracks, first in Adelaide. It made both the odds and the size of winnings depend altogether on the numbers betting. The South Australian government hoped that the totalisator would destroy the business of bookmaking and stop betting on credit. On the other hand, it also threatened to change a game of skill into a game of chance, making betting a pastime for everyone. The latter was what happened. Women, including some who knew nothing about the track, were drawn to bet, struggling and squabbling in hordes at the betting windows. 'The men gather round and watch the mêlée with an amused grin.'[48] The totalisator was banned in Victoria and New South Wales.

Sports of all kinds drew unprecedented numbers, and sport nearly always meant some sort of mathematics. '[W]e carry our worship of muscle', said an anonymous writer, 'to an extravagant and ridiculous extent'.[49] A few sportsmen were turned into national heroes. But if their muscle was worshipped so were their brains. Sportsmen were expected to be 'rational' and 'scientific', and so were spectators, in assessing skill and weighing chance. Scoring was now set out in the newspapers as an unfolding series of ratios, a story in figures. The pages had always been dotted with commercial news and predictions. Now they were filled with sporting detail, including columns of tabulated results. Great expanses were given up to names and numbers.

The result was a new kind of sports journalist, a man like

William Stanley Jevons, who could tell readers how tiny events affected results. Each writer trained himself to be exciting. In cricket, the older kind of newspaper reports had featured run-by-run detail, with not much about the accumulating strategy and drama of each match, but in December 1881 Donald Macdonald of the Melbourne *Argus* pioneered a different style of writing with his report of a game between Victoria and New South Wales. It was packed narrative, with fragments coming staccato like in a telegram:

> A brace to A. Bannerman for a neat cut in the slips off Allen. Palmer then bowled a fast one to the elder Bannerman, which went from the bat to his pad and thence to the wicket – 3-25-75 – … Both the colts were batting well, and the scoring was more rapid than at any other time during the day. Another single to Davis, for a beautiful off-hit along the carpet.

And so on. Is it surprising that some boys kept to their reading lessons so they could read about sport (so the school inspectors said) or to their mathematics so they could do the necessary calculations? Macdonald had developed his style at Corowa, on the River Murray, where he had worked on the *Free Press*, reporting matches – at a slower pace – among neighbouring towns.[50] Writing like this brought the game home. You could imagine yourself there. You shared the excitement, but also the cleverness of the skilled observer. Everyone used their brains.

Traditionally, rugby fields were often invaded from the sidelines, even as late as the 1870s. Gordon Inglis, a sportswriter of the next generation, remembered the chaos. 'Many a try was scored by dodging through spectators, who … did not hesitate to "open the ranks" or "close" them according to their sympathies.' Now, in the last years of the nineteenth century (like the chaotic annual yarding of cattle described in chapter 2), that was unacceptable. In goal kicking, what was the point of the best men developing a wonderful accuracy – the ball, once driven from the point of the toe, was now taken on the instep – when they could be thrown off balance by milling crowds? That long moment before the posts, that studied focus by the man alone, summed up the new attitude to sport.

The training of sportsmen became an occupation in its own right. Gordon Inglis remembered his own boxing lessons at Sydney Grammar School, from 'Sergeant' Morris. 'Twice a week he came to the school and his disciples gathered round him in the "gym".' Morris lectured them on anticipating the opponent's attack. Inglis mocked Morris's plebeian pronunciation – the 'sergeant' jumbled his 'h's – but he had nothing but respect for his theories of probability. 'We learned', he said, 'to appreciate that it was "the quickness of the heye that deceives the 'and"'.[51]

The nerves and muscles of children were central to the whole effort. District athletic competitions started in the late 1890s, partly modelled on the cricket matches played between towns such as those Macdonald had reported on from Corowa. In New South Wales, children took the train, for instance, between Armidale, Tamworth, Maitland and Newcastle, in the north, to run and jump against each other, sometimes drawing crowds of 20,000. According to the school inspector at Armidale, thanks to the resulting 'healthy rivalry', physical training had wonderfully improved. Among the locals, schools were popular as never before.[52]

Much depended on trains running from place to place. By this time railways linked up all areas of substantial settlement, opening the way for meetings and competitions. Where there were no trains it was hard to do much at all. Around Raymond Terrace, a small pocket of settlement to the north of Newcastle, interschool competitions failed because of 'insuperable difficulties in the way of locomotion' – that is, reliance on 'bullock drays and effete spring carts'.[53]

The systematic teaching of swimming started in the 1870s. Within twenty years the movement was far advanced, especially in

New South Wales (where school clubs totalled 10,000 members), although Victoria was not far behind. One of the pioneers was Harriet Elphinstone Dick, an Englishwoman who gave lessons at St Kilda Sea Baths, in Melbourne, besides managing a women's gymnasium. Miss Dick was a champion. In 1876 a large crowd, male and female, came to see her swim against several men in a 2-mile (3-kilometre) race. In the interests of fairness, 'each competitor had to wear a dress similar to that donned by Miss Dick', a costume designed for both modesty and speed. Swimming dress left an unusual amount of flesh uncovered or inadequately disguised, and men and women bathed together only under the strictest regulations. At the private saltwater baths, or 'Natatorium', in Pitt Street, Sydney, mixed bathing was allowed only for members of what was called the Dual Club, which made it possible for men to instruct their wives and children in 'the natatory art'.[54]

Not just the brain but the whole body was a machine, to be primed for fire brigade efficiency. In the schools, at least in theory, every item of juvenile behaviour could be pinned down by 'drill'. The brain's connection with other parts of the anatomy was thereby seriously tightened up. '[I]t is as necessary', a South Australian inspector told his teachers, 'to train the eye to see, the ear to hear, and the hands to execute what the mind conceives and wills, as it is to appeal to the reason or the imagination'. Military drill was taught to boys, making them more orderly in school hours and fitting them for future wars, but also giving them self-awareness in managing their bodies. The girls had gentler exercises, including the use of 'wands' and dumbbells. In the best schools everyone was subject to a rat-a-tat of orders as they moved about the classroom: 'Set methods should be practised in every school, for entering and leaving the room, for taking and leaving the seats, for passing and collecting the material issued during the lessons, for taking positions for writing, &c; and all should be done quickly, quietly, and without flurry'.[55]

Drill, drill, drill. In learning to speak well, said one inspector, we need 'mouth drill' – 'dumb-bell exercises [as it were] for the mouth'. Sewing lessons called for 'thimble drill, needle drill, [and] knitting-pin drill'. This was another way of coping with growing numbers, and with the sheer size of schools, as more and more children were pushed through the system. The old method of teaching sewing involved the teacher sitting down beside each pupil, guiding her stitch by stitch. With drill, as with the mustering of cattle, you could manage large numbers with minimum effort, instructing entire classes all at once.[56]

No sport changed as much as tennis, and in no sport was it easier to think of the brain as the master spring to arms, hands and legs. Tennis (lawn tennis, rather than real, or royal, tennis) was originally played on lawns in large gardens, like croquet. It had been a family game, and ladies set the pace. The inventor of lawn tennis was Major Walter Wingfield, a cavalry officer in England, who drew on the rules of various existing games and in 1875 produced for sale a patented kit, including racquets, net, balls and so on. Sales immediately took off. The educated classes wanted precisely this mixture of discipline and fun. The ladies of the royal family, the inventor boasted, played his tennis, and in Melbourne by the end of the 1880s leading girls' schools competed for 'best four'.[57] But men took up the game too. Public competitions started and a jargon was laid down – 'serving', 'poaching', 'lobbing', 'the rally', 'the volley', 'the smash' – all of it taught to the masses by sports journalists, coaches and miscellaneous experts.

In fact, men threw themselves into tennis. Frequently, everything came down to the man alone, to 'a cool head and steady hand', and skilled men playing singles were said to represent the game at its best. The change from Wingfield's original idea was complete within twenty years. What had once been a ladies' game now (to the male mind, including the minds of sportswriters) only proved how feeble women were. The typical female player rushed at the ball, so the sportswriters said. She was weak and indecisive. In mixed doubles she did best to keep out of the way.[58]

All sports were now more tightly organised – and at every level, from the lofty intricacies of international competition down to bodily contact on the field. Intercolonial tennis matches started in 1885, with New South Wales playing Victoria, and there were soon established groups in several colonies. Intercolonial and international competitions followed. A Lawn Tennis Association of Australasia, including the states of the Federation and New Zealand, was formed in 1903, followed by the Australasian Championship. In 1905 an Australasian team was entered in the new Davis Cup competition (the International Lawn Tennis Challenge).[59]

Within the much smaller space of the field itself every player – brain and body – was trained to share in thrilling combinations of ritual and adventure, like firemen training for crisis. A happy temper mattered. One sportswriter listed a catalogue of ludicrous comments heard on the court when shots went wrong. '[S]ome say, "Oh, dash it all!", or make a peculiar noise … something like "chick"', or, 'I didn't think that was coming over', 'There's too much sun', 'The wind put me off'. Some players – so unladylike had the game become – broke their racquets in exasperation.[60] In tennis, more than in most sports, using your brain to good effect could turn on the fraction of a movement.

V

Brains were well fed in the Australian colonies – with 'profuse liberality', according to William Wilkins, referring specifically to the brains of children. Wilkins had spent thirty years in charge of government schools in New South Wales. Just as governments underwrote water supply for everyone, so they poured money into schools for everyone. From colony to colony, more public money was used on education during the late 1870s and early 1880s, according to Wilkins, than anywhere else in the world. (In fact, other peoples were doing the same. The Germans especially used schools for nation building.) The amount doubled in that time, and throughout the continent numbers of schools and average attendance went up by roughly half, in an effort to make elementary schooling universal.[61]

Among other things, this great movement created a generation of young men and women who could not help but know that they were better educated than their parents (and their parents had felt the same in their time), and whose ideas about self-improvement, about breaking free from what they saw as the archaic rigmarole of previous ages, had real punch.

The colonies housed their own obscure geniuses. Henry Sutton lived all his life in Ballarat, where he made musical instruments. Within two years of Alexander Graham Bell's invention of the telephone, in Boston in 1876, Sutton had worked out twenty variations on Bell's model (using Bell's description in the *Scientific American*) and was trying to link his Ballarat warehouse by telephone with his 'music emporium' in Melbourne. Almost at the same time as Thomas Edison, Sutton invented a carbon filament lamp. In 1885, excited by rapid advances in photography, he designed a piece of machinery with which to watch the Melbourne Cup from Ballarat. It all depended (as with the telephone to start with) on the telegraph wire, which Sutton thought might carry enough data for a proper picture. More theoretically, the challenge, as he put it, was 'to take an optical image, seen as a *surface*, translate it into a *line* of consecutive varying electrical currents, and by means of these produce an effect as a *surface*, having the characteristics of the original image'. This was his 'telephane', an early, but unsuccessful, forerunner of television. His idea was all the more remarkable because photographers in Europe were only just starting to grapple with the question as to whether the imaging of movement was best understood in terms of liquid flow or staged succession. We do not know Sutton's answer.[62]

Sutton's ingenuity was not much used, even in Victoria. When it came to inventions of this kind colonists preferred to look overseas. They asked for international credentials. Maybe Ruth Bond, who had her own commercial laundry at Kent Town, on the edge of Adelaide, had the same problem with her own invention, a laundry iron gas-heated and fitted with a tap for controlling the flow and therefore the temperature.[63] But some antipodean needs were distinctive. In the bush, where men and women depended on themselves and neighbours, several new inventions every year, derived somehow from life on the land, received an official patent in one or other of the colonial capitals.[64] Many others, just as useful, were never patented.

Mina Rawson, who had a succession of homes in central and north Queensland, was a famous inventor. To start with, she had been one of a group of women swapping cooking recipes by mail. 'Everyone who discovered or invented a new dish or cake at once made it known to the others; and in this way each was benefited by the cleverness of the whole number.' This was the principle she always used. The distribution of ideas was a democratisation of knowledge. Mrs Rawson took flight with her *Queensland Cookery and Poultry Book* (1878), which was used across the continent. She liked publicising equipment useful to bush housekeepers. Some she thought up herself. Her bush oven (an oil drum, bricks and 'the bushman's cement of ant-bed and sand') was superior to the standard type, or so she said. She also admired an invention she had seen for keeping food warm. It looked like a tin billy, but it had several compartments, including one shaped to hold a red-hot iron. Thus armed, a woman could carry her husband's dinner to him while he worked, and it was still warm when she got there.[65]

In some places, there was a determined backwardness. But many men and women knew that specialised skills could help life on the land, could help them to understand the country and what it might do for them. They complained when their children came home from school without being able to help them as they had hoped, 'in such matters as areas of land, length of fencing, contents of tanks, quantities of farm produce, &c'.[66] The *Australian Town and Country Journal*, a leading Sydney weekly, filled several columns of each issue with readers' questions on a great miscellany of local topics:

> I have a selection on a lessee's run; there is a dog leg fence on my land. I gave him notice to remove it nine months ago, he has not done so. How am I to act?
>
> W bets T that the sun is seen in the morning in Tambaroora before it is seen in Sydney. Who wins?
>
> Can I obtain in Sydney Judson's gold paint?

The *Town and Country Journal* offered answers on its own inscrutable authority.[67]

In more radical papers, where argument mattered as much as information and where everyone was an expert, editors teased, flattered and abused their correspondents.[68] The Sydney *Bulletin* threw out column on column of sharp irony and hard-hitting, half-hidden jokes, initiating readers into its own brand of wit, most of it directed at life roundabout. Like sportswriters, the *Bulletin* men spread a feeling of shared brilliance. Apparently, we could all decipher the 'ideographic prophecy' written on the face of the continent – if we read the *Bulletin*. The sharing was part of the prophecy.

Everyone deciphered in their own way. Mary Gilmore remembered how the rural poor took advantage of the things of the bush, sometimes instructed by Aborigines and sometimes thinking for themselves, and then broadcast the results. They used the sinews of kangaroos and emus as thread for sewing leather, and the wings of scrub turkeys and brolgas as fans. And again, '[t]he wild hop made yeast; the "sarsaparilla" made naughty little boys good by clearing their "over-crowded" blood; the bottle brush soaked in soft water yielded syrup for sore throats and colds'. The seeds of the white cypress pine were chewed by bushmen to stave off hunger. The same seeds were also boiled and used to flavour treacle beer, and their steam, like eucalyptus vapour, was inhaled as a cure for common ailments.[69]

Mina Rawson, using Queensland experience, recommended the 'ground game' of the Aborigines, including white wood grubs: 'for my own part, I prefer the grubs parched before eating'. She also publicised the medicinal qualities of young eucalyptus leaves, and not just their vapour. They should be cut up 'very very fine', mixed with fat and boiled to make a poultice, which could be applied to local aches.[70] In Brisbane, Dr Joseph Bancroft gave bitterbark (*Alstonia constricta*) to his patients as a tonic. He tried pituri (*Duboisia hopwoodii*), a desert shrub containing nicotine, as a means of reviving the weak, and used extracts from corkwood (*Duboisia myoporoides*), its close relation, for eye problems.[71]

VI

In 1879 Sir Henry Parkes sketched two future nations for continental Australia. One was Queensland. The other was a federation composed of South Australia, Victoria and New South Wales. Parkes thus put his finger on a vital distinction. Australia featured two centres of power and promise, two types of ingenuity gathered in two geographical hotspots, two hubs of invention, North and South, central and south-east Queensland on the one hand, and the Riverina, Melbourne and Sydney on the other.

Trade unionism, with all its ingenious organisation, registered the distinction. Striking shearers in Queensland thought of men brought by employers from the South as 'foreigners'. The southerners, more sedentary and more in touch with towns, tended to think of Queenslanders as brutal and uncouth – as a people 'given over to native rum drinking and nigger-shooting'.[72] Queensland had its own ideographic prophecy. In Queensland, Patrick Robertson Gordon applied himself to the problems associated with livestock and Mina Rawson, Joseph Bancroft and others explored indigenous nature and other problems of raw pioneering. In the South, on the other hand, brains worked in more outward-looking ways. In the South, ingenuity was more in touch with other parts of the world. It was more 'modern', even more rarefied, in the way it asserted itself from above. In the South, imported ideas made a deeper mark. Money was more plentiful, people more tightly packed and talk more complex than in Queensland. Skills were more varied. The city shaped the bush rather than the other way around.

In Brisbane, Frederick Manson Bailey, the leading natural historian, worked on the usefulness of native plants. In Melbourne, his equivalent, Baron Ferdinand von Mueller (famous throughout the colonies and in Europe) was a theorist, mainly interested in taxonomy – collecting, sorting and naming – as a contribution to abstract, worldwide knowledge. In his writing Bailey used English, so as to be understood on the spot, but Mueller, the Melburnian, with a European audience in mind, tended to Latin. Queensland's royal society focussed on plants, the acclimatisation of crops and so on. Equivalent bodies in the South were interested in such matters too – Mueller was a keen acclimatiser – but they were at least as likely to talk about astronomy and physics.[73]

Southern ingenuity imposed itself on the landscape rather than growing out of it. There was a determination to change the country. In the Riverina and northern Victoria a parcel of invention, in land title, control of water, pasture improvement, and the management and breeding of livestock, was brought to bear on problems of climate and soil. The southerners were also good with machinery. Near Corowa, on the Murray, William Creed, a surveyor, invented a wire strainer, a godsend for men who made and fixed fences. With it, you could 'tighten a slack wire without having to join a piece', which made added pieces of wire unnecessary. At Temora, further north in New South Wales, John Dacey, a blacksmith (later a member of parliament and town-planning enthusiast), invented a machine for pulling out stumps and dragging down dead trees. He called it the 'Forest Devil'.[74] South of the Murray, between Echuca and Bendigo, Hugh Mackay, with his father and brother, put together the prototype of the 'Sunshine Harvester', a machine which could strip, thresh and winnow grain all at once. It was to transform farming output here and overseas. At Shepparton, John Furphy, elder brother of Joseph, the writer, invented a grain stripper, a disc harrow, ploughshares and toothed rollers. He worked by keeping a careful eye on all the needs of farmers roundabout.

But it was John Furphy's mobile water tank – akin to the fire cart mentioned by Charles Bean – that made his name. A cylinder of sheet steel and cast iron holding 180 or 250 gallons (810 or 1125 litres) was laid on its side and balanced over a single pair of wheels, so that whether it was full or empty the distribution of weight matched the strength and habits of the horse in front. It was designed for carrying water to stock, but it was also used to fight bushfires. It was to be essential during the Great War in slaking the thirst of soldiers.[75]

The Furphy brothers, Joseph and John, sum up the cleverness of the Riverina, its high learning and mechanical ingenuity. Unhappily, the fragility of the riverine landscape was such that the resulting impact, especially in the areas of irrigation and engineering, did enormous environmental damage in years to come, destroying wetlands and bringing fatal levels of salinity to the soil. To start with, however, it conjured a gilded vision, the final answer to the continent's intractability and the challenge set by water.

Until the 1860s there was still land in the South with river frontage, offering graziers water at their doorstep, though some had been moving the water about for many years, by digging canals and building small dams. More recently expansion meant looking to the back country, where digging and damming were essential. What was 'front' and what was 'back' depended on the reliability of watercourses. Pushing out back – taking up 'backblocks' – called for a particular kind of brainwork.[76] Riverina graziers had been the first with large-scale fencing, partly so as to manage the way their livestock found water. Drought in 1875, when sheep were driven in all directions in an effort to stop them dying of thirst, shocked many into thinking in more fundamental ways about that question.

Could the answer be a machine newly invented by John Wilding and Co., agricultural engineers in Melbourne? Three of Wilding's 'Patent Champion Excavators', combining plough and scoop, appeared near Deniliquin in April 1875, escorted by 'a number of stout hearty fellows, of the real navvy stamp, and a small mob of good serviceable draught horses' – though with these machines bullocks were as good as horses. Some hoped that inventions so splendid would conjure water out of nothing, and when the skies stayed blue and the dams empty purchasers wondered if the whole effort had been useless. '[I]t is hard, indeed, that after spending so much money in preparing to meet bad times, the rain will not come.'[77]

Some took a longer, broader, wiser view. Samuel McCaughey, from the north of Ireland, had started buying pastoral properties in the Riverina in 1860. His experiments with sheep breeding had made a dramatic difference to the yield per head. He used careful subdivision and fencing, and his need for new country which was necessarily without river frontage led him to think about the redirection and conservation of water. In judging country, McCaughey was a genius. His mind moved by shortcuts. It jumped stages of calculation which made others pause and struggle, and still he came to true conclusions, pulling together a host of problems in a moment. His shearing shed on Dunlop Station, on the Darling, was the first to use the mechanical shears invented by Frederick Yorke Wolseley, another grazier, which transformed speed, efficiency and cheapness in shearing. But it was water that intrigued McCaughey. He knew blacksmithing (he had trained himself), and at his head station at Coonong on the Murrumbidgee he designed heavy-duty scoops for digging drains and dams. He used steam engines to pump from the river, and he built a network of concrete channels and weirs for watering pasture.[78]

The largest efforts came from overwhelming need and, as Alfred Deakin knew, relied on government initiative. In Western Australia in 1887–88, alluvial gold had been found at Southern Cross, 370 kilometres east of Perth, leading in 1892 to richer finds at Coolgardie and, richest of all and most remote, at Kalgoorlie in 1893. Soon there were several thousand people in and around Coolgardie alone, roughly half the population of Perth, most of them immigrants from the east. All of a sudden, the rest of the world knew about Western Australia. It already had its North and South, the Kimberley in contrast with the older settled parts. Now, vastly enriched, it was divided west and east, between the first settlements and the goldfields, and the goldfields were where the new money came from.

The government in Perth, already confronted with separatist feeling in the Kimberley, was ready to spend large sums to make sure of a united people, an incipient nation. 'We will never have real prosperity in this country [Western Australia]', the premier Sir John Forrest said, 'until we are of more importance as a producing country'. A harbour was built at Fremantle to handle all the new traffic, plus a railway to the goldfields. But the miners had no water. Their rainfall was sparse and unpredictable, and there were no rivers or subterranean supplies. The smallest shower was met with delirious joy. When Forrest visited in December 1895 he found, he said, 'a numerous population of hard-working men, as dirty as ever they could be. No water to wash in – scarcely enough to drink'. Wandering prospectors died of thirst. Public health was at serious risk. Mining itself was held up because the men had to have water to crush the quartz.[79]

The only fresh water available was in the streams of the Darling Range, near Perth, and in an extraordinary leap of faith – dazzling proof of 'national' energy – during 1894–96, the government's engineer-in-chief made plans for the damming of the Helena and for a steel pipeline capable of carrying 5 million gallons (22.5 million litres) a distance of 600 kilometres eastwards per day. In his ability to see and solve large problems, Charles Yelverton O'Connor was an engineering Samuel McCaughey. For West Australians the pipeline was 'a great national work'. It was the most ambitious engineering project so far attempted in the Antipodes. The distance covered and the problems solved one by one, including the need to pump the water uphill all the way, gave it worldwide uniqueness.[80]

VII

As Sir John Forrest said, Western Australia was so completely cut off from the eastern colonies that it was really like an island in the Indian Ocean. It was as remote from the eastern colonies as New Zealand was in the other direction. And at the same time, it was so big that 'there is room for an empire'.[81] If the pipeline was 'a great national work', how difficult was it to go a step further and imagine, as a great national work on another level, the federation of the continent and outlying islands?

Unitary and vast, the idea, like most ideas of its kind, flourished best in Melbourne. Victoria had been called an intellectual powerhouse. Fundamental to its power was the notion of the 'Australian group', whatever that might be exactly, as one enterprise – one great knowledge-driven project – and there was unusual inclination to comprehend and use great spaces. Charles Henry Pearson was mainly a geographer. His earliest book, *Historical Maps of England* (1869), and his last and best, *National Life and Character* (1893), both dealt with human life in spatial terms. He talked about space – living space, working space, fighting space – as one of the ingredients of power. His turn of thought shaped the minds of some of the best of Melbourne's younger men.

Among Pearson's students was Alfred Deakin. In 1884, as a young parliamentarian, Deakin's efforts in rethinking the management of water involved his chairing a royal commission on Victoria's water supply. He toured California looking at methods there, and taking a historical perspective, as Pearson did, he read about irrigation under the pharaohs and in ancient China, Japan, Mesopotamia, India and Ceylon (now Sri Lanka). He inquired about Spain and British India. In 1887 he visited Egypt and Italy. He made himself an irrigation expert, gathering facts about climate and topography, weaving them through his historical understanding.

To start with, Deakin was mainly interested in Victoria. But, ever the Melburnian, his thinking was easily extended. He could not help extending it, drawn as always towards 'the endless spheres of physical nature' and its productive powers. A particularly remarkable piece of his writing called 'Irrigation in Australia', published in 1892, was unprecedented in pointing out a way for agile minds to imagine the continent as a single landscape and a single source of wealth. Deakin's thoughts ranged without prejudice from colony to colony, from the 'magnificent streams' in the northern parts of Western Australia to the mud springs of southern Queensland, from the flooding of the Clarence River in northern New South Wales to the subterranean moisture which fed South Australia's lucerne crops, from the watering of Chinese market gardens near Melbourne to the vineyards and orchard plots of the irrigated Riverina.[82]

To think such thoughts was one thing. To put them down and have them read and understood by a sufficiently large number was another thing altogether. It was the democratisation of knowledge that did this, plus the worship of system 2. It was literacy, and not just Alfred Deakin's literacy, but the world of literacy in which his mind moved. It was a view easy for later generations, but at this point wonderfully new. It made the larger nation possible.

6

Adding North to South

I

There was a particularly savage war fought among English-speaking peoples during the lifetimes of most of the men and women who populate these pages. In the American Civil War (1861–65), thanks to newly invented repeating rifles and uncompromising hatred, more than a million died. The fighting was about Black slavery, and in the end about four million slaves were freed. But the hatred had other causes too. There was the question of states' rights. The southern states of America believed (most of the time) that the inhabitants of each state should be able to govern themselves without Washington getting in the way. But more important still was the question of race, a racial difference quite apart from Black and White.

In the American Civil War the White people on either side looked much the same. But they did not feel the same. Southerners especially convinced each other that they were of different and better blood than the Yankees. That made killing easier.

The two 'races', they said in the South, were 'entirely separated by climate, by morals, [and] by religion'. A people bred in 'the cold, forbidding crags of the North' had to be different from a people bred on the 'sunny soil of the South'. To the southern mind, Yankees were venal money makers. They themselves were men of 'dignified greatness and natural command', hereditary slave masters, lords of many acres. And yet the Yankees wanted to control them. 'Any nation', they said, 'that defers thus wholly to another is soon emasculated'. Hence the war, which was to keep a masculine people, the nation of the South, free of domination by another.[1]

It was all wind. But it was a type of wind that erupted on this side of the Pacific too. In the American South they dreamt of a 'sisterhood of states' centred on the Mississippi.[2] In Australia, not long after, things of the same sort were said about climate and geography, and about the Murray-Darling as the life stream of one people. We had one continent, but there were real doubts as to whether a single surrounding coastline of such vast length could hold together a single nation-state – better, surely, a fabric of rivers?

Some divisions stood out. An east–west desert barrier several times bigger than the Tasman Sea cut off Western Australia from the main centres of power and population in the east. Even more risky was the distinction between North and South. As in North America, latitude mattered. It meant dissimilarity of temperature, weather and vegetation. It meant different *climates*. 'Climate' was a powerful word, as JSC Elkington, Tasmania's chief health officer, remarked, around which was woven 'a tissue of incorrect inferences, of superstitions, and of prejudices'. From a climatic point of view, Queensland, especially its north, matched the remaining bulk of the continent even less than New Zealand did.[3] With the American Civil War still fresh in living memory, it must have been hard not to wonder whether the latitude question might one day cause bloodshed even within the 'unbroken circle' of Australian skies.

A hot climate, if it did not destroy White men, made them masterful. With this idea, in the 1890s antipodean fiction writers explored the North of Australia as keenly as they did the Centre. In Europe, this was the age of Rudyard Kipling, who had been born in India of a governing race. Those governed were, as Kipling put it, 'new-caught sullen peoples, / Half devil and half child'.[4] It was the age of Joseph Conrad, whose time in the East Indies fed his storytelling, fleshing out for instance that ineffable master of men Lord Jim.

Among antipodean colonists, Ernest Favenc wrote about both the Centre and the North, both regions he knew well. Favenc's usual publisher was the *Bulletin*, and from 1893 he was joined in its pages by his friend Louis Becke, who had worked in the Pacific Islands labour trade. They both told short stories, and Becke was even more popular than Favenc, with titles such as *By Reef and Palm*, *His Native Wife* (his own wife was an islander) and *Wild Life in the Southern Seas*. Stories about the North echoed the mood of Charles Henry Pearson's famous work of prophecy, *National Life and Character*, published around the same time. All were heavy with a sense of fate coming from the North. Favenc liked the image of weathered corpses lying under hard skies. His dead were sometimes storytellers themselves, thanks to journals found in ragged, fading pockets.[5]

The future had to be secured against erratic alien races, types crowding at the continent's edge. Stories about the Centre spoke of a kind of spiritual frontier and of a fearful edge of being. In stories about the North, brutality came in less fantastic forms. The problems there were not inward ones. They came from beyond, in a siege on civilisation itself.

In the South, including the biggest Australian cities, the people who had reached the continent since 1788 were nearly all from Europe. According to the 1901 census, there were just over three million people of non-Aboriginal descent living in New South Wales, Victoria, South Australia and Tasmania. Many of them were native-born, but with family ties going back to Britain and Ireland. Some were from the European mainland, especially Germany. The only significant minority were about 17,000 Chinese, most of whom had come to dig for gold, though many had since taken up other occupations, such as hawking, market gardening, cabinet-making and shopkeeping. There were also some much smaller groups, including Lebanese, who were mainly Christian and who worked as hawkers and shopkeepers; Muslim cameleers, who managed cross-country transportation from Marree, Broken Hill and Alice Springs; and Sikh banana growers on the coast north of Sydney. Others were very few indeed.[6]

The North was different. In Queensland, where the settler population as a whole numbered about half a million, there was a wonderful variety of face and form. Head for head, there were three times as many Chinese as there were in the South, and four times as many people from other parts of Asia (mainly Japan, Malaya and the East Indies). There were also thousands of men from the Pacific, most of them indentured labourers.[7] Near the New South Wales border, around Brisbane, Ipswich and Toowoomba, the people were much like those of other colonies. But in central Queensland the sugar plantations were manned with Pacific Islanders, and further north again, especially along the Cape York coast, nothing was mainstream. The whole northern part of the continent, including the Northern Territory and the Kimberley in Western Australia, was a human medley in amazing contrast with the South. In these regions, the continental shoreline seemed at times to merge in a lawless blur with nearby islands. Along much of the coast, pearl shell and trepang (sea cucumbers or bêche-de-mer), destined for China, drew divers and investors from the western Pacific, Japan and Ceylon. Here and there, a quarter or more of the people were Asian-born. In southern eyes, this was 'the piebald north'.[8]

The people of the North knew they were different. In the low latitudes of Western Australia they felt a common interest with Queensland. It was like the Confederation against the Yankees. At Roebourne, a gold, copper and tin town halfway between Perth and the Kimberley, the *Nor'-West Times* demanded a division of the continent with 'a United North' free of the despotism of the South. Certainly, said Sir Samuel Griffith, Queensland premier, the dividing line, if there must be one, would create two great nations, north and south, a division of latitude and climate.[9]

For CH Pearson the difference between North and South was of fundamental importance. Most people in Melbourne and Sydney assumed that with their numbers and wealth they would always overawe the North. They would take the lead just as the Yankees had done in the United States. But in Pearson's pages it was the North which held the key to the continental future. White men everywhere must wake up to the threat of the Tropics. Indeed, in tropical latitudes a band of alien colour encircled the world. The races living and multiplying in those parts would enrich and arm themselves in coming years, throwing the White man onto the defensive. Think of southern Africa, where Whites were already on guard. The same would happen here: '[t]ransform the Northern half of our continent into a Natal with thirteen out of fourteen belonging to an inferior race, and the Southern half will speedily approximate to the condition of a Cape Colony, where the whites are indeed a masterful minority, but still only as one in four'.[10] Maps, if you read them properly, were prophecies. Pearson read them in large, precise and dramatic terms. Beyond our far headlands and islands the enemy was limitless, just as in Natal.

In the North of the continent, admittedly, women from Asia were scarce, and without women increase was slow and permanence might seem unlikely. But even while Pearson was writing, around Cairns, where nearly a fifth of the people were Chinese, family life was starting to emerge. There had been little sign of it in the 1891 census, but the count ten years later showed, among hundreds of Chinese men, fifteen women and seventy children.[11] By Pearson's logic, families might soon, and suddenly, be found in their thousands. Where would the 'masterful minority' be then?

Northerners had a different view to the horizon. Looking outwards, Queenslanders glimpsed in the mind's eye the islands of the East Indies and, to their east, the ocean. On the other side of the continent, West Australians imagined the same islands northwards and another ocean to their west. Since the 1820s, the west coast settlements had been bound to Cape Town, Calcutta (Kolkata) and Singapore. All were English-speaking ports interlinked by trade and traffic, a network as important from the Perth point of view as the Adelaide–Melbourne–Sydney run. The government in Perth encouraged contact especially with Singapore, and it subsidised a regular steamship service from 1882. Since 1869 the end of convict transportation to Western Australia had created a need for imported workmen, especially among graziers in its North. Several hundred Chinese were brought in each year as bonded labourers, and the northern ones often drifted southward when their time was up – just the kind of movement Pearson was afraid of. By the end of the 1890s nearly half of all West Australian Chinese lived in or near Perth. Here too women were extremely scarce. But a few Chinese men married Europeans.[12]

Elsewhere in the North, as in the South, most Chinese came looking for gold. There was a goldfield at Pine Creek, in the Northern Territory, worked and managed largely by Chinese, and Chinese merchants were central to life nearby in Darwin. In Queensland the Chinese presence went back to the discovery of gold along the Palmer, Mitchell and Gilbert rivers (there were 7000 Chinese on the Palmer in 1875). And at Charters Towers, with all its rhetoric and politicking, the loudest voices declared anathema on the Chinese. Banned by Queensland law from new goldfields, they did well keeping shops and growing bananas. '[I]n the theatre of agriculture', said the *Cairns Post*, 'the Chinese have the front seat while the whites sit behind them and admire their pigtails'.[13]

Until 1890, Western Australia was a Crown colony. Its government was accountable to London rather than to any electorate of its own. Everywhere else there had been democracy (manhood suffrage) since the 1850s, and under democratic pressure ministers did everything they could to keep the Chinese out. Strenuous efforts had been made in Victoria and New South Wales during the early goldmining years, on the grounds that the 'Celestials' were taking too much gold. Those laws had lapsed as the rush abated. Following the Queensland discoveries, old worries revived, although it was now working men in the cities who shouted loudest about the Chinese.

Among White people by the 1880s and '90s there was a keener sense of territory, of geographical encirclement, than there had been hitherto. As usual it was most keen among the young, and it was sharpened too by talk about the Chinese. Taking lower wages, they supposedly put White men out of work, just as they had taken White men's gold. The government statistician in New South Wales Timothy Augustine Coghlan (a disciple of William Stanley Jevons) argued that this was fiction. The cheap Chinaman was a myth. Indeed, he said, as market gardeners the Chinese made an important contribution to Australian diet. Three-quarters of the vegetables grown for sale throughout the continent came from Chinese gardens.[14]

'Is it not fact', said one man to another on this vexed subject, 'that almost everybody purchases vegetables from them?'

'Yes', was the grudging reply. 'I believe there are a lot of vegetables hawked round and sold.' Whoever bought from the Chinese were spineless fools. 'Personally, I have never bought anything from a Chinaman in my life, nor do I intend to.'[15]

The striking shearers in central Queensland in 1891 had the virtues of the Chinese forced on them when they ordered local hotel keepers to stop employing Chinese cooks. Suddenly the meals served to them were inedible. They also asked their union to buy up all the Chinese market gardens and lease them to unionists, 'working on cooperative principles'. But it was hard to find shearers keen to grow cabbages. Food was a delicate issue in the mingling of races. Ideas about cleanliness were culturally conditioned. Even liberal-minded Europeans objected to sitting at table with a people so strikingly different. And yet these various alien peoples were funds of useful information about eating. Mina Rawson, the Queensland inventor, liked the Kanakas' way of cooking fish heads – 'there are nice pickings in the head' – and she had taken, she said, 'a few lessons' in poultry and game from an Indian cook. She also recommended a type of gelatine found only in Chinese shops. 'Doubtless many ladies will know what I mean.'[16]

Indeed, Mrs Rawson lagged somewhat in envisaging a future Australasia, North and South, managed by a master race whose gorge revolted at Chinese gelatine. The priorities of the dinner table, of 'local geography' and of neighbourly negotiation, mattered more to people like her. However, from the late 1870s an apparent consensus at a higher level, fed by a self-conscious literacy and an eager aptitude for maps, echoed the shearers' approach to the Chinese. In November 1880 senior representatives of the governments of New South Wales, Victoria and South Australia met in Melbourne in the first of a series of intercolonial conferences designed to put such ideas into practice. Sir Henry Parkes, premier of New South Wales, led the discussion. They tackled questions of trade and railways, but Parkes also wanted some kind of intercolonial constitution, including a 'Federal Council' to legislate on matters of common interest. He urged, as a top priority, joint action on the immigration of other races.

Colonists, including leading politicians, rarely ventured beyond their own boundaries, and talking face to face like this suddenly sharpened ideas about the wider world and its impact on their own. As with the Australasian Association for the Advancement of Science eight years later, the experience of getting together in one spot, sitting down and comparing notes, raised imagination to a new level. Pushing this advantage, Parkes moved for a second session, in Sydney, in the new year. And, he said, they should bring in the outer circle – Tasmania, Queensland, Western Australia and New Zealand.[17]

These two meetings, in 1880 and 1881 in Melbourne and Sydney respectively, transformed notions of the future, including notions about race. Turning its collective attention to Western Australia (that 'small and remote colony'), the Sydney meeting was astonished to learn that the government in Perth was currently subsidising the immigration of Chinese labourers, and since Western Australia was still ruled directly from Britain a letter was sent to the minister in London demanding that the practice cease.[18] New Zealand mattered too, because New Zealanders were starting to think of themselves as a Pacific power. Besides, the current governor of New Zealand was also high commissioner for the western Pacific, with responsibility for policing the labour trade. The delegates in Sydney wanted to stop islanders killing Europeans. They agreed to ask London for an Australasian federal court to deal with such crimes.[19]

There was also talk of a federal union. Its imagined limits were uncertain, but there was a possibility of including New Zealand and surrounding seas, a scheme flagged by the slogan 'Federation and all the islands'. The delegates wanted a tighter kind of order throughout these spaces. They wanted a network of policing centred on the south-eastern mainland and stretching from the south-west Pacific to the edge of the Indian Ocean.[20]

Fundamental, once again, was North *versus* South. How were the original three, Victoria, New South Wales and South Australia, the heartland of the federal idea, to deal with the subtropical parts of the continent and with the warmer ocean waters? The three, it seemed, were to be the core of a multiform sub-empire, vast and, beyond a certain point, loosely knit. The details were so far vague, but the question was suddenly urgent during the next few years, when the French started to busy themselves in the New Hebrides and New Caledonia.

A Federal Council was set up, by a British act of parliament, as the first step towards the archipelagic vision. However, when it came to the point, not everyone marched in step. Victoria jarred with New South Wales. Even Parkes had second thoughts, and New South Wales never joined the Federal Council. Also, for many the scheme was all too thin and formal. It failed to register a sense of blood. Younger men, especially, just organising their thoughts and coming into power, wanted a more modern type of nation. Policing, courts and councils were beside the point. A generation beyond the American Civil War, they wanted cooperation of like with like, the brotherhood of youth, not the protocols of middle age. They wanted racial purity of the more obvious kind, and the bright symmetry of a single landmass. They did not want a mess of islands. Bred up with maps and with an up-to-date feel for geography, like Jules Michelet in France they wanted boundaries solid, obvious and eternal.

After the 1880–81 meetings all seven colonies passed laws restricting Chinese immigration. Some were harsher than others, but all of them limited the number arriving in any one ship. They imposed taxes at so much per head (£30 in Queensland and £10 everywhere else). With more meetings, each government became steadily more clearly aware of what the others were doing. Step by step, too, legal and bureaucratic niceties were pushed aside in favour of absolute rules about geography and race (a development which the Chinese themselves called 'barbarous'). Earlier laws had let in British subjects whatever their race and origin. By the late 1890s delicacy of this kind was abandoned. Laws passed in New South Wales, New Zealand, South Australia and Tasmania kept out members of every 'coloured race' living within a vast salt circle from the west coast of Africa to the furthest point of the Pacific. Only Aborigines and Maori were exempt.[21]

On the mainland, step by step the sense of urgency shifted, from the far-flung archipelago to the sacred shores of the continent itself, from half-imagined waters to a dry-land home.

II

Among the leaders of public opinion, or the most cogent and anxious of them, something had happened, worldwide, since the 1860s, when the White people of the American South had set their faces against the alien 'race' to their North. Here is another example from these later, larger horizoned days. In 1895 the German Kaiser, Wilhelm II, wrote to his cousin Nicholas II of Russia. That year Wilhelm turned thirty-six. Nicholas was nine years younger and newly crowned, and Wilhelm sent him a piece of political advice in the form of a picture sketched by himself to start with but finished by a professional hand. It showed several female figures, symbolising the peoples of Europe, summoned by the archangel Michael to a headland from which they looked down on the advancing power of heathen Asia. CH Pearson's book *National Life and Character* had penetrated even as far as the imperial palace at Potsdam, and Pearson was apparently Wilhelm's inspiration. He called his picture 'The Yellow Peril', and he advised Nicholas to wake up as he had done. The picture was his argument for 'the *united* resistance of *all* European powers' against the new terror from the east.[22]

The call for White and Christian states to join forces against Asiatic 'barbarism' was worldwide. In Europe the main danger seemed to be Japan. Japanese commercial and military strength had advanced with extraordinary speed since the Meiji Restoration, in 1868, and the sharp edge of Japanese modernisation was felt especially by the Russians as they tried to extend the eastern parts of their own empire into Manchuria and along the Pacific coast. Russia came to blows with Japan within ten years of the Kaiser's warning and was badly beaten – the first defeat of a European national force by an Asiatic one – at the naval Battle of Tsushima, in May 1905.

The mass of Russians, however, still worried more about the Jews who lived among them than about the Japanese. The wide horizons natural to modern emperors, and to assiduous readers such as Pearson, were compromised at the local level. Jews had been a vital part of European civilisation for centuries and were densely scattered among the Christian majority, and now it was Jews above all who suffered from Christian prejudice. There were pogroms – popular onslaughts on Jewish life and property – in Russia in 1881–82 and again in 1903–06, including the murder of thousands.

In Australasia racist feeling (except against Indigenous peoples) was much less brutal, in theory and in practice. Nevertheless, the Chinese were mistreated for global and local reasons combined. To those articulate few who had woken up they were the 'barbarian' power of Wilhelm II's imagination, and their presence rubbed up old anxieties about North and South. For Wilhelm, Europe was the imminent Armageddon, but some European Australians saw their own continent as the likely flashpoint between White and Yellow, 'the Precious Front Buckle', as one man put it (several years later), 'in the White Girdle of Power and Progress encircling the Globe'.[23] At the same time, like the Jews in Europe, the Chinese suffered more intimate suspicions. They were not only part of the global jigsaw of race. Like the Jews, they also belonged to daily life. They were the sly enemy within.

To some extent the Chinese were divided among themselves. In the eastern Australian colonies they came mainly from around Canton (Guangzhou), but labour-recruiting firms in Singapore drew on several of the south-eastern provinces of the Celestial Empire. That meant that in Western Australia dialects and loyalties varied.[24] But any such divisions were flimsy compared with the great divide, real and imagined, between White and Yellow.

The Chinese were deeply loyal to their families and home villages, and they usually came with no intention of staying. But a few made money and became local leaders among their own people, especially in Queensland and the Northern Territory. Their ancient ideas about social distinctions were laid aside, because Chinese of high rank stayed in China, and at the same time the immigrant Chinese worked together in such a way as to make the employer–employee distinction, the 'master and man' idea which meant so much to Europeans, fairly unimportant. They lived in stores, workshops and farmhouses almost as womanless families.[25]

Europeans liked fellowship and cooperation. But Chinese fellowship seemed strange, even vicious. So many celibate men sparked rumours of sodomy. Worse, the Chinese attachment to the past was exactly what many Europeans in Australia, especially the young, were teaching themselves to despise. The Chinese were poles apart from the Aborigines. But as with the Aborigines, European suspicion saw them as facsimiles of a dead way of life. They were not true individuals, not possessed of 'individuality' in the contemporary sense. They existed only in bulk. They were, apparently, a race 'in whom uncounted generations of serf-like toil have developed a capacity for unremitting labor, while killing out every spark of that higher nature which makes men capable of being true citizens of a free state'. Like the Aborigines, they lived, apparently, in endless unreflecting mimicry. As craftsmen, especially in the furniture trade, they were 'exact copyists'. They seemed inscrutable, but also totally predictable. They were like machinery. Their expressions, to European eyes, were vacant of whimsy and liberated thought.[26]

The gentlemen who met at the intercolonial conference in Sydney in 1881 spelt out the problem for the secretary of state in London. Their main aim, they said, was 'to preserve and perpetuate the British type in the various populations'. The trouble with the Chinese presence, they hastened to assure the minister, was 'not altogether one of prejudice of colour or race'. It was cultural – 'language, laws, religion, and habits of life'. Delegates took what they called 'a rational view' of the risk that lay in two such different peoples living together. They also drew attention to the vast population of China itself, 'whose geographical position makes the danger more imminent'.[27] It was their duty, they said, to stop the flood before it became too much for them, before it could wash away all that the Europeans here had achieved.

Confrontation with the Chinese went on at two levels. Keeping them out meant taking a view like Kaiser Wilhelm's, a global view.

But dealing with the Chinese already in these colonies seemed just as urgent. Face-to-face racism was full of contradictions. In Russia men and women of the mainstream people could look into Jewish faces every day, finding in them (if they liked) reflections of their own humanity. But closeness could also sharpen savagery. In the Russian pogroms of 1881–82 and 1903–06 some of the Jews' worst enemies were sometimes their own neighbours. A pogrom was launched against the Chinese in Brisbane in May 1888. No-one was seriously hurt and it was over in one night, but, as in Russia, it was fuelled by an idea that these half-and-half humans had only half-and-half rights.

Police and politicians fed this thinking. So did William Lane, who five years later was to lead the expedition which established 'New Australia' in Paraguay. In 1888 his *Boomerang*, a popular Brisbane weekly, included from his own hand twelve episodes of futurist fiction called *White or Yellow?*. His heroes were the people of Brisbane, angered by the very existence of these strangers among them and 'mad with excitement' at the chance of destroying their shops, houses and gardens, first in Brisbane, then Queensland, then, perhaps, Australasia-wide. The real riot started straight after Lane's story came to its bloody climax. It also came at the end of a parliamentary election campaign thick with anti-Chinese speeches. Although there was no loss of life, there was serious damage in north Brisbane and Fortitude Valley, just as in Lane's story. The leaders were boys and young men banging sticks and throwing stones, but well-dressed followers totalled (apparently) 1000 strong. For four hours city life was chaos, with rioters freely looting and destroying Chinese property, passing from shop to shop, shattering windows and terrifying the few within.[28]

In Germany an anti-Semitic slogan went, '*Kauft nicht von Juden!*' ('Don't buy from Jews!'). In Queensland, William Lane agreed about Jews but he was more concerned about the Chinese. He dwelt on their 'unrestrained sensuality'. It ought to be a flogging offence, he said, to send children to 'a Chinaman's shop'. Altogether, '[i]t is a crime to have dealings with such a race', and they should be shut out even from the ordinary commerce of life. This idea hit home hardest in Queensland and Western Australia. The first concern was mining, especially gold. In Queensland from 1877 there were laws for 'Asiatic and African aliens'. 'Aliens' meant non-British subjects, and Indians and Hong Kong Chinese, for instance, were exempt. Aliens, so defined, had to pay £3 a year instead of the normal ten shillings for the right to dig, and from 1878 the same 'coloured aliens' were barred from all new fields, unless they found them themselves. Rules of the same sort applied in Western Australia from the first discovery of gold, and there Chinese miners were almost non-existent.[29]

During the 1890s attention shifted to other kinds of work and to sharper discrimination, and the various colonies found their way to this point by different tracks. Nothing shows more clearly the difference between North and South. In Queensland racist language was uncompromising. Violence was easy and government action was haphazard. In Victoria everything was more civil, more complicated, more refined, more searching and more self-consciously consistent. Victorians were polished lawmakers. They wanted to wear the Chinese down by regulation rather than by riot.

Victoria was 'protectionist' and the other colonies were all more or less 'free trade'. At first, protectionism was just a question of the way tariffs were set on incoming goods. In Victoria a thoroughgoing tariff system, argued through on a regular basis by David Syme and his writers in *The Age*, encouraged Victorian manufactures. In a territory of limited size, it was said, local efforts had to be given every advantage. In that sense alone, Victorians were used to commercial discrimination and to the favouring of fellow citizens when it came to buying and selling, though how much good this really did for the colonial economy is debatable. But then new laws went further, protecting people as well as profits, and sometimes people above profits. During the summer of 1882–83 the Tailoresses' Union, backed up by *The Age*, succeeded in publicising the long hours and low pay of women in the clothing trade. A thoroughly organised strike led to an increase in wages, but the larger result was a detailed government inquiry focussing on conditions for women and children.[30]

There was already a type of 'rural code' throughout the colonies (chapter 2). Now there was set in place another kind of code, a social and moral code, a far-reaching framework of law centred mainly on cities and towns. The aim was to safeguard and improve what a later age was to call the 'human resources' of the country. During 1885–96 the Victorian parliament passed several Factories and Shops acts, which stopped the employment of children in factories besides imposing a strict regime of pay and conditions for men and women in most kinds of manufacturing – printers, bakers, seamstresses, ironworkers and so on. Employers had to maintain detailed records, they had to keep a careful eye on hygiene and safety, they had to limit hours of labour (ending each weeknight at seven and each Saturday night at ten), and they had to observe a minimum wage.[31]

Normally, the factory laws applied only where there were at least six employees (afterwards four). But where there were Chinese they applied without restriction. In 1896 differentiation went further, pinpointing furniture making. About a third of workmen in that trade were Chinese, specialising in less complicated articles, such as meat safes, kitchen tables and small chests of drawers, and located in one part of central Melbourne (Lonsdale, Little Lonsdale and Exhibition streets). They used nails and glue rather than dovetailing and morticing, and the quality of their work was suspect. In the words of a European, it was 'of the cheap-and-nasty order'.[32]

To start with, European and Chinese makers catered for different markets, but the 1890s depression hit Melbourne manufacturers extremely hard. All suffered, but the Chinese recovered first.

They were soon in a position to expand their share of the trade, and the Europeans demanded help from parliament. Some, typically for Victorians, did so with an uneasy conscience, because they were asking for laws that privileged one group (themselves) over another. This would be 'class legislation', which was anathema for modern egalitarians. And yet, so they said, nothing else could make things genuinely fair. A situation already unequal had to be remedied. Habits of work gave the Chinese an advantage, as they did on the goldfields. Chinese methods were quicker and cheaper, and their product was simpler. They worked like machines rather than real craftsmen.

Were the Chinese really automatons, replicas turning out replicas? Were they incapable of the kind of brainwork prized among White men? Whatever the answer, Chinese workmen seemed dangerous. By the late 1890s, as a government inquiry conceded, the quality and general finish of Chinese work were suddenly improving. Some European makers refused to admit any difference – 'I never saw a Chinese job properly constructed yet' – but the Chinese were undoubtedly skilled in making the best of poor material and in finding a market when everything was against them.[33]

Even when the law did not explicitly discriminate, the Chinese found ways around it, pushing their advantage against European labour. In firms made up entirely of Chinese, workmen were paid by the piece rather than by the hour. That made their labour cheaper. Piecework was illegal for everyone, but the Chinese did it with impunity. The laws were framed by Europeans, and they took it for granted that employer and employee were typically at odds and that workers would report exploitation, but that was not true of the Chinese. According to one inspector, 'When questioned as to rate of payment, they usually said – "Alle same company"; or, "We all same share um profits". It is very difficult to get a truthful answer from them where it concerns their pockets'. They lived together in the workrooms and factories. They would lock up at the right time but then break the law by working on into the night. 'There is no difficulty in getting them to understand anything that is in their own favour', said the same inspector, 'but directly it is the reverse they are as immovable and unimpressible as the Sphinx. You are invariably met with the too familiar expression "Me no savee", which conveys a world of meaning'. He told of a Chinese employer who said that he paid as much as the law required. His men backed him up, but his own books proved otherwise. '[I] asked him if that was his signature, he said – "Yes", and then said – "My flend writee for me; he makee mistake. I no more savee".' The inspector went in search of the friend. 'It was a race as to who would get there first, and finally ended in a dead-heat.' The friend saw what was going on and the inspector went away beaten.[34]

By the late 1890s there were several big, well-equipped Chinese factories, and their success made them more conspicuous and manageable, so that the rules were less frequently flouted. But by that time the law itself was more demanding. All furniture was now supposed to be stamped either 'European labour only' or 'Chinese labour', with the idea that European buyers would avoid the Chinese product.[35] Some Chinese failed to stamp, some stamped in obscure places (under drawers, for instance), and some European retailers sanded off the stamps. On the other hand, some Chinese embellished their stamps with their names and addresses, making a stigma into an advertisement.

The biggest problem was the Chinese manufacturer who worked alone. He was impossible to police:

> In the day time he works hard but intermittently, breaking off to indulge in his own peculiar pleasures, and giving but a few minutes to his meals. Then, when evening arrives, he has to make up for lost time, and, entering the room which he keeps for the purpose, he works by gas or lamp light far on into the night.

Secrecy was the barrier the Chinese raised against an alien authority. These makers were also the ones who used the worst timber, 'concealing its defects with the aid of polish or varnish'. The retailers they used, Chinese or European, were just as shady.[36]

But what was wrong with men making money in their own time and selling wherever they could? They worked alone. Was the law justified in telling them when to stop in the evening? Why should discreet advertising – adding names to stamps – be frowned on? It was all hypocrisy. It was inconsistent with the best principles of Victorian public life. It was also futile. Thomas Holdsworth, a chair maker and president of the Furniture Employees' Union, told a Victorian government inquiry that all Chinese furniture makers should be bought out at a fair price and no new ones allowed to register. We must take some such step, he said, 'and have done with them'.

But this was hypocrisy too. Holdsworth was reprimanded by a member of the committee of inquiry, Arthur Otto Sachse (born in Queensland of a Prussian father). 'Do you consider that a British proposal – to prevent a man from having a licence to work if he wishes to?' Every possible solution contradicted fundamental principles. It was a dilemma nicely suited to the refined sensibilities of the South.

Holdsworth, however, shot back, '[I]f men are not amenable to British laws they must be dealt with in a different manner to Europeans'.[37] In the Australian South, legislators could only torture their consciences and hope for the best. There had once been a chance of the Chinese somehow disappearing. Now they seemed to be doing just the opposite.

III

In 1888 Henry Parkes, in his fourth term as premier of New South Wales, put forward a scheme to rename his own colony 'Australia'.

The change would make it clear to the world that in any future federation the oldest province of European settlement was mother and guide to the rest. Some colleagues liked the idea: 'Before those [other] colonies became our offshoots, as they are, we were Australia; and we only propose to give [ourselves] that title which we always had, before they became our offshoots'.[38] This was roughly how federation had happened in Canada – the original Canada transforming itself butterfly-like and reaching at length to the coast of the Pacific. The name 'New South Wales' was an ugly jumble. It did not reflect Sydney's ancient dignity or its early sweep of power, from the Bay of Islands to King George Sound, from Tasmania to the Tropics.

What was 'Australia'? It was still a word to play with, an ill-defined medley of hopes. Not long after Parkes's short-lived effort, William Lane decided to give the name 'New Australia' to the colony he planned in South America. This time the name was all about snatching back lost opportunity. Lane wanted a type of Australia which he thought could never exist in its original soil. Selfishness and greed had killed his hopes of having everything in common. The people of New Australia would manage their affairs in such a way as to stop the same thing happening there.

Equality was everything. Or was it sameness? In projects such as Lane's, every individual man and woman came in on the same terms and with matching expectations. On the same principle, the other colonies attacked Parkes's idea of making New South Wales into the authentic and original Australia. In any future federation each would have to start on the same footing.

In the cooperative utopias, members chose a committee to work out rules for them, divide up the work, dispose of produce, settle disputes and stop intruders. Success depended on mutual respect between rulers and ruled. In the continental scheme, members of the ruling committee, the federal government, would likewise have to think of the citizens as their masters, but at the same time they would have to have enough power to govern. To keep up this balance all parties had to be high-minded men leading transparent lives. That disqualified Chinese. White women were citizens too, but they were not often thought of as part of the driving formula, and members of government were bound to voters by a frankness best described as 'manly'. In that position of trust, as Alfred Deakin put it, they must, he said, 'speak their sentiments, without the intervention of any other body, or subject to any other influence than the judgment and reason of the manhood of their colony'.[39]

This was how things were done, ideally, in the White man's workplace, and also in the thousands of shared enterprises, including commons, throughout the continent. This was how things were done in all those futuristic novels mentioned in chapter 5. Every man stood up for himself in the light of day. The main point of the factory laws was to create the kind of administrative machinery which would make that happen. The Chinese, supposedly, could never understand those laws and respond to them properly. They were neither rational nor manly. Only uniform citizenship, a single culture and a single language manifest in the workplace, committee room and government, could create a genuine commonwealth – a country held in common.

IV

On the Australian mainland, all those brief utopias, these little models of cooperation and civility such as William Lane wanted, lived and died along southern riverbanks. In the North, though hopes were high and schemes were legion, the only significant effort (Lane's) meant giving up the continent altogether. This was another part of the problem of North and South. Was a true spirit of commonwealth possible in those overheated latitudes?

For a generation hitherto, Queensland had seemed to many to have a separate destiny. In 1879, opening the debate about

Federation, Henry Parkes had published in the *Melbourne Review* his plan for the union of the south-eastern three, New South Wales, Victoria and South Australia, under the heading 'An Australian Nation'. The compact Federation thus established would leave Queensland free, as he put it, to be a 'mighty nation' on its own.[40] This was a year before the same three met in Melbourne, the gathering which led to a much more widely horizoned meeting, in Sydney early in 1881. The union between North and South was then in the balance. It stayed in the balance until the century's end.

In 1877 the Melbourne writer Marcus Clarke had prefigured Parkes's idea in apocalyptic terms. Maybe Parkes was deliberately echoing Clarke. Maybe, too, Clarke was not quite serious. The continent and its adjacent islands, Clarke prophesied, would be divided by a line running east to west. In the North, including Queensland and the islands and peninsulas of the East Indies, there would be, self-sufficient and self-contained, 'a luxurious and stupendous civilisation', a land of dramatic riches and poverty like the old empires of the Egyptians and the Aztecs. The South, both east and west of the Tasman Sea and including South Australia, would be governed as a commercial republic, 'a democracy', Clarke put it, 'tempered by the rate of exchange', a place where all men were on a level. Its fashions would be set on Sydney Harbour but its ideas would come from Melbourne.[41]

In these two great sovereignties climate, as usual, would make the difference. Queensland was hot, like Egypt and Mexico. Hot climates, as in the American South, bred luxury, rank and high emotion. In the cooler parts of Australia, as in the American North, the people would be more equal, more racially uniform, more brotherly, more town-bred, more commercial and more free.

Clarke wrote with his usual wild hyperbole, but it still did seem possible that Australia would follow the two-nation path lately sketched by Confederate Americans, and obvious already as between Canada and the United States. Only during the 1880s and '90s did the distinction between North and South on the Australian mainland start to seem powerfully at odds with the dictates of Providence, and even then it was slow to die. Hear a woman, whose home was near Sydney, mourning in 1907 the death of her daughter, who had gone with her husband to live near Warwick, on Queensland's Darling Downs. Poor Linda had died not just in great pain but 'in a strange land'.[42]

There was an abiding charm in Parkes's early idea of union between the south-eastern three (with Tasmania an easy addition). The result would have been a nation as big as Western Europe, with several rich cities, crisscrossed by railways and rivers, centred on Joseph Furphy's riverine people and embraced by an arc of coastal seas. It could be called 'Australia' as easily as the federation across the Pacific – only part of a continent – was called 'America'.

But by the 1880s, manifest destiny was carrying the eye outwards. At the public service level, negotiation day by day across the Queensland–New South Wales border, including the work of the two chief inspectors of stock, Patrick Robertson Gordon and Alexander Bruce, had helped to make North and South look like two parts of a single whole, to some at least. This possibility was proclaimed in a famous speech by Sir Henry Parkes, at the border town of Tenterfield, in October 1889, as he made his way home to Sydney from talks with ministers in Brisbane. Tired of dealing with the narrower jealousies of the South, and provoked by the report of a British major-general, James Bevan Edwards, on the need for the colonies to join forces against possible attack, he spoke directly to the North: '[I]f two Governments [Queensland and New South Wales] set an example, the others must soon of necessity follow'. It was a trumpet call aimed at listeners on both sides of the North–South border.[43]

It was North plus South, the ultimate calculation.

In the United States the southern vision had not triumphed. Democracy of a spacious continental kind (not the voice of particular states) – Abraham Lincoln's 'government of the people, by the people, for the people' – had been forced on wayward brothers. A great nation had thus been permanently united. Different manners and habits, in other words, and lesser variations of 'race', had been subsumed in the greater, more entirely global question of colour.[44]

In the United States the South had to be forced to match the North, at least on the surface. In Australia, the North had to be forced to match the South. In Queensland and in the Kimberley, said leaders from the South, together with liberal thinkers around Brisbane, bonded labour must cease. Pacific Islanders and Chinese had to be expelled. The coastline of the continent, unbroken by Providence, had to be governed by a single power. Among other things, Victoria's Chinese problem had to be revisited from a continental perspective. Hitherto, the best democracies had flowered in small places, in commons and cooperatives, but the democracy binding North and South would be vast. The journalist Francis Adams, thinking about Marcus Clarke's prophecy, suggested an explosive mingling of democrat and aristocrat, as in America. But maybe, he said, and it was a wonderful prospect, the democracy of the South would manage the North 'as an appanage for its own more adventurous sons'.[45]

In fact, there was a third possibility. It was one feared by labour leaders in the South. Such men were scornful about the chances of a large, complex federal system registering the will of the people. It was a fix. True democracy, they said, could not happen on such a scale. It would go backwards. Standards of protection for factory workers varied from colony to colony. With comprehensive free trade all the factories would soon be moved to one 'Sweater colony' (that is, in the North), where the laws were easiest, and whose 'soiled goods' would be distributed everywhere else. Working men and women, as buyers, their democratic voice ignored, would join in the 'murder [of] their fellows'.[46]

But first, how many colonies were to be brought in? On this

question, South Australia was key. South Australia was one of Parkes's original trinity. And yet South Australia was an outlier compared with Victoria and New South Wales. The worst possibility for South Australians, as a labouring man at Moonta said, was 'the two larger brothers [cooperating] to drain all the wealth from the three smaller ones'. (He left out Queensland.) In fact, given the rivalry of the two larger brothers, such cooperation was unlikely, so that really the main challenge lay in avoiding domination by one of them, as Germany was overawed by Prussia and Italy by Sardinia-Piedmont, and in having both within a system of mutual obligation. Any arrangement which left out New South Wales, South Australians said, would make Melbourne our Berlin.[47] The South Australians managed this challenge with considerable skill.

South Australians had to find allies like themselves, and they were in a good geographical position. With its Northern Territory, South Australia extended across the continent to the edge of Asia. The Centre itself was South Australian. So was the Overland Telegraph, linking all the colonies to the outside world. South Australian interests extended into Queensland by way of the Birdsville Track, and South Australian seaports stood on the main line of traffic to Western Australia – a route much travelled since the gold discoveries at Coolgardie and Kalgoorlie.[48]

At the same time, with Federation, they said, South Australia would still be South Australia. 'We want to see a union of strong colonies', said the South Australian premier, John Alexander Cockburn, at the intercolonial meeting in Melbourne in 1890. Every colony would keep 'its own local traditions ... its own local affections ... its own peculiarities'. We wanted 'a brotherhood of infinite diversity', he said. We did not want 'a homogeneous union'. This was the general idea, at least outside Victoria. Even Sir Henry Parkes said much the same. 'You must go proudly into it,' he told fellow New South Welshmen, 'strongly into it, or your position will be worse than it was before'.[49]

The Tasmanian Andrew Inglis Clark echoed the sentiments of his band of Minerva Club 'boys'. He talked of 'various governments moving in their respective orbits'. '[E]ach must be complete, each must have its independence.' Clark, like Parkes, was an enthusiast for Australian nationality, but even more for what he called 'local public and national life'. He meant down-to-earth 'national' democracy, such as he had helped to build for Tasmanians – an engine for shared justice.[50] The pivot of real government had to be down among the people.

Together, South Australians and Tasmanians worked out how the wheels of the federal machine should intermesh. Clark knew all about the American Constitution and he applied its principles, as he understood them, wherever he could. Through such work, as the South Australian delegate James Howe remarked, 'the mighty brain-power of the great men of America of those days' (he meant the 1770s and '80s) was united to the contemporary brain power of Australasia. Even more important than Clark was Charles Cameron Kingston, South Australian premier during most of the 1890s. For years, Kingston's mind had been exercised by two overlapping visions for his own colony. He had foreseen South Australia growing, he said, 'to a nation'. And, on the other hand, he wanted South Australia to be part of 'a united Australia, numbering many millions'. The first was good but the second was 'better still'.[51] He chased both at once.

V

Charles Cameron Kingston was a brilliant bully, 'a man of great physical size and strength,' as Deakin recalled, 'of fine features and large head with rather small eyes and compressed lips'. He drew all eyes, and all ears. '[H]e delighted in hard adjectives,' said Melbourne's *Punch*, 'those which rang out like a blacksmith's hammer on an anvil, and he had an almost primitive love of combat'.[52] He was also hard to beat in drafting complicated legislation, but his interest in ideas meant that in the process he took pleasure in running his mind backwards and forwards between points of view, building up middle ground. New forms of society meant new ways of government. That called for ingenuity and the leadership of 'big and brainy men', as the Adelaide *Critic* put it. Kingston was big and brainy. He knew how to harness public opinion to get his way. He cut through old conventions and he took the lead however he could. He was inventive. In South Australia in 1894 he introduced votes for women. Then, in 1896, he held a popular referendum on the relationship between the churches and the public schools. Both were experiments in democracy. The second on the back of the first – giving the women of South Australia a direct say in a 'national' matter – was doubly novel.[53]

More than any other leader, Kingston kept the federal cause moving. He was always asking for deadlines and prodding the others.[54] In 1891 he was a delegate at the National Australasian Convention, forty-five men from seven colonies (the original three plus Tasmania, New Zealand, Queensland and Western Australia), who met in Sydney to work out the basic principles of Federation. At that meeting he was one of a committee of three set up to devise a draft bill. The other two members, also from outlier colonies, were Andrew Inglis Clark and Sir Samuel Griffith, premier of Queensland. Griffith was a brilliant lawyer and widely read (he translated Dante from the Italian). Francis Adams described him as a typical 'educated Australian gentleman': 'an open-minded, secular individual, dressing neatly, speaking correctly, moderately plebeian at heart, and moderately attached to his country'. Griffith's mind had lately been exercised by a scheme for the federation of his own colony, with its three sections governed respectively from Brisbane, Rockhampton and Townsville.[55] Among Queenslanders he was also a rare supporter of continental Federation. He had thought in detail about multilayered power.

As for New Zealand, its leaders were keen to sell freely in

Australian markets, but the long trip across the Tasman Sea caused endless complications. A federal army, for instance, headquartered on the mainland would be useless to New Zealanders. On the other hand, New Zealander offerings at early conferences had sometimes shed sudden light on points taken for granted by the others.

The edginess with which New Zealanders sipped at the Federation cup looked ridiculous to those mainlanders who now found themselves high on manifest destiny. West Australians also hesitated. Federation, said a member of parliament in Perth, was 'a subject that almost intoxicates one'. It was so large and so dazzling, and yet it called for much care and much sacrifice.[56] In spite of the reassurances of Cockburn and Clark, the settled character of each colony was at risk, and New Zealanders dared not jeopardise their own 'very complete individuality'. They were 'a distinct national type', they said, because of both climate and history. To old-fashioned minds, Western Australia proved with particular clarity how 'national types' (the older generation might have called them 'races') could emerge on the same continent, as they had done within the United States. The goldrushes in the west had brought about a strange combination of 'sandgropers' (old settlers) and 't'othersiders' (miners from other parts). Joseph Furphy, when he went to live in Fremantle, found himself comparing the somnolent 'Groper spirit' he found there (the men 'amiable, ignorant, extremely lazy', the women self-contained and stately) with 'Eastern restlessness and ambition'. He liked easterners better.[57]

Furphy wanted Federation all the same. Bernard O'Dowd, the best antipodean poet of the day, wanted it too, though it meant marrying his own country, Victoria, with Queensland, the home of 'sugar-planter bloodhounds', and Tasmania, which was full of 'prigs and serfs'. A kinder appraisal of Tasmanians found them '[p]hysically and mentally ... more typical of England than of Australia'. They were said to have personalities to match their broad backs and thick limbs.[58]

How many national types (real or imaginary) could one nation contain and nourish? By his victory in the Civil War, Abraham Lincoln had given the American people a Yankee kind of citizenship, free of slaves. In Australia, people like Furphy and O'Dowd could not see much point in preserving the character of inferior colonies. Everyone had to be raised to the level of the south-eastern three. In O'Dowd's case, the standard of Victoria alone would do. But the scheme for the two houses of the federal parliament, as it was worked out during the 1890s, conceded a good deal of variety – as, indeed, the American Constitution still did. The House of Representatives, the lower house, would be elected by the people as a whole, from shore to shore, in proportion to numbers. (Two-thirds would therefore come from Victoria and New South Wales.) But in the Senate every member state, big and small, would come in on equal terms. Sir Thomas McIlwraith, Griffith's colleague and rival from Queensland, spelt it out at the Sydney meeting:

> What is the reply when the small states say, 'We cannot lose our nationality; we are a unit now, and we must preserve our nationality in any kind of federation that may take place?' They are answered at once, 'Very well, we will allow you to be a unit and will create two houses of legislature; one of which shall be a senate in which each colony as it stands now shall be represented; no matter what its length and breadth and population may be, it shall have the same voice and the same influence in that senate as is enjoyed by the other chamber.' That is a substantial *quid pro quo*; that is something given on each side; that is business.[59]

There would be one nationality woven from various nationalities. That was the essence of the Constitution drafted by the committee of three, the Tasmanian Andrew Inglis Clark, the South Australian Charles Cameron Kingston and the Queenslander Samuel Griffith.

Another problem occurred to labour leaders, though there was nothing they could do about it. Victoria and New South Wales, said a Melbourne man, had managed to build up genuine democracies, in which working people had some chance of being heard. Now they were to be 'handed over to the mercies of an Upper House that is dominated by reactionaries from Western Australia and Tasmania'.[60] His reactionaries also included the masterful sugar growers of Queensland.

Delegates agreed that there had to be free trade among all member states. Tariff barriers had to vanish. But free trade was not enough to make buyers and sellers into a single people. He looked forward to Federation, said the New South Welshman Joseph Palmer Abbott, and to 'brotherly love' among all the colonies, because, '[w]ith our resources, with our coalfields, we shall be able to fight Victoria, not only in her own markets, but in the markets of Australia'. '[W]e must federate', he said (by 'we' he meant New South Wales), 'to get those markets'. Even among the careful civility of the Federation meetings Victorians still sounded like antipodean Prussians, poised to eat up their neighbours. Alfred Deakin might think he was arguing with wonderful politeness about the need for 'a strong government upon the broadest popular basis, and with the amplest national power'. To other ears he was describing a Federation which would be 'a sort of enlarged edition of one of the existing colonies – say, for example, the colony of Victoria'.[61]

And so to Queensland. Paramount in the thinking of the original three was the need to bring in Queensland. The combined riches of North and South, those vast and remote spaces subject to the enterprise of Sydney and Melbourne, made up a truly seductive vision. They could do without New Zealand. Nor was much anxiety spent on Western Australia and Tasmania. Everyone knew that those two could not afford to stay out, and both were mentioned, even in public debate, with cheerful condescension. According to Parkes, the population of his own Sydney suburb was more than two-thirds the population of all Western Australia.[62] This was just before the invasion of easterners looking for gold, but even then, in eastern eyes, nothing much changed.

Queensland was another matter. 'There can be no complete federation without Queensland', said William Lyne, of New South Wales – given 'the possibilities before that great country'.[63] The new regime would be cartographically and economically incomplete without the North. Since military threats were most likely to come from the south-west Pacific, integrated defence would be pointless. Good policy would remedy the 'piebald' mix of races in that part of the world. The combination of North and South, brilliantly begun by public servants such as Gordon and Bruce in the 1860s, was the main task ahead. Even after Federation, that was the pivot on which Commonwealth policy was to turn.

In Queensland itself, the federal cause was pushed hard by Sir Samuel Griffith, a leader of intellectual causes in Brisbane and its hinterland. Even Griffith admitted that climate drove a wedge between Queensland and the rest. '[I]f there is to be a division of Australia', he said in 1891 (and by 'Australia' he meant New Zealand too), 'into more countries than one – that is, in the sense of political divisions – it must be a division between north and south'.[64] And yet Griffith was mainly responsible for the final draft of the federal Constitution, as it emerged from the committee appointed that year.

Cross-currents of opinion in Queensland itself were extremely complicated. Many looked to Federation as a way of ensuring that their colony did not fall victim to the Chinese and other 'aliens'. For quite different reasons, support came also from sugar growers around Townsville and Mackay, who were angry about the long campaign by Liberal politicians in Brisbane (including Griffith) to replace their Pacific Islander workforce with more expensive Europeans. The sugar growers had a poor grasp of opinion in the southeast, and in a wonderful leap of wishful thinking they convinced themselves that a federal government would leave them alone. Their Federation was a sugary confection, a syllabub, a castle in the air – although they did understand, rightly enough, that free trade would help their sales in the South.[65]

Other Queenslanders stuck to their strong belief in Queensland's self-sufficiency. They feared, also rightly enough, that their large-scale manufacturing would be fatally damaged by open competition. It was a campaign that made no sense to sober minds. '[F]ederation', said the editor of Barcaldine's *Western Champion*, 'is the cause of ardent young men who have been screaming to be born again'.[66]

In fact, Queensland was not as self-sufficient as it seemed. It had enormous potential, but the 1890s depression showed just how much Queensland money really belonged to investors in the South and in London. The Queensland National Bank was the only bank with headquarters on the spot, and some of the loudest talk about Queensland nationhood came from men, including premiers, who led the race for loans from abroad.[67] Vastly richer than Tasmania, like Tasmania Queensland needed other people's money.

After the conference of 1891 there was a long pause within the leadership of the Federation movement. But in most of the colonies, with the worst of the 1890s depression over, Federation slowly took fire as a popular cause, as brains adapted to the 'intoxicating' vision. Even then, in New Zealand and in large parts of Queensland the vision failed to catch, and when the leaders met again, in 1897–98, in three sessions (in Adelaide, Sydney and Melbourne), neither New Zealanders nor Queenslanders turned up. As a result the impact of the smaller colonies was less, and big-colony attitudes more easily prevailed. So the idea of a single nationality, embodied in the House of Representatives (as distinct from the Senate, the 'States' House'), was driven home at last.[68]

The great question – should the colonies federate? – was put to the people of the south-east (Victoria, New South Wales, South

Australia and Tasmania) in June 1898 and again in April–July 1899, and finally passed. After a moment of suspense, a pivotal few months, Queensland followed, in September 1899. Western Australia completed the circle ten months later.

Taken colony by colony, the final majorities were clear-cut. Even in 1898 there was a problem only because the New South Wales government had made its own required majority too high. But subdivide Queensland and we find outright rejection in the south and bare approval in the centre. '[D]o not let these political stockmen,' pleaded a writer in a Rockhampton paper, 'with their loud oratorical cracking whips, round you up like so many cattle, and having goaded you to a momentary frenzy, rush you blindly into this Federation paddock'. Many did, in fact, shy at the gate. But voters in north Queensland made up the necessary overall number voting 'yes'. There, the vote turned largely on the theory that a federal government would save the Pacific Islands labour trade.[69] It was a simple mistake, a straightforward breakdown in communications over what was still an enormous distance. It was a piece of fantasy left uncorrected, and it made the difference in joining North and South, thus resolving the single greatest challenge of the Federation process.

INDIVIDUALITY

The relativity of space and time is a startling conclusion ... From the well-worn statement that the speed of light is a constant, we conclude *that space and time are in the eye of the beholder*. Each of us carries our own clock, our own monitor of the passage of time. Each clock is equally precise, yet when we move relative to one another, these clocks do not agree. They fall out of synchronization; they measure different amounts of elapsed time between two chosen events. The same is true of distance. Each of us carries our own yardstick, our own monitor of distance in space. Each yardstick is equally precise, yet when we move relative to one another, these yardsticks do not agree; they measure different distances between the locations of two specified events.[1]

Brian Greene, *The Fabric of the Cosmos*

7

Men and Women

I

In the two least willing colonies, New South Wales and Queensland, between 40 and 50 per cent of those who voted were against Federation. In both Victoria and Tasmania it was rather less than a fifth in the 1898 vote and 6 per cent in 1899. In 1898, when only the four south-east colonies voted, 'no' votes made up a third. In 1899, throughout the continent, they were not much more than a quarter.

How many were against Federation altogether and how many were just holding out for something better no-one can know. But some men and women made it quite clear where they stood.

Among the nay-sayers – but as a woman she had no vote – maybe the angriest and most absolute was Rose Scott, honorary secretary of the Womanhood Suffrage League of New South Wales. Miss Scott was a reformer of prodigious energy, who achieved much for women working in factories and shops, for prostitutes and for female prisoners. In June 1898 voters in the four south-eastern colonies were asked to decide whether they approved of the Federation bill, and Rose Scott made some impassioned speeches, trying to sway the vote. 'Oh, if I had been the Premier of New South Wales', she said (always reading, she echoed the speech Shakespeare's Antony makes for the murdered Caesar), 'with all his influence and eloquence you would have heard an orator that would not only have shown you all the evils of this Bill, but one that would have caused the very stones of Australia to mutiny'.

'Oh you men, you men,' said Rose Scott, 'it is we women that know the least and the worst of you'. This bill, she said, epitomised the least and the worst. It was a parcel of masculine vanity. It had no moral anchor. It had nothing to do with conscience and the needs of suffering humanity. It was all about power and size. In such ways men imposed themselves on women, physically, emotionally, intellectually, and with the noise of their voices: 'Oh, if I had been the Premier ... with all his influence and eloquence'. It followed as night followed day that the women and children of Australia, facing a power they could never hope to manage, would be the victims.[1]

Men often talked about the Federation of Australia as if it was a way of being initiated into the brotherhood of real nations, and Australian historians have done the same since. Men liked this kind of adventure. Moving up, step by step, the task harder and harder, the self-realisation deeper and deeper, finding favour, as Proverbs has it, 'in the sight of God, and man', was the characteristic story of men's lives.[2] For women the same process might look like climbing down in pitch dark, into vacancy. Women had their own customary life changes – marriage, childbirth and widowhood. But theirs, so they idealised, was a divinely choreographed pattern of relationships with other people, of networked initiative, not a self-willed race to the horizon. The difference between male and female agendas was not black and white, but it was real.

Some men had doubts like Rose Scott's. Remember the writer, presumably a man, in the *Western Champion* (quoted in chapter 6) who said that 'federation is the cause of ardent young men who have been screaming to be born again'. The *Capricornian*, in Rockhampton, spoke of voters herded like cattle, jammed through a narrow gate in 'momentary frenzy', a rush impossible to turn.[3] Once reborn, as with our first entry to the world, there was no going back. Such doubts, women's and men's, made a big difference to the Constitution. They were part of a worldwide conflict, which was to distinguish the twentieth century, and which set intellectual power, the power of centralised ideas, high rhetoric, even high ideals, against the particular and the momentary, against narrow horizons and passing emotions, the unexpressed and ordinary.

'I fear those big words', said Stephen Dedalus, in *Ulysses*, 'which make us so unhappy'.[4] James Joyce's *Ulysses*, set in 1904 and written during the Great War, is probably the most ambitious celebration of the unexpressed and ordinary ever tried.

At the federal conference of 1891, in Parliament House, Sydney, when talk had gone on for three weeks with hardly a break, William Russell, a New Zealander, suggested a pause, if not a retracing of their steps. They needed to see how much their thoughts had changed, he said, since they first sat down together. It was good to listen and learn as one among forty-five men from far-flung corners of Australasia, all of great talent and wide experience, talking to a common purpose, as founders of a nation. But maybe their enthusiasm was carrying them in the wrong direction. They had learnt a lot, but who could tell how much more they, let alone people out of doors, had to learn before they could fully grasp the new form and purpose they were imprinting on themselves?[5]

In fact, decisions at this conference were not final. Federation was talked through for several years more, culminating with the bill of 1898. Anxieties like Rose Scott's and William Russell's did make a lasting difference in limiting centralised power. But some of the basic principles were certainly quickly done, and the final arrangement, in the eyes of many, seemed forced and therefore undemocratic, the hurried work of a select few who wanted Federation at any price. It was 'a vile constitution', said WJ Bartlett of Goulburn, New South Wales, a highly regarded local politician, 'born of avarice and arrogance, and had ambition for its Godfather'. A 'Tragic Farce' for his own colony the Melbourne poet Bernard O'Dowd called it, '[a] meaningless, half-considered, wanton Holocaust of hard-won Victorian liberties ... [a] National Dance of Death'. It was 'a downright stampede', said the eminent Sydney lawyer AB Piddington. It entrenched old divisions so that there could never be a 'national Australia'. It was the work, said William Holman, Labor Party leader in New South Wales, of 'a hothouse, artificial moment of enthusiasm', and so we had a 'sham nation'. If we had stood by until the people outdoors really knew what was going on, we could have had a real one.[6]

The New Zealanders, including William Russell, who came to the meetings of 1890–91 were struck with the trans-Tasman contrast. New Zealand boasted a distinctive kind of radical liberalism. Trying to resolve the difference, New Zealanders' minds wandered home. Sir George Grey had been governor of New Zealand long ago (and earlier still governor of South Australia), and then the democratically elected premier. When he came to Sydney as a delegate in autumn 1891 he showed all the brilliant, eccentric radicalism of his reclusive old age. The main concern of Federation should not be the central machinery, he said. It should be democracy. The federal Constitution should start by declaring that 'the electors should have certain powers'. It should focus on the people, not on their rulers. With a certain affinity himself for 'big words', Grey wanted the old colonial governments remodelled in a single sweep, from top to bottom. That would be true rebirth, he argued. Then, 'the people of the states [would] walk forth as free men'.[7]

New Zealand aside, democratic methods were most advanced in South Australia. Everywhere except in New Zealand and South Australia it was still possible for one man to vote in several electorates all at once, not just where he lived but wherever he had property. This 'plural voting' was an insult, Grey said, to the personal dignity of citizens. It meant putting land and houses on a par with men. It would be tragic to build the future on a foundation like that. It would mean forcing men into harness even heavier than they had already, 'a yoke of a most oppressive kind'. In the new morning which Australasian patriots yearned for – the dawn of a larger nationhood and a more expansive manhood – we must be perfect citizens, 'each man with an equal vote'.[8]

Russell, the other New Zealander, took a different tack. His problem with the federal idea was apparently more profound, although he never managed to explain it properly. They seemed to be forgetting about the main questions of the day, the 'social upheaval', Russell called it, which everywhere filled the minds of thinking men and women. These great issues, he said – he might have included the rights of women, race relations, the regulation of industry, the condition of the people, street-level citizenship, governments geared to tangible humanity – were commonplace to New Zealanders. Here was the central difficulty of the Federation movement, the clashing demands of vastness and of intimacy, the different agendas of the mass and of the individual. This and the next two chapters are about Russell's 'social upheaval'. What was its connection with Federation shore to shore?

New Zealanders had no such dilemma themselves, or not much. Their country was never big and their citizenship was always more obviously embedded in the small, separate settlements, in towns and villages, halls and churches, coloured with the protocol of public and private meetings, sober, civil, intricate, personal. But New Zealand tradition was not a flower easily transplanted to desert vacancies, to the great continental vacuum implicit in Australian Federation.

Only a country awake to these questions, said the critics of Federation, a people debating them daily, could be properly democratic. There could be no advance otherwise in 'the true liberties and freedom of the people'. All this hurrying towards centralised, abstract power seriously threatened old principles. We were caught, Russell went on, in a mighty undercurrent of nationalist rhetoric, and we had lost sight of what we were doing. 'We are getting into this absurdly anomalous position – that although we call what we are adopting federation, we are, in reality, drifting into unification' – towards a single government, impersonal and all-powerful over a vast territory, set far above the people's real relationships and concerns.[9]

If old liberties were to be kept safe, the regimes which had built them up had to be preserved. We had to have genuine Federation, a coordinated network of sovereignties, not one. The old governments had to keep enough power and dignity to go on doing what they did best. Like Rose Scott, Russell wanted government with feeling, in step with local, even family, life. In the bigger colonies it was remote enough already. Federation would make it worse.[10]

Alfred Deakin, impatient for union, called Russell (privately) a dilettante. 'If we wander over the whole subject of federation,' Thomas Playford retorted when the New Zealander sat down, 'we shall never finish our labours'. Time was scarce. 'We are doing things on business lines, and we should confine ourselves to the business before us.' But a majority of delegates, especially South Australians (even Playford, but for different reasons), agreed that there were problems with giving too much power to the centre. 'I would like to know', asked JA Cockburn, former premier of South Australia, 'since what time have centralisation and democracy been associated?'[11]

At the 1897–98 conferences there were no New Zealanders, and the defence of place-bound democracy was therefore left mainly to the South Australians. Frederick Holder, sometime mayor of Burra, now a senior minister in the South Australian government, hammered the need for a Constitution in which 'every personal unit of the population shall be recognised [that is, both men and women] and his individuality preserved'. 'Individuality' involved what a later age was to call 'autonomy' or 'identity'. But it was more than either. It also involved mutual respect, and it involved action. As the contemporary English philosopher Thomas Hill Green put it, it meant the 'realisation of self', which was not just thinking (and certainly not just introspection) but also doing.

The notion was first cultivated in Germany, and there dated back to Immanuel Kant. It underpinned the nineteenth-century German intellectual renaissance. Among Germans, as chapter 3 has said, it was called '*Bildung*'. This is where Rose Scott's arguments came in. Rarely thinking about herself in any sense, she was praised all the same as a model of 'strong individuality'. '[T]he secret of all government', said Rose Scott, 'is self government'. She included the way men and women governed their own particular lives and connections. Just as the individual colonies had to keep all possible freedom of action, women, she said, had to stop 'merging their individuality with that of others', and men, who had a habit of governing everything, 'must learn to respect and even to encourage the individuality of women'. In Europe, the poet Rainer Rilke thought the same. Even sex, Rilke argued, should be for each party 'a sublime occasion for the individual to mature, to become something in himself'. In sex, 'two solitudes ... protect, border, and greet each other'. Even in sex there should be nothing like surrender. Rilke might have been unread so far in the Antipodes, but marriages among the advanced few were tending in the same direction. In Adelaide one of the first Australian women to graduate in medicine, Rosamond Benham, took the lead with such arguments in her book *Sense about Sex*, by 'a Woman Doctor' (1905).[12]

A parallel reasoning said that Federation must be opposed. To the extent that it meant union in one centralised nation, it would take us in the wrong direction. It would mean merging and submerging. It would lift power beyond the easy reach of women and of the sort of men who shared women's priorities. It would threaten self, not just states' rights but freedom of soul. It would squeeze to extinction the rights of humanity and the power, little enough already, of women in public affairs. Put another way, Australia might not be too big to be a nation. But it was too big to be a nation-state. 'I broke my heart over federation', said Rose Scott.[13]

Miss Scott deliberately echoed the great Englishman John Stuart Mill, whose books *On Liberty* (1859) and *The Subjection of Women* (1869) shaped her thoughts and the thoughts of her generation. 'The free development of individuality', wrote Mill, 'is one of the leading essentials of well-being'.[14] For some, individuality, *Bildung*, meant a kind of solitary mysticism. Like your own voice, inescapable once you became fully aware of it – self-conscious – it could be a complicated burden, deadlier by the day. 'God strengthen me to bear myself', wrote the English poet Christina Rossetti (1866), 'That heaviest weight of all to bear'.

> If I could set aside myself,
> And start with lightened heart upon
> The road by all men overgone!

It was a burden too, sometimes, for Alfred Deakin, who wanted to merge himself with the will of God, 'in the perfect individuality', as he put it, 'of sacred self surrender'. But men and women like Rose Scott were happy with the weight they had to bear, always taking on more, chasing individuality – more multifarious, more down-to-earth, more self-sufficient but at the same time (as with TH Green) more social.[15]

Frederick Holder came from the only mainland colony (South Australia) where women could vote, a reform that shook up the whole question of individuality. His wife, Julia Holder, was a politician too. She was a leading figure in the South Australian branch of the Women's (or Woman's) Christian Temperance Union, which for years had fought for votes for women. Individuality, measured in the to and fro of their own marriage, was a fact of life for the Holders. Frederick, at least, thought that fruitful individuality could in fact be achieved under the new, continent-wide regime. There would be no absolute self-surrender – only the endless small, mutual sacrifices which were the common stuff of civilised life. '[E]ach State unit', he said, 'shall have its individuality preserved and its independence assured'. So would every citizen.[16]

Men such as Holder, in that age of emerging ideas about women's education, owed a lot to their wives, and the stimulation must have been mutual. In this age, men and women were deliberately experimenting with a new paradox more typical of the twentieth century. Both manhood and womanhood could seem more deeply entrenched if reflections of each could be found in the other. John Stuart Mill was the same. Mill's wife, the feminist Harriet Taylor, shared in his work. 'What was abstract and purely scientific was generally mine', he said; 'the properly human element came from her'. It was hard to disentangle their thinking. But 'in all that concerned the application of philosophy to the exigencies of human society and progress, I was her pupil ... [S]he was much more courageous and far-sighted than without her I should have been'. There was no merging of individuality. There was 'plural work', as one writer has called it.[17] It was like the shared labour being tried out at the same time in communitarian settlements.

Women won the vote first in New Zealand, in 1893, and in South Australia in 1894. Everywhere else, change was slow. Victoria, so progressive in many things, was last of all, in 1908. The Women's Christian Temperance Union, Julia Holder's flagship and a great movement for women's suffrage, was itself built from local democracy – from networks of family and neighbourhood, and from individuality of the sort which in English intellectual life made sense, say, to JS Mill and TH Green. The WCTU began in New York, in 1874, and its evangelisers went from town to town getting neighbours to organise. Two Americans, Mary Clement Leavitt and Jessie Ackermann, started the movement in Australia. Local unions chose delegates who met in the capital cities to set up colony-wide unions and from there reached out beyond colonial boundaries. The fortunes of the WCTU are more proof that the federating instinct was everywhere, pulling kitchen-garden questions into large, interwoven structures, combining the aims of this generation, individuality and collaboration, the one and the many.

The WCTU also showed what genuine, widespread democracy might look like. In South Australia, even before an Adelaide-centred union network was formed, there were twenty-three well-established local unions, averaging nearly fifty members each.[18] With or without centralisation, down-to-earth matters – drunkenness, brutal husbands, mistreated children – always powered debate. This was what Frederick Holder wanted for the whole country. Policy had to start in the smaller places, where so many men and women felt most free.

II

Every married or courting couple faced these questions more or less, all the jarring priorities of male and female individuality pushed together. Take John Monash, in later years Australia's greatest war leader. Monash was just short of seventeen when he started at Melbourne University, in March 1882. He was an introspective young man. Like many such men he wanted to be born again, or at least to remould himself on more imposing lines. He wanted self-realisation. He was as keen as Deakin was to tunnel into the hidden depths of self, but unlike Deakin he encountered granite. 'I cannot understand *myself* at all, though I am ever the subject of my reflections.' Nor was he perfectly serious about university lectures, at least to start with. 'Went into town', he told his diary, '& walked till I found myself at University. Therefore attended Lower Math & Science'. 'Set off with a determination to go to Upper Math, but nothing came of it.'[19]

His first year at university was a transformation all the same. Hitherto a child, within ten months, he said, '[there] were born in me, those sentiments & passions, which enable me to form … opinions of my own'. A few years more and his brainwork was entirely rearranged. He came to understand that joining with other young men in a great mental discipline was a form of drill. He saw the effect in his habits of expression. So, he announced in his fourth year, 'I am essentially a mathematical student … I live in a sea of mathematics ... [M]y mental operations are indissolubly linked with the subject'. From his first year as a student he had dreamt large dreams. He had been sure then that he could conquer the world if he really tried. Now he was settled at last, he said, on 'the upward path'. 'Oh, this is the secret of mental tranquillity, – despise not thyself.'[20]

He joined a volunteer military unit, the University Company of the 4th Battalion, Victorian Rifles, under the command of his professor of mathematics. He was jubilant at his promotion to sergeant, in spring 1889 – a vital step, he said, in 'the race for a position in the world'. With promising employment and always needing women, he was ready to marry, and about this time he met Victoria Moss, who was Jewish, as he was. She was also sensuously good-looking, obviously clever, sometimes an aggressive flirt and sometimes coldly self-contained. Monash was fascinated. This was individuality strangely packaged. 'She is a woman', he said, 'far beyond her years [she was twenty-two], and has a disposition startlingly akin to my own'.[21]

John Monash's usual technique with women was to assert his sheer strength of character. He was in every way an impressive man. With Vic matters went differently. Like others of her generation, she played with authenticity and mood, always setting up barriers. To Monash she had all the appearance of a skilled tactician, asking him for complete frankness ('be yourself'), only to catch him off his guard. 'You have conquered', he told her within three months of meeting. 'Make of me what you wish.' But this was really an ongoing war of attrition, an endless, mutual wearing down, a reshaping of her individuality to fit his, matched by resistance on her part, and granite again. A month further on Monash reported to his diary that he was making progress at last. 'To my extreme delight', he said, 'I find that Vic if properly treated is easily led, & shows growing confidence in me'.[22] But triumph was brief. His most receptive friend remained his diary, not his sweetheart.

She showed an almost childish scorn for his strength.

> In Vic [he said] I see the outward embodiment of my physical ideal. But in her moral nature I have been bitterly deceived & disappointed ... She is no mental companion for me, & has just so much knowledge of the world that she is most difficult to lead & instruct, & repels all my attempts to do so.

They could not do without each other. But together they were always on guard.

The soldier in him saw it all as a military campaign, and it was desperately important that these battles should be won by the civilising party. 'I love her dearly.' Driven by love, he watched, as he put it, 'for the first sign of surrender from her – for I will in the end conquer her & she will be led by me in the life I have planned for both of us. It is the conflict of two strong natures, & I intend to win'. They married, but that only made things worse. He tried and failed to interest her in books. 'Strange is this distaste for intellectual exercise in a woman of such strong intellect and brilliant faculties. To let them lie dormant & inactive is a sin, yet what can I do[?]'

> What a strange girl she is; she is so proud that she prefers to suffer in silence, she seeks no sympathy, & holds herself aloof from it, & yet seems disappointed at the absence of it. Yet how can one show sympathy where it is so plainly written 'My suffering I do not wish you to share in'.

Monash needed to conquer. But he could not stop Vic conquering him. 'I have striven to do everything in the way *she* wishes – and indeed she shows no disposition to allow anything else.'[23] They both gave their tempers full rein. They separated but could not live apart, and settled finally into an uneasy truce.

III

Vic Monash's resistance was like Rose Scott's efforts with Federation. Vic had no time for the verbiage which sweetened submission among married women. She would not be cowed by large ideas. Rose Scott, moving much more easily among men, making use of men's power for her various causes, was exasperated by the thought of men in bulk, of men's talk, but even more of the silences, the deep solidarity, which made the other sex so intractable.

The imagination of some women (Mary Gilmore, for instance) was stirred by the wide horizons and wandering existence of men. Not Rose Scott. She talked about the federalist campaign of the 1890s as 'a glorified cricket match'. It was all cheering and excitement, unconnected with the real priorities of the people. One West Australian, a man, was just as sceptical. Those who revelled in the idea of one nation shore to shore used 'such beautiful language', said Walter James, an ardent democrat and social reformer, that it was hard to pull away the petals and get to the errors underneath.[24] Rose Scott struggled for years to tear up the flower of federalism, even while it was unfolding in full glory.

The coming Australia was often equated with a flower, sometimes the erect waratah, sometimes the gentler wattle or flannel flower. Avant-garde craftsmen and interior decorators argued about which would symbolise the nation best. But it was not an argument that interested Rose Scott. More than a flower, for her the Federation idea was like a bushfire. Trickling at first in tiny flames, by 1898 it was powerful beyond all prediction.

> [L]awyers, politicians and orators are throwing fuel on this fire which, unless you stamp it out ... will go on burning, burning ... till it has consumed the people's money and melted away their liberties, and the voice of the people (as it is in old world countries), smothered in the ashes, can no longer make itself heard.[25]

Newspapers were a ragged free-for-all of large ideas, and they typically supported Federation. But in Sydney the *Daily Telegraph* was on Rose Scott's side, 'fighting', as a federationist put it, 'the battle of provincialism, with an ability and vigour without parallel in the history of Australian journalism'. The *Telegraph* braved the mockery of the young and ardent. 'The "Telegraph" has got 'em bad, got 'em bad, / And Federation drives it mad, drives it mad', sang the young men at Sydney University. 'But what it says is but a gag, / We still will hoist the Fed'ral flag.' According to the *Telegraph*, most women were anti-Federation. (The paper was also a stout supporter of women's suffrage.) Housewives, unlike students, were hard to fool with 'poetical abstractions'. They were not 'dazzled by the national aspect of the question'. More government meant more taxation, more invasion of family budgets.[26]

Ben Tillett, visiting British socialist, speaking before a male audience in Melbourne, agreed. Women ought to have the vote on this. 'Where their honour, where their dignity, where their rights, where their food, were concerned, they would not put up with the damn-nonsense that you put up with.' Certainly, some women would have insisted on proportional voting in elections for the Senate (the system Catherine Helen Spence had worked to improve and which did come much later) so as to break down the tyranny of men-managed parties. But probably most women, like most men, hoped for the best of both worlds. 'I think it will be just splendid to have one Federated Australia', said Elizabeth Jane Ward, Sydney milliner and charity worker, 'with one grand Government for all the colonies'. But she did not want any far-reaching changes. She was sure that the old governments would go on pretty much as before.[27]

There would obviously be new efficiencies. Federation would mean goods, livestock, mail, telegraph messages and people all moving with less hindrance about the continent. There would be a customs union and a single postal system, and maybe a single rail network (that never came). It was sensible to proceed like this, 'on business lines'. Federation would cancel distance among widely scattered families, maybe. It would mean quicker patterns of communication, not just among the colonies but between this continent and the rest of the world. It would match the habits of an up-to-date people. As Francis Adams said, Federation called up a 'modern scientific spirit' – or at least it did in Victoria. New South Wales, according to Adams, 'does not understand this modern scientific spirit – she dreads it, is jealous of it, and admires it! It is so self-reliant, so self-confident!' For him this explained the hesitancy in New South Wales in taking up the cause.[28]

Men and women also liked the idea of *commonwealth*, of the continent as a common – 'Australia for Australians!' For Rose Scott, Australia was like a house. In that house New South Wales was a room, her room. It was full of familiar comforts. Weaken any one colony for the sake of some untried abstraction and all of them would be damaged. '[I]f one room is injured the Home suffers.' But surely if the continent was a house, it could also be a household? The 'federal spirit', as another woman said, was an unselfish spirit. It was a spirit of sacrifice for the greater good. It was like the spirit which shaped good marriages, reconciling individualities. It should make perfect sense to high-minded women.[29] More important still, it meant mutual charity and forbearance, even a comprehensive spirit of social justice. In minds attuned to the teaching of faith, Federation was deeply Christian.

As a household, Australia was too big for Rose Scott. A home was both more and less than a household. The unity she wanted was a shared love of the land and of its familiar beauty. She hated muscle and marching, bluster and bureaucracy. She used the logic of German idealism, manifest in *Bildung*. Something absolute and eternal was to be found in every created thing, including every human being and every nation. Each had a right to shape its own future. For her New South Wales was nation-state enough and,

Australia-wide, the land itself was enough, its beauties ungovernable and ungoverned.

Federation meant overlaying, maybe smothering, the old focal points of social life. It meant a more idealised but also a less humane kind of citizenship, a citizenship of abstractions. Or else, as Rose Scott feared, it meant military regimentation, the citizenship of soldiers. What else was there to fill that desert vacancy but the fellowship of men and warriors, since men alone moved there freely? Scott belonged to a network of propertied and educated families interwoven for generations with the life of their own colony and tied to the thickly populated parts of the land, much of which they owned. It was a fabric embroidered by women like herself. She had her own weekly salon in Sydney's expensive eastern suburbs. She had her own political causes – freeing women and girls from the authority of men, especially in poverty and in prison – in which success depended on her friends in parliament and the public service. Her fears are not surprising.

Miss Scott identified with Sydney but also with the place of her childhood, Glendon on the Hunter River – 'the most loved River,' as she called it, 'which gurgled over pebbles & stones to join forces with the mystical & far off sea'. The Hunter was her watercourse, just as the Murray was Elsie Birks's.[30] She liked richly bounded things, and she took it for granted that everyone had, or ought to have, something equivalent to a childhood river. It was that country childhood, she said, which had taught her to think for herself. From it came her ambition 'to be a sort of Joan of Arc, and do something for my country'. Hers was the small-scale geography of Margaret Browne. Remember too Mary Gilmore (but Gilmore supported Federation), who mourned the passing of Australia's multiple accents and fragmentary ways.

> A gum tree [said Rose Scott] as it flourishes & grows owes much to the Earth, the atmosphere, and the thousand and

> one things that give it life – environment, heredity – but still from first to last it is a gum tree. Its individuality is its own – & so with a human being whose self or spirit may be nourished from outside factors, but is in itself indestructible.[31]

It was typical of Rose Scott to see individuality in every tree, whose elemental opponent was fire.

IV

And yet some eucalypts, such as the Sydney blue gum (*Eucalyptus saligna*), regenerate with fire. In Australia the desire for rebirth, for self-realisation, was everywhere, and everywhere it was at war with ideas like Rose Scott's. Young men of meaner prospects than John Monash created or recreated manhood in their own ways, as men had always done. Sometimes they learnt subversive codes, warring with police. Between Greta and Glenrowan, in north-eastern Victoria, the Greta Mob set themselves apart by wearing their chinstraps under their noses, by habits of cheerful, violent defiance ('flashness') and by first-class horsemanship. There was no self-despising here. Among them, the Kelly brothers, Ned especially, were bright stars. The Kellys and their closest mates specialised in systematic horse and cattle theft, and after murdering three policemen they graduated to bushranging. The pursuit of Ned Kelly and three others during 1878–80, in and out of the Victoria–New South Wales border country, was an extraordinary public drama, covered in breathless detail by the morning papers in both capitals until it climaxed in a fixed battle at Glenrowan, at midwinter 1880.

Like the student John Monash, Ned Kelly sketched out his initiated self, his manhood reborn, on paper. He wrote an essay (later called the 'Jerilderie Letter'), 8300 words long and meant for publication, a mix of wit, blasphemy, anger and ambition. He had killed so far, he said, in self-defence. But, having done it once, now he promised 'wholesale and retail slaughter'. For 'I am a widow's son outlawed, and my orders must be obeyed'.[32] Within two years (November 1880) he was hanged.

'Youth! Youth!' cried Oscar Wilde in his story *Dorian Gray* (1890–91) – though Oscar Wilde and Ned Kelly were chalk and cheese – 'There is nothing in the world but youth!' Youth was the time, all too short, of rebirth, of large ideas. Australia's own Henry Kendall had said the same:

> [S]adder than all is the sense of his losses
> That cometh to one when a sudden age crosses
> And cripples his manhood.

'I felt older', said Kendall, 'at thirty than some do at eighty'.[33] Ned Kelly never came near thirty.

In these colonies the numbers of the young among the White population were multiplying marvellously, as if racing to make death irrelevant. The number aged from fifteen to twenty-nine grew from one in five in the 1870s to one in three in the 1890s. It was a carnival of youth which war would make into a conflagration. They put on their best show on Saturday nights in summer, perambulating the principal streets of the big cities, 'the girls in pairs', so a South Australian said, 'with an air of independence that is but one of the manifestations of the breaking up of old conventions'.[34]

But it was the boys that startled most, all those pale Ned Kellys. In the cities they gathered and drifted like shoals of fish, independent but unamiable, ubiquitous but incomprehensible. 'The colonial boy … is not a *domestic* animal', said someone who knew the species. '[H]ome is much too slow for him. At the same time he is decidedly gregarious, and must have his amusement in the company of others.' In the cities, boys and young men, with the occasional young woman, took possession of alleys and open spaces. These were larrikins, the city equivalent of the Greta Mob. The word 'larrikin' was said, probably incorrectly, to come from 'larking', larking about being the larrikin's way of life. In fact, there was nothing unique about the gregarious habits of the colonial boy. Contemporary English streets were inhabited by 'scuttlers' and 'hooligans'. Paris had its 'apaches'. In every case, the way they spoke was a badge of belonging and added to their mystery. 'The corners of streets,' said the *Sydney Mail*, 'the secluded places of parks, are really out-door clubs, where obscenity and profanity are the staple talk'.[35]

The bravado was threaded through with uncertainty. 'Above all things', a visiting Englishman observed, 'an Australian school boy' – and he might have added many who should have been at school or who had not long left school behind – 'dreads making himself ridiculous. He must be thought a man'.[36] In England, apparently, the young male did not live so much on edge, at the mercy of anxious ambition.

In Sydney and Melbourne each nest of inner-city streets had its gang of larrikins, its 'push'. According to Ned Kelly (possibly not the best authority), even a single 8-stone (50-kilogram) larrikin was enough to terrify a host of Melbourne policemen – though each of the latter, said Ned, might be 'big and ugly enough to lift Mount Macedon out of a crab hole'. In fact, larrikins moved not one at a time but in bulk. Then there were university students, outrageous youth of the kind John Monash knew. They could be very like larrikins, so much so that at one of the Sydney University colleges (St Paul's), students divided into a 'learned push' and a 'sporting push'. At Sydney too the annual Commemoration Day speeches in the university's Great Hall were overwhelmed with the massed catcalls of young men. ('But what have we got voices for / If not to rile the Chancellor?') Indeed, in 1891 the chancellor had to sit down defeated, while the governor's wife, Lady Jersey, met with shouts of 'Come on, Mrs J.!' and 'Trot her out!'[37]

How easily the one was lost in the many. In violence especially we forget ourselves when we are en masse, and it is an experience easiest in youth. According to the German writer Baron von der Goltz, when young, from eighteen to twenty-three, the body feels pain less. 'The grain of heedlessness, a quality peculiar to the freshness of youth, is an excellent incentive to martial achievement.'[38] How sweet it was to feel, among a mass of others, that self-forgetting freshness.

'The use of the foot as an offensive weapon is a noticeable trait of the larrikin', said the *Singleton Argus*. The violent breed of Australian larrikin was notorious for a backstreet sport called 'jumping'. It was another test of manly mettle. The enemy was knocked down and kicked, or else his stomach was jumped on. 'Yes, the larrikin's in heaven when with wild barbaric shout / He can down a man – in numbers – and then – "jump his liver out"'. Note 'numbers'. Numbers mattered. A Sydney paper called jumping a national sport, like riding rough.[39]

It was said that the rising generation, the males that is, were destined for great things, if only they could work together. On this continent, Federation itself depended on them. '[T]he rising youth of Australasia … will be the great factor in bringing about the ultimate union of every portion of its different populations.'[40] For good or bad, for jumping or for nation building, young men worked together. This was what enraged Rose Scott. The tyranny of the other sex, for Miss Scott and for many women, in any generation, was multiplied many times when they moved en masse.

The foot was not the larrikins' only offensive weapon. Some pushes liked rape just as much as they liked jumping. In Sydney during the 1880s there were several famous cases of gang rape, and many more must have gone unrecorded. Under questioning young men talked of rape as the most normal thing in the world, though in law it was a hanging offence. 'The others in the push put me on to her', said a New South Wales youth (the victim was eleven years old), 'and I went for her just the same as anyone else would do'. In some workplaces young men weighed their chances as if for weekend sport.[41]

On a Thursday in September 1886 Mary Jane Hicks, a sixteen-year-old servant girl, was raped on sandhills south-east of Sydney, a place called Mt Rennie, between the university and the sea, by at least a dozen men. She was small even for her age. She had no parents alive and she was new from a rural convent. By her own half-dazed account (she went to hospital vomiting blood), she had been taken and retaken as if by a series of armies, starting with the red-bearded cabman who drove her there. Mary Jane was 'by no means repulsive', in the judgment of a *Sydney Morning Herald* reporter. But she was 'plain, and altogether unattractive'. In earlier days it might have been hard to raise much public interest in such an unremarkable victim. But now, as Rose Scott said, the 'man & woman question' was everywhere. Whatever else she was, Mary Jane Hicks was a female human being. In public debate her rights were placed in balance against the demands of massed manhood.[42]

Massed manhood had highly placed friends. Surely the laws of nature, at their most noble when glimpsed in the passions of men, needed a little leeway? Except for the cabman, who was 'middle-aged' (he was thirty-five), Mary Jane's attackers were all young labouring men, all exemplars of the 'coming man'. All were samples of 'tyrannous freedom' such as William Wetmore Story wrote about. Twelve were brought to trial in the New South Wales Supreme Court and nine were found guilty. The judge, William Charles Windeyer, had a soft spot for the glories of young manhood, having been ardent enough in his own undergraduate days. When at the bar he had acted free of charge for larrikins he liked the look of. But Windeyer, like Frederick Holder, had married a forthright wife, Mary Elizabeth, foundation president of the Womanhood Suffrage League. Like Holder, like John Stuart Mill, Windeyer's mind had been enlarged by marriage. In the Mt Rennie case his priorities were unmistakable, and the trial, having been conducted, some said, with unbecoming speed, resulted in four hangings.[43]

Sir Henry Parkes called the executions 'legal butchery'. The cabman was only given imprisonment. Even that was too hard, said the *Bulletin*. If such a sentence was just, 'where is there "a man of the world" who would go unwhipped?' It was not women who were under siege. It was men. This court case proved it. Women had apparently hit on a new kind of power, a new kind of insolence. First they played on men's weaknesses. Then they swore their lives away in court.[44]

Certainly, girls were not just victims. The great contemporary experiment in educating the whole people changed the way in which girls thought about boys. In the public schools, now that girls sat side by side with boys – or at least in the same room, maybe gathered in particular rows and corners – it was found, to the surprise of many older observers, that the female brain could usually keep up with the male, and even do better. 'Boys are sometimes in advance in arithmetic and grammar,' said one inspector, 'but the girls make up for this by quicker intelligence, pleasanter reading, and neater work'. Surprisingly too, women might make better teachers, even of older children. Men were organisers and disciplinarians. 'Sympathy with the child-nature, liveliness, fertility of resource, and gentleness of manner', all desirable up-to-date aptitudes, were more typical of women.[45]

Women promised a new fund of intelligence. Some men saw this. In Europe, the poet Rilke said that women were 'more human humans' than men. A man, said Rilke, 'undervalues in his arrogance and rashness what he claims to love'. And again, 'A man', wrote William Leonard Courtney, friend of John Stuart Mill and husband of the feminist Janet Courtney, 'habitually underrates the woman's quickness of apprehension, and her delicate and intuitive insight'. Women's superiority could be rational as well as spiritual. When a man and a woman talk together about the same problem and her thinking runs ahead of his, '[h]e admires her', said Courtney, 'in proportion to the seriousness of his own logic, not in reference to her own native powers'. In fact, so Courtney went on, 'the feminine mind is surprisingly quick in assimilating and reproducing thoughts and ideas which have been sympathetically presented to it'. Perhaps, in adapting to 'a new medium', it was even quicker than the male. Men were startled to find women building their own intellectual universe, suitable to the day. Those of us who do not see the great change coming, Rilke warned, 'will end up being taken by surprise and vanquished'. In England, Virginia Woolf was beginning to think the same. In America, the novelist Elizabeth Robins said, 'If I were a man, and cared to know the world I live in, I almost think it would make me a shade uneasy – the weight of that long silence of one-half the world'.[46]

In the project of civilisation, females were creeping ahead of males. In good economic times boys left school early, or at least skipped classes, because they could get paid jobs easily. They sold newspapers, for instance. Girls stayed on. At one point in Victoria's Western District girls in the top two classes outnumbered boys four to one. Unlike boys, girls were not always aching to get out of doors. The government statisticians noticed that men were lagging seriously behind women of the same age in their reading and writing, a difference which in fact went back to the 1850s.[47] During the 1870s and '80s women were admitted for the first time to university lectures. They sat together at the front, and lecturers might find it most productive to direct their remarks mainly to them.

The mass of university students were still men. But female students could hardly fail to notice that the lives of the other sex were a round of casual privilege, of card playing, billiards, football and cricket. Male students, said Ambrose Pratt, 'cared for nothing seriously except sport, cutting lectures, and larking with rowdy girls (not students)'.[48] And yet, as with John Monash, they got ahead somehow, treading roads mapped out for them by their fathers.

For years girls had thought that they were more virtuous than boys. In the 1840s the great coloniser Caroline Chisholm had spoken of 'wives and little children' as 'God's police', sent from above to guide and uplift the men of their families.[49] Now girls, or some of them, thought that they were not just good. They were clever too, and in ways boys could not emulate. Maybe womanhood was the best summing up of modern individuality.

Women novelists were taken especially with the question 'How does a clever woman cope with a dull lover?' In Miles Franklin's *My Brilliant Career* (1901), for instance, Sybylla Melvyn was brains and energy uncontained. She was sparkling individuality. Madly in love with her, Harry Beecham promised Sybylla 'everything'. But his best gift was intellectual submission, when he told her what every self-consciously modern girl – Franklin's intended reader – wanted to hear: '[Y]ou are too clever for me'.[50]

V

This generation was always edgy about invasion and extinction, about being submerged. Charles Darwin, or Darwin's interpreters, had alerted them to that risk. The word 'menace', heard everywhere, summed it up. A menace was not just a nuisance. It was a threat to existence. Take even flower gardens. The bestselling handbook *A Year in My Garden* was written in Melbourne by Margaret Tuckett. When we see our flowers, said Mrs Tuckett, 'drooping under the rays of the fierce sun, scorched with the hot breath of the north wind, and gasping for want of moisture', we naturally take up arms. The fight for our gardens, like every good fight, was continuous, eternal and nearly (not quite) hopeless. 'Gardening is now, and ever shall be, a constant warfare against the forces of Nature. Should the puny efforts of man falter for ever so short a time, Nature, always vigilant, triumphs, and the garden returns to its primeval state of wildness.'[51]

The same lesson lay at the heart of the federated nation. But even before Federation, in each colony the various governments had struggled to unify their peoples, to create a national feeling within their own particular borders. Building, extending, defending, territories were to be kept safe with brain and muscle, ingenuity and drill. In New Zealand settlers had organised from the start against Maori attack, and a regular body of volunteers had been raised there in 1862, during the Maori Wars. On the Australian mainland the main threat was from abroad. Safety lay in 'the unbroken circle of the skies', an intact coastline and secure capital cities. The capitals were the centres of order, the nursery beds of colonial civilisation. Everyone looked to their capital seat for speeches, editorials and expert instructions about building and defending on a national scale.

Rose Scott was right when she said that men liked to be in armies. British regiments stayed in the Australian colonies until 1870, and Henry Parkes had winced at the way the men of New South Wales let other men, from the far side of the world, defend their shore, 'denationalising the country,' he said, 'stripping it of its highest attributes, emasculating it of the British spirit which was its safety'. Even before the British left, local men, feeling the same, had started massing themselves into volunteer units, in the capitals and in a few country towns. These were private bodies, springing up at random from place to place. They bought their own weapons and uniforms, made their own rules and elected their own officers.[52] The volunteer units were part of a far-flung effort, especially by young men keen to test, man to man, their brains and bodies, just as they did in fire brigades, rifle clubs, cricket and football teams, and in city pushes.

In the schools, as I say, drill was used in teaching all kinds of subjects. Children were taught how to sit, stand and move in orderly ways, in and out of class. Out-of-class exercises in stubble-and-dirt playgrounds were easily converted into a kind of military drill. Male teachers' enthusiasm for turning children into soldiers annoyed some parents. Girls slouched their resentment. But some boys, hungry for danger, could not meet their teacher in the street without snapping to a salute.[53]

School cadet units multiplied fast. For a while they had looked like a passing fad, but in the 1890s governments made them into a great centralised movement and boys queued to join. In New South Wales there were enormous cadet camps every year, like athletics competitions, and boys came in uniform from all corners. In Victoria not every schoolboy was judged good enough to sign up, and the lucky ones showed off their uniforms and insignia. In Victoria in 1891 there were 450 male teachers (volunteers) learning about drill and musketry so that they could pass it on to their boys.[54]

At the universities the need for hands-on nation building made engineering courses popular in the 1880s. At Melbourne the volunteer John Monash qualified himself as a civil engineer. He loved the wonderful concentration of intellectual energy that such work involved. It was drill perfected. Also, in their buildings and other projects, civil engineers had to take full advantage of new inventions, besides catering for all sorts of needs, from the everyday habits and susceptibilities of crowds to the esoteric demands of manufacturers, miners, scientists, lighthouse keepers and so on – everyone who used their creations. With civil engineering a man lived at the edge of futurity. Time was money. In his mid-twenties, newly employed on important work, Monash found himself even more fully reborn, a man of business, quite capable, as he boasted to his diary, 'of rapidly passing from one thing to another, with little loss of time or delay in getting a fresh focus'. The shifting and shuffling of thought was pure joy, and work a 'perpetual holiday'.[55] He also loved bushwalking. Like military drill it tightened up body and brain.

Aiming to turn the pleasures of drill to good use, governments appointed drill sergeants for the various volunteer units. They also subsidised the purchase of uniforms and equipment, and the building of drill halls. Companies, squadrons and batteries were formed and commandants named, headquartered in the capital cities.

Regular government allowances were introduced. In New South Wales volunteers were fined if they did not turn up for training and given ten shillings a day if they did.[56]

When the university company at Melbourne was disbanded John Monash moved over to the Garrison Artillery, North Melbourne Battery, with responsibility for the guns defending Port Phillip, and he was promoted lieutenant. Soldiering for Monash was intellectual. It was a building process, creating order among men and things. It was brainwork. While he was building up this drilled life he kept a copious diary, compiling a detailed story of his feelings and achievements, jotting notes from day to day and then, every month or so, writing it all up in large volumes. He also made copies of all letters, including introspective ones, measuring thereby his steps upwards. This is how we know about the progress of his battles with Vic. He sent despatches to the future. At the same time he worked on designing and building Prince's Bridge, over the Yarra at the centre of Melbourne – granite and bluestone, topped by an elegant fabric of timber and iron.

A term even more popular than 'menace' was 'the struggle for existence'. One of the founders of modern psychology, the great American William James, put it like this:

> If this life be not a real fight, in which something is eternally gained for the universe by success, it is no better than a game of private theatricals from which one may withdraw at will. But it *feels* like a real fight – as if there were something really wild in the universe which we, with all our idealities and faithfulnesses, are needed to redeem.[57]

This was exactly Monash's point of view.

The 'real fight' was every day more real. The German and French presence in the western Pacific was a menace on an increasingly large scale, a scale which to Australians seemed cosmic. It called up a keen sense of the great spaces of the world, an understanding such as many young men and women were now starting to manage with ease. Since 1864 French convicts had been transported to New Caledonia. In the 1880s the French took control of Tahiti, the Tuamotus and the Marquesas, and the government in Paris came to uneasy agreement with London about the New Hebrides. From 1884 much of north-east New Guinea and the islands roundabout were under German control, which was from there extended to the Solomons, Nauru and the Marshalls, and so to the Marianas, Carolines and Samoa. At Castlemaine, in Victoria, a school inspector asked if every school could be supplied with a map of those waters, periodically updated so that future citizens could watch from their desks, in their bush classrooms, even as their enemies closed in. '[A]s every fresh claimant to colonial empire was year by year entered upon the maps,' he said, 'the necessity for keeping up a strong militia force would be indelibly imprinted on the minds of the children'.[58]

A minority, their minds attuned to narrower horizons, refused to see the danger. They too could sense menace, but it was the menace of centralised, drill-ridden, undemocratic authority. According to Henry Gyles Turner, a Melbourne banker and historian, the good soldier of the new dispensation was a man drilled to become 'as much like an insensate machine as possible'. He (or it) was brought into being for the sole purpose of 'destroying whatever it is bidden to attack'. People such as Turner and Rose Scott were impossible to bring to heel. They could not be made to see the need to arm. 'It is no use differing from them', said Sir Samuel Griffith. '[T]hey believe that is only a device of a military caste, of persons with military fads, to spend money, and do foolish things'.[59] More than that, to Rose Scott's mind it was feeding fire.

VI

The sceptics were easily beaten. The mass of men and women could in a moment be made to about-turn, whipped up to common action as if by a sudden shifting wind. In February 1885 news came of the death in the Sudan of General Charles Gordon at the hands of Arab insurgents, followers of the Muslim messiah (or Mahdi), Muhammad Ahmad. Gordon was the high-minded epitome of modern manliness, and his death at Khartoum, besieged by evil, shocked the British world. The New South Wales government – first in the Antipodes – straightaway offered artillery, infantry and an ambulance detachment to join avenging forces from Home. Getting the numbers was easy. In Victoria too, ours was 'a restless and migratory community', said Henry Gyles Turner. '[T]here could … be no difficulty in raising a body of five hundred men … ready to fight under any banner in any part of the world.' (But '[t]o claim patriotic virtue', Turner went on, 'for the men who are ready to shoot Arabs, Negroes, Abyssinians, or Egyptians indifferently at 5s. a day is a miserable prostitution of terms'.)[60]

A total of 768 men embarked from Sydney, 'glad', as a more patriotic pen remarked, 'of the chance of proving themselves possessed of manliness and courage'. They were watched with great excitement. A mass of citizens, rich and poor, gave more than £40,000 to support the wives and children they left behind, but the men were too late to be much use. None were killed, but six died on the way home. The usual wit appeared in the *Bulletin*, with a barrage of brilliant cartoons from Livingston Hopkins ('Hop'). We came back from battle, said the paper, like a peacock with our tail plucked.[61]

We had spent hundreds of thousands, Hop said, 'to be took notice of'. And indeed, the premier, William Bede Dalley, imagined with exquisite delight that moment when the imperial forces were joined in the field by 'the representatives of our manhood'. At last, by the very act of joining in, Australia was 'a nation in the eyes of all the world'.[62] But in this case, as with Monash's conquest of Vic, a single triumph was not enough. It had to be repeated over and over. In street fights too, it was never enough for a man to prove himself once. In the contest of nations, the need to repeat and to keep repeating, to go on being noticed, was increasingly urgent in the 1890s.

It was easy to find things to fight about. In 1898 the United States was at war with Spain, aiming, as it seemed, to take over Spanish territory in the West Indies and Pacific. A Sydney member of parliament told a local crowd that rights and wrongs were beside the point. '[T]hey ought to have a brotherly sympathy with the people of the United States.' Together they were Anglo-Saxons. Together they were men.

> He thought that if any of them came across one of their brothers in a fight or a scrimmage in the street they would, if they were men, hardly stop to ask the particulars of the quarrel. The probabilities were that they would off with their coats and rush into the fight.

'Big brother Jonathan' could look after himself, but that was beside the point. A man who wanted to prove himself, who wanted to know himself and to be known, joined in.[63]

Excitement multiplied with continuous trouble in Africa. Gold was found in the Transvaal, where the Boers, descendants of early Dutch settlers, had governed themselves independently of Britain, their former ruler, since 1881. A rich field on alien soil threatened London's supremacy in the gold markets of the world, and British ministers therefore had good reason to reconquer the Transvaal. The attitude in Australia was potentially complicated. The Boers were Christian and White. They were like Australians and they only wanted to be left alone. However, larger loyalties intervened. In July 1899 the colonial secretary in London told the governors of Canada, Victoria and New South Wales that he would like 'spontaneous' offers of support from their colonies. Mayors of capital cities, from Sydney to Perth, had already, on request, used their powers of persuasion at public meetings, but the results had been disappointing. There was only the usual swelling of the ranks of volunteer units, by random men drawn by hopes of blood and adventure. As a New South Welshman put it (like Henry Gyles Turner, a sceptic), '[I]f an expedition to the Antarctic regions in Maori war canoes was proposed, half our fellows would volunteer'. Now there were new pressures. The military hierarchies which had been formed to manage the volunteers wanted something to increase their own reach, and one by one governments gave in. In Tasmania and Western Australia, in particular, the love of drill was still feeble. But there was no possibility of staying out when joining meant so much.[64]

There was war in October. The Boers moved first, suddenly crossing into British territory and bombarding several towns, Mafeking (now Mafikeng), Kimberley and Ladysmith, terrifying and starving the townspeople. The siege of Ladysmith lasted four months, from October to February, and the story of its suffering, like the story of Gordon's encircling, gripped Britons everywhere. This was a country the Europeans in Australia knew from their reading of Henry Rider Haggard's stories. Inspired by his own years in the same part of Africa, in *Cetywayo and His White Neighbours* Haggard had told of the Boers. They were 'a peculiar people', he said.

> They are very religious, but their religion takes its colour from the darkest portions of the Old Testament … [W]hat they delight in are the stories of wholesale butchery by the Israelites of old; and in their own position they find a reproduction of that of the first settlers in the Holy Land.[65]

There was rage among Britons at the thought of being cornered by such people.

For the Europeans in Australia the Boer War was an early lesson in worldwide geopolitics, cast in military terms. With a sudden leap of imagination beyond the old horizons, this quarrel in the heart of Africa was linked to the steady expansion of France and Germany (the latter actively sympathetic with the Boers) into the western Pacific. If the Boers won, all our enemies won. With our weakness exposed those enemies would pounce. The Reverend James Jefferis, one of the most penetrating and sober of public speakers, spoke of a world war which would hurt us here unless Britain conquered. He felt in the air a 'bitter race hatred', fomented in Africa but everywhere contagious.[66]

With uniforms in Australian streets there was eagerness to fight. The Boer War had come too late to affect the vote for Federation, but Federation and the war were born of the same impulse. They involved two great bushfires of imagination and enthusiasm suddenly gathering and quickening, and then, in 1900–01, joined in a brilliant scorching rush. The mass of troops in Melbourne in May, at the opening of the first federal parliament, was beyond anything Australia had ever seen, and men returned from South Africa were given pride of place.[67]

As ever, the shadow of war hung heavily over the schools. What better thing than war to focus lessons about loyalty and moral purpose? Who could doubt now, asked the chief inspector of schools in New South Wales, that the military training of our boys was essential for the defence of 'our country'? And 'our country' now meant not New South Wales, and perhaps not even the empire, but Australia. 'With zeal', reported one of his subordinates, 'the pupils are being taught that the future safety of the Australian State lies in "Her Men! high-minded Men!"'[68]

A few clung to the idea that the Boers were right and we were wrong. No newspaper was more completely committed to the cause of Australian nationalism than the Sydney *Bulletin*, but for many writers in the *Bulletin* the new nationalism was already corrupted. The Boers were just the sort of people we should be, said the *Bulletin* – manly, stiff-backed, contemptuous of other races. This was a fight between the British money market and 'the white democracy of the Transvaal'.[69]

Like the *Bulletin* writers, Rose Scott wanted public order tied to landscape and people, free from bureaucracy and gold braid, and eventually this view started to win friends. The savagery of the British forces after beating the Boers, the deliberate devastation of farms and the wholesale incarceration of families (one child in two died in British concentration camps) were shocking. These facts were exposed mainly by Englishwomen. Emily Hobhouse, a welfare campaigner, was sent from England by the South African Women and Children's Distress Fund to make a tour of the camps, and Millicent Fawcett, whose main interest was women's rights, headed an inquiry unwillingly undertaken by ministers in London. Australians remained unmoved. 'I see no reason', said a Sydney clergyman, 'why we should shed more tears over Boers than over Britons, or why we should put down to British brutality what the doctors of the camps ascribe to maternal ignorance and stupidity'.[70]

VII

Australians were more interested in debating their own involvement in the war. Early in 1902 news broke that George Arnold Wood, professor of history at Sydney University, had told an English newspaper that Australian motives were mixed. A lot of our enthusiasm, said Wood, was amoral, 'the Empire right or wrong'. At Eugowra, west of Bathurst, the professor, if he ever ventured so far, was promised 'rather rough treatment – a bath in the nearest horse trough'. Eugowra men had given their lives for the empire.[71]

Rose Scott ran hard in this debate. By 1902 she was active in the

Australian Anti-War League, the main purpose of which was '[t]o substitute arbitration for war in international disputes'. She went beyond the question of arbitration to the question of freedom of speech. She focussed on the right to speak out against war without being shouted down, or, as she put it, quoting John Milton's *Areopagitica* (1644), the right 'to think, to utter, and to argue according to conscience'. It was the right to refuse to join in. The twentieth century, she said, must be a 'woman's century'. It followed that 'the settlement of disputes between nations must be by reason and moral force'.[72] Men and women of influence such as she was had to hold the ring, keeping clear of bludgeoning words and dispute en masse.

The Boer War coloured public and private conversations during the first years of the federated continent. In 1907, with the war over but with the possibility of a new war ever present, Rose Scott and Alfred Deakin, who was now prime minister of the new Federation, exchanged a series of letters about his scheme for the compulsory military training of boys and young men. She put it to him, and she was not the only woman to do so, that teaching anyone to fight was teaching them violence. It was teaching them not to think. Deakin disagreed, but something about the logic unsettled him. While she kept on writing he kept on answering, even against his better judgment. 'I never can resist replying to you', he said, 'though when you appeal to fundamental principles it becomes impossible to reply by letter'. He admired her 'truly womanly humanitarianism', and he wanted to make her believe that he shared it.[73] For him nationhood and manhood were not interwoven. The individuality of men need not show in blood.

As Australians we would never fight just for the sake of joining in. We would fight only in self-defence. He hoped 'to see the principles of peace and of arbitration in all disputes taught in all schools, preached in all churches and applied universally'. Was Miss Scott impressed? Probably not. Education was not a federal matter. And she was probably even less convinced by the suggestion that military training was really a training in the principles of peace. No-one could enjoy it, said Deakin. It would prove to all recruits 'the pains and penalties of war'. A true modern democracy could be 'a nation in arms', but it could never love war.[74]

Alfred Deakin was the last man in the world to fight for the joy of joining in. He was the last to want to be reborn in blood. He imagined his own civilised virtues easily multiplied among men, although, in fact, the moral capacity of people en masse was still barely understood. Rose Scott's imagination, on the other hand, conjured up 'the least and the worst' of mankind, egging each other on, as they did with Mary Jane Hicks at Mt Rennie. When Deakin said 'military spirit' he thought of countries invading each other, and Australians would never do that. When Miss Scott said 'military spirit' her mind moved among men, women and children living and dealing with each other in much smaller spaces. Again, Australia was an idea, an ill-defined medley of hopes. These two imagined two different Australias.

8

Black and White

I

The Kimberley, in the far north-west of the continent, was and is a world apart. The northern Kimberley, a place of bloodwood and yellow wattle, of ragged inlets, sheer cliffs and spots of mangrove, much of it impenetrable and spectacular, confronts Asia. Inland, the Fitzroy River flows into King Sound to the south-west, and the Ord River into Cambridge Gulf to the north-east. The valleys, cut through with limestone ranges, grey and gold-red, make up an expansive half-circle of grassland. A proclamation of 1832 had included the Kimberley within the colony of Western Australia. But it was separated from the government in Perth by two or three thousand kilometres of largely desert country. A continental point of view, the view of the Melbourne map reader, say, made the Kimberley part of the North, of the territory stretching from the north-eastern islands of the Indian Ocean to the coral reefs of the Pacific. And indeed, livestock moved in a more or less steady stream 'across the top' westward from Queensland. In travelling time – by sea – the Kimberley was closer to south-east Asia than it was to Sydney or Melbourne.

In 1821 Bundell, an Aboriginal man from near Sydney, had visited the northern Kimberley, sailing with Lieutenant Phillip Parker King on the circumnavigation of Australia. Bundell was familiar with European exploration, having already made two lengthy bush trips with parties keen to know about Sydney's hinterland. The Worora at Hanover Bay, halfway between King Sound and

Cambridge Gulf, seeing Europeans for the first time, took them to be ghosts, and Bundell eased relations by displaying his own blackness, standing naked in the prow of the ship's boat as it came in to shore.[1] More than a generation later, in 1865, a similar effort involved another Aboriginal intermediary, from the southern parts of Western Australia. When the Sholls, father and son, arrived with the idea of forming a cattle station, the Jeidji of Cambridge Gulf dealt directly with Billy. As the younger Sholl told his journal, one of the local men 'seemed very much amused by our native Billy – shook hands with him, felt him all over, made him open his mouth and had a look at his teeth'. All the time the probing Jeidji laughed out loud. Inspection inside and out broke the ice. Billy was alive.[2]

Kimberley people already knew that there were outsiders. The coast had been regularly visited by Makasans from the islands to the north, searching for trepang. These latest arrivals, Black and White, vastly extended their view of the world.

The Sholls did not last. Permanent European settlement started only in the early 1880s, at first from the south into the valley of the Fitzroy, then from the east (the Northern Territory and Queensland) along the Ord. Some newcomers wrote in lyrical fashion about travelling into this latest and last unknown. '[W]e rode', said Richard Pilmer, a constable charged with keeping order between Black and White, 'through miles of the delicate pink everlastings, then miles upon miles of the white'. Pilmer was a first-class bushman, and it was his first assignment of this kind. During the next stage, by boat to Derby, '[w]e sailed along on seas of glass under a cloudless sky, and the glory of the dawns and sunsets was beyond telling'.[3]

The sweetness in these descriptions sits strangely beside the terror encountered by the man who wrote them, and beside the terror he created. In the Kimberley, Richard Pilmer traumatised Aboriginal imagination for several generations, and his impact was remembered rightly or wrongly as a holocaust. He and another man, according to later legend,

> was shooting people
> Thousands and thousands of people, they start from eastern state right down
> to north
> right up – to west.[4]

A deadly will-o'-the-wisp, ubiquitous and all-powerful, in memory Pilmer levelled whole tribes. His own story was more modest:

> I knew too well the tragedy of that dwindling race. But they had offended against the law of the white men, and we were mounted police and our mission was to get them. In the early days of Australia's pioneering [Pilmer was writing as an old man, fifty years on], everywhere, in every State, the native was looked upon as a fierce and formidable foe, and there is no doubt that he could, and did, make things lively. Without punitive measures, sometimes drastic, Australia could never have been a white man's country.[5]

On the one hand the race was dwindling. It could not survive. On the other hand, only serious bloodshed could make Australia 'a white man's country'.

In deeper retrospect, the main drama in Pilmer's life seems to be the pursuit of the Black man Tjangamarra (or Jandamarra or Tjandamurra – or Pigeon), who was born in the early 1870s. He was a Bunuba from the valleys of the Lennard and Fitzroy rivers, open country traversed by the almost (for Whites) impenetrable King Leopold Ranges. This was the southern Kimberley, first taken up by pastoralists travelling northwards when Tjangamarra was little. The invaders depended from the start on Aboriginal labour, and Tjangamarra learnt to ride, shear and shoot, all with extraordinary skill, on William Lukin's Lennard River Station. In 1889 he escaped a charge of killing sheep by agreeing to work with the police. He became a native tracker. Tjangamarra's sexual escapades had already made him a refugee from Aboriginal justice. He now helped to round up his own people.

In spring 1894 Tjangamarra and Bill Richardson, a constable, caught sixteen men and chained them together so that they could be taken for trial for killing stock, before the magistrate at Derby, which was the European headquarters for the western Kimberley. Tjangamarra had once saved Richardson's life and they were close. But the sixteen were all Bunuba, including an even older friend, Ellemarra, who was afterwards, like Tjangamarra himself, a brilliant figure in Aboriginal memory.[6]

'Our women / you chase after', the sixteen said to Tjangamarra. '[W]hy don't you shoot him [Richardson]?' Tjangamarra had been an offender against both Black and White, and now he suddenly changed sides again, making himself a leader of his own people. Richardson was killed in his sleep, the others were unchained, and all headed for the fortress of Windjana Gorge, a great limestone channel with walls at some points 330 feet (100 metres) high, which is the passage of the Lennard River, sometimes tearing sometimes trickling through the Napier Range. Now Tjangamarra put it about that he meant to 'kill whites'. He goaded Black stockmen into following him and he trained them to shoot. He killed two White stockmen and butchered their cattle. As Pilmer recalled, 'The lubras ... carried the news [of meat] to the hill-country tribes, who came in for their share of the feast. Pigeon was the hero of the hour, "bulya-man" of the King Leopolds'.[7]

In fact, Tjangamarra was the hero of countless hours. To be a 'bulya-man' was to have a magic immunity, especially against bullets. Such a man was not easily forgotten. '[H]e the one done all the fighting', they said eighty years later, 'this others [his followers] didn't understand him'.[8]

The police in Derby were authorised by telegraph from Perth to spare no expense in putting down what looked like a dangerous rebellion. It was the first example of Aboriginal resistance anywhere which made full use of firearms. No Kimberley Black, it was thought, could be fully trusted, but a few from other parts, including Queensland, were recruited, together with all the weapons and ammunition available, and Whites were sworn in as special constables.[9]

A force of twenty-eight, including Pilmer and a number of Aborigines, tried to storm the gorge. In the hours before daylight – clothed in a silence typically interspersed in those parts with the cape turtle dove's wistful 'where's father?' – they surrounded the spot where they imagined the insurgents to be. The sudden siege at dawn, with the enemy sleeping, was a tactic used by troops and police in Queensland with camps of shearers on strike, but in this case the encirclers were themselves encircled. About fifty Aborigines, expecting the siege, had climbed into caves and cracks surrounding the site, with their rifles, shotguns and revolvers. However, they themselves were surprised by another party, again Black and White, arriving late and firing from even further above. After eight hours' sporadic shooting, Ellemarra was shot and killed, a devastating setback, because he, like Tjangamarra, was supposed to be proof against bullets. In a moment of consternation, Tjangamarra suddenly emerged, pushed back the attackers with a round of gunfire, darted again into the rocks, reloaded and reappeared. He was hit in stomach and chest before vanishing with his followers into a tangle of limestone tunnels.[10]

A day was spent looking for him. Pilmer had a way with words, and in describing these events afterwards he did not stint. 'Some of the caverns', he said, 'were two hundreds yards [180 metres] in, dark as pitch, with wonderful stalactites and stalagmites, and springs of clear water forming deep pools'. Tjangamarra survived the search, and the hunter again became the hunted. Pilmer was now the bulyaman's principal target, or so he (Pilmer) said. 'Wampa (blackfellow) wanta catchem Bil-i-mur [Pilmer]', women warned him. '[H]e bigfella finishem. Bymeby finishem up whitefella altogether.'[11]

Guessing, boasting and sweeping predictions were parts of this kind of war. In fact, conflict was more or less over. For a while Tjangamarra was said to be dead. After two and a half years, most of the time in the hills with his people, he was in fact shot and killed by an Aboriginal tracker from near Roebourne called Mingo Mick. Mick had moved between Black and White like Tjangamarra, gathering skills and breaking the law on both sides. Like Tjangamarra and Ellemarra he was a 'wit[ch] doctor'. It was futile to shoot him.[12]

There was wizardry in moving and in talking beyond old boundaries, as if old boundaries had suddenly evaporated. The Blacks thought Pilmer could manage such miracles too, as a magic worker among White men. Or so he boasted – 'I had greatness thrust upon me'.[13]

Pilmer was not alone among White men, in this generation especially, in wanting notoriety as a master among savages, and he used stories to make his name. They had all read Rider Haggard. Maybe some were acquainted too with Joseph Conrad's *Heart of Darkness*, or at least with *Lord Jim*.

Both sides were dazzled by Tjangamarra's cleverness and his seeming invulnerability. 'As natives go', said Pilmer (who did not want to sound in awe of anyone), he was 'a weed', 'not more than five foot five [165 centimetres], but very intelligent and agile, a leader and a strategist, and not wanting in pluck'. Not wanting in pluck! In Aboriginal judgment, even two generations later, Tjangamarra could 'fly like a bird and disappear like a ghost'. Had he survived,

> he had ta been a
> king of Australia
> and everything would have been come back – right way.[14]

Some Europeans agreed that the business of making the Kimberley, at least, into 'a white man's country' was in jeopardy because of

Tjangamarra. Long before he killed Richardson, pastoralists had a feeling of being under siege by Tjangamarra's people.

Guessing and terror, again, were parts of frontier life – a perception of menace and a longing to get rid of it – but the government in Perth took a broader view. It was always keen to avoid any policy which looked like extermination, which public opinion in Britain would not allow. Aborigines were British subjects, and pastoralists were warned against indiscriminate killing.[15] Until 1890, when self-government came to Western Australia, officials in Perth were accountable to London, and even after that there was an Aboriginal Protection Board, which reported home to the other side of the world, though it was much less useful.

II

Throughout Australasia governments each had their own old ways of dealing with Aboriginal people. In the league table of arbitrary brutality, Tasmania had once set the pace. In Tasmania, Blacks had often been thought of in bulk, cunning perhaps but with nothing like modern individuality, and rarely as beings of separate value. In the 1830s near Perth a visiting Tasmanian had caused a stir when he shot at a group of Blacks without any sort of provocation. 'Damn the rascals', he said. 'I'll show you how we treat them in Van Diemen's Land.'[16]

In those days Tasmania had been an enticing model for impatient White men. Now, however, the model was Queensland. In 1907 an old Queenslander gave his recollections to a Townsville paper under the heading 'Taming the Niggers'. In writing, this man (his name is now lost) hung between guilt and bravado. But on one thing he was clear. He agreed with Richard Pilmer. Aborigines had to be shown that killing cattle was wrong. They had to be 'tamed and taught to obey the law of the white man'. He remembered being in a party which killed in one swoop more than 150 Blacks.

'In that wild, yelling, rushing mob', he said, 'it was hard to avoid shooting the women and babies'. And again, on a night-time raid, '[h]ow those gins and kiddies shrieked when we got amongst them. The blood of the white man was up and nothing with a black hide escaped death that night'. Exaggeration or not, wholesale murder was a bragging matter in Queensland.[17]

In Western Australia there were White men who took gladly to such stories. In 1892 a newspaper editor at Roebourne, a centre of opinion for Kimberley graziers, published a story about local Europeans killed by Aborigines. The aim might be to teach law to the Aboriginal people, but the solution, he said, was not legal process. It was 'abundance of ammunition'. We needed action 'in good old Queensland style'.[18]

Queensland style was already used in managing stock and stockmen, especially in the eastern Kimberley. In other parts of Western Australia the usual way was to take on men like Tjangamarra, from local tribes, but in Queensland such trust was rare. In Queensland the old inhabitants had usually been cleared out of the way, with the idea that stock might be largely unattended. The Queensland Native Mounted Police was crucial. This was a force with White officers, but otherwise using Aborigines from other parts of the continent, armed and mounted. The force in Queensland dated back to the 1840s, and by the 1870s and '80s, when Queensland cattle numbers dramatically increased, it had reached a peak of efficiency. The Native Police had Tasmanian habits. As a sometime premier admitted, they had a policy of shooting every unenlisted Aborigine wandering between their sights. The result, said a grazier on the spot, was 'cold blooded cruelty ... quite unparalleled in the history of these colonies', in impact beyond even Tasmania.[19]

Demands for a native police in Western Australia came to nothing. Old principles of law and humanity prevailed, more or less. The government could turn a blind eye to the misdeeds of settlers. But it did not itself go in for systematic murder.

Also, by the end of the century new principles of law and humanity were overtaking the old ones. We were all being reborn. The minds of the Europeans in Australia, like Europeans elsewhere, were starting to move in a more wide-horizoned, bookish, or mappish, fashion. Again, this is the story told through all these chapters. First the people reimagined one by one each corner of the continent. Then came the single comprehensive view. In coming to terms with the whole space, cartographically conceived, sometimes the Europeans showed a sudden exhilaration, an intoxication, at the vastness available. Maps were common now. They were used in schools and even in newspapers. From the contemplation of maps sprang a driving sense of control, a busy wish to plant and partition, to divide and subdivide, to take a firmer grip on entirety. This busy wish turned Aboriginal lives upside down.

So far, managing the country had been about making journeys, exploring and fetching back information to the colonial capitals. The Kimberley was the last substantial blank. With the Kimberley invaded and its people broken, there were no more lines between known and unknown, no more inner boundaries between us and the others, no frontier.

Now the continent could be seen as a single mass of wealth. It was space for a commonwealth on a vast scale and raw material for a single great idea. It was to be managed by clearing and fencing, by apportioning for a multitude of purposes, by trading and travelling freely, by moving water, like money, from places of superfluity to places of need, by conserving and exploiting as all-embracing minds thought best.

As for the Aboriginal people, the focus of thinking about them shifted from conflict to discipline. Ideas about 'dispersal' (often meaning massacre) were replaced by ideas about mustering and bringing in to specially allocated places. In this too, Queensland set extreme standards. In Queensland extreme violence and extreme idealism lived together. They sometimes overlapped, in a jejune tyranny of bookishness. In Russia not long before, Fyodor Dostoyevsky had written *Crime and Punishment*, in which the hero murders an old woman because he needs her money for nobler purposes than she in her ignorance can ever imagine. It was a 'modern' murder, they said, 'a case characteristic of our time', a time when people deliberately set their brains free from their feelings. 'We're dealing with bookish dreams here, with a heart exacerbated by theories.'[20] Our collective heart, the heart of Australia, was 'exacerbated by theories', and it showed with particular rawness in Queensland.

William Lane's 'New Australia' (chapter 6), a Queensland creation, was a bookish dream. Lane taught mateship and collaboration. But when his party reached Paraguay he became a relentless autocrat. What else can a journalist turned hero-idealist do when his disciples fail him? In Black–White relations a similar figure was Archibald Meston, another journalist and another man of theory, but also a plantation manager and an explorer.

In 1894 Meston was asked by the Queensland government to report on what ought to be done with the Aborigines – those who were left. Meston believed that current practices were unworthy of a civilised country. Treatment of Pacific Islands labourers was regulated by law. According to Meston, we needed similar regulation and protection for the original owners of the soil. 'The work of atonement for some of the dreadful past lies before us', he said. Nothing less than 'the future honour of the nation' (he meant Queensland) depended on how quickly it started and how well it was done.[21]

Sometimes Meston believed that the Aboriginal people were condemned by Providence to die out, but sometimes, depending on what story he wanted to tell, he argued the opposite, declaring that the dying race theory was 'the shameful subterfuge in which strong races have endeavoured to take refuge from their crimes on the weak'. In the 1830s George Augustus Robinson, house builder turned evangelist, had taken the mass of surviving Tasmanian Aborigines to Flinders Island, thereby rescuing them from murder for instruction in European ways. This was Meston's solution, but instead of an island he suggested two (later three) large inland reserves. What was needed most of all, he said, was '*complete isolation of their social life from contact with the white races*'. With isolation secure we only had to be patient. We had to wait for the turnover of generations. The old people, in all charity, should be left alone. The young men and women should be allowed to mix traditional habits with new ways, 'a little work, a little hunting, a little amusement'. But the children should be urged much further.[22]

Meston was a big man. Like Richard Pilmer he was physically fit, and like Pilmer he was a boaster. He saw himself as both a reader and a warrior, and he admired the Aborigines because they had been warriors too. (The Chinese, on the other hand, were to his mind a feeble race, unfit to live.) He had been among Blacks since childhood, or so he said. He could pick up their dialects easily and he could handle weapons like one of them. What he could do was like magic. Aboriginal initiation, the ritual making of men, touched his own sense of what he was and, always a man among men, he had been initiated, he said, among the Blacks. '[I]t was possible', he said, 'for me to establish friendship with even the wildest and most suspicious tribes'.[23]

To the new generation of White bushmen throughout Australia, men like Meston, there was nothing mysterious about the 'ideographic prophecy' written on the face of the country. Reborn, self-realised in the Australian bush, it was child's play. Meston was a hard man. In fact, he was manly in an ideal way because he was also brainy, using the current definition. Like Pilmer in his contest with Tjangamarra, he thought he could beat Aboriginal men at their own game. But unlike Pilmer, at times he saw something in Aboriginal life worth preserving. Tracking skills, so valuable in catching White criminals and finding people lost in the bush, were dying out. Meston wanted a 'training station', jointly funded by all the colonies, to keep up a supply of 'these matchless lynx-eyed detectives'.[24]

Meston idolised the late superb (some said satanic) Lord Byron. Byron had wanted justice for the Greeks. Meston wanted it for the Aborigines. Byron had mourned the feebleness of modern Greeks:

> Fill high the bowl of Samian wine!
> Our virgins dance beneath the shade –
> I see their glorious black eyes shine;
> But, gazing on each glowing maid,
> My own the burning tear-drop laves,
> To think such breasts must suckle slaves.[25]

Meston took the same approach to the Australian Blacks.

However, the Aborigines would need forcible persuasion to make them free. Here Meston relied on his other main source of ideas, that worshipper of heroes Thomas Carlyle, plus a popularised Charles Darwin. In any human crisis there was no alternative to decisive action, plus suffering.

> [T]he old order of things is passing away [Meston said], and they [the Aborigines] must adapt themselves to the changed environment, just as white races, individuals and communities, have to adapt themselves to sudden or gradual changes all over the face of the earth. Their land has been taken from them on no other title than the law of the strongest, and they must make the best of any alternative the strongest chooses to offer.

On the reserves, so Meston imagined, everything would be strictly regulated, with 'a fixed code of laws, sternly enforced at all hazards when necessary'. Troublemakers and backsliders would need to be thrown out, 'for the sake of all the others'.[26] With strong measures and with leaders like himself the manhood of a fighting people would be restored.

III

So isolation was the answer. The idea of being cut off from the rest of creation, or from the rest of your kind, both horrified and enchanted late-nineteenth-century Europeans. Much was epitomised by Alexandre Dumas's Count of Monte Cristo, a favourite character for the pre-War generation (though the story dates from 1844), a man first imprisoned for years in perfect isolation and then gloriously empowered.[27] Isolation meant individuality in extremis. It was an idea that echoed through everything, from penal theory to the origins of the universe and the evolution of species.

It had started to take hold as early as the 1830s – for instance, when Charles Darwin had made his way across the Pacific, in a voyage of discovery among animate and inanimate creation. It had occurred to Darwin then that isolation made islands into big laboratories. Within a single encircling shoreline, if at all remote, animal and human life unfolded alone over thousands of years, moving by infinitesimal steps towards a perfect match of self and circumstance. By the last decades of the nineteenth century, the idea of life finding its way under Providence, each fragment bearing the mark of its own destiny, each quarantined from all the others, was dazzling.

This was 'self-generated motion', orderly but unpredictable, marching with the majesty of the ages. It had been formulated best by the German philosopher Wilhelm von Humboldt (1767–1835), and it had an infinity of applications.[28] Every race and species, like every man and woman, had to find its own irreducible self. Isolation made individuality sublime – but very often cruel. As the *Bulletin* poet put it,

> For life is life, and death is death, and each man 'goes alone',
> And death is a frozen No Man's Land, and life is a torrid
> zone;
> And the way of the world is a curious way, and curious
> creatures thrive,

> And the false man lives and the true man dies, and only the fit survive.[29]

The Australian continent was an island on a large scale. It looked like a forcing ground for the higher evolution of the White race, or of the British type, 'going alone'.

However, different parts of it could be set aside for smaller purposes. In the 1890s there were a number of White communities formed on the principle of intense, complete cooperation (mentioned in chapter 5). With members carefully chosen, they were pools of virtue away from the White Australian mainstream and designed to show, as Elsie Birks said about Murtho, the 'inherent good in human nature'.[30]

Those projects were called 'village settlements'. Archibald Meston planned 'Aboriginal settlements', to bring out the inherent goodness of Black men and women.[31] Like the founders of the village settlements, Meston hit upon mingling kindness and hardness. That involved keeping out, and throwing out, the unworthy, every 'false man'. It was a question of setting firm boundaries and finding a balance, freedom *versus* order.

Meston's theorising was wide-horizoned. He helped to pioneer one of the founding ideas of Australian nationhood. Like the word 'Australia', the word 'Aboriginal' summed up both a great problem and a great solution. You only had to think and write on this sweeping scale, about a mass of human beings well defined and neatly bounded, and the answers came.[32]

Some might still like to find answers by thinking small, even on Aboriginal questions. Take that determined reformer of Queensland race relations the Catholic priest Duncan McNab. Father McNab came from the Scottish Highlands, and he started work in Queensland in 1875. Missionaries in earlier days had tried to teach Christian belief. McNab was more concerned with Christian order, fond, intricate, inward, domestic.

For McNab it all came down to couples, male and female, and to parents and children. As the Queensland minister for lands explained, 'Mr McNab's idea ... is to base his reformation of the blacks on the principle of the family rather than of the communistic or tribal compact'. The old family life of the Aborigines, to McNab's mind, was shaped around 'barbarous customs, superstitions, and certain usages, which, with them, have the form of law, and are incompatible with our civilisation'. These evils had to be fought in cooperation with the people, working from the inside out. Inherent goodness had to be cultivated bit by bit, with infinite pains, by making homes within neighbourhoods. The Aborigines had to be 'domiciled like the whites', he said, 'and not merely preserved like cattle on a run'.[33]

Like Whites, Aborigines had to have their own land – individual holdings, family farms. Title would be held by each husband-father. On the reserves, the land belonged to no-one in particular and it was used in common, which meant that Aboriginal people kept up their old marriage laws. Their 'communism' and their 'polygamy and polyandria' were two sides of the same coin.[34] The regular inheritance of property, on the other hand, depended on state-sanctioned marriage. McNab took it for granted that Aboriginal people were as anxious as Europeans to provide for their children.

This was the key. Land should be given to individual men, inheritable like all other property, even entailed by law within one family, 'on condition of their contracting a regular marriage and having legitimate offspring'. They should be bound to particular spots, generation after generation, just as tribes were bound to bigger spaces. In fact, McNab aimed to make use of ancient attachment. The 'homesteads' he wanted would be carved out of tribal land.

In July 1876 McNab wrote to the minister for lands in Brisbane, arguing for the right of Aboriginal men to leases from the Crown on which they could set up as small farmers. He was acting, he said, '[b]y instructions received from the Aborigines, James Diper,

William Watiman Nilepi, and Charles Diper Ghepara', and on behalf of these three he applied for 640 acres each (1 square mile, or about 260 hectares), to be granted under the terms of the *Crown Lands Alienation Act 1868*, from the homeland of the men concerned. In making their application, the three men

> conceive and maintain [McNab went on] that because they and their ancestors, from time immemorial, have occupied and possessed those lands and appurtenances for their use and benefit, especially of residence, hunting, fishing, and otherwise providing for the necessaries of life, and also always the right of tillage and pasturage, they ought to be acknowledged, without expense, the rightful owners of the specified homesteads.

There were other Aboriginal men ready to give him the same kind of instructions. But the minister must not take fright, 'not in such numbers as to embarrass the Government'.[35]

For McNab, these three men would pioneer a new order of 'common benefit to the colonists and the Aboriginals'. It would be good for the colonists because the Blacks would make money instead of living off charity. They would become a class of well-regulated wage labourers. It meant that the Aborigines would be 'treated as men, and not merely shot down as vermin'. We had to have equal justice. 'Chastise alike, the blacks for killing or maiming the cattle of the colonists, and the latter for destroying the game of the former till they are otherwise provided for.'

The Aborigines, like other free selectors, would have to stay on their land if they wanted to keep it. To start with they would want to graze stock rather than farm. '[M]en who have lived by the chase will not submit to constant toil, such as is required by extensive cultivation', and the best way to begin would be to set aside common land for each collection of homesteads. But livestock should be individual property. Every owner should have his own livestock brand – registered under Patrick Robertson Gordon's new centralised system, started only three years earlier. Aboriginal people were to be subject like Europeans to the rural code, the redefining of the propertied citizen, which Gordon was pioneering.[36] They were not to be 'herded like cattle', 'shot down as vermin' or treated as unfeeling pieces of property.

The scheme had two matching keys. There was attachment to children and attachment to land. The recruitment of labour in Queensland included the wholesale theft of Aboriginal children (see chapter 2). The breakup of Aboriginal families underpinned the settlement of Europeans on the land, and the results were obvious everywhere. 'This isolation of solitary men and women', as Archibald Meston put it, 'and couples, and small groups of old people and children separated widely from friends, family and class relations is a source of much fretting and grief'.[37] Father McNab's system was meant to stop that devastation.

Most of what McNab knew about Aboriginal people at this point he had got out of books or heard second-hand.[38] His own experience so far was scanty, much less than Meston's. The minister for lands showed McNab's proposal to Matthew Hale, Anglican bishop of Brisbane, whose interest in Aboriginal society went back thirty years. Hale had founded and managed a successful church mission at Poonindie, near Port Lincoln, South Australia, and later on, as bishop of Western Australia, he had looked into the Benedictine monastery settlement at New Norcia, north-east of Perth, a great example of patient, small-scale missionising. In Brisbane, Hale had been appointed to chair a royal commission on the condition of Queensland Aborigines. The bishop liked McNab's enthusiasm. But McNab was too optimistic. There was nothing wrong, Hale said, with Aboriginal people having cattle in common. Living and working 'as a large co-operative society' did not make them feel like cattle themselves. McNab was guessing.

> I can assure Mr. McNab [said Hale] that natives have no feeling of this kind when they live together in one large institution and all work for the common good.
>
> The feeling which they have is that it is all theirs, and they talk of the stock and the crops as 'ours' with the greatest interest and satisfaction.[39]

It was just another case of communal livelihood. Hale's verdict was enough to sink McNab as the kind of reformer the Queensland government wanted.

But how could little Poonindies or New Norcias be set up all over Queensland? Where was the bottomless pit of skill and sensitivity which would make Aboriginal people give up their 'barbarous customs, superstitions, and ... usages' and submit to a new order? The answer, as usual, was a single big idea. It was Meston's.

IV

Attractively packaged brainwork, bookish dreams, large, sweeping and apparently pregnant with a final answer, were irresistible. Just as schoolchildren looked for easy ways through the problems of mental arithmetic, governments looked for ideas which could resolve straightaway the problems they now confronted – big problems, tied to large spaces and to populations expanding beyond easy control, and in particular to the poor and ignorant. The main fund of such ideas was in what later generations called the social sciences – sociology, geography, psychology, or, as the poet Robert Browning said,

> cosmogony,
> Geology, ethnology, what not
> (Greek endings, each the little passing-bell
> That signifies some faith's about to die).[40]

Such sciences threw up universal laws far more useful than the laws generated by judges and legislators. Understanding human beings en masse – subdividing, classifying and treating each subset according to need – must cut back risk, the risk of unpredictable variety and deep disorder.

These new laws were not just bigger than the laws of human beings. They were also bigger, or at least they were clearer and more convincing – more promising – than the laws of God as understood for many centuries. As Robert Browning said, they cancelled out the whisperings of conscience, the inner-felt threads of common humanity, which had been the fabric of old Christendom.

Big ideas were a necessary part of deliberate, high-speed nation building. During the 1890s and 1900s, for instance, the English sociologist Charles Booth divided the poor of London into five types. His lowest type, class A (he was radical and his alphabet started at the bottom), was criminally degenerate and beyond hope, but happily it was also very small. At the other end, classes C, D and E were all more or less respectable, and they could look after themselves. For Booth, it was class B, second from the bottom and big, which was the challenge of the day for scientists and statesmen. The problem of class B was all the more intriguing because it was not quite insoluble. It called for manly brainwork such as few could manage. It was work for heroes.

Class B was a conundrum, intellectual, moral and political. Every modern nation had its class B – it was the shirking, shiftless poor, interested only in casual, unskilled work, of questionable morals and irregular habits. Their intermingling dirtied the rest.

Members of London's class B, said Booth, if they could not better themselves by themselves, should be sent to disciplined communities, 'labour colonies'. National welfare depended on '[t]he entire removal of this very poor class out of the daily struggle for existence'.[41] Booth's aim was to chastise this one class so as to free the rest for more perfect citizenship. Unlike class A, class B was not a 'criminal class'. But they might be treated as if they were. With these great truths established, old protocols could be put aside. Old principles of law and humanity, including the rights of the British subject under the law, even the commands of conscience, might give way to a higher rule.

To the reforming eye, the Aboriginal people of Australia resembled a class B. They were both a social category and a race. This formulation, so exciting to the well read, was Queensland's answer to the 'Aboriginal problem'. It quickly became Australia's answer. Like the intractable among London's poor, the Aboriginal people were to be removed, for their own good and for the general good, 'out of the daily struggle for existence'.

Archibald Meston drew these issues together in a masterly fashion. Active also in Queensland was Ernest Gribble. A clergyman like Father McNab (but Church of England), Gribble did not share McNab's faith in the bond between parents and children. Like Meston, Gribble thought that that bond was in fact the problem, not the answer, because it compounded the power of the old over the young. That power had to be broken.

Ernest Gribble ran his own mission at Yarrabah, near Cairns, under the general supervision of the Church of England's Australian Board of Missions. It had been founded by his father, John Gribble, in 1892, but Ernest had been forced to take it over almost straightaway when John was struck down, fatally as it turned out, by malaria. (There is more about Ernest Gribble in chapter 9.) Ernest had a driving sense of duty. In his own life he followed conscientiously in his father's footsteps, but he was driven to destroy the same sense of duty among the Blacks. The old ones, he said, were 'very conservative'. They 'look with a suspicious eye upon everything that threatens their old customs and traditions'. He had to wrestle the young away.[42]

In Cairns the constables were happy to use Gribble's nearby mission to house the town's dispossessed and displaced Aboriginal children, starting with a blind boy called Willie, who arrived at Yarrabah in 1893. During the second half of the nineteenth century 'industrial schools' were set up throughout the colonies for White children deemed to be in moral danger, with negligent and/or vicious parents, or else adrift, to all appearances, in the adult world (living on the streets, for instance). Fated otherwise to belong to class B, or even class A (the criminal class), they were supposed to be trained for work and a useful adulthood. Queensland's *Industrial and Reformatory Schools Act 1865* made special mention of children born of Aboriginal or part-Aboriginal mothers, and for Ernest Gribble this act was providential. Yarrabah was registered as an industrial school in 1900. With or without the requisite magistrate's signature, Gribble took any children the police had to offer.[43]

It seemed a good idea to get these children off the streets. Certainly, a Cairns newspaper called it tyranny – 'In the name of humanity, of religion, and of common sense, we denounce a law under which children may be torn from their parents at the option of any one man' – but this was old-fashioned prejudice. It could not shake the notion of progress underpinned by the highest form of brainwork. In the first year alone Ernest Gribble gathered sixteen children, finding a space for them among his flock, forcing them to speak nothing but English and supervising all they did. 'These Mission children,' he said, 'growing up under Christian teaching, lose all touch with native laws and regulations, and naturally form their own attachments'.[44] Such was progress.

A more sweeping solution had to be found for the men and women. This was left to Archibald Meston. In 1894 he was consulted by the Queensland government, and his detailed answer led to the *Aboriginals Protection and Restriction of the Sale of Opium Act 1897*. This great act – 'great' because it crystallised and perpetuated an extraordinary idea – involved the complete reform of Aboriginal administration in Queensland, and it foreshadowed the same kind of changes in Western Australia, South Australia and the Northern

Territory. It gave the government in Brisbane the power to gather Aboriginal people onto reserves, to confine them because they were Aboriginal, and for life.[45]

In the days of the Native Police, the government had killed large numbers without any kind of legal justification. Now it was committed to a system of abduction and imprisonment which was just as thorough, but anchored in law and in scientific theory.

Meston did not get the three large inland reserves he wanted, but a number of smaller ones were created over time, each with its own character. Under the act, he was appointed protector of Aborigines for southern Queensland, and he based himself on Fraser Island, about 200 kilometres (at its nearest point) north of Brisbane, a relatively small space 120 kilometres long and, though an island, not entirely isolated from Europeans. During the first three years more than 300 men, women and children were transported to Fraser Island from all parts of Queensland. Meston did not hesitate to prevent marriages and to break up families. He was often just playing with power, but he was also driven by hopes of rejuvenating the Aboriginal people, of rediscovering their manhood.[46]

Aboriginal people themselves would soon see the beauty of the plan, so the government believed. And not just Aboriginal people. 'I hope', said the Queensland home secretary, 'the result of this legislation will be to show the civilised world that however black may be the page of history in Queensland on account of the past, there is a bright page to be written'. Meston's dreams went even further. He saw Fraser Island as a kind of paradise. With a little labour and with true leadership (his own leadership), 'it will establish a permanent precedent and the problem of the Aboriginals will be at last near a satisfactory solution'.[47]

Many of Queensland's Black inhabitants, Meston thought, would be keen to come in. They would realise that they were to be trained to take part in the new civilisation, and at the same time allowed to continue their old ways. A few would need a little forcible persuasion. In fact, Meston became more and more forceful. Even within the settlement he had his own way of managing ingratitude and insolence. He continually tested his powers and he revelled in the result. A few words delivered like the touch of a whip left an indelible mark. '[T]hey have a wholesome fear', he said, 'of having to deal with me'. He gloried in the idea of Fraser Island as a place of special discipline, perfect for Aboriginal ex-criminals and others in need of an iron hand, 'especially adapted', as he put it, 'for a station to receive blacks over whom an effective control is a stern necessity'.[48]

By 1900 Meston's callous inefficiency had become so glaringly obvious that the settlement was handed over to the Anglican Church's Board of Missions, in consultation with Ernest Gribble. In 1904 it was closed. The people were moved to Yarrabah and to Durundur, near Brisbane. But Meston's larger solution, his big idea, remained, set out in black and white for Black and White, in the 1897 act.

V

At the bottom of most of the arguments about the Aboriginal people were children, little children and the still unborn, posterity on the brink of being. Meston was mainly interested in warriors, but most reformers looked to children, hung on their voices, assessed their degree of colour and trained their bodies, classifying them for futurity. Much the same happened among White people themselves, but it was more obviously and unflinchingly done for the Blacks.

In 1898 Alexander Sutherland, a Melbourne journalist and sometime schoolmaster, wrote a book called *The Origin and Growth of the Moral Instinct*. Sutherland made everything turn on the feeling of parents for their children, which for him was the origin of all moral instincts. He tied it to biology, but his thoughts also caught at the puzzle now impending for humanity – the moral helplessness which came from confronting, in the newly vast cities, for instance, troubles unlimited. Vastness in numbers led to a kind of moral numbness and confusion. If parents in any species, fish being one obvious example, had too many offspring, their moral instinct could not develop during long-term evolution, because moral instinct could make scant difference to the survival of the species. With small numbers, no more than a few progeny each, as with human beings, affection, and therefore moral instinct, could make all the difference.

True, some 'savage' people, including the Australian Blacks, practised infanticide. But Sutherland put this down to their hard life rather than to feeble moral instinct. He knew that Aboriginal parents idolised their children. They had to travel, and it was impossible, he explained, for parents to cover long distances if their toddlers numbered more than one or two. He owed this insight to the great English anthropologist Edward Tylor. Infanticide, said Tylor, comes from 'hardness of life, rather than hardness of heart'. Imagine, said Sutherland, a mother of three carrying and suckling the smallest, while 'the father bears one child in his arms and drags another worn-out whimperer behind him under a blazing heaven'. It could not be done. Wise parents made their choice. '[W]hile nature', he said, 'would introduce four children only to starve and extinguish three of them, the savage kills two and makes an effort to rear the other two'.[49]

Sutherland saw in this true human ingenuity. He did not think of Black and White as distinct types of creation. The understanding of right and wrong was shaped by circumstances. Some observers took difference for granted and discounted similarity. Others, such as Sutherland, took similarity for granted and made a problem of difference. The first were polygenists, who believed that different races might sometimes amount even to different species, while those on Sutherland's side were monogenists, arguing for humankind's common ancestry at the dawn of time.[50] Sutherland noticed kindness among the Aboriginal people. He saw love more than hatred, sympathy more than violence. He examined, with what he hoped was scientific precision, the way men cooperated with women, the old with the young, and tribal groups with one another, through trade, for instance. That 'warm heart of humanity', that 'inherent good in human nature', which William Lane, Mary Gilmore and Elsie Birks were sure they would find in their little White utopias, observers like Sutherland looked for among the first Australians.

Procreation and babies had another kind of significance. The blood of Black and White was intermingled, not just in killings but also by 'miscegenation', the birth of mixed-race children. Anyone using the 1897 act was easily drawn into the deep puzzle as to just what an Aborigine was. Under the act, 'half-castes' (defined as anyone born of an Aboriginal mother and a non-Aboriginal father) were to count as Aboriginal if they associated with Aboriginal people, and it followed that a 'half-caste' mother could be classed as Aboriginal. Her children were then drawn after her into the same classificatory machinery and so on, in principle, ad infinitum. In fact, Meston ruled that such children, called 'quadroons' (implying one Aboriginal grandparent), might be classed as 'Aboriginal'. They thereby came within the reach of anyone entrusted with administering the act. That included himself. It even included police on the beat.[51]

The label, once attached, could last for life and usually did. Also, under the act the 'Aboriginal' part of the population was given its own criminal code. Of his own discretion, the minister could make rules for the reserves, and anyone breaking them could serve up to three months in gaol. On any reserve, 'aboriginal rites or customs' could be banned. Also, quite apart from the rules sent from Brisbane, any protector could lock up for a fortnight an individual (if Aboriginal) whom he found guilty of anything he deemed 'serious misconduct, neglect of duty, [or] gross insubordination'.[52]

The law was designed for the 'protection' of Aboriginal people.

It established rules for their employment, and it stopped anyone (skin colour unspecified) from taking advantage of them by selling them alcohol or opium.[53] Especially in the South, the 'protection' of Europeans was in progress by this time, including the protection of children and labouring people, the prime example being the Factories and Shops Acts. There had been 'protectors' of Aborigines since the mid-nineteenth century, but nothing like this meticulous bureaucracy which gathered great agglomerations of human beings, scientifically defined and statistically measured. Protection laws, broadly defined, North and South, aimed at far-reaching changes in the way people, White and Black, lived, worked, bought and sold together. They were rigorously policed. In all cases, White and Black, officials at ground level were to be the shock troops of a regime built on a new attitude, on a scientific understanding of humanity.

But there were differences between the two kinds of protection, White and Black. The protection of White people was much better thought through, though faulty in practice. It was part and parcel of the democratisation of knowledge, of self-realisation and rebirth. It was much better funded and it was more accountable to educated opinion. Australian methods sometimes set world standards. The protection of Blacks was to degrade and humiliate, and to narrow and shorten lives for generations to come.

VI

Application of the Aboriginals Protection Act proved the need for a single hard-and-fast idea – an idea uninterrupted by the peculiarities of place – as to what an Aborigine was. How was it really possible to think about 'the Australian Aboriginals' in detail and yet all at once? Where were the finely drawn maps which would show how they were patterned into provinces, population centres, stages of settlement and lines of movement? How were they organised, through space and through time? How could the idea 'Aboriginal' be neatly settled into the modern, modernising brain?

The Europeans had brought with them to this continent some large enough ideas about race, but so far the most pressing problems had evolved piecemeal on the ground. They had grown out of day-to-day dealings, friendly and unfriendly, between real men and women. A few of the invaders had made themselves into experts. Some of them learnt Aboriginal languages. Some managed to force their advice on administrators whose thoughts were generally elsewhere, and some then remained in control of Aboriginal affairs for many years. Policy in Victoria was especially sophisticated, and so were the ways in which ideas were harnessed to governing. A government agency had been set up in Melbourne in 1860, which became the Board for the Protection of Aborigines, overseeing a number of Aboriginal reserves, more or less well managed, and as early as 1871, with typical Victorian ambition, aspiring the establish a model for 'the whole of the Aboriginal population in Australia'. The leading figure on the ground was the Moravian minister Friedrich Hagenauer, who ran the Ramahyuck mission settlement in Gippsland, said to be a model of its kind. From Ramahyuck came Nathaniel Pepper, one the first Aborigines to preach as a baptised Christian among his own people.[54]

In the management of Aborigines the idea that 'protection' was a scientific business, calling for careful information gathering, expert decision-making and rigorous policing, was carried through first and best in Victoria and entrenched in the Half-Caste Act of 1886.[55] For all their theories, at the rough frontier of civilisation Queenslanders such as Meston and McNab fumbled. In Victoria there was more steady collective effort, more reliance on established rules, a better read, all-powerful public service spirit. The three men who managed the board worked, it was said, as a 'small family'.[56]

The New Zealander William Russell, speaking at the federal conference in Melbourne in 1890 (chapter 7), said that in a

Federation the management of native people would need to stay with the constituent colonies. Certainly, New Zealanders, if they came in to Federation, would refuse to hand Maori problems over to a mainland government which, he said, 'cares nothing and knows nothing about native administration, and the members of which have dealt with native races in a much more summary manner than we have ventured to deal with ours'. Even among the mainlanders, few doubted that government was most sensitive, in everything connected with family, property and the delicate underside of common life, when it was near to the people. Aboriginal administration must stay at the lower level. And why should the new national vision be muddied for the sake of a race doomed to extinction, a class B?[57]

There was in fact one good reason for handing Aboriginal affairs to the federal government, but few mentioned it just yet. The main cause of the recent American Civil War had been just this question, the connection between states' rights and race. The southern states had wanted to preserve Black slavery, whereas the government in Washington had wanted to end it. Victory for Washington (that is, for Abraham Lincoln) in 1865 had meant a lasting marriage between continental nationhood and moral purpose. The Europeans in Australia, or some of them, were well aware of the need to make that marriage – the central authority must have a conscience. But Aborigines were no part of their logic.

The Victorian and the Queensland ways of managing Aboriginal people spread outwards and overlapped. With Federation, the management of Aborigines stayed with the states, but Aboriginal people could not be ignored when it came to deciding who had the right to vote in federal elections. In Victoria, New South Wales and South Australia, Aborigines had always had full voting rights. If they were male (or female too in South Australia), and if they cared to enroll – it was not compulsory – they could vote. This arrangement did not carry over to Federation. On the insistence of Queenslanders and West Australians, when it came to passing the *Commonwealth Electoral Act 1902* the new federal parliament excluded Aboriginal people altogether.

And the next question – who was Aboriginal? What definition would set Aboriginal people apart? In Queensland, as with laws relating to the Chinese (chapter 6), not much attention was paid to fixed rules and a good deal was paid to circumstances, including the needs of employers.[58] In Victoria everything was more strictly principled. There, the category 'Aboriginal' included only people of full Aboriginal descent. In Victoria children of mixed background were often taken from their parents so as to be brought up among Europeans as Europeans, but classification itself was an exercise of power. Louisa Briggs, for instance, was the daughter of a sealer in Bass Strait and a Tasmanian Aboriginal woman. She was allowed to live on the reserve at Coranderrk, where she worked as a nursing matron, but when she spoke out about its management in 1886 she and her children were reclassified as half-caste and ejected.[59]

In the Federation-wide electorate, when it came to deciding who was Aboriginal, the Victorian principle prevailed. Anyone of mixed descent, or at least anyone of 'preponderating' European lineage, was classified with the majority, among the White people.[60] They could vote, but with the right to vote went the need to be brought up, and to live, European.

Again, it was all about children. The risk of being taken in childhood to a new kind of initiation, painful beyond expression, was built into the national regime. They were to be born and they were to die within a great idea.

9

God and Humanity

I

It is impossible to understand the years of Australian Federation without taking account of religion. The energy of religious commitment for that generation was a federating energy. The ideas of religion were federating ideas. Religious feeling made Federation possible.

On a winter Sunday in 1892, Ernest Gribble, twenty-three years old, started keeping a diary. He wrote a motto on the title page. 'By the grace of God', it said, 'I am what I am'. It was a quotation from St Paul's first letter to the Corinthians. Ernest was then a Church of England catechist in southern New South Wales. What could such words mean to a man his age, just grown up, obstinate, uncertain, in the last years of the nineteenth century? What was the importance of being Ernest? Day by day, Ernest Gribble's diary echoed with this idea. Through it all runs the theme 'I am in the hands of my maker, to change as he sees fit'. Or maybe, 'Take me as I am; I come finished from the hand of the Lord'. Maybe even God would neglect to change his finished Ernest. After all, for many people then the Almighty had to all appearances withdrawn to the misty edge of his creation, a long way from Ernest or from anyone else.[1]

At about the same age, Ernest's father, John Gribble, had started a diary too. Superficially, it was much the same, and no doubt, as he entered on the business of baring himself to himself, the son was somehow mimicking the father. But the diary of the elder Gribble had been dense with spiritual drama, with none of the self-conscious coolness of this newer, turn-of-the-century man. In his record day by day John Gribble had spoken of God suddenly smothering him with grace and scorching him with infinite power. At a moment of particular blessing, he said, 'The Lord whom I sought came suddenly to the temple of my unworthy heart and filled it with Himself'. From this meeting Gribble senior had sunk exhausted. 'I could do nothing but praise God for some time.' Sometimes, Satan had been just as rough. For a whole day in September 1873 Ernest's father had contended with a sharp pain in his left side while under siege, as he said, from 'the devil and his terrible hosts'. He had won for the time being and he called on God, 'Give me faith to cling to *thyself*, continue as my all in all, as my rock of safety'.[2]

For Ernest, God was never all in all. Son copied father in being sure that the Almighty could answer his prayers, worthily offered. But Ernest, if his diary rings true, was less startled by God's particular attention and less completely grateful. He did not feel the hard breath of the Lord as his father did. While his father, now in late middle age, wrestled with the living forces of good and evil as a missionary at Yarrabah, near Cairns, in one of the most remote parts of European Australia, Ernest stayed near his mother, taking services within a small parish circuit and living in the village of Tumbarumba, in south-west New South Wales.

For Ernest, God moved almost like a distant government official, responsive to his requests (properly couched) but impersonal. On 9 September 1892 he gave his diary the following information:

> Received telegram yesterday saying that my Father was ill with Pleurisy in N. Queensland. After lighting up the Church this evening for Choir practice I made prayer & supplication to God for his recovery, hearing footsteps outside the Church I went to the door & found a boy with a telegram stating that my father was improving & that there was no cause for anxiety.

His prayer had been answered and the divine response telegraphically relayed on the instant. 'I thank thee oh my God for thus hearing the cry of a poor & miserable sinner.'[3]

In fact, John Gribble's health was still precarious, and early in October Ernest set out to see him. As it happened, this was the young man's great initiation. For a while his father had been asking him to come and help, and he had always refused. Now he had to act as deputy at Yarrabah while John Gribble went to Sydney for treatment, even perhaps to take over. He hated it, and agonising about his duty he asked for the bitter cup to be taken away. His father died, and full of doubt Ernest did indeed take up the mission as a sacred trust, snared, as it were, by God.[4] For the rest of his life he struggled to be worthy of both his dead father and his heavenly one. Joined by John Gribble, God's power over Ernest doubled.

'I am what I am.' But what am I? In an age of introspection, the search for self, the journey to the Centre, could be endless, and endlessly perplexing. Remember the experience of Ernest Giles (chapter 1). Would it be diamonds? Would it be water endlessly deep? Would it be saltbush? Ernest Gribble's generation was driven by a hunger for the elemental, and yet the elemental was more elusive than ever. God hid from young Ernest and his contemporaries in ways he had not done in earlier generations. Alfred Deakin, twelve years older, had been through this trouble. '[G]ive me thy guidance', Deakin demanded (we heard this prayer in chapter 3), 'that I may fearlessly pierce into the depths of my own Being and open sanctuaries within its unexplored recesses'. In these internal journeys AD, as Deakin called himself, travelled by pen, writing to himself and God. It was hard ink work, done in silence, not mouth work.[5]

In earlier times God had lived less in unexplored recesses, in our own inner depths, than in the transparent silences binding human beings one to another, in ceremony and in conversation, in the interspersing of ordinary days. God had been much more, even, than a 'rock of safety', to use John Gribble's term. He had been the geological substratum of human thought.

All had changed. JF Archibald, of the *Bulletin*, said that 'every man ... knows things unknown to any other man'.[6] In these later days it was that mystery *between* men, *between* men and women, *between* women, that mattered. It was the mystery of individuality, of *Bildung*, inwardness, that made every man and woman, and the God within each, into an undiscoverable island. In earlier times, ideally anyway, every man and every woman had known about God, and everyone had lived in each other's knowledge. Now God was off limits, beyond the cosmos according to one interpretation, strictly confidential according to another.

In April 1897, in a conference in Adelaide called to piece together the federal Constitution, there was brief talk about including a reference to the Almighty, as the guide and ruler of nations. This was the suggestion of a South Australian lawyer, Patrick McMahon Glynn. The delegates had been debating the Constitution's preamble. The version they had before them stated that the people of the various colonies had 'agreed to unite in one indissoluble federal Commonwealth'. Before the word 'agreed' Glynn wanted three new words: 'invoking Divine Providence'. Some delegates were strongly opposed. 'Nothing', said Adye Douglas, sometime premier of Tasmania, contradicting the experience of eighteen centuries, 'does more damage to religion than to make an outward show of it'.[7] Anyway, what was the point of stating in such a solemn document that God had been at work in the minds of thousands of voters, or that he might be at work later on, when by no objective criteria such a thing could ever be proved?

Edmund Barton, who was to be the first prime minister of the Commonwealth, put it neatly. When the people took up their voting papers to have their say on whether we ought to federate, 'a large number', he said, would no doubt be invoking the Divine. But whether they did so or not, and how many did so, was none of our business. 'We cannot know that anyone will have those feelings before the action has occurred; we should not know the feelings that anyone has had even if the action had already occurred.' We could make none of the assumptions we used to make in earlier generations. If we did inquire, and we had no right to, we would still have to calculate the statistical proportions before we could think of inscribing any relevant statement in our federal Constitution.[8]

There was a basic misunderstanding here. Douglas and Barton were thinking of the dealings individuals had with the Almighty. They were thinking of a God sought by every voter within himself (and herself in South Australia). Glynn was thinking of something different altogether. For him, 'the people' were not single decision-makers, turning minds heavenward as they took up pencil and paper to vote. By 'the people' Glynn understood a united historical being moved by spiritual impulse towards one mighty destiny. Glynn's God was ubiquitous and vast. He was thinking, he said, of a 'great central fact of faith and feeling', the creative effort on which Federation depended. He was thinking about consensus, about something immeasurable, not the sorting of papers and the totting and tabulation which went with assessing votes. He was trying to find words which might express ancient but still living habits of association, not state-of-the-art statistical analysis. He wanted a reminder as to what the people did among themselves, how they existed among themselves, as a body. He was not concerned with the decisions each of them made alone in that little temple of individuality, the modern polling booth.

Glynn spoke of God as 'the Unseen'. He (but Glynn's God was hardly solid enough even to be 'he') was a spirit moving through nations, guiding people, in their tens, their hundreds, their thousands, to higher things. Glynn's God surfaced in innumerable small phenomena, eternal but ephemeral. Our reverence for this spirit, he said, 'is felt in the forms in our courts of justice, in the language of our Statutes, in the oath that binds the sovereign to the observance of our liberties ... in our domestic observances, [and] the offices of courtesy at our meetings and partings'. In public life, Glynn said, human beings had always 'felt the breath of a Divine Being'. They needed to register that feeling somehow. But it was a gentle breath he was talking about, nothing urgent or passionate such as the elder Gribble felt, just the sweet breeze of common conscience.[9]

In his more prosaic moments, Glynn agreed with Douglas, Barton and probably everyone else present at that meeting. He too had decided many years ago that talk about religion could easily be overdone, especially in public. 'A man might really be more Christian', he told his brother in Ireland, 'by going to Church less'. What mattered was private principle and private prayer. And yet, he said, 'I often heartily and sadly wish the dreams of our childhood were true'. These were dreams like the ones the English poet Matthew Arnold recounted in his lines called 'Dover Beach' (1867), when he mourned the ebb tide of '[t]he sea of faith', that ocean of assumption which lay once 'round earth's shore ... like the folds of a bright girdle furled'.[10]

The three words Glynn wanted to put into the federal Constitution hinted at this deep longing. Glynn had come a long way from his Irish childhood, from the big family house in county Galway, from lessons with the Mercy Sisters and the Holy Ghost Fathers, and from undoubting Catholic Christianity. But he still wanted the old certainties. His three words preserved a fragment of sometime truth.

And they did more than that. Those three words, 'invoking Divine Providence', echoed not just a longing for the past. They also expressed another kind of pain. They expressed anxiety about the future, a fretting borne out by the events of the next twenty years, from the Boer War to the apocalyptic conflict of 1914–18. Under a ghastly and increasing shadow the three words invoked light. What was the moral purpose of a good nation? Did nations have moral purpose any more? Were they just glorious combinations of race and manhood, soil and blood? Were they guided only by natural law, by the need to survive in the great struggle for existence? An older and some said a richer ideal had bound Christian rulers to their own people and to the rest of the believing world. International affairs had been anchored then, in theory – a vital theory – in the Christian inclinations of the powerful.

Now conscience was only a private thing. It was no-one else's business. If so, what weight could it have in the governing of nations? If ancient faith was not the glue binding peoples, within nations and among nations, what was there instead, beyond, as a Sydney clergyman put it, 'present and material interests'?[11]

Remember (from chapter 7) the remark by the New South Wales parliamentarian about the duty of Australians to rally to the United States in times of need, without bothering about right and wrong. '[I]f any of them', he said, 'came across one of their brothers in a fight or a scrimmage in the street they would, if they were men, hardly stop to ask the particulars of the quarrel'. 'If they were men.' The global ties of blood, as Charles Henry Pearson put it, made up the only moral code that mattered, especially for men properly reborn to the privileges of manhood.[12] Where did this leave the hope of Christians?

Some saw no problem. Joseph Furphy could find no connection between his own conscience and Christian teaching. 'My own Sunday-school conceptions of heaven, hell, the judgment day, etc., have long ago gone by the board, and without affecting my sense of right and wrong in the slightest degree.'[13] But Furphy was a man of simple life – bullock driver, husband, father, friend. He worked from habit and affection, and from his own inner spring. He might have been less cocky if he had had to decide on the fate of nations.

II

Clergymen, more than anyone else, struggled to pin down an up-to-date, practical distinction between good and bad. Habits of thought being what they were, everyone was always alert to the chance of siege, insult or extinction, always anxious about fighting back. The result was something like Aboriginal understandings of good and bad. Evil comes from being beyond the law, the law governing human existence, and in many late-nineteenth-century European minds that law had now changed.[14] How might we go back to the old law? Or rather, how might we go back to the fundamental teachings 'Thou shalt love the Lord thy God with all thy heart, and with all thy soul, and with all thy mind' and 'Thou shalt love thy neighbour as thyself'?[15] It was men of the cloth who hunted most energetically for the way, and for the moral principles which in this generation might justify and direct an incipient nation.

James Jefferis was a Congregationalist minister who had arrived in South Australia from England in 1859, aged twenty-six. He made a name for himself in Adelaide as a preacher, welfare organiser and public intellectual, and in 1877 he moved with his family to the bigger and more challenging world of Sydney, where, as in Melbourne, a kind of continental power was gathering. In both places he ministered to big city congregations. Many Congregationalists were highly educated. Jefferis was one of the founders of Adelaide University. Also, Congregationalists took the duties of individual citizenship, and the direct relation of every individual with their God, extremely seriously. Crucially, they believed in the strict separation of church and state. However, Jefferis was starting to think that separation had in fact hamstrung the churches at a danger point in the history of civilisation.

The ideas Jefferis brought from England matched local hopes and conditions. He consequently loved Australia. Existence here, he thought, made English memories seem stale. Thirty years of this 'strong free life', as he called it, gave extraordinary ambition to his mental habits.[16] Here, you could restate the great idea at the centre of Christianity. Here, anchored in secular life, was St Paul's notion of individuality and divinity combined. The separate consciousness of every man and woman could be affirmed and electrified by a single great force above and beyond.

Jefferis loved vastness. He was a religious version of the meteorologist-astronomer Henry Chamberlain Russell, who discovered a single drama in the infinite sensations of the weather, shore to shore, ocean to ocean, hemisphere to hemisphere, and who was determined to find running through it all a Providential pattern. In seeing and feeling God at every turn, Jefferis was also like Glynn. But Glynn's God decked himself in civility and order. Jefferis's God was a God of nature, a God like the God discovered 200 years earlier by the philosopher Baruch Spinoza, a God, as Jefferis said, 'who works amid all the ceaseless energies of our being', a God who demonstrates his power 'by the pervading forces ever at work throughout all creation'.

Men and women played with the idea of invisible fields of force, as with gravity and magnets. In the 1870s was born the idea that electricity and light might spread within fields, travelling through space in waves. Joseph Furphy showed a sensibility increasingly common when he said, in *Such Is Life*, that sound consisted of vibrations which 'penetrate and saturate all solids and gases, yet are palpable corporeally only to the tympanum of the ear'. Research in these areas proved God's dazzling reach:

> Think [said Jefferis] of the power of gravitation that sent the worlds spinning on their axes and through their orbits; of the powers of electricity, galvanism, magnetism, chemical affinity, and of light which every day re-creates the world! Think too of the vital energy existent in plants and animals; of the psychic forces that are peculiar to man, and of the more spiritual powers which link him to the Unseen, and to the Divine![17]

Jefferis hoped that astronomers, in particular, stretching their thoughts outward, would explore not just the stars but also the power of God. And not just God's power but also his goodness. 'I know that teaching of this kind is deemed unscientific', he said. But surely God's goodness, his eternal drive to create and sustain, is obvious? So why could it not be appraised with something like the brain-bending methods used to trace other hints of the Almighty, in the vastness of the skies, for instance? Sociology, psychology and so on were proving the multiple uses of scientific method. 'To leave Him out of the count', said Jefferis, 'because He works in secret, because we cannot fully understand His plan or completely divine His purpose, appears to me utterly unscientific'.[18]

Sociologists and psychologists, even the new racism in its aspirations to scientific method, aimed to drive the mystery out of the way human beings dealt with each other. They were designed to make everything predictable. Jefferis wanted the same done with the dealings between God and humanity. To earlier generations this would have seemed chillingly presumptuous. Some thought so still.

Adelaide was a breeding ground for such thought. In the early 1880s Catherine Helen Spence, another South Australian (a Presbyterian turned Unitarian), stated the great dilemma of the day, as far as God was concerned, in a speech in her novel *Gathered In*. In earlier times, said her hero, it was easy to believe in God because he had 'parts and passions' like ours. Because he was like us, the God of those days had dealt with us Person to person.

> Now the difficulty is to believe that in so vast a universe as science discloses to us, there is care and love in the Infinite Creator for his creatures, beyond the ordering of laws working on the whole for the best. We do not question our individual claims on the love of our Heavenly Father, but we are stunned by the sense of infinite space and time, and law and forces, working with solemn and rhythmic precision

> unaffected by our words or efforts. No text will settle that doubt – no key of promise will open that lock.[19]

James Jefferis was stunned too. But God, he said, was patron of 'the divine rights of our manhood'. They included our right, as individuals, to cross old boundaries of thought and action, expanding our sense of place, uprooting prejudice and entering on vastness. He echoed John Milton, the great exemplar of the Congregationalists, who wrote in *Paradise Lost* of the glory of the individual mind, the best compensation for suffering on earth:

> for who would lose,
> Though full of pain, this intellectual being,
> Those thoughts that wander through eternity[?][20]

The astronomer, Jefferis thought, would best apply that right, especially if he was also a man of faith. The devout astronomer was 'the ideal man'. His sweeping intelligence could draw into a single pattern the infinite and the tiny. It could resolve the great puzzle of the day, the puzzle of vastness, so that humanity could start to understand the paradox of the 'condescending' God, the being who was the Almighty but at the same time, as Jefferis put it, 'a household God'.

Addressing young men in Sydney, Jefferis outlined a 'scheme of Divine government which centres in a Prince and Saviour, bone of our bone and flesh of our flesh, and yet seated at the right hand of God with power'. The dilemma lay in that '*and yet*'. It was a great gap for the imagination to cross, but manageable if you took a series of logical steps. It was like the teaching of geography in South Australia, starting with 'local geography' and moving steadily outward to embrace the world (chapter 4).[21]

Charles Dickens had shaped the thoughts of this generation of the Europeans in Australia, and it has been said of Dickens that he married the fate of nations to the treatment of children (Oliver Twist, Nicholas Nickleby and so on). So did James Jefferis and many more like him. Children were the weakest and most defenceless of humanity, so that families were central to the fabric of Providence. Children pointed the way to genuinely Christian government. 'Children must have houses', said Jefferis, and good houses depended on clean and orderly towns. And so on, bigger and bigger, the dictates of conscience led up to the just and orderly state. At the local and family level the divine order needed moral government, or what was now called 'protection'. Jefferis was deeply excited by the sheer scale of the federal project. For Congregationalists, nations were responsible to God as individuals were. We were building 'a vast commonwealth', he said, one 'which realizes the Divine ideal of justice and freedom'. It would be a thing of glory.[22]

Like Rose Scott, Jefferis was also wary of the massive power of the state, so easily 'inflamed with the passions of war'. By getting mixed up with the Sudan campaign, in 1885, he said, we had entered on a heritage of hatred. We had to guard against that. The answer was genuine Federation, in which power would be centralised and distributed at the same time. A state aspiring to perfection was easily tyrannical because freedom came from haphazard, piecemeal detail, not from one big idea entrenched at the beginning. Also, 'small States are more favorable to the development and preservation of liberty than large ones'. The whole point of Federation, as the South Australian Frederick Holder had explained, was to make a fruitful marriage between small and large, between children, say, and the continent's geographical bulk.[23]

Jefferis was Protestant and a dissenter. He hated the power of the Roman Catholic Church, which thought of itself as a utopia but which was focussed on Rome and the pope. Congregationalists defined their ideas of public order against power like the pope's (more concentrated than ever since mid-century, thanks to Pius IX). Jefferis wanted Australian Federation to be underpinned by diversity. Australia was big, like God. A federated Australia, in its bigness, would reflect the goodness of a Being who sustained all creation while 'neither invading our freedom, nor destroying our individuality'. In this country we would have a multitiered commonwealth, driven by a single national and Christian spirit but full of complexity. All at the same time it would centralise and delegate, unite and divide, weave and unravel, affirming 'strong free life' at every level.[24]

In other words, Federation and modern Christianity were two sides of the same coin. They were joint answers to one problem. No wonder, as we now see, modern clergy told voters to say 'yes'.

At precisely the same time, on the other side of the world, Leo Tolstoy, author of *War and Peace* and *Anna Karenina*, was completing his lesser known novel *Resurrection*. Its climax is the revelation, bursting on the hero, Nekhlyudov, that great modern states have their own momentum, expressed in the smallest actions of their humblest officials, in which ordinary human sympathy has no part.[25] The clergy sensed this truth, but in Federation they thought they had the answer.

III

Scattered through the continent, but concentrated in the colonies of the south-east, were men enflamed with the federal idea. They included a good number of clergy. Some clergy were as wildly hopeful as, say, those who wanted an Australian republic, who were vocal especially in the 1880s. For republicans, a continental nation made no sense, it was not *logical*, without separation also from the British Crown. For clergy, a continental nation was not logical without the spiritual underpinning that bound each to each, and each to all, in a spirit of high-minded togetherness.

Making sure of those ties was not just a matter of preaching. It needed ingenuity and persistence, virtues of the few. Some might say that 'church and creed' could have no effect on the federating of the colonies. That was the jaundiced verdict of the visiting English historian James Anthony Froude in 1886.[26] In fact, clergymen still exercised considerable authority in public debate, among their own congregations and more widely. Some congregations, especially inner-city ones in the great metropolises, with the money to provide good salaries, hunted down men of ideas to be their ministers. Jefferis was such a man. High-profile churches produced high-profile preachers, and the newspapers often published their arguments in detail.

How exactly would Federation build on this continent a pattern of collaboration and Christian humanity in all the little things of life? How would Federation match the 'ideographic prophecy' Furphy wrote about, when it came to human feeling? One answer came from Henry Latimer Jackson, rector of St James', King Street, a leading Anglican church in central Sydney and a gathering place for the city's professional families. A bicycle-riding Cambridge scholar, Jackson was a liberal Anglican and a professed Christian Socialist. He stayed too briefly in Australia to have much feel for the land, but long enough to predict here the arrival of the kingdom of God on earth.

Like Jefferis, Jackson made social justice, including the enlightenment of the poor, central to his thinking. He was a hard man to ignore. 'There was something extraordinarily intense in his appearance', his friends recalled. 'He seemed to take a vital interest in many things.' He sensed great promise in the settler people. Drunk on ideals, he wanted to see them running fast towards the future. His was '[a]n alert and somewhat impetuous brain', and not well suited to Sydney, where the atmosphere was 'conservative and conventional, rather than keenly intellectual'.[27] And yet Jackson was not unique, and he had supporters.

Jackson could see the problems Froude pointed to. Large numbers attended church fairly regularly (between a third and a half of all adults), and some form of religious belief was probably almost universal. Churches were still at the social and ceremonial heart of every settled community. But he was pained to find clergymen taken lightly by many, not credited with manly intelligence but classed almost as 'a third sex'. The title 'Reverend', he said, together with the clerical collar, blocked casual communication with 'the type of individual – largely represented – who had been alienated by ignorant and repulsive presentations of religious truth'. But this only made the job more interesting. The clergy had to find other ways and other words for entrenching faith. 'There are numbers', Jackson said, 'to whom the voice of the Church speaks in almost a foreign language'. The church's language had to match this new age, this time of brooding, trembling vacancy, as Jackson thought, the quiet before a storm as big as the European Reformation five centuries before. '[A] great revolution is going on among us', he said, 'a revolution – not only in matters political and social, but also in matters connected with religious thought'. We needed energy. We needed fearless leadership. We needed ideas, not big, sudden ideas, but ideas which made a steady and deep demand on the brains of the people.[28]

Jackson's God was a God of the future, drawing humanity forward. Age by age, he thought, God spoke intricately through the best minds. It was an old theory. A century earlier Johann Wolfgang van Goethe had argued about the duty of civilised men to write their own bibles. 'Physical scientist, politician, sociologist, divine', said Jackson, 'are equally "striving for the light"; now one and now another comes forward with a message which may be, and often is, the voice of God'. The best novelists of the day, men and women, did the same. If Australians were going to think and work together as a nation, said Jefferis, they must have a 'National Church', an 'Australian Church' shaped by the educated, looking to the future and throwing out dead ideas and sectarian difference.[29]

Did women, with their 'fertility of resource', their distinctive human insight, as some contemporary men put it, their remarkable 'readiness ... to adapt to a new medium', take to these possibilities more eagerly than men?[30] It was common knowledge that women now significantly outnumbered men in church congregations, and the Women's Christian Temperance Union, Julia Holder's organisation, was a clear case of religious faith being turned into new and patently useful channels. Did some women sense that the networking that now drove the churches, from the local to the national level, was something like a new medium?

One country should mean one creed. Jackson clung to the Anglican ideas of 'common worship' and 'common faith'. '[S]olitary acts of devotion', he said, the man or woman alone with God, were not enough. Australians needed a creed of broad principle. The detail did not matter, except that it had to be coloured by up-to-date ideas, by the 'new learning'. They would claim it proudly. At the heart of their national church would be the essence of what they were. Its centre would be their Centre.[31]

In 1885, in Melbourne, the former Presbyterian minister Charles Strong did in fact establish an 'Australian Church'. He meant it to prepare the way for a federated nation. Strong believed that among European peoples Australians alone could manage something like a union of Christianity, or at least of Protestant Christianity. For him it was urgent. 'Great nations have all been nursed at the breast of religion.' This nation, especially in its infancy, must have its own church, or its own organisation of churches, tailored to its purpose. We must have a 'Church of Australia', echoing the authority of national churches in England and Scotland.

> Australia [Strong said] seems to want a great national centre of moral and spiritual life – a Church, in short, as the home and nursery of all the best and noblest aspirations of our Commonwealth. What is a Commonwealth without a soul, but a lifeless conglomerate, or a corpse? And must not the soul have nourishment, and find some expression for itself in

> symbol, such as only some form of religious communion or association can afford?

We needed complete religious union, or else some sort of network – 'One Catholic [that is, all-embracing] Church, or a federation of Churches'. Strong would have been happy with either.[32]

The agendas of the clergy and the republicans were different. But they did overlap. The organisation Strong talked about was to be indigenous to the country, the creation of a settler people but obviously antipodean and distinct from empire.

Federation, religious or secular, had to grow from Christian compromise. Remember the Sermon on the Mount: 'Do unto others as you would have them do unto you'. We had to see God in others. As Victor Hugo, a popular author even in English, put it, '[E]very time we come across the infinite in man, whether properly or badly understood, we feel seized with respect'.[33] Federation depended on that act of seeing.

In fact, Hugo was the sort of novelist Henry Jackson talked about, one who inspired a new morality and a new sense of the divine. It all seemed possible here. '[W]e are living', said Strong, 'in the midst of a revolution. A new heaven and a new earth are in the process of formation … [A] new ideal of life has dawned upon us, making all things new'. Old ways were 'often cold and uninteresting', especially in this country.

> [H]owever well suited they may have been to earlier days or to a country congregation in the old country, they are not altogether in harmony with the feelings of a congregation composed of men and women of different nationalities and varied experience in a new country or in a large modern city.

By 'nationalities' he meant ethnic identities, and he was thinking mainly of the persecuted Chinese. Like Strong, Jefferis wanted 'a great Commonwealth ... Asiatic and European ... which realizes the Divine ideal of justice and freedom'.[34]

Plenty of such variety within one communion would keep Christians up to the mark, always testing their charity. When he preached on the story of Jonah, Strong focussed on the sailors, who were aliens. They were not among the chosen people of the Hebrew God, and yet they struggled, conscience-stricken, to avoid throwing Jonah to the storm. So the Chinese, our own aliens, might have lessons to give us about generosity. (This logic enraged some readers.)[35] We should have variety in unity. The Americans had created one out of many ('*e pluribus unum*'). A century later, so Strong and others said, we should have it the other way around, with the many contained and quickened, each in its own way, by a single spirit.

True Christianity depended on the cultivation of 'rational life'. There was a moment in every human existence, Strong said, a moment of initiation, or rebirth, when rational life suddenly grew bigger. 'From shells and pebbles, limpid pools and sea-anemones, and castles in the sand, the sporting child lifts now his eyes, to gaze over the waves to the setting sun and the evening star, and listens to "the mighty waters rolling evermore" – no more a child.' The same things happened to whole peoples. Rational life became national life, and the collective soul stepped outward to a great unity. Looking forward to Federation, Strong glimpsed 'a larger Catholic Australian Church', whose driving idea would be 'mutual helpfulness'.[36] He would have the Sermon on the Mount working on a continental scale.

It was an enormously difficult agenda. In *Resurrection*, Tolstoy made it a tragic impossibility. As a potential program of government and law it challenged both heart and brain. Worldwide, it was to be one of the main issues of the twentieth century, tackled, for instance in the 1930s and '40s, by the Hungarian-German-British scholar Karl Mannheim with his idea of the 'Great Society'. In short, how was it possible to reconcile the life of the soul with the life of the subject, freedom with planning, variety with unity, humanity with technology, especially given the high administrative skill and the vast new technology which since the eighteenth century had been framing and driving human life?

Rose Scott could see no link between Federation and social justice. She sensed, and truly, that however much it might have democratic sanction Federation must be shaped from the top, whereas social justice, as she understood it, was a matter of networking and wire pulling, of multiple individuality. But for clergy such as Jefferis, Jackson and Strong the two were a neat fit. In working out that fit they used religious thought and experience. For them, Federation was like any intellectual challenge. It was like mental arithmetic. It was like serving well in tennis. Except it was much bigger. Define the problem, apply training, skill and method, and the answer came with almost algebraic elegance.

IV

The Christian churches have always been good at throwing themselves across large spaces. Since St Paul, Christianity has had a peculiar, dynamic relationship with geography and distance, working sometimes far ahead of secular powers, and sometimes even ahead of trade networks. In England in the late seventh century there were church councils at Hertford and Hatfield, which created an English church long before there was an English state. That process was fuelled by ideas of English landscape and English history, and broadcast by clergy using a technology – writing – over which they had almost complete control.[37] For centuries without a break the idea of Christendom had shaped the idea of Europe, more than any empire did.

Christians had also been ingenious in working out new forms of order. The various monastic rules (male and female), the sects and national churches springing from the Reformation, and any number of methods of toleration and non-toleration show what they could do when the spirit moved them. In the Australasian colonies in the 1830s 'the New South Wales system' had involved government recognising and subsidising all the main churches. It had meant a new kind of confessional citizenship, a unique answer to the urgent question of the place of faith in modern government, which many Europeans in Europe found a lot harder to answer. (See *The Europeans in Australia*, volume 2.)

This new generation made a new effort. In Tasmania, Bishop Henry Montgomery, echoing Charles Strong in Melbourne, spoke of Federation as 'in a very true sense a religious question, one in which we, as Christians, have a direct concern'. The churches, he said, were in a particularly strong position to treat the continent as a single enterprise. Christians were committed 'steadily to enlarge our ideas of family relationship and mutual helpfulness', an effort involving ever-larger imagination. 'Mutual helpfulness' was the mark of modern faith, and new technology – the telegraph, railways, telephone, the possibility of speaking in unison (same dialect, same accent) – made mutual helpfulness much easier and more comprehensive. The pervasive ambition of the churches, whether apocalyptic or incremental, made eager use of such technology. 'One outcome of our Christian training', Montgomery went on, 'is that we are predisposed for Federation of any kind and are opposed to selfish isolation'.[38] It was another way of using brains better.

Most of the main Christian denominations in Australia had already federated, in piecemeal ways, during the second half of the nineteenth century. As an Anglican remarked in 1900, his church 'some years ago set the example of federation to the State by the organisation of her dioceses under the General Synod'.[39] The need to missionise on a shoestring forced them to be inventive. In the secular world, for federationists the Australian North was a defining challenge. Just so, the condition of the heathen in and around the Gulf drew churchmen together. The Presbyterian Church of

Australia and Tasmania, so called, came into existence in about 1885, aiming to feed the 'Federal spirit', with Queensland Aborigines high on the agenda (mainly a Victorian initiative). The Australian Board of Missions, an Anglican effort which survived (though barely) on funds sent from all dioceses, did its poor best at Yarrabah (John Gribble's mission near Cairns), on the Mitchell River, on Cape York, and on the Roper River, in the Northern Territory.[40]

Everyone said that drawing up a federal Constitution called for a particular effort of humane forbearance and mutual charity. The 'principle of federation', according to the great New Zealander Sir George Grey, was a new discovery, as yet undeveloped. '[A]s is the case with electricity, day by day better modes will be found for administering it – better means for making it useful to men.' Sir George Grey was old enough to remember when it seemed impossible for men of different religions to sit together in the same legislature.

> But it was found [he said] that that was a great mistake … [T]alent and ability can be drawn forth from any religious opinions whatever. The nation [he meant Britain and its empire] has progressed more than ever it has done before in so short a period of time; and its happiness and tranquillity are greater. Now, I think we should establish this principle in reference to federation.

Sir Patrick Jennings from New South Wales, a delegate like Grey at the 1891 federal convention, said the same. In order to build, everyone had to compromise. 'I should prefer, instead of the expression give and take, or take and give, to use the motto of the great German Chancellor [Bismarck], *do ut des*, "We give that you may give us back again"; and that is the true spirit of conciliation and compromise.'[41]

On the other hand, there were men such as Joshua Thomas Bell, a Darling Downs grazier. Speaking among his fellow

Queenslanders in parliament in Brisbane, Bell imagined intercolonial dealings differently. 'I am quite sure', he said, 'that the harder we hit, and the harder we are able to return blows when they are given, the more likely we [he meant Queenslanders] are to become a worthy nation when we are federated' – one nation, that is, within a larger Australia.[42]

Among churchmen too, there was a limit to fellow feeling, especially between Catholics and Protestants (in spite of what Sir George Grey said). Sir Patrick Jennings was Roman Catholic, indeed a papal marquess. Catholics made up a third of the European population, more or less, from colony to colony. Their energies were focussed on old opponents, especially Protestant bigots (the Orange Order was flourishing) and the Anglican establishment (still obvious in government, courts and public service). Catholics also beat back new ideas about the secular, liberal state. Within the Catholic Church, power was concentrated in the bishops, one for each diocese, and in 1900 there were nineteen Catholic dioceses in Australia, including the archdioceses in each capital city. Each bishop ruled his own roost and extended his reach by creating under himself a culture of faith and obedience, especially in the schools. Bishops, coming mainly from Ireland's old towns and cities, worked to build up communities of faith centred on their cathedrals, their high-towered churches, parish priests and parish schools, their guilds, their benefit societies, sodalities and confraternities, their Children of Mary, their young men's clubs, their women's leagues, their ringing of bells and their public processions. As with the old colonial regime, order among the Catholics shone where people gathered, in networks of roads and in hierarchies of villages and towns. These were the icons of belonging.

'[H]ow incomprehensible, wavering and misty are the beings that share with us the sight of the stars and the warmth of the sun.' The speaker is Lord Jim, Joseph Conrad's everyman hero. Conrad cast Jim's destiny in Australian seas, and in the years just before

Federation. Jim was right. For all this spiritual effort among men and women of faith, Catholics included, each of us, man or woman, was an island. 'It is as if', said Jim,'loneliness were a hard and absolute condition of existence; the envelope of flesh and blood on which our eyes are fixed melts before the outstretched hand, and there remains only the capricious, inconsolable, and elusive spirit that no eye can follow, no hand can grasp'.[43] And each had an opinion. How do we knit those opinions together? Each had a story. How do we draw those stories into one story? How do we weave our own opinion and story into the opinion and story of the archetypal person the Christian churchman calls 'our neighbour'? For those who listened in imagination to Lord Jim, throughout the English-speaking world, the only absolute, the only elemental, was self.

What if the self was a vacancy too? Among Catholics, no-one wrestled with emptiness better than Mary MacKillop, St Mary of the Cross, founder with Father Julian Tenison Woods of the first Australian religious order, the Sisters of St Joseph of the Sacred Heart, which started at Penola, north of Mt Gambier, in 1866. Mary made a strange combination between Australia's emptiness and traditional ideas of womanhood, of abnegation and vacancy of self. In establishing her own order, with its distinctive rule, she did battle with some bishops and with the hierarchy of settled places. James Quinn, bishop of Brisbane, called her a 'sentimental young lady'. At thirty-two she had already, he said, 'led a most eventful career', much too eventful for a decent female. Mary balanced individuality (*Bildung*) and obedience. She and her sisters were, she said, 'weak, helpless women, or young girls, possessing nothing of ourselves but a succession of faults and glaring imperfections'. Defined in terms of absolute humility, they could resist their bishops with the power of inventive, persevering womanhood.[44]

'Nothingness' (in algebraic terms, a null space) was what Mary fought for. Using patterns of thought which went back to Francis of Assisi and beyond to the desert fathers of the third century, her mission was also deeply Australian. Members of Catholic religious orders normally took vows of poverty, chastity and obedience, but Mary carried poverty beyond the norm. Even as an institution, her sisterhood was to own nothing. A cell of her own would give each sister 'a *spirit* of *property*'. They were to possess no buildings, no income, not even the means of their own support. They were to live on charity alone. '[T]hey know well', she said, 'that solicitude as to their own temporary wants, necessity of securing beforehand a house to live in and such things, are the greatest possible drawback to a truly missionary spirit'. Owning nothing, they could be tied to no single spot. They were to live in hope and faith, protected by nothing but their nun's habits.[45]

In this way they had to support not just themselves but the inmates of their women's refuges and orphanages. A senior nun, Sister Ignatius, set the pace in pestering well-off citizens for food and clothing. In Adelaide they called her 'Sister Fly'. She was 'indefatigable', 'ever on the move', but 'a merry little lady, with a perpetual smile'. With one companion Ignatius 'begged her way', as one paper put it, around the western hemisphere (Mauritius, South Africa, the United States, Ireland and England) when funds were even lower than usual.[46]

The Sisters of St Joseph busied themselves with the bush poor, with labouring and farming families, especially children. As with so many other great causes during this generation, children were the defining point, children endangered in their Catholic faith by parental indifference and by the menacing outreach of 'godless' government schools. Her sisters 'hold themselves ready', Mary said, 'to go at the shortest notice and without a murmur wherever obedience and the cause of the dear little ones of the Church require it'.[47]

This added up to a new Christian geography, shattering old patterns of points and boundaries. Mary herself, though well educated, was the daughter of a broken family, with a wandering father. She made her sisters' prayerful thoughts rest on the Sacred Heart, a place for weary souls, and on the Holy Family. Heaven was a settled household. And yet, 'Jesus', she said, 'is perfectly detached', and, like themselves, '[h]e dwells as readily in one place as another'. He was part of the hard, bright air. Pivotal also to their world was the sublime manhood they found in their patron, St Joseph, 'Foster Father' of Jesus. Mary told the sisters of Joseph's 'tender solicitude ... for the comfort and welfare of his most pure Spouse', and 'the complete abnegation of his heart, in its total forgetfulness of self, [and] in its death to all human desires', all of which made him, though a man, somehow the perfect model for themselves.[48]

Such were the complications of late-nineteenth-century love.

Mary's earliest concern was 'the neglected poor children of South Australia'. But she was one of the few who, even in the 1870s, was at ease with the idea of Australia in its entirety. Her extraordinary imagination also gave her an anguished sense of the will of God. 'His holy, adorable Will' was an engine, driving her own faith, tantalising, ubiquitous, all-embracing – vast but almost petty, a father's will – pushing the sisters out to the antipodean void, reducing each of them and all together to desert emptiness.[49]

In 1871 Mary was excommunicated by her bishop, on a confused and illegitimate charge of disobedience. Never defiant, she luxuriated in the face-to-face subjection, the amputation of herself from Mother Church, while one of her women collapsed hysterical.

> I really felt [she said] like one in a dream. I think I seemed not to realise the presence of the Bishop and priests, I know I did not see them, but I felt, oh, such a love for their office, a love and sort of reverence for the very sentence which I then knew was being in full force passed upon me.

She knew it was all a horrible mistake. And yet, 'I was intensely happy'. Shut out from the sacraments and from salvation itself, cast into a void, she said, '[I] felt *nearer* to God than I had ever felt before

... I cannot describe the calm beautiful something that was near'.[50]

The sisters had convents, refuges, schools and orphanages. But typically they spent their lives in remote spots. They were often on the move, as small bush communities gathered and dispersed. They boarded little children whose parents lived too far from schools.[51] The daily pattern of their lives was often fragile and unpredictable, and they had to carry church order with them as they shifted in their twos and threes. For long periods they could be out of reach of the priesthood, which meant having to do without the sacraments, a serious matter for any Catholic wanting to live close to God. They saw themselves as groundbreakers. They made their way round any inconvenient bishop and they moved ahead of their male counterparts, the priests, and unlike the priests they made next to no demand on the resources of the people.[52]

Mary McKillop's sisters were remarkable for the way they used their understanding of the Divine to embrace the continent. They owed that to the brainwork of their founder. They read the 'ideographic prophecy', as sketched by Joseph Furphy, in their own way. Several male religious orders among the Anglicans went down the same track between the late 1890s and the outbreak of the Great War. These were the bush brotherhoods, three of them in remote parts of Queensland (the brotherhoods of St Andrew, of St Barnabas and of St Paul) and one each in western New South Wales (the Good Shepherd), in Western Australia (St Boniface) and in South Australia (St Stephen). Like the St Joseph sisters, the brothers made a point of movement and of poverty, with 'the words of Cranmer [in the church's *Book of Common Prayer*]', as one brother put it, 'competing with the blowflies while the sun beats down outside'.[53]

These great projects lived beside the schemes outlined in the first few chapters of this volume. South Australia was the original home of the Sisters of St Joseph. South Australians also led the way with the cooperative village settlements, such as Murtho on the Murray. Queensland led the way with the bush brotherhoods, just as it did with the centralised branding of cattle and the gathering and broadcasting of ideas about native plants. Australia's rural codes were ingenious patterns of order flung across its great spaces during the last decades of the nineteenth century. The order there was secular. But the churches had their rural codes too. Much deep invention, laced with piety, went into sketching citizenship in the Australian bush.

V

'[M]inisters of religion', said the *Sydney Morning Herald*, 'concede first place to no-one in the intensity of their interest in matters pertaining to federation'.[54] Each of the three engine room capitals, Sydney, Melbourne and Adelaide, made its own contribution to religious thinking on the question, and of course with an urban emphasis. Everywhere, certainly, Wesleyans, the leading Methodist sect, drove a sense of community in which government might deal even-handedly with all religious traditions, dismissing the exclusive claims of the Anglicans and Catholics, but otherwise each centre had an edge of its own.

In Sydney, with its hierarchies of power going back in some respects to convict days, Anglicans such as Henry Jackson were the most inventive. They looked to the English model, with professional men, men of the 'new learning', keeping an eye on everyone else. In Sydney, hopes depended on secular and religious idealism mixed together. In Melbourne, a few Presbyterians, pre-eminently Charles Strong, wanted something more democratic, but still clever. Their reference point was Scotland, where for centuries widespread schooling, managed by Presbyterian ministers, had created a well-read respectability unmatched anywhere else in Europe. In both cases there was always a national dimension – English in the first, Scottish in the second.

In Adelaide, it was the Congregationalists, such as James

Jefferis and Frederick and Julia Holder, who set the pace. They worked hardest and they planned best. Congregational ideas about order matched Australian conditions, they were not bound to old forms of secular power, they made women very much part of the answer, they could reach easily beyond colonial boundaries, and they worked as well in small towns as they did in big ones. The South Australian model operated in two directions at once. Congregationalists reached out without any difficulty to other churches, but their church had always worked from the bottom up, through congregations, and they therefore took easily to a new method of public consultation – the referendum. It was this effort, horizontal in one case and vertical in the other, which made it possible for religion to be interwoven in the federating process.

Referendums were a type of direct democracy.[55] They were much discussed in Australia and New Zealand following their introduction into the Constitution of Switzerland in 1874. They were a way of involving the sovereign people directly in government (to break deadlocks between two houses of parliament, for instance), although this was said to be 'un-English'. (The monarch alone was sovereign.)[56] But they had another purpose. Referendums gave authority to the moral citizen, to the man or woman whose judgment, heard en masse, offered a new way of endowing governments with virtue.

Here was another answer to the question as to whether, in the great 'struggle for existence', rulers needed to bother much about the difference between right and wrong. The answer was to be found in the multiple consciences of the people. The moral citizen had to make decisions about the regulation of private life (divorce, child support and so on) and private morals (salacious publications, drunkenness, adultery, birth control). He or she was also duty-bound to speak out on religious matters whenever they affected society as a whole (Sunday trading, prayers in parliament, the Bible in schools).

These were urgent issues. They were matters of feeling, affection, loyalty, family duty, the rights of men, the rights of women, even, embryonically, the rights of children. The great fear of men and women such as Rose Scott was that a federal government would use its centralising power either to drain these issues of their urgency or to interfere from on high, blundering (men often blundered) into the tender underside of daily life. These matters had to be kept at the old colonial and if possible the local level, where women had some say. At that level, particularising sensibilities could be brought to bear. Better still (said some), they should be handed over to the people themselves, through direct democracy, and here the churches saw their chance. Bit by bit churchmen, over the forty years or more covered by this volume, pieced together a scheme for direct action by the mass, a new kind of decision-making by citizens, male and female, even a new kind of citizen. The great aim, as ever, was to link the intimate with the vast, in this case to link souls with modern states.

The South Australians moved first. In 1876 South Australian ratepayers were given the right to veto the licensing of new public houses in their area, a distinctively moral issue. Women ratepayers did not usually vote, although that had sometimes happened (in a municipal election at Port Adelaide in 1864, for instance).[57] Then in 1882 parents of children in government schools were asked in a questionnaire whether they wanted lessons to include Bible reading. The same period saw the signing of mass petitions on such issues, by both men and women. Some believed that signing was another way of voting, because, as with referendums, matters were referred to the people, and the people sent back their answer. It was voluntary, but so was all voting, from registration to the casting of ballots. In July 1892 the question of giving votes to women was tested in a reader survey by the *Adelaide Evening Journal*, with over 600 responses, male and female. A little over half, including many men, approved.[58]

For women, appeals like this were an excellent way of bypassing old protocol. Women's answers and women's signatures were counted with men's. Following the 1892 survey a petition was organised by the local Women's Suffrage League and signed by 11,600 people (two-thirds women) on several thousand sheets, the names being collected by a massive effort from door to door. It was followed by a counter-petition, signed by 2060, said to be from men with an interest in the liquor trade, who believed that if women had the vote they would enforce prohibition. An act of the South Australian parliament followed, in 1894, giving the vote to all women, the first on the continent (but one year behind New Zealand).[59]

When men such as James Jefferis dreamt of a Christian Australia they had their sights on 'the Divine ideal of justice and freedom'. Other churchmen, with narrower imaginations, were more interested in discipline. They wanted God in the federal Constitution as a first step towards a tighter religious order shore to shore. From 29 March 1897 the makers of the Constitution, meeting in Adelaide, confronted an avalanche of demands that the Almighty be enthroned in the preamble. This was when Patrick McMahon Glynn made his bid. On the first day of meeting, seven petitions were presented, signed by over 17,000 people, asking for a statement that 'God is the Supreme Ruler of the world and the ultimate source of all law and authority in nations'. From that much else would surely follow, including especially laws to keep the Sabbath holy. Over the next three days sixteen more petitions followed, with 140,000 signatures, and there were more again during the ensuing week. Everyone from Roman Catholics to members of the Salvation Army signed. And in opposition there were also half-a-dozen petitions against any such centralised regime. It was the weightiest display of feeling about the Constitution apart from the vote itself.[60] It was democracy in action.

It was also Christianity in action, on a continental scale. A feeling lingered that God lived mainly in face-to-face, settled communities. If he was indeed 'a household God' (Jefferis's description), surely he spoke in a 'still, small voice', a voice geared to the individual conscience, to the tenderness of hearth and home, and in small places – suburban churches, for instance – hallowed by memory and habit. Religion should be close to the people, beginning among neighbours and managed by the old, familiar, family-slanted governments. A genuinely federal spirit would make this household God at the same time into an electrified, steam-powered, telephonic God, manifest in rapid travel, instantaneous communication and federated churches – a God of the future. In Victoria in 1892 a Congregationalist minister organised a council in which his own church was to work with Anglicans, Presbyterians, Wesleyans, Baptists, Lutherans, and Primitive and United Methodists. There was talk, at least among the Congregationalists, of a 'Protestant Social Congress', which would lay the foundations for 'a Christian commonwealth', the touchstone of which would be the service of humankind.[61]

With the same thing happening in other colonies, the prospect was wonderfully exciting. This was the way to found a national religion. Maybe, said a Queenslander (another Congregationalist), the great ideal would soon be realised. We would have not just a Federation of the colonies 'but all the churches united in one great Australian church, which would leave behind the old country's past histories of pride, oppression and violence – histories of persecution and wrong which did not belong to us'. But hopes of discipline figured too, especially within the Queensland Council of Churches, which set up a Committee of Public Morals entrusted with keeping an eye on 'public movements and utterances'.[62]

The petitions sent to the 1897 convention were the work of the Council of Churches movement, with the New South Wales council inspiring the others. But the churches went further still. Taking advantage of the new possibilities of transcontinental communication, Joseph King, a Congregationalist minister in Melbourne, suggested in a letter sent to various newspapers, from Perth to Hobart, that all the colonies should observe a 'Federation Sunday', to 'secure the simultaneous advocacy of the Federal cause from a Christian standpoint'.[63] At least in Victoria and South Australia, the idea immediately caught on.

In Victoria, on Federation Sunday, 22 May 1898, 'not only were the sermons distinctly federal, but the Scripture lessons and hymns were of a national and appropriate character'. It was an unusual theme for preaching because it did not relate to personal failings or eternal salvation. Rather, it was about once-and-for-all action, a simple, straightforward decision to be made by each voter in a few weeks' time. The Anglican bishop of Ballarat distributed an extra verse for the national anthem ('God Save the Queen'):

> Lord God of Hosts, we pray
> That this whole people may
> United stand,
> So shall Australia be
> One nation, vast and free,
> Mighty, and serving Thee;
> God bless our land.[64]

The Presbyterian minister at Footscray, Melbourne, set out three reasons to vote 'yes'. One: the proposed Constitution acknowledged God. '[J]ust as far as a nation acknowledges him, so far will that nation be blessed.' Two: Federation meant unity, and 'with unity the brotherhood of man will be more fully recognised'. Three: it was part of God's plan. What was next in that plan? '[T]he federation first of the English speaking peoples and finally the federation of all nations and all classes and creeds.'[65] God, and communications technology, were obviously and inexorably moving us in this last direction.

Catholic clergy were not involved with the councils of churches, but most of them took the same view. The cardinal archbishop of Sydney, Patrick Moran, was strongly in favour of Federation. He stood unsuccessfully for election to the federal convention of 1897, and his influence weighed heavily with priests and people. According to Sydney's main Catholic paper, the *Freeman's Journal*, 'religious people were on the side of the Bill'. It meant Catholics especially, and influence among Catholics meant influence among large numbers of the more-or-less poor.[66]

As Edmund Barton said (he was quoted earlier), no-one can know how many voters had God on their minds when they made their mark, whether 'yes' or 'no'. Of those who did and who voted 'yes', some had hopes of a Christian commonwealth, a country in which compassion and social justice would be ruling virtues, and some were concerned more with religious discipline, such as the better observance of the Sabbath. With many the two purposes must have been mixed in various measures of preference and degrees of doubt.

In legislating for a referendum in New South Wales the government had insisted that in that colony a majority vote for Federation would not be enough. The number saying 'yes' would need to exceed 80,000. It fell short of that number in 1898, though still reached more than 50 per cent. Also, at that point neither Queensland nor Western Australia voted. In 1899 there were referendums in all colonies except Western Australia (which followed in 1900), and another failure in New South Wales would have destroyed the scheme. Just as the vote in Queensland was crucial in securing Australia's North, the vote in New South Wales was crucial in securing the original heartland of European Australia. New South Wales was also the biggest colony in terms of population, and without New South Wales there would be nothing to counter the influence of Melbourne, so that Australia might be Victoria writ large. Without New South Wales, Federation was impossible.

In New South Wales much depended on the clergy. Single-minded nationalists found most traction for their rhetoric in

Victoria, but middle-aged men of the cloth, taking a more internationalist line, seem to have been more typical of New South Wales. In Victoria, the popular movement for Federation had emerged from the Australian Natives' Association (founded 1871), whose defining energy came largely from young or youngish men, locally born, who were nationalists first and foremost and who saw themselves as 'the first generation of the Australian race'.[67] The ANA aimed to duplicate itself and its thinking Australia-wide, and yet, despite having branches in Charters Towers and Kalgoorlie, it failed to flourish in Sydney. In New South Wales the focus was on justice and peace, church priorities. We had to federate, said the Reverend WH Howard, Wesleyan minister at Brushgrove, near Grafton, in the north, 'for the purpose of suppressing wrong and building up what is right and just'. Forced labour, 'the "sweating" system which prevails in our large cities', must be put down, he said, and Federation would do it. His colleague in Grafton itself, the Reverend Robert Allen, preached what the local paper called 'a very strong sermon' arguing that this great change was about 'the Fatherhood of God and the Brotherhood of Man'. It would 'hasten the time when, according to prediction, all nations shall be one, and there shall be universal peace'.[68]

No other pro-Federation organisation or movement was so large or so far-reaching as the churches. No other set of institutions, apart from newspapers (and sermons were well reported), was better placed to catch popular attention. None could offer such easy-to-follow reasons for voting 'yes'. One clergyman preached from Isaiah: 'And in that day seven women shall take hold of one man, saying, We will eat our own bread, and wear our own apparel: only let us be called by thy name, to take away our reproach'. Another from Matthew: '[L]et your communication be yea'. (In fact, Matthew says, '[L]et your communication be, Yea, yea; [or] Nay, nay').[69] In New South Wales there was very little orchestration among the various denominations. And yet, more than in the other colonies, the clergy kept this effort up, piecemeal and yet intense, as outspoken in 1899 as they had been in 1898.

In 1899 the vote in New South Wales was certainly not close, with 107,420 saying 'yes' and only 82,741 saying 'no'. But it was close enough to suggest that the continuing efforts of men of the cloth had made an essential difference. The 'yes' vote was bigger by half than in 1898. Part of that increase must have been due, for instance, to Cardinal Moran, who had become much more vocal. Nothing could bridge the Catholic–Protestant divide, but Moran had long believed in what he called 'a federation of the people', a union based on 'Christian principles and Christian feelings'.[70] In pulpit after pulpit, in town meetings and common talk, clergy of all sorts had drawn the deeper ideas together, injecting them with a moral purpose and a larger logic than anyone else could manage.

It was alleged that the cardinal got to thousands otherwise out of reach of the Federation movement. But the same was true more or less of all clergy. Normand MacLaurin, chancellor of Sydney University and a fiscal expert, had fought hard against the model on offer, which he thought would seriously burden his own colony. His down-to-earth arguments had been routed, he said, by 'the dominant religious bodies'. 'We had to fight the Churches', said Richard Windeyer, a Sydney barrister, who was on the same side, 'and the young voters dominated by sentiment'. Fighting against two such inspiriting antagonists, we had lost.[71]

There is no way of pinpointing exactly why opinion on Federation moved in essential ways in the end, but Patrick McMahon Glynn, it seems, had predicted truly. Voters who mattered did, in fact, 'invoke Divine Providence' when they agreed to federate, and Divine Providence said the time had come. Federation matched in principle the great aims of the churches, and the churches carried the people with them.

THE FOURTH DIMENSION

To accept special and general relativity is to abandon Newtonian absolute space and absolute time. While it's not easy, you can train your mind to do this. When you move around, imagine your *now* shifting away from the *nows* experienced by others not moving with you … Everyday experience … fails to reveal how the universe really works, and that's why a hundred years after Einstein, almost no one, not even professional physicists, feel relativity in their bones … Deep awareness and true understanding therefore require that we diligently use our intellect to fill in the gaps left by our senses.[1]

Brian Greene, *The Fabric of the Cosmos*

10

Conscience and Total Calculation

I

At the moment of Australian rebirth as a federal Commonwealth massive preparations were underway for the invasion of this world from Mars. '[A]cross the gulf of space ... intellects vast and cool and unsympathetic', reported HG Wells, 'regarded this earth with envious eyes, and slowly and surely drew their plans against us'. This sentence is on the first page of Wells's chilling story *The War of the Worlds*, which he placed in the first years of the twentieth century, shortly after the time he wrote.[1] *The War of the Worlds* was originally serialised in *Pearson's Magazine*, a London journal, and it was in this form that Europeans in Australia first read it, during 1897.

Never, at least since John of Patmos described the End Days in his Book of Revelation, had apocalyptic disaster been more graphically portrayed. On the other hand, it was not long at all before stories of equal callousness were to arrive from the edge of fighting during the Great War, 1914–18.

The Martians landed to the west of London, and soon their most potent weapon, the 'Black Smoke', crept across the English landscape, half-solid, half-fluid, instantly poisoning human life (and prefiguring the mustard gas of the War). 'The intellectual side of man', said the author, as he set the scene, 'already admits that life is an incessant struggle for existence'. The Martians had more than an intellectual side. Everything about them was intellectual, and so they carried the struggle for existence to its logical conclusion. If they were capable of mercy they never showed it. The 'cold-blooded reality' of the story (as the Adelaide *Advertiser* put it), its 'engrossing vividness' (*Brisbane Courier*), made it a bestseller.[2]

The extraordinary thing about Wells's story was the way he jammed bigness – enormous distance, vast intellectual reach, the height and bulk of Martian machinery – up against little, fragile, homely, earthly things, the intellectual against the emotional, metallic brain against mere affection. The ordinary world was swept aside by the invaders, all the sweet comforts and the fragile courtesies of daily life. Conscience itself struggled to survive. The approach of Martian intellect reduced humanity to a featureless bulk. The hordes fleeing London were a boiling stream, a torrent, a roaring fire – like Rose Scott's description of Australian Federation itself. '[T]he black heads, the crowded forms, grew into distinctness as they ... hurried past, and merged their individuality again in a receding multitude that was swallowed up at last in a cloud of dust.'[3]

There is a direct line from this story to the one Arthur Koestler told a generation or so later, called *Darkness at Noon*. By that time the menace of mere intellect was everywhere. The evil made itself known as totalitarianism, the deep rule of a single idea. In *Darkness at Noon* the 'intellects vast and cool and unsympathetic' belonged to the Party, or rather there was one intellect, that of the leader, 'No. 1'. Under this regime, the individual subject, the ordinary man, women or child, the 'I' every human being learns to live with from birth – inward, peripatetic, serendipitous, marred and dappled by events, worried by feelings of good and evil – was only, as the Party said, a 'grammatical fiction'.[4] Again, individuality was abolished.

There were ideas about No. 1, but by another name, in this earlier period. In 1909 Melbourne's *Punch* told its readers about Field Marshal Lord Kitchener, who had made his name in the Sudan and in the Boer War, and who was visiting Australia. 'He is pure, unalloyed brain,' said *Punch*, 'unhampered by any other feeling of vice or virtue … superb, magnificent – the finest brain in the British Army'. 'There is no man Kitchener. There is just a brain, and that is why he is called "K".' He took from his men not love, hatred or admiration, so said *Punch*, 'but merely unquestioning acquiescence'.[5]

Raw energy and 'unquestioning acquiescence'. An admiration for the letter 'K' also explains the trade name 'Kodak', chosen in 1888 as a commercial gamble by the American George Eastman for his cameras, and by the turn of the century it was a household word. Advertising, newly understood in these days, called for 'unquestioning acquiescence' just as much as military leadership did. 'The letter "K"', Eastman said, 'had been a favorite with me – it seems a strong, incisive sort of letter'.[6]

Germinating within the fiction of the 'pure, unalloyed brain' – so strong, so incisive – was the great adventure of the twentieth century. Humankind en masse was to follow the great experts, the great brains, into worlds beyond common instinct and intuition, beyond shared custom and the everyday. John Locke's reprimand was a thing of the past. '[N]o definitions that I know,' said Locke, the great philosopher of the early Enlightenment, 'no suppositions of any sect, are of force enough to destroy constant experience'. We know what we perceive, that is, and nothing more.[7] Now, in the opening years of the twentieth century, we were to be rushed by better brains than our own outside common sense as we would normally understand it, beyond good and evil, vice and virtue. The future would be born from the rich work of advanced literacy – scientific literacy, cartographic literacy, technological literacy. Traditional wisdom, embedded in ordinary talk, was no longer enough.

The invasion of the small by the big, the overshadowing of settled, familiar, tactile things by brains vast, cool and unsympathetic, and to most people incomprehensible, was happening everywhere. James Jefferis might wonder at the infinite intelligence of God, but he believed also in God's infinite goodness. But for Catherine

Helen Spence even divine power now seemed too big to share in our 'parts and passions'.[8] Worse again, what would happen if the deeper impact of the Almighty could be best engaged by brains rather than by souls, by 'tyrannous freedom' rather than by worship, by sheer thinking rather than by goodness?

Might there be other realities, known as yet only to God, differently ordered from anything most of us now understood and which only the most incisive, superfine brains might one day reach? What was that brainwork which would be needed to cope with them? Spiritualism – imagination rather than calculation – had lost much of its early promise as the way to find another world. By now the idea of a fourth dimension appealed to the better read. In 1884–86 an English schoolmaster, Charles Hinton, published a series of *Scientific Romances*, of which the most famous was called 'What Is the Fourth Dimension?' It sold for a shilling in Adelaide.

> Now [said Hinton], if there are beings who live in a four-dimensional world, they must feel as habituated to it as we do to ours, and the conceptions which seem so impossible to us must be every-day matters to them. It would be impossible for us to try to enter at once into the serious thoughts of these denizens of higher space.[9]

But what if some of us could in fact join them? What if some of us could share in those 'conceptions', and ourselves produce those 'serious thoughts'? In short, what was the limit to human intelligence? Did it have a limit?

A few claimed the fourth dimension for the Holy Spirit, though they were not sure whether imagining that dimension, if they could ever do it, would mean imagining God or imagining *like* God. It was a deeply important distinction. The *Clarence and Richmond Examiner* reported on a pure mathematician at Cambridge whose friends said that he lived in the fourth dimension, because his extraordinary mathematical insights mixed with his piety had seemingly taken him to some such place. But the *Maitland Mercury* went further (copying, as these all did, from overseas papers), insisting that we were all on the point of entering, in imagination and in fact, on 'a new world', a world which would include the fourth dimension. When that happened, said the *Mercury*, '[m]any attributes, which have hitherto been regarded as the exclusive possession of the Deity, will be shared by His creatures'. That would be an era of true freedom. Imagine, it said: '[t]he past mingles with the present, and the future unfolds its secrets, Death loses its sting and parting its sadness'.[10]

That would be dazzling. But maybe this other reality would be the worst of all worlds. Maybe it would be hell. Humanity would soon lose all contact with 'the simple life', said the *Camperdown Chronicle*, in western Victoria. We would be so completely weighed down by 'tyrannous toys' – steam engines, motor cars, telephones and now even airships, doubtless to be followed by 'some subtler and swifter vehicle' designed for use in the fourth dimension – and by so much complexity and sheer cleverness, that civilisation itself would surely crash.[11]

Soon the term 'fourth dimension' was shorthand for anything badly out of kilter with 'the simple life'. '[T]he fourth dimension in women's apparel' meant embroidered nightgowns and suchlike frippery, priced a lot higher than anyone with any sense would pay. '[L]ike the fourth dimension in mathematics it leads to madness.'[12]

Modernity asked us to live counterintuitively. It did lead to madness, as a few short years were to prove. But it led to other things too. It led to extraordinary scientific discoveries, most notably Albert Einstein's special theory of relativity, in 1905, followed by his general theory of relativity, in 1915, which proposed a new system of physics, absolutely contradicting common experience and common sense, to be followed in due course by quantum mechanics – if possible even more weird.

This was the beginning of an age when the best-prized experiences were gateways, existential openings to another level of the human. It has been called an age of extremes, but it was really an age of absolute newness.[13] What men and women wanted, some of them, was spiritual and intellectual transformation combined. They wanted total rebirth. As Jefferis said, we now understood that God set no limit to the wandering impulses of the brain, no barrier to 'the divine rights of our manhood'. Ernst Jünger, a German army officer, put it another way, having himself crossed an existential borderline under a vast artillery barrage during the Great War. '[W]e had gone over the edge of the world', he said, 'into superhuman perspectives'. On the other hand, an enemy he never knew, Adrian Stephen of Sydney, an artillery officer at about the same time and place, adding his contribution to some such titanic cataclysm, thought himself godlike – carried away, as he put it, with 'a sense of infinite power'.[14]

Extraordinary aspirations, including new ways of seeing, were suddenly realised everywhere. The new automobiles provided more varied vistas of the world, but airships and aeroplanes made such vistas superhuman indeed. The air was not yet the dominion of humanity it was to become in the 1920s, but there were hints of that apotheosis, especially in the musings of Bernard O'Dowd, who imagined 'Australia's untainted blue' as already, in a spiritual sense, 'a crowded aerial highway of trysting souls', an upside-down version of the intricate underground waterways imagined in the decades hitherto.[15]

And what of X-rays – seeing inside humanity itself? Stories of X-ray examinations titillated readers, especially when they were close to home, stories about the discovery of a penny in the abdomen of Denis Maloney of Ballarat (he had been throwing it up and catching it in his mouth), of the false teeth of Kenneth Redmond, a blacksmith in Dungog, New South Wales (swallowed at dinner), and of a bullet from a pea rifle fired by Henry Knight, aged five, of Toora, south-east Victoria, at his sister Charlotte (lodged in her jaw).[16] Thomas Mann, the great German novelist, wrote at length about X-rays in his tale of pre-War life, *The Magic Mountain*. Mann's young hero gazed at a strange animal shape, like a bag but with a slow jellyfish motion, struggling to realise its significance on the screen. 'Good God, it was the heart, it was Joachim's honour-loving heart, that Hans Castorp saw!'

This was invasion! '"I am looking at your heart," he said in a suppressed voice.

'"Go ahead," answered Joachim.'[17]

Myriad such adventures, leaps into the unknown, were sketched in newspapers such as the *Examiner*, the *Mercury* and the *Chronicle*, by Hinton's little books, by pieces of fiction carrying readers into new worlds. All showed what brains could do, eyes could see and ears could hear, uncoupled from human feeling. You were launched like this into a moral vertigo, disengaged from the old signposts of human existence, and fell where nothing seemed to matter except cleverness alone.

II

If brains were the answer, maybe the brain power of many individuals working together would do just as well as No. 1, the single genius. HG Wells called this 'organised intelligence'.[18] Something like it had registered in the research associations and discussion groups of the Australian colonies throughout the nineteenth century, coming to a head in the Australasian Association for the Advancement of Science, in 1888. (At that point, the words 'science' and 'scientists' had a more comprehensive meaning than they were to have later on.) The cooperatives, which became steadily more ambitious during the late nineteenth century, were built on the same hopes. They were all meant to make the most of multiple decision-making.

The new mass of newspapers, so essential to Australian life, pointed in the same direction, especially the more interactive ones, such the *Bulletin* and *Dawn*, which drew in their readers and made them part of the publishing enterprise. In this way, organised intelligence became more and more powerful. The newspaper industry was increasingly interconnected, complex and dynamic. With the submarine cable to Europe, agencies such as Reuters had been established and non-local news was packaged for sale. And newspapers were just one of the manifold types of communication now familiar to many, which were altogether more far-reaching, all-embracing and continuous than anything previously known, thanks to steam-driven traffic, the telegraph, the telephone and good postage. The pioneering American sociologist Albion Woodbury Small made the link with telephones explicit. He argued for 'the unity of social science'. That would happen, he said, when human knowledge stopped running along separate channels, as it had done since the Enlightenment, and lived instead within crisscrossing lines of connection, like a telephone switchboard.[19] It was already happening.

German thinkers idolised this sort of collaboration, though from a more elite perspective. For them, following the great philosopher Johann Gottfried Herder, 'the realm of minds' was the foundation of the state. That idea was now taken up everywhere too. Albion Small argued that intellectual leaders had to work together to set a new agenda for humanity:

> The most reliable criterion of human values which science could propose would be the consensus of councils of scientists representing the largest possible variety of human interests, and co-operating to reduce their special judgments to a scale which would render their due to each of the interests in the total calculation.

This was the great alternative to No. 1.[20] Maybe the 'total calculation' Small talked about was preferable to the sublime sacrifice No. 1 might expect.

Sir Samuel Griffith, the Queenslander, was referring to something like organised intelligence when he talked about a 'general movement' (he called it 'the body politic') whose 'vital processes' sprang from the separate actions of many 'intelligent beings'. As a whole, he said, this movement was 'to a great extent, automatic and unconscious', and yet it was not unconscious by the very fact that Griffith and others were commenting on it.[21] Indeed, HG Wells's organised intelligence was just as magnificently self-aware as any of the 'intelligent beings' who drove it. It was always listening to its own voice and watching its own impact. It was a new, almost animal thing, with, as Griffith said, its own 'vital processes'.

To change the image, it was like a great tide coming in, lifting altogether the manifold boats of late-nineteenth-century idealism, and setting them all more or less to drift, or run, in the same direction, towards a belief in the intellectual possibilities of the nation – any nation.

The spirit of Australian Federation was the spirit of organised intelligence. Some had said that the collective aspect of it should have been pushed a lot further. In 1898 the Launceston businessman Charles Graham Worsley had proposed a provisional federal Constitution rather than a final one, with six years' trial. Then, he said, 'all the intelligence of the *country* would be bent to the task of thrashing out the problem, throwing out suggestions and devising suitable measures for the continuance of the Union' – a collective effort truly national and democratic.[22]

In another of his stories, *The History of Mr Polly* (serialised in the *West Australian* in 1910), HG Wells spent a page or two on this kind of collective effort. The character who argues for it in *Mr Polly* is a 'dome-headed monster of intellect' who has one great diagnosis for every small failure, every dull example of bankruptcy, aimlessness and despair he sees about him. The people of each nation think as one, says this individual, and a rapidly complicating society must think well. If it does not face up to 'the intricate problems of its organization, [it] is in exactly the position of a man who takes no thought of dietary or regimen, who abstains from baths and exercise and gives his appetites free play'. Failing to exert its collective brain, its collective body becomes lazy, fat and miserable, and it dies before its time.[23]

On such matters argument often went back to the beginning, homing in on the manufacture of the human race itself, on the procreation and welfare of babies. This was an urgent issue for organised intelligence, but also of course for the individual parent. The science behind breeding the strongest and brightest forms of humanity, using pseudo-Darwinian principles, was called 'eugenics'. In a public lecture on the West Australian goldfields, Henry Ellis, a local doctor, promised an audience of parents and potential parents that eugenics would be 'almost the greatest of the sciences'. It was a science, he said, 'of national importance, because the welfare of a nation was bound up in the numerical strength and physical and mental fitness of its people'.[24] We must have as many fit babies as possible, and virility and healthy maternal instincts would ensure that abundance, and with it a series of robust, rapidly multiplying generations.

However, current statistics on infant mortality proved, for Ellis, that a large share of men and women in Western Australia were not fit, either physically or mentally, to be parents. This was a question of eugenics and economics combined. Some years earlier, when he was living in Sydney, Ellis had given a paper at a meeting of the local Australian Economic Association, as a contribution to the discussion begun nearly a century earlier by the English clergyman Thomas Robert Malthus, in his *Essay on the Principle of Population* (1798). Malthus had proposed that national populations could not increase beyond a certain point without outstripping resources and bringing about starvation and misery, but experience, as Ellis pointed out, had since proved that human intelligence could break the nexus between population numbers and resources, by multiplying production as well as reproduction. We must look, he said, to 'the excessive vital brain power of individuals' for the solution. Excessive, because the value-adding brain power in such cases would be over and above what each creative genius needed in his own 'struggle for existence'. He would devote his excess to the general good.[25]

At the same time, at Lambrigg, a small property on the Murrumbidgee, William Farrer was doing precisely that. Living on a small inherited annuity – lifted, in other words, above the struggle for existence – he was engaged in the experimental crossbreeding of wheat (in its reliance on generational inheritance a variation on eugenics). After several years of gradual experiment Farrer developed a strain he called 'Federation', which in New South Wales led to a four-fold increase in wheat production by the first year of the War ('marvellous yields ... a beautiful plump smooth grain') and made Australia as a whole for the first time an exporter of wheat.[26] Output had outstripped the growth of population. This is exactly what Ellis meant.

It was not conscience which would decide these struggles but applied intelligence, diligently solving questions of need in its various human dimensions. Jesus might say, '[Y]e have the poor always with you'. In this new age, when even God might defer to human invention, some Christians did better. There was now a particular answer to the problem of the perpetual poor. It was called 'charity organisation', and it was a clear case of organised intelligence. The idea of charity organisation had originated in Germany and had been taken up in England, and then with enormous enthusiasm in the United States.[27] A Charity Organisation Society was founded in Melbourne in 1887 (even before the suffering of the 1890s depression). True to Melbourne's nation-building spirit, its leaders had quickly moved to make it Australia- or even Australasia-wide.

Charity organisation had no obvious horizon. It was charity carried beyond the limits observed for the last nineteen centuries and its catchcry was 'widespread'.[28] Charitable groups of all sorts, from suburb to suburb and from town to town, were to be gathered into one great scheme. Like the Women's Christian Temperance Union, like William Guthrie Spence's trade unions, and like the great sporting competitions and cadet camps, charity organisation was a way of collating human energies and individualities across enormous spaces, using railways and the telegraph. It was sociology with a mission. Psychology offered similar promise. As a country newspaper put it, when we knew everything that psychology could teach us, then we would 'efficiently love our unfortunate brother by knowing how to make him lovable, and how to make life lovable to him'.[29] Charity organisation was about efficient love.

The movement flourished only in Melbourne. Everything depended on 'full inquiry and complete co-operation', said Edward Morris, professor of modern languages and literature at Melbourne University, one of the two instigators in Australia, at the intercolonial conference called to get it all started. Morris wanted a 'network of societies' uniformly collecting information about the poor for a central register. '[The] interchange of records and information', he said, 'would checkmate even the cleverest of those who prey on society, and – this tribute is at least their due – some of them are remarkably clever'. We must be cleverer still.[30]

Charity organisation might seem to lack some of the divine spirit of the Sermon on the Mount. Some called it 'a cold-blooded thing'. 'I utterly deny that charity organization is un-Christian', Morris said. The great aim was to wipe out poverty altogether, a dream now within reach for the first time. Random acts of kindness meant 'heedless giving'. They carried no chance of lasting good.[31]

(Morris had a scholar's sense of humour. His great compendium of *Austral English*, a list of terms distinctive to the Antipodes, included 'jump', and he offered a usage obviously originating in the goldrushes, as in 'You have jumped my pew'. In the same dilemma, Morris added, one might also say, 'Excuse me, sir, but you are occu-pewing my py'.[32])

The Reverend Henry Latimer Jackson, of St James', King Street, Sydney, tried to start a Charity Organisation Society in Sydney. It was hard going. 'We are', he said, 'sadly conservative in many things'. When it came to looking after the poor, 'there is plenty of limb-activity', of good neighbourliness, of going from door to door, of sitting and listening endlessly to sufferers. '[But] brain-activity is, on the other hand, exceedingly rare.'[33] It was brain activity which would lead us to a new revelation, to knowledge counterintuitive like the fourth dimension, knowledge contradicting everything believed so far, including the Word of God, and yet weirdly true.

III

In Western Australia, Henry Ellis also argued for a tax on bachelors, an idea which raised a clap from the women in his audience. The money forthcoming would support expectant mothers so that they need not work, the better to preserve the health of their offspring. He also wanted equal pay for women. A lack of equality all round reduced the productivity of women as units of society, or, as some put it, 'members of the state'. Similarly, their ignorance as parents was a great obstacle to public health. There were mothers, said Ellis, who thought that sickness and health were acts of God. 'The person who got knowledge by the grace of God', he said, 'generally ended up killing their kiddies'.[34]

Some might mock. The *Geraldton Guardian* carried a piece about marriages planned for their eugenic consequences, called 'Eugenic Courting':

> She (after seeing his physician's certificate): 'And you will always be my genetic and eugenic mate, sweet chromosome?'

> He (Darwiningly): 'Yes, my darling little natural selection.'
>
> She: 'Then you will take me as your co-operative worker in the process of evolution?'
>
> And putting on their rubber gloves, they went out hand in hand in search of a disinfected minister.[35]

Maybe, even in the bearing of children, the grace of God would make way for 'the greatest of the sciences'.

Thirza Morgan, wife of Thomas Morgan, bootmaker of Goodwood, Adelaide, accumulated children as usual, and on one day, 17 December 1898, she gave birth in quick succession to two sons and two daughters. First reports said that mother and babies were all well ('No mention was, however, made of the physical or mental condition of the surprised father'), and the *Advertiser* joked that this lady had obviously been moved to respond to a recent report by the local health officer, which included 'some doleful statistics' on the decline of the birthrate in his municipality. France was a byword for small families, and the figure reported for the municipality of Unley (24.2 births per thousand) was nearly as bad as France. Clearly, Mrs Morgan 'has decided that this reproach to the important municipality shall be wiped away, at least as far as her family is concerned'.[36]

Most of the doctors in Adelaide came to see the Morgan phenomenon, as Tommy Morgan all his life proudly recalled. However, within a few days all four babies were dead. Another of Mrs Morgan's children had died some years earlier, but she and her husband managed to raise two sons and six daughters, beginning at Goodwood and finishing up at Port Pirie, so she had nothing to be ashamed of.[37] By this multiple birth in 1898 she also made her own passing contribution to a debate about the South Australian birthrate which had been urged now and again for several years by the two leading papers, the *Advertiser* and the *Register*.

The argument touched all the colonies, but differently. In Melbourne the moral implications had been developed in detail by the leading surgeon-gynaecologist Walter Balls-Headley. In a book published in 1894 called *The Evolution of Diseases in Women*, Balls-Headley underpinned his argument with statistics. Victoria, he said, was highly urbanised, and that meant its marriage rate was low because men and women always married later in towns than in the country. 'Native races', he added, married earliest of all, and in most animals too sexual relations started with maturity. Among ourselves, we must allow, he said, for 'late physical development because of mental education'.

However, with us such delay had lately passed beyond all natural and healthy limits. Women who were still single at twenty-five, their physical needs blocked by 'the influences of civilisation', were at serious risk, from cervicitis, for instance, and from vaginal congestion, such problems being exacerbated by mental stress – by unrequited longing for 'marital functions'.

> The selection of the fittest [he argued] has resulted in a race of women of such extraordinary physical growth and beauty as has probably never before existed, but whose sexual growth is liable to be so affected by mental culture, mode of dress, and delayed or non-marriage, that never before were uterine abnormalities of development, disease, and difficulty in parturition so prevalent.

And at the same time, he said, 'the developing brain of man is probably increasing the size of the head in birth', making childbirth, if and when it happened, even harder for women. In such ways, among highly cultured peoples, or at least among those given to excessive brainwork, were 'Nature's arrangements' frustrated.[38]

Statistics, as I have said already, had always been central to the way the Europeans in Australia understood themselves, and by the time of Federation 'birthrate' was a household term among the leaders of public opinion. There was a real concern, when the nation needed them so much, that potential parents were not doing their duty. The modern decline of France and, worse, the ancient collapse of Rome set alarming precedents. In the case of Rome, said the Sydney *Truth*,

> [h]ordes of lusty Goths and Huns and Vandals, from whose loins could spring children, whose wives were pure and faithful, whose ignorance of the unnatural vices and strange passions of the Romans was as complete as their ignorance of art and letters, swooped down upon the rich homes of the feeble men and impure women and swept Roman civilisation off the face of the earth.[39]

In that case, in short, uncultivated brains had triumphed. What would happen in ours?

Here was an extraordinary dilemma. Intellectual progress seemed to carry with it the seeds of its own destruction. Many thought that the answer lay with a great cleansing war which would call up fundamental virtues, vision, chivalry, physical courage, fortitude, patriotism and self-sacrifice. But attention turned also to the failings of modern women.

Girls and women might think that they had an aptitude for learning sometimes superior to men's. The Englishman WL Courtney had suggested that women might be better than men in adapting to 'a new medium', surely an important ability in an age of change.[40] And yet there were men convinced that too much education hindered a woman's purpose. This was most obvious in the way calculating wives decided for themselves, or with colluding husbands, whether or not to bring new souls into the world. The 'divine rights of manhood' were not enough. Women were claiming divine rights too, including a 'tyrannous freedom' which seemed to set aside God himself.

'[T]he existence and formation of females', said Balls-Headley, 'are for the purpose of the propagation of their kind'. And yet, 'high mental culture is antagonistic to healthy sexual development and child-bearing'. It was therefore time to assert an awkward truth. A man might be complimented by saying that he was 'all brain'. Alfred Deakin called Sir Henry Parkes (not to his face) 'a full-blooded, large-brained, self-educated Titan'.[41] Lord Kitchener was 'pure, unalloyed brain'. Blood and brain, flesh and intelligence, made up one compound. This was the new type of perfect manhood. But when a woman's brain took over like that she risked everything, in this world and in the world to come.

This was in spite of the fact that women's brains were making a productive impact as never before. Between 1891 and 1911 the number of breadwinners described by the government statisticians as in some sense catering for public culture in the broadest sense increased by about one-fifth. These were the men and women 'mainly engaged in the government and defence of the country, and in satisfying the moral, intellectual, and social wants of its inhabitants'. In some areas in particular (music, the fine arts, publications, the sale of paper and stationery) the increase was mainly female. Also, most schoolteachers now were women.[42] Many more women than hitherto were bringing money home. Many women were not just balancing income and expenditure in new ways, and thereby linking their fiscal fortunes to the larger world, but also stitching and weaving HG Wells's organised intelligence in whatever patterns they liked.

Balls-Headley's logic was typical of his generation. There never was an age better prepared to swallow, all at once, vast theories. There was an abiding temptation to look to tiny, common things ('instinct' was a particularly popular word) as keys to the vast secrets of creation. But in its hunger for large laws this generation ran very fast, sidestepping scientific method as it had been worked out over the previous three centuries and cutting straight from the particular to the general. The world was full of what Andrew Garran, eminent Sydney journalist and public intellectual, called 'single cause philosophers', social theorists who used one factor to explain vast complexity. Though more sophisticated than most, Alexander Sutherland, in his book *The Origin and Growth of the Moral Instinct*, argued that moral instinct had evolved from parents' feeling for their children. Balls-Headley said that the progress of the human race could be put down to 'the power of sexual attraction'. In France the influential writer Jean-Marie Guyau asserted that the painful gap the newborn discovered between need and satisfaction, mouth and mother, explained the notion of time itself.[43]

Some found the answers in statistics. The colonial governments of the Australasian archipelago had always done so. In earlier times the most remarkable of the government statisticians had been William Archer (chapter 5). At the turn of the century it was Timothy Augustine Coghlan, government statistician in Sydney. Coghlan was the epitome of a new generation of public servants, eager, intelligent, of democratic temperament, a nation builder. His statistical concerns were brilliantly wide-ranging and he was the supreme authority on all the quantitative dimensions of humanity in New South Wales. His main contribution to the discussion of the birthrate was his 1899 pamphlet *Childbirth in New South Wales: A Study in Statistics*, which added a mass of statistical detail to logic like Balls-Headley's.[44] But not many were as subtle as Coghlan.

Print, said the leaders of the Bolshevik Revolution, in Russia, 'is the strongest and sharpest weapon of our party'. But also, said Joseph Conrad in *Lord Jim*, there remained 'a weird power in the spoken word'.[45] Side by side with the accumulating literature about how men and women should procreate, and the 'total calculation' which underpinned it, was another body of knowledge living in the world of talk, especially talk in families, the chat, the chaffing, the cheek, the chastising, the endless quiet comfort and instruction that went on within the walls of ordinary homes. And the two were interconnected. Scientific writing used 'Nature's laws' plus intimate observation, and on the other hand family talk, even ordinary desire, was shadowed by reading. In managing their lives men and women were trusting more and more to imported books on family limitation, to cheap pamphlets and to newspaper advertisements – advertisements, say, for the No More Worry Company's 'patent pessary' (pessaries were women's contraceptives), for Nemia Tonic (among other things, apparently, an abortifacient), and for books such as *The Naked Truth*, which linked 'sexual weakness' in men to 'boyish folly', while giving all who read it hope of 'brighter days to come' (the coarse slang of the street suddenly insinuated into print).[46]

Talk among parents and children was changing too. The great educational effort since the goldrushes, for boys and girls equally, which had speeded up in the 1880s, was transforming the soundscape of domestic life. English visitors found Australian children remarkably free in addressing their parents. 'The growth of a spirit of lawlessness is painfully apparent.' Conversation in novels such as Miles Franklin's *My Brilliant Career* (1901) catches the transformation (and what better book than *My Brilliant Career* to show the divine rights now claimed for women?). There was less room for overbearing fathers. '[C]hildren are better educated now', said Edward Riley, a Sydney plasterer, who had seven of them. 'There used to be one way of keeping children under some control, by frightening them with some bogie-man or something like that, but all that has disappeared.'[47]

There was even talk about the rights of children. '[E]very child', said *Harper's Monthly*, which was read by men and women of advanced literacy in the United States, 'has the right to premeditated existence, subsequent happiness, and individuality'. 'They had clamoured for men's rights,' said Littleton Groom, lately federal attorney-general, 'and women's rights, and now there was a popular cry for children's rights'. He was all in favour, especially in light of the current movement to set up kindergartens.[48] Here was an agenda absolutely new, and with large implications for the twentieth century. Even Rose Scott, in her talk about the individuality of women and men, never included the individuality of children.

The equal individuality of husbands and wives was certainly more than an idea. Thomas Hardy's stories, mentioned in chapter 3, showed sensuality, including the sensuality of voices, felt equally by men and women, which could easily mean husbands and wives. Women, especially those with some literacy, had a new command of information, including information about their bodies. By the 1880s, for instance, various editions of Charles Knowlton's scandalous and highly informative text, *Fruits of Philosophy; or, The Private Companion of Young Married People*, had reached Australia (one of them, by Annie Besant, with the daunting title *The Law of Population, Its Consequences, and Its Bearing upon Human Conduct and Morals*). In a single newspaper advertisement in 1891 a Sydney bookseller listed *Book of Nature and Illustrated Marriage Guide*, *Plain Home Talk about the Human System*, *The Fruits of Philosophy*, *The Law of Population* and, also by Mrs Besant, *Marriage: As It Was, as It Is, and as It Should Be*.

With such texts speaking boldly to them (and also, in the same notice, *The Male Generative Organs, Their Use and Abuse*), women were no longer prepared to be 'merely patient bearers of children'. 'Comprehension of the laws and phenomena of reproduction', said a Rockhampton paper, 'is not now confined to a limited number of medical students. The modern woman does not confine her studies to domestic affairs: there is no limit to their range'. With this new knowledge, 'the modern woman' talked differently – with her friends, with her doctor, with the chemist who sold her the new paraphernalia of birth control, and with her husband.[49]

A secret island was suddenly annexed to the continent of democratised knowledge. 'The time had passed when knowledge had to be regarded as the exclusive privilege of caste or class', said

William Windeyer from the bench of the Supreme Court of New South Wales. This was part of his judgment in the prosecution of *The Law of Population* for obscenity, in 1888, two years after the Mt Rennie case, in which Windeyer had ordered the hanging of four men for rape.[50] Such events were straws in the wind, but the wind was blowing in one obvious direction.

'How few women', said Rose Scott, 'ever discuss the vital realities of life with men', including 'the very things that most concern their mutual happiness'.[51] But that was already starting to change. The new freedom, bursting forth in ordinary conversation, could be startling. In Sydney the chief supplier of contraceptives was Washington H Soul Pattinson, of Pitt Street, a pharmacy so successful that in 1903 it was listed on the local stock exchange. Soul Pattinson employed a saleswoman known as 'the Nurse', who kept a room stocked, as she explained to a state royal commission, with pessaries and safety sponges, plus 'enemas, douches, elastic goods, belts, accouchement sheets, sanitary towels, breast pumps, [and] trusses', and where she offered advice to married women who came with a doctor's note. Such advice might involve some practical skill. A Newcastle doctor, John Harris, told the same commission that homemade pessaries were common. 'They [young wives] use quinine and sulphate of zinc, and make them up with cocoa-butter themselves.' And the know-how came back full circle to other retailers. 'You see,' said George Stephens, chemist of Newtown, in Sydney's south, 'there is a peculiar thing about women; they will tell one another, and they simply come along and ask for them'.[52]

Offered these flashes of X-ray insight into women's intimacies, so unlike older days, medical men might be taken aback. '[T]here seems to be a twist in them that way', said Dr Robert Scot Skirving. He meant a kind of moral warp, seen suddenly even in good women. Nowadays, said Scot Skirving, 'a woman will talk to me of the most inner sexual relations with as much *sang froid* as if she were talking about having lunch'. Similarly, a man would tell his workmates, quite frankly, that he had decided against having any more children because he was 'full up' with them taking the food from his table. The Presbyterian minister William Dill Macky was struck with the casual tone of a father who brought him a baby for christening. There was a seven-year gap since the last. They had stopped for a while, the man explained, 'but the mother took a fancy that she would rather have another child, so we brought it about'.[53] Just like that.

In most houses, bed was one of the few places available for such husband–wife consultations. '[T]hey generally discuss the matter,' said Dr Ralph Worrall, 'and make up their minds'. It was often on the grounds of expense. '[T]hey say they cannot afford to rear and educate their children.' Some couples, said a mother of sixteen, 'made a sort of agreement on marrying'. And so, said Scot Skirving, 'both the husband and the wife fall into any methods to dodge conception'. And then some, said Dr Stanhope MacCulloch, 'come to me after a time and say they have been married for two or three years, and now want children'. Perhaps they needed him to remind them how to manage it. More often, couples started early, or after a brief interval, and then stopped when they had enough.[54]

In spite of the passion for vast ideas which has coloured these pages, the moral economy of husband, wife and children, their happiness together, now had a dynamic all its own. It was itself, indeed, a vast idea, with as yet untold implications. By the standards of family life all would be judged.[55] The change was led, as usual, by the better educated, both men and women, and probably less in the bush, where the domains of family and small community easily merged, than in the cities. Emotional closeness meant a tighter sharing of family resources, and that led to fewer children. Women who spoke openly about family limitation were speaking as calculating, far-sighted wives, in consultation with their men. They were accountable to no-one else.

To some men and women this new understanding seemed dangerously selfish. Australia's population had to grow in order for the nation to survive in the global 'struggle for existence', and to some, including medical men such as Balls-Headley, the decline in the birthrate since the 1880s was a national emergency. It justified the royal commission of 1903–04 mentioned earlier, headed by Charles Mackellar, a member of the Legislative Council and former president of the New South Wales Board of Health (and father of Dorothea Mackellar, who at the same time, in London, wrote the lovely patriotic lines 'I love a sunburnt country').

For many clergy (there were exceptions), interfering with procreation meant interfering with the prerogative of God, but among lay people, including those who went to church (Protestants, at least), Christian conscience was working in new ways. 'There is a tendency to greater tolerance of social sins', said the Rockhampton *Morning Bulletin*, 'which meet with the severe approbation of all the churches'. Men and women might heed the advice of clergy where the outcomes were long term and more or less mysterious, such as Federation. But, except among the Catholics, it was another matter where the outcomes were obvious, urgent and personal. 'They [women, that is] only admit the religious sense', said the Reverend John Howell Price, Church of England minister at Richmond, near Sydney, 'insofar as it may touch them in other directions – absolutely not in this'.[56]

Sometimes you could get through to them. Price once gave a strong sermon on the wickedness of birth control. A childless couple, married for seven years, heard him, he said, and 'within twelve months after the preaching of that sermon a child was born to them and was brought to me, and I christened it'. But for most clergy birth control was not a subject to be mentioned in a sermon, in front of people of all ages and both sexes. Besides, it could make no difference, and they risked their authority in other matters, and also their income, which in most churches depended on voluntary donation.[57]

Talking privately could be just as awkward. Clergy came up against a well-informed, self-sufficient world of female conversation, and of husband–wife consultation. It was a world they could not enter as they had once been able to do, let alone control, and it embodied a morality they could not fathom. Few clergy now were scientists, as many of them had been not so long before, and they had no feel for the moral issues the new science was throwing up. Medical men themselves were divided. Some took Balls-Headley's line, but some, as 'the Nurse' at Soul Pattinson said (and those, she said, of 'the very highest standing'), sent women to buy her products. 'I thought I was doing right when the medical men ordered them.'[58]

Many couples now, said the mother of sixteen (who thought differently), 'think it is wrong to bring children into the world and not be able to provide for them'. Her own large family had managed by living carefully, but even her adult sons were taking a more prudent line, and not marrying at all.[59] Families now needed not just economic independence but also emotional independence. The two were powerfully interconnected.

This approach was sanctioned at the highest level, in a celebrated case heard before the Commonwealth Court of Conciliation and Arbitration, founded in 1904 to assess the competing claims of employers and employees, with Henry Bournes Higgins, a Victorian and friend of Alfred Deakin, as president. The spirit of 'New Protection', initiated before Federation in Victoria, was ripe for extension throughout the continent and in 1906 the federal government, led by Deakin, had legislated accordingly, forcing certain types of employers to pay their workmen 'a fair and reasonable wage' in return for tariff protection. Higgins's subsequent judgment in the Harvester Case (1907) was an example of the learned idealism which was Melbourne's finest contribution to the federal cause, and it was to make a deep impact on Australian households and workplaces for most of the twentieth century.[60]

In the 1890s Higgins had been one of a small number of leading men who had argued hard against Federation, in the form presented to voters. He called it 'provincial federation'. It was too rigid, he said, and too difficult for the people as a whole to change when they felt the need. They should have 'a flexible Constitution', one that 'the sun might play freely about'. They should have a Constitution which would recognise the common interests of Australians and their ability to make up their own minds as members of one great community, free of provincial considerations. He was thinking first of railways and river traffic, but more elaborate questions occurred to him in due course. Higgins was not an orator (he stuttered) but a man of painstaking, orderly, prosaic detail. Sometimes, going on at length, he was heckled, as at the federal convention debates in 1897. 'Let him alone or he will never dry up', said a man of the majority.[61]

In his own court, Higgins ended formalities which made the law seem alien and inaccessible.[62] In the same spirit, in the Harvester Case he set out on his own, without any obvious precedent, to define 'a fair and reasonable wage'. Such a wage, he said, had to meet 'the normal needs of the average employee, regarded as a human being living in a civilized community' and in 'a condition of frugal comfort'. He was thinking of the great body of male unskilled labour, not just the employees in the Harvester Case. Each man of this class must have a basic or living wage.[63]

Victorian idealism of this sort was geared to male individuality, and Higgins was not concerned with the wages of women, including even those of lone mothers. But he was thinking of families, as the world now valued families. It must be presumed, he said, that every 'average employee' would have a family, and the Harvester Judgment established the idea of the family with fair and reasonable needs as one made up of a husband, as breadwinner, a wife and three dependent children. Most families ended up bigger than that, but according to Australian statisticians the number at any one time who were not yet old enough to leave school (under fourteen in most states) averaged between two and three. Parents, relying on the man's wage alone, should not be afraid of being impoverished by that number. 'The main impulse in the movement for better wages', said Higgins, 'comes from the wonderful family instinct, the desire of parents to build up sound, sane, and well-nourished children'. Three such children, still at school or younger, would make sense to fair, reasonable, well-informed, self-regulating men and women.[64]

However, in Higgins's imagination all this was infrastructure. More clearly than anyone else, perhaps, Higgins represents the deeply human and at the same time practical side of the federal impulse, the hope of doing good in detail, and of enlarging lives. What he really enjoyed was the thought of the man at home, released from worry so as to be part of the to and fro of family life, the man ready, in the words of Henry Ellis, to apply the 'excessive vital brain power' happily left over from the struggle for existence. '[G]ive them reasonable certainty', said Higgins, 'that their essential material needs will be met by honest work, and you release infinite stores of human energy for higher efforts, for nobler ideals'. You free them for their families, and for that time each day, he said (quoting the poet Robert Browning), when 'body gets its sop and holds its noise / And leaves soul free a little'.[65]

IV

Among Aboriginal people declining birthrates were a sign of the crumbling of family life. Throughout the various parts of the continent falling numbers dated more or less from the arrival of the Europeans, and the impact was much more sudden and dramatic, and much more clearly linked to demoralisation, compounding diarrhoea and respiratory diseases, than anything the Europeans found among themselves.[66] The Aboriginal people were now the subject of 'total calculation' too. Their case presented challenges which the statisticians were barely starting to comprehend, but in one way the issue was the same. How was 'total calculation' consistent with conscience? Indeed, what was conscience, now that moral priorities seemed to slip so awkwardly between the needs of the nation and the needs of family, of public and of private life?

The New South Welshman Robert Hamilton Mathews turned sixty in the year of Federation. Even as a child he had been interested in Aboriginal experience. Working in the bush as a government surveyor, he had watched and listened, but he had made no effort to sort out what he saw and heard until he was in his fifties. By then he was living within reach of meetings of the learned in Sydney, including the Royal Society of New South Wales. He started to think of himself as an anthropologist, and yet his methods always showed the delicate reverence of a child, plus the sense of etiquette taught him when he was little by Aboriginal men and women.

Mathews's ideas about the sacred in Aboriginal life lacked the chill of scientific objectivity. He was a private man who kept secrets. He badly wanted to be taken seriously as a scholar, here and overseas, but the intimacies and trust of Aboriginal people mattered more. He collected no stone blades, woven baskets or sacred items, because such things were tied to the ongoing lives of others.[67]

Mathews was interested in art, imagery, language and intellect, and in moral instinct. His story of the making of bark canoes has a typical ring: 'The tree from which the bark is taken is chosen according to the size one wants to give the canoe'. With the word 'one', the White reader identified with the Black canoe maker. He explored thoughts, putting himself in the place of the man or woman in the bush. 'The thick smooth trunks of the eucalyptus trees in Australia might easily have suggested to the minds of the natives the use of the bark for huts and canoes.' He called their rock paintings 'curious', 'remarkable', 'excellent'. Their byzantine marriage rules were 'wonderful'. The Aboriginal people were an underestimated race, and it was the European knowledge of them that was 'rudimental'. There was a long way to go, Mathews said. We had no chance of a true sense of the intricacies of Aboriginal thought 'until a very much larger amount of information has been brought together'.[68]

In 1900, the year before Federation, when a single nation looked like a kind of ultimate truth, Mathews drew a map showing 'Boundaries of the Several Nations of Australia'.[69] The more boundaries the better. His mind was always running along boundaries, brokering difference, pinpointing connections, exploring 'the real joints of nature' where the best energies of humanity seemed to be (possibilities already mentioned in chapter 3). He spent his life at edges, looking or listening over. Mathews focussed on landscape and place. He was probably the first European to sense, though vaguely, that Aboriginal marriage rules involved not just the categorisation of men and women but also a kinship with particular sites. Rose Scott, remembering her own bush childhood, said (I repeat this from chapter 7):

> A gum tree as it flourishes & grows owes much to the Earth, the atmosphere, and the thousand and one things that give it life – environment, heredity – but still from first to last it is a gum tree. Its individuality is its own – & so with a human being whose self or spirit may be nourished from outside factors, but is in itself indestructible.

This was something like the position from which Mathews tried to understand Aboriginal people, but perhaps he sensed that their priorities were the other way around. Their 'self or spirit' was embedded in particular sites, so that its individuality was not in fact its own. He wrestled especially with the individuality of sacred places, as he gathered evidence from the elderly.[70]

He picked up languages, Black and White, including the learned jargon which took him into new intellectual worlds. He was quick to adopt the protocols of debate used by the Royal Society of New South Wales just as he was interested in the paths with which Aboriginal people crossed similar borders. He noticed other scientists defeating their own ends by the way they talked, from White to Black. Questioned about totems, for instance, Aboriginals avoided a straight answer. Mathews could hear them dodging the White man's assumption that they thought they could change by magic, as he said, into 'rats, chicks, grubs &c'.[71]

Mathews also sensed the distinction between sounds and letters, which schoolteachers had to pursue, and he struggled to transform into writing the sounds which came from Aboriginal mouths. Even more slippery was the world of ideas those sounds encapsulated. These were obviously a people, or peoples, with an unfathomable collective individuality. The women too had a distinctive knowledge and sense of what was right, which for Mathews was even more mysterious, and even more baffling, than the womanly priorities which clergy now encountered among the settler population.[72] The sociological approach to Aboriginal people, built on a global union of knowledge, gave no glimpse of wonders of this sort.

In the 1870s Mary Cameron (afterwards Mary Gilmore) and Joseph Furphy had luxuriated in the variety of White habits of speech in Australia – '[t]hat mixture of Scotch, Irish, county-and-shire-English,' as Gilmore put it, 'with its interlarding of aboriginal words, its sprinkling of Californian Spanish and its Red Indian hunting and gold-digging terms'. Mathews heard similar patterning among the Blacks, having picked his way through thickets of meaning over many years. Sprinkling and interlarding impressed him as something essential to humanity.[73]

Unfortunately for his wider reputation, Mathews had no big idea of his own and not much engagement with big ideas at all. Building on the work of Charles Darwin was the great intellectual enterprise of the day, and for those who did it the Aboriginal people were an inexhaustible source of data, as a human type which had come to a halt early in the march towards modernity. Gathering evidence about the Aboriginal way of life was therefore almost as good as collecting by time machine. No-one was so keen in this task as Walter Baldwin Spencer, professor of biology at Melbourne University. Spencer had come from England in 1887 as a zoologist, and all his life he had a zoologist's taste for classifying, and for large spatial and chronological patterns. His great concern to start with had been the distribution of animal species, matched with climate and ecology, and he took the lead in the zoological mapping of Australia, defining three great ecoregions – Bassian, Torresian and Eyrean, classifications still in use today.[74]

Spencer had travelled as a zoologist with the great expedition from Adelaide to Central Australia in 1894, financed by William Austin Horn, mentioned in chapter 1. At Alice Springs he had met Frank Gillen, the local post and telegraph master, and sub-protector of Aboriginals, whose discerning knowledge of the local people fired his interest. Gillen gave Spencer the term 'dream times', and he showed him Chambers Pillar, a sandstone formation set 34 metres high south of Alice Springs which local legend said was the body of a great warrior. Spencer often glimpsed a deep, illusive life of the mind among Aboriginal people, and his insights, like Mathews's, linked people and place. But the intellectual conquest of the whole continent was always his chief ambition. From now on his main subject was not animal species but the Aboriginal people.[75]

Spencer wanted Aboriginal Australia to be a neat dominion within the empire of Darwinian science. Horn had thought of the Aboriginal people as 'the living representative of a stone age', and Spencer agreed. Blacks were caught within one continent. They had no discernible past because they had always been much the same, and they had no future because, he was sure, they were dying out. They were therefore isolated, in both space and time. In their pristine, 'uncontaminated' state, especially in Central Australia, they represented a rich and fragile deposit of scientific truth. In these circumstances the needs of intellect seemed to fully justify any invasion.

Spencer was guided by *The Golden Bough: A Study in Magic and Religion*, a book by James Frazer, a Cambridge ethnographer, which was published first in 1890, in an enlarged edition in 1900, and enlarged again (to twelve volumes), as Frazer's ideas became more elaborate, in 1906–15. Stage by stage, according to Frazer's grand theory, human beings had laboured through increasingly sophisticated forms of religious belief, until in the nineteenth century they had burst the surface so as to achieve a state of pure reason. He gathered his evidence worldwide, and while Spencer relied for his facts and artefacts on Gillen in Alice Springs, Frazer relied on Spencer, whose offerings he fitted more or less easily into his theory. Eventually, every Australian tribal group which kept its old ways would be examined and given its place in the whole. '[I]t is a grand piece of work we are asking you ... to do,' he told Spencer, 'probably the finest piece of anthropological work that could be done in the world'.[76]

Spencer's assignment called for a sweep of intellect matching the vastness of the continent, uniform and uncorrupted by any special attachment to place, and from his lofty position in the world of science he despised Mathews with a peculiar vehemence. Mathews simply reported what he found, from place to place. He was 'utterly unreliable', Spencer said, 'a perfect fraud', and Spencer's allies and followers all said the same. Mathews was 'a true parasite', according to Walter Roth, protector of Aboriginals in the northern half of Queensland, and perfectly marginal to the main intellectual endeavours of the day.[77]

Mathews offended especially by insisting that ideas about inheritance patterns did not all match the scheme Frazer and Spencer were developing. Frazer and Spencer themselves relied on a book by the American anthropologist Lewis Henry Morgan, *Ancient Society; or, Researches in the Lines of Human Progress from Savagery, through Barbarism to Civilization* (1877). The subtitle shows how

Morgan and Frazer agreed on the human march to modernity. Social organisation, said Morgan, evolved from the matriarchal to the patriarchal. Long-term improvement could be traced from the localised and family concerns of women, which were essentially primitive, to the more expansive, abstract, generalised and perfectible thoughts of men. Primitive societies vested power and property in the female. They privileged womanly priorities. Rational and sophisticated societies looked to the male.

The key to a society's position on the historical scale, and to its participation in modernity, in the great trajectory of human civilisation, was therefore to be found in its inheritance patterns. Were they matrilineal or patrilineal? Both arrangements were to be found among Aboriginal people, and it followed that skilled study across the continent should show how humanity made the great leap from one to the other. A crucial moment of social evolution would thus emerge, with a line drawn through the continent dividing old from new. But the scheme worked only if Mathews's evidence could be set aside.[78]

V

Meanwhile, alongside the demands of science, and sometimes in collaboration with it, churchmen struggled to assert the power of conscience on a continental scale. They aimed to make themselves its arbiters, and their effort with the Indigenous populations in the North was especially keen. The Anglicans now had the largest ideas. In 1898 missionary bishops were appointed to two new Anglican dioceses – New Guinea, with a cathedral planned at Dogura, on the north coast, and Carpentaria (including north Queensland and the Northern Territory), with a cathedral on Thursday Island, in Torres Strait – two of the most remote outposts it was possible to imagine. This effort was managed through the Australian Board of Missions.[79]

In 1901 Walter Baldwin Spencer met the new bishop of Carpentaria, Gilbert White, by chance near the Centre of Australia. They both had a strong interest in the Australian landscape, which Spencer indulged by buying some of the best new paintings (of the Heidelberg School in particular: see chapter 11), while the bishop wrote verse, about a Queensland storm, for instance:

> Like a skin of purple wine
> Filled to overflowing,
> Trembling hung the cloud awhile
> O'er the earth's dry glowing.
>
> Came a glare of yellow fire,
> All too swift for wonder,
> Reeled the earth beneath the shock
> Of that awful thunder.

In each case, a sense of place underwrote a sense of nation. Bishop White had inherited the curiosity of his forebear, another Gilbert White, 'the gentle curate of Selborne', England's first ecologist and phenologist. Pursuing geological, botanical and anthropological research on the track between Darwin and Adelaide, the current Gilbert White found much to talk about with Spencer, so that curiosity overlapped with conscience, and all within large horizons.[80]

In New Guinea, White's brother bishop was Montagu Stone-Wigg. In 1903 they took a step which followed naturally from the program outlined by the churches for Australian Federation, with the published suggestion that the federal government assume 'national' responsibility for Aboriginal welfare – national in the sense of a responsibility embedded in the great train of historical events which had created the continental nation. It was a responsibility for each Australian as an Australian, they said, not just for the good churchman but also for 'the hardened man of the world who cannot enter into the enthusiasm of the Gospel'.[81] In some ways this idea was not new. Concerned about a brutal past, in 1895 Archibald Meston had urged Queenslanders to look to 'the future honour of the nation' (meaning Queensland), and in 1902 Hugh Mahon, a West Australian Labour member of the federal parliament, had talked of 'the national honour' (Australia this time). Some of the states had 'failed in their duty', said Mahon. Some had 'deliberately sought the enslavement of the natives' (a reference to the Protection Acts). As in the United States since Abraham Lincoln, our 'good name' depended on the moral awareness of centralised power.[82] However, the bishops, finding God in all the glories of creation, talked about conscience rather than honour and good name.

In England itself 'national conscience' had long been a concern of members of the national (Anglican) church. Originally, this meant the conscience of king and/or government.[83] But by now conscience could be worked into the organised intelligence of the nation by enlightened public opinion – the so-called national or even the international mind. There could be a 'conscience of the world', stopping war, for instance, or limiting wartime savagery (as with the first Geneva Convention, 1864).[84] Australian Federation had been the result of organised intelligence. But could the Federation have a conscience?

To draw on the moral sense of a population mass still settling into shape was a big challenge. To do it from the northern and western edges of the continent, as White and Stone-Wigg wanted, rather than from some large centre of public opinion, was even harder. In Melbourne at the same time, the poet Bernard O'Dowd did argue that a 'national or communal conscience' was more important than democracy itself, but he was not clear what he meant by it, beyond 'the average opinion of what is right or wrong', or what it would be for.[85] The bishops were thinking about spiritual community, not an average. They could recall, in England, their church, as the church of government, leading public opinion, and sometimes doing particularly well at the edges – in island monasteries, for instance, long ago.

The bishops' proposal slept until January 1910. It was then revived by Charles Lefroy, general secretary of the Australian Board of Missions and former archdeacon of Perth. Before Federation, like the others, Lefroy had argued for 'a national Church of Australia'. He had suggested a union of all the English-origin churches (Anglicans, Methodists, Congregationalists and so on) to create an 'Anglo-Saxon Christianity' for the continent. The 'national character' thus created would, he said, be the basis of a 'national conscience'. With some such logic, Lefroy now urged the federal government to take responsibility for the rights of 'native peoples' across the continent, and also in New Guinea.[86]

The Lefroys were an imperial family. Some were senior public servants in Perth, and one had governed Bermuda and Tasmania. Another, a bishop in India, had worked for a national (Anglican) church there.[87] And yet the ideals of clergy families such as the Lefroys sprang from small places, from the hierarchies of the English countryside, and from the parochial workings of conscience manifest, for instance, in Jane Austen's stories a century before, and lately those of Anthony Trollope (*The Barchester Chronicles*). A Lefroy, later lord chief justice in Ireland, had courted Jane Austen while she was writing *Pride and Prejudice*. The same field-and-coppice moral refinement ran down through the Whites, from Selborne to Torres Strait.

Lefroy's campaign started with a Sydney meeting of the Australasian Association for the Advancement of Science, in January 1911. He gave a paper on the Aboriginals, who were a people, he said, of marked intelligence, at first held back by their natural environment and now demoralised and decimated by Europeans. 'Relatively', he said, 'they were gentle and moral beings. Their tribal and family laws were of considerable ethical value'. The only solution to their degradation lay in 'making the whole of the remnant a national responsibility under national control'. A Welfare of Aborigines Committee was formed straightaway by the AAAS, 'to save this most interesting race, in the interests both of humanity and of science'.[88]

The prime minister himself, Andrew Fisher, apparently agreed. 'Anything that this Government can do to protect the natives within Australia will be done.' A public meeting was called in Sydney and a plan of action drawn up, including hopes for a federal inquiry to define 'the native obligations of the Commonwealth', and for a new government department, 'with oversight of Aborigines, Papuans and other native races'. This scheme was presented to Fisher by Lefroy, accompanied by Bishop Stone-Wigg and several scientists.[89]

They also asked the prime minister to take action in the Northern Territory, which was about to be transferred from South Australian to federal jurisdiction. As it turned out, this was all that Fisher would take on. Spencer was sent with a team to the territory to report on its economic potential, and he was then appointed chief protector and special commissioner. As chief protector, Spencer's main achievement was a set of elaborate recommendations on the government of the Aborigines of the territory prepared in consultation with White and endorsed by Lefroy's association. Here at last was a chance for the national conscience. Unluckily, before anything could be done the War turned all eyes elsewhere.[90]

Rose Scott had made one mistake. It is true that the new federal system, unlike the old colonial ones, was out of the reach of women like herself – out of the reach of those settled networks which were the stock-in-trade of ordinary dealers in social justice. But it was not heartless. Protection on the Victorian model (of human beings as well as industry) was recycled at the higher level. Also, with women voting federally, from 1902, the new national government had to think about the needs of households. To Higgins's basic wage of 1907 was added the *Invalid and Old-Age Pensions Act 1908*. Among other things, that helped families to look after members too old to work, with a pension at about a quarter of the basic wage.[91] The *Maternity Allowance Act 1912* likewise gave mothers £5 at the birth of each child, roughly equal to five weeks' wages for a working woman.

In this way, ideas about Australian citizenship and about sharing in commonwealth were explored, expanded and methodically applied. Family and household were in principle tied to the new authority even more tightly than to the old, at the same time shaping its actions. But none of these affirming and reinforcing advantages were extended to Aboriginal families. Both acts deliberately excluded 'Aboriginal natives of Australia', as well as Indigenous people from Papua and the Pacific. While intellect was drawing them together as a single sociological and scientific challenge, from a moral point of view they were still the responsibility of the states.

Until Aboriginals themselves started to create national organisations, in the 1920s and '30s, there could be no national conscience in this respect.[92] They were a people bound to exist, as it were, within a pre-federated Australia, the Australia of half-a-dozen nations, where an earlier sense of right and wrong, the work of public servants, churchmen and leading figures such as Rose Scott, lived on especially in the old capital cities.

11

The Voice of the Country

I

My father's father was born in 1864 and he died in 1946. Arthur Atkinson's mind mirrored several Federation ideals. His first home was Melbourne. His father, who worked in the postmaster-general's department, was eulogised at his death as a former printer who had invented the combined chase and frisket for printing postage stamps. John Atkinson was also a man of Quaker background and secularist associations, with strong opinions about slavery and the rights of working men.

Arthur's mother kept a series of ladies' schools. Eliza Atkinson might have done more in her line of work if she had not been caught at the start of her biggest venture by Arthur's arrival, and she applied her skills all the more thoroughly to him. All his life he took pleasure, as a well-taught lady might do, in reading French, playing the piano and listening to women singing. He was a great admirer of Nellie Melba. He was also egocentric, sometimes overbearing and too much mothered.

At eighteen Arthur joined the public service, as a junior clerk in the lunatic asylum at Yarra Bend. Yarra Bend was full of object lessons in humanity, or the lack of it, in a public institution, matters which always interested him. For instance, he might have been the young man who attended to David McKinlay, a labouring man from Warrnambool, who visited the asylum at Christmas 1884.

McKinlay asked to see his 21-year-old daughter, Elizabeth. Directed to a chair, he waited, as he later recalled, gazing out at a verandah, where there was an open doorway. Then,

> at that door [said the unfortunate father] there appeared a most miserable terror-stricken object, its two hands stretched out before it, and so terrified that it did not appear to know which way to go to get away from a voice which I heard behind it calling, 'Come back'. At this time I recognised this miserable creature as my daughter. The owner of the voice, a strong young woman, appeared and grabbed my daughter by the back, pushed her violently into the door, where she was joined by an older woman, who at once began to scold and call her names; they went out of my sight; I heard a slap, but did not see it given.[1]

Those noises, partly out of sight, ending with the unseen slap, had the sound of moral chaos. For Arthur, with a Quakerish attitude to violence and super-solicitous about the treatment of women, Yarra Bend must have been a shock. The asylum was a showpiece of old ways of government, government disorganised in its primary task, as Arthur thought, which was the care of vulnerable creatures such as Elizabeth McKinlay. He was one of the coming generation, whose ideas about justice under government had moved forward a step. For men such as Arthur, Federation was a great good.

His parents separated, and, living with his mother (who had been a clerk of sorts in her father's business), Arthur picked up the principles of domestic economy, the ecology of the household. They gave method to his whole life. Yarra Bend might be a kind of anti-household from an ethical point of view, but at Yarra Bend he perfected his skills with double-entry bookkeeping, which meant balancing debit and credit, and registering the passage of resources in and out. Passage in and out defines an economy – a moral economy as well as a commercial one. In a proper system of book-keeping there were several concurrent books of accounts. The day book was the main volume of record, including all transactions in both directions. It carried detail over from the cash book, which was a record of all money paid and received, and it sent that detail on via the journal to the ledger, which showed all accounts of debtors and creditors.[2] From the ledger came letters of either payment or demand.

It was all about money and goods, incoming and outgoing. At Yarra Bend this traffic mirrored the entry and exit (sometimes escape) of inmates. Government funding sprang from the needs, proved or imagined, of men and women such as Elizabeth McKinlay.

Arthur mastered such matters as a variation of women's work at home. Eliza's methods as wife and mother, carefully watched, were easily applied to this new complexity. Fresh fruit, such as good hard apples, stood for sound housekeeping, and as a young man Arthur admired the hawking greengrocers who carried their goods straight from market gardens to the shopper. In the Melbourne markets few things pleased him more, he said, than the long lines of 'attractively-laden fruit trucks' attended by 'cleanly and civil men'. These included Chinese, who were typically gardeners themselves. '[B]ut for their industry,' said my grandfather, 'vegetables – life fruit – would be an unprocurable luxury for the working class'. The system in Melbourne let these hawkers thrive. And yet in free enterprise Sydney, as he found later on, the Chinese were harassed by 'the authorities', so that retailing greengrocers, who charged more, controlled the market. So 'an alien class of shopkeepers [he meant Italians], infinitely of less value to the community', were favoured above 'the persecuted and industrious Chinaman', while 'the children of men drawing moderate salaries can never know the taste of fruit unless it be rubbish fit for pig's feed'. Everything, he thought, should turn on civility, on 'the care and welfare of the public', and on good housekeeping at every level.[3]

National housekeeping must be driven by this spirit. 'National' might mean Victoria and New South Wales to start with, but by the end of the century it was starting to mean the continent which was to house a Commonwealth. The idea of housekeeping on such a scale was deeply exciting. At twenty-four, having perfected his elementary skills at Yarra Bend, Arthur was moved to the finance branch of the Chief Secretary's Office, at twice the salary. Three years later he was promoted to Trade and Customs, and to a desk in its weighty, white, colonnaded building in Flinders Street. This was early in the 1890s depression, when a public servant was lucky to keep his job, let alone see his pay increased. In control of his life as never before, at the same time Arthur was given permission to teach (or to continue teaching) shorthand on the side.

Customs was central to the task of preparing for the Federation of Australia, and the department's acquisition of Arthur seems to have been a direct result of the appointment of the dynamic Harry Wollaston as its head, or secretary of Trade and Customs. Wollaston was like Timothy Coghlan in New South Wales, a public servant of a new breed, dynamic, clever, fully capable of driving a nation-building agenda within his own domain, and happy to extend that domain wherever he could. He might have sensed a little of the same energy in Arthur, who knew all about rules but would not be bound by them. A man with a monocle, Wollaston had spent several years in charge of the department's Correspondence branch, and by 1891 he had overhauled office procedure, acquired a doctor of laws degree from Melbourne University and published a compendium of customs law. In the same year he was also asked by the West Australian government to report on Customs there so that it might be reshaped on the Victorian model. On his own Wollaston was the customs equivalent of the meteorologists and inspectors of stock mentioned in chapters 1 and 2, and of the various government statisticians as well, all of whom drew together the infrastructure of Federation before Federation happened. As Wollaston's acolyte,

Arthur worked as his chief had done in Correspondence, at the administrative heart of the office.

In 1901 Customs became a federal responsibility. Its headquarters was the office in Melbourne, but Arthur was sent to what was now the branch office in Sydney, in charge of Correspondence. There was some initial confusion, and Wollaston also travelled to Sydney, in order to sort things out and to reassure local businessmen of their continuing importance in the great scheme of things. He could not help telling them that in Melbourne the introduction of the continental tariff had been very smooth. 'You see, down there they understand all its characteristics.'[4]

In Victoria, thanks to the interventionist spirit of protection, Customs had long been a separate department, and Harry Wollaston had a high profile, whereas in the other colonies it was just part of Treasury. In Victoria, Customs officers were given a great variety of work which was done elsewhere by others (mainly police), regulating the standard of liquor sold in pubs, controlling the use of explosives, looking after lighthouses, gathering trade statistics and so on. In Victoria, as Wollaston said, Customs was

> the 'handy man' of the Government ... If the police wanted to search some suspected premises without a warrant, the Customs would be invited to make use of its powers to enable them to do so. If an officer were wanted for any special services, the Customs would be applied to.

Before 1901, Wollaston had been the right hand of a focussed, proactive state. He was less obvious at the federal level, where he had a minister just as energetic as himself (CC Kingston). But still, as in Melbourne, this was a separate portfolio, one of the two most important federal portfolios for the time being, the other being that of the postmaster-general.[5] Without Customs, and the income therefrom, the new government would have been too impoverished to work at all.

His, said Wollaston, was 'a live department', and its flexibility gave it an edge in changing times. Government could be confident that Customs 'would not hesitate', as he put it, 'to push the law to its utmost extent in the public interest'.[6] From 1901, when he became comptroller-general, the great vacancy of the continent and the still-untested capacity of the new Constitution gave men like Wollaston room to move. Australia's variety of resources, and therefore the complexity of its trading networks, was vast. In a tour of Queensland, for instance, he received a deputation which quizzed him, among many other things, on the excise on jelly crystals, whether determined on raw weight or on the likely subsequent quantity of jelly. On a later visit he looked into the packing of bananas for the South, the need for more lighthouses and the main direction taken by seaborne rats.[7]

Before 1901, Victorian Customs had also looked after birds, animals and fish as public assets. In these matters too Wollaston's eye had been everywhere. Since the 1870s most colonies had had Game Protection Acts, mainly to conserve kangaroos for hunting.[8] There were also laws to protect birdlife because birds ate insects, including those dangerous to orchards and crops. There was a famous case of a Mitcham strawberry grower who complained to the secretary in Melbourne that magpies ate more grain than insects did. To uphold the system Wollaston gave permission for two magpies to be shot and cut open (otherwise against the law). Happily, they contained 'grubs, beetles, and other insect pests', and no grain at all. He then asked the Field Naturalists Club to go to Mitcham to find more evidence against the doubters.[9]

To start with creatures such as magpies were valued because they were useful. They were to be looked after just as water was to be looked after, and water management had been one of the main points of late-nineteenth-century ingenuity in Australia. However, the focus of conservation laws was starting to shift to humanitarianism and long-term preservation. The Animals' Protection

Society of New South Wales, an early exemplar, had secured an Animals Protection Act by 1879, and its inspectors moved around Sydney and the countryside looking for cases of cruelty, with an eye especially to horses (starved, overloaded, or worked when wounded or lamed). By the end of the 1890s they had secured about 4000 prosecutions.[10] Conservation of this sort looked to the interests of animals themselves. From capital to capital, within each state regime, this movement was gathering pace. On a transcontinental scale it was still barely imaginable, but Arthur Atkinson's story shows that even that was not altogether out of the question.

Harry Wollaston worked, it was said, 'without fuss, yet with much energy'.[11] Bright and pleasant, he thrived on variety, and there was a type of mighty destiny in the work he did. His fellow Melburnian John Monash, as a young man, had found what a joy it was to be surrounded with a massed diversity of work, and to feel the sweet sense of control involved, as he put it, in 'rapidly passing from one thing to another, with little loss of time or delay in getting a fresh focus'.[12] The 'genial Secretary for Customs' flourished similarly, and in his successive departments, before and after Federation, the same skill of rapid transition and decision-making was concentrated especially in the Correspondence branch. As Wollaston explained, under his system each day started with the morning mail, 'and its dissection for treatment by various officers, according to the importance of the items'. Some were trivial, but

> a large proportion are of such importance that they require a great deal of thought … A letter cannot be judged by its bulk or its apparent insignificance; for the most trivial-looking communication – on the surface – may involve some vital principle, and a careless decision may establish a precedent which may lead to further complications.

This was the work my grandfather managed in Sydney from 1901. In Melbourne, at head office, there were several hundred letters a day, and in Sydney there cannot have been many fewer. In all the capitals of the Commonwealth these letters composed themselves as a minutely shifting mimicry of Federation in action. And new technology added more, not just 'the telegrams that drop in continuously', as Wollaston said, but also 'the telephone that buzzes all day long'.[13]

Better methods and tighter classification were the only useful responses to 'the crisis of abundance' which was the main challenge of the day. During not much more than a generation before the outbreak of the Great War, namely 1870–1914, the population of Europe itself grew by nearly 70 per cent. In the same period the total living in what the new Constitution defined as 'Australia', Wollaston's domain, more than tripled, from about 1.6 million to about 4.9 million. At the same time the continent's gross domestic product, as it was later called, roughly doubled. The main population expansion had been in the late 1870s and early 1880s, partly because of the size of families but also reflecting, at a generation's remove, the great inrush of the 1850s. Married women, many born themselves in the years of gold, had on average six or seven children each, which explains the concern about the decline of the birthrate later on, because that brief abundance was taken as the norm. But immigration from Britain boomed too, until the beginning of the 1890s depression and afterwards, because relatively speaking life in the Australian colonies was enormously attractive. On average the settler population earnt and spent more per head than the population of any other country in the world.[14]

Australian Customs therefore belonged to a worldwide network of vastly increasing wealth. Within this scene of jostling abundance, the department was concerned with keeping some things from entering the continent, through immigration restriction, tariffs and quarantine, and with introducing others, in a properly regulated and documented fashion. During 1870–1914 the quantity of pig iron and of coal produced by Europe's three great industrial powers, Britain, France and Germany, increased about three times over. Steel, relatively light but remarkably strong, and mass-produced for the first time thanks to the ingenuity of the Englishman Henry Bessemer, was one of the defining products of the age. It had a profound impact on Australia and was a principal import.

> Without steel [the *Clarence and Richmond Examiner* told its readers in far north-eastern New South Wales] there would be no fast trains nor cheap means of freight ... there would be no 14,000 ton ships covering the distance between the mother country and her possessions in a month ... there would be no steel cruisers, and therefore no British Navy of the present proportions, and of course there would be no great span bridges and no sky-scrapers of the American pattern of 'all steel'.[15]

In the end the most conspicuous thing about steel was its quantity. The sheer bulk now available was capable of containing, protecting, transporting and, as weaponry, destroying vast numbers of humanity. And also employing them. In Australia, though steel was largely imported, in 1907 an ambitious new blast furnace was built at Lithgow, west of Sydney, and another at Newcastle, in 1915. Before too long, said Thomas Waddell, New South Wales treasurer, the Lithgow works might provide jobs for everyone who wanted them. So, he said, we would 'prevent money to the extent of hundreds of thousands of pounds going elsewhere annually, to working men in other parts of the world'.[16]

In and out of government, this was the world of the 'business man'. 'Business man', only now being shortened to 'businessman', was an American term and it encapsulated certain vital modern virtues. It was a label for the mass of men who coordinated the national economies created by the Industrial Revolution, sorting and distributing capital, opportunity, information and goods for sale, including steel. In an age of introspection, the business man, or man of business, could sense the power of his own intelligence. As the *Queanbeyan Age* put it, he was 'possessed of method, [and] can arrange what he has collected'.[17] The young Monash, an engineer, working largely with steel and concrete, had felt the thrill of making decisions quickly and at the edge of futurity. Some said, in these remarkable days, that that thrill was the feel of humanity at its finest. With this ultimate engine, we find modernity. We ride time, and the harder we ride, said the great French philosopher Henri Bergson, 'the more we feel the different parts of our being enter into each other, and our whole personality concentrate itself in a point, or rather a sharp edge, pressed against the future and cutting into it unceasingly'.[18]

Thus the 'divine rights of manhood', in the words of James Jefferis, were fully exercised. Intense sport had the same effect, and sport was now organised with unprecedented enthusiasm. So it was with efficient business, including office work under a regime like Wollaston's. The discipline was tight and the pace could be nerve-racking, but it was in such work under pressure, as Bergson said, that 'life and action are free'.[19]

The noise of the telephone, constantly buzzing, breaking into conventional labour, into conversation, into every simple routine, summed it all up. Thanks to telephones, said the Canadian writer Herbert Casson, 'life has become more tense, alert, vivid'. The frequent ringing raised the quick-shifting focus of men such as Monash to another gear. Breaking willy-nilly into whatever was going on, it also cut through the more stately pace of letter writing.

> The brain [Casson explained in his *History of the Telephone*] has been relieved of the suspense of waiting for an answer, which is a psychological gain of great importance. It receives its reply at once and is set free to consider other matters.

> There is less burden upon the memory and the *whole mind* can be given to each new proposition.

The result was what Casson called '[a] new instinct of speed', a greed for the ensuing moment. Automobiles had the same effect, and yet some understood that telephones and cars were both in fact symptomatic of something much bigger. The historian Oswald Spengler wrote of the 'unsurpassably intense Will to the Future', which he saw all around him.[20] Telephones and cars, in short, were the tools of a new kind of humanity.

The office shorthand in which Arthur was adept was suddenly everywhere, and the papers carried stories of top speeds (up to 200 or 300 words a minute) as they did sporting records. Business colleges specialising in typing and shorthand were started in Australia and New Zealand by Sydney Stott, a native of Ballarat, who also brought in Australia's first typewriters (Remingtons) for his students. In Sydney, a few years afterwards, the pioneer was Dora Armitage, with her Ladies' Typewriting Association. Typewriters were exciting objects. John Monash, at twenty-four years old, was 'fascinated', as he put it, with the prospect of having his own, as an 'aid to my vis via' (his way through life).[21] The women who learnt to type at the new colleges were soon to be found throughout the business world. In 1903 a seventeen year old, 'smart, self-reliant, full of zest and "go"', was interviewed for the Melbourne *Argus* about her life as a clerk. Her course in bookkeeping, typing and shorthand, she said, had cost her mother £26, an excellent investment given that her commencing salary was £1 a week, soon to go up to £2. She worked with three others.

> Each girl has a thick mat under her feet, and there's an asbestos stove to be lighted if required. Each of us has a table, at which we sit comfortably with our shorthand notes, carbons, &c., arranged round the typewriter ... I just love my

> little machine [she said], and would rather be a typist than a princess.

Certainly it was noisy and rushed. 'There are a dozen girls scattered through our chambers, and we all type "at speed," so naturally there's a clatter.'

Such women found themselves dealing differently with men. This seventeen year old said that the experience of officework made flirting easier after hours. '[B]usiness girls', the female equivalent of business men, she reported, 'are not too shy and scared to chat, laugh, and be themselves when they meet men at little gaieties'. After a while, however, they were hardened. 'I come in contact,' said an older clerk, 'sometimes into collision, with all sorts of men … Were I a man, I might permit myself to boil over occasionally … As it is, my experience doesn't make me any fonder of brother Man'. She regretted that.[22]

Arthur Atkinson, if not a business man, was an inhabitant of offices and of the business world. He was a man of precise emphasis, in voice and manner, and assertive eccentricity, and a man torn, as his world was torn, between the pleasures of living at the edge of a momentous future, working like this, and the need to escape backwards, to the bush, the mountains and the sea, between the noise of the telephone and the noises of old Australia. 'Banjo' Paterson's verse 'Clancy of the Overflow' (1889) catches the contrast, but with clear preference for the bush ('the murmur of the breezes and the river on its bars'). With extraordinary application Arthur crammed both experiences into each day. In his last Melbourne years he made his home two hours away from work in a boarding house at Yarra Glen ('A Lovely Home among the Mountains', 'Unequalled situation, magnificent views'). In Sydney, still unmarried, he lived first at Manly, across the harbour, and then further north, in a beach cottage so remote that sometimes the morning was half-gone when he reached the Customs House at Circular Quay. Later still it was the Blue Mountains, and again two hours each way by train.[23]

Trains made such things just possible. For Arthur trains were the epitome of public service. They were vehicles in which a representative miscellany of citizens, crammed at close quarters, went about every possible purpose. Ignoring rules which banned public agitation by public servants, from Yarra Glen he got up a monster petition to the Victorian minister for railways about an 'entirely inadequate' rail service. From Leura in the Blue Mountains he complained to the Sydney press that the morning trains were too few and so full that passengers had to stand, sometimes at risk of falling out. Uncivil staff were a fair symptom of what he called a 'simply disgraceful' service.[24]

The humanising impulse of Federation came in various forms. Alfred Deakin dreamt of 'a temple to Thee & to Thy glory'. Julia and Frederick Holder hoped that the new Australia would be a rainbow of individuality, feeding the self-sufficiency of women, of men, and of every community, large and small. Churchmen worked for 'a Christian Commonwealth', and for some of them that meant a network of 'mutual helpfulness', for others a citadel of social justice on Christian principles, and for others again strict Sundays and no public houses. Henry Bournes Higgins used his arbitration court to make the federal regime a guarantor of civilised family life.

My grandfather wanted an end to 'official autocracy and tyranny'.[25] A public servant himself, he wanted power combined with civility, including polite words from ticket collectors. He wanted well-ordered, forward-thinking human sympathy, as exemplified by Harry Wollaston. It happened in Melbourne. Why not Sydney? He wanted the genuine spirit of 'protection' to infiltrate government everywhere, spreading from its Victorian heartland so as to settle from shore to shore.

II

In rapidly changing times, as in fast-moving vehicles, when we seem to be hurtling into the unknown, there is a tendency to hang on hard. In the age of Federation there was a hunger not just for places of quietness, such as Yarra Glen, but also for accumulating and preserving fragments of the past and of apparently timeless things. This was an age of autobiography. Men and women everywhere stored up snatches of recollection, in the form of reminiscences, autographs, stamps, postcards and photographs. The advertising of albums and scrapbooks doubled in Australian newspapers between the 1870s and the 1880s, and while it fell off thereafter the habit of collection and recollection was entrenched. 'JUST ARRIVED. – Comic ALBUMS and Dance ALBUMS for 1900. Howard's, Dean's, Feldman's, Francis and Day's.' 'ALBUMS, ALBUMS – A magnificent supply of albums, many patterns and prices.' Everything was collectable – the pictures, for instance, to be found in Capstan cigarette boxes (suitable albums might be bought at tobacconists) and even picture scraps, which the shops sold in packets.[26]

For Adelaide, or Addy, Suttor, in late middle age (she was born in 1837), images and voices of girlhood near Bathurst and Orange recurred as miscellaneous scraps to be gathered and written out as they rose to memory's surface – a new home in the bush, for instance, during her adolescence. 'I can picture so plainly the small bark hut and slab walls and rugs hung at the openings instead of doors and windows.' Her father, convalescing from a bullet wound in the leg and lying on an air bed to ease the pain – that image (or echo) too, was gathered in the wildflower field of imagination Mrs Suttor carefully preserved. Addy, the child, kept the bed blown up. 'I was some distance from the house and I heard Mother calling me in great distress. Of course I ran as fast as possible and found the air had escaped from one portion of the bed.' Her father was in agony. 'I have often laughed since at my efforts to blow up that bed before I had recovered breath from my long run. Mother stood on one side holding up Father's leg to make it lighter for me and poor Father's distressful saying – blow my child, blow.'[27]

Rosa Praed, remembering her girlhood in Queensland, set out on paper a stream of 'shifting glimpses' and voices from the past, each 'dimly photographed on the memory page' – the page of an imagined album. Once, after a dose of opium, she was overcome with 'the most curious sense of dual personality'. There was a child (herself) perched on sliprails, red braid on her overalls, blue lilies floating on a nearby lagoon, and voices from within and without. '"Yes, it is all just like that," the inert, mature self, watching the child, seemed to be saying, while the child-self swung herself from the sliprails ... and jabbered to the piccaninny who came up from the lagoon.'[28]

For Alfred Deakin, such experiences suggested a vast power within. From God, he said, came 'the divine stream feeding every soul'. Releasing that stream was like opening a floodgate. As Ralph Waldo Emerson, the American essayist, said – and everyone of mystical temperament read Emerson – when a man unlocks his 'human doors' and allows 'the ethereal tides to roll and circulate through him; then he is caught up into the life of the Universe, his speech is thunder, his thought is law'.[29] Who would not want to collect and recall such deeply reassuring experience? By such unlocking, trivialities became sublime.

The process shared by Adelaide Suttor and Rosa Praed was to reach its apotheosis in Europe with two extraordinary novels, both searching ever inward and both started just before the War: James Joyce's *Ulysses* (first published 1918–20) and Marcel Proust's *À la recherche du temps perdu* (Remembrance of Things Past, first published in the French 1913–27). Proust has been called 'the Shakespeare of the inner world'.[30]

Civilised freedom, this freedom of modern men and women, involved a connection with eternal things. When he played his piano in his house by the sea (a wall had to be broken up to get it in) my grandfather was unlocking 'human doors'. He was also an energetic walker, for the same sort of reason. In Britain and Australia long-distance walking had for many years been a respectable pastime. Samuel Johnson and James Boswell had walked in the Hebrides, collecting experiences, and William Wordsworth had walked in the English Lake District. Arthur's uncle, a leather worker, had walked from Melbourne to Kyneton and back, 85 kilometres each way, in the 1850s, finding the scenery magnificent beyond description. But not until the 1870s did organised walking and cycling become delights for large numbers, who typically took with them Kodak cameras, to capture and hold salient sensations. In 1899, for instance, on a bicycle trip across the Darling Range east of Perth, a party of men and women, having reached a likely summit, 'lamented the absence of a kodak, for an excellent snapshot might have been taken and entitled "The Holiday Makers"' – though it was all so strenuous, they said, that 'The Workers' might have been better.[31] Like organised mass sport, touring pushed individuals to their physical limit, an effort worth recording.

Outdoor photography, possible now because of the invention of dry plate processing, was used to promote tourism. John Beattie, a member of Andrew Inglis Clark's Minerva Club, led the effort in Tasmania, as government photographer. 'I love the bush,' he said, 'and nothing gives me greater delight than to stand on the top of some high land and look out on a wild array of our grand mountains. I am struck dumb, but oh! my soul sings'.[32] His pictures drew others to the same spots.

In Victoria, Mt Buffalo, nearly 350 kilometres north-east of Melbourne, was a prime spot for walking, climbing, and wondering at and recording views. An Alpine Club was formed on the model of the fashionable Alpine clubs in Europe, with the idea of making it into 'the Switzerland of Australia'. John Monash climbed Mt Buffalo with a friend in summer 1890–91 and found it 'almost frightening in its immensity', and from 1910 the mountain had a two-storey government chalet, which according to one visitor catered for 'visitors from all stations in life'. 'If you are willing, every day brings its picnic, and no one dare tell his friends of the city his tally of mountain miles under pain of inclusion with the fisherman.'[33]

It was common now, when imagining Australia, to imagine and memorise the sublime, even the sacred. You could be sure you heard the country speak. The effort to uncover the 'ideographic prophecy', as Joseph Furphy called it, the deep message living within its landscape, was attempted, or at least pretended, by 'all stations in life', and often, and the effort to record and broadcast such discoveries also multiplied. RH Mathews had been among the first Europeans to grasp the importance of place for Aboriginal people, and to glimpse the patterning of the landscape vital to their sense of self. But some of the novelists mentioned in chapter 1 invented ancient sacred places, just as they invented a system of rivers beneath the country's dry surface. There was Rosa Praed's Maianbar, or 'the Deep Tank', for instance, in *Fugitive Anne* (1902). The poet Bernard O'Dowd, in his esoteric way, had tried to do the same with Chambers Pillar, in the Centre. It should be, he said, 'the Olympus of the Australian dispensation'.[34]

The message was clearest in children's books – books, in other words, where whimsy and insight could be tried with straightforward freshness and imprinted for life on young minds. Some such stories were lessons about looking and listening to the bush, as a 'deep tank' of sensation resounding with voices. 'At first', wrote Ethel Pedley, in her story of *Dot and the Kangaroo*, which began with a child opening her ears,

> it seemed like hearing sounds in a dream, they were so faint and distant, but soon the talking grew nearer and nearer, louder and clearer, until the whole bush seemed filled with talking ... They [the voices] came from the earth, from the bushes, from the trees, and from the very air.

Miss Pedley was a trained violinist and soprano. With a friend she founded and conducted the St Cecilia Choir, a chorus of forty to seventy women in some demand in Sydney, and itself a remarkable novelty when it started, in the 1880s. So she was attuned to sound. *Dot and the Kangaroo* is set in a place called Gabblebabble and within the massed hubbub of the bush. Music runs through it. 'Only music can quiet my nerves', said the platypus. 'I will sing a little threnody composed by myself.' '[W]ithout music it would be very dull', said the satin bird.[35]

This new articulation, detailed and published in multiple forms, was largely women's work, and that says something. '[T]hat long silence of one-half the world' which the American Elizabeth Robins noticed in 1907 was starting to break up.[36] Writing about France many years before, Jules Michelet had described his country as a woman to be adored and defended. In Australia, by the time of Federation, women writers were also starting to give a female individuality to Australia, but much less passive than Michelet's France. It was 'her beauty and her terror' that appealed to the multilingual Sydney-born Dorothea Mackellar, in exile in London. Miss Mackellar thought of Australia as a woman free in all respects:

> An opal-hearted country,
> A wilful, lavish land –
> All you who have not loved her,
> You will not understand[.]

Ethel Pedley translated this for children. The kangaroo which rescued Dot is turn-of-the-century womanhood, assertive but serene within small horizons. She has a 'gentle, soft voice' but also an individuality which would have made sense to Rose Scott.[37]

Dot and the Kangaroo sold all over the continent. In Sydney, Grace Stafford, a music and drama director, rewrote it as a children's play, woven through as Ethel Pedley would have wanted with dance and song.[38] Mystery, beauty and terror in childlike portions, including fear of being lost for good in the bush, gave the story its power. Its principal message, relayed by the kangaroo, was that human violence consisted of nothing but terror.

> Humans have become so cruel [the kangaroo told Dot] that they kill, and kill, not even for food, but for the love of murder ... The black Humans kill and devour us; but they, even, are not so terrible as the Whites, who delight in taking our lives, and torturing us just as amusement. Every creature in the bush weeps that they should come to take our beautiful bush away from us.[39]

Arthur Atkinson had something like this visceral dislike of violence.

Such men and women built a world of feeling in which they imagined animal thought and sensation. My grandfather's friend the naturalist David Stead, father of the future novelist Christina Stead, wrote to him, for instance, about a galah he had seen in Singapore tied to its wire perch with a 2-inch (5-centimetre) chain. 'Think of that', Stead told Arthur. 'Day in and day out this bird is chained to that thin piece of metal, and never has the satisfaction of grasping, even for a moment, a piece of wood that might remind it of its days of freedom.'[40]

With a little more effort, thanks to such sensibility, a connection could be made with Aboriginal thinking about birds and animals. Katie Langloh Parker, a grazier's wife on the Narran River near Walgett, New South Wales, learnt local languages and collected stories, and she published two volumes of 'legendary tales', loosely adapted for children. Again, there are voices. Dinewan the mother emu, when she was offended by the wild turkey, Goomblegubbon, 'would flap her wings and begin booing in her pride, not the loud booing of the male bird, but a little, triumphant, satisfied booing noise of her own'. Goomblegubbon, in reaction, Medea-like, killed her own children. Given that the stories were meant for reading aloud, Dinewan's booing, the song of Gooloo the magpie (whose voice was like children sobbing, said Mrs Parker), and the mimicry of Weedah the lyrebird became part of the soundscape of numerous families.[41]

III

Such noise had large echoes. In August 1902 there began in Melbourne the *New Idea*, a monthly for Australian mothers and children, soon selling from Christchurch to Perth. With narrow aims to start with, the *New Idea* was almost immediately covering everything from recipes to child rearing, from work in factories, hospitals and telephone exchanges to swimming, including a piece on 'How to Dive', by Annette Kellerman, 'the Champion Lady-Swimmer of Australasia'. It linked the individuality of women with what was understood to be the womanly individuality of Australia itself.[42]

The other world which was now discoverable in the Australian bush, the concert of voices, proved nature's dynamic interconnectedness, reflecting above ground the unplumbed voiceless network of artesian and subartesian streams. This was ecology. It was a step beyond the mere classification of species. A sense that Australian wildlife was a mingling of non-human households, economies of need and feeling within an almost limitless network, went back to the writing of Louisa Anne Meredith, including, as a late example, *Tasmanian Friends and Foes, Feathered, Furred and Finned* (1880). Now it gathered pace. Every fragment of evidence helped – Harry Wollaston's inquiry into the feeding habits of the magpie, David Stead's published remark that net fishing in rivers was destroying platypuses ('The nets were baited, and attracted prawns, and the prawns attracted the platypus') and so on.[43] The perverse challenges offered by this 'wilful, lavish land' – the fire, the floods, the disastrous drought of 1895–1903 (which destroyed half the continent's sheep) – added to a sense of nature's independent power. A disastrously expensive rabbit plague in the eastern colonies gave the message a peculiar twist, since rabbits were imported. Spreading westward at a speed hitherto unmatched among mammals, the rabbits were met with the world's longest fence, built in 1901–07 north–south across Western Australia. It failed to keep them out.

The idea of so many secrets still to be uncovered gave the whole movement an innovative, intellectual edge. Throughout much of the twentieth century curiosity and research in Australia were to focus especially on the life sciences, on organisms and their environments, on biology, agriculture and connections between climate and public health. By comparison, astronomy, which had been a leading area in the colonies through much of the nineteenth century – and in which Henry Chamberlain Russell, for example, had made great strides – fell a little into the background, especially as it drew apart from meteorology.[44] So did geology, the science of the goldrushes. Even eugenics could be considered a cutting-edge science of life.

In 1903 Annie Rentoul, aged nineteen, sent to the *New Idea* four stories for children. The line drawings by her younger sister, Ida, in these and in later efforts (some in watercolour), made the Rentoul sisters famous. The 'delicate feats of color and imagination', said Sydney's *Sunday Times* in 1916, 'hover up towards the ecstasies'. But Annie's stories were the initial trigger for both careers. Her first sentence in the *New Idea* was 'If the Kookaburra hadn't said "Stop!" Dorothy would never have gone down the ravine', a ravine which stood for the ecology of the bush. There was an enticing danger in the articulation of birds and danger too, an otherworldliness, in the 'uncanny harp-strings' which Bernard O'Dowd said decked Australian trees. Their threatening power opened up imagination. In the Rentouls' third story, 'How Music Came to Australia', the fairy originator bestowed sound on landscape and birds. 'The bush shall ring with music; the earth and the trees shall exhale it', the breezes will carry 'soft melodies', but among the trees the symphony of storms will be wild.[45]

The 'ideographic prophecy' thus revealed, the ecology, was music but also light. In Melbourne a school of Impressionist artists evolved from the late 1880s, working with the Australian light. Like JF Archibald, of the *Bulletin*, and others hunting for new ways of expressing Australia, they looked partly to France, to Manet, Renoir, Cézanne, Toulouse-Lautrec and so on. Tom Roberts, Frederick McCubbin, Charles Conder, Arthur Streeton and others holidayed in tents while they painted around Heidelberg, at the north-east edge of the city, in a burning mixture of purple, tawny-gold and blue. Roberts and Streeton afterwards moved to a camp between bush and beach at Sirius Cove, on the northern shore of Sydney Harbour. There was 'great need', said McCubbin's student Norman St Clair Carter, 'for the sun to be let shine into some minds as well as on some bodies for the mental and physical welfare'. Artists, especially, said Carter, 'would have to abandon the city for the country'.[46] Heidelberg and Sirius Cove represented a remarkable flowering in the bush, but they worked their way less into common imagination than stories such as Ethel Pedley's and Katie Parker's.

Even Melbourne and Sydney were small worlds. In Melbourne the Rentouls' father, John Laurence Rentoul, Presbyterian theologian and publicist, was a close friend of HB Higgins and went fishing with him in the wildernesses of Tasmania and New Zealand. Arthur Atkinson's sister knew the Rentouls too, and Norman Carter, having moved from Melbourne to Sydney, was one of Arthur's groomsmen when he married at Manly in 1905.[47] With the poet Hugh McCrae, Carter had just published *The Australian Alphabet* for children:

E stands for Emu
With wonderful legs

Who'd think that they ever
Were folded in eggs.

Ruby Seed, Arthur's bride, was twenty-four to his forty-one, and her grandfather, William Seed, had been the New Zealand equivalent of Harry Wollaston. Free of female timidity, long-suffering but cheerful, strong-minded but pliable, she suited his opinionated middle age, though she found herself increasingly put upon. They honeymooned in the tangled depths of the Blue Mountains, at the spectacular Jenolan Caves, to which the government had lately built a road. It was a track so hazardous that Arthur, having hired two places in a tourist automobile, stood all the way on the running board poised to snatch his wife from the steep drop on the far side.[48]

IV

Meanwhile, in the cities, managing the world of mass production and mass distribution called for distinctive method. 'Taylorism', or 'scientific management' in industry, is remembered as a phenomenon of the 1920s, and as an early stage of 'Fordism' (the production method invented by Henry Ford for his Ford Motor Company in Detroit, turning out cheap cars in bulk). In fact, Frederick Winslow Taylor's book *The Principles of Scientific Management* was published in 1911 and immediately crossed the Pacific. Taylorism, like Fordism, was about time and motion. Taylor taught efficiency in the workplace. Elaborating on the forms of drill already used, or attempted, in many modern classrooms, even in 1911 it expanded trains of thought already well underway.

In the United States itself, during the last thirty years or so, said a returning Australian, Edward Swain of the New South Wales Forestry Department, 'efficiency engineering [had] spread its productive influence over the whole business and industrial organisation of the States, and [now] promises to revolutionise the world'.

Efficient communication spread the message everywhere. 'Briefly stated,' the *Northern Miner* at Charters Towers told its readers in September 1911, distilling Taylor's argument, 'every operation [is] made up of a series of motions on the part of the worker'. The point was to abolish waste, and at present, the *Miner* went on, '[i]n nine cases out of ten, 10 to 50 per cent. of these motions were unnecessary, and many of the remaining motions were so made that much time was wasted'. If the movements of men and machinery could be perfectly integrated the result would be 'an efficiency ... hitherto undreamed of in most industrial work'.[49]

This language of machines drew on new work in thermodynamics, and on the conservation and dissipation of energy within contained systems. *The Treatise on Natural Philosophy* (1867), by the Scottish scientists William Thomson (Lord Kelvin) and Peter Tait, had established physics on a new foundation, opening the way from Isaac Newton to Albert Einstein. As with Darwin's *Origin of Species*, scientific work which had never been intended as a way of understanding humanity was quickly carried over to the affairs of men and women. Engineers, in particular, had to be both physicists and business men, and their intellectual training shaped their business methods.

There was handy imagery here too for economists. In Sydney, the economist Arthur Duckworth used '[t]he modern doctrine of conservation of energy' to explain how effete civilisations in the past had collapsed, when hit simultaneously from below by the 'potential energy' of disgruntled masses and from without by the 'kinetic energy' of barbarian invasion.[50]

Psychology was useful too, promising as it did a full understanding of 'the laws of aesthetics, of education, of ethics and of every human faculty', and indeed scientific management was drill underpinned by psychology. Better organised training in sport had already fixed attention on the micromanagement of the body. Taylorism did the same in the workplace.

> Under the new system [wrote one of Taylor's American disciples], the management is working from below [like democracy itself], lifting up the workman. The superior officers of the management are planning out his work, coordinating it with the work of others; the inferior officers are standing beside the workbench or the machine, teaching him 'how to do it' on scientific lines, and seeing that he obeys the teaching.

The best managers, like sports trainers, and like men mustering cattle for that matter, also took account of the natural inclinations of each subject. Better output meant better wages all round, so that the ultimate instructor in scientific management, said the same authority, was Jesus of Nazareth, because, after all, the great aim was 'satisfied stomachs, shod feet, light hearts, untroubled souls', such as every true Christian longed to see.[51]

In Australia, drill and time-and-motion ideas had been prefigured in curious ways over several decades. In the 1880s, for instance, women throughout the colonies had been offered advice on efficiency in domestic organisation, in a book by 'An Old Housekeeper'. The tongue-in-cheek title, *Men and How to Manage Them*, was symptomatic of a people only half, and only half willingly, absorbed in a mechanised, managerial world. Advice varied from precise timing in the use of ovens to servant discipline, from the correct sequence of weekly duties to the question of life insurance. '[I]f your husband is suddenly killed, the sum of money thus secured is the only thing that has to be deducted from the irreparable pecuniary loss you sustain by his death.' While living, however, he was to be regarded 'as a plastic, invertebrate, manageable animal, indocile and intractable undoubtedly, seldom to be led, driven, or persuaded, but usually to be cajoled and circumvented, and always, from his cradle to his grave, to be reached through his stomach'.[52]

Something like Taylorism coloured the ideas of Henry Bournes

Higgins as president of the Commonwealth Court of Conciliation and Arbitration, and his notions of protection included ideas about efficiency. Building on his Harvester Judgment of 1907, Higgins applied time-and-motion principles in further adjusting the employer–employee relationship. The right pay and conditions benefited both parties. For instance, there was, said Higgins, 'a positive increase in efficiency and in results arising from well-regulated pauses in muscular exertion'. More serious than the Old Housekeeper, Higgins's intention was in some sense much the same. 'A man', he said, 'wants to feel that he is not a tool, but a human agent finding self-expression in his work'. Satisfy that feeling and everyone will be better off.[53]

In America, Frank and Lillian Gilbreth, a celebrated husband-and-wife team, added several more elements to scientific management. The workers themselves, they said, might have useful thoughts – they too had brains – and they should be consulted about waste. Also, said the Gilbreths, the filming of work could reduce its analysis to one-thousandth of a second. Time and motion was tried on the twelve Gilbreth children, probably the first case anywhere of family management by stopwatch. In Britain too the most up-to-date couples were 'obsessed', as HG Wells put it, with the agglomeration of human assets they had manufactured together, and with getting each baby started, as he said, 'on the best lines, with the best methods, training and preparing it – presumably for a cleaned and chastened world'.[54]

In Australia parents struggled with the same need, to give their children 'mental and physical efficiency'. Among other things, this meant the better regimented care of babies. 'Always hold a baby in your arms when feeding it', the Adelaide *Chronicle* told its readers. 'Regular habits, proper food, and long hours of sleep are necessary conditions to a healthy infant.' Taken up by leading women, the movement for infant welfare was to be one of the great lifesavers of the twentieth century.[55]

David Stead, already mentioned, deliberately used scientific management for his own household. Christina, his eldest, was to recall the experience in her novel *The Man Who Loved Children*. Washing dishes, for instance. The boiling of the water and the scraping and rinsing of dishes had to be simultaneous actions. Then, 'all extra grease should be removed and the plates can then be dipped and stacked without extra work. A little scientific method', the children in the story were told by their father (the man who loved them), 'would eliminate all work from the household, so to speak'. My grandfather admired David Stead – he found whimsical ebullience plus efficiency an intoxicating combination – and he too took pride in the smart classification of cutlery as he dried up, an aptitude passed to his sons.[56] It was like the way Harry Wollaston had taught him to sort the mail in Customs. I still remember my father's neat manipulation at the sink.

V

For efficiency's sake there had to be an intimate relationship between managers and managed, rulers and ruled. They had to know and trust each other, on the pattern of parents and children. This was another reason for racial and ethnic uniformity from shore to shore. Racial differences precluded trust, and in many minds the scheme for Federation was a scheme for a White Australia. Some wanted to get rid of competition from Chinese shopkeepers in country towns and from Chinese fruit sellers and furniture makers in Melbourne, who could undersell everyone else by banding together to keep the cost of labour low.[57] Others were more angered by the cheap Pacific Islands labour in the Queensland cane fields, which looked like slavery and offended free enterprise liberals as well as labour organisers.

An efficient nation classified and graded its people, and disposed of waste. As I say in earlier chapters, it aimed at purity and uniformity, a maximum sameness of appearance, language and habit, and rational and manly citizenship. The Chinese, said the Country Storekeepers' Association of New South Wales, should be forced to conform to 'the customs and usages of white citizens'. Better still, they should not be here at all. Their customers, including housewives, might think differently. Remember Mina Rawson's comment on the quality of the gelatine found in the shops of the 'Chinamen': '[d]oubtless many ladies will know what I mean'.[58] In the larger scheme of things, such opinion mattered little.

The federal government had made an emphatic statement on Asian immigration at the first sitting of parliament, although the states already had restrictive regimes in place. In Melbourne before Federation every such immigrant had been interviewed by Harry Wollaston himself and his chief clerk, through an interpreter, and the answers checked against the papers on hand. Now, under pressure from the Labour Party, which had suddenly emerged as a dynamic force at state and federal level, Edmund Barton's ministry legislated to allow for a dictation test for all new arrivals at Australian ports. Labour wanted an explicit ban on particular races, so as to trumpet to the world the principle of a White Australia, but the British government suggested instead the more tactful but also more dishonest process already used in the colony of Natal, in south-east Africa. New arrivals thought undesirable might be administered a test in a language they could not possibly know and excluded when they failed.[59]

Under similar pressure from Labour, Barton's government ruled that all Queensland's Pacific Islands labourers were to be returned home by 1906. Henceforth, the national population was to be as uniform as federal governments could make it. As Barton put it, the federated nation was to be 'one people and remain one people without the admixture of other races'. We would be, in the words of a Queensland paper, the Gympie *Truth*, 'a white and clean Australia'.[60]

Scientific management and the whole ethos of efficiency were drawn into the government of nations, as we see with HB Higgins. Armed with such ideas, ministers thought in more radical, expansive ways about managing both people and things. Two great prime ministers, Alfred Deakin and Andrew Fisher, dominated the period from 1903 to the opening years of the Great War, Deakin first and Fisher towards the end. Thanks largely to Deakin the protectionist vision worked out in Victoria now became central to the larger project, and Fisher followed through. That and other familiar concerns, including democracy and individuality, were all interwoven with the need for efficiency, which also meant tighter coordination from the centre.

It might have meant deeper, wider, more intricate habits of communication too. But better communication at the popular level, through cheap postage (one penny for a half-ounce or ordinary letter), was not a high priority with the federal government, in defiance, as the Melbourne *Argus* said, 'of the growth of public opinion, and regardless of the expansion of business that follows a reduction in the charges'. Penny postage, continent-wide, was delayed until 1911, by which time most of the empire was stuck together, so it was said, with penny stamps, as were Britain and the United States.[61] Australian Federation, however benign, had so far concentrated on its own centralised machinery, as the New Zealander Sir George Grey had predicted. The energy of the federal postmaster-general paled beside that of federal Customs, and cheap transcontinental postage came long after the federal tariff.

As examples of such machinery, in 1906 three laws (and others later on) linked the tariff to minimal wages, which were to be Higgins's concern at the new Court of Conciliation and Arbitration. Deakin also enlarged the new High Court, and he gave the continental regime a fact-finding edge, with a Bureau of Meteorology and a Bureau of Census and Statistics. Fisher, who was Queensland Labour, took protectionism further with the *Manufacturers*

Encouragement Act 1908 and a maternity allowance (1912). He also initiated a national currency (pounds but not pounds sterling) and a Commonwealth Bank, partly modelled on the Queensland National Bank – a people's bank promising security for depositors but also capital for governing, which meant more freedom from British investors. In the same years the government took over both British New Guinea (Papua) and the Northern Territory, and a site for a national capital was finalised in southern New South Wales.[62]

All this activity notwithstanding, authority on the continental scale barely touched most lives. The federal Constitution, after all, was designed to protect the continuing sovereignty of the old governments. But a powerful undercurrent came of the understanding that national efficiency called for one pervasive power. The South Australian Thomas Playford had been right when he spoke of the plans to federate. 'We are doing things', he said, 'on business lines, and we should confine ourselves to the business before us'.[63] There was a momentum here that was long term but ineluctable.

In Australia as elsewhere, the more people multiplied, and the more they multiplied their possessions, the more they feared annihilation. In 1893 the Melbourne *Argus* had remarked on the suddenly popular notion 'of an approaching Armageddon, in which the military forces of the whole civilised world may be engaged and destroyed'. All the hopes and fears of many, it said, even at that early stage, 'are being directed to the possibility of a tremendous war'. A sense of impending doom hung at the edge of popular consciousness for the next twenty years, and indeed, through most of the coming century.[64] Under its influence, combined with a hunger for efficiency, many of the vaguer hopes of pre-Federation times were to dwindle fast.

Deakin and Fisher both contributed to the founding of the Australian navy, which by the outbreak of the War included a 19,200-ton (19,500-tonne) battlecruiser (*Australia*), three light cruisers, three torpedo destroyers and two submarines. This was on top of

Deakin's invitation in August 1908 to a touring American naval fleet, 'the Great White Fleet', to put in at Port Phillip and Sydney Harbour. As the massive armaments of a rising and friendly power, the fleet received a rapturous welcome.[65] But efficiency had to involve the individual human being too. For instance, the Maxim Silencer for machine-guns was a parallel development with the muffler for automobiles. Both were invented in Britain soon after the turn of the century. Automatic rapid-fire guns themselves dated back to the American Civil War, and they had been used by the British against the amaNdebele (or Matabele) people in Africa in 1896–97 and against the Boers. They had been imported by the colonial governments for training from 1897. Mass-produced, they destroyed en masse. Fitted with Hiram Maxim's silencer, machine-guns were adapted to the individual soldier as a thinking, feeling being, on genuine efficiency principles. Unlike older forms of machine-gun the noise of each shot was now muffled, it was said, so that '[t]he nervous strain and subsequent fatigue of the soldier due to the ... noise of firing is abolished'. The recoil was also less, and he no longer dodged as he pulled the trigger, which was 'conducive to better marksmanship'. Altogether, 'the soldier is less likely to yield to panic'.[66] This was good industrial psychology carried into battle.

Rose Scott had protested to Deakin, when he was prime minister, about militarising the lives of young men with mass conscription, but she was out of step with the large agenda of continental nationhood. A democratic people, as Deakin told her, had to be organised for its own defence.[67] He did not see this as militarisation. An instinct for fighting in an organised, intelligent way, and a familiarity with up-to-date weapons, such as the machine-gun, were part of good citizenship. A national program of military service, in other words, took war out of the hands of those who were no good at anything else and made everything accountable to those in the electorate at large who loved peace. In this increasingly interconnected world there was a direct line now between the soldier and the business man, and even between the soldier and the woman voter.

In earlier generations, university students had been contemptuous of soldiering. Now war in a great cause, such as defence of your country, summed up the main aspirations of high-minded manhood, including the right relationship between brain and body. Remember again Melbourne *Punch*'s description of Lord Kitchener, who made his name in the Boer War: 'unalloyed brain ... the finest brain in the British Army'.[68] Australian universities began their own regiments. In Sydney the University Volunteer Rifle Corps, soon renamed the Sydney University Scouts, started in 1900. In Melbourne the University Company of the Victorian Rifles, which had been John Monash's unit, became the Melbourne University Rifles.

Thanks to the Boer War, where men had learnt to negotiate kopje and veldt, soldiering was also associated with the clever use of landscape, with seeing and hearing better. 'Scouting' had started as an American idea, associated with the novels of James Fenimore Cooper and Edward Ellis. Even my grandfather, for all his dislike of violence, read his children Ellis's stories of Deerfoot the Shawanoe, wise friend of the pale-face, and the American play *Davy Crockett; or, The Backwoodsman's Bride* had been playing in Australian theatres as early as the 1870s.[69] Organised scouting for boys, invented in England by Robert Baden-Powell, reached Australia in 1907–08 (immediately mimicked with an equivalent for girls) and the military implications were obvious. 'Success in warfare today', said the *Sydney Morning Herald*, 'depends on outclassing the enemy in the scholarship of war'. That meant tactics, but also keen individual observation. The good soldier, said the *Herald*, must 'read the books of the running brooks, the warnings in stones, and news of the enemy's movements in everything'.[70] Clearly, in war, as in business, the life of each man was to be 'more tense, alert, vivid'. Like any reader of *Dot and the Kangaroo*, he was to make himself part of the landscape, with ears pricked. In war too, we felt ourselves, our whole personality, in Henri Bergson's words, 'pressed against the future'.

The federal government's *Defence Act 1909* made Australia the first country in the British empire to impose universal military training in peacetime. All boys and men from twelve to twenty-six were required to train, and Kitchener himself was invited to come to Australia to give initial advice. The country was divided into Military Districts, then into Battalion Areas and then in turn into Training Areas. At the centre of the scheme were the battalions of senior cadets, aged fourteen to eighteen, who were expected to go on to be members of the Citizen Military Forces. As part-time soldiers they would be trained to defend Australia and at the same time to be more efficient as men, by taking drill and mental focus into their civilian lives. Cadets had four full days of training each year, interspersed with shorter periods. Training in the field was the ideal, but most units used the easier option of parade-ground drill. The authorities were pleased with the result, but genuine brainwork was found to be impossible on such a scale.[71]

One result of compulsory training was to divide the willing and worthy, who did what the law asked for and more, from the 'loafers' and 'shirkers', who held back. Visiting Australia in 1912, Major-General Baden-Powell treated a Sydney audience to a classification of 'loafers': the car-driving type ('healthy fellows who do little more than loll like ladies behind a steering wheel'), the 'racing loafer' and the 'woman loafer' ('fingering a piano [in this world] ... does not help you to play a harp in the next'). As a related taxonomy he distinguished the idle rich, the idle middle class and the idle poor. Waste was the opposite of efficiency, and these all constituted a waste of what Baden-Powell called 'human material', a term popular now as never before.[72]

All-inclusive programs needed ever more intense classification. Who deserved to belong to the nation and who did not? When war came, in 1914, to start with there was an emphasis on using only the best 'human material'. This war would be a trial for heroes, and something like physical perfection was called for. In England, to start with, Winston Churchill asked for 'the flower of our manhood, nothing but the best', and in Australia it was said that the medical men responsible for choosing recruits in the early months seemed to be 'selecting models for a Rodin or a Bertram Mackennal [the distinguished Australian sculptor] rather than troops for war'. 'Many a man', said the Sydney journalist Tom Heney, 'stumbled out of the barrack gates unable to answer the greetings of his friends, with unaccustomed tears in his eyes, as he knew himself rejected'.[73]

VI

When HG Wells wrote about organised intelligence he spoke of it as the work of a brainy elite. It had nothing much to do with democracy. In fact, Wells thought that the triumph of organised intelligence would mean the end of genuine government by the masses. '[W]hen organised intelligence', he said, 'differs from the majority, the majority will have no adequate power of resort'. This was not what happened in Australia, for much of the twentieth century at least.[74] Here, at least, we see an impulse of inclusion.

The Europeans in Australia, more and more, were a people of energetic literacy. For most, newspaper reading was already second nature. Between 1891 and 1911, according to the government statisticians, the number of breadwinners involved in government and defence, or in 'satisfying the moral, intellectual, and social wants' of the people, increased by about a fifth. In every state the increase was much the same, and this was on top of significant increases in the twenty years beforehand. In the years just before the War the same category accounted for 7 or 8 per cent of the total in employment. It was an expansion of power the older generation could not have failed to notice.[75]

Half were teachers so that, HG Wells notwithstanding, the opinions of the majority were in fact receiving the deliberate imprint of organised intelligence. The vast investment in schools during the late nineteenth century was justified at the time by the near certainty, as a leading education official in South Australia put it, that 'radical social changes' were nearly upon us. Soon, given the progress of democracy, the people themselves would be in charge. 'It will be highly dangerous to the State', he said, 'if the boys and girls are not educated in such a manner as to enable them rationally to use the increased power that soon must be exercised by the masses'. The generation reaching adulthood between Federation and the War had followed the lead of its teachers. The enthusiasm for school cadets, among male teachers and among boys, is one example of that.[76]

In short, organised intelligence was creating its own majority. It was opening a road for the population at large to use, together with any number of esoteric paths interesting only to itself. At the same time visits from international figures such as Lord Kitchener and Major-General Baden-Powell, and the massive importing of international literature, including learned journals and periodicals such as the *World's Work* (a highly influential New York monthly which taught scientific management), drew the colonies into a global organised intelligence, just as they were being drawn more thoroughly into the ups and downs of what might be called the world economy. Newspaper editors sorted through these imports and broadcast the best items far and wide. The Europeans in Australia had never been less independent than at the time they became a continental nation.

The intellectual leadership also made itself responsible for the efficient preservation of national assets, whether artefacts, landscape or living creatures. They fought against random destruction. 'On my last excursion', one of its members told a gathering of the Field Naturalists Club of Victoria, 'I came across a party of four or five boys with guns … I asked them what they intended to shoot? "Oh, anything!" was the prompt reply'.[77] The moral of this story needed no emphasis. Leaders like themselves had to bring to an end such happy abandon, a process calling for complicated and often expensive methods. They needed popular support, which meant getting the word out. Except in managing defence, the federal government was powerless in this area. Only organised intelligence could create the necessary networks, reaching out from the old capital cities so as to link up across the continent and beyond.

Historical societies were one way. It was necessary to collect, sort, preserve and defend the evidence of the past. There were already numerous antiquarian groups in Britain and the United States, and in Sydney the government had set in train the copying and publication of the *Historical Records of New South Wales*. An educational campaign across the continent was the next step. In 1897 a group in Sydney proposed an Australian Historical Society, 'to collect and preserve the remaining fragments, on which might be built the materials of a reliable History of Australia'. It was founded in time for Federation, but it never reached beyond New South Wales, and only in Sydney did it do much for public debate.[78]

The work of the Australian Historical Society ('Royal' from 1918) could not compare with the campaign for Australian wildlife. It was wildlife more than anything else which seemed to give the God-given land a characteristic voice large numbers wanted to hear. First we had to know what was there. The classification and publication process had started in earnest some years before. In Melbourne, Ferdinand von Mueller had published vast compilations, including *Eucalyptographia: A Descriptive Atlas of the Eucalypts of Australia and the Adjoining Islands* (1879–84) and *Key to the System of Victorian Plants* (1886–88). The work of Frederick Manson Bailey, Queensland government botanist, was mentioned in chapter 2: *Handbook to the Ferns of Queensland* and so on. Their

Sydney equivalent, Joseph Maiden, responded with *The Useful Native Plants of Australia* (1889), following up with *The Flowering Plants and Ferns of New South Wales* (1895–98), *A Manual of the Grasses of New South Wales* (1898), *The Forest of New South Wales* (1901), *A Critical Revision of the Genus Eucalyptus* (1903, improving on von Mueller's work with 366 species), and many more.[79]

Working in New South Wales Fisheries, David Stead did the same, with *Fishes of Australia* (1906), *The Edible Fishes of New South Wales* (1908) and *A Brief Review of the Fisheries of New South Wales* (1910), all full of photographs, a technique startling in its precision and novelty. As an educator, Stead went far beyond his own children. He helped to found a Naturalists' Club and an Aquarium Society in Sydney, and he gave talks – on 'The Life and Troubles of the Oyster', for instance.[80] Experts such as Stead were not content with making lists. They wanted action from their various governments. Arguing for the 'immense national value' of fisheries in Australia, Stead described North American hatcheries to show what could be done through interventionist protection.[81]

In 1907–08, in Victoria, Walter Baldwin Spencer tried to set up an expert committee to advise the state government on all matters of nature conservation, but that came to nothing. Almost immediately, however, the newly established Gould League of Bird Lovers, with its appeal directly to children, was suddenly and wonderfully successful, and largely because it looked not to government but to public opinion and to individual commitment. The Gould League was modelled on the Audubon Society, founded in New York in 1905. In a direct challenge to the habits of boys, both groups asked members to sign a pledge not to molest birds or to raid their nests. Picked up by schoolteachers in their nature study classes, there were soon Gould Leagues also in Tasmania, South Australia and New South Wales, and 'Bird Day' was authorised by the various state governments. At the school at Ultimo, in Sydney, on Bird Day 1911, '[l]ittle tots, some of them just able to toddle, sang bird songs (little human birds, the chairman called them) and went through action songs with a sweetness and vivacity that captured all'.[82]

In two years Gould League membership had reached 7000 in New South Wales alone. The pledge was a type of national enlistment, designed to impose new notions of manhood – notions of gentleness and restraint. Then, in the winter of 1909, in Sydney, David Stead started the equally successful Wild Life Preservation Society of Australia. It was to be partly a pressure group, but it too threw itself into education, linking up with other bodies, including the Gould League, and experimenting with ways of getting the word out beyond the state. It also had an international edge. Stead worked first with the Swedish consul Birger Mörner, naturalist and poet, and the United States consul-general was also involved.[83]

The Preservation Society had unprecedented impact. In Sydney the governor and chief justice both gave their active support, and the government agreed to put more birds on the protected list and make a better effort to publicise restrictions. The state's postmaster-general approved lists being stuck up in post offices, and the inspector-general of police said he would do more to stop the killing of platypuses. A cinema screening was planned to spread awareness of the destruction of bird and seal rookeries in Bass Strait, and the governors of Dutch and German New Guinea were asked to stop the destruction of birds of paradise, something already underway in the Australian-ruled Papua.[84]

The entire campaign was meant to make a feeling for animals and birds characteristic of Australia. The control of a continent, and the great hopes attached thereto, meant that the 'love of murder', as Ethel Pedley called it, must end. Several distinguished women were among the founders of the Preservation Society (Rose Scott joined later), but women were its targets too. Women's hats included feathers from the most beautiful of birds, such as herons and ospreys, and this was now a frontline issue in the battle for women's sensibility. The society's secretary, the zoologist Launcelot Harrison, was married to Amy Mack, author of *Bushland Stories* and *Scribbling Sue*, and women's editor at the *Sydney Morning Herald*. The *Herald*'s women's page therefore gave the cause good publicity. The 'fashionable woman' must understand, Mack told her thousands of readers, that when she decks herself with feathers she has 'the blood of slaughtered innocents upon her head'.[85]

Habitat came next. In 1910 a society was proposed in Tasmania by the local branch of the Australian Natives' Association, the organisation for native-born men, to push for the better management of native forests. The idea spread quickly, and the Australian Forest League, partly modelled on the Society of American Foresters (a body of experts), was formed with branches in all states. Feeling concentrated originally on the fact that forests are 'the natural home of fauna worthy of preservation' and that they 'govern water supply, preventing erosion ... moderating floods, and maintaining in periods of drought regular stream flow'. But there was also an interest in the future national supply of timber, possibly including wood pulp (an invention of the 1840s). With such materialist concerns, the Forest League never possessed the eccentric energy of its wildlife counterpart.[86]

With business booming, Arthur Atkinson, who had been one of the original council of the Preservation Society, agreed to act as Launcelot Harrison's assistant. Harrison was an educator, specialising in lantern slide lectures and school visits. Atkinson, a man of the office, managed things instead from his desk in the Customs House or from Manly, sending statements, meticulous and passionate, to men and women of substance, and making a case in the press. Soon he took over altogether, and from now on this was his obsession and his life's work. As a pleasant early duty he composed a letter to his admired Nellie Melba, and other respected actresses and singers, about the cruelty involved in wearing feathers, and about 'the claims of the birds as our best friends'.[87]

Melba continued to wear feathers. Wilful and lavish in her

own way, she nevertheless supported the cause with a statement for Bird Day 1911 about her love for 'the chatter and song of birds'. Myriad and disparate, they were the voice of the continent intricately distilled. 'As a girl', she told Australia's children, 'I knew all their notes'.[88]

12

War

I

South Grafton was a village on the Clarence River, whose brown waters separated it from Grafton proper, in the far north-east corner of New South Wales. At the census of 1901 its population numbered 976, 'exclusive of Aborigines', and its houses 168. For sixty years it was the home of Henrietta Burghardy. Mrs Burghardy was an immigrant of the immediate post-goldrush period. By the early years of the twentieth century she had been twice widowed and had also lost several children, but she had seen eight grow up, and grandchildren were multiplying fast. Albert Schwinghammer, second son of her first marriage, was a long-time mayor of South Grafton, and she was herself a woman of some property and standing. She had donated a chalice and cross to the new weatherboard Anglican church (St Matthew's), and the *Clarence River Advocate*, published downriver at Maclean, thought it worth printing some of her many memories of that flourishing part of the world.[1]

Charles Schwinghammer, Mrs Burghardy's first husband, had been a saddler. Together they had made money. They had invested (unsuccessfully) in goldmines, and Schwinghammer had led the effort to plant trees in Grafton's main street (hence Grafton's famous jacarandas, a flood of purple in early summer). When he died the shopkeepers of South Grafton did him the honour of partial closure as his long funeral procession moved down the main street. His widow and children had turned for support to William Burghardy, a publican, but this second marriage was unhappy and debt-ridden.

Burghardy held the pub licence (the Post Office Hotel), but his wife did all the work and she also owned the building. In 1890 he had disappeared.[2]

Dignified self-reliance in the mother of a large family was bound to make an impression on a small community. Also, the Burghardy-Schwinghammers were the sort of townspeople who joined and contributed. They were musical too, and in small towns and bush settlements sharing such pleasures was a process especially rich and easy. George Schwinghammer, the third son, featured in local concerts and singalongs. As postmaster at Drake, on the Tenterfield road (he had taken with him a farewell address from Grafton and South Grafton friends, in a 'massive' gold frame), he sang the new American ballad 'Frankie and Albert':

> Frankie and Albert were lovers, O Lordy how they could love.
> Swore to be true to each other, true as the stars up above:
> He was her man, but he done her wrong.

So she shot him, 'root-a-toot-toot'. George's young wife, the daughter of Scottish immigrants at Maclean, had 'a fund of talent' too, said the *Clarence and Richmond Examiner*, and 'a perfect control of her facial muscles'. His brother Albert named his fourth-born George Verdi (known as Verdi), probably in honour of 'Signor George Verdi' (real name William Green), 'Australia's Favourite Baritone'.[3]

News of Britain's declaration of war against Germany reached all of the more accessible centres of Australian population on 5 August 1914. At Grafton, the *Examiner* forecast the ruin of civilisation, with weapons efficient and cunning as never before and with 'the greatest battles the world has ever seen'. The slaughter, it said, would be immense. But everywhere the mood to start with was a mixture of prudence and enthusiasm, the latter in spite of all the horrors foretold. At Echuca, on the River Murray, '[m]uch cheering was indulged in by the crowd at the military tournament and the Rangers Band played the National Anthem'. At Cohuna, 64 kilometres upriver, the Anglican and Methodist clergymen joined forces to form a local association 'to consider what steps should be taken to meet local contingencies arising from the war in Europe'. In Perth, together with some cheering, two boys, eight or nine years old, marched along St George's Terrace shouldering broom handles and whistling 'Soldiers of the Queen'. Again, at Grafton, the wife of the manager of the Bank of New South Wales organised a sewing bee, 'to provide comforts for our soldiers'.[4]

Enlisting was immediate. Men crowded the main depots and by the end of the month 16,000 or 17,000 had signed up. By then an expeditionary force had gone to take over German New Guinea, and on 14 September news came back of its success, but with four Australians dead.[5] A month later a combined Australian and New Zealand fleet sailed with troops for Egypt, as a halfway house to Europe. By now the Ottoman empire, with its capital at Constantinople (since named Istanbul), had entered the War in support of Germany and Austria-Hungary. These (the Central Powers) confronted Britain and France to the west, but also the Russian empire to the east (these three were the Triple Entente). Russia was linked with its western allies through a waterway, consisting of the Sea of Marmara and two straits, the Dardanelles and Bosporus, and the Ottoman empire lay across that waterway. In order to take control of this vital passage, the bulk of the Australians and New Zealanders, combined as the Australian and New Zealand Army Corps, or ANZAC (no strong, incisive 'K', as with Kodak, but very close) were ordered from the Middle East to join British, French and Indian forces in a landing in the Dardanelles, in April 1915.

However, for the armies of the British empire the main centre of action during the War was to be the Western Front, mainly Artois and Picardy, in France's northern corner, and Flanders, in Belgium. The Australians first arrived there in April 1916. Six of Henrietta

Burghardy's grandsons fought on the Western Front. At Pozières in August 1916, at the mid-point of the Battle of the Somme, flying shrapnel wrecked the right wrist of the youngest of them, Charles Smith, and he was sent home early, while Verdi Schwinghammer's brother Charles succumbed to mustard gas at Villers-Bretonneux in May 1918. Charlie Schwinghammer had already been in hospital with 'trench feet', caused by long periods standing in cold, deep mud, and he was now invalided out, with bad burns and damaged lungs. Another grandson, Bernie Johnson, was shot twice, once in the leg and once in the lower back. He returned to the line twice, but he was killed near Albert, just across the River Somme from Villers-Bretonneux, in June 1918. '[Those] who knew Bernie', said the *Byron Bay Record*, 'and watched him grow from a bright and promising boyhood to stalwart youth and manhood', would grieve with all his family.[6]

This pleasant remark conceals a tangled story. The long lists of dead which started to appear after Australian troops landed at Gallipoli, in the Dardanelles in April 1915, had given the War a new kind of purpose at home. It made some ask who was Australian and who was not. From June 1915 a new Sydney weekend paper, the *Mirror of Australia*, urged readers to look out for Germans in their midst, and to stop speaking German, buying German, listening to German music and drinking German beer (meaning Resch's, but all lager was suspect). The federal government was already interning Australians with German names and whose sympathies were doubted. The *Mirror* claimed credit for increasing vigilance and it hunted down Germans from town to town: 'Hun Spies at Moss Vale', '206 Justices of the Peace with Hun Names Gazetted in Queensland', 'Newcastle Hun Doctor', 'Hun Ladies Tailor', 'A Hun at Barrenjoey'.[7]

Mrs Burghardy and her first husband had both been born in Württemberg, then an independent kingdom but now part of the German empire. They had come in a shipload of immigrants from

Bremen, and Grafton, where most settled together, was sometimes called Germantown, though they had freely intermarried with other families. With good reason then the attention of the *Mirror* shifted in May to Grafton, with the heading 'Grafton Huns. The Schwinghammer Scandal'. For four months it kept up demands that all of that particular 'nest of Huns' should be placed behind barbed wire.[8]

There were neighbours in Grafton keen to allege that Kaiser Wilhelm was toasted at Burghardy-Schwinghammer family gatherings and that they made a habit of hoisting the German flag, black, white and red. One made the peculiar accusation that Albert Schwinghammer had tried to get his son into the army by telling him to use his mother's surname, Saul, which was English. This was probably Verdi Schwinghammer, altogether (as friends said) 'a decent young fellow' and, like his uncle George, 'a clever and obliging musician', who, after two tries, and with some strings pulled by his father's colleagues, eventually got in under his proper name. But Verdi's brother Charlie enlisted as 'Swinghammer' ('Sw' was more English than 'Schw'), and in Brisbane, where nobody knew him.[9]

The War was energised and justified by the newspapers, however narrow their circulation. Driving home the facts of the family's contribution, Verdi's parents frequently sent to the papers his postcards and letters from the front, and one of them devoted two issues to his long account of the Battle of Villers-Bretonneux and the bombing of Calais. Verdi had a bright generosity of spirit which, when you knew him, made his exotic names irrelevant. It shows in his painstaking hunt for the grave of his cousin Bernie Johnson. 'I buried a little bunch of pressed flowers, that his Mother had posted over to me, on the grave, and got a little tobacco tin of earth ... which I posted back.' Whenever a piano turned up in a captured French village Verdi played on it. He was also an eloquent writer. Besides the pieces published in the local papers, he wrote love letters for an illiterate Queensland bushman and he won third prize for an essay about the fighting at Broodseinde, a curtain-raiser for Passchendaele, in October 1917, in an Armistice competition among the troops.[10]

When Henrietta Burghardy died, at South Grafton, six weeks after the Armistice, a lengthy newspaper tribute noted the number of her soldier grandsons. Instead of Württemberg, it also kindly made her a native of Alsace, the borderland which the Allied triumph had just won back from Germany for France.[11]

II

Throughout the small towns and rural centres, as well as the capital cities, and even before the War began, myriad newspapers established the complexities of war, moral, ideological, political, logistical. Each in its own way had woven the wonder and banality of an increasingly frightening world into ordinary conversation – and had taken back from ordinary conversation all the little prejudices and suppositions which made people want to read the newspapers in the first place.

In January 1910, for instance, the *Colac Herald*, published 150 kilometres north-west of Melbourne, carried news of the arrival of futurism in England, in the form of Filippo Tommaso Marinetti's pamphlet 'The Futurist Manifesto'. Futurism was an artistic and literary movement with political pretensions, which aggressively set aside the past and all settled virtues. Soon Marinetti himself reached London from his native Italy – an elegantly moustachioed personification of 'the love of danger, [and] the habit of energy and rashness'. He would, as he put it in his 'Manifesto', 'glorify war – the only cure for the world – militarism, patriotism, the destructive gesture of the anarchists, the beautiful ideas which kill, and contempt for women'.[12]

Gradually, at second hand, Australians became aware of futurism, as a typical curiosity of the day. One of its principles, so the

Melbourne *Argus* reported, is that '[n]oise ... is the spirit of the age'. Futurists wanted to push nouns ahead of other parts of speech because of their 'dynamic properties'. We must have strings of them, as in 'smoke, smoke, whirlwind, stench, blood, groans, shrieks, victory, death!' Dress had to change too. In fact by 1914 in Australia futurism seemed to be mainly about fashion. 'A suggestion for a "Futurist" gown', said the *Bendigo Advertiser*, 'is given in our illustration'. Attractive shades might include 'tango yellow and various startling reds and purples'.[13]

This lurch from the apocalyptic to the à la mode sums up the deeper quarrels. So does the vexed debate which broke, also in 1910, around the writing of the British journalist Norman Angell, exacerbated by his book *The Great Illusion* (1911). Angell attacked the cult of violence which the futurists fed on, and specifically the belief that the progress of nations depended on the survival of the fittest. If war did really bring the best men to the fore, said Angell, it also destroyed them, which in fact meant the survival of the least fit. And those it did not kill it forced into sameness. Modern warfare involved, he said, 'an artificial barrack life, a highly mechanical uniformity and centralization tending to crush individuality, and accentuating a drift towards a centralized bureaucracy already too great'.[14]

Surely, said Angell, civilisation, wealth and learning moved forward when there was less violence, and more forbearance and cooperation? Indeed, what could be more blindingly obvious? A minute's clear thinking showed that, in spite of this obsession with destruction, cooperation was now more intense and multifarious among human beings, and more widespread, than it had ever been before.

Norman Angell was interested mainly in international trade, the network which drove the vast increase of production and consumption obvious on every side. As the great internationalist Richard Cobden had taught a generation or two earlier, trade grew out of interdependence. In fact, quite apart from trade, the last half-century had been full of examples of keen, self-conscious, deliberate cooperation. It was organised intelligence. In Australia, as I have said, such cases ranged from the little communes along the Murray to the Federation movement itself.

Angell was right, but he was also out of his depth. He was in territory as new and strange as that which Allan Quatermain, Henry Rider Haggard's hero, found in *King Solomon's Mines*, as bleak and morbid as Jonathan Harker and his friends discovered in *Dracula* (recall chapter 1). The English journalist Charles à Court Repington put the issue better. Writing in December 1914 in the London *Times* (a piece copied all over Australia, from the *Cairns Post* to Perth's *Western Mail*), Repington called the War an event which 'transcends all limits of thought, imagination and reason' (a quality the futurists had revelled in, even before fighting started).

> We little creeping creatures [said Repington] cannot see more than a fraction of it. Even if we climb painfully to the top of the highest ladder of thought we are still pygmies, and the war still towers high above us ... We look, gasp, wonder, and are dumb. We do not know. Nobody knows. This war, for once, is bigger than anybody. No one dominates it. No one even understands it. Nobody can ... The forces at work – forces moral, material, religious, fanatical – defy analysis and investigation.

Marshal Ferdinand Foch, the great French commander, said the same: 'The Armies have outgrown the brains of the people who direct them'.[15] No wonder, during the War, there were so many massive and tragic mistakes.

Clergy sensed this immeasurability, and most missed their way in it. In Australia, the authority they had apparently won during the Federation campaign they now compromised. For most, but for

Catholics much less than for Protestants, the War was so far beyond ordinary understanding that it could only be the work of an angry God, and from start to finish they held to this point, struggling to make it stick in the Australian conscience. The cause of nations had become the cause of the Almighty. The Reverend Charles Strong might vigorously condemn this 'religion of the State', which was so different from his hoped-for national church and from true Christian brotherhood. Under the regime of war, 'the State', said Strong and eight other ministers, in a powerfully dissenting manifesto, 'replaces God and the national flag replaces the Cross'. This new and ghastly teaching meant that 'supreme law is not the law of God but the military safety of the country'.[16] But this was the opinion of a very few.

Most clergy were confident that the War was designed by God to cleanse the country. It was about righteousness. Germans were God's enemies but we ourselves were not yet righteous in his sight, and the War was meant to make us so. In 1916, when millions had died, the Anglican archbishop of Brisbane told his congregation that he wanted no peace until Australians were ready for it. That would be when '[o]ur moral and spiritual condition' was certain, and there was no sign of that yet. In a Salvation Army gathering, after four years and with no hint (and a disappearing memory) of peace, a woman asked the agonising question 'Why does not God stop the War?' God would not stop the War, the Army's preacher replied, until 'right should triumph over wrong and that not until we ourselves were right'. However, a soldier in France, Roy Berry, also from Queensland and a clerk before the War, was one of a large number of his kind who felt differently. The fighting surely must end soon, he said, in a letter home, because it was destroying 'all that is beautiful in civilised life'.[17]

At the opening of this volume I spoke of the journalist Charles Bean, who reported from the front and who was afterwards Australia's great historian of the War. Before the War, writing from the

River Darling for the *Sydney Morning Herald* in 1909, Bean had found something 'strangely simple', an element engaging and mysterious, in the men he met there. In wartime Bean ignored Charles Repington's immeasurability, except to find it in the character of the typical Australian soldier. He was not interested in machines and he did not wait for any kind of redemption, national or individual. In the Australian national story which Bean did most to create, the mystery – and the glory – were within each man at the front. He was a volunteer, a citizen-soldier, making his own jokes and his own decisions, drawing on his own kind, and with a determined understanding as to who his kind were. It was a remarkable image. The simplicity and ingenuity of the typical man, his nonchalance and his daring, his earnestness and his jokes, his literacy and his slang, his fierceness and his gentleness, his cunning and his sacrifice, gathered on paper by Bean, were altogether worth a century of reflection. As Bean said himself, 'the big thing in the war for Australia was the discovery of the character of Australian men'.[18]

This War gave immeasurability to everyman, though not to everywoman. It was individuality raised to a shining ideal. In England, the poet Wilfred Owen wrote about training recruits. 'For 14 hours yesterday', he said, 'I was at work – teaching Christ to lift his cross by numbers, and how to adjust his crown ... With a piece of silver I buy him every day, and with maps I make him familiar with the topography of Golgotha'.[19] This was the English way of discovering everyman. Bean's type was more sharp-edged.

The horror remained. According to Norman Angell, the habits of association built up during the nineteenth century meant that 'the biological division of mankind into independent and warring States [was] a scientific ineptitude'. It was a deeply seductive ineptitude all the same, which even the men of God succumbed to. An officer in the German army used an explanation which was common on both sides. 'A long period of law and order,' said Lieutenant Ernst Jünger, who was wounded fourteen times between 1915 and the

Armistice, 'such as our generation had behind it, produces a real craving for the abnormal, a craving that literature stimulates'.[20]

Jünger explained how he and his kind used to ask themselves, '[W]hat does it look like when there are dead lying about?' Now they knew. Every day at the front there were dead lying about, often several layers deep, sunk in mud, in varying degrees of mutilation and decomposition. The stench and lurid colour of death, all the colours of the butcher's shop, were commonplace. An Australian, Jimmy Downing (of the 57th Battalion, Australian Imperial Force), spoke of digging trenches. 'The deeper one dug, the more bodies one exhumed. Hands and faces protruded from the slimy, toppling walls of trenches. Knees, shoulders, and buttocks poked from the foul morass, as many as the pebbles of a brook.' 'So it was [at first]', said Ernst Jünger, 'that we had to stare again and again at these things we had never seen before, without being able to give them any meaning ... as though we walked in a dream through a garden full of strange plants'. Soon, they took no notice.[21]

They got used to killing too. Downing wrote of Germans driven back against their own barbed-wire defences near Bullecourt, on the Western Front, in the northern spring of 1917. 'There was a horrible scene', he said, 'as the Australians [of the 1st Division] grimly pumped bullets as fast as they could work their bolts into a mass of Germans demented with terror, running to and fro along the front, screaming and screaming'.[22]

Here was futurism. Here, on the Western Front, was a 'sea of craters' (Jünger again), mass-produced, the apparently limitless product of an industrial age, a 'fantastic desert ... [with] the sameness of the machine-made article'. Each battlefield was itself a superhuman machine, capable of being thrown into action as if with an electric switch. 'A thousand guns roar out on the instant, and at a touch, driven by innumerable levers, the work of annihilation goes pounding on its way.' The impact was vast. 'With springing step', said Downing, describing the conflict at Bullecourt, 'the light of youth in their eyes, one brigade after another, our men went into the line in battalions of six hundreds. Dull-eyed, shambling, half-crazed, the wrecked battalions came out, after four days or a week, two hundred strong or less'. And there was mud, along the Somme a chalky subsoil churned with the topsoil to create yellow-grey glue metres deep, and smelling of putrefaction. 'It was mud, mud, mud all the way', said Downing. Mud to live in and mud to die in. '[T]he armies', he said, 'thought mud, ate mud, lived in a sea of hundreds of square miles of it'.[23]

This experience converted the Europeans in Australia into the Australians in Europe. At one level the Australian soldier fought for king and empire, or, as some said, 'in God's cause for God's principles', to decide 'whether spiritual principles or military despotism will control this world of ours'. One man gave a comprehensive assortment of reasons: 'for all that Christianity stands for, for the Liberty we've always talked about and for the Country we live in and are proud of, and of [*sic*] the traditions of the English race for centuries back'. And, said one, 'think of what might be should Germany win!' It was commonly understood that Australia itself would be a prize of war, that 'England would have to disgorge her colonies in the terms for peace'.[24] But on both sides men also fought, as Lieutenant Jünger put it, for the abnormal – for the alien, for the faraway itself, for vast abstractions steeped in mud. For the 60,000 Australians who died, of the 331,000 who served overseas, this was what they knew last.

III

The landing at Gallipoli by the Australian and New Zealand Army Corps under William Birdwood, an English lieutenant-general, was made on 25 April 1915, remembered as Anzac Day. Writing home shortly beforehand, Colonel John Monash predicted that the action then imminent would redound 'to the eternal glory of

Australia and all who have participated'. The word was already out. 'It is going to be Australia's chance', said Alan Henderson, a twenty-year-old lieutenant, as he waited in tremulous excitement the night before, 'and she makes a tradition out of this one. God grant it will be a great one'. The campaign lasted until December, when troops were withdrawn, the main object unmet. Among the Allies the total killed was about 44,000, with Australian deaths making up one-fifth, Henderson himself being fatally wounded on the first day. His elder brother was killed a fortnight later. This campaign, and the sudden mighty slaughter, had, as I say, a profound effect on public opinion in Australia and New Zealand – and also in Turkey, where national pride, newly quickened, eventually led to the fall of the Ottoman empire and the founding of the Turkish republic.[25]

'Are not nations like individuals?' a Catholic priest in Sydney asked his congregation on the first anniversary of the Gallipoli landing. 'If the nation is to be born, if the nation is to live, someone must die for it.'[26]

Details of the landing, including the names of men killed and wounded, had reached home within a month. The flag at the town hall at Wallaroo, in South Australia, was flown half-mast for Arthur Elphick, a labourer, the only son of Sarah Elphick, a widow. 'He always took a keen interest in military matters', and while his mother had stopped him going to the Boer War she had failed this time. The *Kalgoorlie Miner* wrote of the wounding of Rupert Finlason of Boulder, 'a sluicer on the Golden Horseshoe mine at the outbreak of the war', and the Launceston *Examiner* reported the death of Barrett Taylor, who had worked in an orchard at Trevallyn. Taylor's glasses, a tobacco pouch and knife, a leather-bound notebook, a tapestried 'perfume bag' (perhaps a present from one of his younger sisters – the eldest was a nurse at the front) and a gunmetal watch were found on him and, as in all such cases, were sent back to his family.[27]

Pressure, official and unofficial, redoubled on men to enlist.

At a recruitment gathering in Sydney a man in his twenties felt the sharp end of a woman's umbrella.

> 'Now, young fellow ... what about you – you've cold feet?'
>
> 'I'm married with one child.'
>
> 'Well, that's nothing to stop you! Why, I gave my only son, and he got killed. Go and enlist now!'

A great surge of enthusiasm took the War into homes hitherto untouched.[28]

The original German impulse sprang from the belief that war was needed to give Germany its proper weight in the world, on which depended global enlightenment. By land and by sea Germany was hemmed in by substantial powers, including Britain and its empire, unrivalled as a global network of settlement and trade. When this War was won, said the German chancellor, Germany would be able to build up its strength indefinitely, and the apocalyptic mission of the German people could be fulfilled. But having failed to break through their encirclement in the west, the Germans found themselves both blocked and besieged, unable to go forward but also unable to go back without being overrun. In that sense Germany lost the War in the first few months.[29]

This was the stalemate in which Australians were embedded. Travelling to the front by train from Marseille in the northern summer of 1916, after a spell in the sands of Egypt, Corporal (afterwards Lieutenant) Dick Williams looked out the window onto 'fields ablaze with scarlet poppies, blue cornflowers and white marguerites', in which women waved, and shouted, '*Vive l'Australie!*' 'An old seaman, well past the romantic age, said to me: "A man would gladly die for a country like this".'

Recall Richard Pilmer's journey from Perth to the Kimberley twenty-two years before (chapter 8), to confront Aboriginal people under Tjangamarra. Pilmer had similarly exulted at the endless pink and white everlastings which crowded him in on the way. Is this the feel of impending danger? Certainly, Dick Williams was alert to such things. Later, talking of the night before fighting at Villers-Bretonneux, in 1918, he was enchanted by the interval between eating and sleep, when 'in all the little dugouts, honeycombing the bank like birds' nests, candle-lights appeared, and men about them lifted up their voices in song'. It was always the same, he said, in the moments of peace before battle.[30]

The long period of sacrifice on the Western Front had two parts to it, and the Australians missed most of the first. During 1914–16 the British government was building up troop numbers, from a peacetime army of ten divisions to an empire-wide one of more that sixty. British industry was turned over to a new kind of mass production, including weapons completely unknown when the War started, and the British workforce was mobilised accordingly. British bureaucracy reached out to link up the various branches of the national and imperial effort, and British commanders in the field started, in a fumbling fashion, to see what all this meant, not just for strategy but also for the way every soldier lived and moved. Now, during 1916–18, with more than six million British subjects under arms (the whole Australian population was not yet five million), and drawn from several continents, the second phase was vast.[31]

By the time the Australians arrived at the Western Front it was clear that the Gallipoli experience was not an aberration. Old methods of fighting were obsolete. Forming, charging, wheeling and retreating were no longer the main point, much less the bushcraft of scrub and plain perfected during the Boer War. Digging was more common than running. Staying in one place, in trenches, was more usual than moving, either forwards or backwards. The great aim, having dug in, was to wear down the other side, by sheer abundance of effort and weight of firepower, as each kept up attack and counterattack, replete with invention and ingenuity. One side, national economies included, had to collapse exhausted before there could be peace.[32]

Organised intelligence, the new dispensation described by HG Wells, meant brains interconnecting in a deliberate, focussed way for one shared purpose. This was how the new warfare worked, though not always well. The French, fighting on their own territory, learnt quickly. They were also the first to grasp fully that the War would last a long time. The British, wary of centralised power and with a much smaller trained army to start with (three-quarters of a million compared with France's three and a half million), and engaged on various fronts, all of them a long way from London, found the articulation of authority, the application of scientific management, the link between government and gunfire, much harder to manage.[33]

From top to bottom, everything depended on drawing together a vast mass of small movements, a number of tactical layers beyond any kind of easy comprehension, into something like a single strategy. The self-conscious use of brains, typical of the time, was urgent now. Major-General Cyril Brudenell White, the Australian commander, according to Charles Bean, was a man of 'wonderfully quick intellect and wide, swift grasp' of affairs, a man with the essential combination of 'brain' and 'force of character'.[34] Everyone needed that combination more or less.

Firepower was a symptom of brain power, and all the way through the ranks. As methods settled, more and more initiative passed down from the battalion level to the company, and from the company to the platoon, and so even to the section, to the corporals and lance-corporals, and to the men with no rank at all. Lieutenant Jünger's attitude to ordinary personal risk was common to both sides. 'I have always made it a rule', he said, 'to let any one [*sic*] carry his own skin to market as he pleases'. The War's main vortex, the Western Front, from Ypres to the Rhine, was in peacetime one of the most productive and technologically sophisticated places in the world, dense with the railways which were now to sustain all the traffic of battle, the massive to and fro of manpower, ammunition, weapons, food and so on.[35] In this landscape new patterns of ingenuity unfolded.

For men adept with big ideas and complicated technology the War was a thrilling challenge. Besides the bafflement Charles Repington spoke of, there was intoxication with its sheer size, with what such size could do, and with the enormous results which came from enormous causes. Enlistment was a chance to see at first hand not just new places but also the clashing of titanic powers, and to stretch mental capacity beyond anything the world could otherwise provide. It was like flying inside a thunderstorm. The great Austrian writer Karl Kraus, one of those who spelt out best the moral dimensions of the War, said that 'man has invented the machine only to be overpowered by it'. '[We] outdo the madness of having invented it', he said, 'with the worse madness of letting ourselves be killed by it'.[36] Men proud of their own brain power were not so gloomy.

Condescending British opinion smiled at the Australian soldier, tall, broad, wilful, unflinching and childlike. It was also said, rightly or wrongly, that among Allied troops few were more murderous with their prisoners of war. The British journalist Philip Gibbs regaled his readers with a story of an Australian he met in France who had been drinking with mates in an estaminet, or bistro, when at the third round the landlady suddenly put the price up. It was his shout. Paying under protest he coolly broke the glasses and then, apprehended by an *agent de police*, called out to Gibbs, who spoke French. 'I should be very glad if you would explain the case to this little Frenchman,' the man said. 'If he does not take his hand off my wrist I shall have to kill him.'

Gibbs obliged. 'I ... pointed out that the Australian was a very large-sized man, and that in spite of his quietude he was a man in the habit of killing Germans. He also had a curious dislike of policemen.'

The soldier, set free, was grateful, and in the simple, unselfconscious way which Gibbs thought typical of his kind. 'Thanks for your trouble', he said. 'It was the injustice I couldn't stick. I always pay the right price. I come from Australia.'[37]

The estaminet (the men called it 'staminay') was a place to find women, and also a testing place for French. It featured in stories by trench poets:

> Up came the tart to get the glass,
> So Bill most gravely said,
> 'Mam'selle vous promenade with moi' –
> She laughed and tossed her head.

Bill persisted: '"Deux beer, encore, please, sil vous plait, / I'm talkin' French tonight"'. And so did she: '"Yes, Bill, apres la guerre"'.[38]

In fact, Australian soldiers were in most ways more astute than the English. They were not so ready to leave everything to their officers (thereby resembling the French and Americans). '[W]e do not take much notice of orders when we are in a tight [spot]', said one man (an Australian born in Worcestershire), 'as it is each man for himselfe [*sic*] different to the home lads [his English compatriots] who do not know what freedom is like we are used to in the bush'. '[T]he Tommies', said an Australian lieutenant, 'don't seem to take much interest in the war outside their own part of it ... whereas our chaps are always speculating on this, arguing on that or giving biscuit tin orations on something else'. 'The British', so said a sergeant (he had served before the War in the Royal Warwickshire Regiment), 'seem to be all boots, and gapes, but the Australian usually looks as if he knew what he was after'.[39]

'There is no doubt', an ambulance man told his diary, 'that our men are hard and even cruel'. Battle weary, said Dick Williams, their 'hard, fierce-looking faces' made Australians look like birds of prey compared with other men. Jimmy Downing thought that for fierceness Australians could not match the French Canadians. '[But] the special excellence of the Australian soldier', so he said, 'lay ... in his mental resources', and that virtue went beyond the few who were thoroughly educated. The Australian soldier, said Downing, and others said the same, was easy to lead if you appealed to his intelligence. And he was hard to mislead, 'for long before the matter has been officially presented to him, he will have wind of it and formed his own conclusions'.[40]

Again, the Great War, though it looks like a carnival of stupidity, was really a contest of intelligence. Each side struggled to understand and control the mighty phenomenon thus created. The process brought out a clear distinction between collective ingenuity, organised for vast purposes, and the keenness of the man alone, or at least of the man working hands-on with half-a-dozen like himself, 'forming his own conclusions'. In 1914 the Germans had aimed to win with the former, with a single swift strike, using enormous manpower and matériel, plus first-class organisation. But with less planning and preparation to start with, by 1917 the British and French were in a better position to adapt to battle methods no-one had foreseen. The Germans then gave up relying on what they called 'the brainless piling up of war material' and boasted instead of the living genius of one man alone, meaning Field Marshal Paul von Hindenburg.[41]

Starting late, the Australian effort was a mix. It was a bridging of big and small, aggregation and individuality, democratised knowledge and select expertise, like much else in this third volume of *The Europeans in Australia*. John Monash, promoted major-general, testified to the 'intellectual gifts' of the Australian in the field – on the one hand, the 'avidity' each man showed in handling new weapons, on the other, his imagination and 'political sense', the keen, critical way he had with the orders which shaped his life. 'He was always mentally alert to adopt new ideas and often to invent them.' All this gave him, so Monash said, 'a personal dignity all his own'.[42]

Brains mattered, including the handy individual aptitude so much valued in Australia. Norman Angell had predicted bureaucratic sameness in wartime. In fact, industrial warfare, like the most subtle forms of scientific management in peacetime, gave new chances to the individual. Men at the bottom had to absorb tactics of which they were part as they had never done in warfare before. Their thoughts had to be deeply engaged as they fought or prepared to fight. Women too, working in the hospitals near the front, at casualty clearing stations and in hospital ships and trains, made life and death decisions, for themselves and for the men they looked after. About 2500 women enlisted, most of them in the Australian Army Nursing Service. Of these, eight received the Military Medal for bravery and twenty-one were killed.[43]

The War also hastened invention, and all the new machinery at the front, from flamethrowers to tanks, from poison gas to fighter and bomber aircraft, required adaptability in those who used it, plus keenness in being at the end point of the business of invention. During the Battle of the Somme, from July to November 1916, which was the turning point of the War, the machine-gun was established at last as a determining feature of battle. Also, with the Somme there was a new focus on superiority in the air. Control of the sky above the front line meant that troops could be forewarned of enemy movement. For soldiers with any sense of the War as a chance to use their brains, the vehicles overhead represented an entirely new age, 'somersaulting, nose-diving, twisting right over from left to right', said Lieutenant Willie Mann. 'You could hardly believe it possible.'[44]

The machine-gun made by Vickers, armament manufacturers of Sheffield (who also produced Wolseley motor cars and the powered sheep shears well known in Australia), was the type most used by the Allies. Properly mounted and in good conditions, machine-guns could fire 500 rounds a minute, sweeping an area more than 400 metres across and 2000 metres deep. Anyone could use them, and they were soon more tactically important than the rifles of the infantry, first of all among the Germans. Following British practice, the Australians created machine-gun companies. These used Vickers, but Australians were particularly fond of the Lewis guns, invented in the United States and made in Birmingham, which were light weapons a man could move with.[45]

Everywhere there was a chance to learn, including from the enemy. Pushing forward into German trenches in March 1917, for instance, Dick Williams noticed the way machine-guns had been mounted, 'evidently as anti-aircraft defence'. 'This system', he said, 'had yet to be adopted by our artillery; we were still learning from the enemy the use of machine-guns'.[46] In no previous war had learning, and initiative built on it, been so much part of fighting.

Infantrymen also carried hand grenades. Again, German stormtroopers set the pace, but here British and Australian troops learnt from German excesses. They were told to rely on their rifles and bayonets instead of forcing their way forward with grenades. The bayonet, said Downing, was the Australians' favourite weapon. The heavy machine-gun on the one hand and the bayonet on the other summed up this War. The right tactical relationship between the two, mass slaughter being followed up by killing face to face, was the secret to success.[47] This was the nightmare world which only the most vivid pessimist could have predicted of the fourth dimension.

Ingenuity, plus complex metallurgical and chemical skills, were also applied to heavy artillery, usually involving 18-pounder (8-kilogram) field guns. By the end of the War British factories were producing over eight million shells a month, either shrapnel, high explosive, smoke or chemical. Poison gas was a by-product of chemical manufacturing. Debilitating and fatal gases were used from 1915, beginning with chlorine, followed by phosgene, which was more potent and not so easily seen, and finally mustard gas, which had the advantage of being excruciatingly painful. On the

Eastern Front, among the Russian army, gas casualties ran to half a million.[48]

A good knowledge of the qualities of steel, gas and explosives, and of the way they could be maximally destructive, drew top scientists into the War. The University of Western Australia, which had taken its first students only the year before fighting started, had two professors, Norman Wilsmore (chemistry) and Hubert Whitfield (mining and engineering), who moved over to the local War Munitions Supply Company. Whitfield went on to work in the United States and England, perfecting explosives. Medical skills were also in high demand. Nearly 6000 Australian doctors and nurses had enlisted by 1915, said to represent a third of the country's medical profession.[49]

More than this, the leading figures at Australian universities, as in Britain, took it upon themselves to educate public opinion in the large aims of the War, and to crystallise the difference between German *Kultur*, which they described as essentially militarist and authoritarian, and the civic and spiritual freedoms maintained by the Allies. 'War committees' were formed in each university and set themselves to make the mass of the people grasp the ideological dimensions of the conflict.[50]

This was the first war anywhere in which university students and graduates thought they must fight. Before this, fighting and brainwork had been quite different vocations. The Melburnian Henry Gyles Turner had said of the soldiers who went to the Sudan in 1885 that they came of 'a restless and migratory community'. They were men, said Turner, 'ready to shoot Arabs, Negroes, Abyssinians, or Egyptians indifferently at 5s. a day'. They could hardly be called patriotic.[51] Now university men, with brains like Turner's, signed up in enormous numbers and no-one doubted their patriotism. Throughout the War the fatality rate for men from Oxford and Cambridge was twice the national British average, thanks partly to the fact that many joined the infantry, where young officers were most at risk, but partly also to the enormous number joining up. The same feeling gripped Australian students. Even before Gallipoli 160 undergraduates had signed up from Melbourne University, and twice that number of former students. Many more followed. At Sydney University a list of nearly 1300 enlisted men was put together at the War's end, about equal to the male part of a single year group before it had all started.[52]

Adrian Stephen, aged twenty-two, newly graduated in law at Sydney University, went to England to join the Royal Artillery, which could promise more advanced machines than its Australian equivalent. He was enchanted with the 18-pounder. He thought it 'a beautiful weapon'. It made precision firing 'a fascinating game'. 'Brain, Brain, that is our need,' said Stephen, 'and, of course, ammunition and organisation'. It was brain that invented the weapons, and only brain could use them well.

Stephen had been an acclaimed student playwright and actor. He had liked the new realism of Henrik Ibsen and George Bernard Shaw, and in his own productions witty dialogue, à la Shaw, met with plentiful chortling. Now he was absorbed by battlefield tumult. 'I have discovered a thrill in mere noise', he said, 'such as Wagner could never give me'. In July 1916, a year before his death, he described for his parents the opening of the Battle of the Somme (really a series of battles in which over a million died). 'The bark of the 18-pounders, the cough of the howitzers, the boom of heavy guns, and the lightning rush of naval guns, swelled and merged into a jerky rumble. It was wonderful music, the mightiest I have ever heard.' It was gorgeous, pure joy. 'Somehow', he said, 'one felt inclined to laugh with the exhilaration of it'.[53] A month later the propaganda film *The Battle of the Somme* opened in London and three months later again in Australian cinemas. 'Here is war – the real thing', said the Adelaide *Advertiser*, 'war with its horror, glamour, confusion, realism, and majesty'. Thousands saw it, and the applauding, as good as at a football match, was usually enough to drown the piano accompaniment (films were still silent). At Blackboy Hill, however, the military camp near Perth, the pianist managed to soften scenes of excessive violence with the new parlour song 'When You Come to the End of a Perfect Day'.[54]

At the front, how many laughed, or felt like laughing, as Stephen did? You could gasp, wonder and be dumb, as Charles Repington said. Or you could laugh. Philip Gibbs said that joking was sparked by a ghastly mismatch, between the sweet ideals of pre-War days and the current horror. 'Men who had been brought up to Christian virtues', he said, 'found themselves compelled to live and act like ape-men; and it was abominably funny'. 'The more revolting it was', he said, 'the more, sometimes, they shouted with laughter'.[55]

Australians had their own sense of humour, often intensely black. Jimmy Downing described an attack on a German trench and his men throwing grenades, with 'Share that among you'.

> The appeal of 'Mercy, kamarad', was dismissed with a curt 'No kamarad of mine, son!' or the sardonic, 'You're just two years too late'. Knobkerries [clubs] and bayonets were hard at work. A cry was heard, 'No, no, Englander, I haaf seven kinder'. 'That's to make sure you won't have seven more.'

At Bullecourt in May 1917 the shooting of Germans as they jumped from shell hole to shell hole, edging closer and closer but in the end all killed, one by one, by Australians with cigarettes hanging from their bottom lips, seemed at the time 'irresistibly funny'.[56]

The never-ending jokes, salted with irony and insubordination, seemed typically antipodean. After Gallipoli a number of light horsemen were left behind in Egypt to defend it against the Turks, when the bulk of Australian and New Zealand troops moved on to the Western Front. It was this group which staged the famous cavalry charge at Beersheba, in October 1917, and which participated in the fall of Gaza and with it, finally, the defeat of the Ottoman empire. It included a camel corps, in which some of the roughest men served. Lost one day on patrol in the desert a cameleer lieutenant asked his men where they were. The answer, whispered cruelly in the officer's ear: 'Sir, something tells me we are on active service abroad'.[57]

IV

In October 1915 Andrew Fisher, prime minister since just after the outbreak of the War, gave way to William Morris Hughes. Hughes was a man apart from the old political establishment – energetic, abrasive, flamboyant, and a man of the people. Visiting England in 1916, he gave such electrifying speeches that for the English he became the sword-bearer of imperial solidarity. He was even spoken of as the right man to take over from Herbert Asquith, their urbane and gentlemanly prime minister. By this time there was weariness everywhere, and despair with the regimes responsible for such suffering, regimes which seemed to belong now to another age. Asquith was in fact replaced, in December 1916, by David Lloyd George, like Hughes a better medium for the fierce energy of new ways. At the same time in Germany the Kaiser was marginalised because Hindenburg seemed a more suitable idol for a people fighting to the death. In Russia the monarchy was abolished, and soon the whole Russian war effort collapsed with the Bolshevik Revolution. But in France Georges Clemenceau, 'the Tiger', became prime minister, declaring 'total war'.[58]

For Australia total war, as it was now played out, meant several things. It meant more authority for the federal government over the states. Given that this was a war for the empire, that process was helped by the presence of an able and strong-minded governor-general, Sir Ronald Munro Ferguson.[59] For Hughes it meant, in particular, the end of voluntary enlistment and a more thorough form of conscription. Hughes was determined that, as in other countries involved, all Australian men liable for military service at home (all aged between eighteen and sixty) should also be available for the front. He organised two plebiscites to test opinion on what he knew would be a difficult political move within his own Labor Party, and he failed both times.

The non-Catholic churches were behind him. In fact, their clergy had demanded something like total war from the start. As a form of moral cleansing this conflict could not be half-hearted. 'Christianity was not peace', said the Anglican rector of Moree, in north-west New South Wales, 'but ruthless, uncompromising war, war to a finish … war to the knife against selfishness, and greed and lust'. This War, he said, had to be understood on those terms. The conscription campaigns were to split the Labor Party, for some of whom this was a conflict of capital. And they split the country. The bitterness ran very deep, dividing the Australian population as it had never been divided before. This went far beyond the business of finding Huns in our midst, and it meant venomous criticism of all men of a fighting age who for various reasons chose not to fight. Many families depended on their men for sheer survival, and for everyone the test of priorities, household or nation, was always hard. It was an impossible choice, say, for many farmers, whose family livelihoods would have collapsed without them.[60]

It also set Protestant against Catholic, in a conflict of loyalties which divided the empire itself. The Easter Rising in Dublin, in 1916, demanding Irish independence from Britain, was the work of a few. But it was savagely repressed, which further complicated the allegiance of men and women everywhere of Irish background, who were mainly Catholic, adding in turn to Protestant suspicions.

At the front, on the other hand, national solidarity flourished. In December 1917 the two Anzac corps were rearranged to create a single Australian Army Corps, in a powerful assertion of unified national purpose. From this time, as far as possible, the various Australian divisions were all under one commander, first Birdwood and then Monash. The Australian Corps was a vanguard force in Britain's Fourth Army, under General Sir Henry Rawlinson.[61]

Army corps were an arrangement which came into its own during this War. A vast, slow-moving contest called for unified control over more or less fixed areas, and army corps were the answer. Within the dominion of an army corps webs of expertise and authority were built up. Within each area clerks, draughtsmen, intelligence analysts, cartographers, photographers, printers, drivers, cooks, cyclists, grooms, storekeepers, ambulance and medical staff, telegraphists, mechanics (there were hundreds of lorries), electricians, engineers and labourers were linked by roads, rail, telegraph, telephone, dispatch riders, carrier pigeons and messenger dogs. They all had to be fed and housed as well as possible. The trenches alone, reinforced as much as they could be, were a network as complicated as a town.[62]

With five divisions Monash had the biggest army corps ever assembled, increasing to 200,000 men (roughly a third of the population of Melbourne), and his command also included a squadron of the Australian Flying Corps. All were assembled at a crucial point on the Western Front, along the Somme to the east of Amiens. Monash now reached the extraordinary climax of what, at twenty-four years old, he had called his 'race for a position in the world'. He had just the right parcel of abilities, and he was qualified, if anyone was, to lead others into the fourth dimension, into the cataclysm of modernity. According to the most authoritative military commentator of the time, the Englishman Basil Liddell Hart, he was better suited to the new mass fighting than any other commander in the War, thanks to his 'great constructive and organising brain'. 'Monash', said a member of the federal parliament who visited the front line during the War, 'is one of the "biggest" and brainiest men I have ever met'.[63]

Monash had spent the years before the War working with concrete, which for modern building was as important as steel.

Reinforced concrete came to Australia in the 1890s, and as a contracting engineer Monash had taken the lead in new methods of building bridges (with T-girders), silos and water tanks. He learnt to argue and educate through maps and diagrams, and during the War he took great pride in the work done in France by his Topographical Section, which kept up a steady stream of maps, so that everyone would think as their commander did, fitting future movements into the landscape. His air squadron similarly gathered and printed air photographs of the enemy lines. Thousands of maps and photographs were distributed to the troops before each action, and Monash boasted about the result on the day before each battle: 'numerous small groups of men [could be seen] gathered around their sergeant or corporal, eagerly discussing these maps and the photographs and the things they disclosed, the lie of the land, the wire, the trenches, the probable machine-gun posts, the dug-outs and the suspected enemy strong points'.[64] He built on mass schooling and on all those lessons in geography which had been part of the buzz of classroom work for at least a generation.

Monash was vain, but his was partly the vanity of a teacher who sees other brains answering his own. He knew how intractable deep contests of will and intelligence could be. His own marriage had been good training. At the front line he made a point of staging large conferences of senior men, including the technical services (heavy artillery, tanks, aircraft), where he explained, debated and settled every detail of imminent battles. These gave an unusual dynamic to the written orders. The meetings were highly effective, Monash said, because they meant 'an exhaustive and educative interchange of views'. He was extremely lucid, if long-winded, and he enjoyed the argument likely to follow from bold proposals. Senior staff might object, as one of them recalled. '"That can't be done, you can't do it that way." And he'd say "General, I think it can you know," in his smiling way. He ... never showed any personal animosity.' It was wonderful to watch. '[Y]ou could see the brain-work in it.'[65]

Monash saw in fellow Australians, as he put it, 'a curious blend of a capacity for independent judgment with a readiness to submit to self-effacement in a common cause'. He brought that out in argument. By talking with everyone together he set up what he called 'a responsive spirit of competition'. It was an appeal to individuality, which his subordinates copied. 'A perfected modern battle plan', he said, 'is like nothing so much as the score for an orchestral composition'. The timing had to be perfect. 'Every individual unit must make its entry at precisely the proper moment, and play its phrase in the general harmony.'[66]

On both sides, ordinary soldiers were encouraged to wear wristwatches, which like tennis had once been thought unmanly. Verdi Schwinghammer had a luminous watch, to which he was riveted during the half-hour before each battle, but he dropped it on night patrol. 'I felt lost', he said, 'without the time on me'.[67] With Monash, watches were synchronised to the second before battle. This was time and motion, this was scientific management, to perfection. 'The very magnitude of his plans', said Dick Williams, 'were doubted by some seasoned soldiers, so used had they become to the old type of attack set with a very limited objective', but magnitude plus precision, and the inclusion of all ranks in a perfect system of scientific management, proved him right. John Scott, from Sydney, was in the front line at Amiens on 8 August 1918. 'Oh the wonderfulness of the organisation', Scott said. 'You could simply feel it, it permeated the whole atmosphere and was splendid.'[68]

Monash came into his own during the climactic period of the War. He found the work all-absorbing. It was like a vast machine, with your own brain at the centre of everything. There were 'always some loose screws somewhere that want tightening up, and some stiff bearings that want oiling, and the furnaces need constant stoking, or else the fire will go out'. With so much to do, when the action was hot, it was vital to keep 'one's thinking machinery cool'.[69]

Especially at corps level, everything depended on good

communications, and here too ingenuity made great strides during the War. To start with there was a complete mismatch between the sudden mass of objects and humanity on the one hand and information technology on the other. No-one knew what anyone else was doing. By 1917 all this was greatly improved. Aeroplanes came into their own, not only for fighting from the air with machine-guns and for bombing, but also for carrying documents, dropping them, for instance, at convenient places wrapped in or trailing coloured streamers for identification purposes, in response to variously coloured flares on the ground. The enemy used fireworks to illuminate their targets. The Germans, said Verdi Schwinghammer, 'had the contract for lighting up nomansland [the space between the trenches] thereby saving us the trouble and expense'.[70]

But communication could still be very slow. Information about the other side, gleaned from prisoners and from sorties by air, could be skilfully collated and analysed, but it still had to be distributed. The telephone was a vital link among senior officers, but they were often a long way from each other and also from the front line, where no telephones existed. Coordinating men and machines could be particularly hard.[71]

Monash won when he did because he was so careful with communications. Among his great triumphs, the Battle of Hamel, on 4 July 1918, depended on persuading the troops that the tanks they had were an improvement on the previous model, itself an effort in communication. But the scheme at Hamel also brought together infantry, artillery, tanks and aircraft much more tightly than had ever been tried before, and it became a model for British army tactics. Expert in getting the word out wherever it helped, Monash also took real pleasure in concealing his intentions from the other side. At Hamel he used a range of subtle subterfuges beforehand, under extreme secrecy and tight control, and everything took place as intended down to the last detail, with a prize of 1600 prisoners. The capture of Mont-St-Quentin and Péronne, on 1–2 September

1918, was even more remarkable, the single greatest feat of the War, according to General Rawlinson. Monash always said that engineering was basic to modern warfare, and in this case everything depended on his engineers repairing bridges as they went, so that his forces could swoop on the enemy stronghold unawares.[72]

V

After months at the front, let alone years, said Dick Williams, it was hard sometimes to remember what home and family meant. The other men were everything. 'Away from the company any one of us felt like a lost dog and on return was greeted with yells and what would be regarded in other walks of life as obscene insults.' That was what it meant to be 'pals' and 'cobbers'. Even when it was all over and men prepared to go home, it might be hard to pull yourself away. John Scott, waiting to go, spoke of 'hankering to be back' at the front. '[W]hen you are in the line', he said, 'facing the same enemies fear, death & other horrors you are absolutely one'. Lost in that deep solidarity, a state of complete self-sacrifice, Scott told his family, 'one gets momentary glimpses of that truer and greater democracy which is opening out to solve all human problems'.[73] Thanks to the deep divisions, especially in the debate on conscription, it was a democracy fading from view in Australia itself.

Scott's feeling was a genuine mystery, and it goes to the heart of Charles Bean's typical soldier. It had in it that 'something beyond' which Bean sensed for a moment among a circle of passengers on board the steamship on the River Darling, and also a little of that 'inherent good' which Elsie Birks's people looked for at their sweeter intervals beside the River Murray. From this circle of closeness Scott's family at home was shut out.

Certainly, on both sides of the front line there were quarrels all the way down. The British and French commanders grated on each other. The Bavarians resented the Prussians, whose aggressive ideological energy they did not always share. The Australians resented the British. Among the Australians themselves the relief roster could be a seriously vexed issue, the men of one division objecting to another getting more than its share of rest.[74] Each AIF (Australian Imperial Force) battalion came from a particular state, and local loyalties were strong. Hence the battle cry of one Maitland man at Gallipoli: '[W]e will show them what sunny N.S. Wilshmen [*sic*] can do'. But that lessened with time. A man's battalion remained all-important. It was his home base. But the hard years on the Western Front meant that state-by-state feeling was merged more completely in being Australian. As a nurse (unnamed) from Ararat, Victoria, said of the wounded men she looked after, 'One seems to have a fellow-feeling for the Victorians, but it makes no difference, they are all Australians. In fact my best friends [among them] are from New South Wales and Queensland'.[75] John Scott's feeling of being 'with "the boys"' took on national dimensions.

Before and during the period of the Australian Army Corps the men lived in cities of trenches and connecting tunnels. Sometimes inoperative through water, mud and slippage, at best they could be highly elaborate. 'The tunnels', said Edward Lynch, a soldier, 'all connect up with each other and are called streets, bearing the name plates like real streets, and are lit by electricity and have gas-proof doors'.[76] In these cities, as among street dwellers in Sydney and Melbourne, there grew up a language, perfected among the mud, although some terms had originated in the sand of Egypt and some went back to the Boer War. Each man had his temporary piece of real estate, his 'possie', from which he could 'hop over' when called on to fight. There was a certain amount of military bureaucratese, the language of the 'business man' at war. Men learnt and used words such as 'camouflage', a new term, taken from French. They spoke of being 'entrained', 'detrained', or 'disentrained'. 'Arrived Bailleul', John Scott told his diary, 'detrained and marched to Meteren'. But even officers could ridicule such pretentious lingo.

Terms embedded in ordinary conversation were much more robust, though they could convey falsehood as easily as truth. Truth varied. Rumours ('the latrine wireless', 'the oil') ran continuously up and down the trenches. Some were true – 'dinkum', 'the good oil', 'good guts'. Others were 'furphies'.[77]

There was a widespread belief that men could feel before a battle whether they would be wounded or killed. 'Alright – I know I'm going to die, even if I stop here', said a man forced to fight when he felt (rightly) he would be killed. 'I expect my career to be a very short one in France and will end one day or another very soon now', so another man told his father. His two brothers had already died. He too was correct.[78]

While the world of home might seem barely real, less real than death, it too haunted the subconscious. Adrian Stephen spoke of hearing of the bleat of a French sheep, and of finding his mind suddenly shift, as he put it, to 'the sunlit plains extended', to the silent heat and vast horizon of the country beyond Sydney. At Fromelles a man hit with a German shell started suddenly raving, shouting out to his mother to 'shut the gate', as if the oncoming enemy was livestock rushing into the wrong paddock – 'until, exhausted, he moaned in a way horrible to hear'.[79]

After Gallipoli maimed men started to come home from battle, confronting listeners with their distinctive talk. 'Now you young fellows, look at me; I'm going back. I left an eye over there, but that's nothing. I won't have to close one now to take aim to pop a Turk over.' In some minds, men of fighting age still at home were 'shirkers', 'mongrels', barely men, who left the work of national defence to others. The papers started publishing lists of 'Killed in Action' and 'Rolls of Honour', schoolteachers kept a record of former pupils who had fallen, and there was talk of an 'Australian roll of honour'. The idea of dying 'for Australia' took hold. It was possible still, sometimes, in the 'mighty nation' in the North of the continent, for men to give their lives 'for Queensland'. But everywhere, more or less, the talk of national sacrifice now took continental form, driving, for instance, the anger about conscription.[80]

When Ellen Ward, mother of a farming family at Carboor East, near Wangaratta, heard of the death of her son, Grenville, in June 1917, as a granddaughter recalled, '[s]he just lay on the bed for days and days and sobbed and sobbed'. Grenville was one of three boys abroad, and two were lost.[81] It was impossible to write down that feeling, but many tried. When Drummer Ted Heydon died, in France, aged twenty-three (blue eyes, fresh complexion, smoked a pipe), ten notices were sent in all at once, like a sudden burst of tears. From an aunt and uncle: 'A hero laid beneath French sod, / With honour has returned to God'. From his Grannie: '[D]ead in the prime of his lovely manhood and glory; far from them that loved him so dear'. From his girlfriend, Mattie:

> He marched away so bravely
> His young head proudly held,
> His footsteps never faltered,
> His courage never failed.

And from his poor mother:

> He fought, and for Australia
> Lasting glory won,
> And so, tho' sore at heart, we say
> 'O Lord, Thy will be done.'

Mrs Heydon gave in more to her feelings when it came to choosing something for the battlefield gravestone:

> A grave in France
> With the grass o'ergrown,

A grave in the heart of his Mother,
His form lies lifeless and lone in one,
But he lives in the heart of the other.

But this was way beyond the limit a standard stone could hold.[82]

In neighbouring columns, headed 'Births', the papers went on callously announcing the future. My other grandfather, my mother's father, joined the AIF in March 1916. He was a civil engineer, five years out from graduation, and the second of three brothers. He had spent eighteen months in the Intelligence Corps before the war broke out, and he then moved on to the Intelligence Section of the Australian Engineers. There he was, still in Sydney, at the start of 1916. Meanwhile, his younger brother had enlisted, lingered in hospitals in India and Egypt with dysentery and enteritis, fought at Gallipoli, come home, and gone off again to France. His elder brother had followed in February. Finally, Tom Wilkins himself, though five weeks married, began the brief training which would make him fit for engineering work in the field. He sailed in July, leaving his young wife with her family. Sufficiently brave but the least aggressive of men, he was what those already at the front called, with typical sarcasm, a 'deep thinker', implying that he had paused too long.[83]

During his four months in France, on the Somme with the 1st Field Company of Engineers, he was knocked over three times by explosions, once in December (the month Ted Heydon was killed), and twice in January. The trauma, described in his case as shellshock (though that soon came to mean long-term disability), was the result of men meeting, in an instant, all the vast mechanical and scientific impact of war, the full weight, as it were, of the twentieth century. Another soldier said it was like the kick of a draughthorse. 'My mouth was open and rigid, my hands clutched my stomach, and my limbs felt as if they had been petrified ... [F]or days afterwards my senses were as if I had been stunned.' Tom Wilkins ended up in hospital in London, physically and emotionally smashed, his body shaking, racked with headaches (which lasted all his life) and dreaming 'horrid dreams'. In April his younger brother was killed at Hermies, aged twenty-four, one of 353 lost on the Allied side alone in a single morning.[84]

In the midst of this fatal cataclysm a telegram reached him. It had been originally tapped out in the telegraph office at Dubbo, a wool and wheat town in central-western New South Wales (estimated population 4710), near where Ina, his wife, was living. It was from her parents and it read, 'INA DAUGHTER BOTH WELL'.[85] The daughter was my mother, from whom, in powerful ways, comes this book.

Such is death. Such is life.

Afterword

I

Ernst Jünger, the German stormtrooper, spoke of the way total war, with its massive suffering and death, gave him a new feeling for Germany. In spite of all the high language beforehand, the Fatherland had long been for Jünger 'an empty thought veiled in symbols'. Now, from within the immensity of conflict, in its last stages, Germany's 'clearer and brighter essence' emerged. The old clutter of duchies and kingdoms was a nation at last. The Australian Adrian Stephen perceived for his own country too, buried in tragedy, some such 'clearer and brighter essence'.[1] Felt among young men on both sides, and set out by skilled writers, this was a twentieth-century enthusiasm. This was what happened when refined self-awareness managed to digest appalling violence.

Adrian Stephen had no time for men who would not enlist, or for any anti-conscription verbiage. '[I]t is not a case for argument or reason', he said. 'It it a question of right or wrong, of patriotism or unpatriotism – which is beyond argument.' It was not just that defeat would be unbearable. We had discovered an unfathomable source of life at our Centre, which a man ignored at his peril. 'Australia has at last found a "soul"', said Stephen. Compared with that great revelation, 'the life of a man is as nothing'.[2]

At the same time, the life of the individual man at the front, his particular attachments, his quirks and comforts, his pain and fear, were everything. Enormous efforts were made to look after him. The telegram mentioned at the end of the previous chapter, announcing to Tom Wilkins the birth of his daughter, had passed through the Postal Unit established by the Australian Imperial Force in Islington, London, along with a mass of other mail to and from men serving in Europe. During a single six-month period at this stage of the War the women of the Postal Corps, sitting in their regimented rows, handled more than 101 million letters, plus parcels, packets and newspapers – averaging more than fifty letters per soldier per month.[3] In that sense, the life of each man, fragile and cherished, was wrapped around with paper.

Greatly improved standards of general literacy, far beyond that in any previous war, meant that each man could be given the utmost attention, by the Defence bureaucracy, by writers in home papers, by the many periodicals the troops themselves produced in the trenches, and by distant family and friends. When Charles Bean said that 'the big thing in the war for Australia was the discovery of the character of Australian men', he subsumed them as a type. But he was also thinking of them as individuals, because individuality was for him their richest virtue.[4]

In hospitals the testimony of nurses and medical men said the same, though among the pull of competing priorities it was frequently necessary for them to sacrifice the one to the many, and the apparently hopeless case to those with better chances. The scale of conflict was eternally complicating. Between a third and a half of all mail passing through the Islington exchange had to be redirected, and the business of tracing recipients, in light of constant movement from unit to unit, from place to place, in and out of hospital and on and off leave – and with some men vanished, either dead or missing – was a mighty challenge. Meanwhile, the Base Records Office at Victoria Barracks in Melbourne tracked soldiers' movements as far as it could and kept inquiring families informed as to where it thought they were.[5]

The Europeans in Australia had been bureaucratic from the moment of first settlement. The mounting and management of the First Fleet in 1786–88, plus the few years of mere survival which followed, made up an administrative achievement unique in its day. (See volume 1 of this book.) The movement in the other direction now, the shipping of so many Australians to Europe, was just as remarkable. It juggled the individual in a mighty mass.

The staff at the Department of Defence, at its headquarters in Melbourne, multiplied between five and six times during the War, ending at nearly 1500. Their work penetrated the depths of life in Australia itself, though it might be represented there by men who were not public servants, by the doctors who checked the fitness of aspiring soldiers, and by the clergy who had the task of calling on families to tell them that their men were dead.[6] The department created hundreds of thousands of individual soldiers' files (now to be seen online), a mass of official jargon picked out with the most painful human detail, tedium linked with heroism, intricate certainty with vague doubt, in a galaxy of interconnected stories.

At the same time other monuments, carrying name after name, adding up to many thousands, were being put up out of doors. The rolls of honour which had started to appear in newspapers after Gallipoli were transferred to permanent war memorials, as communities everywhere set themselves to remember every individual who served. The great memorials in the capital cities stood only for each state, but they were called 'national war memorials' all the same, perhaps because when it came to raw emotion the sense of smaller, older nationhood and closer kin lived on. Only in the 1930s were they to be followed by an Australian War Memorial in Canberra, the federal capital (opened 1941).[7]

Almost as soon as possible, however, a standard ceremony for the newer and larger nation was designed to mark Anzac Day, 25 April. Its sacred flame and its focus on young heroes had a pagan feel, like the opening ceremony of the revived Olympic Games. But it drew on the hopes of clergy, expressed during the debates on Federation, for a national faith. In the 1890s Charles Strong had wanted an Australian church which would be 'the home and nursery of all the best and noblest aspirations of our Commonwealth', and Archdeacon Lefroy had spoken of a new form of worship, distilling the 'national character'. In 1916 the Reverend David Garland, of Brisbane, proposed that 25 April be 'Australia's All Souls Day', a day when all could meet in one faith.[8] Anzac Day thus matched Anglican tradition in particular, but from the start outgrew it.

Australia had found a soul, as Adrian Stephen said, but a way had also been found to embrace all souls. Was even this enough? In 1901, when a 'national memorial' was first suggested for Melbourne to mark the sacrifice of Victorians in the Boer War, the *Coburg Leader* had noticed some opposition. 'It is true', said the *Leader*, 'that monuments cannot materially benefit the fallen, but they can help to keep alive the sense of duty and patriotism of a people'. Doubts continued after the Great War, though war memorials were starting to dot the landscape. 'I am not in favour of all this kind of thing,' said Rebecca Hinds, whose invalid husband died years after his return, 'as we wives and mothers do not need them to remind us of those we have lost'. She struggled for a livelihood. 'Why worry over the dead', she said. 'I'm sure they would not wish it, if they only knew how we who are left are treated.'[9]

II

Priorities of this sort, largely but not wholly women's priorities, priorities arising from the absolute importance of small places, from the merest households and the most straightforward feelings, never quite fitted the higher agendas. Such issues of local geography and local talk have run right through this volume. During the War there was also a women's bureaucracy, which tended to each man. The Australian Red Cross, formed in Melbourne at the start of the War, was led by Lady Helen Munro Ferguson, wife of the governor-general. Helen Ferguson was an energetic woman with 'a mind', as her husband said, 'quite unrivalled for business'. With headquarters in her drawing room, the wartime Red Cross eventually had 2200 self-managing branches throughout Australia, from town to town, staffed with volunteers, who coordinated local efforts and took in donations. Altogether it raised nearly £5 million, an enormous sum, spent largely on soldier comforts.[10]

From 1915 it took on the problem of lost men, with a Wounded and Missing Enquiry Bureau, set up first in Egypt but then in London. This part of the work was led by Vera Deakin, Alfred Deakin's daughter. Taking hundreds of inquiries from Australia every week, Miss Deakin's volunteers wrote to officers, chaplains, hospital matrons and German prisoner-of-war camps, and travelled themselves all over Britain and the Front. They made 10,000 reports a year on missing men. Often they could only confirm the worst fears of families, but they used a human touch that Defence staff lacked. They passed on every shred of detail, including regular hospital reports, believing, as they told the brother of Corporal Kenton Moore, that 'you would be anxious to have every particular which comes to hand'. The Moore case was one of dead or missing. Defence made detailed inquiries too, but it was the Red Cross which assured Angus Moore, in half-a-dozen additional words, that they understood 'a little of your great anxiety'.[11]

Defence did not always like it. '[W]e were often met with suspicion', Vera Deakin said, 'and eventually jealousy, as we had made ourselves felt as a sort of court of appeal for relatives who were unsuccessful in obtaining satisfaction from the military authorities'. For some men Lady Helen Munro Ferguson was also an irritant. She insisted on chairing her own finance committee meetings. 'Lady H ... likes to have a finger in every pie ... I am sure we could do better work, if we had a man in the chair.'[12]

Women were deeply entangled in the conflict, much more than in any previous war. At the front, the solidarity of men might make home ties seem unreal, as they said themselves. Nevertheless, in the minds of many, perhaps most, the War made sense because of family. Four-fifths of enlisted men were unmarried, but a war of citizen soldiers was at least a war of sons and brothers. They felt that.

Private feeling, and what HB Higgins called 'the wonderful family instinct', were things of final weight for this generation. The War posed grave public duties. But the private man, the man caught in a network of feeling, mattered now as much or more than the public man.[13] Soldiers used their family letters to set out their duty, as if family alone could justify and judge it. The War destroyed many families, but family needs – an accountability to kin – wove themselves tightly through it.

The usual form of leadership among women at the time has been called 'maternalist'. Its purpose was to give public weight to good womanhood by making the priorities of the home the main drivers of public life.[14] During the War many men showed attitudes like this. They were fighting, they said, for small things as well as for big things, 'for Australia and home', as one of them put it, or (to his family) 'for you and my country'. In the middle of this network of feeling were the nurses who looked after wounded men at the front and in dedicated hospitals in England. Anne Donnell, in Normandy in 1917–18, discovered that the men she cared for made her a substitute 'for the time being [for] their dearest ones', which was, she said, a very hard part to play. 'Sister', a man, on hearing that he was maimed for life, told her, 'but you're worth fighting for'. Two hundred million letters a year, backwards and forwards, wove the same story. In October 1915 the English nurse Edith Cavell was executed by a German firing squad for organising the escape of British and French soldiers caught in Belgium. The case of Nurse Cavell – skilled, adventurous, high-minded, self-sufficient, steadfast, a type of the new womanhood – made the same point. Empire-wide, her death was a powerful reason for enlisting.[15]

More and more women were trained, and were training each other, to work in networks and teams. Was this 'a new medium', as predicted for women by the Englishman WL Courtney? It certainly meant new ways of friendship. 'We sit in a row and scream laughing', wrote Kitty McNaughton, another nurse on the Western Front, about the women's lavatory arrangements. Ida Mockridge, her hut-mate, was Kitty's particular friend. During brief hours of rest, she said, 'we [she and Ida] sit by the fire & write, read & smoke & tell tales to each other', forgetting altogether 'the rest of the crowd'. It was always talk, plus deep reliance, one on the other, among life and death, and among demands utterly new to both of them: 'What I would do without Ida I do not know'.[16]

As the First Fleet approached Botany Bay in January 1788 and as the first dim outline of land came into view, one of the more ebullient officers, fear and apprehension notwithstanding, could hardly contain his excitement.

> The wind was now fair [he said], the sky serene, though a little hazy, and the temperature of the air delightfully pleasant: joy sparkled in every countenance, and congratulations issued from every mouth. Ithaca itself was scarcely more longed for by Ulysses, than Botany Bay by the adventurers who had traversed so many thousand miles to take possession of it.

That quotation appears at the beginning of volume 1 of this book. In February 1919 Anne Donnell, aboard the troopship *Margha*, approached the coast of Western Australia in a similar state of heightened excitement. 'I can't sleep', she said, 'for the anticipated pleasure of meeting my own folk in Perth, and seeing that part of God's own country again'. She smelt it before she saw it, 'an uncommon scent, and we fancy it savours of trees so we just call it "the smell of Australia"'. There was deep disappointment when only the West Australians were allowed to disembark, and at the fact that only one message of welcome reached the ship before it turned south, from the Red Cross ('but the Red Cross has always done the nicest things').[17]

Although she had relations in Perth, Anne Donnell's own home was Adelaide. Port Adelaide was reached on 28 February. 'It was a perfectly glorious day. I look towards the Adelaide hills, and listen to the music of the band that is welcoming us from the shore. Flags are flying, crowds are on the wharf.' And now, not the smell but the noise. '[T]here are shouts of greetings and Sammy Lunn's voice is louder than all the rest, but I can't stop to listen to what he is saying.' Sammy Lunn was everyone's friend, a centre of jokes, impersonations, admiration and thanks in Adelaide, one of those enigmatic men who always attract attention and always add happiness. Over four years he had worn himself out looking after soldiers' interests and, with no bureaucracy at all, had collected over £8000 for the cause, 'mostly in coppers and small silver coins'.

'Cameras', said Anne Donnell, 'seem to be everywhere. I eagerly see one dear familiar face, another, and another, and as I go up the gangway to them and set my foot on my own native land again I inwardly breathe a word of thanksgiving'.[18]

Notes

Where multiple sources are cited in a note, they are arranged in order of creation date.

Abbreviations

ADB *Australian Dictionary of Biography* (18 vols), Melbourne
Age *The Age* (Melbourne)
AMM Archives of Mary MacKillop and the Sisters of St Joseph of the Sacred Heart, Sydney
Argus *Argus* (Melbourne)
ATCJ *Australian Town and Country Journal* (Sydney)
ML Mitchell Library, State Library of New South Wales, Sydney
NLA National Library of Australia, Canberra
NSW *RMPI* New South Wales, Public Instruction Department, *Report of the Minister of Public Instruction upon the Condition of Public Schools Established and Maintained under the Public Instruction Act of 1880*, Sydney (to be found in the relevant annual volumes of the New South Wales Legislative Assembly *Votes and Proceedings*)
RBE South Australia, Central Board of Education, *Report of the Board of Education*, Adelaide (exact title varies; to be found in the relevant annual volumes of the *Parliamentary Papers of South Australia*)
RMCE South Australia, Education Department, *Report of the Minister Controlling Education with Appendices*, Adelaide (to be found in the relevant annual volumes of the *Parliamentary Papers of South Australia*)
SMH *Sydney Morning Herald*
Vic. *RMPI* Victoria, Education Department, *Report of the Minister of Public Instruction*, Melbourne (to be found in the relevant annual volumes of the Victorian Legislative Assembly *Votes and Proceedings*)

Foreword

1 Tim Rowse, 'Mabo and Moral Anxiety', *Meanjin*, vol. 52, 1993, pp. 229–52.
2 Nicholas Brown, 'Government, Law and Citizenship', in Alison Bashford & Stuart Macintyre (eds), *The Cambridge History of Australia* (2 vols), vol. 2, Melbourne 2013, p. 427.
3 James R Flynn, *What Is Intelligence? Beyond the Flynn Effect*, Cambridge 2009 (2007), pp. 1–2; Siew Ching Ang, Joseph Lee Rodgers & Linda Wänström, 'The Flynn Effect within Subgroups in the U.S.: Gender, Race, Income, Education, and Urbanization Differences in the NLSY-Children Data', *Intelligence*, vol. 38, 2010, pp. 367–84.
4 Walter J Ong, *Orality and Literacy: The Technologizing of the Word*, London 1982, p. 105; Alan Atkinson, *The Commonwealth of Speech: An Argument about Australia's Past, Present and Future*, Melbourne 2002, pp. xiv–xv.

5 Flynn, pp. 24–9; Steven Pinker, *The Better Angels of Our Nature: The Decline of Violence in History and Its Causes*, London 2011, pp. 175–7, 580–92, 689–90.

6 Benedict Anderson, *Imagined Communities: Reflections on the Origin and Spread of Nationalism*, London 1983.

7 Alan Atkinson, *The Europeans in Australia* (3 vols), vol. 1, Melbourne 1997, pp. ix, x.

8 Michael Polanyi, *Personal Knowledge: Towards a Post-Critical Philosophy*, New York, NY, 1962 (1958), pp. 3–4; Flynn, p. 34.

9 Peter Brown, *The Rise of Western Christendom*, Oxford 2003, p. 1.

10 ibid., pp. 14–15.

11 *Barrier Miner* (Broken Hill), 2 June 1898.

12 James Bryce, *The American Commonwealth* (2 vols), vol. 1, New York, NY, 1898 (1888), p. 15; *Official Record of the Proceedings and Debates of the Australasian Federation Conference, 1890*, Melbourne 1890, p. 34 (Andrew Inglis Clark); *Official Report of the National Australasian Convention Debates: Sydney, 2 March to 9 April, 1891*, Sydney 1891, p. 253 (Andrew Inglis Clark).

13 Rowse, p. 231 (quoting Hobbles Danyarri, 1980).

14 *The Letters of John Keats* (2 vols), vol. 1, ed. Hyder Edward Rollins, Cambridge 2011, p. 264 (John Keats to Benjamin Haydon, 8 April 1818).

15 Meg Vivers, 'Dealing with Difference: Evidence of European Women in Early Contact History', *Journal of Australian Colonial History*, vol. 4, 2002, pp. 72–96; Margaret Vivers [Meg Vivers], 'Female Perspectives: A Study of the Colonial Texts of Adelaide Bowler and Lucy Gray', PhD thesis, University of New England 2007; Meg Vivers, *Castle to Colony: The Remarkable Life and Times of Lucy Sarah Gray (1840–1879)*, Hughenden 2011; Meg Vivers, 'Landscapes or Inscapes? Alternative Perspectives on Frontier Life', *Journal of Australian Colonial History*, vol. 13, 2011, pp. 151–82.

16 Bain Attwood, *The Making of the Aborigines*, Sydney 1989; Deborah Bird Rose, *Dingo Makes Us Human: Life and Land in an Australian Aboriginal Culture*, Cambridge 2000 (1992); Bain Attwood, 'The Law of the Land or the Law of the Land? History, Law and Narrative in a Settler Society', *History Compass*, vol. 2, 2004, pp. 1–30; Bain Attwood, *Possession: Batman's Treaty and the Matter of History*, Melbourne 2009.

17 Anne Coote, 'Imagining a Colonial Nation: The Development of Popular Concepts of Sovereignty and Nation in New South Wales with Particular Reference to the Period between 1856 and 1860', *Journal of Australian Colonial History*, vol. 1, 1999, pp. 1–37; Anne Coote, 'Space, Time and Sovereignty: Literate Culture and Colonial Nationhood in New South Wales up to 1860', PhD thesis, University of New England 2005; Anne Coote, 'Out from the Legend's Shadow: Re-thinking National Feeling in Colonial Australia', *Journal of Australian Colonial History*, vol. 10, 2008, pp. 103–22; Anne Coote, 'Science, Fashion, Knowledge and Imagination: Shopfront Natural History in 19th-Century Sydney', *Sydney Journal*, vol. 4, 2013, pp. 1–18.

18 Raymond Evans, *Fighting Words: Writing about Race*, Brisbane 1999; Raymond Evans, *A History of Queensland*, Cambridge 2007.

19 Henry Reynolds, 'The Island Colony: Tasmania – Society and Politics 1880–1900', MA thesis, University of Tasmania 1963; Henry Reynolds, *The Other Side of the Frontier: Aboriginal Resistance to the European Invasion of Australia*, Townsville 1981; Henry Reynolds, *North of Capricorn: The Untold Story of Australia's North*, Sydney 2003. See also Henry Reynolds, *A History of Tasmania*, Cambridge 2012.

20 Graeme Davison, 'Sydney and the Bush: An Urban Context for the Australian Legend'; and John B Hirst, 'The Pioneer Legend', *Historical Studies*, vol. 18, 1978, pp. 191–209, 316–37.

21 Stuart Macintyre, *A Colonial Liberalism: The Lost World of Three Victorian Visionaries*, Melbourne 1991; Frank Bongiorno, *The People's Party: Victorian Labor and the Radical Tradition, 1875–1914*, Melbourne 1996; Frank Bongiorno, *The Sex Lives of Australians: A History*, Melbourne 2012. Some of Bongiorno's other work is listed in the Bibliography.

22 Sylvia Lawson, *The Archibald Paradox: A Strange Case of Authorship*, Melbourne 1983; Ann Moyal, *Clear across Australia: A History of Telecommunications*, Melbourne 1984; Ann Moyal, 'Invention and Innovation in Australia: The Historian's Lens', *Prometheus: Critical Studies in Innovation*, vol. 5, 1987, pp. 92–110.

23 Marilyn Lake, 'Mission Impossible: How Men Gave Birth to the Australian Nation; Nationalism, Gender and Other Seminal Acts', *Gender and History*, vol. 4, 1992, pp. 305–22; Marilyn Lake, *Getting Equal: The History of Australian Feminism*, Sydney 1999; Marilyn Lake & Henry Reynolds, *Drawing the Global Colour Line: White Men's Countries and the Question of Racial Equality*, Melbourne 2008.

24 John B Hirst, *The Sentimental Nation: The Making of the Australian Commonwealth*, Melbourne 2000; Bob Birrell, *Federation: The Secret Story*, Sydney 2001.

25 Roger Chickering & Stig Förster (eds), *Great War, Total War: Combat and Mobilization on the Western Front, 1914–1918*, Cambridge 2000; William Philpott, *Three Armies on the Somme: The First Battle of the Twentieth Century*, New York, NY, 2010.

26 Bill Gammage, *The Broken Years: Australian Soldiers in the Great War*, Melbourne 1975 (1974); Stephen Garton, *The Cost of War: Australians Return*, Melbourne 1996; KS Inglis, *Sacred Places: War Memorials in the Australian Landscape*, Melbourne 1998; Joy Damousi, *The Labour of Loss: Mourning, Memory, and Wartime Bereavement in Australia*, Cambridge 1999.

27 John A Moses, 'Was There an Anzac Theology?', *Colloquium*, vol. 35, 2003, pp. 3–13; John A Moses, 'Anglicanism and Anzac Observance: The Essential Contribution of Canon David John Garland', *Pacifica*, no. 19, February 2006, pp. 58–77; Joan Beaumont, *Broken Nation: Australians and the Great War*, Sydney 2013.

28 Richard Sennett, *The Fall of Public Man*, Cambridge 1977 (1976); Stephen Kern, *The Culture of Time and Space, 1880–1918*, Cambridge, Mass., 1983; Ann Curthoys & John Docker, *Is History Fiction?*, Sydney 2010.

29 CMH Clark, *A History of Australia* (6 vols), Melbourne 1962–87; Mark McKenna, *An Eye for Eternity: The Life of Manning Clark*, Melbourne 2011; Bashford & Macintyre.

30 Yvonne Preston, 'Moral Issues and Mass Democracy in Australasia 1890–1914', unpublished report, February 2009.

31 Atkinson, *Commonwealth of Speech*, pp. 23–6.

Exploring

1 Brian Greene, *The Fabric of the Cosmos: Space, Time, and the Texture of Reality*, London 2004, pp. 9–10.

1 The Elements

1 CEW Bean, *The 'Dreadnought' of the Darling*, London 1911, pp. 34–8; CEW Bean, 'Account for Effie', 1924, Australian War Memorial, Canberra, 3DRL/3520/10a.

2 CH Kirmess, *The Australian Crisis*, London 1909, p. 144; Bean, *'Dreadnought'*, pp. 3–8.

3 Bean, *'Dreadnought'*, pp. 4–5; Valerie Fletcher, 'The Northern Territory, 1895 to 1900: The Royal Commission of 1895 and Its Results', MA Qual. thesis, University of Queensland 1988, p. 5.

4 John Milton, *Paradise Lost* (1667), in *The Poems of John Milton*, ed. John Carey & Alasdair Fowler, London 1968, p. 612.
5 Dennis Butts, 'Introduction', in Henry Rider Haggard, *King Solomon's Mines*, Oxford 1989 (1885), pp. vii–viii.
6 *Age*, 9 December 1876.
7 Joseph Conrad, *Lord Jim: A Romance*, New York, NY, 1905 (1899–1900), p. 56; Stephen Kern, *The Culture of Time and Space, 1880–1918*, Cambridge, Mass., 1983, pp. 190–1; Melissa Bellanta, 'Mobilising Fictions; or, Romancing the Australian Desert, 1890–1908', *History Australia*, vol. 1, 2003, pp. 15–30; Melissa Bellanta, 'Fabulating the Australian Desert: Australia's Lost Race Romances, 1890–1908', *Philament*, no. 3, *Offbeat*, April 2004, viewed 16 December 2013, <sydney.edu.au/arts/publications/philament/issue3_Critique_Bellanta.htm>.
8 Honoré de Balzac, 'Colonel Chabert' (French 1832), in Honoré de Balzac, *The Atheist's Mass and Other Stories*, trans. Clara Bell, London 1896, p. 125.
9 Nathaniel Hawthorne, *The Marble Faun; or, The Romance of Monte Beni*, London 1910 (1860), p. 274.
10 *Advertiser* (Adelaide), 10 August 1894; Eleanor Hogan, 'Dreaming State', *Meanjin*, no. 2, 2013, p. 6.
11 Bernard O'Dowd, 'Australia' (1900), in *The Poems of Bernard O'Dowd*, ed. Walter Murdoch, Melbourne 1941, p. 35; Bean, *'Dreadnought'*, p. 142; Arthur Conan Doyle, *The Lost World and Other Stories*, Ware, Herts., 1995 (*The Lost World*, 1912), p. 134.
12 WA Horn, 'Introduction', in Walter Baldwin Spencer (ed.), *Report on the Work of the Horn Scientific Expedition to Central Australia* (4 parts), part 1, London 1896, p. ix; Joseph McCabe, 'Australia: A Museum of Living Antiquities', *Lone Hand* (Sydney), November 1910; Libby Robin, *How a Continent Created a Nation*, Sydney 2007, pp. 32–4.
13 *Argus*, 18 December 1880.
14 WH Willshire, *The Land of the Dawning*, Adelaide 1896, p. 34.
15 Charles Todd, *Meteorological Observations Made at the Adelaide Observatory during the Year 1878*, Adelaide 1878, p. x.
16 EC Stirling, 'Anthropology', in Spencer, part 4, London and Melbourne 1906, p. 83; David H Turner, *Life before Genesis: A Conclusion; An Understanding of the Significance of Australian Aboriginal Culture*, New York, NY, 1987 (1985), pp. 53–85; Deborah Bird Rose, *Dingo Makes Us Human: Life and Land in an Australian Aboriginal Culture*, Cambridge 2000 (1992), pp. 106–24.
17 Robert Graham & Peter Thorley, 'Central Australian Aboriginal Stone Knives: Their Cultural Significance, Manufacture and Trade'; and RG (Dick) Kimber, 'The Dynamic Century before the Horn Expedition: A Speculative History', in SR Morton & DJ Mulvaney (eds), *Exploring Central Australia: Society, the Environment and the 1894 Horn Expedition*, Sydney 1996, pp. 83, 99–100.
18 RG (Dick) Kimber, 'Smallpox in Central Australia: Evidence for Epidemics, and Postulations about the Impact', *Australian Archaeology*, vol. 27, 1988, pp. 63–8; Kimber, 'Dynamic Century', pp. 93–4.
19 DJ Mulvaney, 'The Chain of Connection', in Nicolas Peterson (ed.), *Tribes and Boundaries*, Canberra 1976, pp. 72–94; Luise A Hercus, '"How We Danced the Mudlunga": Memories of 1901 and 1902', *Aboriginal History*, vol. 4, 1980, pp. 17, 19–21 (quoting Mick McLean Irinjili); Erich Kolig, 'Post-Contact Religious Movements in Australian Aboriginal Society', *Anthropos*, vol. 82, 1987, pp. 254–5; Tony Swain, *A Place for Strangers: Towards a History of Australian Aboriginal Being*, Cambridge 1993, pp. 219–33; Kimber, 'Dynamic Century', pp. 95–6; Iain Davidson,

Isabel Tarrago & Tom Sullivan, 'Market Forces', in Val Donovan & Colleen Wall (eds), *Making Connections: A Journey along Central Australian Aboriginal Trading Routes*, Brisbane 2004, pp. 12–23. Iain Davidson and Luise Hercus kindly helped with this material.

20 Luise A Hercus, 'Mick McLean Irinjili', *Australian Institute of Aboriginal Studies Newsletter*, n.s., no. 7, 1977, pp. 27–8.

21 Richard Colyer, 'Welsh Cattle Drovers in the Nineteenth Century' (3 parts), part 3, *National Library of Wales Journal*, vol. 19, summer 1975, p. 6; Swain, pp. 229–32.

22 Peter Taylor, *An End to Silence: The Building of the Overland Telegraph Line from Adelaide to Darwin*, Sydney 1980, p. 147; Graham & Thorley, pp. 74–89; Kimber, 'Dynamic Century', pp. 94, 99; Lesley Head & Richard Fullagar, 'Hunter-Gatherer Archaeology and Pastoral Contact: Perspectives from the Northwest Northern Territory, Australia', *World Archaeology*, vol. 28, 1997, pp. 418–28.

23 Milton, p. 583.

24 Ernest Giles, *Australia Twice Traversed: The Romance of Exploration* (2 vols), vol. 1, London 1889, p. lv.

25 Andrew Barton Paterson, *An Outback Marriage*, Sydney 1906, pp. 12–13.

26 Peter Bell, 'Three Tracks across the Desert', in Donovan & Wall, pp. 94–5.

27 In Canada in 1891 the population of Montreal was 216,650 and of Toronto 181,000.

28 Conrad, p. 263.

29 James M Osborn, *Young Philip Sidney*, New Haven, Conn., 1972, p. 515 (quoting Fulke Greville, *The Life of the Renowned Sir Philip Sidney*, London 1652, pp. 129–30).

30 Giles, vol. 1, p. 81.

31 *Australasian* (Melbourne), 23 January, 6 February 1875. For an example of the last image mentioned, see *Queenslander* (Brisbane), 9 May 1891.

32 *Australasian* (Melbourne), 23 January 1875.

33 Mary Gilmore, *Old Days, Old Ways: A Book of Recollections*, Sydney 1934, pp. 245–6.

34 Mrs Campbell Praed [Rosa Campbell Praed], *My Australian Girlhood: Sketches and Impressions of Bush Life*, London 1902, p. 104; Gilmore, p. 220.

35 *Riverine Herald* (Echuca), 28 November 1874.

36 *Illustrated London News*, 2, 9 January 1875; *ATCJ*, 6 March, 27 November 1875; 'The Loss of the Scotch Patrick', in Patrick Shuldham-Shaw & Emily B Lyle (eds), *The Greig-Duncan Folk Song Collection* (7 vols), vol. 1, Aberdeen 1981, p. 77.

37 *ATCJ*, 6 March 1875; Geoffrey Raby, AP Kershaw & Marcel Van Dijk, 'Climate', in Wray Vamplew (ed.), *Australians: Historical Statistics*, Sydney 1987, pp. 68–9.

38 Michael McKernan, *Drought: The Red Marauder*, Sydney 2005, p. 5.

39 TK Abbott, 'On Wells in Liverpool Plains', *Journal and Proceedings of the Royal Society of New South Wales*, vol. 14, 1880, pp. 281–92; WH Williamson, 'Water: From Tank Stream to Snowy Scheme', in Council of the Royal Society of New South Wales (ed.), *A Century of Scientific Progress: The Centenary Volume of the Royal Society of New South Wales*, Sydney [1968], pp. 55–7.

40 Samuel Taylor Coleridge, 'Xanadu' (1816), in *The Complete Poetical Works of Samuel Taylor Coleridge* (2 vols), vol. 1, ed. Ernest Hartley Coleridge, Oxford 1912, p. 297; William James, 'Is Life Worth Living?', in William James, *The Will to Believe and Other Essays in Popular Philosophy, and Human Immortality*, New York, NY, 1956 (*The Will to Believe and Other Essays in Popular Philosophy*, 1896), p. 62.

41 JD Hennessey, *An Australian Bush Track*, London 1896, pp. 208–10; George Firth Scott, *The Last Lemurian: A Westralian Romance*, London 1898, pp. 38–46; Mrs Campbell Praed [Rosa Campbell Praed], *Fugitive Anne: A Romance of the Unexplored Bush*, London 1902, pp. 103, 161.

42 Miles Franklin, *Joseph Furphy: The Legend of a Man and His Book*, Sydney 1944, pp. 147–8 (quoting Joseph Furphy).
43 Abbott, pp. 284, 288–9; Noela Corfield, 'The Development of the Cattle Industry in Queensland 1840–1890', BA thesis, University of Queensland 1959, p. 105.
44 Kern, p. 228.
45 *Argus*, 14 December 1881; Harley Wood, *Sydney Observatory, 1858 to 1958*, Sydney Observatory Papers no. 31, Sydney 1958, pp. 14–15.
46 Bernard O'Dowd, *Conscience and Democracy*, Melbourne 1902, p. 3; HG Wells, *An Englishman Looks at the World: Being a Series of Unrestrained Remarks upon Contemporary Matters*, Hazleton, Penn., 2004 (1914), pp. 9–10; Richard R Yeo, 'Scientific Method and the Rhetoric of Science in Britain, 1830–1917', in John A Schuster & Richard R Yeo (eds), *The Politics and Rhetoric of Scientific Method: Historical Studies*, Dordrecht 1986, pp. 264–73; Frank Bongiorno, 'Bernard O'Dowd's Socialism', *Labour History*, no. 77, November 1999, p. 102.
47 HG Wells, 'The Star' (1897), in HG Wells, *Tales of Time and Space*, London 1900, pp. 51–2.
48 HC Russell, 'Anniversary Address', *Journal and Proceedings of the Royal Society of New South Wales*, vol. 11, 1877, pp. 14–15; *SMH*, 5 February 1877. See also Victoria, Legislative Assembly, *Votes and Proceedings*, 1877–78, vol. 2, p. 690 (Robert Ellery).
49 *SMH*, 9 February 1877.
50 HC Russell, 'Anniversary Address', *Journal and Proceedings of the Royal Society of New South Wales*, vol. 16, 1882, pp. 13–14, 17, 20–1; Clark C Spence, *The Rainmakers: American 'Pluviculture' to World War II*, Lincoln, Nebr., 1980, pp. 9–18.
51 *Minutes of Proceedings of the Intercolonial Meteorological Conference Held at Sydney on 11th, 13th, 14th November 1879*, Sydney 1880, p. 6 (transactions, 13 November 1879).
52 ibid.
53 Kern, pp. 11–12; Mark Monmonier, *Air Apparent: How Meteorologists Learned to Map, Predict, and Dramatize Weather*, Chicago, Ill., 1999, pp. 39–54.
54 *Intercolonial Meteorological Conference Held at Sydney*, p. 6 (transactions, 13 November 1879); *Minutes of Proceedings of the Intercolonial Meteorological Conference Held at Melbourne on the 21st, 22nd, 25th, 26th, and 27th of April 1881*, Melbourne 1881.
55 HC Russell, 'Meteorological Periodicity', *Journal and Proceedings of the Royal Society of New South Wales*, vol. 10, 1876, p. 166; HC Russell's answers to Dr Ross's questions, 16 December 1898, ML, MS Ar 19/1.
56 Russell, 'Meteorological Periodicity', pp. 151–77.

2 Australia's Rural Code

1 George Main, *Heartland: The Regeneration of Rural Place*, Sydney 2005, p. 144.
2 Mary Gilmore, *Old Days, Old Ways: A Book of Recollections*, Sydney 1934, pp. 103, 105, 106.
3 WG Blomfield, 'Pioneering Days of Miriam Vale and District, Queensland, etc.', n.d., ML, A3076, p. 46 (Blomfield was born in 1869, near Armidale, and died in 1955); Gilmore, pp. 183–4.
4 Andrew Barton Paterson, 'Saltbush Bill' (1896), in *The Collected Verse of A.B. Paterson*, Sydney 1923, p. 37; Tom Collins [Joseph Furphy], *Such Is Life*, Sydney 1962 (1903), p. 6; Gilmore, pp. 137–43.
5 Tom L McKnight, *The Long Paddock: Australia's Travelling Stock Routes*, Armidale 1977, pp. 23, 26, 29, 42–70; Julian Croft, *The Life and Opinions of Tom Collins: A Study of the Works of Joseph Furphy*, Brisbane 1991, pp. 127–31.

6 Terry L Anderson & PJ Hill, 'The Evolution of Property Rights: A Study of the American West', *Journal of Law and Economics*, vol. 18, 1975, pp. 168–72; R Taylor Dennen, 'Cattlemen's Associations and Property Rights in Land in the American West', *Explorations in Economic History*, vol. 13, 1976, pp. 424–8.

7 Jeremy Adelman, *Republic of Capital: Buenos Aires and the Legal Transformation of the Atlantic World*, Stanford, Calif., 1999, pp. 193–250.

8 Samuel Amaral, *The Rise of Capitalism on the Pampas: The Estancias of Buenos Aires, 1785–1870*, Cambridge 1998, pp. 140–56.

9 Adam Lindsay Gordon, 'The Sick Stockrider' (1870), in *The Poetical Works of Adam Lindsay Gordon*, London 1913, p. 132.

10 *Historical Records of Australia*, ed. Frederick Watson, series 1, *Governors' Despatches to and from England*, vol. 21, *October 1840 – March 1842*, Sydney 1924, p. 127 (Sir George Gipps to Lord John Russell, 19 December 1840).

11 Miles Franklin, *Joseph Furphy: The Legend of a Man and His Book*, Sydney 1944, p. 95 (quoting Joseph Furphy to Cecil Winter, 1901).

12 Oswald Spengler, *The Decline of the West* (2 vols), vol. 1, *Form and Actuality*, trans. CF Atkinson, New York 1926 (German 1918), p. 62 (original emphasis); Stephen Kern, *The Culture of Time and Space, 1880–1918*, Cambridge, Mass., 1983, pp. 138–9, 223–9.

13 Frank M Turner, *The Greek Heritage in Victorian Britain*, New Haven, Conn., 1981, pp. 213–44.

14 SG Butlin, *Foundations of the Australian Monetary System, 1788–1851*, Sydney 1953, pp. 340–5.

15 Sir William Blackstone, *Commentaries on the Laws of England* (4 vols), vol. 2, London 1825 (1765–69), pp. 391–5.

16 Kern, pp. 132–9 (quoting Ernst Mach, *Space and Geometry in Light of Physiological, Psychological, and Physical Inquiry*, trans. Thomas J McCormack, Chicago 1906 [German 1901]).

17 NG Butlin, *Investment in Australian Economic Development, 1861–1900*, Cambridge 1964, pp. 72–5, 79.

18 Sir Walter Scott, 'The Two Drovers' (1827), in Sir Walter Scott, *Waverley Novels* (25 vols), vol. 20, Edinburgh 1853, p. 364. For borders in this period, see Frank Bongiorno, '"The Men Who Made Australia Federated Long Ago": Australian Frontiers and Borderlands', in Paul Readman, Cynthia Radding & Chad Bryant (eds), *Borderlands in World History, 1700–1914*, Chapel Hill, NC, 2014 (kindly shown to me before publication by Frank Bongiorno).

19 SG Butlin, pp. 44–5, 96–7; Bruce Davidson, 'Agriculture', in Wray Vamplew (ed.), *Australians: Historical Statistics*, Sydney 1987, pp. 80–1.

20 Alexander Bruce, 'Agricultural Societies and Their Work', *New South Wales Agricultural Gazette*, vol. 2, part 1, October 1891, p. 17; Stephen Dando-Collins, *Pasteur's Gambit: Louis Pasteur, the Australasian Rabbit Plague and a Ten Million Dollar Prize*, Sydney 2008, p. 185.

21 Geoffrey Serle, *The Rush to Be Rich: A History of the Colony of Victoria, 1883–1889*, Melbourne 1971, pp. 192, 315–16, 320–6.

22 New South Wales, Legislative Council, *Votes and Proceedings*, 1845, vol. 1, p. 3 (Select Committee on the Lien on Wool Act); AR Buck, '*Attorney General v Brown* and the Development of Property Law in Australia', *Australian Property Law Journal*, vol. 2, 1994, pp. 133–8.

23 Queensland, Parliament, *Debates*, vol. 9, 15 June 1869, p. 336. See, for this and other matters, Noela Corfield, 'The Development of the Cattle Industry in Queensland 1840–1890', BA thesis, University of Queensland 1959.

24 Queensland, Parliament, *Debates*, vol. 9, 15 June 1869, p. 336; vol. 12, 10 May 1871, p. 188; vol. 13, 18 January 1872, p. 493; Queensland, Legislative Assembly, *Votes and Proceedings*, 1875, vol. 1, pp. 559–62 (Case of McAndrew: offence under the Brands Act); Anderson & Hill, pp. 173–5.

25 Queensland, Legislative Assembly, *Votes and Proceedings*, 1875, vol. 2, p. 1327 (PR Gordon); 1878, vol. 3, p. 1013 (PR Gordon).

26 ibid., 1881, vol. 2, p. 966 (PR Gordon, quoting Alfred Compigné).

27 PR Gordon, *Fencing as a Means of Improving Our Pasture Lands, and Its Advantages to the Stock-Owners and the Colony*, Sydney 1867, pp. 23, 26–7.

28 NG Butlin, pp. 73–5.

29 FM Bailey & PR Gordon, *Plants Reputed Poisonous and Injurious to Stock*, Brisbane 1887, pp. 13, 17, 65, 67.

30 Peter King, 'Gleaners, Farmers and the Failure of Legal Sanctions in England', *Past and Present*, no. 125, November 1989, pp. 123–31, 137–40.

31 Queensland, Parliament, *Debates*, vol. 11, 9 December 1870, p. 211; Western Australia, Parliament, *Debates*, n.s., vol. 8, 12 September 1895, p. 968 (Sir John Forrest); Bruce Baskerville, 'Creating Arcadia? A History of Nature Conservation in Colonial Western Australia 1870–1914', BA thesis, University of Western Australia 1992, pp. 43–55 (quoting, pp. 45–6, EH Laurence to Roger Goldsworthy, 16 June 1880; Commissioner for Crown lands, memorandum, 22 June 1880). Dongara's name was then Dongarra Flats.

32 *Argus*, 26 April 1860.

33 *New South Wales Government Gazette*, 23 August 1870, pp. 1822–3; 24 January 1873, p. 260.

34 Application for extension of an existing common and accompanying papers, 15 September 1879, Victorian Public Record Office, Melbourne, 44/P/494/Benalla and Winton Common, 1860–79.

35 Victoria, Legislative Assembly, *Votes and Proceedings*, 1870, vol. 1, pp. 205–12 (commons areas). The figures include town commons and/or goldfields commons and amalgamated town and goldfields commons. For quantity to free selectors, see Stuart Macintyre, *A Colonial Liberalism: The Lost World of Three Victorian Visionaries*, Melbourne 1991, p. 101.

36 David Gaunson to Francis Longmore, 30 May 1877; and minute, 6 June 1877, Victorian Public Record Office, Melbourne, 44/P/432/G7932.

37 Trustees were not to behave like landowners. They were barred from offering leases, and, on the other hand, events proved that the government was quite ready to redistribute common land for sale.

38 *New South Wales Government Gazette*, 9 November 1866, p. 2713; *SMH*, 9 May 1873; *Armidale Chronicle*, 22, 29 January 1874. See *Commons Regulation Act 1873* (NSW) (36 Vic. no. 23), s. 3.

39 CEW Bean, *The 'Dreadnought' of the Darling*, London 1911, p. 318.

40 New South Wales, Legislative Assembly, *Votes and Proceedings*, 1875, vol. 4, pp. 461–2 (Conference of the Chief Inspectors of Stock for the Australian Colonies).

41 NG Butlin, pp. 16–24, 35–6.

42 Richard W Slatta, 'Rural Criminality and Social Conflict in Nineteenth-Century Buenos Aires Province', in John J Johnson, Peter J Bakewell & Meredith D Dodge (eds), *Readings in Latin American History* (2 vols), vol. 2, *The Modern Experience*, Durham, NC, 1985, pp. 218–27; Amaral, pp. 150, 159–81.

43 Blomfield, pp. 140–5.

44 ibid., pp. 142–3 (original emphasis); Andrew Barton Paterson, 'Clancy of the Overflow' (1896), in *The Collected Verse of A.B. Paterson*, Sydney 1923, p. 16.

45 South Australia, Parliament, *Parliamentary Papers*, 1891, vol. 3, p. 123 (FJ Gillen); Robert Foster, 'Rations, Coexistence, and the Colonisation of Aboriginal Labour in the South Australian Pastoral Industry, 1860–1911', *Aboriginal History*, vol. 24, 2000, pp. 1–2.

46 Deborah Bird Rose, *Hidden Histories: Black Stories from Victoria River Downs, Humbert River and Wave Hill Stations*, Canberra 1991, pp. 49–53; Mary Anne Jebb, *Blood, Sweat and Welfare: A History of White Bosses and Aboriginal Pastoral Workers*, Perth 2002, pp. 27–46.

47 Knut Dahl, *In Savage Australia: An Account of a Hunting and Collecting Expedition to Arnhem Land and Dampier Land*, London 1926 (Norwegian 1897), pp. 254–5; South Australia, Parliament, *Proceedings of the Parliament of South Australia*, 1899, vol. 2, no. 77, pp. 83–4 (William Russell, quoting Paul Foelsche, in questions put to JL Parsons before Select Committee on Aborigines Bill); Rose, pp. 49–53.

48 Foster, pp. 1–26; Tracey Banivanua & Penelope Edmonds, 'Indigenous and Settler Relations', in Alison Bashford & Stuart Macintyre (eds), *The Cambridge History of Australia* (2 vols), vol. 1, Melbourne 2013, p. 352.

49 Sir Anthony Musgrave to Lord Derby, 17, 27 December 1884, National Archives, London, CO 234/45, fols 147–52, 173–9; Queensland, Royal Commission Appointed to Inquire into the Circumstances under Which Labourers Have Been Introduced into Queensland from New Guinea and Other Islands, etc., *Report: With Minutes of Evidence Taken before the Royal Commission*, Brisbane 1885, p. 828.

50 Queensland, Royal Commission, p. 866 (Ro-bah-he); Kay Saunders, *Workers in Bondage: The Origins and Bases of Unfree Labour in Queensland, 1824–1916*, Brisbane 1982, pp. 20–6.

51 Queensland, Legislative Assembly, *Votes and Proceedings*, 1876, vol. 3, pp. 118 (William Matson), 130 (JL Kirby); W Gray, 'The Kanaka Labour Traffic in the New Hebrides', *South Australian Register* (Adelaide), 10 August 1893; Saunders, pp. 26–33; Michael Quinlan, 'Australia, 1788–1902: A Workingman's Paradise?', in Douglas Hay & Paul Craven (eds), *Masters, Servants, and Magistrates in Britain and the Empire, 1562–1955*, Chapel Hill, NC, 2004, pp. 232–3, 238–9; Raymond Evans, *A History of Queensland*, Cambridge 2007, pp. 132–4; Marilyn Lake, 'Colonial Australia and the Asia-Pacific Region'; and Cindy McCreery & Kirsten McKenzie, 'The Australian Colonies in a Maritime World', in Bashford & Macintyre, vol. 1, pp. 553–5, 580–2.

52 Adrian Merritt, 'The Historical Role of Law in the Regulation of Employment: Abstentionist or Interventionist?', *Australian Journal of Law and Society*, vol. 1, 1982, pp. 56–8; Frank Bongiorno, *The People's Party: Victorian Labor and the Radical Tradition, 1875–1914*, Melbourne 1996, pp. 14–16.

53 John Merritt, *The Making of the AWU*, Melbourne 1986, p. 138.

54 William Guthrie Spence, *History of the A.W.U.*, Sydney 1961, p. 16.

55 HJ Gibbney, 'Howe, John Robert (1861–1920)', *ADB*, vol. 9, 1983, p. 379.

56 Jillian Oppenheimer, 'Shearing "Difficulties" in New England in 1888', *Australia 1888*, no. 11, May 1983, pp. 62–4.

57 Spence, pp. 17–18; Lee Kelly, '"Knights of the Blade": Shearers in 1888', *Australia 1888*, no. 8, September 1981, p. 52; Ellen McEwen, 'Moving around New South Wales', *Australia 1888*, no. 14, September 1986, pp. 38–9.

58 *Queenslander* (Brisbane), 21 February 1891; RJ Sullivan, 'The Maritime Strike, 1890', in DJ Murphy (ed.), *The Big Strikes: Queensland 1889–1965*, Brisbane 1983, pp. 65–79.

59 *Queenslander* (Brisbane), 28 February, 2 May 1891.

60 ibid., 14 March, 9 May 1891.

61 ibid., 21 February, 14 March 1891.

62 RJ Sullivan & RA Sullivan, 'The London Dock Strike, the Jondaryan Strike and the Brisbane Bootmakers' Strike, 1889–1890', in Murphy, *Big Strikes*, pp. 56–7; Elizabeth Morrison, *Engines of Influence: Newspapers of Country Victoria, 1840–1890*, Melbourne 2005, pp. 290–9.

63 DJ Murphy, 'Queensland', in DJ Murphy (ed.), *Labor in Politics: The State Labor Parties in Australia, 1880–1920*, Brisbane 1975, p. 136; Sullivan & Sullivan, pp. 50–3.

64 *Queenslander* (Brisbane), 2 May 1891.

65 Frank Bongiorno, 'The Origins of Caucus 1856–1901'; and Stuart Macintyre, 'The First Caucus', in John Faulkner & Stuart Macintyre (eds), *True Believers: The Story of the Federal Parliamentary Labor Party*, Sydney 2001, pp. 3–16, 17–29.

3 The Commonwealth of Speech

1 Mary Gilmore, *Old Days, Old Ways: A Book of Recollections*, Sydney 1934, p. 217.

2 William Westgarth, *Half a Century of Australasian Progress: A Personal Retrospect*, London 1889, p. 21.

3 William Shakespeare, *The First Part of the History of Henry IV*, Cambridge 1958 (1598), p. 52 (act 3, scene 1, lines 52–4).

4 1 Kings 19:12; *Argus*, 5 February 1878.

5 *Cornwall Chronicle* (Launceston), 1 April 1878; Telecom Australia, *'The Palace of Winged Words': The Development of Telephone Exchanges in Australia*, Melbourne [1980], p. 3; Ann Moyal, *Clear across Australia: A History of Telecommunications*, Melbourne 1984, pp. 72–3.

6 *Brisbane Courier*, 1 February 1878; Queensland, Legislative Assembly, *Votes and Proceedings*, 1878, vol. 2, p. 542 (WJ Cracknell).

7 *Cornwall Chronicle* (Launceston), 1 April 1878; Stephen Kern, *The Culture of Time and Space, 1880–1918*, Cambridge, Mass., 1983, pp. 187–8 (quoting Arnold Bennett, *Your United States: Impressions of a First Visit*, Plainview, NY, [1912]).

8 Frank A Soden, Reuban Phillip Watson, Bruce Whitehead & Neilma E Watson (comps), *100 Years of the Telephone*, private limited edn, Melbourne 1976, pp. 24–41; Jim Bateman, *History of the Telephone in New South Wales*, Sydney 1980, pp. 13–17.

9 *Australasian Sketcher* (Melbourne), 29 January 1881; *ATCJ*, 10 September 1887.

10 *ATCJ*, 10 September 1887; Myra S Merfield, 'The Australian Telephone-Girl', *New Idea* (Melbourne), 1 January 1903; Edwin J Houston & AE Kennelly, *The Electric Telephone*, New York, NY, 1906, pp. 249–50.

11 *ATCJ*, 10 September 1887.

12 *Worker* (Brisbane), 24 February 1906; *West Gippsland Gazette* (Warragul), 6 March 1906.

13 Ralph Waldo Emerson, 'The Poet' (1844), in Ralph Waldo Emerson, *Essays and Lectures*, 2nd series, ed. Joel Porte, New York, NY, 1983, pp. 449, 465.

14 Tom Collins [Joseph Furphy], *Such Is Life*, Sydney 1962 (1903), pp. 155, 207, 316. Julian Croft points out that Tom Collins was not Joseph Furphy, but Furphy's creation. Nevertheless, Collins is sometimes also Furphy's mouthpiece. See Julian Croft, *The Life and Opinions of Tom Collins: A Study of the Works of Joseph Furphy*, Brisbane 1991.

15 Collins, p. 321; Lynda C Mugglestone, *Talking Proper: The Rise of Accent as Social Symbol*, Oxford 2003, pp. 17–49.

16 HC Russell, 'Meteorological Periodicity', *Journal and Proceedings of the Royal Society of New South Wales*, vol. 10, 1876, p. 166.

17 CEW Bean, *The 'Dreadnought' of the Darling*, London 1911, p. 279; CEW Bean, 'Account for Effie', 1924, Australian War Memorial, Canberra, 3DRL/3520/10a.

18 Bean, *'Dreadnought'*, pp. 326–7. See also Vic. *RMPI* for 1886–87, p. 141 (Alfred C Williams).
19 *RBE* for 1876, p. 11 (Edward Dewhirst); Vic. *RMPI* for 1899–1900, p. 80 (James Livingstone).
20 *RMCE*, for 1885, p. 15 (Alexander Clark).
21 Vic. *RMPI* for 1886–87, p. 141 (Alfred Curlewis); for 1889–90, p. 205 (Charles Tynan); for 1890–91, p. 80 (James Livingstone).
22 *RMCE* for 1898, p. 20 (George Gill); Andrew Barton Paterson, *An Outback Marriage*, Sydney 1906, pp. 8–9.
23 Knut Dahl, *In Savage Australia: An Account of a Hunting and Collecting Expedition to Arnhem Land and Dampier Land*, London 1926 (Norwegian 1897), p. 255.
24 T Nicklin, *The Sounds of Standard English*, Oxford 1925, pp. 10–11.
25 Alexander J Ellis, *On Early English Pronunciation, with Especial Reference to Shakespere and Chaucer*, London 1869, pp. 263–6; Lynda C Mugglestone, 'A.J. Ellis, "Standard English" and the Prescriptive Tradition', *Review of English Studies*, vol. 39, 1988, pp. 87–92 (quoting, p. 88, AM Bell, *A New Elucidation of the Principles of Speech and Elocution*, Glasgow 1849).
26 *RMCE* for 1880, p. 4 (Edward Dewhirst); for 1889, p. 3 (Edward Dewhirst).
27 Vic. *RMPI* for 1884–85, p. 134 (Alfred Curlewis); for 1885–86, pp. 156–8 (Colin Campbell); for 1896–97, pp. 47–8 (William Hamilton); Mugglestone, *Talking Proper*, pp. 186–9.
28 *RMCE* for 1887, pp. xv–xvi (John Hartley); for 1888, p. 3 (Edward Dewhirst); Vic. *RMPI* for 1890–91, p. 116 (J Summers); Edward E Morris, *Austral English: A Dictionary of Australasian Words, Phrases and Usages*, London 1898, p. 224.
29 Vic. *RMPI* for 1886–87, p. 142 (James Holland).
30 ibid. for 1889–90, pp. 240–5 (Alfred Jackson).
31 *RMCE* for 1885, p. 11 (Alexander Clark); for 1887, p. 27 (Alexander Clark); *Advertiser* (Adelaide), 17 March 1913.
32 *Argus*, 21 December 1893; *RMCE* for 1897, p. 17 (IA Plummer).
33 EW Hornung, *A Bride from the Bush*, London [1890], pp. 29–31; Mrs Campbell Praed [Rosa Campbell Praed], *Nulma*, London 1898, p. 309; Mrs Campbell Praed [Rosa Campbell Praed], *My Australian Girlhood: Sketches and Impressions of Bush Life*, London 1902, p. 215; *West Australian* (Perth), 23 September 1911.
34 *Bulletin* (Sydney), 6, 13 January 1894.
35 Valerie Desmond, *The Awful Australian*, Sydney 1911, p. 16; Mugglestone, *Talking Proper*, pp. 84–5.
36 Vic. *RMPI* for 1890–91, p. 1065 (James Holland); for 1899–1900, p. 65 (William Hamilton).
37 David Stow, *The Training System of Education, for the Moral and Intellectual Elevation of Youth*, Edinburgh 1846, pp. 78–82; *RBE* for 1870, p. 213 (JS Jones); Derek Phillips, 'The State and the Provision of Education in Tasmania, 1839 to 1913', PhD thesis, University of Tasmania 1988, pp. 321–6; William R Johnson, '"Chanting Choristers": Simultaneous Recitation in Baltimore's Nineteenth-Century Primary Schools', *History of Education Quarterly*, vol. 34, 1994, pp. 14–16, 22.
38 *RMCE* for 1898, p. 14 (Alexander Clark).
39 ibid. for 1899, p. 13 (Alexander Clark).
40 *RBE* for 1873, p. 7; NSW *RMPI* for 1884, p. 404 (James McCredie); Vic. *RMPI* for 1887–88, p. 162 (FH Renwick); for 1889–90, p. 225 (FH Renwick).
41 Vic. *RMPI* for 1882–83, pp. 224–5 (Frederick Gladman); for 1883–84, pp. 212–13 (Frederick Gladman); for 1885–86, pp. iii–xxiv (CH Pearson); for 1886–87, pp. 145

(Alexander Stewart), 155 (John Dennant); for 1888–89, p. 215 (Peter Carmichael).

42 Samuel McBurney, *Victoria: A School Cantata Composed and Dedicated to the Singing Masters of the Victorian State Schools*, Melbourne 1875, p. 2; 'SCR', 'School Songs', *New South Wales Educational Gazette*, 1 September 1891, p. 77.

43 JE Southcott, 'Music in State-Supported Schooling in South Australia to 1920', PhD thesis, Deakin University 1997, pp. 58–62, 77–9, 107–38, 214–17.

44 *South Australian Weekly Chronicle* (Adelaide), 29 October 1859; *South Australian Chronicle* (Adelaide), 31 January 1891; *South Australian Register* (Adelaide), 9 September 1897; Southcott, p. 78.

45 *Thomas Hardy's Personal Writings: Prefaces, Literary Opinions, Reminiscences*, ed. Harold Orel, Basingstoke, Hants., 1990, p. 76 (quoting Thomas Hardy, 'Preface', in *Select Poems of William Barnes*, Oxford 1908).

46 Thomas Hardy, *Desperate Remedies: A Novel*, London 1975 (1871), p. 164.

47 Thomas Hardy, *The Return of the Native*, ed. James Gindin, New York, NY, 1969 (1878), pp. 91, 99–107.

48 Collins, pp. 314–25.

49 Victoria, *Report of the Board of Education*, Melbourne, for 1871 (Archibald Gilchrist); CH Pearson, *Report on the State of Public Education in Victoria and Suggestions as to the Best Means of Improving It*, Melbourne 1878, p. 61; Vic. *RMPI* for 1881–82, p. 215 (Alexander T Lewis); for 1896–97, p. 1853 (William Gates).

50 Mary MacKillop to Monsignor Tobias Kirby, 17 July 1873, AMM, Mary MacKillop Letters, vol. 6. Thanks to the staff at the archives for help with this material.

51 Catherine Helen Spence, *Clara Morison: A Tale of South Australia during the Gold Fever*, Adelaide 1971 (1854), p. 92 (for the final quotation – from a fictional character, but an example of Spence using characters to state her own views); Catherine Helen Spence, *Mr Hogarth's Will*, Melbourne 1988 (1865), p. 243; Catherine Helen Spence, *An Autobiography*, Adelaide 1910, pp. 28, 45, 53; Susan Magarey, *Unbridling the Tongues of Women: A Biography of Catherine Helen Spence*, Adelaide 1985, pp. 62–7. Susan Magarey gave me useful advice on this material.

52 Geoffrey C Bolton, *A Thousand Miles Away: A History of North Queensland to 1920*, Canberra 1970, pp. 54–8.

53 *Bulletin* (Sydney), 15 May 1897 (see also *West Australian Worker* [Perth], 1 February 1901, citing *Bulletin* [Sydney]); *Sunday Times* (Perth), 14 July 1907; E Jaggard, 'Bread and Democracy: F.C.B. Vosper in the Roaring Nineties', *Westerly*, no. 4, December 1977, pp. 29–46.

54 *SMH*, 20 January 1891; *Queenslander* (Brisbane), 21 February, 9 May 1891.

55 *Queenslander* (Brisbane), 21, 28 February, 14 March, 2 May 1891; Adrian Muir, 'The Trials of the Queensland Shearers, 1891', BA thesis, University of Sydney 1986, pp. 29–35 (quoting Mr Justice Harding's notebook, vol. 5, 1891, p. 48, Queensland State Archives, Brisbane).

56 *Queenslander* (Brisbane), 2, 9 May 1891; John Bastin & June Stoodley, 'F.C.B. Vosper: An Australian Radical', *University Studies in History*, vol. 5, no. 1, 1967, p. 41 (quoting *Australian Republican*, 21 February 1891); Raymond Evans, *A History of Queensland*, Cambridge 2007, pp. 121–3.

57 *Queenslander* (Brisbane), 7 March 1891.

58 Muir, pp. 36–43, 44, 46.

59 Victor Hugo, *Les Misérables*, trans. Julie Rose, London 2008 (French 1862), p. 202; Rick Rylance, *Victorian Psychology and British Culture, 1850–1880*, Oxford 2000, pp. 8, 111, 130.

60 William B Carpenter, *Principles of Mental Physiology*, London 1896 (1874), pp. xx–xxi (quoting unnamed informants).

61 Peter Watson, *The German Genius: Europe's Third Renaissance, the Second Scientific Revolution and the Twentieth Century*, London 2010, pp. 240–1 (citing Friedrich Schelling, *Ideas for a Philosophy of Nature*, [German 1797]; Friedrich Schelling, *The Grounding of Positive Philosophy*, [German 1841]).

62 Thomas Hardy, *A Laodicean: A Story of Today*, London 1951 (1881), p. 5.

63 Jens Peter Jacobsen, *Niels Lyhne*, trans. Tiina Nunnally, Minneapolis, Minn., 2008 (Danish 1880), p. 82; George Gissing, *Born in Exile*, Hasscocks, Sussex, 1978 (1892), pp. 71, 316; *Bendigo Advertiser*, 28 May 1894.

64 Will H Ogilvie, *My Life in the Open*, London 1908, p. 7.

65 Catherine Martin, *An Australian Girl*, ed. Rosemary Campbell, Brisbane 2002 (1891), p. 347.

66 Alfred Deakin, 'Boke of Praer and Praes', 19 October, 7 December 1884, 27 November 1887, NLA, MS 1540/5/7; Alfred Deakin, 'Personal Experiences of Spiritism', [1895], NLA, MS 1540/5/1189–92.

67 John Stuart Mill, *Autobiography*, London 1873, pp. 273–4.

68 Deakin, 'Boke of Praer and Praes', 26 October 1884, 21 November 1887, 19 October 1888, 6 September 1890.

69 ibid., 3 August 1884, 25 October 1885, 2 March 1890; Deakin, 'Personal Experiences of Spiritism', MS 1540/5/1277, 1540/5/1278; Alfred Deakin, autobiographical notes, 4 September 1913, NLA, MS 1540/3/30.

70 Bernard Rainbow, *Music in Educational Thought and Practice: A Survey from 800 BC*, Aberystwyth 1989, p. 212 (quoting John Curwen, 'Lessons on Singing, in Letters to a Friend Who Had Undertaken to Train a Class of Children', *Independent Magazine*, 1842, pp. 23–4 [original emphasis]).

71 Vic. *RMPI* for 1888–89, p. 226 (J Summers); Mitford M Mathews, *Teaching to Read: Historically Considered*, Chicago, Ill., 1966, pp. 77–81.

72 James C Scott, *Seeing Like a State: How Certain Schemes to Improve the Human Condition Have Failed*, New Haven, Conn., 1998, p. 153.

73 Victoria, *Ninth Report of the Board of Education*, Melbourne, for 1870, pp. 49–50 (JSC Elkington); *RMCE* for 1880, p. ix (Thomas King).

74 New South Wales, *Report of the Council of Education upon the Condition of the Public Schools*, Sydney, for 1870, pp. 213 (JS Jones), 272 (William McIntyre); for 1871 (Edwin Johnson & James W Allpass); *RMCE* for 1878, p. 22 (James Hosking).

75 Vic. *RMPI* for 1890–91, pp. 63–5 (Walter Gamble); NSW *RMPI* for 1898, p. 80 (HD McLelland).

76 Vic. *RMPI* for 1881–82, p. 718 (John Kevin); for 1898–99, pp. 48–54 (Robert Russell); Tasmania, *Annual Report of the Tasmanian Council of Education*, Hobart, for 1892, pp. 13–14 (SO Lovell); for 1894, p. 11 (SO Lovell).

77 *RMCE* for 1885, p. xviii (John Hartley); for 1886, p. 4 (Edward Dewhirst); John Barnes, *The Order of Things: A Life of Joseph Furphy*, Melbourne 1990, p. 26 (quoting Joseph Furphy, 'A Boy of the Old Brigade', n.d.).

78 Vic. *RMPI* for 1886–87, pp. 140 (Alfred Curlewis), 174–5 (JE Laing), 186 (Thomas Brodribb).

A JIGSAW FOR A CONTINENT

1 Brian Greene, *The Fabric of the Cosmos: Space, Time, and the Texture of Reality*, London 2004, p. 16.

4 Tyrannous Freedom

1 Joseph G Witton to Grace Clark, 11 August 1885, University of Tasmania Library Special and Rare Materials Collection, Hobart, C4/C346.

2 William Wetmore Story, 'Cleopatra' (1858), in Charles Dudley Warner (ed.), *A Library of the World's Best Literature, Ancient and Modern* (45 vols), vol. 35, New York, NY, 1896, p. 14,063.

3 Alfred Deakin, *The Federal Story: The Inner History of the Federal Cause, 1880–1900*, ed. JA La Nauze, Melbourne 1963 (*The Federal Story*, 1944), p. 32.

4 Joseph G Witton to Andrew Inglis Clark, 19 January 1886, University of Tasmania Library Special and Rare Materials Collection, Hobart, C4/C350; Max O'Rell [Léon Paul Blouet], *John Bull & Co.: The Great Colonial Branches of the Firm; Canada, Australia, New Zealand and South Africa*, London 1894, p. 68; Geoffrey Serle, *The Rush to Be Rich: A History of the Colony of Victoria, 1883–1889*, Melbourne 1971, p. 270.

5 *Mercury* (Hobart), 11 November 1882.

6 George B Edwards to Andrew Inglis Clark, 15 July 1883, University of Tasmania Library Special and Rare Materials Collection, Hobart, C4/C57.

7 *Official Record of the Proceedings and Debates of the Australasian Federation Conference, 1890*, Melbourne 1890, p. 36 (Andrew Inglis Clark); Andrew Inglis Clark, 'The Future of the Australian Commonwealth: A Province or a Nation?', [1902], in Marcus Haward & James Warden (eds), *An Australian Democrat: The Life, Work and Consequences of Andrew Inglis Clark*, Hobart 1995, pp. 219–20 (quoting Wendell Phillips); Alan Atkinson, 'Tasmania and the Multiplicity of Nations', *Tasmanian Historical Research Association Papers and Proceedings*, vol. 52, 2005, pp. 199–200.

8 Jack Cato, *I Can Take It*, Melbourne 1947, p. 22; Jack Cato, *The Story of the Camera in Australia*, Melbourne 1955, pp. 80–7; Henry Reynolds, 'The Island Colony: Tasmania – Society and Politics 1880–1900', MA thesis, University of Tasmania 1963, p. 46.

9 REN Twopeny, *Town Life in Australia*, London 1883, pp. 2–3; Francis Adams, *Australian Essays*, Melbourne 1886, p. 6.

10 Adams, *Australian Essays*, p. 61; Tom Collins [Joseph Furphy], *Such Is Life*, Sydney 1962 (1903), p. 8; NG Butlin, *Investment in Australian Economic Development, 1861–1900*, Cambridge 1964, pp. 129–30; Serle, pp. 3, 49.

11 Peter Watson, *The German Genius: Europe's Third Renaissance, the Second Scientific Revolution and the Twentieth Century*, London 2010, pp. 204–5.

12 Story, p. 14,065.

13 Stuart Macintyre, *A Colonial Liberalism: The Lost World of Three Victorian Visionaries*, Melbourne 1991, pp. 89–90 (quoting *Age*, 1860).

14 Vic. *RMPI* for 1874–75, p. 170 (Joseph Baldwin).

15 Henry Parkes, 'Bismarck', in Henry Parkes, *The Beauteous Terrorist and Other Poems*, Sydney 1885, p. 23; John B Hirst, *The Sentimental Nation: The Making of the Australian Commonwealth*, Melbourne 2000, pp. 9–10.

16 RA Swan, *Australia in the Antarctic: Interest, Activity and Endeavour*, London 1961, pp. 46–60; Serle, pp. 47, 48–50, 68; DJ Mulvaney & JH Calaby, *'So Much That Is New': Baldwin Spencer, 1860–1929; A Biography*, Melbourne 1985, pp. 110–13.

17 Adams, *Australian Essays*, p. 1; Vic. *RMPI* for 1888–89, p. 229 (J Main & Charles A Topp, report 'on the Schools of New South Wales, South Australia and Victoria'); *Argus*, 13 December 1893; Kathleen Fennessy, *A People Learning: Colonial Victorians and Their Public Museums, 1860–1880*, Melbourne 2007, pp. 15–16.

18 Macintyre, pp. 85–7; Marilyn Lake, 'The White Man under Siege: New Histories of Race in the Nineteenth Century and the Advent of White Australia', *History Workshop Journal*, no. 58, 2004, pp. 41–62; Marilyn Lake & Henry Reynolds, *Drawing the Global Colour Line: White Men's Countries and the Question of Racial Equality*, Melbourne 2008, pp. 75–94.

19 Alfred Deakin, 'Boke of Praer and Praes', 3 August 1890, NLA, MS 1540/5/7; Francis Adams, *The Australians: A Social Sketch*, London 1893, p. 34; Serle, p. 311 (quoting *Age*, 3 May 1888).

20 Twopeny, p. 2; Geoffrey Bartlett, 'Berry, Sir Graham (1822–1904)', *ADB*, vol. 3, 1969, pp. 151–6; Serle, pp. 8–9.

21 Victoria, Parliament, *Debates*, vol. 45, 24 June 1884, p. 231 (CH Pearson); Marian Quartly, 'A History of the Australian Natives Association, 1871–1900', PhD thesis, Monash University 1970.

22 CH Pearson, *National Life and Character: A Forecast*, London 1893, pp. 16, 182; Oscar J Falnes, 'European Progress and the "Superior" Races: As Viewed by a *Fin-de-Siècle* Liberal, Charles H. Pearson', *Journal of the History of Ideas*, vol. 15, 1954, pp. 312–21.

23 *Argus*, 10 January 1884.

24 *Official Report of the National Australasian Convention Debates: Sydney, 2 March to 9 April, 1891*, Sydney 1891, pp. 191 (Sir Thomas McIlwraith), 731 (Adye Douglas).

25 Reynolds, 'Island Colony', pp. 63 (quoting *Tasmanian News* [Launceston], 12 January 1886), 186–7.

26 *Daily Telegraph* (Launceston), 14, 21 August 1888; William Westgarth, *Half a Century of Australasian Progress: A Personal Retrospect*, London 1889, pp. 31–2; *SMH*, 1 January 1901; Reynolds, 'Island Colony', p. 267.

27 Deakin, 'Boke of Praer and Praes', 25 October 1885; Queensland, Parliament, *Debates*, vol. 75, 8 July 1896, p. 237 (Joshua Thomas Bell).

28 Mary Gilmore, *Old Days, Old Ways: A Book of Recollections*, Sydney 1934, p. 103.

29 Sir Samuel Walker Griffith, 'The Political Geography of Australia', *Proceedings and Transactions of the Queensland Branch of the Royal Geographical Society of Australasia: 6th Session, 1890–91*, vol. 6, part 1, Brisbane 1891, p. 72.

30 JS Mertle, 'The Origin and Development of Photolithography', *Australasian Printer*, April 1951, p. 30; Julie Brown, 'Versions of Reality: The Production and Function of Photographs in Colonial Queensland 1880–1900', PhD thesis, University of Queensland 1984.

31 Rolf Boldrewood [Thomas Alexander Browne], *A Sydney-Side Saxon*, Sydney 1925 (1888–89), pp. 12, 18, 32, 140–1.

32 William Guthrie Spence, *History of the A.W.U.*, Sydney 1961, p. 20.

33 Mrs Rolf Boldrewood [Margaret Maria Browne], *The Flower Garden in Australia: A Book for Ladies and Amateurs*, Melbourne 1893, pp. 2, 31–2, 98.

34 Deakin, 'Boke of Praer and Praes', 19, 21 October 1888.

35 Charles Howard Hinton, 'The Education of the Imagination', in Charles Howard Hinton, *Scientific Romances*, 2nd series, London 1896, p. 7; Daniel H Calhoun, 'Eyes for the Jacksonian World: William C. Woodbridge and Emma Willard', *Journal of the Early Republic*, vol. 4, 1984, pp. 14–26; Avril MC Maddrell, 'Discourses of Race and Gender and the Comparative Method in Geography School Texts 1830–1918', *Environment and Planning D: Society and Space*, vol. 16, 1998, pp. 84–5. Anne Coote kindly helped with this material.

36 Victoria, *Report of the Board of Education*, Melbourne, for 1870, p. 22; JJ Fletcher, 'Teaching Geography in the National Schools of New South Wales 1848–1866', in S Murray-Smith (ed.), *Melbourne Studies in Education, 1973*, Melbourne 1973, p. 194.

37 *RBE* for 1874, p. 13 (Emil Jung).

38 ibid. for 1876, p. 11 (Edward Dewhirst); *RMCE* for 1880, p. 11 (Edward Dewhirst); Hinton, p. 19.

39 NSW *RMPI* for 1881 (M Willis); for 1882 (JH Murray).

40 Victoria, *Report of the Board of Education*, Melbourne, for 1871, p. 38 (Charles A Topp); Charles E Lyne, *Life of Sir Henry Parkes, G.C.M.G.: Australian Statesman*, London 1897, p. 366 (quoting Sir Henry Parkes, speech, n.d.).

41 Keith Sinclair, *A History of New Zealand*, London 1969, pp. 88–90, 105–11, 152–5.

42 Henry Reynolds, '"Men of Substance and Deservedly Good Repute": The Tasmanian Gentry 1856–1875', *Australian Journal of Politics and History*, vol. 15, 1969, pp. 68–71; Henry Reynolds, 'Regionalism in Nineteenth Century Tasmania', *Tasmanian Historical Association Papers and Proceedings*, vol. 17, 1969, pp. 16–19; Shayne Breen, *Contested Places: Tasmania's Northern Districts from Ancient Times to 1900*, Hobart 2001, pp. 116–20, 132–50.

43 *Mercury* (Hobart), 15 September 1864; Reynolds, 'Island Colony', p. 62 (quoting *Tasmanian News* [Launceston], 11 January 1884).

44 Reynolds, 'Island Colony', pp. 51–5, 140–57, 193–258; Henry Reynolds, 'Clark, Andrew Inglis (1848–1907)', *ADB*, vol. 3, 1969, pp. 399–400; Atkinson, pp. 189–200.

45 Reynolds, 'Island Colony', pp. 44–5.

46 Sir Henry Parkes, 'An Australian Nation', *Melbourne Review*, vol. 4, 1879, p. 327.

47 Queensland, Parliament, *Debates*, vols 61–4, 1890–92.

48 PR Schlencker, 'The National Agricultural and Industrial Association of Queensland 1875–1900', BA thesis, University of Queensland 1973, pp. 43–6.

49 Deakin, 'Boke of Praer and Praes', 6 September 1890.

50 *Royal Readers: Second Series or Sequels*, no. 4, 1883, pp. 264–5. Stephen Innes of the University of Auckland Library (Special Collection) kindly helped with this material.

51 John B Hirst, *Sense and Nonsense in Australian History*, Melbourne 2009, p. 200 (quoting William Gay, 'Federation', [early 1890s]).

52 Queensland, Parliament, *Debates*, vol. 61, 9 July 1890, p. 186 (Charles Powers).

53 HC Russell, 'Anniversary Address', *Journal and Proceedings of the Royal Society of New South Wales*, vol. 11, 1877, pp. 4, 6.

54 Sally Gregory Kohlstedt, 'Australian Museums of Natural History: Priorities and Scientific Initiatives in the 19th Century', *Historical Records of Australian Science*, vol. 5, no. 4, 1983, pp. 1–29.

55 *Journal and Proceedings of the Royal Society of New South Wales*, vol. 23, 1889, pp. 46–7 (report of meeting, 5 June 1889); HC Russell, 'On Meteorite No. 2 from Gilgoin Station', *Journal and Proceedings of the Royal Society of New South Wales*, vol. 27, 1893, pp. 361–2; Ian Inkster & J Todd, 'Support for Scientific Enterprise', in RW Home (ed.), *Australian Science in the Making*, Melbourne 1988, pp. 113–15.

56 Russell, 'Anniversary Address', p. 7.

57 Richard Threlfall, 'Anniversary Address', *Journal and Proceedings of the Royal Society of New South Wales*, vol. 29, 1895, pp. 11–12; RW Home, 'First Physicist of Australia: Richard Threlfall at the University of Sydney, 1886–1898', *Historical Records of Australian Science*, vol. 6, 1984, pp. 335–8, 346 (quoting, p. 338, HS Carslaw to JJ Thomson, 31 October 1932).

58 ME Hoare, 'The Intercolonial Science Movement in Australasia 1870–1890', *Records of the Australian Academy of Science*, vol. 3, no. 2, 1975, pp. 11–15, 22–7; RW Home, 'The Problem of Intellectual Isolation in Scientific Life: W.H. Bragg and the Australian Scientific Community, 1886–1909', *Historical Records of Australian Science*, vol. 6, 1984, pp. 19–30; John Gascoigne & Sara Maroske, 'Science and Technology', in Alison Bashford & Stuart Macintyre (eds), *The Cambridge History of Australia* (2 vols), vol. 1, Melbourne 2013, p. 458.

59 Adams, *Australian Essays*, pp. 52–60; 'MUU' to the editor, *Hermes* (University of Sydney), 21 July 1887.

60 Edmond Marin la Meslée to 'the gentlemen of the Postal Conference, Sydney', 14 May 1883, ML, A2664, fol. 13; Edmond Marin la Meslée, 'Preliminary Meeting to Establish a Geographical Society' (speech, 2 April 1883), in AC Macdonald, JH Maiden & JH Myring (eds), *Special Volume of the Proceedings of the Geographical Society of Australasia*, Sydney 1885, p. 3; Gascoigne & Maroske, p. 450.

61 Jules Michelet, *Histoire de France* (4 vols), vol. 1, Paris 1880 (1833–67), p. i (preface to 1869 edn): '*Le premier je la vis comme une âme et une personne*'.

62 Jules Michelet, *The History of France* (2 vols), vol. 1, trans. WK Kelly, London 1884 (French 1833–67), pp. 264, 331, 336; Edmond Marin la Meslée, *The New Australia*, ed. and trans. Russel Ward, London 1973 (French 1883), pp. 32, 33; Edmond Marin la Meslée to Harrie Wood, 26 April 1883; and to John Shillinglaw, 28 April 1883, ML, A2664, fols 5–6, 8–9; Marin la Meslée, 'Preliminary Meeting', p. 4.

63 Michelet, *History of France*, vol. 1, p. 331; Eugen Weber, *Peasants into Frenchmen: The Modernization of Rural France, 1870–1914*, London 1977, pp. 310–13, 333–5.

64 Edmond Marin la Meslée to John Shillinglaw, 28 April 1883, ML, A2664, fols 8–9; George D Meudell, 'An Australian Protest against Imperial Federation', *Melbourne Review*, July 1885, p. 249.

65 Adams, *Australian Essays*, p. 33; *Boomerang* (Brisbane), 28 July 1888; Bruce Scates, *A New Australia: Citizenship, Radicalism and the First Republic*, Cambridge 1997, pp. 29, 153; Hugh Anderson, 'Introduction', in Hugh Anderson (ed.), *Tocsin: Contesting the Constitution, 1897–1901*, Melbourne 2000, p. xxiii. See also KS Inglis, *The Rehearsal: Australians at War in the Sudan*, Adelaide 1985, pp. 63–71.

66 Michelet, *History of France*, vol. 1, p. 323.

67 Peter Ackroyd, *Albion: The Origins of the English Imagination*, London 2004, pp. 208–15.

68 Edmond Marin la Meslée to 'the gentlemen of the Postal Conference, Sydney', 14 May 1883, ML, A2664, fol. 13; Marin la Meslée, 'Preliminary Meeting', p. 3.

69 Marcel Aurousseau, 'Notes on Geographical Associations Formed in Australia', typescript, March 1960 – April 1961, NLA, Npf 910.6294 AUR; Hoare, pp. 19–21; Tom Griffiths, *Hunters and Collectors: The Antiquarian Imagination in Australia*, Cambridge 1996, pp. 200–2.

70 Regular notice in the *Bulletin* (Sydney), from 1892; Sylvia Lawson, *The Archibald Paradox: A Strange Case of Authorship*, Melbourne 1983, p. 154; Bob Birrell, *Federation: The Secret Story*, Sydney 2001, p. 123.

71 O'Rell, p. 189; Lawson, pp. 72, 79–80, 103, 123, 212–13.

72 Adams, *The Australians*, p. 55.

73 ibid., pp. 54–5.

5 The Significance of Brain

1 *Maitland Mercury*, 13 February 1886; *Brisbane Courier*, 1 March 1887.

2 Edward Bellamy, *Looking Backward: If Socialism Comes, 2000–1887*, London 1888, p. 93; *Worker* (Brisbane), 1 March 1890; *Clarence and Richmond Examiner* (Grafton), 4 October 1890; *Brisbane Courier*, 13 October 1890; *Windsor and Richmond Gazette*, 22 November 1890.

3 Edward Bellamy, *Equality*, Sydney 1943 (1897), pp. 208–16.

4 Alfred Deakin, 'Irrigation in Australia', in *The Year-Book of Australia for 1892*, Sydney 1892, p. 91.

5 *ATCJ*, 8 May 1875.

6 *Burra Record*, 9 May 1890.

7 *ATCJ*, 2 January 1875.

8 CEW Bean, *On the Wool Track*, London 1916, pp. 124–7.

9 See also John B Hirst, *The Strange Birth of Colonial Democracy: New South Wales, 1848–1884*, Sydney 1988, pp. 203–4, 214–15.
10 Robert Yezerski, 'Burning Desires: Fighting Fires and Masculinities in Nineteenth Century Victoria', BA thesis, University of Sydney 2001, pp. 3–4.
11 *South Australian Register* (Adelaide), 26 May 1879.
12 ibid., 14 March 1878, 14 March 1884.
13 ibid., 31 May 1877.
14 Deakin, 'Irrigation in Australia', pp. 86–7, 95.
15 Victoria, Parliament, *Debates*, vol. 51, 24 June 1886, p. 447 (Alfred Deakin).
16 Sir William Blackstone, *Commentaries on the Laws of England* (4 vols), vol. 2, London 1825 (1765–69), p. 18.
17 Deakin, 'Irrigation in Australia', p. 91; SD Clark, 'Australian Water Law: An Historical and Analytical Background', PhD thesis, University of Melbourne 1971, pp. 159–86.
18 Bruce Smith, *Our Commonwealth: A Handbook of the Australian Constitution*, Sydney 1904, pp. 20–1; Martha Rutledge, 'Smith, Arthur Bruce (1851–1937)', *ADB*, vol. 11, 1988, pp. 637–9.
19 [William Lane], 'The Gospel of Organisation', *Worker* (Brisbane), 1 March 1890; Lloyd Ross, *William Lane and the Australian Labour Movement*, Sydney 1937, p. 180.
20 William Morris, *News from Nowhere; or, An Epoch of Rest*, London 1912 (1890), pp. 79, 122, 167, 170, 176, 177.
21 Tom Collins [Joseph Furphy], *Such Is Life*, Sydney 1962 (1903), p. 125.
22 Frank Bongiorno, *The People's Party: Victorian Labor and the Radical Tradition, 1875–1914*, Melbourne 1996, p. 94 (quoting Alfred Deakin, 1893); Bob Birrell, *Federation: The Secret Story*, Sydney 2001, pp. 70–1.
23 Shirley Adamson, 'The Queensland Sugar Industry', BA thesis, University of Queensland 1953, pp. 48–51; Erik Eklund, 'Building the "Kingdom of Freedom": Co-operatives and the Co-operative Movement in Australia', paper presented at the United Kingdom / Australian Comparative Labour History Conference, Manchester, July 2003, pp. 6–8. Erik Eklund kindly gave me a copy of this paper.
24 Gavin Souter, *A Peculiar People: The Australians in Paraguay*, Sydney 1968, pp. 23, 162–4, 175–6, 282–7.
25 William Pember Reeves, *State Experiments in Australia and New Zealand* (2 vols), vol. 1, Melbourne 1969 (1902), pp. 312–15.
26 David Mack, *The Village Settlements on the Murray in South Australia, 1894–1909: A Chronicle of Communal Life and Hardship*, Adelaide 1994, pp. 3–5.
27 Elsie Birks to a friend (name illegible), 27 February 1897; and Elsie Gilmour to Elizabeth George, 29 April 1945, State Library of South Australia, Adelaide, D 2861. For George Birks, see Melissa Bellanta, 'The Manliness of Radical Sentiment: The Case of George Napier Birks', *Australian Historical Studies*, vol. 39, 2008, pp. 322–37.
28 Reeves, vol. 1, pp. 299–312; RB Walker, 'The Ambiguous Experiment: Agricultural Co-operatives in New South Wales, 1893–1896', *Labour History*, no. 18, May 1970, pp. 19–31; Bruce Scates, *A New Australia: Citizenship, Radicalism and the First Republic*, Cambridge 1997, pp. 117–35; Gary Lewis, *The Democracy Principle: Farmer Co-operatives in Twentieth Century Australia*, Wamboin 2006.
29 Elsie Birks to Blanche Vivian, 5 October 1894, State Library of South Australia, Adelaide, D 2861; Souter, p. 138 (quoting Henry Connelly); Mack, pp. 44–52.
30 Oscar Wilde, *De Profundis*, London 1912 (1905), pp. 97–8.
31 Elsie Birks to a friend (name illegible), 24 August 1895, State Library of South Australia, Adelaide, D 2861 (original emphasis); W Michael Ryan,

Lieutenant-Colonel Charles à Court Repington: A Study in the Interaction of Personality, the Press, and Power, New York, NY, and London 1987, p. 18 (quoting Duke of Cambridge).

32 Daniel Kahneman, *Thinking, Fast and Slow*, London 2011, pp. 36–7.

33 Rick Rylance, 'Convex and Concave: Conceptual Boundaries in Psychology, Now and Then (But Mainly Then)', *Victorian Literature and Culture*, vol. 32, 2004, p. 452 (quoting Alfred Marshall).

34 *Portland Guardian*, 17 January 1896; Frank Fox, *From the Old Dog: Being the Letters of the Hon. ——, ex Prime Minister to His Nephew*, Melbourne 1908, p. 87; Scates, pp. 21, 75.

35 Assessment from search of the NLA's newspapers online, Trove, <trove.nla.gov.au/newspaper>.

36 *Official Report of the National Australasian Convention Debates: Sydney, 2 March to 9 April, 1891*, Sydney 1891, p. 380 (Sir Henry Parkes); *Maitland Mercury*, 22 December 1891; Alfred Deakin, *The Federal Story: The Inner History of the Federal Cause, 1880–1900*, ed. JA La Nauze, Melbourne 1963 (*The Federal Story*, 1944), p. 28.

37 NSW *RMPI* for 1894, p. 72 (Frederick Bridges); for 1900, p. 81 (WH Johnson); Scates, p. 36.

38 Vic. *RMPI* for 1891–92, p. 81 (J Livingstone); for 1899–1900, p. 62 (Alfred Jackson).

39 NSW *RMPI* for 1892, p. 53 (RF Russell).

40 William Stanley Jevons, 'On Clouds: Their Various Forms, and Producing Causes', *Sydney Magazine of Science and Art*, vol. 1, 1858, pp. 163–76; JA La Nauze, *Political Economy in Australia: Historical Studies*, Melbourne 1949, pp. 26–44; *Papers and Correspondence of William Stanley Jevons* (7 vols), vol. 1, ed. RD Collison Black & Rosamond Konekamp, London 1972, pp. 26–32.

41 *Autumn: From the Journal of Henry D. Thoreau*, ed. HGO Blake, Boston 1892, p. 208 (3 November 1861).

42 William Stanley Jevons, *The Theory of Political Economy*, London 1879 (1871), pp. 9, 10–11; Peter L Bernstein, *Against the Gods: The Remarkable Story of Risk*, New York, NY, 1996, pp. 190–1. I owe this reference to Jim Franklin.

43 TA Coghlan, *The Decline in the Birth-Rate of New South Wales and Other Phenomena of Child-Birth: An Essay in Statistics*, Sydney 1903, p. 47.

44 Cecily Close, 'Archer, William Henry (1825–1909)', *ADB*, vol. 3, 1969, pp. 41–3.

45 Alain Desrosières, *The Politics of Large Numbers: A History of Statistical Reasoning*, trans. C Naish, Cambridge, Mass., 1998 (French 1993), pp. 167–9.

46 ibid., pp. 188–94.

47 'Sporting', in *The Official Directory and Almanac of Australia for 1884*, Sydney 1884, pp. 137–8.

48 *South Australian Register* (Adelaide), 20 October 1879; Jessie Ackermann, *Australia from a Woman's Point of View*, Sydney 1981 (1913), p. 53 (ostensibly quoting *Evening Post*, 30 September 1911, a report on the 1911 Melbourne Cup, but in 1911 the race was run as usual in November, and the totalisator was not then allowed in Victoria); Sonia Jennings, 'Women and Gambling in Australia: Attitudes and Practices, 1860–1950', *Australian Society for Sports History Bulletin*, no. 27, December 1997, pp. 3–5.

49 'Sporting', p. 136.

50 *Argus*, 27 December 1881 (compare *Corowa Free Press*, 3 December 1880); Vic. *RMPI* for 1889–90, p. 230 (FC Eddy); ES Cunningham, 'Donald Macdonald: An Appreciation', *Newspaper News* (Sydney), 1 December 1932; *SMH*, 3 December 1932.

51 Gordon Inglis, *Sport and Pastime in Australia*, London 1912, pp. 141–2, 191.

52 NSW *RMPI* for 1896, pp. 69 (Frederick Bridges), 71 (JD Bradley), 91 (CO Flashman).

53 ibid. for 1900, p. 91 (John Kevin).

54 *Age*, 15 December 1876; *Bulletin* (Sydney), 4 April 1891; NSW *RMPI* for 1896, p. 69 (Frederick Bridges).

55 *RMCE* for 1881, p. 15 (Thomas Burgan); for 1885, p. 17 (Alexander Clark).

56 Vic. *RMPI* for 1895–96, p. 53 (Sub-committee on Plain Needlework); *RMCE* for 1897, p. 20 (Blanche McNamara); for 1900, p. 25 (Allen Martin).

57 Ray Crawford, 'Imitation, Need, Necessity: Muscular Christianity for Girls and the Emergence of the Sports Mistress in the Private Schools of Melbourne', paper presented at 'History in the Community', Australian Historical Association Conference, Adelaide, 25–29 August 1986.

58 *Queenslander* (Brisbane), 19, 26 May 1894; Bradley Blaschak, '"The Ignorant Labelled It a Ladies' Game": Masculinity in Australian Tennis in the Late Nineteenth Century', in Ian Warren (ed.), *Gender, Theory and Sport: The Formative Years of Tennis and Snowboarding*, Australian Studies for Sports History no. 16, Melbourne 2005, pp. 10–11, 16–17.

59 Anthony F Wilding, 'Lawn Tennis', *Lone Hand* (Sydney), 1 November 1909; Blaschak, pp. 24–5.

60 *Queenslander* (Brisbane), 19 May, 23 June 1894; Blaschak, pp. 15–17.

61 William Wilkins, 'Education in Australia', in *The Year-Book of Australia 1885*, Sydney 1885, p. 458; Lance E Davis & Robert A Huttenback, *Mammon and the Pursuit of Empire: The Political Economy of British Imperialism, 1860–1912*, Cambridge 1986, pp. 123–5, 134–5; Kathleen Fennessy, *A People Learning: Colonial Victorians and Their Public Museums, 1860–1880*, Melbourne 2007, p. 11.

62 *Argus*, 22 February 1878; Henry Sutton, 'Tele-photography', *Telegraphic Journal and Electrical Review*, 7 November 1890, pp. 549–50; Austin McCallum, 'Sutton, Henry (1856–1912)', *ADB*, vol. 6, 1976, pp. 226–7; Stephen Kern, *The Culture of Time and Space, 1880–1918*, Cambridge, Mass., 1983, pp. 20–2.

63 Ann Moyal, *Clear across Australia: A History of Telecommunications*, Melbourne 1984, pp. 77–8; Ian B Bates, '"Necessity's Inventions": A Research Project into South Australian Inventors and Their Inventions from 1836 to 1886', MA thesis, University of Adelaide 2000, p. 20.

64 See, for instance, *Index to New South Wales Letters of Registration of Inventions from 1854 to 31st July, 1887*, Sydney 1891.

65 Mrs Lance Rawson [Mina Rawson], *Australian Enquiry Book of Household and General Information*, Melbourne 1894, pp. 14, 15–16, 29, 78–9, 98–9.

66 NSW *RMPI* for 1896, p. 67 (Frederick Bridges).

67 *ATCJ*, 10, 17 July 1880.

68 Scates, p. 60.

69 Mary Gilmore, *Old Days, Old Ways: A Book of Recollections*, Sydney 1934, pp. 4, 9, 17.

70 Mrs Lance Rawson [Mina Rawson], *The Antipodean Cookery Book and Kitchen Companion*, Melbourne 1907 (1895), pp. 54–6.

71 IM Mackerras & Elizabeth N Marks, 'The Bancrofts: A Century of Scientific Endeavour', *Proceedings of the Royal Society of Queensland*, vol. 84, no. 1, 1973, pp. 5–6. Similar scientific inquiry in New South Wales was spoken of as a thing of the past in the late 1880s: William Wools, 'Plants of New South Wales Having Medicinal Properties', *Victorian Naturalist*, vol. 3, 1886–87, pp. 103–5.

72 John L Shattock, 'A City of the Sun', *Victorian Review*, 1 February 1883, p. 367.

73 HG Clements, 'Science and Colonial Culture: Scientific Interests and Institutions in Brisbane, 1859–1900', PhD thesis, Griffith University 1999, pp. 66, 201–42.

74 'Creed's Portable Wire Strainer', patent registrations issued to William Creed for South Australia, New South Wales, Victoria, Queensland, Canada and the USA, 1884–86, ML, A689; *Cootamundra Herald*, 2 August 1884; *Index to New South Wales Letters of Registration of Inventions*, p. 37 (Dacey's patent, 6 September 1884).

75 John Barnes, *Made in Shepparton: The History of J. Furphy & Sons, 1873–1998*, Shepparton 1998, pp. 14–24.

76 Daniel Connell, 'Managing Climate for the Murray-Darling Basin (1850–2050)', in Tim Sherratt, Tom Griffiths & Libby Robin (eds), *A Change in the Weather: Climate and Culture in Australia*, Cambridge 2005, pp. 82–3; Daniel Connell, *Water Politics in the Murray-Darling Basin*, Sydney 2007; Robyn Ballinger, 'Frontier and Homeland on the Northern Plains of Victoria 1841–1869', *Journal of Australian Colonial History*, vol. 13, 2011, pp. 49–64.

77 *ATCJ*, 27 March, 3, 10, 17 April, 1 May, 12 June 1875; NG Butlin, *Investment in Australian Economic Development, 1861–1900*, Cambridge 1964, pp. 65–80.

78 Archibald Crowley, 'The Life and Work of Sir Samuel McCaughey', *Journal of the Royal Australian Historical Society*, vol. 40, 1954, pp. 305–9, 311.

79 Western Australia, Parliament, *Debates*, vol. 8, 9 October 1895, p. 1289 (Sir John Forrest); vol. 9, 21 July 1896, p. 131 (Sir John Forrest); Vera Whittington, *Two Fevers: Gold and Typhoid; A Social History of Western Australia during the Decade 1891–1900 under the Particular Influence of These and Other Related Factors, People in Events*, Perth [1982], pp. 67–108.

80 Western Australia, Parliament, *Debates*, vol. 9, 21 July 1896, p. 143 (Sir John Forrest); AG Evans, *C.Y. O'Connor: His Life and Legacy*, Perth 2001, pp. 156–78.

81 *Official Report of the National Australasian Convention Debates: Adelaide, March 22 to May 5, 1897*, Adelaide 1897, pp. 251, 253 (Sir John Forrest).

82 Deakin, 'Irrigation in Australia', p. 82; John Rutherford, 'Interplay of Australian and American Ideas for Development of Water Projects in Northern Victoria', *Annals of the Association of American Geographers*, vol. 54, 1964, pp. 88–106.

6 Adding North to South

1 Joseph T Rainer, 'The "Sharper" Image: Yankee Peddlers, Southern Consumers, and the Market Revolution', *Business and Economic History*, vol. 26, no. 1, 1997, p. 42 (quoting EL Schwaab, *Travels in the Old South: Selected from Periodicals of the Times* (2 vols), vol. 2, Lexington, Ky., 1973, p. 470); James M McPherson, *Is Blood Thicker than Water? Crises of Nationalism in the Modern World*, New York, NY, 1999, pp. 40–61 (quoting Charles C Jones, jr, to his father, 28 January 1861; *Southern Literary Messenger* [Richmond, Va.], 19 June 1861; *De Bow's Review*, November–December 1863); Robert B Bonner, 'Roundheaded Cavaliers? The Context and Limits of a Confederate Racial Project', *Civil War History*, vol. 48, 2002, pp. 34–59; James Belich, *Replenishing the Earth: The Settler Revolution and the Rise of the Angloworld, 1783–1939*, Oxford 2009, p. 246.

2 McPherson, p. 55 (quoting *Southern Literary Messenger* [Richmond, Va.], 1860–61).

3 JSC Elkington, *Tropical Australia: Is It Suitable for a Working White Race?*, Melbourne 1905, p. 4; H Macqueen, R Cilento & C Lack, *Triumph in the Tropics*, Brisbane 1959; DJ Murphy, 'Queensland's Image and Australian Nationalism', *Australian Quarterly*, vol. 50, no. 2, 1978, pp. 77–91; Ross Fitzgerald, *From the Dreaming to 1915: A History of Queensland*, Brisbane 1982; Geoffrey C Bolton & Duncan Waterson, 'Queensland', in Helen Irving (ed.), *The Centenary Companion to Australian Federation*, Cambridge 1999, pp. 94–5.

4 Rudyard Kipling, 'The White Man's Burden' (1899), in *Rudyard Kipling's Verse 1885–1926*, London 1927, p. 320.

5 Ernest Favenc, *Tales of the Austral Tropics*, Sydney 1997, pp. xxii, xxviii; Libby Robin, *How a Continent Created a Nation*, Sydney 2007, pp. 124–5, 146–7.

6 James Jupp (ed.), *The Australian People: An Encyclopedia of the Nation, Its People and Their Origins*, Cambridge 2001, pp. 164, 428, 554–6, 682.

7 Wray Vamplew (ed.), *Australians: Historical Statistics*, Sydney 1987, p. 13.

8 Commonwealth of Australia, Parliament, *Debates*, vol. 1, 22 May 1901, p. 184 (John Watson); Henry Reynolds, *North of Capricorn: The Untold Story of Australia's North*, Sydney 2003, pp. ix–xv; Raymond Evans, *A History of Queensland*, Cambridge 2007, pp. 131–2.

9 Sir Samuel Walker Griffith, 'The Political Geography of Australia', *Proceedings and Transactions of the Queensland Branch of the Royal Geographical Society of Australasia: 6th Session, 1890–91*, vol. 6, part 1, Brisbane 1891, pp. 76–7; *Nor'-West Times* (Roebourne), 22 October 1893.

10 CH Pearson, *National Life and Character: A Forecast*, London 1893, pp. 16–17; Marilyn Lake, 'The White Man under Siege: New Histories of Race in the Nineteenth Century and the Advent of White Australia', *History Workshop Journal*, no. 58, 2004, pp. 41–62.

11 Cathie R May, *Topsawyers: The Chinese in Cairns, 1870–1920*, Townsville 1984, p. 54.

12 Jan Ryan, *Ancestors: Chinese in Colonial Australia*, Perth 1995, pp. 18–21, 26–31, 42–58, 61, 79–81.

13 Geoffrey C Bolton, *A Thousand Miles Away: A History of North Queensland to 1920*, Canberra 1970, pp. 54–8; Reynolds, p. 64 (quoting *Cairns Post*, 22 May 1889).

14 TA Coghlan, *Labour and Industry in Australia: From the First Settlement in 1788 to the Establishment of the Commonwealth in 1901* (4 vols), vol. 3, London 1918, pp. 1331–4. (Coghlan apparently means grown for sale, though he does not say so.)

15 Victoria, *Evidence Taken by the Royal Commission Appointed to Investigate and Report on the Operation of the Factories and Shops Law of Victoria*, Melbourne 1903, p. 499 (Archibald Dobson).

16 *Queenslander* (Brisbane), 10 January 1891; Mrs Lance Rawson [Mina Rawson], *Australian Enquiry Book of Household and General Information*, Melbourne 1894, pp. 30, 37, 40.

17 *Minutes of Proceedings of the Intercolonial Conference Held at Melbourne, December 1880*, Melbourne 1880, pp. 7–8.

18 *Minutes of Proceedings of the Intercolonial Conference Held at Sydney, January 1881*, Melbourne 1881, pp. 17, 62.

19 PJ Stewart, 'New Zealand and the Pacific Labor Traffic, 1870–1874', *Pacific Historical Review*, vol. 30, 1961, pp. 53–7.

20 Geoffrey Serle, 'The Victorian Government's Campaign for Federation, 1883–1889', in AW Martin (ed.), *Essays in Australian Federation*, Melbourne 1969, p. 4 (quoting James Service to Sir Thomas McIlwraith, 1883); Roger C Thompson, *Australian Imperialism in the Pacific: The Expansionist Era, 1820–1920*, Melbourne 1980, pp. 68–131.

21 *Argus*, 28 June 1888; *Coloured Races Restriction and Regulation Act 1896* (NSW) (60 Vic. XLI); Marilyn Lake & Henry Reynolds, *Drawing the Global Colour Line: White Men's Countries and the Question of Racial Equality*, Melbourne 2008, pp. 42–3.

22 Wilhelm II to Nicholas II, 26 September 1895, in *Letters from the Kaiser to the Czar*, ed. Isaac Don Levine, New York, NY, 1920, pp. 16–19; Niall Ferguson, *The War of the World: History's Age of Hatred*, London 2006, pp. 43–4 and illus. 2; Lake & Reynolds, pp. 289–90.

23 CH Kirmess, *The Australian Crisis*, London 1909, p. 335 (original all in capitals); Robert A Huttenback, 'The British Empire as a "White Man's Country": Racial

Attitudes and Immigration Legislation in the Colonies of White Settlement', *Journal of British Studies*, vol. 13, 1973, pp. 108–37.

24 Ryan, p. 42.

25 May, pp. 57, 68–71, 101.

26 *Brisbane Courier*, 26 November 1878; 'The Yellow Species of Mankind', *Australasian Anthropological Journal*, no. 5, 31 March 1897, p. 93; Kathryn Cronin, 'From Plodding "Paddy" to the "Ching-Chong Chinaman": The Chinese Rural Labourer', in Raymond Evans, Kay Saunders & Kathryn Cronin, *Race Relations in Colonial Queensland: A History of Exclusion, Exploitation and Extermination*, Brisbane 1988, p. 244; Marilyn Lake, 'Equality and Exclusion: The Racial Constitution of Colonial Liberalism', *Thesis Eleven*, no. 95, 2008, pp. 20–32.

27 *Intercolonial Conference Held at Sydney*, p. 353 (conference members to Earl of Kimberley, draft, n.d.).

28 'The Sketcher' [William Lane], *White or Yellow? A Story of the Race-War of A.D. 1908*, serialised in *Boomerang* (Brisbane), 18 February – 5 May 1888; Raymond Evans, *Fighting Words: Writing about Race*, Brisbane 1999, pp. 79–94.

29 *Gold Fields Act Amendment Act 1877* (Qld) (41 Vic., no. 12), further amended 1878 (42 Vic., no. 2); *Goldfields Act 1886* (WA) (50 Vic., no. 18).

30 Victoria, Employés in Shops Commission, *Second Progress Report of the Commission of Enquiry into the Best Means of Regulating and Shortening the Hours of Employés in Shops and Wholesale and Retail Trading Establishments, etc.*, Melbourne 1883; Victoria, Royal Commission of Employés in Shops, *Final Report: Courts of Conciliation; With Minutes of Evidence, Appendix, etc.*, Melbourne 1884; Victoria, Royal Commission of Employés in Shops, *Report on the Operation of the Victorian Factory Act 1874: Together with Minutes of Evidence, Appendix, etc.*, Melbourne 1884; Geoffrey Serle, *The Rush to Be Rich: A History of the Colony of Victoria, 1883–1889*, Melbourne 1971, pp. 69–77, 100–6.

31 Serle, *Rush to Be Rich*, pp. 104–5.

32 Victoria, *Report of the Royal Commission Appointed to Investigate and Report on the Operation of the Factories and Shops Law of Victoria*, Melbourne 1903, p. l.

33 Victoria, *Evidence Taken by the Royal Commission*, pp. 442 (David Fallshaw), 445, 446 (David Fallshaw, quoting WH Ellis), 485 (Thomas Holdsworth); Victoria, *Report of the Royal Commission*, p. l.

34 Victoria, *Evidence Taken by the Royal Commission*, pp. 445, 446 (David Fallshaw, quoting WH Ellis).

35 *Factories and Shops Act 1890* (Vic.) (54 Vic., no. 1091); *Factories and Shops Amendment Act 1896* (Vic.) (60 Vic., no. 1445).

36 Victoria, *Evidence Taken by the Royal Commission*, pp. 445, 447 (David Fallshaw); Victoria, *Report of the Royal Commission*, p. li.

37 Victoria, *Evidence Taken by the Royal Commission*, p. 491 (Thomas Holdsworth).

38 *The Colony of Australia: Views of Sir Alfred Stephen and Sir John Robertson*, Sydney 1887; New South Wales, Parliament, *Debates*, 1st series, vol. 29, 23 November 1887, p. 1505 (Thomas O'Mara); Serle, 'Victorian Government's Campaign', pp. 34–6.

39 *Official Report of the National Australasian Convention Debates: Sydney, 2 March to 9 April, 1891*, Sydney 1891, p. 74 (Alfred Deakin).

40 Sir Henry Parkes, 'An Australian Nation', *Melbourne Review*, vol. 4, 1879, p. 327.

41 Marcus Clarke, *The Future Australian Race*, Melbourne 1877, pp. 20, 22.

42 Jill Roe, *Stella Miles Franklin*, Sydney 2008, p. 126 (quoting Susannah Franklin to Stella Miles Franklin, 30 August 1907, ML, MLMSS 364/48).

43 Bernhard Ringrose Wise, *The Making of the Australian Commonwealth, 1889–1900:*

A Stage in the Growth of the Empire, London 1913, pp. 5–7 (quoting Sir Henry Parkes, speech, 24 October 1889).

44 Lake & Reynolds, pp. 56–74, 112, 150–1.

45 Francis Adams, *The Australians: A Social Sketch*, London 1893, p. 38.

46 Hugh Anderson (ed.), *Tocsin: Contesting the Constitution, 1897–1901*, Melbourne 2000, p. 7 (quoting 'Gavah' [Bernard O'Dowd], 'Federation and Factories', *Tocsin* [Melbourne], 2 December 1897).

47 *Advertiser* (Adelaide), 17 August 1893, 29 March, 4 June 1898.

48 JC Bannon, 'South Australia', in Irving, pp. 134–5, 144.

49 New South Wales, Parliament, *Debates*, 1st series, vol. 29, 23 November 1887, p. 1516 (Sir Henry Parkes); *Official Record of the Proceedings and Debates of the Australasian Federation Conference, 1890*, Melbourne 1890, p. 45 (JA Cockburn).

50 *Australasian Federation Conference, 1890*, p. 34 (Andrew Inglis Clark); *Australasian Convention Debates: Sydney*, p. 253 (Andrew Inglis Clark).

51 *South Australian Register* (Adelaide), 25 March 1881; *Official Report of the National Australasian Convention Debates: Adelaide, March 22 to May 5, 1897*, Adelaide 1897, pp. 252–3 (JH Howe); Margaret Glass, *Charles Cameron Kingston: Federation Father*, Melbourne 1997, p. 26.

52 *Punch* (Melbourne), 21 May 1908; Alfred Deakin, *The Federal Story: The Inner History of the Federal Cause, 1880–1900*, ed. JA La Nauze, Melbourne 1963 (*The Federal Story*, 1944), p. 37.

53 Paris Nesbit, 'Impressions of C.C. Kingston', *Register*, 15 February 1927; Glass, p. 47; Bannon, p. 170 (quoting *Critic* [Adelaide], 14 May 1898).

54 Bannon, p. 156.

55 Adams, p. 73; RB Joyce, 'Griffith, Sir Samuel Walker (1845–1920)', *ADB*, vol. 9, 1983, pp. 112–19; Katherine McConnel, '"Separation Is from the Devil while Federation Is from Heaven": The Separation Question and Federation in Queensland', *New Federalist*, no. 4, December 1999, pp. 14–21.

56 Western Australia, Parliament, *Debates*, vol. 10, 17 August 1897, p. 12 (Richard W Pennefather); Geoffrey C Bolton, *Land of Vision and Mirage: Western Australia since 1826*, Perth 2008, pp. 72, 92.

57 *Australasian Federation Conference, 1890*, p. 41 (William Russell); Joseph Furphy to Kate Baker, 27 March 1905, NLA, MS 2022/1/27; Miles Franklin, *Joseph Furphy: The Legend of a Man and His Book*, Sydney 1944, pp. 104–7.

58 Herbert Nicholls, 'The Struggle in Tasmania', in Wise, p. 354; Frank Bongiorno, 'From Republican to Anti-Billite: Bernard O'Dowd and Federation', *New Federalist*, no. 4, December 1999, p. 56 (quoting *Tocsin* [Melbourne], 2 June 1898); Bernard O'Dowd, 'Federation as Proposed', in Anderson, p. 9.

59 *Australasian Convention Debates: Sydney*, p. 62 (Sir Thomas McIlwraith).

60 Anderson, p. 13 (quoting 'Federal', *Tocsin* [Melbourne], 12 February 1898).

61 *Australasian Convention Debates: Sydney*, pp. 86 (Alfred Deakin), 144–5 (Arthur Rutledge), 299 (Joseph Palmer Abbott), 657 (Andrew Inglis Clark).

62 *Australasian Federation Conference, 1890*, p. 88 (Sir Henry Parkes); *Australasian Convention Debates: Adelaide*, pp. 514–15 (Alfred Deakin).

63 *Official Record of the Debates of the Australasian Federal Convention, Third Session: Melbourne, 20th January to 17th March, 1898*, Melbourne 1898, p. 704 (W Lyne).

64 Griffith, p. 76.

65 Duncan Waterson, 'The Absentees from North of the Tweed', *New Federalist*, no. 1, June 1998, pp. 29–38; Kay Saunders, 'The North Comes In: The 1899 Referendum Campaigns in North Queensland', *New Federalist*, no. 4, December 1999, pp. 7–13.

66 *Western Champion* (Barcaldine), 5 September 1899; JD Stanford, *The Long-Term*

Effect of Federation on the Queensland Economy, London 1988, p. 107; Bolton & Waterson, pp. 96, 100.

67 Evans, *History of Queensland*, pp. 111–18, 123–4.

68 Bolton & Waterson, p. 105.

69 *Capricornian* (Rockhampton), 26 August 1899; Alan Jenkins, 'Attitudes towards Federation in North Queensland', MA Qual. thesis, University of Queensland 1969, pp. 1–2; Lorna McDonald, *Rockhampton: A History of City and District*, Rockhampton 1995, p. 546; McConnel, p. 20; Evans, *History of Queensland*, pp. 141–2.

INDIVIDUALITY

1 Brian Greene, *The Fabric of the Cosmos: Space, Time, and the Texture of Reality*, London 2004, p. 47.

7 Men and Women

1 Rose Scott, draft speeches, [1898], ML, MLMSS 38/27, pp. 112–13, 173.

2 Proverbs 3:4.

3 AB Piddington to HB Higgins, 17 April, 8 June 1898, NLA, MS 1057/1/1; *Dubbo Liberal*, 30 April 1898; *Capricornian* (Rockhampton), 26 August 1899; *Western Champion* (Barcaldine), 5 September 1899.

4 James Joyce, *Ulysses*, London 1960 (1922), p. 38.

5 *Official Report of the National Australasian Convention Debates: Sydney, 2 March to 9 April, 1891*, Sydney 1891, pp. 826–7 (William Russell).

6 AB Piddington to HB Higgins, 17 April, 8 June 1898; and WJ Bartlett to HB Higgins, 24 June 1899, NLA, MS 1057/1/1; *Barrier Miner* (Broken Hill), 15 May 1905; Hugh Anderson (ed.), *Tocsin: Radical Arguments against Federation, 1897–1900*, Melbourne 1977, pp. 31–2, 136 (quoting *Tocsin* [Melbourne], 17 March, 28 April 1898).

7 *Australasian Convention Debates: Sydney*, pp. 890, 925 (Sir George Grey).

8 ibid., p. 926 (Sir George Grey).

9 ibid., pp. 66 (William Russell).

10 ibid., p. 826 (William Russell).

11 ibid., pp. 707 (JA Cockburn), 828 (Thomas Playford); Alfred Deakin, *The Federal Story: The Inner History of the Federal Cause, 1880–1900*, ed. JA La Nauze, Melbourne 1963 (*The Federal Story*, 1944), p. 45.

12 Rose Scott, literary notes, n.d., ML, MLMSS 38/26, p. 380; and draft speech, [1897], ML, MLMSS 38/27, p. 179; *Queenslander* (Brisbane), 12 July 1902; Rainer Maria Rilke to Franz Kappus, 14 May 1904, in Rainer Maria Rilke, *Letters to a Young Poet*, ed. and trans. Mark Harman, Cambridge, Mass., 2011 (German 1929), pp. 65, 70–1; Alison Mackinnon, *Love and Freedom: Professional Women and the Reshaping of Personal Life*, Cambridge 1997, pp. 40–1. Thanks to Frank Bongiorno for help with this.

13 'Sydney's Leading Political Lady: A Chat with Rose Scott', *New Idea* (Melbourne), 1 January 1903.

14 John Stuart Mill, *On Liberty*, New Haven, Conn., 2003 (1859), p. 122; 'Sydney's Leading Political Lady', p. 430; Andrea Nye, *Feminism and Modern Philosophy: An Introduction*, New York, NY, 2004.

15 Christina Rossetti, 'Who Shall Deliver Me?', *Argosy*, vol. 1, midsummer 1866, p. 288; Alfred Deakin, 'Boke of Praer and Praes', 7 November 1885, NLA, MS 1540/5/7.

16 *Official Report of the National Australasian Convention Debates: Adelaide, March 22 to May 5, 1897*, Adelaide 1897, p. 144 (Frederick Holder).

17 John Stuart Mill, *Autobiography*, London 1873, pp. 241–8; Jo Ellen Jacobs, '"The Lot of Gifted Ladies Is Hard": A Study of Harriet Taylor Mill Criticism', *Hypatia:*

A Journal of Feminist Philosophy, vol. 9, 1994, pp. 132–62; Melissa Bellanta, 'The Manliness of Radical Sentiment: The Case of George Napier Birks', *Australian Historical Studies*, vol. 39, 2008, pp. 322–37.

18 Isabel McCorkindale (ed.), *Torch-Bearers: The Women's Christian Temperance Union of South Australia, 1886–1948*, Adelaide 1949, pp. 55–6; Marilyn Lake, *Getting Equal: The History of Australian Feminism*, Sydney 1999, pp. 23–7.

19 John Monash, diary, 5, 12 September 1882, NLA, MS 1884/137/1019 (original emphasis).

20 John Monash, diary, 20 March, 13 August, 31 December 1882, NLA, MS 1884/137/1018; and to BW Pulver, 8 September 1885, NLA, MS 1884/50/1.

21 John Monash, diary, 22 July 1889, NLA, MS 1884/138; and to Annie Gabriel, 2 September 1889, NLA, MS 1884/51.

22 John Monash, diary, 16 July 1889, NLA, MS 1884/138; 9 November 1889, NLA, MS 1884/138/1025; Victoria Moss to John Monash, [24], 27 August, 6 October 1889, NLA, MS 1884/104; John Monash to Victoria Moss, October 1889, NLA, MS 1884/1.

23 John Monash, diary, 26 January 1890, NLA, MS 1884/137/1018; 2 March 1890, NLA, MS 1884/138/1925; 8 April 1890, NLA, MS 1884/138.

24 *Australasian Convention Debates: Adelaide*, p. 546 (Walter James); Rose Scott, draft speech, June 1899, ML, MLMSS 38/27, p. 187; Lyall Hunt, 'James, Sir Walter Hartwell (1863–1943)', *ADB*, vol. 9, 1983, pp. 466–9.

25 Rose Scott, draft speech, [1898], ML, MLMSS 38/27, pp. 35–8; Anne Watson, 'The Legacy of a Vision: From Lucien Henry to R.T. Baker', in Ann Stephen (ed.), *Visions of a Republic: The Work of Lucien Henry; Paris, Noumea, Sydney*, Sydney 2001, pp. 111–23; Libby Robin, *How a Continent Created a Nation*, Sydney 2007, pp. 13–18.

26 RA Harris, 'Federation' (sung at the University of Sydney Commemoration, 1898), notebooks, ML, MLMSS 1588/1/2, p. 9; *Daily Telegraph* (Sydney), 3 May 1899; Bernhard Ringrose Wise, *The Making of the Australian Commonwealth, 1889–1900: A Stage in the Growth of the Empire*, London 1913, pp. 272–3; Audrey Oldfield, *Woman Suffrage in Australia: A Gift or a Struggle?*, Cambridge 1992, p. 79; Helen Irving, 'Fair Federalists and Founding Mothers', in Helen Irving (ed.), *A Woman's Constitution? Gender and History in the Australian Commonwealth*, Sydney 1996, pp. 7–15.

27 *Evening News* (Sydney), 8 February 1897; *Argus*, 28 April 1898.

28 Francis Adams, *Australian Essays*, Melbourne 1886, p. 60.

29 Rose Scott, draft speech, n.d., ML, MLMSS 38/27, p. 25; *Evening News* (Sydney), 8 February 1897.

30 Rose Scott, draft speech, [April 1921], ML, MLMSS 38/27, p. 315.

31 Rose Scott, literary notes, n.d., ML, MLMSS 38/26, p. 367; 'Sydney's Leading Political Lady', p. 429.

32 Justin Corfield, *The Ned Kelly Encyclopaedia*, Melbourne 2003, pp. 241–6 (quoting Ned Kelly, 'Jerilderie Letter', 10 February 1879).

33 Henry Kendall, 'Narara Creek' (1872), in Henry Kendall, *Songs from the Mountains*, Sydney 1880, p. 113; Oscar Wilde, *The Picture of Dorian Gray*, London 2000 (1890–91), p. 25 (the character quoted being Lord Henry Wotton).

34 Gerald O'Collins, *Patrick McMahon Glynn: A Founder of Australian Federation*, Melbourne 1965, p. 149 (quoting Patrick McMahon Glynn, diary, 31 December 1898).

35 Vic. *RMPI* for 1877–78, p. 195 (Charles Tynan). In fact, the word was English rural dialect: Jon Savage, *Teenage: The Creation of Youth Culture*, New York, NY, 2007, pp. 34–48; Melissa Bellanta, *Larrikins: A History*, Brisbane 2012, pp. 2–3. Bellanta

(p. 3) says that the word was first used by the press in February 1870, but in fact there is an isolated instance in the *Empire* (Sydney), 16 October 1867.

36 Edward Kinglake, *The Australian at Home: Notes and Anecdotes of Life at the Antipodes*, London [1891], p. 20.

37 Kelly, p. 244; *SMH*, 20 April 1891; *Hermes* (University of Sydney), 29 April 1891; RA Harris, 'Varsity Songs and Solos' (this one from Commemoration Day 1900), ML, MLMSS 1588/1/2; Ambrose Pratt, *The Great 'Push' Experiment*, Sydney 1902, pp. 103–4; [Francis Russell], 'Paul's in the Early 'Nineties', *Pauline* (magazine of St Paul's College), 1927, p. 54; James Murray, *Larrikins: 19th Century Outrage*, Melbourne 1973, pp. 189–90.

38 Baron Colmar von der Goltz, *The Nation in Arms: A Treatise on Modern Military Systems and the Conduct of War*, trans. PA Ashworth, London 1906 (German 1883), p. 7; Savage, p. 17.

39 *Singleton Argus*, 14 January 1885; *Kerang Times and Swan Hill Gazette*, 23 November 1888; Murray, pp. 24, 91–3; Alan Atkinson, *The Europeans in Australia* (3 vols), vol. 2, Melbourne 2004, pp. 22–3.

40 *Official Record of the Proceedings and Debates of the Australasian Federation Conference, 1890*, Melbourne 1890, p. 150 (William McMillan [NSW]).

41 David Walker, 'Youth on Trial: The Mt Rennie Case', *Labour History*, no. 50, May 1986, p. 33; Judith Allen, *Sex and Secrets: Crimes Involving Women since 1880*, Melbourne 1990, p. 54.

42 *SMH*, 13 September 1886; Juliet Peers, 'The Tribe of Mary Jane Hicks: Imaging Women through the Mount Rennie Rape Case 1886', *Australian Cultural History*, no. 12, 1993, pp. 128–30, 134.

43 *Evening News* (Sydney), 27 April 1886; Murray, pp. 123, 161; Allen, p. 56; JS Sheldon, *The Big School Room at Sydney Grammar School: With an Account of the Decline and Fall of Sydney College*, Sydney 1997, p. 145 (quoting William Charles Windeyer, journal, 11 October 1852); Bellanta, *Larrikins*, pp. 92–8. Thanks to Frank Bongiorno for help with this.

44 *Bulletin* (Sydney), 7 September 1895; Walker, p. 38; Peers, pp. 133–4.

45 *RMCE* for 1885, p. xx (John A Hartley); Vic. *RMPI* for 1899–1900, p. 77 (James Livingstone).

46 WL Courtney, *The Life of John Stuart Mill*, London 1889, pp. 117–18; Rainer Maria Rilke to Franz Kappus, 14 May 1904, in Rilke, pp. 69–70; Elizabeth Robins, *Woman's Secret*, Letchworth, Herts., 1907, p. 6.

47 *RMCE* for 1881, p. 58 (James HH Vockins); Vic. *RMPI* for 1884–85, p. 146 (J Dennant); *Census of New South Wales, 1891 (Statistician's Report)*, Sydney 1894, pp. 197, 199–203; NSW *RMPI* for 1894, p. 69 (Frederick Bridges); *Census of the Commonwealth of Australia, 1911* (3 vols), vol. 1, Melbourne 1911, pp. 168–9; Alan Atkinson, '"He Filled Us Full of Laughter": Contact and Community in Australian Experience', in Richard White & Hsu-Ming Teo (eds), *Cultural History in Australia*, Sydney 2003, pp. 44–7.

48 Pratt, pp. 104–7.

49 Eneas Mackenzie, *Memoirs of Mrs. Caroline Chisholm, with an Account of Her Philanthropic Labours, in India, Australia, and England*, London 1852, p. 115.

50 Miles Franklin, *My Brilliant Career*, Sydney 1965 (1901), p. 220; Catherine Martin, *An Australian Girl*, ed. R Campbell, Brisbane 2002, p. 202.

51 Mrs Arthur Tuckett [Margaret Tuckett], *A Year in My Garden*, Melbourne 1905, pp. 4–5, 27.

52 *SMH*, 21 December 1859; KS Inglis, *The Australian Colonists: An Exploration of Social History, 1788–1870*, Melbourne 1974, p. 234.

53 Victoria, *Report of the Board of Education*, Melbourne, for 1870, pp. xliii (Board), 41 (Joseph Geary); *RMCE* for 1885, p. 17 (Alexander Clark); for 1887, p. 28 (Alexander Clark); Vic. *RMPI* for 1891–92, pp. 57–9 (Colin H Campbell).

54 NSW *RMPI* for 1885, pp. 415–16 (WJ Trickett); for 1895, p. 107 (John Dettman); Vic. *RMPI* for 1890–91, p. 117 (WH Snee & DL Henry); for 1891–92, p. 82 (WH Snee & DL Henry); Paul Kitney, 'The History of the Australian School Cadet Movement to 1893', *Defence Force Journal*, no. 12, 1978, pp. 53–60.

55 Geoffrey Serle, *John Monash: A Biography*, Melbourne 1982, p. 82.

56 Craig Wilcox, *For Hearths and Homes: Citizen Soldiering in Australia 1854–1945*, Sydney 1998, pp. 19–20, 22–3.

57 William James, 'Is Life Worth Living?', in William James, *The Will to Believe and Other Essays in Popular Philosophy, and Human Immortality*, New York, NY, 1956 (*The Will to Believe and Other Essays in Popular Philosophy*, 1896), p. 61.

58 Vic. *RMPI* for 1884–85, p. 139 (Ross Cox).

59 Henry Gyles Turner, 'Australia Militant', *Melbourne Review*, vol. 10, 1885, p. 152; *Australasian Federation Conference, 1890*, p. 10 (Sir Samuel Walker Griffith).

60 Turner, p. 153.

61 ibid., p. 152; *Bulletin* (Sydney), 20, 27 June, 4 July, 26 September 1885; George Meudell, 'An Australian Protest against Imperial Federation', *Melbourne Review*, July 1885, pp. 251–2; KS Inglis, *The Rehearsal: Australians at War in the Sudan*, Adelaide 1985, pp. 36, 43, 83.

62 *SMH*, 15 April 1885; Inglis, *Rehearsal*, p. 104.

63 *SMH*, 23 April 1898.

64 *Advertiser* (Adelaide), 29 September 1899; CN Connolly, 'Manufacturing "Spontaneity": The Australian Offers of Troops for the Boer War', *Historical Studies*, vol. 18, no. 70, 1978, pp. 108–15.

65 Henry Rider Haggard, *Cetywayo and His White Neighbours; or, Remarks on Recent Events in Zululand, Natal, and the Transvaal*, London 1882, p. 46. The passage also appears in Haggard's *The Last Boer War*, London 1900, p. 10.

66 James Jefferis, *The Federation of the British People*, Adelaide 1901, p. 17.

67 *Argus*, 11 May 1901.

68 NSW *RMPI* for 1899, p. 72 (Frederick Bridges); for 1900, pp. 72 (J Dawson), 95–6 (George H Hunt).

69 *Bulletin* (Sydney), 28 February 1903.

70 'Clericus' to the editor, *SMH*, 4 February 1902.

71 *SMH*, 25, 28 April 1902.

72 ibid., 28 May 1898, 7 (but Milton said 'argue freely'), 13, 14 February 1902; *Advertiser* (Adelaide), 28 October 1904.

73 Alfred Deakin to Rose Scott, 14 January, 20 February, 10 May 1907, ML, A2281.

74 Alfred Deakin to Rose Scott, 14 January, 20 February, 10 May 1907, ML, A2281; Margaret Levi, *Consent, Dissent, and Patriotism*, Cambridge 1997, pp. 73–4.

8 Black and White

1 Ian Crawford, *We Won the Victory: Aboriginals and Outsiders on the North-West Coast of the Kimberley*, Perth 2001, pp. 98–105. Bundell has been identified with the boy who attached himself to Captain William Hill of the New South Wales Corps in 1790–91 and also with a man who lived during the 1820s–1840s around Camden: *Bundle (c.1787–c.1844)*, Journeys in Time, Macquarie University, n.d., viewed 17 January 2014, <www.lib.mq.edu.au/all/journeys/people/profiles/bundle.html>. However, it seems strange that a native of Port Jackson should have identified himself in adulthood with a quite different people, the D'harawal.

2 Christopher Richards, *There Were Three Ships: The Story of the Camden Harbour Expedition 1864–65*, Perth 1990, pp. 110, 126; Crawford, pp. 142–3 (quoting and discussing Trevarton Charles Sholl, journal, 24 April 1865, State Library of Western Australia, Perth, Q B/SHO).

3 RH Pilmer, *Northern Patrol: An Australian Saga*, ed. Cathie Clement & Peter Bridge, Perth 1998, pp. 14, 32.

4 Stephen Muecke, Alan Rumsey & Banjo Wirrunmarra, 'Pigeon the Outlaw: History as Texts', *Aboriginal History*, vol. 9, 1985, p. 92 (quoting Banjo Wirrunmarra, as told to Alan Rumsey, August 1984; the editors of this article use capitals for 'shooting people', 'Thousands' and 'thousands' to represent emphasis); Erich Kolig, *The Noonkanbah Story*, Dunedin 1987, p. 19.

5 Pilmer, pp. 17–18.

6 Howard Pedersen & Banjo Woorunmurra, *Jandamarra and the Bunuba Resistance*, Broome 1995, pp. 69–78, 94–117.

7 ibid., p. 152 (quoting Banjo Woorunmurra [*sic*], as told to Howard Pedersen, n.d.); Muecke, Rumsey & Wirrunmarra, pp. 88, 96 (quoting Banjo Wirrunmarra, as told to Stephen Muecke, 1977; and as told to Alan Rumsey, August 1984); Pilmer, p. 52.

8 Muecke, Rumsey & Wirrunmarra, pp. 88, 96 (quoting Banjo Wirrunmarra, as told to Stephen Muecke, 1977; and as told to Alan Rumsey, August 1984; the editors of this article use capitals for 'fighting' and 'others' to represent emphasis).

9 Pedersen & Woorunmurra, pp. 118–27.

10 ibid., pp. 127–30; Pilmer, p. 52.

11 Pilmer, pp. 57, 70.

12 Muecke, Rumsey & Wirrunmarra, pp. 91–2 (quoting Banjo Wirrunmarra, as told to Alan Rumsey, August 1984); Pilmer, pp. 71–5.

13 Pilmer, pp. 22–3.

14 Muecke, Rumsey & Wirrunmarra, p. 94 (quoting Banjo Wirrunmarra, as told to Alan Rumsey, August 1984); Pedersen & Woorunmurra, pp. 152–3 (quoting Banjo Woorunmurra [*sic*], as told to Howard Pedersen, n.d.); Pilmer, p. 75.

15 Paul Hasluck, *Black Australians: A Survey of Native Policy in Western Australia, 1829–1897*, Melbourne 1942, pp. 122, 206.

16 George Fletcher Moore, *Diary of Ten Years Eventful Life of an Early Settler in Western Australia*, London 1884, p. 183.

17 AJ Vogan, *The Black Police: A Story of Modern Australia*, London 1890, p. 141; Henry Reynolds, *Why Weren't We Told? A Personal Search for the Truth about Our History*, Melbourne 1999, pp. 106–8 (quoting 'H7H', 'Taming the Niggers', *Townsville Herald*, 2 February 1907); Raymond Evans, *A History of Queensland*, Cambridge 2007, pp. 135–9.

18 *Nor'-West Times* (Roebourne), 9 July 1892.

19 Gideon Scott Lang, *The Aborigines of Australia, in Their Original Condition and in Their Relations with the White Men*, Melbourne 1865, pp. 45–6; Susan Barnett, 'A Study of the Queensland Native Mounted Police in the 1870s', BA thesis, University of Queensland 1975; Alan Atkinson, *The Europeans in Australia* (3 vols), vol. 2, Melbourne 2004, pp. 328–30; Evans, *History of Queensland*, pp. 94–7.

20 Fyodor Dostoyevsky, *Crime and Punishment*, trans. David Magarshak, London 1951 (Russian 1866), p. 467.

21 Archibald Meston, *Queensland Aboriginals: Proposed System for Their Improvement and Preservation*, Brisbane 1895, p. 4.

22 ibid., pp. 22, 25–7 (original emphasis); Archibald Meston, *Report on the Aboriginals of Queensland*, Brisbane 1896, p. 14.

23 Meston, *Report on the Aboriginals*, p. 1; William Thorpe, 'Archibald Meston and the

Aboriginals: Ideology and Practice, 1870–1970; An Exploration in Social History', BA thesis, University of Queensland 1978, pp. 55–7.

24 Meston, *Queensland Aboriginals*, p. 25; Thorpe, pp. 67–72.

25 George Gordon, Lord Byron, 'Greek Song' (1821), in *The Select Poetical Works of Lord Byron*, Boston 1852, p. 321.

26 Meston, *Report on the Aboriginals*, p. 8; Thorpe, pp. 41–53.

27 *Daily Herald* (Adelaide), 30 April 1913: 'There are probably very few people who have not read that remarkable book "The Count of Monte Christo [*sic*]"'.

28 Peter Watson, *The German Genius: Europe's Third Renaissance, the Second Scientific Revolution and the Twentieth Century*, London 2010, pp. 86–7.

29 Samuel Cliall White, 'The Ballad of Stuttering Jim (Illustrating the Survival of the Fittest)' (1894), in *The Bulletin Reciter: A Collection of Verses for Recitation from 'The Bulletin', 1880–1901*, Sydney 1901, p. 103.

30 Elsie Birks to Blanche Vivian, 5 October 1894, State Library of South Australia, Adelaide, D 2861.

31 Meston, *Report on the Aboriginals*, p. 13.

32 Chris Healy, *Forgetting Aboriginals*, Sydney 2008, pp. 206–10.

33 Queensland, *Report of the Board of Inquiry Appointed by the Secretary for Lands to Inquire into and Report upon the State of the Aboriginal Reserve at Mackay*, Brisbane 1876, pp. 3 (Duncan McNab to colonial secretary [Arthur Macalister], 9 May 1876), 10 (Duncan McNab to minister for lands [John Douglas], 2 September 1876), 12 (minister for lands [John Douglas] to Bishop [Matthew] Hale, 11 September 1876); Mark Cryle, 'Duncan McNab's Mission to the Queensland Aboriginals 1875–1880', BA thesis, University of Queensland 1989, p. 62.

34 Queensland, *Report of the Board of Inquiry*, pp. 3–4 (Duncan McNab to minister for lands [John Douglas], 24 July 1876).

35 ibid., p. 3 (Duncan McNab to minister for lands [John Douglas], 24 July 1876).

36 ibid., pp. 8–10 (Duncan McNab to minister for lands [John Douglas], 2 September 1876); Cryle, pp. 30–47. My account owes a good deal to Cryle, though Cryle gives less emphasis to McNab's interest in family relations.

37 Raymond Evans, *Fighting Words: Writing about Race*, Brisbane 1999, pp. 180–200 (quoting, p. 193, Archibald Meston, 'Report on Aborigines West of Warrego', 19 July 1900, Queensland State Archives, Brisbane).

38 Cryle, pp. 23–6.

39 Queensland, *Report of the Board of Inquiry*, pp. 12–13 (Bishop [Matthew] Hale to minister for lands [John Douglas], 15 September 1876).

40 Robert Browning, *Bishop Blougram's Apology* (1855), in *Browning: Selected Poems*, ed. John Woolford, Daniel Karlin & Joseph Phelan, Abingdon, Oxfordshire, 2010, p. 323.

41 John Brown, 'Charles Booth and Labour Colonies, 1889–1905', *Economic History Review*, n.s., vol. 21, 1968, pp. 349–61 (quoting, p. 351, Charles Booth, *Life and Labour of the People of London*, series 3, (17 vols), vol. 1, London 1902 [1889–91], p. 154); Albert Fried & Richard M Elman (eds), *Charles Booth's London: A Portrait of the Poor at the Turn of the Century; Drawn from His 'Life and Labour of the People of London'*, London 1969, pp. 295–8.

42 Noel Loos, 'The Australian Board of Missions, the Anglican Church and the Aboriginals, 1850–1900', *Journal of Religious History*, vol. 17, 1992, pp. 200–1; Christine Halse, *A Terribly Wild Man*, Sydney 2002, pp. 16–47 (quoting, p. 29, ERB Gribble, journal, *Missionary Notes of the Australian Board of Missions*, December 1895, p. 104).

43 Halse, pp. 31, 51–5.

44 ERB Gribble, *The Problem of the Australian Aboriginal*, Sydney 1932, p. 39; Halse, p. 53 (quoting *Cairns Morning Post*, 31 October 1902).

45 John Chesterman & Brian Galligan, *Citizens without Rights: Aborigines and Australian Citizenship*, Cambridge 1997, pp. 37–44.

46 Thorpe, pp. 61–2, 90–3.

47 Queensland, Parliament, *Debates*, vol. 78, 15 November 1897, pp. 1541–2 (Horace Tozer); Raymond Evans & Jan Walker, '"These Strangers, Where Are They Going?": Aboriginal–European Relations in the Fraser Island and Wide Bay Region 1770–1905', *Occasional Papers in Anthropology*, no. 8, 1977, pp. 77–83 (quoting Archibald Meston, 'Report on the Aboriginal Station Recently Formed on Fraser's Island', March 1897, Queensland State Archives, Brisbane).

48 Evans & Walker, pp. 81–4 (quoting Archibald Meston to home secretary, 21 August 1901, 22 April 1902, Queensland State Archives, Brisbane).

49 Edward Tylor, *Anthropology: An Introduction to the Study of Man and Society*, New York, NY, 1899 (1881), p. 427; Alexander Sutherland, *The Origin and Growth of the Moral Instinct* (2 vols), vol. 1, London 1898, pp. 114–17.

50 Russell McGregor, *Imagined Destinies: Aboriginal Australians and the Doomed Race Theory, 1880–1939*, Melbourne 1997, p. 20.

51 Chesterman & Galligan, pp. 53–6.

52 *The Aboriginals Protection and Restriction of the Sale of Opium Act 1897* (Qld) (61 Vic. no. 17), s. 31.

53 Regina Ganter & Ros Kidd, 'The Powers of Protectors: Conflicts Surrounding Queensland's 1897 Aboriginal Legislation', *Australian Historical Studies*, vol. 25, 1993, pp. 536–45.

54 Bain Attwood, *The Making of the Aborigines*, Sydney 1989, pp. 79–103, 105; Tess De Araugo, 'Pepper, Nathaniel (1841–1877)', *ADB*, supp. vol., 2005, p. 319; Robert Kenny, *The Lamb Enters the Dreaming: Nathaniel Pepper and the Ruptured World*, Melbourne 2007.

55 *An Act to Provide for the Protection and Management of the Aboriginal Natives of Victoria 1886* (Vic.) (50 Vic. no. 912).

56 Attwood, p. 87.

57 *Official Record of the Proceedings and Debates of the Australasian Federation Conference, 1890*, Melbourne 1890, p. 126 (William Russell); Russell McGregor, *Indifferent Inclusion: Aboriginal People and the Australian Nation*, Canberra 2011, pp. xvii–xxiv.

58 Chesterman & Galligan, pp. 40–1, 53–4, 88–92.

59 Tracey Banivanua Mar & Penelope Edmonds, 'Indigenous and Settler Relations', in Alison Bashford & Stuart Macintyre (eds), *The Cambridge History of Australia* (2 vols), vol. 1, Melbourne 2013, pp. 354–7.

60 Chesterman & Galligan, pp. 92, 111–15.

9 God and Humanity

1 ERB Gribble, diary, title page, 9 September 1892, ML, MLMSS 4503 Add-on 1822/Box 10/1.

2 JB Gribble, diary, 9 June, 7 July, 29 September 1873, ML, MLMSS 4503 Add-on 1822/Box 1/1 (original emphasis).

3 ERB Gribble, diary, 9 September 1892, ML, MLMSS 4503 Add-on 1822/Box 10/1.

4 Christine Halse, *A Terribly Wild Man*, Sydney 2002, pp. 16–21.

5 Alfred Deakin, 'Boke of Praer and Praes', 19 October 1884, NLA, MS 1540/5/7; Al Gabay, *The Mystic Life of Alfred Deakin*, Cambridge 1992, pp. 63–4, 66, 77, 82.

6 Regular notice in the *Bulletin* (Sydney), from 1892.

7 *Official Report of the National Australasian Convention Debates: Adelaide, March 22 to May 5, 1897*, Adelaide 1897, p. 1186 (Adye Douglas).
8 ibid., pp. 1186–7 (Edmund Barton).
9 ibid., pp. 1184–6 (Patrick McMahon Glynn).
10 Matthew Arnold, 'Dover Beach', in Matthew Arnold, *New Poems*, Boston 1867, pp. 95–6; Gerald O'Collins, *Patrick McMahon Glynn: A Founder of Australian Federation*, Melbourne 1965, pp. 190–2 (quoting Patrick McMahon Glynn to his brother James, March 1886).
11 *SMH*, 2 November 1887; Walter Phillips, *James Jefferis: Prophet of Federation*, Melbourne 1993, p. 163.
12 *SMH*, 23 April 1898.
13 Miles Franklin, *Joseph Furphy: The Legend of a Man and His Book*, Sydney 1944, p. 110 (quoting Joseph Furphy to Cecil Winter, n.d.).
14 Tony Swain, *A Place for Strangers: Towards a History of Australian Aboriginal Being*, Cambridge 1993, pp. 129–30.
15 Matthew 22:37–9.
16 James Jefferis, *A Free Church in a Free State: Its Claims and Conflicts*, Sydney 1878, p. 4.
17 James Jefferis, *Our Bible and Our Belief: Six Lectures Delivered in the Congregational Church, Pitt Street, Sydney, as a Help to Young Men of Free Thought*, Sydney 1882, pp. 4, 7; James Jefferis, 'The Highest Teachings of Astronomy', *Sydney Quarterly Magazine*, vol. 1, no. 3, April 1884, pp. 242–3; Tom Collins [Joseph Furphy], *Such Is Life*, Sydney 1962 (1903), p. 316; Stephen Kern, *The Culture of Time and Space, 1880–1918*, Cambridge, Mass., 1983, p. 154.
18 James Jefferis to the editor, *SMH*, 2 September 1880; Jefferis, 'The Highest Teachings of Astronomy', pp. 244–5; Phillips, *James Jefferis*, p. 138.
19 Catherine Helen Spence, *Gathered In: A Novel*, Sydney 1977 (1881–82), pp. 137–8.
20 John Milton, *Paradise Lost* (1667), in *The Poems of John Milton*, ed. John Carey & Alasdair Fowler, London 1968, p. 514.
21 James Jefferis, *Reply to the Joint-Pastoral of the Roman Catholic Archbishop and Bishops of New South Wales*, Sydney 1879, p. 3; Jefferis, *Our Bible and Our Belief*, p. 5; Jefferis, 'The Highest Teachings of Astronomy', pp. 244–5; Phillips, *James Jefferis*, pp. 242–3.
22 James Jefferis, 'Australia Christianised', *South Australian Register* (Adelaide), 23 June 1880; Phillips, *James Jefferis*, p. 169; Lionel Trilling, 'Little Dorrit', in Harold Bloom (ed.), *Charles Dickens*, New York, NY, 2006, p. 77. I owe this last reference to Aaron Davis.
23 Jefferis, *Reply to the Joint-Pastoral*, pp. 3–4; James Jefferis, *Australia Confederated*, Sydney 1880, p. 19.
24 Jefferis, *Reply to the Joint-Pastoral*, p. 4; Jefferis, *Australia Confederated*, pp. 5, 17, 19; Jefferis, *Our Bible and Our Belief*, p. 7; Phillips, *James Jefferis*, p. 150.
25 Leo Tolstoy, *Resurrection*, trans. Anthony Briggs, London 2009 (Russian 1899–1900), pp. 399–400.
26 James Anthony Froude, *Oceana; or, England and Her Colonies*, New York, NY, 1886, pp. 167–8.
27 W Hey Sharp, 'Henry Latimer Jackson', in *Historical Sketch of S. James' Sydney*, Sydney 1919, p. 23; *Times* (London), 24 March 1926.
28 Henry Latimer Jackson, 'The Church and Modern Thought', *Centennial Magazine*, December 1889, pp. 353–62; Henry Latimer Jackson, 'At the Antipodes', [1925], p. 26, ML, PXn 932; Walter Phillips, 'Religious Profession and Practice in New South Wales, 1850–1901: The Statistical Evidence', *Historical Studies*, vol. 15, 1972,

pp. 385–400; Hugh Jackson, *Churches and People in Australia and New Zealand, 1860–1930*, Sydney 1987, pp. 30–2, 57–76.

29 *South Australian Register* (Adelaide), 13 May 1873; *SMH*, 2 November 1887.

30 *RMCE* for 1885, p. xx (John A Hartley); WL Courtney, *The Life of John Stuart Mill*, London 1889, pp. 117–18.

31 Henry Latimer Jackson, 'The Church and Modern Thought', pp. 360–2 (citing William Robertson Smith, the Old Testament scholar and Jackson's contemporary at Christ's College, Cambridge); Robert D Richardson, *First We Read, Then We Write: Emerson on the Creative Process*, Iowa City, Iowa, 2009, p. 82.

32 'The Re-union of Christendom', *Australian Herald* (Melbourne), February 1892, p. 114; CR Badger, 'Strong, Charles (1844–1942)', *ADB*, vol. 6, 1976, pp. 208–9.

33 Victor Hugo, *Les Misérables*, trans. J Rose, London 2008 (French 1862), p. 422; 'An Australian Church', *Our Good Words* (Melbourne), June 1888, p. 2; 'Reunion of Churches', *Our Good Words* (Melbourne), October 1888, p. 17. (This periodical was run by Charles Strong.)

34 *SMH*, 23 January 1888; Charles Strong, *Concerning Women*, Melbourne 1895, p. 2.

35 'CS' [Charles Strong], 'The Book of Jonah', *Presbyterian Review*, October 1879, p. 157; *Presbyterian Review*, November 1879, pp. 212–13.

36 Charles Strong & Francis Anderson, *The Australian Church: Report MDCCCLXXXVII; and, Sermons*, Melbourne 1887, pp. 21–2; *Our Good Words* (Melbourne), October 1892, pp. 49–50; Strong, p. 3.

37 Peter Ackroyd, *Albion: The Origins of the English Imagination*, London 2004, p. 39; Diarmaid MacCulloch, *A History of Christianity: The First Three Thousand Years*, London 2009, p. 340.

38 *Mercury* (Hobart), 20 April 1898.

39 'Presb. Eccles. Aust.' to the editor, *Church Commonwealth* (Melbourne), 25 October 1900, p. 119; Graeme Davison, 'Religion', in Alison Bashford & Stuart Macintyre (eds), *The Cambridge History of Australia* (2 vols), vol. 2, Melbourne 2013, p. 219.

40 John Harrison, 'Missions, Fisheries and Government in Far North Queensland 1891–1919', BA thesis, University of Queensland 1974, pp. 1–4.

41 *Official Report of the National Australasian Convention Debates: Sydney, 2 March to 9 April, 1891*, Sydney 1891, pp. 124 (Sir Patrick Alfred Jennings); 140 (Sir George Grey).

42 Queensland, Parliament, *Debates*, vol. 75, 8 July 1896, p. 237 (Joshua Thomas Bell).

43 Joseph Conrad, *Lord Jim: A Romance*, New York, NY, 1905 (1899–1900), p. 167.

44 Mary MacKillop to Bishop Laurence Bonaventure Sheil, 10 September 1871, AMM, Mary MacKillop Letters, vol. 4; Mary MacKillop, 'Circular for St Joseph's Day', 19 March 1893, AMM, Mary MacKillop Letters, vol. 14; Daniel Lyne, *Mary MacKillop: Spirituality and Charisms*, Sydney 1982, p. 147 (quoting Bishop James Quinn to Bishop John Cani, 2 March 1875).

45 Mary MacKillop, 'Submission of Mother Mary to Prop. Re. Rule', 18 May 1873 (copy from Irish College Archives, Rome); and Mary MacKillop, Manuscript C, August 1873, AMM, Mary MacKillop Letters, vol. 6; MacKillop, 'Circular for St Joseph's Day'.

46 MacKillop, 'Submission of Mother Mary'; *South Australian Register* (Adelaide), 17 January 1883; *Mail* (Adelaide), 24 January 1914.

47 MacKillop, Manuscript C.

48 MacKillop, 'Circular for St Joseph's Day'; Lyne, pp. 161, 178 (quoting Julian Tenison Woods, 'Book of Instructions for the Sisters', 1870).

49 Mary MacKillop to Monsignor Tobias Kirby, 22 May 1873, AMM, Mary MacKillop

Letters, vol. 6; Lyne, p. 89 (quoting Mary MacKillop to Bishop Laurence Bonaventure Sheil, 10 September 1871).

50 Mary MacKillop to Julian Tenison Woods, [September 1871] (original emphasis); and to her mother, 10 October 1871, AMM, Mary MacKillop Letters, vol. 4; Mary MacKillop to Monsignor Tobias Kirby, 22 May 1873, AMM, Mary MacKillop Letters, vol. 6; Paul Gardner, *Mary MacKillop: An Extraordinary Australian*, Sydney 1994, pp. 104–5.

51 Beverley Zimmerman, *The Making of a Diocese: Maitland, Its Bishop, Priests and People, 1866–1909*, Melbourne 2000, pp. 166–7, 194–8.

52 ibid., pp. 106–18; Marie Crowley, *Women of the Vale: Perthville Josephites, 1872–1972*, Melbourne 2002, pp. 15–16.

53 RM Frappell, 'The Australian Bush Brotherhoods and Their English Origins', *Journal of Ecclesiastical History*, vol. 47, 1996, pp. 82–97 (quoting GW Lovejoy, *In Journeyings Often: Being a Bush Brother's Record of Five Years Spent in the Australian Bush as a Member of the Brotherhood of the Good Shepherd, Dubbo*, Dubbo 1940); Hilary Carey, 'Bushmen and Bush Parsons: The Shaping of a Rural Myth', *Journal of Australian Colonial History*, vol. 14, 2011, pp. 1–26.

54 *SMH*, 9 April 1898.

55 Here I owe a debt to the research assistance and arguments of Yvonne Perkins.

56 *Argus*, 16 February 1880.

57 *South Australian Register* (Adelaide), 18 January 1864.

58 *South Australian Advertiser* (Adelaide), 26, 27 September 1882, 4, 5, 9 October 1886; Helen Jones, *In Her Own Name: A History of Women in South Australia*, Adelaide 1994, p. 149.

59 Jones, pp. 148–67.

60 For petitions for, see *Australasian Convention Debates: Adelaide*, pp. 203, 261, 349, 398, 404; and for petitions against, pp. 405, 429; Anne Winckel, 'Almighty God in the Preamble', *New Federalist*, no. 4, December 1999, pp. 78–83.

61 Jefferis, *Reply to the Joint-Pastoral*, p. 4; *South Australian Register* (Adelaide), 27 October 1886, 27 August, 17 October 1890; *Argus*, 12 October, 10 December 1892.

62 *Brisbane Courier*, 26 October 1892, 11 October 1895; *South Australian Register* (Adelaide), 6 June 1896.

63 *Advertiser* (Adelaide), 3 March 1897, 24 March 1898; *South Australian Register* (Adelaide), 19 March 1897; *Argus*, 24 March 1898; *Mercury* (Hobart), 30 March 1898; *West Australian* (Perth), 1 April 1898.

64 *West Australian* (Perth), 1 April, 21 May 1898; *Argus*, 16, 23 May 1898; Bob Birrell, *Federation: The Secret Story*, Sydney 2001, p. 179.

65 *Independent* (Footscray), 28 May 1898.

66 *Freeman's Journal* (Sydney), 24 June 1899, p. 15; Richard G Ely, *Unto God and Caesar: Religious Issues in the Emerging Commonwealth, 1891–1906*, Melbourne 1976, p. 109; Birrell, p. 139.

67 Marian Aveling [Marian Quartly], 'A History of the Australian Natives Association, 1871–1900', PhD thesis, Monash University 1970, pp. 42–4, 100–4.

68 *Clarence and Richmond Examiner* (Grafton), 27 May, 20 June 1899.

69 *Warragul Guardian*, 14 June 1898; A Williams to HB Higgins, 24 July 1899, NLA, MS 1057/1/1. A count of paired words 'federation' and 'church' in digitised issues of colonial newspapers suggests that, unlike in the other colonies, New South Wales clergy were just as active during the second vote.

70 *Argus*, 6 February 1888, 12 April 1898; Ely, pp. 108–10.

71 Ely, pp. 105–9; Phillips, *James Jefferis*, pp. 238–40; AG Eagar to HB Higgins, 21 June 1899, NLA, MS 1057/1/1; Richard Windeyer to the editor, *Times* (London),

16 August 1899; AE Cahill, 'Cardinal Moran, Bathurst, and the Achievement of Federation', in David Headon & Jeff Brownrigg (eds), *The People's Conventions: Corowa (1893) and Bathurst (1896)*, Papers on Parliament no. 32, Canberra 1998, pp. 94–102; John B Hirst, *The Sentimental Nation: The Making of the Australian Commonwealth*, Melbourne 2000, pp. 5–7.

THE FOURTH DIMENSION

1 Brian Greene, *The Fabric of the Cosmos: Space, Time, and the Texture of Reality*, London 2004, p. 77.

10 Conscience and Total Calculation

1 HG Wells, *The War of the Worlds*, Melbourne 2009 (1897–98), p. 7.
2 ibid., pp. 8–9; *Advertiser* (Adelaide), 28 March 1898; *Brisbane Courier*, 21 June 1898.
3 Wells, *War of the Worlds*, p. 98.
4 Arthur Koestler, *Darkness at Noon*, New York, NY, 1941 (1940), pp. 112, 126, 152, 259.
5 *Punch* (Melbourne), 23 December 1909.
6 Jon Miller & David Muir, *The Business of Brands*, Chichester, Sussex, 2004, p. 125 (quoting Samuel Crowther, 'Slow Profits Today, but Sure Profits Tomorrow: An Interview by Samuel Crowther with George Eastman', *System: The Magazine of Business*, vol. 38, October 1920, p. 710).
7 John Locke, *An Essay Concerning Human Understanding*, London 1836 (1690), p. 59.
8 James Jefferis, *Reply to the Joint-Pastoral of the Roman Catholic Archbishop and Bishops of New South Wales*, Sydney 1879, p. 3; Catherine Helen Spence, *Gathered In: A Novel*, Sydney 1977 (1881–82), pp. 137–8.
9 *South Australian Register* (Adelaide), 12 October 1885; Charles Howard Hinton, 'Casting out the Self', in Charles Howard Hinton, *Scientific Romances*, 1st series, London 1886, p. 224; *Queenslander* (Brisbane), 4 October 1890.
10 *Maitland Mercury*, 8 June 1893; *Clarence and Richmond Examiner* (Grafton), 21 January 1896.
11 *Camperdown Chronicle*, 10 February 1910.
12 *Goulburn Evening Penny Post*, 26 August 1915.
13 Eric Hobsbawm, *The Age of Extremes: The Short Twentieth Century, 1914–1991*, London 1994.
14 Jefferis, *Reply to the Joint-Pastoral*, p. 3; Adrian Consett Stephen, *An Australian in the R.F.A.*, ed. Alfred Consett Stephen, Sydney 1918, p. 108; Ernst Jünger, *The Storm of Steel: From the Diary of a German Storm-Troop Officer on the Western Front*, trans. Basil Creighton, New York, NY, 1975 (German 1920), p. 254.
15 Bernard O'Dowd, 'Morgana Mine and Other Realities', *Heart of the Rose*, December 1907, pp. 8–10; Ann Douglas, *Terrible Honesty: Mongrel Manhatten in the 1920s*, London 1977, pp. 434–5, 454–61; Alan Atkinson, *The Commonwealth of Speech: An Argument about Australia's Past, Present and Future*, Melbourne 2002, pp. 60–1.
16 *Evening News* (Sydney), 15 September 1906, 11 December 1907; *Argus*, 10 April 1912.
17 Thomas Mann, *The Magic Mountain*, trans. HT Lowe-Porter, London 1979 (German 1924), p. 217.
18 HG Wells, *An Englishman Looks at the World: Being a Series of Unrestrained Remarks upon Contemporary Matters*, Hazleton, Penn., 2004 (1914), pp. 9–10.
19 Albion Woodbury Small, *The Meaning of Social Science*, Chicago, Ill., 1910, pp. 58–62; Elizabeth Morrison, *Engines of Influence: Newspapers of Country Victoria, 1840–1890*, Melbourne 2005, pp. 204–13.

20 Small, p. 242 (original in italics); William W Lowrance, *Modern Science and Human Values*, Oxford 1985, p. 9; Peter Watson, *The German Genius: Europe's Third Renaissance, the Second Scientific Revolution and the Twentieth Century*, London 2010, pp. 126–7.

21 Sir Samuel Walker Griffith, 'A Plea for the Study of the Unconscious Vital Processes in the Life of Communities', in *Report of the Sixth Meeting of the Australasian Association for the Advancement of Science, Held at Brisbane, Queensland, January, 1895*, Sydney 1895, p. 659.

22 C Graham Worsley to HB Higgins, 10 June 1898, NLA, MS 1057/1/1/35 (original emphasis).

23 HG Wells, *The History of Mr Polly*, London 2010 (1910), pp. 107–8. Elsewhere, Wells himself argued for 'a National Plan for our social and economic development which everyone may understand and which will serve as a unifying basis for all our social and political activities': Wells, *Englishman Looks at the World*, p. 56.

24 *Kalgoorlie Miner*, 11 June 1912.

25 HA Ellis, 'The Theory of Malthus', *Australian Economist*, vol. 2, no. 4, June 1890, pp. 40–1; Neville Hicks, *This Sin and Scandal: Australia's Population Debate, 1891–1911*, Canberra 1978, pp. 82–3.

26 *Kadina and Wallaroo Times*, 30 January 1907; Archer Russell, *William James Farrer: A Biography*, Melbourne 1949, pp. 34–5.

27 Matthew 26:11 (also Mark 14:7); Robert Humphreys, *Poor Relief and Charity, 1869–1945: The London Charity Organization*, New York, NY, 2002, pp. 1–2, 23–59.

28 Edward E Morris & Jacob Goldstein, 'Preface', *Proceedings of the First Australasian Conference on Charity, Held in Melbourne, from 11th to 17th November, 1890, Convened by the Charity Organization Society of Melbourne*, Melbourne 1891, p. v.

29 *Bacchus Marsh Express*, 9 August 1902.

30 Edward E Morris, 'Organized Charity', *First Australasian Conference on Charity*, p. 5.

31 ibid., pp. 6, 9, 11; *First Australasian Conference on Charity*, p. 44 (Catherine H Spence).

32 Edward E Morris, *Austral English: A Dictionary of Australasian Words, Phrases and Usages*, London 1898, p. 224.

33 Henry Latimer Jackson, 'Pauperism: Its Nature, Causes, and Remedies', *First Australasian Conference on Charity*, pp. 36–43.

34 *Kalgoorlie Miner*, 11 June 1912; Geoffrey C Bolton, 'Ellis, Henry Augustus (1861–1939)', *ADB*, vol. 8, 1981, pp. 433–4.

35 *Geraldton Guardian*, 2 November 1918.

36 *Advertiser* (Adelaide), 19 December 1898.

37 ibid., 22 December 1898, 25 March 1948; *Chronicle* (Adelaide), 16 March 1929; *Recorder* (Port Pirie), 21 August 1937. Thomas Morgan and Thirza Louise Richards had been married at Goodwood in 1889, and their son Roy had died aged nine months in 1892: *Advertiser* (Adelaide), 4 April 1889; *South Australian Chronicle* (Adelaide), 16 April 1892.

38 Walter Balls-Headley, *The Evolution of the Diseases of Women*, London 1894, pp. 12–13, 22–3, 29, 53; Janet McCalman & Rebecca Kippen, 'Population and Health', in Alison Bashford & Stuart Macintyre (eds), *The Cambridge History of Australia* (2 vols), vol. 1, Melbourne 2013, pp. 304–8.

39 *Truth* (Sydney), 17 September 1899.

40 WL Courtney, *The Life of John Stuart Mill*, London 1889, pp. 117–18.

41 Balls-Headley, pp. 2, 22; Alfred Deakin, *The Federal Story: The Inner History of the Federal Cause, 1880–1900*, ed. JA La Nauze, Melbourne 1963 (*The Federal Story*, 1944), p. 28; Hicks, pp. 33–5.

42 *Census of New South Wales, 1901*, Sydney 1901, pp. 630, 633–4; Desley Deacon,

Managing Gender: The State, the New Middle Class and Women Workers, 1830–1930, Melbourne 1980, pp. 152–74.

43 Andrew Garran, 'A Criticism of Malthus' Doctrine', *Australian Economist*, vol. 2, no. 6, 20 August 1890, p. 61; Balls-Headley, p. 2; Stephen Kern, *The Culture of Time and Space, 1880–1918*, Cambridge, Mass., 1983, p. 102 (quoting Jean-Marie Guyau, *La genèse de l'idée de temps*, Paris 1890, p. 44).

44 Hicks, p. 141; Deacon, pp. 104–27.

45 Joseph Conrad, *Lord Jim: A Romance*, New York, NY, 1905 (1899–1900), p. 161; Randall L Bytwerk, *Bending Spines: The Propagandas of Nazi Germany and the German Democratic Republic*, East Lansing, Mich., 2004, p. 52 (quoting Fred Oelßner, *Über die Verbesserung der Arbeit der Presse und des Rundfunks*, Berlin 1953, who was ostensibly quoting Lenin and Stalin).

46 *Liverpool Herald*, 2 June 1906; *Burrowa News*, 27 January 1911; Hicks, pp. 62–3; Deana Heath, *Purifying Empire: Obscenity and the Politics of Moral Regulation in Britain, India and Australia*, Cambridge 2010, pp. 132–4.

47 REN Twopeny, *Town Life in Australia*, London 1883; Henry Latimer Jackson, *Parents and Children*, Sydney 1888, p. 5; New South Wales, Royal Commission on the Decline of the Birth-Rate and on the Mortality of Infants in New South Wales (2 vols), vol. 2, *Minutes, Evidence, Exhibits, Index*, Sydney 1904, p. 198 (Edward Riley).

48 New South Wales, Royal Commission, vol. 2, p. 110 (WA Holman, quoting *Harper's Monthly*); *Brisbane Courier*, 14 May 1909.

49 *ATCJ*, 17 October 1891; *SMH*, 9 September 1899; *Capricornian* (Rockhampton), 23 September 1899; Carl N Degler, 'What Ought to Be and What Was: Women's Sexuality in the Nineteenth Century', *American Historical Review*, vol. 79, 1974, pp. 1467–90; Alison Mackinnon, *Love and Freedom: Professional Women and the Reshaping of Personal Life*, Cambridge 1997, pp. 22–46; Frank Bongiorno, *The Sex Lives of Australians: A History*, Melbourne 2012, p. 66. Thanks to Frank Bongiorno for help with this detail.

50 *Evening News* (Sydney), 14 December 1888.

51 Rose Scott, literary notes, n.d., ML, MLMSS 38/26, p. 407.

52 New South Wales, Royal Commission, vol. 2, pp. 45 (George Stephens), 57 ('Nurse A'), 58 ('Nurse B'), 125 (John Harris); Hicks, p. 63.

53 New South Wales, Royal Commission, vol. 2, pp. 98 (Robert Scot Skirving), 196 (Edward Riley), 203 (Rev. WM Dill Macky); Hugh Jackson, 'Fertility Decline in New South Wales: The Mackellar Royal Commission Reconsidered', *Australian Historical Studies*, vol. 23, 1989, pp. 260–73.

54 New South Wales, Royal Commission, vol. 2, pp. 71 (Stanhope MacCulloch), 89 (Ralph Worrall), 98 (Robert Scot Skirving), 189 ('Witness E'); McCalman & Kippen, pp. 306–8.

55 Richard Sennett, *The Fall of Public Man*, Cambridge 1977 (1976), pp. 19–20.

56 *Morning Bulletin* (Rockhampton), 18 September 1899; New South Wales, Royal Commission, vol. 2, p. 214 (Rev. John Howell Price); Walter Phillips, 'Religious Profession and Practice in New South Wales, 1850–1901: The Statistical Evidence', *Historical Studies*, vol. 15, 1972, pp. 378–400; Hugh Jackson, *Churches and People in Australia and New Zealand, 1860–1930*, Sydney 1987, pp. 143–6.

57 New South Wales, Royal Commission, vol. 2, p. 214 (Rev. John Howell Price).

58 ibid., pp. 58 ('Nurse B'), 125 (John Harris), 208 (Rev. NMcL Hennessy), 215 (Rev. John Howell Price), 223 (Ven. JD Langley); Hicks, pp. 56, 67.

59 New South Wales, Royal Commission, vol. 2, p. 189 ('Witness E').

60 *Ex parte HV McKay* (Harvester Case) (1907) 2 CAR 1; Stuart Macintyre, 'Arbitration in Action', in Joe Isaac & Stuart Macintyre (eds), *The New Province for Law and*

Order: 100 Years of Australian Industrial Conciliation and Arbitration, Cambridge 2004, pp. 62–8. This was the *Excise Tariff (Agricultural Machinery) Act 1906* (Cwlth) (no. 16 of 1906).

61 *Daily News* (Perth), 10 September 1897; *Bacchus Marsh Express*, 14 May 1898; *SMH*, 20 July 1898.

62 Macintyre, 'Arbitration in Action', p. 64.

63 *Ex parte HV McKay* (Harvester Case) (1907) 2 CAR 1, Justice Henry Bourne Higgins, Judgment, 8 November 1907, pp. 3–4.

64 Australia, Commonwealth Court of Conciliation and Arbitration, *Commonwealth Arbitration Reports*, vol. 10, Melbourne 1916, pp. 482–4 ('In the Matter of Industrial Disputes between W Angliss and Co. Pty Ltd and Others and the Australasian Meat Industry Employees' Union [etc.]'); PG McCarthy, 'Justice Higgins and the Harvester Judgment', in Jill Roe (ed.), *Social Policy in Australia: Some Perspectives 1901–1975*, Sydney 1976, pp. 46–53; John Rickard, *H.B. Higgins: The Rebel as Judge*, Sydney 1984, pp. 171–5; Marilyn Lake, *Getting Equal: The History of Australian Feminism*, Sydney 1999, pp. 55–6; Bob Birrell, *Federation: The Secret Story*, Sydney 2001, pp. 205–6; WM Robbins, I Harriss & R Macklin, 'Fact and Myth: Reflections on Why Higgins Made the Harvester Decision', in Marian Baird, Rae Cooper & Mark Westcott (eds), *Reworking Work: AIRANZ 05; Proceedings of 19th Conference of the Association of Industrial Relations Academics of Australia and New Zealand* (2 vols), vol. 1, Sydney 2005, pp. 489–90.

65 Robert Browning, *Bishop Blougram's Apology*, in Robert Browning, *Men and Women*, Boston, Mass., 1856, pp. 146–7; HB Higgins, 'A New Province for Law and Order', *Harvard Law Review*, vol. 26, 1915–16, p. 39.

66 McCalman & Kippen, p. 302.

67 Martin Thomas (ed.), *Culture in Translation: The Anthropological Legacy of R.H. Mathews*, with translations from the French by Mathilde de Hauteclocque and from the German by Christine Winter, Canberra 2007, pp. 190–1.

68 RH Mathews, 'The Rock Paintings and Carvings of the Australian Aboriginals', *Journal of the Anthropological Institute of Great Britain and Ireland*, vol. 25, 1896, p. 152; Thomas, *Culture in Translation*, pp. 16, 46, 56–7 (RH Mathews, 'Contributions to the Ethnography of the Australians' [German 1907]); Martin Thomas, *The Many Worlds of R.H. Mathews: In Search of an Australian Anthropologist*, Sydney 2011, pp. 59–60. I am very largely indebted here to Martin Thomas's work.

69 Thomas, *Many Worlds of R.H. Mathews*, p. 10.

70 Rose Scott, literary notes, n.d., ML, MLMSS 38/26, p. 367; Thomas, *Many Worlds of R.H. Mathews*, pp. 59–60.

71 Thomas, *Culture in Translation*, pp. 17, 32 (quoting RH Mathews to Daisy Bates, 29 August 1905), 18, 28; Thomas, *Many Worlds of R.H. Mathews*, p. 39.

72 Thomas, *Many Worlds of R.H. Mathews*, pp. 3–4, 12, 18.

73 Mary Gilmore, *Old Days, Old Ways: A Book of Recollections*, Sydney 1934, p. 217; Thomas, *Culture in Translation*, pp. 26, 33, 156–64.

74 DJ Mulvaney & JH Calaby, *'So Much That Is New': Baldwin Spencer, 1860–1929; A Biography*, Melbourne 1985, pp. 152, 153, 156–7.

75 ibid., pp. 188–9.

76 ibid., pp. 189, 208 (quoting James Frazer to Walter Baldwin Spencer, 4 June 1900), 190, 212. In its first edition (1890), Frazer's book was called *The Golden Bough: A Study in Comparative Religion*.

77 Mulvaney & Calaby, pp. 195, 215 (quoting WB Spencer to Sir James Frazer, 15 August 1904), 446 (quoting WB Spencer to WE Roth, 30 January 1903; and

WE Roth to WB Spencer, 8 February 1903); Martin Thomas, 'RH Mathews and Anthropological Warfare: On Writing the Biography of a "Self-Contained Man"', *Aboriginal History*, vol. 28, 2004, pp. 2–7; Thomas, *Culture in Translation*, p. 9 (quoting Walter Baldwin Spencer to AW Howitt, 15 August 1907).

78 Thomas, *Culture in Translation*, pp. 9–10, 90–2; Thomas, *Many Worlds of R.H. Mathews*, pp. 6–9, 37–44, 257–72, 325–49.

79 Noel Loos, *White Christ Black Cross: The Emergence of a Black Church*, Canberra 2007, pp. 56–7.

80 Gilbert White, 'Gairloch' (1897), in Gilbert White, *The World's Tragedy and Other Poems*, Thursday Island 1910, p. 13; *Argus*, 7 March 1919; Mulvaney & Calaby, pp. 274–5, 454; Ruth Teale, 'White, Gilbert (1859–1933)', *ADB*, vol. 12, 1990, p. 466; John Gascoigne & Sara Maroske, 'Science and Technology', in Bashford & Macintyre, vol. 1, p. 507.

81 Diane Langmore, 'Stone-Wigg, Montagu John (1861–1918)', *ADB*, vol. 12, pp. 103–4; Loos, p. 64, n. 20.

82 Archibald Meston, *Queensland Aboriginals: Proposed System for Their Improvement and Preservation*, Brisbane 1895, p. 4; Hugh Mahon, 'The Native Races under the New Constitution', *Austral Light: A Catholic Magazine* (Melbourne), 1 March 1902, pp. 198–201. See also Fiona Paisley, 'Federalising the Aborigines? Constitutional Reform in the Late 1920s', *Australian Historical Studies*, vol. 29, 1998, p. 248. A search of the NLA's newspaper digital copying scheme (Trove, <trove.nla.gov.au/newspaper>) suggests that the terms 'national conscience' and 'public conscience' began to be common in Australian newspapers from the 1860s.

83 Robert Hindmarsh, *Letters to Dr. Priestley: Containing Proofs of the Sole, Supreme, and Exclusive Divinity of Jesus Christ*, London 1792, p. 215; 'Crambo Chantor', *The Modern Independent Whig*, Dublin 1792, p. 13; Walter Moyle, *Democracy Vindicated*, Norwich 1796, p. 8. 'Public conscience', where it did not equate with 'national conscience', meant an individual sense of public duty or, by the late eighteenth century, 'the sentiment of enlightened men' without regard to nationhood: George Anderson, *A Remonstrance against Lord Viscount Bolingbroke's Philosophical Religion*, Edinburgh 1756, p. 216; J-P Brissot de Warville, *J.P. Brissot, Deputy of Eure and Loire, to His Constituents, on the Situation of the National Convention*, Dublin 1794, p. 21.

84 Jo-Anne Pemberton, 'New Worlds for Old: The League of Nations in the Age of Electricity', *Review of International Studies*, vol. 28, 2002, pp. 311–36; Mark Mazoer, *Governing the World: The History of an Idea*, London 2012, pp. 75, 90.

85 Bernard O'Dowd, *Conscience and Democracy*, Melbourne 1902, pp. 13–14.

86 *West Australian* (Perth), 19 October 1899; *Daily News* (Perth), 15 January 1910.

87 See 'Lefroy, Sir John Henry (1817–1890)'; and GC Lefroy, 'Lefroy, Anthony O'Grady (1816–1897)', *ADB*, vol. 5, pp. 77–8; Catherine Cameron, 'Lefroy, Sir Henry Bruce (1853–1930)', *ADB*, vol. 10, 1986, pp. 62–3; Wendy Birman, 'Lefroy, Sir Anthony Langlois (1881–1958)', shared entry with 'Lefroy, Sir Edward Bruce Henry (1887–1966)', *ADB*, vol. 15, 2000, pp. 74–5. For George Alfred Lefroy, Bishop of Calcutta, see Jeffrey Cox, 'Lefroy, George Alfred (1854–1919)', *Oxford Dictionary of National Biography*, Oxford University Press 2004, viewed 4 February 2014 (subscription necessary for full text), <www.oxforddnb.com/view/article/46439>.

88 *SMH*, 14 January 1911.

89 ibid., 16, 25 January 1911; Mulvaney & Calaby, p. 274; Bain Attwood & Andrew Markus, *The 1967 Referendum: Race, Power and the Australian Constitution*, Canberra 2007, p. 89.

90 *SMH*, 25 January 1911; Mulvaney & Calaby, pp. 264–75, 296.

91 John Murphy, *A Decent Provision: Australian Welfare Policy, 1870 to 1949*, Farnham, Surrey, 2011, pp. 94–106.

92 John Chesterman & Brian Galligan, *Citizens without Rights: Aborigines and Australian Citizenship*, Cambridge 1997, pp. 85–6; Marilyn Lake, 'Fellow Feeling: A Transnational Perspective on Conceptions of Civil Society and Citizenship in "White Men's Countries", 1890–1910', in Karen Hageman, Sonya Michel & Gunilla Budde (eds), *Civil Society and Gender Justice: Historical and Comparative Perspectives*, New York, NY, 2008, pp. 277–81; Anna Haebich & Steve Kinnane, 'Indigenous Australia', in Bashford & Macintyre, vol. 2, pp. 339–42.

11 The Voice of the Country

1 *Argus*, 6 February 1885, 10 March 1891.

2 CC Marsh, *The Science of Double-Entry Book-Keeping*, New York, NY, 1851, pp. 11–12.

3 Arthur W Atkinson to the editor, *SMH*, 12 January 1914.

4 *SMH*, 16, 28 October 1901.

5 John B Hirst, 'Nation Building, 1901–14', in Alison Bashford & Stuart Macintyre (eds), *The Cambridge History of Australia* (2 vols), vol. 2, Melbourne 2013, p. 16.

6 HNP Wollaston, 'Trade and Customs: The Interesting History of a Great Department', *Life* (Melbourne), 15 November 1907, pp. 445–6; DI McDonald, 'The Former Customs Clerks: Wollaston and Lockyer', *Canberra Historical Journal*, n.s., no. 20, September 1987, p. 32.

7 *Brisbane Courier*, 25 June 1902; *SMH*, 24 June 1908.

8 *Colac Herald*, 27 September 1892; *Argus*, 4 March 1893; *Evening News* (Sydney), 9 May 1895; *Warragul Guardian*, 23 July 1897.

9 *Argus*, 7, 27 August 1894; *Horsham Times*, 17 August 1894; *South Australian Chronicle* (Adelaide), 18 August 1894.

10 *SMH*, 13 March 1875, 31 March 1894, 4 March 1895; *Bathurst Free Press*, 2 May 1891; *Memorandum and Articles of Association of the Animal Protection Society of New South Wales*, Sydney 1895; Andrea Gaynor, 'Environmental Transformations', in Bashford & Macintyre, vol. 1, p. 285.

11 *Argus*, 15 June 1912.

12 Geoffrey Serle, *John Monash: A Biography*, Melbourne 1982, p. 82 (quoting John Monash to Will Steele, August–September 1888, NLA, MS 1884, but seen by Serle while Monash's papers were still in private hands).

13 Wollaston, pp. 446–7.

14 Neville Hicks, *This Sin and Scandal: Australia's Population Debate, 1891–1911*, Canberra 1978, pp. 18–21; Stephen Kern, *The Culture of Time and Space, 1880–1918*, Cambridge, Mass., 1983, pp. 8–9; Janet McCalman & Rebecca Kippen, 'Population and Health'; and Lionel Frost, 'The Economy', in Bashford & Macintyre, vol. 1, pp. 299–301, 317–21.

15 *Clarence and Richmond Examiner* (Grafton), 24 August 1901; Martin van Creveld, *Supplying War: Logistics from Wallenstein to Patten*, Cambridge 1977, pp. 109–10.

16 *SMH*, 17 November 1908.

17 *Queanbeyan Age*, 20 July 1871; NSB Gras, 'Behaviour of Business Men in a Changing World: Rise of Business Statesmanship', *Bulletin of the Business Historical Society*, vol. 23, 1949, pp. 3, 6–7, 21–2.

18 Henri Bergson, *Creative Evolution*, trans. Arthur Mitchell, New York, NY, 1910 (French 1907), p. 201.

19 ibid., p. 220.

20 Herbert N Casson, *The History of the Telephone*, Chicago, Ill., 1910, pp. 231–2

(original emphasis); Oswald Spengler, *The Decline of the West* (2 vols), vol. 1, *Form and Actuality*, trans. CF Atkinson, New York, NY, 1926 (German 1918), p. 137; Kern, pp. 91, 94–103.

21 John Monash, diary, 17 July 1889, NLA, MS 1884/138; *Daily News* (Perth), 1 July 1901; Sydney Stott, 'Condition and Demands in Australia', *Typewriter Topics*, 1917, copy in Robert Messenger, *Australian Typewriter Trade: The Stott Story*, OzTypewriter, 24 February 2013, viewed 18 August 2013, <oztypewriter.blogspot.com.au/2013/02/australian-typewriter-trade-stott-story.html>; *SMH*, 8 October 1927; Desley Deacon, *Managing Gender: The State, the New Middle Class and Women Workers, 1830–1930*, Melbourne 1980, pp. 162–5; MR Hill, 'Armitage, Dora Elizabeth (1858–1946)', *ADB*, vol. 13, 1993, p. 70.

22 *Argus*, 5 May 1906; Marie Docherty, 'An Historical Background to the Predominance of Women in Clerical Employment', in Convenors (eds), *Second Women and Labour Conference Papers*, Melbourne 1980, pp. 41–51.

23 Andrew Barton Paterson, 'Clancy of the Overflow' (1889), in *The Collected Verse of A.B. Paterson*, Sydney 1923, p. 16; *Argus*, 3 December 1898, 21 March 1903; John Wheeler, 'The Memoirs of John Wheeler, Customs Officer New South Wales 1905–1951', *Customs House Magazine*, December 1970, p. 5.

24 *Evelyn Observer*, 9 February 1900; *Healesville and Yarra Glen Guardian*, 19 July 1901; Arthur W Atkinson to the editor, *SMH*, 2 January 1909, 12 January 1914; Dustin Halse, '"Citizens Who Serve": The Political Rights of Victorian Public Servants, 1856–1916', *Labour History*, no. 102, May 2012, pp. 157–76.

25 Arthur W Atkinson to the editor, *SMH*, 8 October 1921.

26 *Argus*, 22 January 1891, 28 May 1904; *SMH*, 26 August 1899; *Brisbane Courier*, 11 June 1908.

27 'Memories of Adelaide Suttor (born Bowler)', 1886, typescript copy in the possession of Meg Vivers (original the property of Lin Gourlay), pp. 2, 6; Margaret Vivers [Meg Vivers], 'Female Perspectives: A Study of the Colonial Texts of Adelaide Bowler and Lucy Gray', PhD thesis, University of New England 2007, pp. 34–5, 38–40. Meg Vivers kindly helped with this material.

28 Mrs Campbell Praed [Rosa Campbell Praed], *My Australian Girlhood: Sketches and Impressions of Bush Life*, London 1902, pp. 54–8.

29 Ralph Waldo Emerson, 'The Poet' (1844), in Ralph Waldo Emerson, *Essays and Lectures*, 2nd series, ed. Joel Porte, New York, NY, 1983, p. 459; Alfred Deakin, 'Boke of Praer and Praes', 12, 19 October, 23 November 1884, NLA, MS 1540/5/7.

30 Stephen Breyer, 'On Reading Proust', *New York Review of Books*, 7 November 2013, p. 30.

31 Thomas Atkinson to William Atkinson, 3–9 September 1858, State Library of Victoria, Melbourne, MS BOX 3421/3-3A (the writer's second name, Bogue, being wrongly recorded as 'Boyne'); *Western Mail* (Perth), 28 April 1899; Gaynor, p. 291.

32 Jack Cato, *The Story of the Camera in Australia*, Melbourne 1955, pp. 82–5 (quoting, p. 82, John Beattie); Michael Roe, 'Beattie, John Watt (1859–1930)', *ADB*, vol. 7, 1979, pp. 232–3.

33 *Independent* (Footscray), 6 May 1911; Melissa Harper, *The Ways of the Bushwalker: On Foot in Australia*, Sydney 2007, pp. 26–31.

34 Bernard O'Dowd, 'Morgana Mine and Other Realities', *Heart of the Rose*, December 1907, pp. 5–11; Frank Bongiorno, 'Aboriginality and Historical Consciousness: Bernard O'Dowd and the Creation of an Australian National Imaginary', *Aboriginal History*, vol. 24, 2000, pp. 43–4.

35 Ethel Pedley, *Dot and the Kangaroo*, Sydney 1991 (1899), pp. 4, 40, 89; *SMH*,

5, 12 June 1909; M Norst, 'Pedley, Ethel Charlotte (1859–1898)', *ADB*, vol. 11, 1988, pp. 193–4.

36 Elizabeth Robins, *Woman's Secret*, Letchworth, Herts., 1907, p. 6.

37 Pedley, p. 4; Dorothea Mackellar, 'My Country' (1908), in George Mackaness (ed.), *An Anthology of Australian Verse*, Sydney 1952, p. 227. By arrangement with the Licensor, The Dorothea Mackellar Estate, c/- Curtis Brown (Aust) Pty Ltd.

38 *SMH*, 19 August, 7, 14, 25 December 1916.

39 Pedley, pp. 24–5.

40 *Argus*, 29 August 1922.

41 Katie Langloh Parker, *Australian Legendary Tales: Folklore of the Noongahburrahs as Told to the Piccaninnies*, London 1897 (1896), pp. 1, 18.

42 *New Idea* (Melbourne), 1 August, 1 November 1902, 1 March, 1 April 1903.

43 Mrs Charles Meredith [Louisa Anne Meredith], *My Home in Tasmania: During a Residence of Nine Years*, London 1852; *SMH*, 26 November 1909; Martin Mulligan & Stuart Hill, *Ecological Pioneers: A Social History of Australian Ecological Thought and Action*, Cambridge 2001, pp. 166–7.

44 Alison Bashford & Peter Hobbins, 'Science and Medicine', in Bashford & Macintyre, vol. 2, pp. 267–72.

45 Bernard O'Dowd, 'Australia' (1900), in T Inglis Moore (ed.), *Poetry in Australia*, vol. 1, *From the Ballads to Brennan*, Berkeley and Los Angeles, Calif., 1965, p. 187; 'Billabong' [Annie Rentoul], 'The Fairies of Fern Gully', *New Idea* (Melbourne), 6 August 1903; 'Billabong' [Annie Rentoul], 'How Music Came to Australia', *New Idea* (Melbourne), 6 October 1903; *Sunday Times* (Sydney), 3 December 1916; Diane Langmore, 'Outhwaite, Ida Sherbourne (1888–1960)', *ADB*, vol. 11, pp. 109–10.

46 Terence Lane, *Australian Impressionism*, Melbourne 2007, esp. Mary Eagle, 'Streeton in the City of Laughing Loveliness', pp. 201–23; Alex Taylor, *Perils of the Studio: Inside the Artistic Affairs of Bohemian Melbourne*, Melbourne 2007, p. 76 (quoting Norman St Clair Carter to Sidney Ure Smith, 28 January 1940, ML, MLMSS 31/2/216).

47 *SMH*, 20 May 1905; Stuart Macintyre, 'Rentoul, John Laurence (1846–1926)', *ADB*, vol. 11, pp. 363–5.

48 Hugh McCrae, *The Australian Alphabet*, illus. Norman Carter, Sydney [1903], n.p. Robert Holden gives the date of the McCrae-Carter publication as 1905: *Twinkle, Twinkle, Southern Cross: The Forgotten Folklore of Australian Nursery Rhymes*, Canberra 1992, pp. 20–1. In fact, it was published for Christmas 1903: *Advertiser* (Adelaide), 5 December 1903. Thanks to the granddaughters of Hugh McCrae for copyright permission.

49 *Northern Miner* (Charters Towers), 20 September 1911; *SMH*, 23 June 1916.

50 Arthur Duckworth, 'The Territorial Environments of Men', *Australian Economist*, vol. 1, 1889, p. 150.

51 *Bacchus Marsh Express*, 9 August 1902; Will Irwin, 'The Awakening of the American Business Man' (3 parts), part 1, 'The New Science of Management'; and part 2, 'The Human Side of Scientific Management', *Century Magazine*, vol. 81, March 1911, pp. 689–90, 692; and April 1911, p. 950.

52 'An Old Housekeeper', *Men and How to Manage Them: A Book for Australian Wives and Mothers*, Melbourne 1885, pp. 17, 119 (serialised in the Melbourne *Herald*, 1882).

53 HB Higgins, 'A New Province for Law and Order II', *Harvard Law Review*, vol. 32, 1918–19, pp. 197, 203.

54 HG Wells, *Marriage*, London 1912, p. 188; FB Gilbreth, Jr, & EG Carey, *Cheaper by the Dozen*, Boston 1948; Brian Price, 'Frank and Lillian Gilbreth and the

Motion Study Controversy', in Daniel Nelson (ed.), *A Mental Revolution: Scientific Management since Taylor*, Columbus, Ohio, 1992, pp. 58–64.

55 *Chronicle* (Adelaide), 3 December 1904; Kerreen M Reiger, *The Disenchantment of the Home: Modernizing the Australian Family, 1880–1940*, Melbourne 1985, pp. 128–31.

56 David Stead to Christina Stead, 15 November 1922 (extract in notes by Hazel Rowley), NLA, MS 9244, box 7; Christina Stead, *The Man Who Loved Children*, Sydney 1994 (1940), pp. 372–3; Hazel Rowley, *Christina Stead: A Biography*, Melbourne 1993, pp. 9, 17, 19–21.

57 *SMH*, 18, 31 August 1904; *Clarence and Richmond Examiner* (Grafton), 30 August 1904.

58 Mrs Lance Rawson [Mina Rawson], *Australian Enquiry Book of Household and General Information*, Melbourne 1894, p. 30; *SMH*, 18 August 1904.

59 *Argus*, 4 December 1891, 12 July 1894, 31 January, 15 June 1895, 12 April 1898; Huang Tsen-ming, *The Legal Status of the Chinese Abroad*, Taipei 1954 (1936), p. 131; Robert A Huttenback, 'The British Empire as a "White Man's Country": Racial Attitudes and Immigration Legislation in the Colonies of White Settlement', *Journal of British Studies*, vol. 13, 1973, pp. 108–37; Marilyn Lake & Henry Reynolds, *Drawing the Global Colour Line: White Men's Countries and the Question of Racial Equality*, Melbourne 2008, pp. 145–50, 162; Hirst, pp. 21–3.

60 David Day, *Andrew Fisher: Prime Minister of Australia*, London 2008, p. 85 (quoting *Truth* [Gympie], 25 March 1898).

61 *Argus*, 9 January 1901.

62 Bob Birrell, *Federation: The Secret Story*, Sydney 2001, pp. 76–7, 82, 207; Day, pp. 187, 249–52, 273; Hirst, pp. 24–37.

63 *Official Report of the National Australasian Convention Debates: Sydney, 2 March to 9 April, 1891*, Sydney 1891, p. 828 (Thomas Playford).

64 *Argus*, 26 December 1893.

65 Arthur W Jose, *Official History of Australia in the War of 1914–1918* (12 vols), vol. 9, *The Royal Australian Navy, 1914–1918*, Sydney 1941 (1928), p. 1; Day, pp. 185–6, 275–6; Lake & Reynolds, pp. 195–208; Hirst, pp. 31–3.

66 *SMH*, 10 May 1897; *Inquirer* (Perth), 27 August 1897; *Mercury* (Hobart), 4 August 1898; JS Gregory, 'New Things in War', *The World's Work*, September 1914, p. 102.

67 Alfred Deakin to Rose Scott, 14 January, 20 February, 10 May 1907, ML, A2281.

68 *Punch* (Melbourne), 23 December 1909.

69 *Brisbane Courier*, 26 March 1879. This seems to be identical with Frank Murdock's *Davy Crockett; or, Be Sure You're Right, Then Go Ahead*, first performed in the United States in 1872: Don B Wilmeth & Christopher Bigsby (eds), *The Cambridge History of American Theatre* (3 vols), vol. 2, Cambridge 1999, pp. 244–5.

70 *SMH*, 23 February 1905; Shurlee Swain, 'Society and Welfare', in Bashford & Macintyre, vol. 2, p. 295.

71 John Barrett, *Falling In: Australians and 'Boy Conscription', 1911–1915*, Sydney 1979, pp. 159–69; Craig Stockings, *The Torch and the Sword: A History of the Army Cadet Movement in Australia*, Sydney 2007, pp. 60–84.

72 *Chronicle* (Adelaide), 25 May 1912.

73 WS Churchill, speech, Liverpool, 21 September 1914, in *The Times Documentary History of the War* (11 vols), vol. 3, London 1917, p. 203; Ernest Scott, *Official History*, vol. 11, *Australia during the War*, Sydney 1941 (1936), pp. 209, 211 (quoting TW Heney); John F Williams, *Anzacs, the Media and the Great War*, Sydney 1999, p. 58.

74 HG Wells, *An Englishman Looks at the World: Being a Series of Unrestrained Remarks upon Contemporary Matters*, Hazleton, Penn., 2004 (1914), pp. 9–10. For the possible

failure of consensus by the end of the century, see James Walter, 'Growth Resumed, 1983–2000', in Bashford & Macintyre, vol. 2, p. 185 (citing Peter Saunders, *The Ends and Means of Welfare: Coping with Economic and Social Change in Australia*, Melbourne 2002).

75 *Census of the Commonwealth of Australia, 1911* (3 vols), vol. 3, Melbourne 1911, pp. 1285–96.

76 *RMCE* for 1890, p. 4 (Lewis G Madley).

77 AJ Campbell, 'The Advisability of Petitioning the Government to Impose a Gun Tax', *Victorian Naturalist*, vol. 8, 1890–91, p. 176.

78 *SMH*, 15 September 1897, 25 April 1900; Tom Griffiths, *Hunters and Collectors: The Antiquarian Imagination in Australia*, Cambridge 1996, pp. 203–10.

79 CM Finney, *Paradise Revealed: Natural History in Nineteenth-Century Australia*, Melbourne 1993, pp. 123–30; Ian R Tyrrell, *True Gardens of the Gods: Californian-Australian Environmental Reform, 1860–1930*, Berkeley, Calif., 1999, pp. 26–35.

80 *SMH*, 8 June, 4 December 1908.

81 David Stead to the editor, *SMH*, 16 July 1901.

82 *SMH*, 12 October 1911.

83 ibid., 18 June, 17 November 1909; *Gundagai Times*, 25 October 1912; DJ Mulvaney & JH Calaby, *'So Much That Is New': Baldwin Spencer, 1860–1929; A Biography*, Melbourne 1985, pp. 261–3; Drew Hutton & Libby Connors, *A History of the Australian Environmental Movement*, Melbourne 1999, pp. 35, 49; Mulligan & Hill, pp. 137, 142.

84 *SMH*, 7 October 1909.

85 ibid., 2, 21 July 1909.

86 *Mercury* (Hobart), 21 November 1910, 15 February 1911, 26 June 1912, 4 October 1913; *Examiner* (Launceston), 5 December 1911; *Land* (Sydney), 21 June 1912; *West Australian* (Perth), 23 December 1912; *Register* (Adelaide), 27 September 1913; *Queenslander* (Brisbane), 13 December 1913; J Dargavel, 'In the Wood of Neglect', in M Agnoletti & S Anderson (eds), *Forest History: International Studies on Socioeconomic and Forest Ecosystem Change*, Durham, NC, 2000, pp. 273–4.

87 *SMH*, 5 May 1910, 12 October 1911; *Evening News* (Sydney), 21 September 1911, 13 September 1913; *Register* (Adelaide), 1 July 1912; Arthur W Atkinson to AT Latham, 23 March 1923, NLA, MS1009/25/104. He had his own assistant in 1913, Mrs Ramsay.

88 *Gundagai Times*, 13 October 1911; Ann Blainey, *I Am Melba: A Biography*, Melbourne 2009, p. 493.

12 War

1 *Census of New South Wales, 1901*, Sydney 1901, p. 553 ('Habitations', table 28); *Clarence and Richmond Examiner* (Grafton), 15 April 1909; *Daily Examiner* (Grafton), 25 November 2008.

2 *ATCJ*, 15 June 1872; *Clarence and Richmond Examiner* (Grafton), 12 May 1877, 17 October 1885, 19 March 1887, 6 December 1890, 20, 29 November 1898; *Maitland Mercury*, 17 May 1877; *SMH*, 4 June 1940.

3 *Clarence and Richmond Examiner* (Grafton), 1 January 1887, 19 February 1889, 6 February 1892, 23 December 1893, 13 October 1900; *Lakeland Ledger* (Florida), 29 May 1975; 'Frankie and Albert', reproduced and discussed in *Bluesletter: The Monthly Magazine of the St Louis Blues Society*, July 2013, pp. 4–11. For more on George Verdi, see *Age*, 24 February 1910; *Sunday Times* (Sydney), 24 September 1911, 28 July 1912. He had sung in Australia with Lyster's Opera Company and later with the Emelie Melville and Montague-Turner companies.

4 *Clarence and Richmond Examiner* (Grafton), 6, 11 August 1914; *Riverine Herald*

(Echuca), 6 August 1914; *Bendigo Advertiser*, 7 August 1914; *Sunday Times* (Perth), 9 August 1914.

5 *Argus*, 14 September 1914; *SMH*, 14 September 1914; CEW Bean, *Official History of Australia in the War of 1914–1918* (12 vols), vol. 1, *The Story of ANZAC from the Outbreak of War to the End of the First Phase of the Gallipoli Campaign, May 4, 1915*, Sydney 1941 (1921), pp. 37–45. For enlistment numbers see Joan Beaumont (ed.), *The Australian Centenary History of Defence* (7 vols), vol. 6, *Australian Defence: Sources and Statistics*, Melbourne 2001, p. 108 (no figures for New South Wales and Western Australia; estimated in light of the others).

6 *Byron Bay Record*, 9 June 1917, 6 July 1918.

7 John McQuilton, *Rural Australia and the Great War: From Tarrawingee to Tangambalanga*, Melbourne 2001, pp. 161–72; John F Williams, *German Anzacs and the First World War*, Sydney 2003, pp. 6–7, 67–102.

8 *Mirror of Australia* (Sydney), 25 March, 6, 20, 27 May, 12, 26 August 1916.

9 *Northern Star* (Lismore), 25 December 1912; *Byron Bay Record*, 4 January 1913; Verdi Schwinghammer, journal, 6 May 1916 – 26 September 1919, ML, MLMSS 1683, p. 9; *Mirror of Australia* (Sydney), 13, 27 May 1916.

10 Verdi Schwinghammer, journal, 6 May 1916 – 26 September 1919, ML, MLMSS 1683, pp. 21, 28, 37, 56, 58; Verdi Schwinghammer, 'A Soldier's Experience', said to have appeared 'over two days in the Grafton [Daily] Examiner, late 1918', but original unfound, Unofficial History of the Australian & New Zealand Armed Forces, n.d., viewed 17 February 2014, <www.diggerhistory.info/pages-battles/ww1/france/somme-1918.htm>. Note that in Grafton the *Daily Examiner* had replaced the *Clarence and Richmond Examiner* in 1915.

11 *Northern Star* (Lismore), 31 December 1918.

12 Filippo Tommaso Marinetti, 'The Futurist Manifesto' (Italian 1909), in Stanislao G Pugliese (ed. and trans.), *Fascism, Anti-Fascism, and the Resistance in Italy: 1919 to the Present*, Lanham, Md., 2004, pp. 27, 28.

13 *Colac Herald*, 14 January 1910; *Globe* (Sydney), 12 October 1912; *Argus*, 27 December 1913; *Bendigo Advertiser*, 5 September 1914; Eugene Goodheart, *Culture and the Radical Conscience*, New Brunswick, NJ, 2001, pp. 142–3.

14 Norman Angell, *The Great Illusion: A Study of the Relation of Military Power in Nations to Their Economic and Social Advantage*, London 1911, pp. 183–8.

15 *West Australian* (Perth), 25 January 1915; *Western Mail* (Perth), 29 January 1915; *Argus*, 30 January 1915; *Cairns Post*, 5 February 1915; *Catholic Press* (Sydney), 11 February 1915; *Northern Star* (Lismore), 15 February 1915; *Bathurst Times*, 20 February 1915; *Clarence and Richmond Examiner* (Grafton), 20 February 1915; W Michael Ryan, *Lieutenant-Colonel Charles à Court Repington: A Study in the Interaction of Personality, the Press, and Power*, New York, NY, and London 1987, pp. 150–1 (quoting *Times* [London], 15 December 1914); Hew Strachan, 'From Cabinet War to Total War: The Perspective of Military Doctrine, 1861–1918', in Roger Chickering & Stig Förster (eds), *Great War, Total War: Combat and Mobilization on the Western Front, 1914–1918*, Cambridge 2000, pp. 24–6; William Philpott, *Three Armies on the Somme: The First Battle of the Twentieth Century*, New York, NY, 2010, p. 525 (quoting Ferdinand Foch).

16 CR Badger, *The Reverend Charles Strong and the Australian Church*, Melbourne 1971, pp. 145–7 (quoting, pp. 146–7, anti-conscription manifesto, December 1917); Michael McKernan, *Australian Churches at War: Attitudes and Activities of the Major Churches, 1914–1918*, Canberra 1980, pp. 23, 68–9, 75–6, 77, 89, 110–11, 153.

17 *Brisbane Courier*, 5 March 1915; *Hawthorn, Kew, Camberwell Citizen*, 23 August 1918; Bill Gammage, *The Broken Years: Australian Soldiers in the Great War*,

Melbourne 1975 (1974), p. 182 (quoting Roy Berry, letter, 24 January 1917).

18 CEW Bean, *In Your Hands, Australians*, London 1918, p. 90; KS Inglis, 'The Anzac Tradition', *Meanjin*, vol. 24, 1965, pp. 25–44 (quoting Bean, *In Your Hands, Australians*, p. 25); David A Kent, '*The Anzac Book* and the Anzac Legend: C.E.W. Bean as Editor and Image-Maker', *Historical Studies*, vol. 21, 1985, pp. 376–90; Jane Ross, *The Myth of the Digger: The Australian Soldier in Two World Wars*, Sydney 1985, pp. 11–24; Alistair Thomson, '"Steadfast until Death"? C.E.W. Bean and the Representation of Australian Military Manhood', *Australian Historical Studies*, vol. 23, 1989, pp. 462–77; Jenny Macleod, *Reconsidering Gallipoli*, Manchester 2004, pp. 5–15; Graham Seal, *Inventing Anzac: The Digger and National Mythology*, Brisbane 2004, pp. 1–35.

19 Paul Fussell, *The Great War and Modern Memory*, Oxford 1975, pp. 119, 137–44 (quoting Wilfrid Owen to Osbert Sitwell, July 1918).

20 Angell, p. 188; Ernst Jünger, *The Storm of Steel: From the Diary of a German Storm-Troop Officer on the Western Front*, trans. Basil Creighton, New York, NY, 1975 (German 1920), p. 23.

21 WH Downing, *To the Last Ridge*, Sydney 1998 (1920), p. 17; Jünger, p. 23.

22 Downing, pp. 55–6.

23 ibid., pp. 21, 65; Jünger, pp. 109, 118; Philpott, pp. 356–7.

24 *SMH*, 23 October 1915; Willie Mann to his parents, 27 April 1917, Australian War Memorial, Canberra, 2DRL/0105/2; HR Williams, *The Gallant Company: An Australian Soldier's Story of 1915–18*, Sydney 1933, p. 274; Gammage, pp. 15 (quoting RD Mulvey, letter, 19 September 1915), 60 (quoting W Davidson, letter, 22 April 1915), 150 (quoting Hubert Howard, letter, 2 July 1916).

25 Alan Henderson to his parents, 24 April 1915, Australian War Memorial, Canberra, 1DRL/0339 (his brother was Rupert Henderson); 'Alan Dudley Henderson'; and 'Rupert Howard Henderson', World War One service records, National Archives of Australia, Canberra, B2455/5315012, B2455/5338767; *SMH*, 26 April 1917; *War Letters of General Monash*, ed. FM Cutlack, Sydney 1934, p. 32 (John Monash to Vic Monash, 23 April 1915).

26 *SMH*, 26 April 1917.

27 'Elphick, Arthur Thomas'; 'Finlason, Rupert'; and 'Taylor, Barrett Leach', World War One service records, National Archives of Australia, Canberra, B2455/3541656, B2455/3900720, B2455/1928397; *Kalgoorlie Miner*, 12 May 1915; *Examiner* (Launceston), 18, 26 May 1915, 11 January 1923; *Register* (Adelaide), 25 May 1915; *Bendigonian*, 27 May 1915.

28 *Democrat* (Sydney), 30 October 1915; Beaumont, pp. 108–9. Between May and August 85,000 men signed up.

29 Philpott, pp. 26, 32.

30 HR Williams, pp. 42, 214–15.

31 Paddy Griffith, *Battle Tactics of the Western Front: The British Army's Art of Attack, 1916–18*, New Haven, Conn., and London 1994, pp. 10–17; Philpott, pp. 129–31.

32 Strachan, pp. 24–6; Philpott, pp. 29–30.

33 JG Fuller, *Troop Morale and Popular Culture in the British and Dominion Armies, 1914–1918*, Oxford 1990, p. 41; Griffith, p. 17; Roger Chickering, 'World War I and the Theory of Total War', in Chickering & Förster, pp. 40–3; Philpott, pp. 38, 72–3, 125, 142, 144, 166.

34 *Advertiser* (Adelaide), 23 May 1918.

35 Jünger, p. 194; Griffith, pp. 21–4, 31; Strachan, p. 27.

36 Karl Kraus, *The Last Days of Mankind: A Tragedy in Five Acts*, ed. Frederick Ungar, trans. Alexander Gode & Ellen Wright, New York, NY, 1974 (German 1919), p. 67.

37 Philip Gibbs, *Now It Can Be Told*, New York, NY, 1920, pp. 131, 300–1; Robert Graves, *Goodbye to All That*, Melbourne 2009 (1929), p. 154; Peter Stanley, *Bad Characters: Sex, Crime, Mutiny, Murder and the Australian Imperial Force*, Sydney 2010, pp. 138–9.

38 'The School for French', *Yandoo* (trench newspaper), July 1917, in David A Kent (ed.), *From Trench and Troopship: The Experience of the Australian Imperial Force, 1914–1919*, Sydney 1999, pp. 143–5.

39 Leonard Bibbs to Kit (sister), 20 February 1915; Robert Adam to his mother, 1 October 1915; and Willie Mann to his parents, 21 June 1916, Australian War Memorial, Canberra, 1DRL/118, 1DRL/0003, 2DRL/0105/2; CEW Bean, *Official History*, vol. 6, *The Australian Imperial Force in France during the Allied Offensive, 1918*, Sydney 1942, pp. 259–61; Gammage, pp. 85–7, 231–2 (quoting George Mitchell, diary, 19 October 1916), 233–4 (quoting Roger Morgan, diary, 1 April 1914); Fuller, pp. 166–8; Philpott, p. 441.

40 Downing, pp. 165–8; Sir John Monash, *The Australian Victories in France in 1918*, London 1920, pp. 291–2; HR Williams, p. 163; Gammage, p. 98 (quoting Thomas Richards, diary, 11 June 1915).

41 John F Williams, *Anzacs, the Media and the Great War*, Sydney 1999, p. 170 (quoting *Münchner Neueste Nachrichten*, April 1917); Chickering, pp. 48–53.

42 Monash, *Australian Victories in France*, p. 291.

43 Strachan, pp. 30–1; Beaumont, pp. 366–7; Philpott, pp. 147–8, 153.

44 Willie Mann to his parents, 1 December 1917, Australian War Memorial, Canberra, 2DRL/0105/2; Philpott, pp. 129–31, 261.

45 Griffith, pp. 122–4, 129–34; Jeffrey Grey, *The Australian Army*, Melbourne 2001, pp. 66–7.

46 HR Williams, p. 117; Dennis E Showalter, 'Mass Warfare and the Impact of Technology', in Chickering & Förster, p. 87.

47 Downing, p. 50; Gammage, p. 98; Griffith, pp. 38–9, 67–9, 120–4; Philpott, pp. 166–7, 260.

48 Griffith, pp. 138–9; Rolf-Dieter Müller, 'Total War as a Result of New Weapons?: The Use of Chemical Agents in World War I', in Chickering & Förster, pp. 102–3.

49 *Chronicle* (Adelaide), 19 December 1914; *Cairns Post*, 16 June 1915; Fred Alexander, *Campus at Crawley: A Narrative and Critical Appreciation of the First Fifty Years of the University of Western Australia*, Perth 1967, pp. 92–3; Fred Alexander, 'Whitfield, Hubert Edwin (1875–1939)'; and BK de Garis, 'Wilsmore, Norman Thomas Mortimer (1868–1940)', *ADB*, vol. 12, 1990, pp. 475, 517–18.

50 John A Moses, 'Australia's Academic Garrison 1914–1918', *Australian Journal of Politics and History*, vol. 36, 1990, pp. 366–72; RJW Selleck, *The Shop: The University of Melbourne, 1850–1939*, Melbourne 2003, pp. 528–30; John A Moses, 'An Australian Empire Patriot and the Great War: Professor Sir Archibald T. Strong (1876–1930)', *Australian Journal of Politics and History*, vol. 53, 2007, pp. 407–19.

51 Henry Gyles Turner, 'Australia Militant', *Melbourne Review*, vol. 10, 1885, p. 153.

52 JM Winter, 'Britain's "Lost Generation" of the First World War', *Population Studies*, vol. 31, 1977, pp. 460–3; Keith Jones, 'The Sydney University Union Records of World War One', *Record* (Sydney University Archives), no. 2, 1991, p. 4 (thanks to Nyree Morrison for help with this); Selleck, p. 528.

53 Adrian Consett Stephen, *An Australian in the R.F.A.*, ed. Alfred Consett Stephen, Sydney 1918, pp. 8, 19, 101, 108, 119, 120, 121. Compare Monash, *Australian Victories in France*, p. 121.

54 *Argus*, 16 October 1916; *Sunday Times* (Perth), 5 November 1916; *Advertiser* (Adelaide), 6 November 1916; Philpott, pp. 265–6. The words and music of 'When

You Come to the End of a Perfect Day', by Carrie Jacobs-Bond, were published in 1909.

55 Gibbs, p. 131.

56 *Advertiser* (Adelaide), 3 July 1917; Downing, pp. 27–8; Gammage, pp. 251–5.

57 Gammage, p. 141 (source not given); Seal, pp. 36–46.

58 Chickering, pp. 38–9, 44–7, 50; Martin van Creveld, 'World War I and the Revolution in Logistics', in Chickering & Förster, pp. 66–9; Showalter, pp. 80–2; Strachan, p. 32; Philpott, pp. 295–7, 450.

59 Ernest Scott, *Official History*, vol. 11, *Australia during the War*, Sydney 1941 (1936), pp. 168–90; David Day, *Andrew Fisher: Prime Minister of Australia*, London 2008, pp. 326–7.

60 *Moree Gwydir Examiner*, 28 March 1916; LF Fitzhardinge, *William Morris Hughes: The Little Digger, 1914–1952*, Sydney 1979, pp. 171–215, 279–99; McQuilton, pp. 110–12; Day, pp. 138–9.

61 Monash, *Australian Victories in France*, pp. 96, 180–1, 192, 235–6, 241, 273–5; PA Pedersen, 'General Sir John Monash: Commander on the Western Front', in DM Horner (ed.), *The Commanders: Australian Military Leadership in the Twentieth Century*, Sydney 1992, p. 109; Philpott, pp. 426, 504.

62 Monash, *Australian Victories in France*, pp. 10–11; *War Letters of General Monash*, pp. 155–60 (John Monash to Vic Monash, 11 April 1917), 172 (John Monash to John Gibson, 29 April 1917).

63 *Brisbane Courier*, 10 October 1931; Geoffrey Serle, *John Monash: A Biography*, Melbourne 1982, pp. 306 (quoting PP Abbott), 373–5.

64 Monash, *Australian Victories in France*, pp. 112–13; Lesley Alves, Alan Holgate & Geoff Taplin, *Monash Bridges: Typology Study; Reinforced Concrete Bridges in Victoria, 1897–1917*, Melbourne 1998, p. 8; Alan Holgate, *John Monash: Tanks and Silos*, Melbourne 2000, pp. 8–16.

65 Monash, *Australian Victories in France*, pp. 112–13; John Thompson, *On Lips of Living Men*, Melbourne 1962, p. 144 (quoting General Sir Julius Bruche).

66 Monash, *Australian Victories in France*, pp. 51, 56, 150–1, 291; CEW Bean, *Official History*, vol. 5, *The Australian Imperial Force in France during the Main German Offensive, 1918*, Brisbane 1941 (1937), p. 177; Serle, pp. 305–6, 378–9, 380–1.

67 Verdi Schwinghammer, journal, 6 May 1916 – 26 September 1919, ML, MLMSS 1683, pp. 22, 23, 53; Stephen Kern, *The Culture of Time and Space, 1880–1918*, Cambridge, Mass., 1983, pp. 288–90.

68 John Scott to his family, 5 November 1918, ML, MLDOC 2476; HR Williams, pp. 207, 214, 219.

69 Monash, *Australian Victories in France*, p. 16; Serle, p. 306 (quoting Sir John Monash to Lady Monash, 15 March 1918); Philpott, pp. 138–9, 152, 192–3, 359–61.

70 Verdi Schwinghammer, journal, 6 May 1916 – 26 September 1919, ML, MLMSS 1683, p. 21; Monash, *Australian Victories in France*, pp. 125, 171–2; Martin van Creveld, *Supplying War: Logistics from Wallenstein to Patten*, Cambridge 1977, pp. 110–13; Griffith, p. 12.

71 Monash, *Australian Victories in France*, pp. 41–2, 112, 124; Griffith, pp. 23–4; Van Creveld, 'World War I', p. 67.

72 Monash, *Australian Victories in France*, pp. 57–8, 94–5, 192; Serle, pp. 330, 334; Pedersen, pp. 105–8.

73 John P Scott to his family, 5 November 1918, ML, MLDOC 2476; HR Williams, p. 146; Gammage, pp. 101–2, 118, 205, 216, 267.

74 *Times* (London), 5 November 1914, 8 July 1916; *Mercury* (Hobart), 1 August 1916; Monash, *Australian Victories in France*, p. 144; Philpott, pp. 52, 368.

75 *Ararat Advertiser*, 11 January 1916; Gammage, p. 228; Philpott, p. 392.
76 EPF Lynch, *Somme Mud: The War Experiences of an Australian Infantryman in France, 1916–1919*, ed. Will Davies, Sydney 2006, p. 195.
77 Verdi Schwinghammer, journal, 6 May 1916 – 26 September 1919, ML, MLMSS 1683, pp. 19, 54; John P Scott, diary, 9 January 1918, ML, MLDOC 2476; Griffith, p. 26; Seal, pp. 18–33.
78 HR Williams, pp. 118–19; Gammage, pp. 260–2 (quoting Ernest Allen, letter, 26 March 1918); Seal, pp. 34–5.
79 Stephen, p. 56; HR Williams, p. 61.
80 *Democrat* (Sydney), 30 October 1915; *Brisbane Courier*, 7, 27 September, 2 October 1917, 2 February 1923; HR Williams, pp. 65, 66; McKernan, pp. 72–3; McQuilton, pp. 149–60.
81 Graham Jones, *Memories of Oxley*, Wangaratta 1995, p. 136 (quoting Ellen Ward's granddaughter, Eunice Smith; and see *Albury and Wodonga Express*, 4 November 1938, which shows that Eunice Smith was the daughter of Austin Ward, another of Ellen Ward's sons).
82 'Heydon, Edward Lynes [Lyons]', World War One service record, National Archives of Australia, Canberra, B2455/5481669; *SMH*, 27, 29 January 1917.
83 'Wilkins, Laurence George'; 'Wilkins, Thomas'; and 'Wilkins, Phillip', World War One service records, National Archives of Australia, Canberra, B2455/8389367, B2455/8389392, B2455/8389379; Amanda Laugesen, *Diggerspeak: The Language of Australians at War*, Melbourne 2005, p. 60.
84 HR Williams, p. 127; David Wilkins, *From Brecon to Broken Hill: The History of a Wilkins Family*, Sydney 2007, pp. 222–3.
85 *Dubbo Liberal*, 14 July 1916; Perry family to Thomas Wilkins (telegram), 28 December 1916, University of New England Regional Archives, Atkinson Box 31 (thanks to David Kent for help with this).

Afterword

1 Adrian Consett Stephen, *An Australian in the R.F.A.*, ed. Alfred Consett Stephen, Sydney 1918, pp. 152–3; Ernst Jünger, *The Storm of Steel: From the Diary of a German Storm-Troop Officer on the Western Front*, trans. Basil Creighton, New York, NY, 1975 (German 1920), p. 316.
2 Stephen, pp. 152–3.
3 *Argus*, 16 January 1917; *SMH*, 4 March 1918; Ernest Scott, *Official History of Australia in the War of 1914–1918* (12 vols), vol. 11, *Australia during the War*, Sydney 1941 (1936), pp. 231–2. The number of redirected items shows that the great bulk was personal.
4 CEW Bean, *In Your Hands, Australians*, London 1918, p. 90.
5 *Argus*, 24 April 1917.
6 Scott, p. 231; Michael McKernan, *Australian Churches at War: Attitudes and Activities of the Major Churches, 1914–1918*, Canberra 1980, p. 73.
7 KS Inglis, *Sacred Places: War Memorials in the Australian Landscape*, Melbourne 1998, pp. 46, 66–7, 333–47. The term 'national memorial' or 'national war memorial' had been first used in Australia for the Boer War, as in 'national memorial in Victoria', 'South Australian National War Memorial' and, in Tasmania, 'a national memorial for the whole island', together with talk of a 'Federal Australian memorial' which would also be 'national': *Sunday Times* (Sydney), 27 May 1900; *Barrier Miner* (Broken Hill), 11 September 1900; *Evening News* (Sydney), 20 October 1900; *Register* (Adelaide), 20 October 1902; *Examiner* (Launceston), 6 January 1905.

8 'The Re-union of Christendom', *Australian Herald* (Melbourne), February 1892, p. 114; *West Australian* (Perth), 19 October 1899; John A Moses, 'Was There an Anzac Theology?', *Colloquium*, vol. 35, 2003, pp. 3–13; Janice Pavils, 'The Emergence of South Australian Anzac Culture 1915–1925', *Journal of the Royal Australian Historical Society*, vol. 89, 2003, pp. 123–44; John A Moses, 'Anglicanism and Anzac Observance: The Essential Contribution of Canon David John Garland', *Pacifica*, no. 19, February 2006, pp. 58–77.

9 *Coburg Leader*, 14 September 1901; Jay Winter, *Sites of Memory, Sites of Mourning: The Great War in European Cultural History*, Cambridge 1995, p. 50 (quoting Rebecca Hinds, letter, 22 October 1941).

10 John McQuilton, *Rural Australia and the Great War: From Tarrawingee to Tangambalanga*, Melbourne 2001, pp. 120–6; Melanie Oppenheimer, '"The Best PM for the Empire in War?": Lady Helen Munro Ferguson and the Australian Red Cross Society, 1914–1920', *Australian Historical Studies*, vol. 33, 2002, pp. 108, 116–19; Stephen Garton & Peter Stanley, 'The Great War and Its Aftermath, 1914–22', in Alison Bashford & Stuart Macintyre (eds), *The Cambridge History of Australia* (2 vols), vol. 2, Melbourne 2013, p. 61.

11 'Moore, Kenton Clifford', World War One service record, National Archives of Australia, Canberra, B2455/3006436; *Chronicle* (Adelaide), 24 August 1918; Winter, pp. 36–8, 40–1; John Rickard, 'White, Vera Deakin (1891–1978)', *ADB*, vol. 16, 2002, pp. 535–6.

12 Oppenheimer, pp. 121–2 (quoting Frederick Fairbairn to James Murdoch, 13 December 1917); Rickard, p. 535 (quoting Vera White).

13 Richard Sennett, *The Fall of Public Man*, Cambridge 1977 (1976), pp. 19–20; Joan Beaumont (ed.), *The Australian Centenary History of Defence* (7 vols), vol. 6, *Australian Defence: Sources and Statistics*, Melbourne 2001, p. 116.

14 Marilyn Lake, 'Mission Impossible: How Men Gave Birth to the Australian Nation; Nationalism, Gender and Other Seminal Acts', *Gender and History*, vol. 4, 1992, pp. 305–22; Marilyn Lake, *Getting Equal: The History of Australian Feminism*, Sydney 1999, pp. 28–36, 49–51, 53–6.

15 Anne Donnell, *Letters of an Australian Army Sister*, Sydney 1920, p. 218 (Anne Donnell to friends, 1 May 1918); Bill Gammage, *The Broken Years: Australian Soldiers in the Great War*, Melbourne 1975 (1974), pp. 60 (quoting Reginald Donkin, diary, 16 May 1915), 157 (quoting George Gordon McCrae, letter, 19 July 1916); Peter Rees, *The Other Anzacs: Nurses at War, 1914–1918*, Sydney 2008, pp. 238–44.

16 WL Courtney, *The Life of John Stuart Mill*, London 1889, pp. 117–18; Janet Butler, *Kitty's War: The Remarkable Wartime Experiences of Kit McNaughton*, Brisbane 2013, pp. 87, 159, 161 (quoting Kit McNaughton).

17 Donnell, pp. 288–90 (Anne Donnell to friends, 16 February 1919); Watkin Tench, *A Narrative of the Expedition to Botany Bay* (1789); and Watkin Tench, *A Complete Account of the Settlement at Port Jackson* (1793), in LF Fitzhardinge (ed.), *Sydney's First Four Years*, Sydney 1979, pp. 30–1.

18 *Daily Herald* (Adelaide), 4 August 1915, 3 September 1918, 20 February 1920; Donnell, pp. 290–1 (Anne Donnell to friends, 28 February 1919); *Barrier Miner* (Broken Hill), 16 March 1921; *Register* (Adelaide), 6 September 1923.

Bibliography

Books and Published Documents from the Period

Abercromby, Ralph (ed.), *Three Essays on Australian Weather*, Sydney 1896.

Ackermann, Jessie, *Australia from a Woman's Point of View*, Sydney 1981 (1913).

Adams, Francis, *Australian Essays*, Melbourne 1886.

—— *The Australians: A Social Sketch*, London 1893.

Anderson, Hugh (ed.), *Tocsin: Radical Arguments against Federation, 1897–1900*, Melbourne 1977.

—— (ed.), *Tocsin: Contesting the Constitution, 1897–1901*, Melbourne 2000.

Angell, Norman, *The Great Illusion: A Study of the Relation of Military Power in Nations to Their Economic and Social Advantage*, London 1911.

Bailey, FM & PR Gordon, *Plants Reputed Poisonous and Injurious to Stock*, Brisbane 1887.

Balls-Headley, Walter, *The Evolution of the Diseases of Women*, London 1894.

Bean, CEW, *The 'Dreadnought' of the Darling*, London 1911.

—— *On the Wool Track*, London 1916.

—— *Official History of Australia in the War of 1914–1918* (12 vols), vol. 1, *The Story of ANZAC from the Outbreak of War to the End of the First Phase of the Gallipoli Campaign, May 4, 1915*, Sydney 1941 (1921).

—— *Official History of Australia in the War of 1914–1918* (12 vols), vol. 5, *The Australian Imperial Force in France during the Main German Offensive, 1918*, Brisbane 1941 (1937).

—— *Official History of Australia in the War of 1914–1918* (12 vols), vol. 6, *The Australian Imperial Force in France during the Allied Offensive, 1918*, Sydney 1942.

—— *War Aims of a Plain Australian*, Sydney 1943.

—— *Anzac to Amiens*, Melbourne 1983 (1946).

—— *Two Men I Knew: William Bridges and Brudenell White, Founders of the A.I.F.*, Sydney 1957.

—— (ed.), *The Anzac Book*, London 1916.

Bellamy, Edward, *Looking Backward: If Socialism Comes, 2000–1887*, London 1888.

—— *Equality*, Sydney 1943 (1897).

Bergson, Henri, *Creative Evolution*, trans. Arthur Mitchell, New York, NY, 1910 (French 1907).

Blackstone, Sir William, *Commentaries on the Laws of England* (4 vols), London 1825 (1765–69).

Boldrewood, Mrs Rolf [Margaret Maria Browne], *The Flower Garden in Australia: A Book for Ladies and Amateurs*, Melbourne 1893.

Brough Smyth, R, *The Aborigines of Victoria*, Melbourne 1878.

Bryce, James, *The American Commonwealth* (2 vols), New York, NY, 1898 (1888).

The Bulletin Reciter: A Collection of Verses for Recitation from 'The Bulletin', 1880–1901, Sydney 1901.

Carpenter, William B, *Principles of Mental Physiology*, London 1896 (1874).

Casson, Herbert N, *The History of the Telephone*, Chicago, Ill., 1910.

Census of New South Wales, 1891 (Statistician's Report), Sydney 1894.

Census of New South Wales, 1901, Sydney 1901.

Census of the Commonwealth of Australia, 1911 (3 vols), Melbourne 1911.

Clarke, Marcus, *The Future Australian Race*, Melbourne 1877.

Coghlan, TA, *Childbirth in New South Wales: A Study in Statistics*, Sydney 1899.
—— *The Decline in the Birth-Rate of New South Wales and Other Phenomena of Child-Birth: An Essay in Statistics*, Sydney 1903.
—— *Labour and Industry in Australia: From the First Settlement in 1788 to the Establishment of the Commonwealth in 1901* (4 vols), London 1918.
Courtney, WL, *The Life of John Stuart Mill*, London 1889.
Curr, Edward M, *The Australian Race: Its Origin, Languages, Customs, Place of Landing in Australia, and the Routes by Which It Spread over That Continent*, Melbourne 1886–87.
Dahl, Knut, *In Savage Australia: An Account of a Hunting and Collecting Expedition to Arnhem Land and Dampier Land*, London 1926 (Norwegian 1897).
Dawson, James, *Australian Aborigines: The Languages and Customs of Several Tribes in the Western District of Victoria, Australia*, Melbourne 1881.
[Deakin, Alfred] *A New Pilgrim's Progress*, Melbourne 1877.
Deakin, Alfred, *Irrigated India: An Australian View of India and Ceylon, Their Irrigation and Agriculture*, London 1893.
—— *Temple and Tomb in India*, Melbourne 1893.
—— *The Federal Story: The Inner History of the Federal Cause, 1880–1900*, ed. JA La Nauze, Melbourne 1963 (*The Federal Story*, 1944).
Desmond, Valerie, *The Awful Australian*, Sydney 1911.
Downing, WH, *To the Last Ridge*, Sydney 1998 (1920).
Elkington, JSC, *Tropical Australia: Is It Suitable for a Working White Race?*, Melbourne 1905.
Ellis, Alexander J, *On Early English Pronunciation, with Especial Reference to Shakespere and Chaucer*, London 1869.
Emerson, Ralph Waldo, *Essays and Lectures*, 2nd series, ed. Joel Porte, New York, NY, 1983.
Fewster, Kevin (ed.), *Gallipoli Correspondent: The Frontline Diary of C.E.W. Bean*, Sydney 1983.
—— (ed.), *Frontline Gallipoli: C.E.W. Bean, Diaries from the Trenches*, Sydney 1990.
—— (ed.), *Bean's Gallipoli: The Diaries of Australia's Official War Correspondent*, Sydney 2009.
Fox, Frank, *From the Old Dog: Being the Letters of the Hon. — —, ex Prime Minister to His Nephew*, Melbourne 1908.
Franklin, Miles, *Joseph Furphy: The Legend of a Man and His Book*, Sydney 1944.
Fraser, John Foster, *Australia: The Making of a Nation*, London 1910.
Fried, Albert & Richard M Elman (eds), *Charles Booth's London: A Portrait of the Poor at the Turn of the Century, Drawn from His 'Life and Labour of the People of London'*, London 1969.
Froude, James Anthony, *Oceana; or, England and Her Colonies*, New York, NY, 1886.
Gibbs, Philip, *Now It Can Be Told*, New York, NY, 1920.
Giles, Ernest, *Australia Twice Traversed: The Romance of Exploration* (2 vols), London 1889.
Gilmore, Mary, *Old Days, Old Ways: A Book of Recollections*, Sydney 1934.
Gordon, David J, *The Central State: South Australia; Its History, Progress and Resources*, Adelaide 1903.
—— *The 'Nile' of Australia: Nature's Gateway to the Interior; A Plea for the Greater Utilization of the Murray and Its Tributaries*, Adelaide 1906.
Gordon, PR, *Fencing as a Means of Improving Our Pasture Lands, and Its Advantages to the Stock-Owners and the Colony*, Sydney 1867.
Graves, Robert, *Goodbye to All That*, Melbourne 2009 (1929).
Gribble, ERB, *The Problem of the Australian Aboriginal*, Sydney 1932.

Griffith, Sir Samuel Walker, *Notes on Australian Federation: Its Nature and Probable Effects*, Brisbane 1896.
—— *Australian Federation and the Draft of the Commonwealth Bill*, Brisbane 1899.
Haggard, Henry Rider, *The Last Boer War*, London 1900.
Hardy, Thomas, *Thomas Hardy's Personal Writings: Prefaces, Literary Opinions, Reminiscences*, ed. Harold Orel, Basingstoke, Hants., 1990.
Hinton, Charles Howard, *Scientific Romances* (2 series), London 1886 and 1896.
Historical Sketch of S. James' Sydney, Sydney 1919.
Houston, Edwin J & AE Kennelly, *The Electric Telephone*, New York, NY, 1906.
Inglis, Gordon, *Sport and Pastime in Australia*, London 1912.
Jackson, Henry Latimer, *Parents and Children*, Sydney 1888.
James, William, *The Will to Believe and Other Essays in Popular Philosophy, and Human Immortality*, New York, NY, 1956 (*The Will to Believe and Other Essays in Popular Philosophy*, 1896).
Jefferis, James, *A Free Church in a Free State: Its Claims and Conflicts*, Sydney 1878.
—— *Reply to the Joint-Pastoral of the Roman Catholic Archbishop and Bishops of New South Wales*, Sydney 1879.
—— *Australia Confederated*, Sydney 1880.
—— *Our Bible and Our Belief: Six Lectures Delivered in the Congregational Church, Pitt Street, Sydney, as a Help to Young Men of Free Thought*, Sydney 1882.
—— *The Federation of the British People*, Adelaide 1901.
Jevons, William Stanley, *The Theory of Political Economy*, London 1879 (1871).
—— *Papers and Correspondence of William Stanley Jevons* (7 vols), ed. RD Collison Black & Rosamond Konekamp, London 1972.
Jünger, Ernst, *The Storm of Steel: From the Diary of a German Storm-Troop Officer on the Western Front*, trans. Basil Creighton, New York, NY, 1975 (German 1920).
Kent, David A (ed.), *From Trench and Troopship: The Experience of the Australian Imperial Force, 1914–1919*, Sydney 1999.
Kinglake, Edward, *The Australian at Home: Notes and Anecdotes of Life at the Antipodes*, London [1891].
Kirmess, CH, *The Australian Crisis*, London 1909.
Lang, Gideon Scott, *The Aborigines of Australia, in Their Original Condition and in Their Relations with the White Men*, Melbourne 1865.
Lynch, EPF, *Somme Mud: The War Experiences of an Australian Infantryman in France, 1916–1919*, ed. W Davies, Sydney 2006.
Lyne, Charles E, *The Industries of New South Wales*, Sydney 1882.
—— *Life of Sir Henry Parkes, G.C.M.G.: Australian Statesman*, London 1897.
McBurney, Samuel, *Victoria: A School Cantata Composed and Dedicated to the Singing Masters of the Victorian State Schools*, Melbourne 1875.
McCrae, Hugh, *The Australian Alphabet*, illus. Norman Carter, Sydney [1903].
Macdonald, AC, JH Maiden & JH Myring (eds), *Special Volume of the Proceedings of the Geographical Society of Australasia*, Sydney 1885.
Mackenzie, Eneas, *Memoirs of Mrs. Caroline Chisholm, with an Account of Her Philanthropic Labours, in India, Australia, and England*, London 1852.
Marchant, James, *Birth-Rate and Empire*, London 1917.
Marin la Meslée, Edmond, *The New Australia*, ed. and trans. R Ward, London 1973 (French 1883).
Marsh, CC, *The Science of Double-Entry Book-Keeping*, New York, NY, 1851.
Marsland, LW (ed.), *The Charters Towers Gold Mines*, London 1892.
Mathew, J, *Eaglehawk and Crow: A Study of the Australian Aborigines Including an Inquiry into Their Origin and a Survey of Australian Languages*, London 1899.

Memorandum and Articles of Association of the Animal Protection Society of New South Wales, Sydney 1895.

Meredith, Mrs Charles [Louisa Ann Meredith], *My Home in Tasmania: During a Residence of Nine Years*, London 1852.

Meston, Archibald, *Queensland Aboriginals: Proposed System for Their Improvement and Preservation*, Brisbane 1895.

—— *Report on the Aboriginals of Queensland*, Brisbane 1896.

Michelet, Jules, *Histoire de France* (4 vols), Paris 1880 (1833–67).

—— *The History of France* (2 vols), trans. WK Kelly, London 1884 (French 1833–67).

Mill, John Stuart, *On Liberty*, New Haven, Conn., 2003 (1859).

—— *The Subjection of Women*, New York, NY, 1869.

—— *Autobiography*, London 1873.

Monash, Sir John, *The Australian Victories in France in 1918*, London 1920.

—— *War Letters of General Monash*, ed. FM Cutlack, Sydney 1934.

Morris, Edward E, *Austral English: A Dictionary of Australasian Words, Phrases and Usages*, London 1898.

Morris, William, *News from Nowhere; or, An Epoch of Rest*, London 1912 (1890).

Nicklin, T, *The Sounds of Standard English*, Oxford 1925.

O'Dowd, Bernard, *Conscience and Democracy*, Melbourne 1902.

The Official Directory and Almanac of Australia for 1884, Sydney 1884.

Ogilvie, Will H, *My Life in the Open*, London 1908.

'An Old Housekeeper', *Men and How to Manage Them: A Book for Australian Wives and Mothers*, Melbourne 1885 (serialised in the Melbourne *Herald*, 1882).

O'Rell, Max [Léon Paul Blouet], *John Bull & Co.: The Great Colonial Branches of the Firm; Canada, Australia, New Zealand and South Africa*, London 1894.

Parker, Katie Langloh, *Australian Legendary Tales: Folklore of the Noongahburrahs as Told to the Piccaninnies*, London 1897 (1896).

Paterson, Andrew Barton, *Happy Dispatches*, Sydney 1980 (1934).

Pearson, CH, *Report on the State of Public Education in Victoria and Suggestions as to the Best Means of Improving It*, Melbourne 1878.

—— *National Life and Character: A Forecast*, London 1893.

Pilmer, RH, *Northern Patrol: An Australian Saga*, ed. C Clement & P Bridge, Perth 1998.

Praed, Mrs Campbell [Rosa Campbell Praed], *My Australian Girlhood: Sketches and Impressions of Bush Life*, London 1902.

Pratt, Ambrose, *The Great 'Push' Experiment*, Sydney 1902.

Proceedings of the First Australasian Conference on Charity, Held in Melbourne, from 11th to 17th November, 1890, Convened by the Charity Organization Society of Melbourne, Melbourne 1891.

Rawson, Mrs Lance [Mina Rawson], *Mrs. Rawson's Australian Poultry Book*, Sydney 1893.

—— *Australian Enquiry Book of Household and General Information*, Melbourne 1894.

—— *The Antipodean Cookery Book and Kitchen Companion*, Melbourne 1907 (1895).

Reeves, William Pember, *State Experiments in Australia and New Zealand* (2 vols), Melbourne 1969 (1902).

Report of the Sixth Meeting of the Australian Association for the Advancement of Science, Held at Brisbane, Queensland, January, 1895, Sydney 1895.

Rilke, Rainer Maria, *Letters to a Young Poet*, ed. and trans. Mark Harman, Cambridge, Mass., 2011 (German 1929).

Robins, Elizabeth, *Woman's Secret*, Letchworth, Herts., 1907.

Small, Albion Woodbury, *The Meaning of Social Science*, Chicago, Ill., 1910.

Smith, Bruce, *Our Commonwealth: A Handbook of the Australian Constitution*, Sydney 1904.

Spence, Catherine Helen, *An Autobiography*, Adelaide 1910.
Spence, William Guthrie, *History of the A.W.U.*, Sydney 1961.
Spencer, Walter Baldwin (ed.), *Report on the Work of the Horn Scientific Expedition to Central Australia* (4 parts), London 1896.
Spengler, Oswald, *The Decline of the West* (2 vols), trans. CF Atkinson, New York, NY, 1926 (German 1918).
Stephen, Adrian Consett, *An Australian in the R.F.A.*, ed. Alfred Consett Stephen, Sydney 1918.
Stephen, Sir Alfred & Sir John Robertson, *The Colony of Australia: Views of Sir Alfred Stephen and Sir John Robertson*, Sydney 1887.
Stow, David, *The Training System of Education, for the Moral and Intellectual Elevation of Youth*, Edinburgh 1846.
Strong, Charles, *Concerning Women*, Melbourne 1895.
—— & Francis Anderson, *The Australian Church: Report MDCCCLXXXVII; and, Sermons*, Melbourne 1887.
Sutherland, Alexander, *The Origin and Growth of the Moral Instinct* (2 vols), London 1898.
Thoreau, Henry, *Autumn: From the Journal of Henry D. Thoreau*, ed. HGO Blake, Boston 1892.
Tuckett, Mrs Arthur [Margaret Tuckett], *A Year in My Garden*, Melbourne 1905.
Twopeny, REN, *Town Life in Australia*, London 1883.
Tylor, Edward, *Anthropology: An Introduction to the Study of Man and Society*, New York, NY, 1899 (1881).
Vogan, AJ, *The Black Police: A Story of Modern Australia*, London 1890.
von der Goltz, Baron Colmar, *The Nation in Arms: A Treatise on Modern Military Systems and the Conduct of War*, trans. PA Ashworth, London 1906 (German 1883).
Ward, Elizabeth Jane, *Womanhood Suffrage from a Christian Standpoint*, Sydney n.d.
—— *Out of Weakness Made Strong: Being a Record of the Life and Labours of Mrs E.J. Ward*, Sydney 1903.
Wells, HG, *Marriage*, London 1912.
—— *An Englishman Looks at the World: Being a Series of Unrestrained Remarks upon Contemporary Matters*, Hazleton, Penn., 2004 (1914).
Westgarth, William, *Half a Century of Australasian Progress: A Personal Retrospect*, London 1889.
Williams, HR, *The Gallant Company: An Australian Soldier's Story of 1915–18*, Sydney 1933.
Willshire, WH, *A Thrilling Tale of Real Life in the Wilds of Australia*, Adelaide 1895.
—— *The Land of the Dawning*, Adelaide 1896.
Wise, Bernhard Ringrose, *The Making of the Australian Commonwealth, 1889–1900: A Stage in the Growth of the Empire*, London 1913.

Books by Modern Scholars

Ackroyd, Peter, *Albion: The Origins of the English Imagination*, London 2004.
Adam-Smith, Patsy, *The Anzacs*, Melbourne 1978.
Adelman, Jeremy, *Republic of Capital: Buenos Aires and the Legal Transformation of the Atlantic World*, Stanford, Calif., 1999.
Agnoletti, M & S Anderson (eds), *Forest History: International Studies on Socioeconomic and Forest Ecosystem Change*, Durham, NC, 2000.
Alexander, Fred, *Campus at Crawley: A Narrative and Critical Appreciation of the First Fifty Years of the University of Western Australia*, Perth 1967.
Allen, Judith, *Sex and Secrets: Crimes Involving Women since 1880*, Melbourne 1990.
—— *Rose Scott: Vision and Revision in Feminism*, Melbourne 1994.

Alves, Lesley, Alan Holgate & Geoff Taplin, *Monash Bridges: Typology Study; Reinforced Concrete Bridges in Victoria, 1897–1917*, Melbourne 1998.
Amaral, Samuel, *The Rise of Capitalism on the Pampas: The Estancias of Buenos Aires, 1785–1870*, Cambridge 1998.
Anderson, Benedict, *Imagined Communities: Reflections on the Origin and Spread of Nationalism*, London 1983.
Atkinson, Alan, *The Commonwealth of Speech: An Argument about Australia's Past, Present and Future*, Melbourne 2002.
——, JS Ryan, Iain Davidson & Andrew Piper (eds), *High Lean Country: Land, People and Memory in New England*, Sydney 2006.
Attwood, Bain, *The Making of the Aborigines*, Sydney 1989.
—— *Possession: Batman's Treaty and the Matter of History*, Melbourne 2009.
—— & Andrew Markus, *The 1967 Referendum: Race, Power and the Australian Constitution*, Canberra 2007.
—— & SG Foster (eds), *Frontier Conflict: The Australian Experience*, Canberra 2003.
Badger, CR, *The Reverend Charles Strong and the Australian Church*, Melbourne 1971.
Baird, Marian, Rae Cooper & Mark Westcott (eds), *Reworking Work: AIRANZ 05; Proceedings of the 19th Conference of the Association of Industrial Relations Academics of Australia and New Zealand* (2 vols), Sydney 2005.
Baker, SJ, *The Australian Language: The Meanings, Origins and Usage; From Convict Days to the Present*, Sydney 1978 (1945).
Barnes, John, *The Order of Things: A Life of Joseph Furphy*, Melbourne 1990.
—— *Made in Shepparton: The History of J. Furphy & Sons, 1873–1998*, Shepparton 1998.
Barrett, John, *Falling In: Australians and 'Boy Conscription', 1911–1915*, Sydney 1979.
Bashford, Alison & Stuart Macintyre (eds), *The Cambridge History of Australia* (2 vols), Melbourne 2013.
Bateman, Jim, *History of the Telephone in New South Wales*, Sydney 1980.
Bayly, CA, *The Birth of the Modern World 1780–1914*, Malden, Mass., 2004.
Beaumont, Joan (ed.), *The Australian Centenary History of Defence* (7 vols), Melbourne 2001.
Belich, James, *Replenishing the Earth: The Settler Revolution and the Rise of the Angloworld, 1783–1939*, Oxford 2009.
Bellanta, Melissa, *Larrikins: A History*, Brisbane 2012.
Bernstein, Peter L, *Against the Gods: The Remarkable Story of Risk*, New York, NY, 1996.
Birrell, Bob, *Federation: The Secret Story*, Sydney 2001.
Blainey, Ann, *I Am Melba: A Biography*, Melbourne 2009.
Blainey, Geoffrey, *The Tyranny of Distance*, Melbourne 1966.
Blouet, Brian W, *Halford Mackinder: A Biography*, College Station, Tex., 1987.
Bolton, Geoffrey C, *A Thousand Miles Away: A History of North Queensland to 1920*, Canberra 1970.
—— *Land of Vision and Mirage: Western Australia since 1826*, Perth 2008.
Bongiorno, Frank, *The People's Party: Victorian Labor and the Radical Tradition, 1875–1914*, Melbourne 1996.
—— *The Sex Lives of Australians: A History*, Melbourne 2012.
Bonyhady, Tim, *The Colonial Earth*, Melbourne 2000.
—— & Tom Griffiths (eds), *Words for Country: Landscape and Language in Australia*, Sydney 2002.
Breen, Shayne, *Contested Places: Tasmania's Northern Districts from Ancient Times to 1900*, Hobart 2001.
Brown, Peter, *The Rise of Western Christendom*, Oxford 2003.
Brumby, Michael, *Muskets and Mantlets: A Brief History of the Life and Times of the*

Charters Towers Rifle Range, 1885–1994, Charters Towers 1996.
Butler, Janet, *Kitty's War: The Remarkable Wartime Experiences of Kit McNaughton*, Brisbane 2013.
Butlin, NG, *Investment in Australian Economic Development, 1861–1900*, Cambridge 1964.
Butlin, SG, *Foundations of the Australian Monetary System, 1788–1851*, Sydney 1953.
Buxton, GL, *The Riverina 1861–1891: An Australian Regional Study*, Melbourne 1967.
Carlyon, Les, *Gallipoli*, Sydney 2002.
Cato, Jack, *I Can Take It*, Melbourne 1947.
—— *The Story of the Camera in Australia*, Melbourne 1955.
Chesterman, John & Brian Galligan, *Citizens without Rights: Aborigines and Australian Citizenship*, Cambridge 1997.
Chickering, Roger & Stig Förster (eds), *Great War, Total War: Combat and Mobilization on the Western Front, 1914–1918*, Cambridge 2000.
Connell, Daniel, *Water Politics in the Murray-Darling Basin*, Sydney 2007.
Council of the Royal Society of New South Wales (ed.), *A Century of Scientific Progress: The Centenary Volume of the Royal Society of New South Wales*, Sydney [1968].
Crawford, Ian, *We Won the Victory: Aboriginals and Outsiders on the North-West Coast of the Kimberley*, Perth 2001.
Crisp, LF, *Federation Prophets without Honour: A.B. Piddington, Tom Price, H.B. Higgins*, Canberra 1980.
—— *Charles Cameron Kingston: Radical Federationist*, Canberra 1984.
Croft, Julian, *The Life and Opinions of Tom Collins: A Study of the Works of Joseph Furphy*, Brisbane 1991.
Crook, Paul, *Darwinism, War and History: The Debate over the Biology of War from the 'Origin of Species' to the First World War*, Cambridge 1994.
Crotty, M & DA Roberts (eds), *The Great Mistakes of Australian History*, Sydney 2006.
—— (eds), *Turning Points in Australian History*, Sydney 2009.
Crowley, Marie, *Women of the Vale: Perthville Josephites, 1872–1972*, Melbourne 2002.
Curthoys, Ann & John Docker, *Is History Fiction?*, Sydney 2010.
Daly, John A, *Elysian Fields: Sport, Class and Community in Colonial South Australia*, Adelaide 1982.
Damousi, Joy, *Colonial Voices: A Cultural History of English in Australia 1840–1910*, Cambridge 2010.
Dando-Collins, Stephen, *Pasteur's Gambit: Louis Pasteur, the Australasian Rabbit Plague and a Ten Million Dollar Prize*, Sydney 2008.
Davis, Lance E & Robert A Huttenback, *Mammon and the Pursuit of Empire: The Political Economy of British Imperialism, 1860–1912*, Cambridge 1986.
Davison, Graeme, JW McCarty & Ailsa McLeary (eds), *Australians, 1888*, Sydney 1987.
Day, David, *Contraband and Controversy: The Customs History of Australia from 1901*, Canberra 1996.
—— *The Weather Watchers*, Melbourne 2007.
—— *Andrew Fisher: Prime Minister of Australia*, London 2008.
Desrosières, Alain, *The Politics of Large Numbers: A History of Statistical Reasoning*, trans. C Naish, Cambridge, Mass., 1998.
Dixson, M, *The Real Matilda: Woman and Identity in Australia, 1788 to the Present*, Melbourne 1976.
—— *The Imaginary Australian: Anglo-Celts and Identity, 1788 to the Present*, Sydney 2009.
Donovan, Val & Colleen Wall (eds), *Making Connections: A Journey along Central Australian Aboriginal Trading Routes*, Brisbane 2004.
Dyrenfurth, N & F Bongiorno, *A Little History of the Australian Labor Party*, Sydney 2011.
Ekins, Ashley (ed.), *1918: Year of Victory; The End of the Great War and the Shaping of*

History, Wollombi, 2010.
Ely, Richard G, *Unto God and Caesar: Religious Issues in the Emerging Commonwealth, 1891–1906*, Melbourne 1976.
Evans, AG, *C.Y. O'Connor: His Life and Legacy*, Perth 2001.
Evans, Raymond, *Fighting Words: Writing about Race*, Brisbane 1999.
—— *A History of Queensland*, Cambridge 2007.
——, Kay Saunders & Kathryn Cronin, *Race Relations in Colonial Queensland: A History of Exclusion, Exploitation and Extermination*, Brisbane 1988.
Faulkner, John & Stuart Macintyre (eds), *True Believers: The Story of the Federal Parliamentary Labor Party*, Sydney 2001.
Fennessy, Kathleen, *A People Learning: Colonial Victorians and Their Public Museums, 1860–1880*, Melbourne 2007.
Ferguson, Niall, *The War of the World: History's Age of Hatred*, London 2006.
Finney, CM, *Paradise Revealed: Natural History in Nineteenth-Century Australia*, Melbourne 1993.
Fitzgerald, Ross, *From the Dreaming to 1915: A History of Queensland*, Brisbane 1982.
Fitzhardinge, LF, *William Morris Hughes: The Little Digger, 1914–1952*, Sydney 1979.
Flynn, James R, *What Is Intelligence? Beyond the Flynn Effect*, Cambridge 2009 (2007).
Frame, TR, *A Church for a Nation: A History of the Anglican Diocese of Canberra and Goulburn*, Sydney 2000.
Fuller, JG, *Troop Morale and Popular Culture in the British and Dominion Armies, 1914–1918*, Oxford 1990.
Fussell, Paul, *The Great War and Modern Memory*, Oxford 1975.
Gabay, Al, *The Mystic Life of Alfred Deakin*, Cambridge 1992.
Gammage, Bill, *The Broken Years: Australian Soldiers in the Great War*, Melbourne 1975 (1974).
Gardner, Paul, *Mary MacKillop: An Extraordinary Australian*, Sydney 1994.
Gerster, Robin, *Big-Noting: The Heroic Theme in Australian War Writing*, Melbourne 1987.
Glass, Margaret, *Charles Cameron Kingston: Federation Father*, Melbourne 1997.
Goodheart, Eugene, *Culture and the Radical Conscience*, New Brunswick, NJ, 2001.
Grattan, Michelle, *Back on the Wool Track*, Sydney 2004.
Grey, Jeffrey, *The Australian Army*, Melbourne 2001.
Griffith, Paddy, *Battle Tactics of the Western Front: The British Army's Art of Attack, 1916–18*, New Haven, Conn., and London 1994.
Griffiths, Tom, *Hunters and Collectors: The Antiquarian Imagination in Australia*, Cambridge 1996.
Hageman, Karen, Sonya Michel & Gunilla Budde (eds), *Civil Society and Gender Justice: Historical and Comparative Perspectives*, New York, NY, 2008.
Halse, Christine, *A Terribly Wild Man*, Sydney 2002.
Harper, Melissa, *The Ways of the Bushwalker: On Foot in Australia*, Sydney 2007.
Hasluck, Paul, *Black Australians: A Survey of Native Policy in Western Australia, 1829–1897*, Melbourne 1942.
Haward, Marcus & James Warden (eds), *An Australian Democrat: The Life, Work and Consequences of Andrew Inglis Clark*, Hobart 1995.
Hay, Douglas & Paul Craven (eds), *Masters, Servants, and Magistrates in Britain and the Empire, 1562–1955*, Chapel Hill, NC, 2004.
Haynes, Roslyn D, *Seeking the Centre: The Australian Desert in Literature, Art and Film*, Cambridge 1998.
Headon, David & Jeff Brownrigg (eds), *The People's Conventions: Corowa (1893) and Bathurst (1896)*, Papers on Parliament no. 32, Canberra 1998.

Healy, Chris, *Forgetting Aboriginals*, Sydney 2008.

Heath, Deana, *Purifying Empire: Obscenity and the Politics of Moral Regulation in Britain, India and Australia*, Cambridge 2010.

Hicks, Neville, *This Sin and Scandal: Australia's Population Debate, 1891–1911*, Canberra 1978.

Hirst, John B, *The Strange Birth of Colonial Democracy: New South Wales, 1848–1884*, Sydney 1988.

—— *The Sentimental Nation: The Making of the Australian Commonwealth*, Melbourne 2000.

—— *Sense and Nonsense in Australian History*, Melbourne 2009.

Hobsbawm, Eric, *The Age of Extremes: The Short Twentieth Century, 1914–1991*, London 1994.

Holden, Robert, *Twinkle, Twinkle, Southern Cross: The Forgotten Folklore of Australian Nursery Rhymes*, Canberra 1992.

Holgate, Alan, *John Monash: Tanks and Silos*, Melbourne 2000.

Home, RW (ed.), *Australian Science in the Making*, Melbourne 1988.

Hood, Robert & Ray Markey (eds), *Labour and Community: Proceedings of the Sixth National Conference of the Australian Society for the Study of Labour History*, Wollongong 1999.

Horner, DM (ed.), *The Commanders: Australian Military Leadership in the Twentieth Century*, Sydney 1992.

Huang Tsen-ming, *The Legal Status of the Chinese Abroad*, Taipei 1954 (1936).

Humphreys, Robert, *Poor Relief and Charity, 1869–1945: The London Charity Organization*, New York, NY, 2002.

Hutton, Drew & Libby Connors, *A History of the Australian Environmental Movement*, Melbourne 1999.

Hynes, Samuel, *A War Imagined: The First World War and English Culture*, London 1990.

Inglis, KS, *C.E.W. Bean, Australian Historian*, Brisbane 1970.

—— *The Australian Colonists: An Exploration of Social History, 1788–1870*, Melbourne 1974.

—— *The Rehearsal: Australians at War in the Sudan*, Adelaide 1985.

—— *Sacred Places: War Memorials in the Australian Landscape*, Melbourne 1998.

Irving, Helen (ed.), *A Woman's Constitution? Gender and History in the Australian Commonwealth*, Sydney 1996.

—— (ed.), *The Centenary Companion to Australian Federation*, Cambridge 1999.

Isaac, Joe & Stuart Macintyre (eds), *The New Province for Law and Order: 100 Years of Australian Industrial Conciliation and Arbitration*, Cambridge 2004.

Jackson, Hugh, *Churches and People in Australia and New Zealand, 1860–1930*, Sydney 1987.

Jebb, Mary Anne, *Blood, Sweat and Welfare: A History of White Bosses and Aboriginal Pastoral Workers*, Perth 2002.

Johnson, DH, *Torres Strait to Coral Sea: The Defence of North Queensland*, Charters Towers 1992.

Johnson, John J, Peter J Bakewell & Meredith D Dodge (eds), *Readings in Latin American History* (2 vols), Durham, NC, 1985.

Jones, Graham, *Memories of Oxley*, Wangaratta 1995.

Jones, Helen, *In Her Own Name: A History of Women in South Australia*, Adelaide 1994.

Jose, Arthur W, *Official History of Australia in the War of 1914–1918* (12 vols), vol. 9, *The Royal Australian Navy, 1914–1918*, Sydney 1941 (1928).

Jupp, James (ed.), *The Australian People: An Encyclopedia of the Nation, Its People and Their Origins*, Cambridge 2001.

Kahneman, Daniel, *Thinking, Fast and Slow*, London 2011.
Kenny, Robert, *The Lamb Enters the Dreaming: Nathaniel Pepper and the Ruptured World*, Melbourne 2007.
Kern, Stephen, *The Culture of Time and Space, 1880–1918*, Cambridge, Mass., 1983.
Kirkpatrick, Rod, *The Life and Times of Thadeus O'Kane*, Townsville 2003.
Knowles, Rob, *Political Economy from Below: Economic Thought in Communitarian Anarchism, 1840–1914*, New York, NY, and London 2004.
Kolig, Erich, *The Noonkanbah Story*, Dunedin 1987.
La Nauze, JA, *Political Economy in Australia: Historical Studies*, Melbourne 1949.
—— *Alfred Deakin: A Biography* (2 vols), Melbourne 1965.
Laidlaw, Zoe, *Colonial Connections, 1815–1845: Patronage, the Information Revolution and Colonial Government*, Manchester 2005.
Lake, Marilyn, *Getting Equal: The History of Australian Feminism*, Sydney 1999.
—— & Henry Reynolds, *Drawing the Global Colour Line: White Men's Countries and the Question of Racial Equality*, Melbourne 2008.
Lane, Terence, *Australian Impressionism*, Melbourne 2007.
Laugesen, Amanda, *Diggerspeak: The Language of Australians at War*, Melbourne 2005.
Lawson, Sylvia, *The Archibald Paradox: A Strange Case of Authorship*, Melbourne 1983.
Lawton, William James, *The Better Time to Be: Utopian Attitudes to Society among Sydney Anglicans, 1885 to 1914*, Sydney 1990.
Levi, Margaret, *Consent, Dissent, and Patriotism*, Cambridge 1997.
Lewis, Gary, *The Democracy Principle: Farmer Co-operatives in Twentieth Century Australia*, Wamboin 2006.
Lightman, Bernard, *Victorian Science in Context*, Chicago, Ill., and London 1997.
Loos, Noel, *White Christ Black Cross: The Emergence of a Black Church*, Canberra 2007.
Lowrance, William W, *Modern Science and Human Values*, Oxford 1985.
Lyne, Daniel, *Mary MacKillop: Spirituality and Charisms*, Sydney 1982.
Lyons, Mark, *Cooperatives in Australia: A Background Paper*, ACCORD Paper no. 1, Sydney 2001.
McCalman, Janet, *Struggletown: Portrait of an Australian Working-Class Community 1900–1965*, Melbourne 1984.
McCorkindale, Isabel (ed.), *Torch-Bearers: The Women's Christian Temperance Union of South Australia, 1886–1948*, Adelaide 1949.
MacCulloch, Diarmaid, *A History of Christianity: The First Three Thousand Years*, London 2009.
McDonald, Lorna, *Rockhampton: A History of City and District*, Rockhampton 1995.
McDougall, R & I Davidson (eds), *The Roth Family, Anthropology, and Colonial Administration*, Walnut Creek, Calif., 2008.
McGrath, Ann & Kay Saunders (eds), *Aboriginal Workers*, with J Huggins, Sydney 1995.
McGregor, Russell, *Imagined Destinies: Aboriginal Australians and the Doomed Race Theory, 1880–1939*, Melbourne 1997.
—— *Indifferent Inclusion: Aboriginal People and the Australian Nation*, Canberra 2011.
Macintyre, Stuart, *A Colonial Liberalism: The Lost World of Three Victorian Visionaries*, Melbourne 1991.
Mack, David, *The Village Settlements on the Murray in South Australia, 1894–1909: A Chronicle of Communal Life and Hardship*, Adelaide 1994.
McKernan, Michael, *Australian Churches at War: Attitudes and Activities of the Major Churches, 1914–1918*, Canberra 1980.
—— *The Australian People and the Great War*, Sydney 1980.
—— *Drought: The Red Marauder*, Sydney 2005.
—— & M Browne (eds), *Australia: Two Centuries of War and Peace*, Canberra 1988.

Mackinnon, Alison, *Love and Freedom: Professional Women and the Reshaping of Personal Life*, Cambridge 1997.

McKnight, Tom L, *The Long Paddock: Australia's Travelling Stock Routes*, Armidale 1977.

Macleod, Jenny, *Reconsidering Gallipoli*, Manchester 2004.

McPherson, James M, *Is Blood Thicker than Water? Crises of Nationalism in the Modern World*, New York, NY, 1999.

Macqueen, H, R Cilento & C Lack, *Triumph in the Tropics*, Brisbane 1959.

McQuilton, John, *Rural Australia and the Great War: From Tarrawingee to Tangambalanga*, Melbourne 2001.

Magarey, Susan, *Unbridling the Tongues of Women: A Biography of Catherine Helen Spence*, Adelaide 1985.

Main, George, *Heartland: The Regeneration of Rural Place*, Sydney 2005.

Manion, John, *Irish Settlements in Eastern Canada: A Study of Cultural Transfer and Adaptation*, Toronto 1974.

—— *Paper Power in North Queensland: A History of Journalism in Townsville and Charters Towers*, Townsville 1982.

Martin, AW (ed.), *Essays in Australian Federation*, Melbourne 1969.

Mathews, Mitford M, *Teaching to Read: Historically Considered*, Chicago, Ill., 1966.

May, Cathie R, *Topsawyers: The Chinese in Cairns, 1870–1920*, Townsville 1984.

Mayer, Henry, *The Press in Australia*, Melbourne 1964.

Mazoer, Mark, *Governing the World: The History of an Idea*, London 2012.

Merritt, John, *The Making of the AWU*, Melbourne 1986.

Miller, Jon & David Muir, *The Business of Brands*, Chichester, Sussex, 2004.

Monmonier, Mark, *Air Apparent: How Meteorologists Learned to Map, Predict, and Dramatize Weather*, Chicago, Ill., 1999.

Morrison, Elizabeth, *Engines of Influence: Newspapers of Country Victoria, 1840–1890*, Melbourne 2005.

Morton, SR & DJ Mulvaney (eds), *Exploring Central Australia: Society, the Environment and the 1894 Horn Expedition*, Sydney 1996.

Moses, John A, *Prussian-German Militarism 1914–18 in Australian Perspective: The Thought of George Arnold Wood*, Berne 1991.

Moyal, Ann, *Clear across Australia: A History of Telecommunications*, Melbourne 1984.

Mugglestone, Lynda C, *Talking Proper: The Rise of Accent as Social Symbol*, Oxford 2003.

Mulligan, Martin & Stuart Hill, *Ecological Pioneers: A Social History of Australian Ecological Thought and Action*, Cambridge 2001.

Mulvaney DJ & JH Calaby, *'So Much That Is New': Baldwin Spencer, 1860–1929; A Biography*, Melbourne 1985.

Munro, Keith, *Have You Finished? The History of the Country Telephonists, Especially Those in the New England Tablelands*, Armidale 1989.

Murphy, DJ (ed.), *Labor in Politics: The State Labor Parties in Australia, 1880–1920*, Brisbane 1975.

—— (ed.), *The Big Strikes: Queensland 1889–1965*, Brisbane 1983.

Murphy, John, *A Decent Provision: Australian Welfare Policy, 1870 to 1949*, Farnham, Surrey, 2011.

Murray, James, *Larrikins: 19th Century Outrage*, Melbourne 1973.

Murray-Smith, S (ed.), *Melbourne Studies in Education, 1973*, Melbourne 1973.

Nelson, Daniel (ed.), *A Mental Revolution: Scientific Management since Taylor*, Columbus, Ohio, 1992.

Nettlebeck, Amanda & Robert Foster, *In the Name of the Law: William Willshire and the Policing of the Australian Frontier*, Adelaide 2007.

Nye, Andrea, *Feminism and Modern Philosophy: An Introduction*, New York, NY, 2004.
O'Collins, Gerald, *Patrick McMahon Glynn: A Founder of Australian Federation*, Melbourne 1965.
Oldfield, Audrey, *Woman Suffrage in Australia: A Gift or a Struggle?*, Cambridge 1992.
Ong, Walter J, *Orality and Literacy: The Technologizing of the Word*, London 1982.
Palmer, Vance, *National Portraits: 25 Australian Lives*, Melbourne 1960 (1940).
Pedersen, Howard & Banjo Woorunmurra, *Jandamarra and the Bunuba Resistance*, Broome 1995.
Peters, Margot, *Bernard Shaw and the Actresses*, New York, NY, 1980.
Peterson, Nicolas (ed.), *Tribes and Boundaries*, Canberra 1976.
Phillips, Walter, *Defending 'a Christian Country': Churchmen and Society in New South Wales in the 1880s and After*, Brisbane 1981.
—— *James Jefferis: Prophet of Federation*, Melbourne 1993.
Philpott, William, *Three Armies on the Somme: The First Battle of the Twentieth Century*, New York, NY, 2010.
Pinker, Steven, *The Better Angels of Our Nature: The Decline of Violence in History and Its Causes*, London 2011.
Polanyi, Michael, *Personal Knowledge: Towards a Post-Critical Philosophy*, New York, NY, 1962 (1958).
Prior, Robin, *Gallipoli: The End of the Myth*, Sydney 2009.
—— & Trevor Wilson, *Command on the Western Front: The Military Career of Sir Henry Rawlinson, 1914–18*, Oxford 1992.
Rainbow, Bernard, *Music in Educational Thought and Practice: A Survey from 800 BC*, Aberystwyth 1989.
Readman, Paul, Cynthia Radding & Chad Bryant (eds), *Borderlands in World History, 1700–1914*, Chapel Hill, NC, 2014.
Rees, Peter, *The Other Anzacs: Nurses at War, 1914–1918*, Sydney 2008.
Reiger, Kerreen M, *The Disenchantment of the Home: Modernizing the Australian Family, 1880–1940*, Melbourne 1985.
Reynolds, Henry, *The Other Side of the Frontier: Aboriginal Resistance to the European Invasion of Australia*, Townsville 1981.
—— *Why Weren't We Told? A Personal Search for the Truth about Our History*, Melbourne 1999.
—— *North of Capricorn: The Untold Story of Australia's North*, Sydney 2003.
Richards, Christopher, *There Were Three Ships: The Story of the Camden Harbour Expedition 1864–65*, Perth 1990.
Richardson, Robert D, *First We Read, Then We Write: Emerson on the Creative Process*, Iowa City, Iowa, 2009.
Rickard, John, *H.B. Higgins: The Rebel as Judge*, Sydney 1984.
Robin, Libby, *How a Continent Created a Nation*, Sydney 2007.
Robson, LL, *The First A.I.F.: A Study of Its Recruitment*, Melbourne 1970.
Roe, Jill, *Stella Miles Franklin*, Sydney 2008.
—— (ed.) *Social Policy in Australia: Some Perspectives 1901–1975*, Sydney 1976.
Roe, Michael, *Nine Australian Progressives: Vitalism in Bourgeois Social Thought, 1890–1960*, Brisbane 1984.
Rose, Deborah Bird, *Hidden Histories: Black Stories from Victoria River Downs, Humbert River and Wave Hill Stations*, Canberra 1991.
—— *Dingo Makes Us Human: Life and Land in an Australian Aboriginal Culture*, Cambridge 2000 (1992).
Rosewater, Victor, *History of Cooperative News-Gathering in the United States*, New York, NY, 1930.

Ross, Jane, *The Myth of the Digger: The Australian Soldier in Two World Wars*, Sydney 1985.
Ross, Lloyd, *William Lane and the Australian Labour Movement*, Sydney 1937.
Rowley, Hazel, *Christina Stead: A Biography*, Melbourne 1993.
Rowse, Tim, *White Flour, White Power: From Rations to Citizenship*, Cambridge 1998.
Russell, Archer, *William James Farrer: A Biography*, Melbourne 1949.
Ryan, Jan, *Ancestors: Chinese in Colonial Australia*, Perth 1995.
Ryan, W Michael, *Lieutenant-Colonel Charles à Court Repington: A Study in the Interaction of Personality, the Press, and Power*, New York, NY, and London 1987.
Rylance, Rick, *Victorian Psychology and British Culture, 1850–1880*, Oxford 2000.
Saunders, Kay, *Workers in Bondage: The Origins and Bases of Unfree Labour in Queensland, 1824–1916*, Brisbane 1982.
Savage, Jon, *Teenage: The Creation of Youth Culture*, New York, NY, 2007.
Scates, Bruce, *A New Australia: Citizenship, Radicalism and the First Republic*, Cambridge 1997.
Schuster, John A & Richard R Yeo (eds), *The Politics and Rhetoric of Scientific Method: Historical Studies*, Dordrecht 1986.
Scott, Ernest, *The Official History of Australia in the War of 1914–1918* (12 vols), vol. 11, *Australia during the War*, Sydney 1941 (1936).
Scott, James C, *Seeing Like a State: How Certain Schemes to Improve the Human Condition Have Failed*, New Haven, Conn., 1998.
Seal, Graham, *Lingo: Listening to Australian English*, Sydney 1999.
—— *Inventing Anzac: The Digger and National Mythology*, Brisbane 2004.
—— *The Soldiers' Press: Trench Journals in the First World War*, Basingstoke 2013.
Selleck, RJW, *The Shop: The University of Melbourne, 1850–1939*, Melbourne 2003.
Sennett, Richard, *The Fall of Public Man*, Cambridge 1977 (1976).
Serle, Geoffrey, *The Rush to Be Rich: A History of the Colony of Victoria, 1883–1889*, Melbourne 1971.
—— *John Monash: A Biography*, Melbourne 1982.
Sheldon, JS, *The Big School Room at Sydney Grammar School: With an Account of the Decline and Fall of Sydney College*, Sydney 1997.
Sherratt, Tim, Tom Griffiths & Libby Robin (eds), *A Change in the Weather: Climate and Culture in Australia*, Cambridge 2005.
Sinclair, Keith, *A History of New Zealand*, London 1969.
Soden, Frank A, Reuban Phillip Watson, Bruce Whitehead & Neilma E Watson (comps), *100 Years of the Telephone*, private limited edn, Melbourne 1976.
Souter, Gavin, *A Peculiar People: The Australians in Paraguay*, Sydney 1968.
—— *Mosman: A History*, Melbourne 1994.
Spence, Clark C, *The Rainmakers: American 'Pluviculture' to World War II*, Lincoln, Nebr., 1980.
Stanford, JD, *The Long-Term Effect of Federation on the Queensland Economy*, London 1988.
Stanley, Peter, *Bad Characters: Sex, Crime, Mutiny, Murder and the Australian Imperial Force*, Sydney 2010.
Stead, Christina, *The Man Who Loved Children*, Sydney 1994 (1940).
Stephen, Ann (ed.), *Visions of a Republic: The Work of Lucien Henry; Paris, Noumea, Sydney*, Sydney 2001.
Stockings, Craig, *The Torch and the Sword: A History of the Army Cadet Movement in Australia*, Sydney 2007.
Swain, Tony, *A Place for Strangers: Towards a History of Australian Aboriginal Being*, Cambridge 1993.
Swan, RA, *Australia in the Antarctic: Interest, Activity and Endeavour*, London 1961.

Taylor, Alex, *Perils of the Studio: Inside the Artistic Affairs of Bohemian Melbourne*, Melbourne 2007.
Taylor, Peter, *An End to Silence: The Building of the Overland Telegraph Line from Adelaide to Darwin*, Sydney 1980.
Telecom Australia, *'The Palace of Winged Words': The Development of Telephone Exchanges in Australia*, Melbourne [1980].
Thomas, Martin, *The Many Worlds of R.H. Mathews: In Search of an Australian Anthropologist*, Sydney 2011.
—— (ed.), *Culture in Translation: The Anthropological Legacy of R.H. Mathews*, with translations from the French by Mathilde de Hauteclocque and from the German by Christine Winter, Canberra 2007.
Thompson, John, *On Lips of Living Men*, Melbourne 1962.
Thompson, Roger C, *Australian Imperialism in the Pacific: The Expansionist Era, 1820–1920*, Melbourne 1980.
Thomson, Alistair, *Anzac Memories: Living with the Legend*, Melbourne 1995.
Tyrrell, Ian R, *True Gardens of the Gods: Californian-Australian Environmental Reform, 1860–1930*, Berkeley, Calif., 1999.
Vamplew, Wray (ed.), *Australians: Historical Statistics*, Sydney 1987.
van Creveld, Martin, *Supplying War: Logistics from Wallenstein to Patten*, Cambridge 1977.
Vincent, Andrew (ed.), *The Philosophy of T.H. Green*, London 1986.
Vivers, Meg, *Castle to Colony: The Remarkable Life and Times of Lucy Sarah Gray (1840–1879)*, Hughenden 2011.
Walker, RB, *The Newspaper Press in New South Wales, 1803–1920*, Sydney 1976.
Warren, Ian (ed.), *Gender, Theory and Sport: The Formative Years of Tennis and Snowboarding*, Australian Studies for Sports History no. 16, Melbourne 2005.
Watson, Don, *Death Sentence: The Decay of Public Language*, Sydney 2003.
Watson, Peter, *The German Genius: Europe's Third Renaissance, the Second Scientific Revolution and the Twentieth Century*, London 2010.
Weber, Eugen, *Peasants into Frenchmen: The Modernization of Rural France, 1870–1914*, London 1977.
White, Richard & Hsu-Ming Teo (eds), *Cultural History in Australia*, Sydney 2003.
Whittington, Vera, *Two Fevers: Gold and Typhoid; A Social History of Western Australia during the Decade 1891–1900 under the Particular Influence of These and Other Related Factors, People in Events*, Perth [1982].
Wilcox, C, *For Hearths and Homes: Citizen Soldiering in Australia 1854–1945*, Sydney 1998.
Wilkins, David, *From Brecon to Broken Hill: The History of a Wilkins Family*, Sydney 2007.
Williams, John F, *Anzacs, the Media and the Great War*, Sydney 1999.
—— *German Anzacs and the First World War*, Sydney 2003.
Winter, Jay, *Sites of Memory, Sites of Mourning: The Great War in European Cultural History*, Cambridge 1995.
Wood, Harley, *Sydney Observatory, 1858 to 1958*, Sydney Observatory Papers no. 31, Sydney 1958.
Zimmerman, Beverley, *The Making of a Diocese: Maitland, Its Bishop, Priests and People, 1866–1909*, Melbourne 2000.

Articles in Learned Journals

Allen, Judith, '"Our Deeply Degraded Sex" and "The Animal in Man": Rose Scott, Feminism and Sexuality, 1890–1925', *Australian Feminist Studies*, nos 7–8, 1988, pp. 64–91.
Anderson, Terry L & PJ Hill, 'The Evolution of Property Rights: A Study of the American West', *Journal of Law and Economics*, vol. 18, 1975, pp. 163–79.

Atkinson, Alan, 'Tasmania and the Multiplicity of Nations', *Tasmanian Historical Research Association Papers and Proceedings*, vol. 52, 2005, pp. 189–200.

—— 'Federation, Democracy and the Struggle against a Single Australia, *Australian Historical Studies*, vol. 44, 2013, pp. 262–79.

Attwood, Bain, 'The Law of the Land or the Law of the Land? History, Law and Narrative in a Settler Society', *History Compass*, vol. 2, 2004, pp. 1–30.

Ballinger, Robyn, 'Frontier and Homeland on the Northern Plains of Victoria 1841–1869', *Journal of Australian Colonial History*, vol. 13, 2011, pp. 49–64.

Bastin, John & June Stoodley, 'F.C.B. Vosper: An Australian Radical', *University Studies in History*, vol. 5, no. 1, 1967, pp. 38–53.

Bellanta, Melissa, 'Mobilising Fictions; or, Romancing the Australian Desert, 1890–1908', *History Australia*, vol. 1, 2003, pp. 15–30.

—— 'Fabulating the Australian Desert: Australia's Lost Race Romances, 1890–1908', *Philament*, no. 3, *Offbeat*, April 2004, viewed 16 December 2013, <sydney.edu.au/arts/publications/philament/issue3_Critique_Bellanta.htm>.

Bongiorno, Frank, 'Bernard O'Dowd's Socialism', *Labour History*, no. 77, November 1999, pp. 97–116.

—— 'From Republican to Anti-Billite: Bernard O'Dowd and Federation', *New Federalist*, no. 4, December 1999, pp. 49–57.

—— 'Aboriginality and Historical Consciousness: Bernard O'Dowd and the Creation of an Australian National Imaginary', *Aboriginal History*, vol. 24, 2000, pp. 39–61.

—— 'Love and Friendship: Ethical Socialism in Britain and Australia', *Australian Historical Studies*, vol. 32, 2001, pp. 1–19.

—— 'A Short History of New Thought in Australia, 1890–1914', *Australian Cultural History*, no. 23, 2004, pp. 25–42.

—— & Grant Mansfield, 'Whose War Was It Anyway? Some Australian Historians and the Great War', *History Compass*, vol. 6, 2008, pp. 62–90.

Bonner, Robert B, 'Roundheaded Cavaliers? The Context and Limits of a Confederate Racial Project', *Civil War History*, vol. 48, 2002, pp. 34–59.

Bridges, Dorven, 'Music in Australian Education: Origins and Backgrounds', *Australian Journal of Music Education*, no. 15, July 1974, pp. 11–13.

Brown, John, 'Charles Booth and Labour Colonies, 1889–1905', *Economic History Review*, n.s., vol. 21, 1968, pp. 349–561.

Buck, AR, '*Attorney General v. Brown* and the Development of Property Law in Australia', *Australian Property Law Journal*, vol. 2, 1994, pp. 128–38.

Calhoun, Daniel H, 'Eyes for the Jacksonian World: William C. Woodbridge and Emma Willard', *Journal of the Early Republic*, vol. 4, 1984, pp. 1–26.

Carey, Hilary, 'Bushmen and Bush Parsons: The Shaping of a Rural Myth', *Journal of Australian Colonial History*, vol. 14, 2011, pp. 1–26.

Chakrabarty, Dipesh, 'The Public Life of History: An Argument out of India', *Public Culture*, vol. 20, 2008, pp. 143–68.

Collins, CW, 'Matters of Social Conscience: Western Australia 1829–1890', *University Studies in History*, vol. 5, 1968, pp. 1–22.

Colyer, Richard, 'Welsh Cattle Drovers in the Nineteenth Century' (3 parts), *National Library of Wales Journal*, vol. 17, winter 1972, pp. 392–409; vol. 18, summer 1974, pp. 312–44; vol. 19, summer 1975, pp. 1–13.

Connolly, CN, 'Manufacturing "Spontaneity": The Australian Offers of Troops for the Boer War', *Historical Studies*, vol. 18, no. 70, 1978, pp. 106–17.

Coote, Anne, 'Imagining a Colonial Nation: The Development of Popular Concepts of Sovereignty and Nation in New South Wales with Particular Reference to the Period between 1856 and 1860', *Journal of Australian Colonial History*, vol. 1, 1999, pp. 1–37.

—— 'Out from the Legend's Shadow: Re-thinking National Feeling in Colonial Australia', *Journal of Australian Colonial History*, vol. 10, 2008, pp. 103–22.

Cox, Gordon, 'Towards the National Song Book: The History of an Idea', *British Journal of Music Education*, vol. 9, 1992, pp. 239–53.

Crowley, Archibald, 'The Life and Work of Sir Samuel McCaughey', *Journal of the Royal Australian Historical Society*, vol. 40, 1954, pp. 293–316.

Degler, Carl N, 'What Ought to Be and What Was: Women's Sexuality in the Nineteenth Century', *American Historical Review*, vol. 79, 1974, pp. 1467–90.

Dennen, R Taylor, 'Cattlemen's Associations and Property Rights in Land in the American West', *Explorations in Economic History*, vol. 13, 1976, pp. 423–36.

Elkin, AP, 'Social Organization in the Kimberley Division, North-Western Australia', *Oceania*, vol. 2, 1932, pp. 297–333.

Ely, Richard G, 'Andrew Inglis Clark and Church–State Separation', *Journal of Religious History*, vol. 8, 1974–75, pp. 271–89.

Evans, Raymond, 'Queensland's First Aboriginal Reserve' (2 parts), *Queensland Heritage*, vol. 2, no. 4, 1971, pp. 26–38; no. 5, 1971, pp. 3–15.

—— & Jan Walker, '"These Strangers, Where Are They Going?": Aboriginal–European Relations in the Fraser Island and Wide Bay Region 1770–1905', *Occasional Papers in Anthropology*, no. 8, 1977, pp. 39–105.

Falnes, Oscar J, 'European Progress and the "Superior" Races: As Viewed by a *Fin-de-Siècle* Liberal, Charles H. Pearson', *Journal of the History of Ideas*, vol. 15, 1954, pp. 312–31.

Finnis, HJ, 'Village Settlements on the River Murray', *Proceedings of the Royal Geographical Society of Australasia, South Australian Branch*, vol. 60, 1958–59, pp. 87–106.

Foster, Robert, 'Rations, Coexistence, and the Colonisation of Aboriginal Labour in the South Australian Pastoral Industry, 1860–1911', *Aboriginal History*, vol. 24, 2000, pp. 1–26.

Frappell, RM, 'The Australian Bush Brotherhoods and Their English Origins', *Journal of Ecclesiastical History*, vol. 47, 1996, pp. 82–97.

Ganter, Regina & Ros Kidd, 'The Powers of Protectors: Conflicts Surrounding Queensland's 1897 Aboriginal Legislation', *Australian Historical Studies*, vol. 25, 1993, pp. 536–54.

Gras, NSB, 'Behaviour of Business Men in a Changing World: Rise of Business Statesmanship', *Bulletin of the Business Historical Society*, vol. 23, 1949, pp. 1–65.

Green, B, P Cormack & A Paterson, 'Re-reading the Reading Lesson: Episodes in the History of Reading Pedagogy', *Oxford Review of Education*, vol. 39, 2013, pp. 329–44.

Green, Bill & Jo-Anne Reid, 'A New Teacher for a New Nation? Teacher Education, "English", and Schooling in Early Twentieth-Century Australia', *Journal of Educational Administration and History*, vol. 44, 2012, pp. 361–79.

Grimshaw, Patricia, 'Federation as a Turning Point in Australian History', *Australian Historical Studies*, vol. 33, 2002, pp. 25–41.

Halse, Dustin, '"Citizens Who Serve": The Political Rights of Victorian Public Servants, 1856–1916', *Labour History*, no. 102, May 2012, pp. 157–76.

Head, Lesley & Richard Fullagar, 'Hunter-Gatherer Archaeology and Pastoral Contact: Perspectives from the Northwest Northern Territory, Australia', *World Archaeology*, vol. 28, 1997, pp. 418–28.

Hercus, Luise A, 'Mick McLean Irinjili', *Australian Institute of Aboriginal Studies Newsletter*, n.s., no. 7, 1977, pp. 27–8.

—— '"How We Danced the Mudlunga": Memories of 1901 and 1902', *Aboriginal History*, vol. 4, 1980, pp. 5–31.

Hoare, ME, 'The Intercolonial Science Movement in Australasia 1870–1890', *Records of the Australian Academy of Science*, vol. 3, no. 2, 1975, pp. 7–28.

Hogan, Eleanor, 'Dreaming State', *Meanjin*, no. 2, 2013, pp. 6–9.

Home, RW, 'First Physicist of Australia: Richard Threlfall at the University of Sydney, 1886–1898', *Historical Records of Australian Science*, vol. 6, 1984, pp. 333–57.

—— 'The Problem of Intellectual Isolation in Scientific Life: W.H. Bragg and the Australian Scientific Community, 1886–1909', *Historical Records of Australian Science*, vol. 6, 1984, pp. 19–30.

Huttenback, Robert A, 'The British Empire as a "White Man's Country": Racial Attitudes and Immigration Legislation in the Colonies of White Settlement', *Journal of British Studies*, vol. 13, 1973, pp. 108–37.

Hyams, BK, 'The Teacher in South Australia in the Second Half of the Nineteenth Century', *Australian Journal of Education*, vol. 15, 1971, pp. 278–85.

Inglis, KS, 'The Anzac Tradition', *Meanjin*, vol. 24, 1965, pp. 25–44.

Irving, Terry & Sean Scalmer, 'Labour Intellectuals in Australia: Modes, Traditions, Generations, Transformations', *International Review of Social History*, vol. 50, 2005, pp. 1–26.

Jackson, Hugh, 'Fertility Decline in New South Wales: The Mackellar Royal Commission Reconsidered', *Australian Historical Studies*, vol. 23, 1989, pp. 260–73.

Jacobs, Jo Ellen, '"The Lot of Gifted Ladies Is Hard": A Study of Harriet Taylor Mill Criticism', *Hypatia: A Journal of Feminist Philosophy*, vol. 9, 1994, pp. 132–62.

Jaggard, E, 'Bread and Democracy: F.C.B. Vosper in the Roaring Nineties', *Westerly*, no. 4, December 1977, pp. 29–46.

Jennings, Sonia, 'Women and Gambling in Australia: Attitudes and Practices, 1860–1950', *Australian Society for Sports History Bulletin*, no. 27, December 1997, pp. 1–9.

Johnson, William R, '"Chanting Choristers": Simultaneous Recitation in Baltimore's Nineteenth-Century Primary Schools', *History of Education Quarterly*, vol. 34, 1994, pp. 1–23.

Kelly, Lee, '"Knights of the Blade": Shearers in 1888', *Australia 1888*, no. 8, September 1981, pp. 51–64.

Kennedy, REW, 'The Leongatha Labour Colony: Founding an Anti-Utopia', *Labour History*, no. 14, May 1968, pp. 54–8.

Kent, David A, '*The Anzac Book* and the Anzac Legend: C.E.W. Bean as Editor and Image-Maker', *Historical Studies*, vol. 21, 1985, pp. 376–90.

Kimber, RG (Dick), 'Smallpox in Central Australia: Evidence for Epidemics, and Postulations about the Impact', *Australian Archaeology*, vol. 27, 1988, pp. 63–8.

King, Peter, 'Gleaners, Farmers and the Failure of Legal Sanctions in England', *Past and Present*, no. 125, November 1989, pp. 116–50.

Kitney, Paul, 'The History of the Australian School Cadet Movement to 1893', *Defence Force Journal*, no. 12, 1978, pp. 53–60.

Kohlstedt, Sally Gregory, 'Australian Museums of Natural History: Priorities and Scientific Initiatives in the 19th Century', *Historical Records of Australian Science*, vol. 5, no. 4, 1983, pp. 1–29.

Kolig, Erich, 'Post-Contact Religious Movements in Australian Aboriginal Society', *Anthropos*, vol. 82, 1987, pp. 251–9.

Lake, Marilyn, 'Mission Impossible: How Men Gave Birth to the Australian Nation; Nationalism, Gender and Other Seminal Acts', *Gender and History*, vol. 4, 1992, pp. 305–22.

—— 'The White Man under Siege: New Histories of Race in the Nineteenth Century and the Advent of White Australia', *History Workshop Journal*, no. 58, 2004, pp. 41–62.

—— 'Equality and Exclusion: The Racial Constitution of Colonial Liberalism', *Thesis Eleven*, no. 95, 2008, pp. 20–32.
Loos, Noel, 'The Australian Board of Missions, the Anglican Church and the Aboriginals, 1850–1900', *Journal of Religious History*, vol. 17, 1992, pp. 194–209.
McConnel, Katherine, '"Separation Is from the Devil while Federation Is from Heaven": The Separation Question and Federation in Queensland', *New Federalist*, no. 4, December 1999, pp. 14–21.
McDonald, DI, 'The Former Customs Clerks: Wollaston and Lockyer', *Canberra Historical Journal*, n.s., no. 20, September 1987, p. 32.
McEwen, Ellen, 'Moving around New South Wales', *Australia 1888*, no. 14, September 1986, pp. 16–44.
McGregor, Russell, 'The Necessity of Britishness: Ethno-cultural Roots of Australian Nationalism', *Nations and Nationalism*, vol. 12, 2006, pp. 493–511.
Mackerras, IM & Elizabeth N Marks, 'The Bancrofts: A Century of Scientific Endeavour', *Proceedings of the Royal Society of Queensland*, vol. 84, no. 1, 1973, pp. 1–34.
MacLeod, Roy, 'On Visiting the "Moving Metropolis": Reflections on the Architecture of Imperial Science', *Historical Records of Australian Science*, vol. 5, 1982, pp. 1–16.
MacPherson, James, '"Ireland Begins in the Home": Women, Irish National Identity, and the Domestic Sphere in the *Irish Homestead*, 1896–1912', *Éire-Ireland*, vol. 36, 2001, pp. 131–52.
Maddrell, Avril MC, 'Discourses of Race and Gender and the Comparative Method in Geography School Texts 1830–1918', *Environment and Planning D: Society and Space*, vol. 16, 1998, pp. 81–103.
Markey, Ray, 'Explaining Union Mobilisation in the 1880s', *Labour History*, no. 83, November 2002, pp. 19–42.
Merritt, Adrian, 'The Historical Role of Law in the Regulation of Employment: Abstentionist or Interventionist?', *Australian Journal of Law and Society*, vol. 1, 1982, pp. 56–82.
Mertle, JS, 'The Origin and Development of Photolithography', *Australasian Printer*, April 1951, pp. 27–30.
Morphy, Howard & Frances Morphy, 'The "Myths" of Ngalakan History: Ideology and Images of the Past in Northern Australia', *Man*, n.s., vol. 19, 1984, pp. 459–78.
Morris, Jeremy, 'The Strange Death of Christian Britain: Another Look at the Secularization Debate', *Historical Journal*, vol. 46, 2003, pp. 963–76.
Moses, John A, 'Australia's Academic Garrison 1914–1918', *Australian Journal of Politics and History*, vol. 36, 1990, pp. 361–76.
—— 'Australian Anglican Leaders and the Great War, 1914–1918: The "Prussian Menace", Conscription and National Solidarity', *Journal of Religious History*, vol. 25, 2001, pp. 306–23.
—— 'Was There an Anzac Theology?', *Colloquium*, vol. 35, 2003, pp. 3–13.
—— 'Anglicanism and Anzac Observance: The Essential Contribution of Canon David John Garland', *Pacifica*, no. 19, February 2006, pp. 58–77.
Moyal, Ann, 'Invention and Innovation in Australia: The Historian's Lens', *Prometheus: Critical Studies in Innovation*, vol. 5, 1987, pp. 92–110.
Muecke, Stephen, Alan Rumsey & Banjo Wirrunmarra, 'Pigeon the Outlaw: History as Texts', *Aboriginal History*, vol. 9, 1985, pp. 81–100.
Mugglestone, Lynda C, 'A.J. Ellis, "Standard English" and the Prescriptive Tradition', *Review of English Studies*, vol. 39, 1988, pp. 87–92.
Murphy, DJ, 'Queensland's Image and Australian Nationalism', *Australian Quarterly*, vol. 50, no. 2, 1978, pp. 77–91.

Oppenheimer, Jillian, 'Shearing "Difficulties" in New England in 1888', *Australia 1888*, no. 11, May 1983, pp. 62–77.
Oppenheimer, Melanie, '"The Best PM for the Empire in War?": Lady Helen Munro Ferguson and the Australian Red Cross Society, 1914–1920', *Australian Historical Studies*, vol. 33, 2002, pp. 108–34.
Paisley, Fiona, 'Federalising the Aborigines? Constitutional Reform in the Late 1920s', *Australian Historical Studies*, vol. 29, 1998, pp. 244–66.
Paterson, Alistair, 'Early Pastoral Landscapes and Culture Contact in Central Australia', *Historical Archaeology*, vol. 39, 2005, pp. 28–48.
Pavils, Janice, 'The Emergence of South Australian Anzac Culture 1915–1925', *Journal of the Royal Australian Historical Society*, vol. 89, 2003, pp. 123–44.
Peers, Juliet, 'The Tribe of Mary Jane Hicks: Imaging Women through the Mount Rennie Rape Case 1886', *Australian Cultural History*, no. 12, 1993, pp. 127–44.
Pemberton, Jo-Anne, 'New Worlds for Old: The League of Nations in the Age of Electricity', *Review of International Studies*, vol. 28, 2002, pp. 311–36.
Phillips, Walter, 'Religious Profession and Practice in New South Wales, 1850–1901: The Statistical Evidence', *Historical Studies*, vol. 15, 1972, pp. 378–400.
Quartly, Marian, 'Mothers and Fathers and Brothers and Sisters: The AWA and the ANA and Gendered Citizenship', *Journal of Australian Studies*, no. 37, special issue, *Women and the State: Australian Perspectives*, 1993, pp. 22–30.
Rainer, Joseph T, 'The "Sharper" Image: Yankee Peddlers, Southern Consumers, and the Market Revolution', *Business and Economic History*, vol. 26, no. 1, 1997, pp. 27–44.
Reynolds, Henry, '"Men of Substance and Deservedly Good Repute": The Tasmanian Gentry 1856–1875', *Australian Journal of Politics and History*, vol. 15, 1969, pp. 61–72.
—— 'Regionalism in Nineteenth Century Tasmania', *Tasmanian Historical Association Papers and Proceedings*, vol. 17, 1969, pp. 14–28.
—— 'Australian Nationalism: Tasmanian Patriotism', *New Zealand Journal of History*, vol. 5, 1971, pp. 18–30.
Robson, LL, 'The Origin and Character of the First A.I.F., 1914–18: Some Statistical Evidence', *Historical Studies*, vol. 15, 1973, pp. 737–49.
Rose, Deborah Bird, 'Aboriginal Life and Death in Australian Settler Nationhood', *Aboriginal History*, vol. 25, 2001, pp. 148–62.
Rowse, Tim, 'Mabo and Moral Anxiety', *Meanjin*, vol. 52, 1993, pp. 229–52.
Rutherford, John, 'Interplay of Australian and American Ideas for Development of Water Projects in Northern Victoria', *Annals of the Association of American Geographers*, vol. 54, 1964, pp. 88–106.
Rylance, Rick, 'Convex and Concave: Conceptual Boundaries in Psychology, Now and Then (But Mainly Then)', *Victorian Literature and Culture*, vol. 32, 2004, pp. 449–62.
Saunders, Kay, 'The North Comes In: The 1899 Referendum Campaigns in North Queensland', *New Federalist*, no. 4, December 1999, pp. 7–13.
Sherington, Geoffrey, 'Athleticism in the Antipodes: The AAGPS of New South Wales', *History of Education Review*, vol. 12, 1983, pp. 16–22.
Spillman, Lyn, '"Neither the Same Nation nor Different Nations": Constitutional Conventions in the United States and Australia', *Comparative Studies in Society and History*, vol. 38, 1996, pp. 149–81.
Stewart, PJ, 'New Zealand and the Pacific Labor Traffic, 1870–1874', *Pacific Historical Review*, vol. 30, 1961, pp. 47–59.
Taylor, Cheryl, 'Constructing Aboriginality: Archibald Meston's Literary Journalism, 1870–1924', *Journal of the Association for the Study of Australian Literature*, vol. 2, 2003, pp. 121–39.

Thomas, Martin, 'RH Mathews and Anthropological Warfare: On Writing the Biography of a "Self-Contained Man"', *Aboriginal History*, vol. 28, 2004, pp. 1–32.

Thomson, Alistair, '"Steadfast until Death"? C.E.W. Bean and the Representation of Australian Military Manhood', *Australian Historical Studies*, vol. 23, 1989, pp. 462–78.

Thorpe, William, 'Archibald Meston and Aboriginal Legislation in Colonial Queensland', *Historical Studies*, vol. 21, 1984, pp. 52–67.

Vivers, Meg, 'Dealing with Difference: Evidence of European Women in Early Contact History', *Journal of Australian Colonial History*, vol. 4, 2002, pp. 72–96.

—— 'Landscapes or Inscapes? Alternative Perspectives on Frontier Life', *Journal of Australian Colonial History*, vol. 13, 2011, pp. 151–82.

Walker, David, 'Youth on Trial: The Mt Rennie Case', *Labour History*, no. 50, May 1986, pp. 28–41.

Walker, RB, 'The Ambiguous Experiment: Agricultural Co-operatives in New South Wales, 1893–1896', *Labour History*, no. 18, May 1970, pp. 19–31.

Waterson, Duncan, 'The Absentees from North of the Tweed', *New Federalist*, no. 1, June 1998, pp. 29–38.

Wieck, GF, 'The Volunteer Movement in Western Australia', *Early Days*, vol. 5, 1961, pp. 49–64.

Winckel, Anne, 'Almighty God in the Preamble', *New Federalist*, no. 4, December 1999, pp. 78–83.

Winter, JM, 'Britain's "Lost Generation" of the First World War', *Population Studies*, vol. 31, 1977, pp. 449–66.

Yeo, Richard R, 'Science and Intellectual Authority in Mid-Nineteenth-Century Britain: Robert Chambers and Vestiges of the Natural History of Creation', *Victorian Studies*, vol. 28, 1984, pp. 5–33.

Unpublished Research

Abbott, Kellie, '"A Woman's Own Concern?": Pregnant Bodies in Western Australia, 1900–1916', BA thesis, University of Western Australia 1998.

Adamson, Shirley, 'The Queensland Sugar Industry', BA thesis, University of Queensland 1953.

Aurousseau, Marcel, 'Notes on Geographical Associations Formed in Australia', March 1960 – April 1961, typescript, National Library of Australia, Canberra, Npf 910.6294 AUR.

Aveling, Marian [Marian Quartly], 'A History of the Australian Natives Association, 1871–1900', PhD thesis, Monash University 1970.

Barnett, Susan, 'A Study of the Queensland Native Mounted Police in the 1870s', BA thesis, University of Queensland 1975.

Barnett-Spies, Pamela, 'The Early Years of the Preservation Movement in New South Wales 1900 to 1939', MA thesis, University of Sydney 1987.

Baskerville, Bruce, 'Creating Arcadia? A History of Nature Conservation in Colonial Western Australia 1870–1914', BA thesis, University of Western Australia 1992.

Bates, Ian B, '"Necessity's Inventions": A Research Project into South Australian Inventors and Their Inventions from 1836 to 1886', MA thesis, University of Adelaide 2000.

Bavin-Mizzi, Jill, 'Raping Matilda: Sexual Assault in Late-Nineteenth-Century Australia', PhD thesis, University of Western Australia 1993.

Blaschak, Bradley, '"The Ignorant Labelled It a Ladies' Game": Masculinity in Australian Tennis in the Late Nineteenth and Early Twentieth Centuries', BA thesis, University of Queensland 2003.

Brooklyn, Bridget, 'Something Old, Something New: Divorce and Divorce Law in South Australia, 1859–1918', PhD thesis, University of Adelaide 1988.

Brown, Julie, 'Versions of Reality: The Production and Function of Photographs in Colonial Queensland 1880–1900', PhD thesis, University of Queensland 1984.

Bruce, Peter, 'William Lane: Personality and Politics', BA thesis, University of Adelaide 1970.

Byrne, Neil J, 'Robert Dunne, 1830–1917, Archbishop of Brisbane: A Biography', PhD thesis, University of Queensland 1989.

Cameron, MB, 'W.H. Groom: Agrarian Liberal', BA thesis, University of Queensland 1965.

Carnell, Ian, 'A History of Gympie, 1867–1900', BA thesis, University of Queensland 1976.

Choo, Christine, 'Aboriginal Women in Catholic Missions in the Kimberley, Western Australia, 1900–1950', PhD thesis, University of Western Australia 1995.

Clark, KN, 'An Examination of Queensland Attitudes to the Federal System 1900–1920', BA thesis, University of Queensland 1960.

Clark, SD, 'Australian Water Law: An Historical and Analytical Background', PhD thesis, University of Melbourne 1971.

Clements, HG, 'Science and Colonial Culture: Scientific Interests and Institutions in Brisbane, 1859–1900', PhD thesis, Griffith University 1999.

Cook, M, 'Cable and Co-operation? A Study of the Development of Submarine Cables to Australia and the Concomitant Expansion of Land Telegraphy within the Continent between 1859 and 1910, with Special Reference to Queensland', BA thesis, University of Queensland 1969.

Coote, Anne, 'Space, Time and Sovereignty: Literate Culture and Colonial Nationhood in New South Wales up to 1860', PhD thesis, University of New England 2005.

Corfield, Noela, 'The Development of the Cattle Industry in Queensland 1840–1890', BA thesis, University of Queensland 1959.

Crawford, Ray, 'Imitation, Need, Necessity: Muscular Christianity for Girls and the Emergence of the Sports Mistress in the Private Schools of Melbourne', paper presented at 'History in the Community', Australian Historical Association Conference, Adelaide, 25–29 August 1986.

Cryle, Mark, 'Duncan McNab's Mission to the Queensland Aboriginals 1875–1880', BA thesis, University of Queensland 1989.

Dalton, JB, 'The Queensland Labour Movement 1889–1915', BA thesis, University of Queensland 1961.

Daly, JA, 'Sport, Class and Community in Colonial South Australia', PhD thesis, University of Illinois at Urbana-Champaign 1977.

Davis, Angela, 'Public Policies towards Motherhood and Infant Care in Western Australia 1900 to 1922', BA thesis, University of Western Australia 1983.

Denholm, TMZ, 'James Tyson 1819–1898: A Man in His Environment', MA thesis, University of Queensland 1969.

Diamond, Marion, 'Ideas of Landed Property in Australia and Other Settler Societies in the 19th Century', paper presented at the Sir Robert Menzies Centre for Australian Studies, London, November 1988.

Eklund, Erik, 'Building the "Kingdom of Freedom": Co-operatives and the Co-operative Movement in Australia', paper presented at the United Kingdom/Australian Comparative Labour History Conference, Manchester, July 2003.

Elliott, Ross, 'Children in Queensland 1900–1920: A Study of Children's Culture and Their Place and Purpose in Adult Queensland Society', BA thesis, University of Queensland 1985.

Evans, Raymond, 'Loyalty and Disloyalty: Social and Ideological Conflict in Queensland during the Great War', PhD thesis, University of Queensland 1980.

Fletcher, Valerie, 'The Northern Territory, 1895 to 1900: The Royal Commission of 1895 and Its Results', MA Qual. thesis, University of Queensland 1988.

Green, Bill & Phillip Cormack, 'Reading, in the Nation: Literacy, Modernity and Australian Schooling', paper presented at the International Invitational Conference, Zurich, February–March 2007.

Green, Louis, 'The Queensland Attitude to Federation', BA thesis, University of Queensland 1951.

Grimes, John, 'The Importance and Meaning of Birth and Death in the Anzac Experience and Tradition', BA thesis, University of Queensland 1974.

Gugenburger, Louis, 'The National and Imperial Image in the Teaching of History of Queensland State Primary Schools 1875 to 1975 with Historical Notes', MA Qual. thesis, University of Queensland 1975.

Halse, Christine M, 'The Reverend Ernest Gribble and Race Relations in Northern Australia', PhD thesis, University of Queensland 1992.

Hamley, Helen, 'The Limits of Choice: White Women, Their Work and Labour Activism in Queensland Factories and Shops 1880s to 1920', MA Qual. thesis, University of Queensland 1992.

Hardy, Margaret, 'Digger Conservatism: A Study in the Development of Ideas', BA thesis, University of Adelaide 1970.

Harrison, John, 'Missions, Fisheries and Government in Far North Queensland 1891–1919', BA thesis, University of Queensland 1974.

Hoskin, Graham, 'The Aboriginal Reserves in Queensland 1871–85, and the Movement to Ameliorate and Improve the Condition of the Aborigines 1870–79', BA thesis, University of Queensland 1967.

Howell, Andrea R, 'The Australian Sugar Industry, 1850–1939', BA thesis, University of Queensland 1986.

Jenkins, Alan, 'Attitudes towards Federation in North Queensland', MA Qual. thesis, University of Queensland 1969.

—— 'Attitudes towards Federation in Queensland', MA thesis, University of Queensland 1979.

Johnson, Murray, '"Leaning on the Lamp-Post": A Study of Larrikinism in South Queensland, 1880–1920', BA thesis, University of Queensland 1998.

Johnson, WR, 'Role of the Legal Profession in Queensland in the Federation Movement, 1890–1900', MA Qual. thesis, University of Queensland 1963.

Lee, Pauline, 'Broome, 1900 to 1940: Local Interaction in the Pearling Industry', BA thesis, University of Western Australia 1969.

Muir, Adrian, 'The Trials of the Queensland Shearers, 1891', BA thesis, University of Sydney 1986.

O'Leary, PJ, 'Queensland Baptists: The Development of Baptist Evangelicalism, 1846–1926', MA thesis, University of Queensland 1992.

Perkins, Yvonne, 'Moral Issues and Mass Democracy in Australasia 1890–1914', report, February 2009.

Phillips, Derek, 'The State and the Provision of Education in Tasmania, 1839 to 1913', PhD thesis, University of Tasmania 1988.

Rayner, Keith, 'The History of the Church of England in Queensland', PhD thesis, University of Queensland 1962.

Reynolds, Henry, 'The Island Colony: Tasmania – Society and Politics 1880–1900', MA thesis, University of Tasmania 1963.

Rickertt, Jeffrey, 'Resistance on the Line: A History of Australian Telephonists and Their Trade Unions, 1880–1988', PhD thesis, University of Queensland 2006.

Schlencker, PR, 'The National Agricultural and Industrial Association of Queensland 1875–1900', BA thesis, University of Queensland 1973.

Southcott, JE, 'Music in State-Supported Schooling in South Australia to 1920', PhD thesis, Deakin University 1997.

Spearitt, Katie, 'The Poverty of Protection: Women and Marriage in Colonial Queensland, 1870–1900', BA thesis, University of Queensland 1988.

Thorpe, W, 'Archibald Meston and the Aboriginals: Ideology and Practice, 1870–1970; An Exploration in Social History', BA thesis, University of Queensland 1978.

Turner, Kaye, 'Yarrabah, a Mission for Aboriginal People in North Queensland: The Effect of Government and Church Policies, 1900–1912', Postgrad. Dip. Arts thesis, University of Queensland 1994.

Vivers, Margaret [Meg Vivers], 'Female Perspectives: A Study of the Colonial Texts of Adelaide Bowler and Lucy Gray', PhD thesis, University of New England 2007.

Voss, VR de V, 'Separatist Movements in Central Queensland in the Nineteenth Century', BA thesis, University of Queensland 1964.

Yezerski, Robert, 'Burning Desires: Fighting Fires and Masculinities in Nineteenth Century Victoria', BA thesis, University of Sydney 2001.

Ziino, Bart, 'Journeys to War: Experiences of Australian Recruits in the Great War', MA thesis, University of Melbourne 1999.

Index

FSC
www.fsc.org
MIX
Papier | Fördert
gute Waldnutzung
FSC® C083411

Zeitfracht Medien GmbH
Ferdinand-Jühlke-Straße 7
99095 Erfurt, Deutschland
produktsicherheit@kolibri360.de